DEVELOPMENTAL LANGUAGE DISORDERS: FROM PHENOTYPES TO ETIOLOGIES

DEVELOPMENTAL LANGUAGE DISORDERS: FROM PHENOTYPES TO ETIOLOGIES

Edited by

Mabel L. Rice
Steven F. Warren
University of Kansas

LEA LAWRENCE ERLBAUM ASSOCIATES, PUBLISHERS
2004 Mahwah, New Jersey   London

Lawrence Erlbaum Associates, Inc., Publishers
10 Industrial Avenue
Mahwah, New Jersey 07430

Cover design by Kathryn Houghtaling Lacey

Library of Congress Cataloging-in-Publication Data

Developmental language disorders : from phenotypes to etiologies / edited by Mabel L.
Rice and Steven F. Warren.
 p.   cm.
 Includes bibliographical references and index.
 ISBN 0-8058-4662-X (cloth : alk. paper)
 1. Language disorders in children—Congresses.   2. Language disorders in
children—Etiology—Congresses.   3. Child development deviations—Congresses.
4. Phenotype—Congresses.   5. Children—Language—Congresses.   I. Rice, Mabel.
II. Warren, Steven F.
RJ496.L35D485   2004
618.92'855—dc22   2004040430
                                                                          CIP

Books published by Lawrence Erlbaum Associates are printed on acid-free paper,
and their bindings are chosen for strength and durability.

Printed in the United States of America
10   9   8   7   6   5   4   3   2   1

Contents

Preface   ix

1   Introduction   1
Mabel L. Rice and Steven F. Warren

**I: PHENOTYPES OF LANGUAGE IMPAIRMENTS
WITHIN CLINICAL DIAGNOSES**

2   Trajectory of Language Development
in Autistic Spectrum Disorders   7
Catherine Lord, Susan Risi, and Andrew Pickles

3   Do Autism and Specific Language Impairment
Represent Overlapping Language Disorders?   31
Helen Tager-Flusberg

4   Dimensions of Individual Differences in Communication
Skills Among Primary Grade Children   53
*J. Bruce Tomblin, Xuyang Zhang, Amy Weiss, Hugh Catts,
and Susan Ellis Weismer*

5 Language, Social Cognition, Maladaptive Behavior,
and Communication in Down Syndrome
and Fragile X Syndrome   77
Leonard Abbeduto and Melissa M. Murphy

6 Investigating Knowledge of Complex Syntax: Insights
From Experimental Studies of Williams Syndrome   99
Andrea Zukowski

7 Research on Fragile X Syndrome and Autism:
Implications for the Study of Genes, Environments,
and Developmental Language Disorders   121
Donald B. Bailey, Jr., Jane E. Roberts, Stephen R. Hooper,
Deborah D. Hatton, Penny L. Mirrett, Joanne E. Roberts,
and Jennifer M. Schaaf

II: INVESTIGATING LANGUAGE IMPAIRMENTS ACROSS DIAGNOSTIC CATEGORIES

8 Cross-Etiology Comparisons of Cognitive
and Language Development   153
Carolyn B. Mervis

9 Intervention as Experiment   187
Steven F. Warren

10 Growth Models of Developmental Language Disorders   207
Mabel L. Rice

11 Linguistics and Linking Problems   241
Colin Phillips

III: NEURAL, GENETIC, AND BEHAVIORAL ELEMENTS OF INHERITED FACTORS

12 Genes, Language Disorders, and Developmental
Archaeology: What Role Can Neuroimaging Play?   291
Ralph-Axel Müller

13   Localization and Identification of Genes Affecting
        Language and Learning   329
        Shelley D. Smith

14   Genotype–Phenotype Correlations: Lessons
        From Williams Syndrome Research   355
        Colleen A. Morris

**IV: RESEARCH ACTION STEPS FOR THE SHORT
AND LONG TERM**

15   Next Steps in the Study of Genetics
        and Language Disorders   373
        Peggy McCardle and Judith Cooper

Author Index   381

Subject Index   405

Preface

The chapters in this volume are the product of a conference sponsored by the Merrill Advanced Studies Center of the University of Kansas. This volume joins other books in the Merrill series on topics of import for a better understanding of various disabilities and research methods across the lifespan:

- *Toward a Genetics of Language* (1996)—edited by Mabel L. Rice;
- *Constraints on Language: Aging, Grammar, and Memory* (1999)—edited by Susan Kemper and Reinhold Kliegl;
- *Aging, Communication, and Health: Linking Research and Practice for Successful Aging* (2001)—edited by Mary Lee Hummert and Jon F. Nussbaum;
- *Self-Injurious Behavior: Gene-Brain-Behavior Relationships* (2002)—edited by Stephen R. Schroeder, Mary Lou Oster-Granite, and Travis Thompson;
- *The Connections between Language and Reading Disabilities* (forthcoming)—edited by Hugh W. Catts and Alan G. Kamhi.

The conference was motivated by the observation that in the last 10 years there have been important advances in our understanding of inherited and environmental components of language disorders in children.

This involves significant research in behavioral phenotypes, associated neurocortical processes, and the genetics of language disorders. These advances, in turn, can provide a foundation for further breakthroughs in understanding the reasons for overlapping etiologies as well as the truly unique aspects of some phenotypes. The potential is limited, however, by the fragmented way that current findings are disseminated in a scientific literature partitioned by diagnostic categories of affectedness.

The authors are scholars with active programs of research funded by the National Institutes of Health (NIH) involving diverse clinical groups of children with language impairments. They convened in Tempe, Arizona, in May 2002 to summarize discoveries from their ongoing programs of research, capture the converging outcomes and common scientific gaps or challenges, and suggest new directions of research for enhancing our understanding of the nature and etiology of developmental language disorders. As the chapters in this volume attest, there are vital and exciting new discoveries underway, along with substantive reworking of old assumptions, as the study of language impairments moves toward better behavioral description, brain imaging, genetics, and intervention technologies. For many of the participants, it is both enlightening and exciting to realize how much discovery is now underway. At the same time, we are aware that discoveries do not have a common pathway for dissemination, and it is difficult in the press of an active research program to stay abreast of the wide range of literatures and emerging conceptualizations. This volume provides an example of a common pathway in the hope that it will inspire others to follow.

In a time of e-mail communication, we are also reminded that it is a valuable experience to bring scholars together for actual discussions and reactions to each other's work in a relaxed setting. The logistics require the assistance of many people. We wish to express our deep appreciation to Fred and Virginia Merrill for their generous support of the Merrill Advanced Studies Center, their personal interest in the proceedings, and their far-sighted vision of the future needs of discovery research on the topic of disabilities across the lifespan. We thank the members of the Board of the Merrill Advanced Studies Center for their oversight and good advice: Melinda Merrill; Richard Schiefelbusch, Distinguished Professor Emeritus; Robert Barnhill, Vice Provost for Research, University of Kansas; Kathleen McCluskey-Fawcett, Senior Vice Provost, University of Kansas; and Kim Wilcox, Dean of the College of Liberal Arts and Sciences, University of Kansas. Joy Simpson provided gracious and highly effective assistance with the organization of the conference, communication with the participants, and oversight of the many details that ensure a conference proceeds in a way that allows people to focus on the discussions and not the logistics. She also provided technical editing for the preparation of the manuscripts. Patsy Woods, among her other duties, manages the budget and pays the bills to the great appreciation of all involved.

—*Mabel L. Rice*
Steven F. Warren

1

Introduction

Mabel L. Rice
Steven F. Warren
University of Kansas

The investigation of language impairments in children has an extensive record. With the exception of the condition now classified as specific language impairment (SLI), much of the literature has focused on the clinical conditions in which language impairment appears as a concomitant condition, such as Down syndrome, Williams syndrome, mental retardation, autism, and, more recently, fragile X syndrome. Funding for research and the associated culture of review has, within the United States at least, been defined more by the clinical categories than the common elements of language impairment. This separation of effort has led to important and fundamental discoveries and has had many advantages, not the least of which is the successful advocacy of funding according to diagnostic category.

This approach to scholarship is less effective in the modern era because advances in genetics necessitate precision in the measurement of the behavioral phenotypes, and the fact that language impairments cross many diagnostic categories and can obscure the genetics of intellectual impairment, social competencies, or other related attributes. Furthermore, language is a key predictor of developmental outcomes and a salient way for families to note affectedness. New insights about genetic effects bring increased recognition of the finely tuned interactions of neurocortical, genetic, and behavioral elements of inherited factors, and the role of environmental events such as intervention. On the other hand, new developments in linguistic theory and application to children with language

1

impairments have added substantively to what is known about the capacity for human language. Yet this line of work is not fully incorporated into other areas of inquiry.

In this context, knowledge of new discoveries across a wide array of studies is essential. This is particularly so when large collaborative efforts, both expensive and time-consuming, are mounted to explore the interface of genetics, the brain, and the environment. Just as efforts are ongoing to ensure that new findings on the human genome are made available quickly to inform the work of others, there is the need to bring together current and converging outcomes of research across behavioral phenotypes with areas of shared variance.

This volume provides such a collection from a group of investigators who each have ongoing programs of investigation that have met the peer review standards of the National Institutes of Health (NIH). The clinical categories in this volume were selected because there is a healthy momentum of currently funded inquiry into those categories. They are: autism spectrum disorders, SLI, Down syndrome, fragile X syndrome, and Williams syndrome. This is not, of course, an exhaustive list of clinical conditions in which language impairment appears, but it does provide a beginning for examining common issues across conditions.

Section I provides a series of chapters that address the phenotypes of language impairments (i.e., the ways in which language impairments are manifest in different conditions), including brief overviews of the clinical category and some of the investigators' current work. The two opening chapters cover recent findings on autism spectrum disorders. Catherine Lord, Susan Risi, and Andrew Pickles (chap. 2) provide an overview of the condition, highlight the range of language abilities of diagnosed children, and discuss developmental questions about language acquisition in these youngsters, including evidence of apparent regression in language abilities. Helen Tager-Flusberg (chap. 3) examines the question of possible overlap of autism and SLI as diagnostic categories, with particular reference to the similarity of language symptoms at the boundaries of the two conditions. Bruce Tomblin, Xuyang Zhang, Hugh Catts, Susan Ellis Weismer, and Amy Weiss (chap. 4) discuss the issue of individual differences among children with developmental language disorders and compare factor analytic outcomes to previously proposed taxonomic systems in a search for best-fit subgrouping criteria. Leonard Abbeduto and Melissa Murphy (chap. 5) compare the symptoms of language impairment and related developmental domains in children with Down syndrome and fragile X syndrome. Andrea Zukowski (chap. 6) describes her recent investigation of complex syntax knowledge in children with Williams syndrome to make a case for fine-grained linguistic investigation to document the linguistic knowledge and limitations of affected children. Donald Bailey, Jane Roberts, Stephen Hooper, Deborah Hatton, Penny Mirrett, Joanne Roberts, and Jennifer Schaaf (chap. 7) summarize their program of research on fragile X and autism, as well as the implications for our understanding of the role of genes and environmental elements in developmental language disorders.

Section II includes issues that bridge different diagnostic categories. This includes methodological issues involved in studies comparing different clinical groups (Carolyn Mervis, chap. 8); intervention as an experimental means to investigate the phenotypes and gene/environment interactions (Steve Warren, chap. 9); growth and related timing mechanisms as a central feature of language impairment across conditions (Mabel Rice, chap. 10); and linguistic issues in language impairments (Colin Phillips, chap. 11).

Section III extends the perspective to brain development and plasticity related to language impairments (Ralph-Axel Müller, chap. 12); methods of genetic investigation (Shelley Smith, chap. 13); and discussion of the complexities of genotype/phenotype relationships in Williams syndrome (Colleen Morris, chap. 14).

Section IV ends the volume with a look toward the future; it offers a synthesis of the content in terms of the perceived needs for the next steps in research and inquiry. Peggy McCardle, of the National Institute of Child Health and Human Development (NICHD), and Judith Cooper, of the National Institute on Deafness and Other Communication Disorders (NIDCD), bring their extensive experience with NIH research sponsorship to these remarks.

Each chapter in this volume stands on its own merits. Yet we believe the whole of the volume is greater than the sum of the parts. Taken together, these chapters reflect an emerging convergence in terms of conceptual approaches, methods, and measures; this enhances our understanding of the role language plays in the gene–brain–behavior–environment interactions that ultimately determine development. As an accurate reflection of the knowledge level of the field, these chapters tend to raise more questions than they answer. This is as it should be. The right questions and the methods to answer them will invariably lead us in exactly the direction we want to go.

I

---

*PHENOTYPES OF LANGUAGE
IMPAIRMENTS WITHIN
CLINICAL DIAGNOSES*

Trajectory of Language Development in Autistic Spectrum Disorders

Catherine Lord
Susan Risi
University of Michigan

Andrew Pickles
University of Manchester

ROLES OF LANGUAGE DELAY

Language delay plays a critical role in understanding autistic spectrum disorders. In the following, we discuss theoretical and methodological implications of different trajectories of expressive and receptive language development in autistic spectrum disorders.

Although the emphasis on autism as a language disorder has changed (Rutter, 1978), speech delays continue to be the most common cause of initial referral in autism clinics (Siegel, Pliner, Eschler, & Elliott, 1988). In our longitudinal studies, following two groups of children who were referred for possible autism at age 2, parents' primary concern was delayed language, followed by delay in developmental milestones other than language and medical problems (such as seizures). Language skills are also the best predictor of later outcome in terms of adaptive skills, school achievement, and independence in adulthood (Howlin & Goode, 1998; Lord & Pickles, 1996; Lord & Schopler, 1989; Venter, Lord, & Schopler, 1992). Language skill remains a predictor whether measured by parent report, spontaneous production (e.g., number of words used on a daily basis, use of phrases), standardized measures of receptive or expressive vocabulary (e.g., the Peabody Picture Vocabulary Test–Third Edition [PPVT–III]; Dunn, 1997), or more sophisticated measures of complex syntax.

Language delays relative to other skills in individuals with autism may not be as consistent over time as we might expect. A recent article compar-

ing cross-sectional groups of children who were administered the Preschool Differential Abilities Scales and the School-Age Differential Abilities Scales (DAS; Elliott, 1990) showed significant differences in the
distribution of language delay relative to verbal and nonverbal scores at
the two different age periods (Joseph, Tager-Flusberg, & Lord, 2002), as
shown in Fig. 2.1. Although this was not a longitudinal comparison, it
suggests the need to look carefully at changes in relationships among
skills over time. Other studies have indicated that differentiating diagnostic groups, such as Asperger's syndrome and high-functioning autism on
the basis of early measures of language delay, does not yield much useful

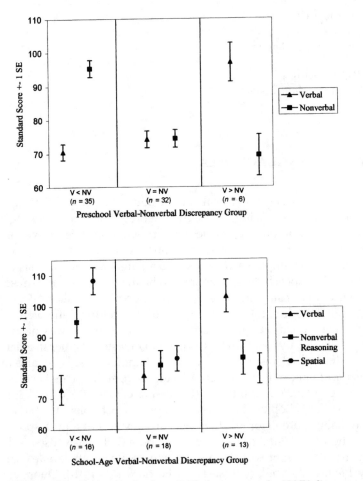

FIG. 2.1.   Preschool and school-age DAS cluster scores by V-NV discrepancy groups.

information regarding outcome (Eisenmajer et al., 1998). In the past, psychometrically strong measures of early language (i.e., under the 12- to 15-month-old level) were not always available (Howlin & Goode, 1998; Howlin, Mawhood, & Rutter, 2000; Lotter, 1978). However, in more recent studies, use of the Reynell Scales (which provide age equivalents down to 12 months; Reynell & Gruber, 1978), the Mullen Scales of Early Learning (MSEL; Mullen, 1995), and the Vineland Adaptive Behavior Scales (VABS; Sparrow, Balla, & Cicchetti, 1984), which both provide age equivalents down to 1 month, now allow more direct tests of the power of early language and communication skills to predict later behavior.

Another important use of simple characterizations of language delay in understanding autistic spectrum disorders has been as a factor in genetic subtypes. Recently, several different studies (Alarcón et al., 2002; Bradford et al., 2001; Buxbaum et al., 2001; Folstein & Mankoski, 2000) have found evidence of genetic specificity (e.g., higher LOD scores [i.e., the logarithm of the odds of linkage versus not linkage] on Chromosomes 2 and 7) when samples included only subjects who had both autism and a history of language delay. This approach ("segregating" groups by early language delay) was initially taken because the first full genome screening of autism included only affected sibling/relative pairs in which one of the children had a significant language delay prior to age 3 (defined by a delay in first meaningful words and/or phrases acquired, respectively, at age 24 or 33 months or later), met autism criteria, and was not profoundly mentally retarded (International Molecular Genetic Study of Autism Consortium [IMGSAC], 1998). When other sites failed to replicate the original findings (e.g., the relatively high LOD score on Chromosome 7 found by IMGSAC), investigators sought to make their samples as similar as possible to the IMGSAC sample. Thus, they attempted to increase the homogeneity of their participants by requiring that children with autism have an early language delay and sometimes by requiring a history of speech or language problems in relatives as well.

Because the investigators had access to exactly the same data and standardized measures, it should have been possible to use the same variable, but that was not the case. To yield significant results, the definition of early language delay had to vary across studies that used language delay as a grouping factor (Alarcón et al., 2002; Bradford et al., 2001; Buxbaum et al., 2001; Folstein & Mankoski, 2000). Nevertheless, the general strategy resulted in findings of increased specificity (e.g., higher LOD scores on Chromosome 7), although not in identical regions. From this point of view, the specific demarcation of what constitutes an early language delay has not been replicated across these studies. Although these findings have been interpreted to mean that language delay may play a role in increasing genetic specificity, as research through IMGSAC has proceeded, stronger results (e.g., even higher LOD scores) on Chromosome 7 have been found when the original IMGSAC sample was broadened to include affected pairs in which neither child had a language delay (International Molecular Genetic Study of Autism Consortium, 2001). There is still a great deal we do not understand about the contribution of language skill and history to the genetics of autism.

The systematic telescoping of how parents report age of first words and first phrases is one possible way to interpret the difference in results across studies. In our longitudinal data, we were able to show with samples of children referred for possible autism and with samples of children with developmental disorders (not referred for possible autism) that in repeated administrations of the Autism Diagnostic Interview–Revised (ADI–R; Lord, Rutter, & Le Couteur, 1994) to the same parents, the ages that parents provided as age of first word and age of first phrases increased consistently with the age of the child at the time of the interview (see Figs. 2.2 and 2.3). This means that when their children are older, parents of children with autism or other developmental delays are more likely to describe their children's early language as delayed than they did when their children were younger. Research samples vary in recruitment and selection strategies. These factors differentially affect the chronological ages and levels of functioning (including language) of the children in the samples. Because the determination of language milestones are affected by methodological factors, simple measures of language delay may serve as markers for other factors that have potential implications for genetics research, such as certainty of

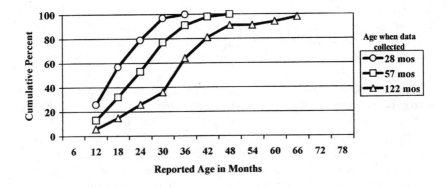

Note: Includes only children who were reported to use some words at each interview.

FIG. 2.2.   Telescoping of how parents of children referred for possible autism report age of first words.

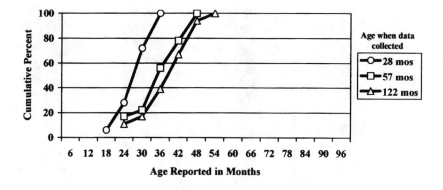

Note: Includes only children who were reported to use some spontaneous phrases at each interview.

FIG. 2.3. Telescoping of how parents of children referred for possible autism report age of first phrases.

caseness, parental education, or dysmorphology even more than they serve as assessments of language skill.

Interpreting the role of language delay in genetics studies may also be complicated by missing data. In any broad sample of individuals with autism, a certain proportion of participants will have language so limited in quantity and complexity that their language cannot be judged in terms of abnormalities. Sometimes missing data for these individuals is simply ignored with the assumption that low-functioning individuals will score as more abnormal on all other measures as well (see Lord, Rutter, & Le Couteur, 1994, regarding the ADI–R). Other times nonverbal children may be given *most abnormal* codes on verbal items, such as delayed echolalia or pronoun reversal, even though they do not speak at all (see Tadevosyan-Leyfer et al., 2003). Both of these approaches clearly distort quantitative meanings of language abnormality. This phenomenon may have contributed to the recent findings that, in verbal children with autism, the severity of their disorder (as computed by a total item score across the ADI–R algorithm) was related to the number of affected relatives, whereas there was no such relation found for nonverbal subjects (Bolton et al., 1994). Ranges for the nonverbal children may have been restricted by the fact that only nonverbal items could be scored, and by ceiling effects on nonverbal items (e.g., such as gestures) related to severe developmental language delay and the absence of the contexts typically provided by verbal interaction in which these behaviors often occur. This kind of pattern could result in a restriction in language scores that would

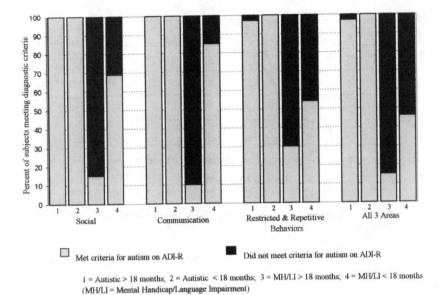

Met criteria for autism on ADI-R   Did not meet criteria for autism on ADI-R

1 = Autistic > 18 months; 2 = Autistic < 18 months; 3 = MH/LI > 18 months; 4 = MH/LI < 18 months
(MH/LI = Mental Handicap/Language Impairment)

FIG. 2.4.   Proportion of verbal and nonverbal subjects meeting *DSM–IV/*
ICD–10 criteria for autism in one or all domains.

limit the potential relationship with other variables such as number of affected relatives.

There are strong associations between scores on autism diagnostic instruments, level of impairment as measured by verbal and nonverbal IQ, and language delay. This occurs because the most common research measures used in diagnosing autism include a number of developmental items intended to assess behaviors consistently present in most children by 18 months of age (Szatmari et al., 2002). For example, for each domain on the ADI–R (social reciprocity, communication, restricted and repetitive patterns of behaviors), as shown in Fig. 2.4, more than half of preschool children without autistic spectrum disorders, but with moderate to severe mental handicap and language delay, met criteria for autism; less than 10% of children with milder language delays and/or mental handicap met criteria for autism (Lord, Storoschuk, Rutter, & Pickles, 1993). When full ADI–R diagnostic criteria were applied to this sample of preschool children, about 40% of severely language-impaired, moderately to severely retarded children, all of whom had nonverbal mental ages below 18 months, met ADI–R criteria for autism. In contrast were much smaller numbers of false positives in children with better verbal skills. Similar findings have been reported with samples of older children with mental retardation as well (Nordin & Gillberg, 1996).

UNIVERSALITY OF LANGUAGE DELAYS
IN AUTISTIC SPECTRUM DISORDERS

Delays in language are not sufficient or unique for all autistic spectrum disorders despite the crucial importance of language delay in consideration of the disorders. The lack of concordance for broadly defined language skill, as measured by verbal IQ, within twin pairs and family members with autism has been a particularly interesting finding. As shown in Fig. 2.5 (Le Couteur et al., 1996), the concordance between monozygotic twins in verbal IQ was no greater than the concordance between twins randomly paired with unrelated children from the same sample. In Fig. 2.5, visual perusal suggested there was in fact quite high agreement (less than a 10-point discrepancy) for about half of the sample, but the remaining half showed IQ discrepancies from 25 to 80 points. Depending on the tests used to measure verbal skill, it is also possible that floor effects accounted for some of the lack of difference in the subjects at the lower end of IQ ranges.

In addition, when growth in receptive and/or expressive language from ages 2 to 5 years, measured by either direct assessment (i.e., Mullen Scales of Early Learning) or parent report (i.e., Vineland Adaptive Behav-

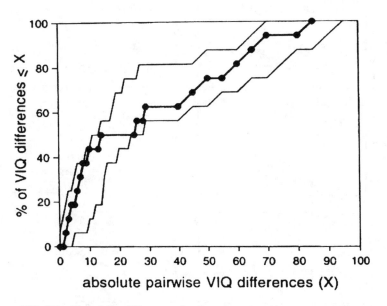

FIG. 2.5. Verbal IQ differences for monozygotic twins versus random pairs.

ior Scales), was observed in our sample of children referred for possible autism at age 2, the variability in language progress was significant when children were grouped by initial clinical diagnosis (see Figs. 2.6 and 2.7). However, as shown in Fig. 2.7, the variability in these growth curves decreased significantly when the children were grouped by diagnosis at age 5. At least for these diagnosticians, language skill at age 5 had a significant effect on diagnosis. Children who initially received autism diagnoses, but who had made particularly strong progress in expressive (and generally receptive) language, tended to receive a 5-year-old diagnosis of Pervasive Developmental Disorder-Not Otherwise Specified (PDD-NOS). Children who had initially received an autism or PDD-NOS diagnoses, but who made little progress in language, tended to receive a diagnosis of autism at age 5.

These groupings were based on clinicians' judgments, either as part of a clinical protocol or a best estimate consensus procedure, in which the diagnosticians were asked to place children into diagnostic categories. However, when measures are used that allow the possibility of continuous dimensions, such as the Social-Communication scale of the Autism Diagnostic Observation Schedule (ADOS; Lord et al., 2000), it is clear that

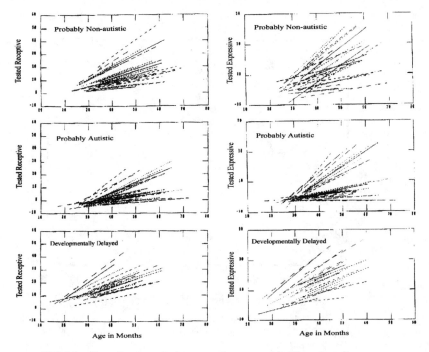

FIG. 2.6.   Growth curves for language from ages 2 to 5 based on diagnoses at age 2.

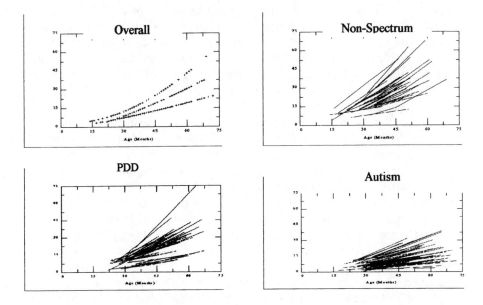

FIG. 2.7.   Growth curves for language from ages 2 to 5 based on diagnoses at age 5.

there are continuous dimensions that characterize children within autistic spectrum disorder (see Fig. 2.8). For example, in Module 1 of the ADOS, which is the module given to children who do not yet speak or are just beginning to use a few words, almost 80% of the children without autism (most of whom had other handicaps such as language delay and mental retardation) received total scores of 4 points or less. A score of 4 was also

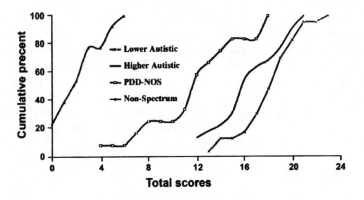

FIG. 2.8.   Cumulative distribution of total ADOS algorithm scores for Module 1.

the lowest score of a child with a clinical diagnosis of PDD-NOS. More striking, however, was that the scores of about two thirds of the children with a diagnosis of PDD-NOS overlapped with the scores of higher functioning children with autism and children with autism who were not high functioning. Children, at least on these measures, did not fall easily into separable categories except autism spectrum disorder and not autism spectrum disorder.

Given the increasing prevalence estimates of autistic disorders, it is particularly important to also consider children who do not meet classic criteria for autism, but still have many of the same behavioral difficulties. As the prevalence estimates have increased, the proportion of children with autistic spectrum disorders who are considered nonverbal has changed, as has the proportion of children with autism who do not have mental retardation. In Fig. 2.9, the prevalence rates for autism showed an increase around the time of the release of *DSM–III–R* and an additional increase in the last 5 years. Some of the increase may be accounted for by further shifts in the diagnostic criteria for autism (i.e., greater broadening of the definition) and some by the inclusion of other disorders under the umbrella of autistic spectrum disorders. However, the full explanation is not yet clear.

HOW MANY CHILDREN WITH AUTISTIC SPECTRUM DISORDERS ARE NONVERBAL?

Although earlier studies described about half of the children with autism as *nonverbal*, recent estimates suggest this is no longer the case (McGee, Morrier, & Daly, 1999). The increased prevalence of autistic spectrum disorders has been accounted for by children with less obvious and/or less severe language delays who are often not mentally retarded and who in many cases, although not all, show milder symptoms of autism (Yeargin-Allsopp et al., 2003). Part of the difficulty in interpreting this change is due to the fluctuating definition of *nonverbal*. This term has been used to include children who may have some words, but do not use words as a primary method of communication, or children who do not have enough language to speak intelligibly to strangers, or children with few or no words. Nonetheless, it has been reiterated in many papers that 50% of children with autism are nonverbal (Lord & Rutter, 1994).

Using data from several different studies, we used the categories of language level from the ADOS, an observational scale, and the ADI–R, a parent report measure, to characterize the language level of participants in our longitudinal research. In the ADOS, because it is based on direct observation, the tasks that are deemed appropriate are in part determined by

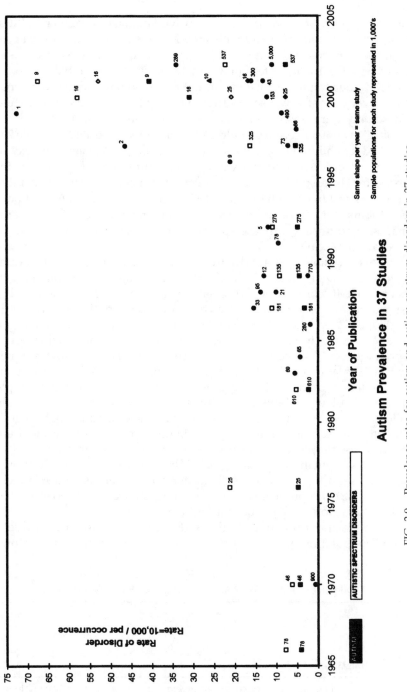

FIG. 2.9. Prevalence rates for autism and autism spectrum disorders in 37 studies.

17

the child's level of spontaneous expressive language using general discriminations. Children are administered Module 1 if they do not yet produce spontaneous, nonroutinized phrases of two or more words consistently. Module 1 is used for children who are truly nonverbal (i.e., have limited understanding or use of words) and who have single words but do not yet consistently use nonroutinized sentences. Therefore, a child whose only phrase is, "I want cookie," but who cannot use "want" or "cookie" in another context would be administered Module 1. Module 2 is intended for children who have some phrase speech and some syntax but are not yet producing complex multiclausal utterances. Module 3 is intended for children who have fluent complex speech. As shown in Table 2.1, of 164 children receiving the ADOS modules at age 10, 63% of both longitudinal cohorts of children (one in Chicago and one in North Carolina) were producing sufficient spontaneous phrase speech to be administered either Module 2 or 3.

It is also possible to group children from the same study by ADI–R categories. The ADI–R makes distinctions within a more narrow range, such that an ADI–R score of 2 on the "overall level of language" item is used to describe a child who does not use words on a daily basis. A score of 1 is used for children who produce single words and some phrases, but do not produce flexible three-word phrases including a verb. Thus, in this case, a score of 2 would be considered nonverbal and includes a lower upper threshold of language (i.e., less than five words used on a daily basis) than the children receiving Module 1 on the ADOS (who may use simple phrases). Looking at Table 2.2, the reader can see that 64% to 68% of the children in these studies would have been considered nonverbal at age 2, although some of them did have some single words on the basis of parent report. These proportions dropped greatly by age 3. By age 9, only 14% to 20% of this population, consisting of children referred for possible autism at age 2, could have been considered nonverbal even using a relatively conservative conception of verbal (so treating children who spoke as nonverbal, but who may have used a few words a day).

These are not population studies and so do not necessarily represent the full population of children with autistic spectrum disorders. How-

TABLE 2.1
Proportion of Children With ASD Receiving ADOS Modules at Age 9

Module	North Carolina	Chicago
ADOS Module 1	36.6	32.4
ADOS Module 2	24.4	26.5
ADOS Module 3	39.0	41.2

Note. These children comprised consecutive referrals for possible autism at age 2 to two different clinics.

TABLE 2.2
Proportion of ADI–R Language Classifications at Different Ages

Classification	Age 2		Age 3		Age 5	Age 9	
ADI–R Overall Level of Language	North Carolina	Chicago	North Carolina	Chicago	North Carolina	North Carolina	Chicago
Flexible three-word phrases or more	9.2	6.1	26.2	48.7	58.1	66.7	76.2
Use of five single words on a daily basis or more	26.7	25.6	24.3	17.9	12.1	13.5	9.5
Less than five words used on a daily basis	64.1	68.3	49.5	33.3	29.8	19.8	14.3

ever, because the children were referred for possible autism when they were very young, it is quite likely that they represent a more severe subset of children than a population obtained at older ages or a population obtained through broader surveillance methods than this clinical sample. Given that this sample is likely to have particularly severe difficulties, it seems clear that we can no longer conclude that 50% of children with autism are nonverbal. These conclusions are summarized in Table 2.3. This is also a lesson in the need to be quite specific about what we mean by the term *nonverbal*, which may be interpreted in different ways in different contexts (e.g., even in two diagnostic instruments by some of the same authors). Integrating information from the ADOS and ADI–R resulted in only 14% to 20% of these samples not using five or more words on a daily basis.

A further question arising from these data is whether there are "sticky ceilings" associated with particular measurements of the language abilities of children with autism (Lord, Pickles, DiLavore, & Shulman, 1996; Taylor, Pickering, Lord, & Pickles, 1997). That is, are there age or language

TABLE 2.3
Percentages of Children With ASD by Expressive Language Level
at Age 9 Based on Combinations of ADI–R and ADOS Scores

Category	North Carolina	Chicago
Fluent language (ADOS Module 3)	43.0	40.9
Phrases but not "fluent" (ADI–R = 0, but ADOS Module 2)	23.4	35.3
Words but not three-word phrases (ADI–R = 1; ADOS Module 1 or 2)	10.5	13.8
No consistent words (ADI–R = 2; ADOS Module 1)	14.3	19.8

levels that most children do not exceed because of particular characteristics of the measurement tool or because of the specific nature of the language deficit in autism? For example, at least in the North Carolina sample, the number of children who had flexible phrases did not increase between the ages of 5 to 9 (see Table 2.2), although there were increases in the number of children who used single words and simple phrases. Here we have used extremely gross characterizations of language. Nevertheless, these results raise the question of whether, given existing treatment methods, there are specific points of language development that some children with autism cannot get beyond even with intense intervention. Much more knowledge is needed about the natural history and specific nature of language acquisition in response to treatment in autistic spectrum disorders.

DEVELOPMENTAL QUESTIONS ABOUT LANGUAGE ACQUISITION

Two other particularly interesting questions concerning the acquisition of language for children with autism are: How can we best describe what occurs in children with autism who fail to acquire speech? How do we account for the phenomenon of word loss usually in the second year of life?

For these questions, we took a somewhat different approach than we had in addressing how many children were nonverbal. In this case, we looked at the developmental trajectories of children in our longitudinal studies and considered the characteristics of children who have particular outcomes. We focused on one outcome that occurred in children who were nonverbal, as defined by a parent's description of a child using fewer than five words expressively at 5 years of age. From our North Carolina longitudinal sample, we were particularly interested in those children whose scores on nonverbal tasks suggested they have a sufficient general developmental capability to learn language, and yet they made little progress in language development. Of the 33 children who had fewer than five words used on a daily basis at age 5 (out of a population of 104 children with ASD), 21 of them had nonverbal mental age scores below 24 months. During their preschool years, there was a verbal–nonverbal discrepancy of about a standard deviation for almost all children in the sample. This meant that language delay could be accounted for by general nonverbal delays, as well as an additional overlay of autistic features (which would account for the additional standard deviation of delay) in about two thirds of children without use of words (see Figs. 2.10a, 2.10b).

However, this still left about 12% of the sample (12 children with autism or PDD-NOS) who still had no words at age 5, although their nonver-

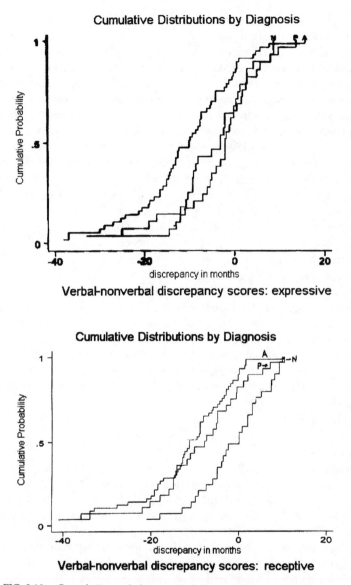

FIG. 2.10.   Cumulative verbal–nonverbal discrepancy scores by diagnosis:
Expressive and receptive.

bal mental ages were 24 months or higher. These children had nonverbal–verbal discrepancies of greater than 30 to 40 points. Looking at their
developmental milestones from 2 to 5 years, they were not different from
any of the other children referred for ASD (grouped by language level) at
age 2 except that they had higher nonverbal skills (by definition) than the

most profoundly retarded group of children. This group of children with greater nonverbal–verbal discrepancies was of particular interest in the Joseph et al. (2002) article as well. In terms of social skills, these children did not differ from the group that had more delayed nonverbal skills. They were more abnormal than children with comparable nonverbal skills. What was most interesting was the parallel between receptive and expressive language. Although these groups were defined purely on the basis of expressive delay, children with significant expressive language delay also showed significant receptive language delay independent of level of nonverbal problem solving. We did not have measures of apraxia or speech-motor problems that we also might expect to contribute to these patterns. However, we were surprised to discover that children who had limited productive expressive language in the face of relatively strong nonverbal skills also had significant receptive language problems, thus indicating that this was not just a motor-speech problem.

Another way to look at this is to plot nonverbal mental age by expressive language mental age for children with autism, other autistic spectrum disorders (primarily PDD-NOS), and nonspectrum disorders as shown in Fig. 2.11. This indicates that children with autism are generally at a higher nonverbal level before they acquire single words than are children with other disorders. It also supports a relationship between nonverbal skills and language, and it provides a nonverbal parallel to the findings discussed by Happé (1995), who suggested that children with autism need higher verbal ability to reach particular ability levels on theory of mind tasks.

Overall, these findings suggest the need for theories to describe the deficits of autism in terms of social cognitive patterns specific to this disorder. Such deficits would account for delayed language in most children early on, but also allow for differential rates of change in language skill across subsets within the disorder. A somewhat similar approach with higher functioning older children with autism and SLIs has been proposed by Tager-Flusberg (Kjelgaard & Tager-Flusberg, 2001; Tager-Flusberg, chap. 2, this volume).

Another interesting trajectory in language development in autism is a pattern of acquisition of a small number of single words in the beginning of the second year of life that are then lost and may be replaced later on or may never recur (see Fig. 2.12). For this study, preliminary data are again based on subjects from our North Carolina sample. We characterized about 20% of the children as a language loss group defined by use of at least three meaningful, spontaneous words besides *Momma* and *Dada* for at least 1 month, followed by no spoken words used for at least 1 month. This category (described in more detail in Lord, Shulman, & DiLavore, in press) was developed primarily to achieve reliability on interview ratings

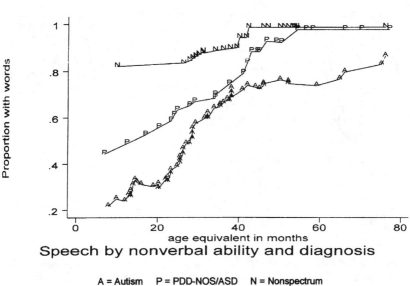

Kernel smooth estimator of proportion

Speech by nonverbal ability and diagnosis

A = Autism   P = PDD-NOS/ASD   N = Nonspectrum

FIG. 2.11.   Speech by nonverbal ability and diagnosis.

of parents' reports across time (during repeated administrations of the ADI–R) and consistency within the interview (from the early questions concerning language loss to the later questions concerning loss of other skills). Figure 2.12 shows the ages that children with autistic spectrum disorders with and without losses acquired first words.

In general, children who later lost skills, as shown in Fig. 2.12, used their first words around their first birthday, similar to the normal controls and the developmentally delayed children. Children who lost words tended to regain them at ages that were similar to the ages when children who had never lost words gained their first words.

Although previous studies found no differences between children who showed a pattern of early word loss and those who did not (Fombonne & Chakrabarti, 2001), we found differences in our sample of children first assessed at age 2 (Lord et al., in press). These differences occurred at this early point in development and did not necessarily become stable differences in later preschool years. Thus, parents of children with autistic spectrum disorders who reported that the child had early word loss also reported that they first became concerned about their child at a later age (at 19 months), compared with parents of children who did not report any history of word loss who indicated that they were first concerned at an earlier age (at about 15 months; see Table 2.4).

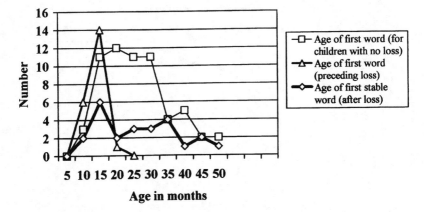

FIG. 2.12.   Age of first words according to loss categories for children with
ASD who used words by age 5.

By combining information from parents' description of language development at age 2 with a detailed interview about language development and loss at about age 7, we were able to classify children into three
groups. These groups were: children whose parents consistently said
they had a word loss or regression, children whose parents consistently
said they had no word loss or regression, and children whose parents'
descriptions of loss or no loss changed between the time the children
were 2 years old to the later interview (Luyster et al., in press). In doing
this, we also showed that parents who initially reported that their child
had no word loss, but later described such a loss, reported later ages of
onset than in the previous interview. Parents who had initially described
an early loss of words, but who later did not report such a loss, reported
an earlier age of onset of autism (associated with no word loss). A small
number of parents provided more detailed and accurate data, with hind-
sight at the later interview, as compared with the interview when their
children were 2 years old.

TABLE 2.4
Age When Parents Reported First Concerns in the ADI–R

Concern	Mean Age in Months	Range	Standard Deviation
Word loss	19.26	8–36	6.38
No word loss	15.3	2–43	10.19
No word loss → Word loss	21.5	14–34	6.00
Word loss → No word loss	14.8	6–24	8.32

Using a modified version of the MacArthur Communicative Development Inventory (Fenson, 1989), we were also able to show, according to parents' reports of how much their children understood, that children who had word loss did not differ in how many words they understood compared to children who had no word loss before 24 months. There were significant differences, however, in how many words each group used expressively. Parents of children who had a word loss said they understood both more single words and more phrases at age 2 than children who did not show a word loss. By age 3, the children with word loss were described as understanding fewer words and phrases than the children without losses (Luyster et al., in press).

It is also important to note that the majority of parents whose children reported a word loss also reported losses or abnormalities in social skills—a finding that replicates several other studies (Goldberg et al., 2003; Kurita, 1985; Luyster et al., in press). Early social abnormalities or losses were most common in children who lost words or who showed a fluctuating pattern of losses, but they also occurred in children who lost nonword vocalizations and had no words at all (Lord et al., in press).

Researchers have attempted to explain this regression in a number of ways. Children who had some words that they lost may have failed to shift from using initial words as associations to using communicative intent and developing symbolism. These children may have failed to develop toddler equivalents of theory of mind or executive function, or failed to develop beginning working memory strategies. More neurologically oriented proposals, primarily by analogy, have suggested that there may be a failure of cortical, specifically frontal lobe, development that could actively support higher order processing beyond the acquisition of first words. A beginning attempt has been made to link these regressive changes, or more general changes in social behavior without specific word loss, to changes in brain volume or to the development of the cerebellum in the first few years of life in children with autism (Courchesne et al., 2001).

Probably the most well-known proposal to explain developmental regression has been the attempt to link what is referred to as *regressive autism* to toxicities—namely, a response to a vaccination or accumulating levels of toxins. However, neither the phenomenon of regression nor the diagnosis of autism has been carefully defined in these studies (see Fombonne & Cook, 2003). In addition, there are methodological issues, such as parents' interpretation of changes, most of which are described as gradual, but which may also be solidified in memory by particular occasions (remembering their child's behavior on a particular vacation or the birth of a sibling). Nevertheless, with the use of retrospective videotapes (Goldberg et al., 2003; Osterling & Dawson, 1994; Werner, Dawson, Osterling, & Dinno,

2000), research suggests that this phenomenon of word loss is real and not something that is confabulated by parents. At this point we are limited in our understanding of it because we must rely on retrospective reports.

SUMMARY AND CONCLUSIONS

Overall, there are many aspects of language delay that have significant implications for our understanding of autistic spectrum disorders. To date most research (with a few important exceptions such as Kjelgaard & Tager-Flusberg, 2001) on the relation between language and autism has used general measures of verbal functioning. However, studies that have incorporated numerous measures have shown high correlations between receptive and expressive language measures as well as with early developmental measures such as the Mullen Scales of Early Learning (Taylor et al., 1997; Venter et al., 1992). Methodologically, it is a challenge to measure change in skills using standardized measures that necessarily shift as the skills reconfigure, and this has limited our knowledge about trajectories of language development over time. However, there are currently a number of creative attempts to develop methods that minimize these difficulties. It is also important to distinguish between the effect of the level of language impairment (e.g., verbal IQ or standard scores) and the effects of absolute language level—either expressive or receptive, or both—on other behaviors because this affects how we view the relation between language and behaviors associated with autism (Happé, 1995). Recently, many of the studies on language and autism primarily control the effect of language development to address the broader conceptualizations of cognition and social development such as theory of mind or central coherence. This strategy has been important in improving our understanding of the specificity of various cognitive deficits in autism. However, it now seems time to step back and take a more serious look at the unique trajectories of language development that may occur in autistic spectrum disorders. These trajectories may have important implications for understanding the etiology, nature of change, and potential response to treatment in autistic spectrum disorders.

REFERENCES

Alarcón, M., Cantor, R. M., Liu, J., Gilliam, T. C., the Autism Genetic Resource Exchange Consortium (AGRE), & Geschwind, D. H. (2002). Evidence for a language quantitative trait locus on chromosome 7q in multiplex autism families. *American Journal of Human Genetics, 70,* 60–71.

Bolton, P., Macdonald, H., Pickles, A., Rios, P., Goode, S., Crowson, M., Bailey, A., & Rutter, M. (1994). A case-control family history study of autism. *Journal of Child Psychology and Psychiatry and Allied Disciplines, 35,* 877–900.

Bradford, Y., Haines, J., Hutcheson, H., Gardiner, M., Braun, T., Sheffield, V., Cassavant, T., Huang, W., Wang, K., Vieland, V., Folstein, S., Santangelo, S., & Piven, J. (2001). Incorporating language phenotypes strengthens evidence of linkage to autism. *American Journal of Medical Genetics, 105,* 539–547.

Buxbaum, J. D., Silverman, J. M., Smith, C. J., Kilifarski, M., Reichert, J., Hollander, E., Lawlor, B. A., Fitzgerald, M., Greenberg, D. A., & Davis, K. L. (2001). Evidence for a susceptibility gene for autism on chromosome 2 and for genetic heterogeneity. *American Journal of Human Genetics, 68,* 1514–1520.

Courchesne, E., Karns, C. M., Davis, H. R., Ziccardi, R., Carper, R. A., Tigue, Z. D., Chisum, H. J., Moses, P., Pierce, K., Lord, C., Lincoln, A. J., Pizzo, S., Schreibman, L., Haas, R. H., Akshoomoff, N. A., & Courchesne, R. Y. (2001). Unusual brain growth patterns in early life in patients with autistic disorder: An MRI study. *Neurology, 57,* 245–254.

Dunn, L. M. (1997). *Peabody Picture Vocabulary Test* (3rd ed.). Circle Pines, MN: American Guidance Service.

Eisenmajer, R., Prior, M., Leekam, S., Wing, L., Ong, B., Gould, J., & Welham, M. (1998). Delayed language onset as a predictor of clinical symptoms in pervasive developmental disorders. *Journal of Autism and Developmental Disorders, 28,* 527–533.

Elliott, C. D. (1990). *Differential Abilities Scale.* San Antonio, TX: The Psychological Corporation.

Fenson, L. (1989). *The MacArthur Communicative Development Inventory: Infant and toddler versions.* San Diego, CA: San Diego State University.

Folstein, S. E., & Mankoski, R. E. (2000). Chromosome 7q: Where autism meets language disorder? *American Journal of Human Genetics, 67,* 278–281.

Fombonne, E., & Chakrabarti, S. (2001, October). No evidence for a new variant of measles-mumps-rubella-induced autism. *Pediatrics, 108,* e58. Retrieved from http://www.pediatrics.org/content/vol108/issue4/index.shtml.

Fombonne, E., & Cook, E. H. (2003). MMR and autistic enterocolitis: Consistent epidemiological failure to find an association. *Molecular Psychiatry, 8,* 133–134.

Goldberg, W. A., Osann, K., Laulhere, T. M., Strauss-Swan, R., Filipek, P. A., & Spence, M. A. (2003, April). *Use of home videotapes to confirm parental reports of regression in autism.* Poster session presented at the biennial meeting of the Society for Research in Child Development, Tampa, FL.

Happé, F. G. (1995). The role of age and verbal ability in the theory of mind task performance of subjects with autism. *Child Development, 66,* 843–855.

Howlin, P., & Goode, S. (1998). Outcome in adult life for people with autism and Asperger's syndrome. In F. R. Volkmar (Ed.), *Autism and pervasive developmental disorders* (pp. 209–241). New York: Cambridge University Press.

Howlin, P., Mawhood, L., & Rutter, M. (2000). Autism and developmental receptive language disorder—A follow-up comparison in early adult life: II. Social, behavioural, and psychiatric outcomes. *Journal of Child Psychology and Psychiatry and Allied Disciplines, 41,* 561–578.

International Molecular Genetic Study of Autism Consortium (IMGSAC). (1998). A full genome screen for autism with evidence for linkage to a region on chromosome 7q. *Human Molecular Genetics, 7,* 571–578.

International Molecular Genetic Study of Autism Consortium (IMGSAC). (2001). Further characterization of the autism susceptibility locus AUTS1 on chromosome 7q. *Human Molecular Genetics, 10,* 973–982.

Joseph, R. M., Tager-Flusberg, H., & Lord, C. (2002). Cognitive profiles and social-communicative functioning in children with autism spectrum disorder. *Journal of Child Psychology and Psychiatry and Allied Disciplines, 43,* 807–821.

Kjelgaard, M. M., & Tager-Flusberg, H. (2001). An investigation of language impairment in autism: Implications for genetic subgroups. *Language and Cognitive Processes, 16,* 287–308.

Kurita, H. (1985). Infantile autism with speech loss before the age of thirty months. *Journal of the American Academy of Child Psychiatry, 24,* 191–196.

Le Couteur, A., Bailey, A., Goode, S., Pickles, A., Robertson, S., Gottesman, I., & Rutter, M. (1996). A broader phenotype of autism: The clinical spectrum in twins. *Journal of Child Psychology and Psychiatry and Allied Disciplines, 37,* 785–801.

Lord, C., & Pickles, A. (1996). Language level and nonverbal social-communicative behaviors in autistic and language-delayed children. *Journal of the American Academy of Child and Adolescent Psychiatry, 35,* 1542–1550.

Lord, C., Pickles, A., DiLavore, P. C., & Shulman, C. (1996). *Longitudinal studies of young children referred for possible autism.* Paper presented at the biannual meeting of the International Society for Research in Child and Adolescent Psychopathology, Los Angeles, CA.

Lord, C., Risi, S., Lambrecht, L., Cook, E. H., Jr., Leventhal, B. L., DiLavore, P. C., Pickles, A., & Rutter, M. (2000). The Autism Diagnostic Observation Schedule–Generic: A standard measure of social and communication deficits associated with the spectrum of autism. *Journal of Autism and Developmental Disorders, 30,* 205–223.

Lord, C., & Rutter, M. (1994). Autism and pervasive development disorders. In E. Taylor (Ed.), *Child and adolescent psychiatry: Modern approaches* (Vol. 3, pp. 569–593). Oxford, England: Blackwell.

Lord, C., Rutter, M., & Le Couteur, A. (1994). Autism Diagnostic Interview Revised: A revised version of a diagnostic interview for caregivers of individuals with possible pervasive developmental disorders. *Journal of Autism and Developmental Disorders, 24,* 659–685.

Lord, C., & Schopler, E. (1989). The role of age at assessment, developmental level, and test in the stability of intelligence scores in young autistic children. *Journal of Autism and Developmental Disorders, 19,* 483–499.

Lord, C., Shulman, C., & DiLavore, P. (in press). Regression and word loss in autistic spectrum disorders. *Journal of Child Psychology and Psychiatry and Allied Disciplines.*

Lord, C., Storoschuk, S., Rutter, M., & Pickles, A. (1993). Using the ADI–R to diagnose autism in preschool children. *Infant Mental Health Journal, 14,* 234–252.

Lotter, V. (1978). Follow-up studies. In M. Rutter & E. Schopler (Eds.), *Autism: A reappraisal of concepts and treatment* (pp. 475–496). New York: Plenum.

Luyster, R., Richler, J., Risi, S., Hsu, W., Dawson, G., Bernier, R., Dunn, M., Hyman, S. L., McMahahon, W. M., Goudie, J., Minshew, N., Rogers, S., Sigman, M., Spence, M. A., Tager-Flusberg, H., Volkmar, F., & Lord, C. (in press). Early regression in social communication in autistic spectrum disorders. *Developmental Neuropsychology.*

McGee, G. G., Morrier, M. J., & Daly, T. (1999). An incidental teaching approach to early intervention for toddlers with autism. *Journal of the Association for the Severely Handicapped, 24,* 133–146.

Mullen, E. (1995). *Mullen Scales of Early Learning.* Circle Pines, MN: American Guidance Service Inc.

Nordin, V., & Gillberg, C. (1996). Autism spectrum disorders in children with physical or mental disability or both: II. Screening aspects. *Developmental Medicine and Child Neurology, 38,* 314–324.

Osterling, J., & Dawson, G. (1994). Early recognition of children with autism: A study of first birthday home videotapes. *Journal of Autism and Developmental Disorders, 24,* 247–257.

Reynell, J., & Gruber, C. (1978). *Reynell Developmental Language Scales—US edition.* Los Angeles: Western Psychological Services.

Rutter, M. (1978). Diagnosis and definition. In M. Rutter & E. Schopler (Eds.), *Autism: A reappraisal of concepts and treatment* (pp. 1–26). New York: Plenum.

Siegel, B., Pliner, C., Eschler, J., & Elliott, G. R. (1988). How children with autism are diagnosed: Difficulties in identification of children with multiple developmental delays. *Journal of Developmental and Behavioral Pediatrics, 9,* 199–204.

Sparrow, S., Balla, D., & Cicchetti, D. (1984). *Vineland Adaptive Behavior Scales*. Circle Pines, MN: American Guidance Service.

Szatmari, P., Merette, C., Bryson, S. E., Thivierge, J., Roy, M. A., Cayer, M., & Maziade, M. (2002). Quantifying dimensions in autism: A factor-analytic study. *Journal of the American Academy of Child and Adolescent Psychiatry, 41*, 467–474.

Tadevosyan-Leyfer, O., Dowd, M., Mankoski, R., Winklosky, B., Putnam, S., McGrath, L., Tager-Flusberg, H., & Folstein, S. (2003). A principal components analysis of the Autism Diagnostic Interview–Revised. *Journal of the American Academy of Child and Adolescent Psychiatry, 42*, 864–872.

Taylor, A., Pickering, K., Lord, C., & Pickles, A. (1997). Mixed and multilevel models for longitudinal data: Growth curve models of language development. In G. Dunn (Ed.), *Recent advances in medical statistics* (pp. 1–15). London: Edward Arnold.

Venter, A., Lord, C., & Schopler, E. (1992). A follow-up study of high functioning autistic children. *Journal of Child Psychology and Psychiatry and Allied Disciplines, 33*, 489–507.

Werner, E., Dawson, G., Osterling, J., & Dinno, N. (2000). Brief report: Recognition of autism spectrum disorder before one year of age: A retrospective study based on home videotapes. *Journal of Autism and Developmental Disorders, 30*, 157–162.

Yeargin-Allsopp, M., Rice, C., Karapurkar, T., Doernberg, N., Boyle, C., & Murphy, C. (2003). Prevalence of autism in a US metropolitan area. *Journal of the American Medical Association, 289*, 49–55.

3

Do Autism and Specific Language Impairment Represent Overlapping Language Disorders?

Helen Tager-Flusberg
Boston University School of Medicine

Autism is diagnosed on the basis of impairments in three behavioral domains: communication, social interaction, and repetitive and stereotyped patterns of behavior, interests, and activities (American Psychological Association, 1994). Within the domain of communication, deficits in both verbal and nonverbal aspects of communication are considered key symptoms, and these are frequently the first signs of disorder noted by parents or clinicians (Kurita, 1985; Lord & Paul, 1997). In recent years, much of the focus of research into communication deficits has been on those aspects that are both specific and universal across the spectrum of people with autistic disorder (Tager-Flusberg, 1996). There is a general consensus that pragmatic deficits, especially in conversational discourse and understanding language as a system for communicating intended meaning, are the key universal impairments that define autism (Lord & Paul, 1997; Tager-Flusberg, 1999). At the same time, the majority of individuals with autism also suffer language deficits that go beyond impairments in pragmatics, although these deficits have been relatively understudied by autism researchers (Kjelgaard & Tager-Flusberg, 2001). In this chapter, I explore the hypothesis that among children with autism there is a subgroup that has language impairments that are parallel to those that characterize children with specific language impairment (SLI). I review evidence from our recent behavioral and brain imaging studies, which suggest that this subgroup within the autism spectrum has SLI. In the final section, I consider the implications of this research for genetic studies of both autism and SLI.

BACKGROUND

One of the earliest hypotheses about the underlying cognitive deficits in autism, proposed by Rutter (1965) and Churchill (1972), was that autism is an extreme variant of developmental dysphasia, as SLI was called then. On this view, autism was caused by profound deficits in language and communication leading to significant social impairment and a restricted repertoire of behavior and interests. This hypothesis led to an important series of studies by Rutter and his colleagues comparing a group of boys with autism to an age- and IQ-matched group of boys with SLI (Bartak, Rutter, & Cox, 1975, 1977). The children in both groups were selected on the basis of significant problems in both receptive and expressive language. Among the key findings, both similarities (e.g., on measures of expressive language and grammatical complexity) and differences (e.g., presence of echolalia and pronoun reversals in the children with autism) were reported for language and other related measures. In addition, there was a small group of boys (about 10% of the sample) who were classified as "mixed," in that they showed atypical language disorder with some autism features. By the time the children reached middle childhood, the boys with autism showed more severe language problems than the boys with SLI (Cantwell, Baker, Rutter, & Mawhood, 1989). The original hypothesis—that autism is an extreme variant of SLI—was not supported given the many unique features in both language and social behavior among the boys with autism. Nevertheless, these studies were the first to suggest that there is some overlap in the populations of autism and SLI in terms of deficits in expressive language and in the presence of the mixed group who shared characteristics of both autism and SLI.

Following these seminal studies, psycholinguistic researchers studying autism turned their attention toward the unique characteristics of children with autism compared with children with other kinds of language disorders. This led to the focus in autism research on pragmatic and communicative aspects of language (Baltaxe, 1977). Much is now known about the range of pragmatic impairments that define autism, which include a restricted range of speech acts (Loveland, Landry, Hughes, Hall, & McEvoy, 1988; Wetherby, 1986), conversational and narrative deficits (Loveland & Tunali, 1993; Tager-Flusberg & Anderson, 1991; Tager-Flusberg & Sullivan, 1995), an inability to consider the listener's perspective (Paul & Cohen, 1984), and difficulties understanding nonliteral language (Happé, 1994). These deficits clearly distinguish between children with autism and children with SLI, although studies have identified milder pragmatic difficulties in the latter group (e.g., Craig & Evans, 1993; Hadley & Rice, 1991). These are typically interpreted as secondary to the main linguistic deficits that are the key to the diagnosis of SLI. In contrast, because in autism severe pragmatic deficits are found across the spectrum of children and adults with autism, they are viewed as orthogonal to impairments in linguistic knowledge, which are more variable and not among the defining criteria.

OVERLAP BETWEEN AUTISM AND SLI

The potential overlap between subgroups of children with autism and nonautistic children with language disorders has become a topic of interest and controversy among speech-language clinical researchers. Allen and Rapin (1980, 1992) reviewed a large sample of unselected children with autism or language disorder and identified three major subtypes in preschool-age children: mixed receptive and expressive disorders, higher order/pragmatic processing disorders, and dyspraxic/phonological disorders. About two thirds of the children with autism in their samples had mixed receptive/expressive disorders, and one third had primarily pragmatic disorders without significant linguistic deficits. The autistic children with mixed receptive/expressive disorders had deficits in phonological processing and syntax as well as impoverished vocabularies, and these children were comparable to about half the nonautistic children with a language disorder who fit the profile for SLI. In Allen and Rapin's studies, no children with autism were classified with verbal dyspraxia or other purely expressive phonology disorders (Allen, 1989; Rapin, 1996; Rapin & Dunn, 2003). At the same time, about 15% of nonautistic children with a language disorder were classified with higher order processing disorders, including a subtype referred to as *semantic-pragmatic* disorder, reminiscent of the mixed group identified in the studies by Bartak and his colleagues (Bartak et al., 1975, 1977).

Semantic-pragmatic disorder, now referred to as pragmatic language impairment (PLI; Conti-Ramsden & Botting, 1999), was also identified as a subtype of SLI by Bishop and her colleagues in England (Bishop & Rosenbloom, 1987). This diagnosis became quite controversial, with numerous researchers claiming that PLI is no different from high-functioning autism or Asperger syndrome (e.g., Brook & Bowler, 1992; Shields, Varley, Broks, & Simpson, 1996). In a recent study, Bishop and Norbury (2002) used rigorous and objective measures, including the Autism Diagnostic Interview (Lord, Rutter, & LeCouteur, 1994) and the Autism Diagnostic Observation Schedule (Lord et al., 2000), to assess whether children with PLI met the diagnosis for autism spectrum disorder. They found that although some children with PLI did meet criteria for an autism spectrum disorder on one or both of these instruments, others exhibited no clear autism symptoms outside the communication domain. This latter group used stereotyped language with abnormal prosody, but they were sociable, did not have restricted or repetitive behaviors, and had no deficits in nonverbal communication. Bishop (2000) argued that PLI is a distinct subtype of language disorder that can be differentiated from autism. At the same time, she emphasizes that there are no clear boundaries among autism, SLI, and PLI. Instead these are overlapping heterogeneous disorders that lie on a continuum.

HETEROGENEITY IN LANGUAGE ABILITY IN AUTISM

The studies by Allen and Rapin (1992; Rapin & Dunn, 2003) on different language subtypes in autism, and Bishop's emphasis on a continuum between autism and other language disorders, highlight what has been known since Kanner's (1943) original description of autism: There is enormous variability in language skills among children with this disorder. Almost half the population has no functional language skills, many show significant delays in the onset and developmental course of language acquisition, and some children attain superior linguistic skills especially on measures of single word vocabulary (Bailey, Phillips, & Rutter, 1996; Lord & Paul, 1997). Until recently, there has been little direct investigation of this heterogeneity in language among children with autism.

As part of a larger interdisciplinary investigation of language, communication, and social cognition in autism, Margaret Kjelgaard and I conducted a systematic analysis of the performance of a large group of children and adolescents with autism on a set of standardized language tests (Kjelgaard & Tager-Flusberg, 2001). The study included 89 participants (80 boys and 9 girls) between the ages of 4 and 14, all of whom had functional language (able to produce at least some two-word phrases). The participants met *DSM–IV* criteria for autism confirmed by the Autism Diagnostic Interview (ADI) and Autism Diagnostic Observation Schedule (ADOS). In addition to the language assessment, the participants' IQ scores were assessed using the Differential Ability Scales. The average IQ score was 68, and the range was from 25 to 141. Thus, we included a sample that varied widely in cognitive ability.

Each child was administered a battery of standardized language tests over the course of two sessions. The battery included the Goldman–Fristoe Test of Articulation (GF; productive phonology skills), Peabody Picture Vocabulary Test–III (PPVT; receptive one-word vocabulary), Expressive Vocabulary Test (EVT; expressive one-word vocabulary), the Clinical Evaluation of Language Fundamentals (CELF; receptive and expressive morphology, syntax, semantics and working memory for language), and the Repetition of Nonsense Words from the NEPSY (NWRT; phonological processing). Because of the wide range of language skills among this heterogeneous sample, about half the children could not be tested on the CELF and NWRT. In general, the children with higher IQ scores were more likely to have the attention and memory skills needed to complete these more complex and demanding language tests.

Children's performance was assessed using standard scores (mean of 100 and standard deviation of 15). Figure 3.1 presents the data averaged across all the children able to complete the tests. Thus, it includes children who could only be tested on the GF, PPVT, and EVT (who would be at floor on the CELF and NWRT), as well as those more able children who received the full battery. The most interesting finding was that basic articulation is quite spared among children with autism, as evidenced by the average scores obtained on the GF test. This supports Allen and Rapin's finding that verbal children with autism were never classified with ex-

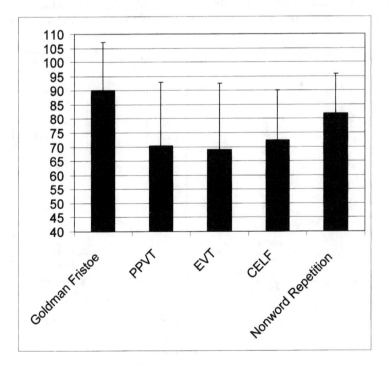

FIG. 3.1.   Profile of language test performance for children with autism.

pressive phonology disorders (Allen, 1989; Rapin, 1996). The large standard deviations included in this graph for all the tests illustrate the wide variability in language skills in this sample.

We divided the children into those whose language test scores were normal, scores between 1 and 2 standard deviations below the mean (borderline), or scores more than 2 standard deviations below the mean (impaired). Here I present the data based on the 44 children on whom all test scores were available, most of whom had nonverbal IQ scores in the normal range. For this analysis, the groups were divided on the basis of their CELF total scores into normal, borderline, and impaired groups. The profiles for the normal and impaired groups are shown in Fig. 3.2, combining PPVT and EVT scores into an average Vocabulary score. About 25% of the children were in the normal group, whereas almost 50% of these higher functioning children with autism fell in the impaired group. The graph shows that these groups have distinctive profiles of language scores. For the normal group, scores on all the language measures were all within the normal range, representing a relatively flat profile. In contrast, the impaired group scored quite differently across the various tests. As before, articulation skills were within the normal range. Higher order grammatical and semantic skills, as measured by the CELF, were most impaired,

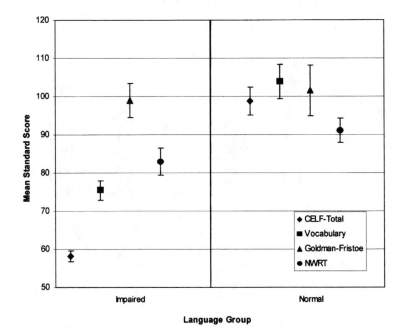

FIG. 3.2.   Profiles of language test scores for normal and impaired children with autism.

and vocabulary and nonword repetition were below average, but somewhat higher than CELF scores. This profile of relative strengths and weaknesses is similar to what has been reported for children with SLI (Tomblin & Zhang, 1999).

This study confirmed the heterogeneity in language skills found among verbal children with autism. About half of our high-functioning children were significantly impaired in language, and their pattern of scores across different language tests mirrored the pattern found for children with SLI.

CLINICAL MARKERS FOR SLI

The studies reviewed thus far suggest parallels between a subgroup of children with autism and children with SLI; however, it is not clear whether these parallels are superficial or whether they reflect more substantive overlap in the phenotypes of these syndromes. Like autism, SLI represents quite a heterogeneous population with different kinds of profiles found among children (Tomblin & Zhang, 1999). The diagnosis of SLI can be quite variable. For example, some children have problems in both receptive and expressive language; others, only in expressive language. There are no clear diagnostic guidelines, including specific instruments or measures, that are used either clinically or in research studies. Nevertheless, in recent years, some consensus has been reached about core language deficits that may be viewed as central to this disorder. Two such deficits have been highlighted: phonological processing and morphosyntax (Tager-Flusberg & Cooper, 1999). Impairments in these aspects of language are now considered important clinical markers that define the phenotype of SLI.

Deficits in phonological processing are measured by nonword repetition tasks. These tasks tap the ability to analyze and reproduce phonological knowledge by asking the child to repeat nonsense words of different syllable lengths that are presented on an audiotape. Numerous studies have shown that children with SLI perform poorly on these kinds of tasks (e.g., Bishop, North, & Donlan, 1996; Dollaghan & Campbell, 1998; Gathercole & Baddeley, 1990; Weismer, Tomblin, Zhang, Buckwalter, Chynoweth, & Jones, 2000). Performance on such tasks differentiates children with SLI from unimpaired children with high sensitivity, specificity, and accuracy even when language impairments appear to have resolved on other standardized language tests (Conti-Ramsden, Botting, & Faragher, 2001; Montgomery, 1995; Stothard, Snowling, Bishop, Chipcase, & Kaplan, 1998). Studies suggest that the problem with nonword repetition for children with SLI lies in forming accurate phonological representations in working memory (Edwards & Lahey, 1998).

A second clinical marker for SLI involves measures of children's knowledge and processing of finite verb morphology. Long after their age-matched peers have stopped making errors, children with SLI continue to omit grammatical morphemes in obligatory contexts. Work by Rice and her colleagues has shown that for English-speaking children with SLI, a composite reflecting children's degree of use of several finite verb-related morphemes in obligatory contexts distinguishes preschool children with SLI from unimpaired children (e.g., Rice & Wexler, 1996; Rice, Haney, & Wexler, 1998; Rice, Wexler, & Cleave, 1995). Oetting and McDonald (2001) found that this measure could also be applied to children speaking various dialects of American English, and Jones, Weismer, and Schumacher (2000) showed that it is still useful for distinguishing SLI in school-age children (see also Conti-Ramsden et al., 2001).

Much of the research on omitting tense in obligatory contexts has been done using natural language samples (e.g., Bedore & Leonard, 1998; Leonard, Miller, & Gerber, 1999; Rice et al., 1998). Experimental production tasks have also been used in which children are asked to respond to prompts designed to elicit either third-person present or past-tense morphology, and children with SLI perform significantly worse on these tasks than age- or language-matched peers, usually producing bare-stem rather than inflected verbs (Rice et al., 1995).

There have been a number of different interpretations of this deficit in marking tense in finite clauses. Rice and Wexler (1996) argued that it reflects an extended period in which children with SLI consider tense as an optional rather than obligatory grammatical feature. Thus, they argued for a grammatical basis of this impairment. Leonard (1998) argued for a processing explanation, claiming that children with SLI have deficits in using grammatical morphemes with low phonetic substance or weak stress patterns especially in contexts with higher cognitive demand. Despite the lack of consensus about why children with SLI have difficulty with grammatical morphology, there is agreement that SLI involves fundamental impairments in these aspects of morphosyntax.

SLI DEFICITS IN AUTISM

In our recent work, we have followed up on our original study that identified a group of language-impaired children with autism (Kjelgaard & Tager-Flusberg, 2001) by exploring whether these children have deficits in nonword repetition and finite verb morphology that are the same as in

SLI. These studies were conducted on the same children who had been part of our earlier investigation in later years of the project.

One reason that we argued that the language-impaired children with autism may represent an overlap with SLI is because of their poor performance on the nonword repetition task (Kjelgaard & Tager-Flusberg, 2001). This was a surprising finding given that children with autism are often *echolalic*, defined as the ability to repeat speech they have heard out of context without apparent reference to meaning. Nonword repetition tasks also require repetition of speech that is meaningless, but importantly, they do not depend on rote memory skills in the way that echolalia does. Although language-impaired children with autism have difficulty with nonword repetition, are their difficulties the same as for children with SLI?

To address this question, we conducted a follow-up study with 35 children from the earlier study (Condouris, Smith, Arin, & Tager-Flusberg, 2001). The average age of this group was 10 years 4 months, and their mean IQ score was 77. This time we used a different standardized nonword repetition task taken from the Comprehensive Test of Phonological Processing (CTOPP; Wagner, Torgesen, & Rashotte, 1999). We administered all 18 nonsense words on the CTOPP subtest and digitally recorded each child's responses. Two trained clinicians then transcribed the responses using a narrow phonetic transcription and then analyzed the error patterns made by the children.

Two thirds of the children received a standard score of 6 or below, which is in the impaired range. The error analysis showed that all the children maintained the overall syllable structure of the stimulus words (97.7% of responses had the same number of syllables as the target stimuli). There was also a strong effect of syllable length, with more errors occurring on the longer nonsense words. Not surprisingly, the children who performed in the impaired range made more errors. The majority of these errors were phoneme substitutions. However, about 20% of the errors made by the impaired children were single phoneme-deletion errors. This pattern of performance mirrors what has been reported in the literature for children with SLI (Dollaghan & Campbell, 1998) and underscores the similarities in phonological processing deficits in a subgroup of autism and SLI.

We also conducted two studies investigating tense marking in children with autism. In the first study, we included 62 children from the original autism sample who were given two experimental tasks to elicit past-tense and third-person present-tense morphology (Roberts, Rice, & Tager-Flusberg, 2000). These tasks were taken from Rice et al. (1995), who found that they differentiated between children with SLI and unimpaired children. On the past-tense task, children were shown pictures of people engaged in activities and were then asked questions such as, "What happened?" or "What did he do with the rake?" There were 11 trials designed to elicit regular past-tense forms on lexical verbs (e.g., wash, color) and eight intermixed trials to elicit irregular forms (e.g., catch, fall). On each trial, the experimenter first modeled the verb and then asked the probe questions. For the third-person task, 12 pictures depicting people in various occupations (e.g., doctor, painter) were presented to the children. They were asked questions such as: "Tell me what a doctor does," "What does a painter do?" Children were probed until they produced a verb in the third person (e.g., He help(-s) people).

The children were divided into normal language ($N = 25$) and language impaired ($N = 20$) on the basis of performance on a standardized language test. The children in the normal language subtype gave almost twice as many correct responses as those in the impaired subtype, whose performance was only between 30% and 40% correct on both tasks. The most common error pattern was to omit any morphological marking on the verb stem—the error that is also most frequently reported for children with SLI. The children in the impaired subtype produced significantly more of these errors than the language-normal children. On the past-tense task, the children were equally likely to produce these bare-stem errors on the regular and irregular verbs and made few overregularization errors (e.g., falled). Again studies on children with SLI report similar findings (Marchman, Wulfeck, & Weismer, 1999; Rice, 1999).

In a second study exploring finite-verb morphology, we coded natural language samples for the use of grammatical morphemes in obligatory contexts (Condouris, Evancie, & Tager-Flusberg, 2002). We included 29 children with autism, divided into those with normal language ($N = 9$) and impaired language ($N = 20$), as well as 13 children with SLI. All three groups were matched on age (mean = 7 years 5 months; range = 4;2–13;1). The language-impaired children with autism and the children with SLI were also well matched on nonverbal IQ and mean length of utterance (MLU). However, the children with autism and normal language had higher IQ and MLU scores than the other children. The language samples were taken from a parent–child play interaction and an examiner–child interaction collected during the administration of the ADOS. The samples, which we combined for each child, were transcribed and coded using SALT (Miller, 2001). Following the methods of earlier studies (Leonard et al., 1999; Rice & Wexler, 1996), we tallied the obligatory contexts and presence/absence of morphemes in these contexts for two sets of grammatical morphemes: finite-verb morphemes (third-person singular present -s, past tense -ed, BE as copula and auxiliary, and auxiliary DO) and control morphemes (plural -s, prepositions in/on, third-person progressive -ing, and articles a/an/the).

Our main predictions were that the language-impaired children (both autism and SLI) would be impaired on the finite-verb morphemes compared with the normal language children with autism. This prediction was confirmed, but only for the third-person singular -s. For the other finite-verb morphemes, all three groups provided the correct morpheme in over 90% of obligatory contexts, which was considered mastery. This is perhaps not surprising given that most of the children were fairly old. We also found that all the children had mastered the control morphemes, confirming the specificity of the deficit to finite verb morphology, particularly third-person singular -s. Across all the morpheme analyses, the children with SLI were indistinguishable from the language-impaired children with autism.

In all the studies presented here, we found that language-impaired children performed in strikingly similar ways to children with SLI on tasks and measures that tap the core deficits associated with SLI: nonword repetition and finite-verb morphology. The poor performance and error patterns suggest that the same deficits in phonological processing and morphosyntactic knowledge underlie the impairments found in these groups of children. At the same time, some aspects of language are relatively spared in both groups. These include articulation (Kjlegaard & Tager-Flusberg, 2001) and verbal fluency (Evancie, Condouris, McGrath, Joseph, & Tager-Flusberg, 2002), suggesting that the overall pattern of language skills is the same in a subgroup of children with autism and children with SLI.

BRAIN IMAGING STUDIES OF AUTISM AND SLI

Thus far, we have shown parallels in the language phenotype of SLI and language-impaired children with autism. To what extent do these behavioral findings reflect parallels in the underlying neuropathology associated with a language disorder in these groups?

Studies investigating brain morphology in the general population have consistently found that the language regions in the inferior frontal cortex, Broca's area, and in the *planum temporale* are larger in the left hemisphere than in the right (Falzi, Perrone, & Vignolo, 1982; Foundas, Leonard, & Heilman, 1995; Foundas, Eure, Luevano, & Weinberger, 1998; Galaburda, Corsiglia, Rosen, & Sherman, 1987; Kulynych, Vladar, Jones, & Weinberger, 1993; Watkins et al., 2001; Zetzsche et al., 2000). In contrast, studies of children and adults with SLI have found reduced or reversed asymmetry patterns in these areas. For example, the *pars triangularis* of the inferior frontal cortex is smaller in the left hemisphere in children with SLI relative to control subjects (Gauger, Lombardino, & Leonard, 1997). Boys with SLI have atypical perisylvian asymmetries due to a larger right perisylvian area compared with normal controls (Plante, Swisher, Vance, & Rapcsak, 1991). A study of the members of the KE family, about half of whom have profound speech and language impairments, found that the affected family members had less grey matter in the left inferior frontal cortex than the unaffected family members (Watkins et al., 2002).

In two recent studies, we explored whether the same abnormal asymmetries are found among children with autism using magnetic resonance imaging (MRI). The first study compared 16 boys with autism (all with normal nonverbal IQ scores) to 15 age- (7 to 11 years old) and handedness-matched controls (Herbert et al., 2002). Using the segmentation and parcellation methods developed by Caviness and his colleagues (Caviness, Meyer, Makris, & Kennedy, 1996; Rademacher, Galaburda, Kennedy, Filipek, & Caviness, 1992), left–right asymmetries in the language-related inferior lateral frontal and posterior superior temporal regions (*planum temporale*) were measured. The main findings were that the boys with autism had significant reversed asymmetry in the frontal language-related cortical areas, corresponding to Broca's area (27% larger in the right hemisphere), compared with the control boys (17% larger in the left hemisphere). The posterior language region, specifically the *planum temporale*, was larger in the left hemisphere in the boys with autism, suggesting exaggerated left asymmetry.

The second study used similar methods on a different sample of children (De Fossé et al., 2002). We obtained high-quality MRI images from 22 boys with autism (whose diagnoses were confirmed on the basis of ADI and ADOS scores), 9 boys with SLI, and 11 unimpaired controls. The autism group was divided, on the basis of language test scores, into those with normal language (ALN; $N = 6$) and those with language impairment (ALI; $N = 16$) using the same definitions as Kjelgaard and Tager-Flusberg (2001). The groups were matched on age and handedness (all the participants were right-handed). The SLI and ALI groups were also matched on nonverbal IQ and language. However, the ALN group and controls had higher IQ and language test scores than the language-impaired groups.

The analyses focused on the hemispheric asymmetries in frontal and posterior language regions. Here I present the data from the frontal areas including the *pars triangularis* and *pars opercularis* in the inferior frontal gyrus and from the posterior *planum temporale*. The asymmetry indexes were calculated using a formula that computed the ratio of the volumes for the specific brain region from the left and right hemispheres. Positive values indicate that the brain area is larger in the left hemisphere, whereas negative values indicate that the brain area is larger in the right hemisphere. The data for each group are presented in Fig. 3.3. Statistical analyses of the data from the frontal areas confirmed that the two language-

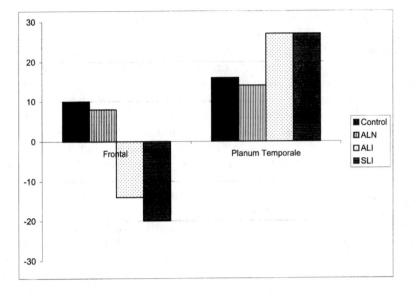

FIG. 3.3. Asymmetry indexes for language regions in the brain.

impaired groups (ALI and SLI) had significant right-hemisphere asymmetry compared with both the ALN and control groups. The language-impaired groups also had larger left-hemisphere asymmetry in the *planum temporale*; however, this was not statistically significant.

These data confirmed our earlier findings (Herbert et al., 2002). However, because this time we also had behavioral data on the children in this study, we were able to demonstrate that the atypical asymmetries we found in the language regions of the brain among children with autism were specifically related to their language impairment. These findings provide strong support for the hypothesis that there is a common neurobiological basis for language impairment in autism and SLI. These atypical asymmetries in both frontal and posterior language regions may be an important biological marker for language impairment across different populations, specifically for SLI and a subgroup of children with autism.

GENETIC IMPLICATIONS

The psycholinguistic evidence and the neuropathological findings presented here support the claim that there is a subtype among children with autism who have a neurocognitive phenotype that is the same as has been reported in the literature for SLI (Tager-Flusberg & Joseph, 2003). Children with autism in the language-impaired subtype performed poorly on standardized and experimental language tests that are sensitive to deficits that specifically characterize SLI, and they showed the same atypical asymmetry patterns in frontal and posterior language regions of the brain. In this section, I consider whether the identification of this language-impaired subtype in autism has significant implications for genetic studies of autism and SLI and, more generally, for finding genes for language.

Both SLI and autism are considered to be disorders with a relatively strong genetic basis. They are both disorders with heterogeneous phenotypes that are likely to have a complex genetic basis. Evidence from family and twin studies shows that SLI clusters in families (Bishop, 2001; Fisher, Lai, & Monaco, 2003; Tomblin & Zhang, 1999). The prevalence rate in parents and siblings of SLI probands is about four times higher than in the general population (Tomblin, 1996). Furthermore, concordance rates among monozygotic (MZ) twins are significantly higher than among dizygotic (DZ) twins (Bishop, North, & Donlan, 1995; Lewis & Thompson, 1992; Tomblin & Buckwalter, 1998). For example, in the Bishop et al. (1995) study, the concordance rate for MZ twins was about 70% compared with close to 50% for DZ twins. Even when family members do not meet criteria for an SLI diagnosis, studies have found that language-related deficits (e.g., reading or spelling disorders) are significantly more common in SLI families, suggesting that traits related to language impairment aggregate in these families.

Similar findings have been obtained for autism, although it is a much rarer disorder than SLI. The risk recurrence rate in families that have had a child with autism is about 6% to 8% compared with less than 0.1% in the general population (Santangelo & Folstein, 1999). Twin studies have also found significantly higher concordance rates for MZ twins—about 70%—compared with 3% for DZ twins (Bailey et al., 1995; Folstein & Rutter, 1977; Steffenburg, Gillberg, & Hellgren, 1989), which suggests a heritability rate of over 90%. Finally, numerous studies have demonstrated that parents and siblings of children with autism are more likely to exhibit traits that are conceptually similar but milder in form to the symptoms that define autism—known as the "broader autism phenotype" (Santangelo & Folstein, 1999).

Some behavioral genetic studies have found interesting and significant overlap between families with an autistic child and families with an SLI child. For example, studies of the broader autism phenotype have found that among first-degree relatives of children with autism, there are significantly elevated rates of documented histories of language delay and language-based learning deficits that go well beyond pragmatic difficulties (Bailey, Palferman, Heavey, & Le Couteur, 1998; Bolton et al., 1994; Fombonne, Bolton, Prior, Jordan, & Rutter, 1997; Piven, Palmer, Landa, Santangelo, Jacobi, & Childress, 1997). Twin studies have also reported that co-twins discordant for autism had increased rates of language deficits that resemble the pattern described as SLI (Folstein & Rutter, 1977; Le Couteur, Bailey, Goode, Pickles, Robertson, Gottesman, & Rutter, 1996). Thus, in families identified on the basis of a probands with autism, there are unusually high rates of language impairment. One recent study identified a similar pattern in families that have children with SLI. Tomblin and his colleagues compared rates of autism among the siblings from a large epidemiological sample of children with SLI and normal age-matched controls (Tomblin, Hafeman, & O'Brien, 2003). All the siblings found to be at risk for autism ($N = 11$) on the basis of a parental questionnaire came from families where the probands had low language scores. Among the children at risk for autism, at the follow-up, four siblings attained confirmed diagnoses on the ADI and ADOS, three of whom came from the SLI families, representing an autism rate of 1% among SLI families compared with 0.1% in the general population. Taken together, these studies indicate familial co-morbidity for autism and SLI, providing evidence for the hypothesis that there is some shared genetic etiology for these disorders.

In addition to the behavioral evidence, recent genetic linkage and association studies may offer further clues to some shared genetic basis for these disorders. The KE family in England has been intensively investigated because they represent a large multigenerational pedigree in which a severe speech and language disorder has been transmitted in a manner suggesting a single dominant gene. The locus of the gene was found on Chromosome 7q31 (Fisher, Vargha-Khadem, Watkins, Monaco, & Pembrey, 1998), and it has now been identified as the *FOXP2* gene (Lai, Fisher, Hurst, Vargha-Khadem, & Monaco, 2001). Tomblin and his colleagues took their population-based sample of children with SLI and found a significant association between SLI and an allele of the *CFTR* gene (O'Brien, Zhang, Nishimura, Tomblin, & Murray, 2003). This gene is within the 7q31 region where *FOXP2* is located, although more recent studies have not found an association between SLI and *FOXP2* (Meaburn, Dale, Craig, & Plomin, 2002; Newbury et al., 2002). Nevertheless, there is some evidence from O'Brien et al. (2003) that there is a gene (or genes) located in this region on the long arm of Chromosome 7 that contributes to SLI. A second locus for a gene associated with SLI has been found recently on Chromosome 13 (13q21) based on the analysis of five large pedigrees (Bartlett et al., 2002).

Studies have consistently identified 7q31 as a region that is likely to include a susceptibility gene (or genes) for autism (e.g., International Molecular Genetic Study of Autism Consortium, 1998), and additional studies indicate overlap between autism and SLI in this region (Ashley-Koch et al., 1999; Warburton et al., 2000). It does not appear, however, that *FOXP2* is a candidate autism gene (Newbury et al., 2002; Wassink et al., 2002). Another locus for a susceptibility gene for autism has been found on 13q21 (Collaborative Linkage Study of Autism, 1999), the same region found in the study of SLI by Bartlett and colleagues (2002). Yet, as noted earlier, all the genome scans conducted thus far have found only modest signals in all studies using linkage analysis.

The parallels between the loci that have been linked to autism and SLI are striking, and recently the Collaborative Linkage Study of Autism (CLSA) explored the possibility of incorporating a phenotypically defined subgroup in their genetic analysis (Collaborative Linkage Study of Autism, 2001). Using only the subgroup of probands with autism who had no language or clearly impaired language and whose parents had a history of language difficulties, the linkage signals on both 7q and 13q were significantly increased, suggesting that these signals were mainly attributable to the language-impaired subtype within autism. Similar findings were obtained by the Autism Genetic Resource Exchange Consortium (AGRE) using different definitions of *language impaired* in an independent sample of autism families (Alarcon, Cantor, Liu, Gilliam, Geschwind, AGRE, 2002). These genetic findings hold out some promise that defining language phenotypic subtypes within the autism population may provide important benefits to genetic studies (cf. Dawson et al., 2002).

CONCLUSIONS

Studies investigating the behavioral and neurobiological phenotypes and genetic etiology of two distinct neurodevelopmental disorders—autism and SLI—are beginning to suggest some striking overlaps at least for some subgroups within each population. The research is still in the early stages, and many of the findings reported here require replication by independent groups of investigators. We still have not identified specific genes associated with elevated risk for either SLI or autism, although it is likely that within a few years several such genes, in addition to *FOXP2*, will be found. These will not only inform our understanding of these disorders, but will provide clues to the genetic basis, neurobiological pathways, and perhaps also the evolutionary history of our uniquely human capacity for language (Fisher et al., 2003; Pinker, 1994).

ACKNOWLEDGMENTS

Preparation of this chapter was supported by grants from the National Institutes of Health (PO1/U19 DC 03610 and RO1 NS 38668).

REFERENCES

Alarcon, M., Cantor, R., Liu, J., Gilliam, T. C., Geschwind, D., & AGRE Consortium. (2002). Evidence for a language quantitative trait locus on chromosome 7q in multiplex autism families. *American Journal of Human Genetics, 70,* 60–71.

Allen, D. (1989). Developmental language disorders in preschool children: Clinical subtypes and syndromes. *School Psychology Review, 18,* 442–451.

Allen, D., & Rapin, I. (1980). Language disorders in preschool children: Predictors of outcome. A preliminary report. *Brain and Development, 2,* 73–80.

Allen, D., & Rapin, I. (1992). Autistic children are also dysphasic. In H. Naruse & E. Ornitz (Eds.), *Neurobiology of infantile autism* (pp. 73–80). Amsterdam: Excerpta Medica.

American Psychological Association. (1994). *DSM–IV: Diagnostic and statistic manual of mental disorders* (4th ed.). Washington, DC: American Psychiatric Association.

Ashley-Koch, A., Wolpert, C., Menold, M., Naeem, L., Basu, S., Donnelly, S., Ravan, S., Powell, C., Qumsiyeh, M., Aylsworth, A., Vance, J., Gilbert, J., Wright, H., Abramson, R., DeLon, G., Cuccaro, M., & Pericak-Vance, M. (1999). Genetic studies of autistic disorder and chromosome 7. *Genomics, 61,* 227–236.

Bailey, A., Le Couteur, A., Gottesman, I., Bolton, P., Simonoff, E., Yuzda, E., & Rutter, M. (1995). Autism as a strongly genetic disorder: Evidence from a British twin study. *Psychological Medicine, 25,* 63–77.

Bailey, A., Palferman, S., Heavey, L., & LeCouteur, A. (1998). Autism: The phenotype in relatives. *Journal of Autism and Developmental Disorders, 28,* 369–392.

Bailey, A., Phillips, W., & Rutter, M. (1996). Autism: Towards an integration of clinical, genetic, neuropsychological, and neurobiological perspectives. *Journal of Child Psychology and Psychiatry, 37,* 89–126.

Baltaxe, C. A. M. (1977). Pragmatic deficits in the language of autistic adolescents. *Journal of Pediatric Psychology, 2,* 176–180.

Bartak, L., Rutter, M., & Cox, A. (1975). A comparative study of infantile autism and specific developmental receptive language disorder: I. The children. *British Journal of Psychiatry, 126,* 127–145.

Bartak, L., Rutter, M., & Cox, A. (1977). A comparative study of infantile autism and specific developmental receptive language disorders: II. Discriminant function analysis. *Journal of Autism and Childhood Schizophrenia, 7,* 383–396.

Bartlett, C., Flax, J., Logue, M., Vieland, V., Bassett, A., Tallal, P., & Brzustowicz, L. (2002). A major susceptibility locus for specific language impairment is located on 13q21. *American Journal of Human Genetics, 71,* 45–55.

Bedore, L. M., & Leonard, L. B. (1998). Specific language impairment and grammatical morphology: A discriminant function analysis. *Journal of Speech, Language, and Hearing Research, 41,* 1185–1192.

Bishop, D. V. M. (2000). Pragmatic language impairment: A correlate of SLI, a distinct subgroup, or part of the autistic continuum? In D. V. M. Bishop & L. Leonard (Eds.), *Speech and language impairments in children: Causes, characteristics, intervention and outcome* (pp. 99–113). Hove, UK: Psychology Press.

Bishop, D. V. M. (2001). Genetic and environmental risks for specific language impairment in children. *Philosophical Transactions of the Royal Society of London, Series B, 356,* 369–380.

Bishop, D. V. M., & Norbury, C. (2002). Exploring the borderlands of autistic disorder and specific language impairment: A study using standardized diagnostic instruments. *Journal of Child Psychology and Psychiatry, 43,* 917–929.

Bishop, D. V. M., North, T., & Donlan, C. (1995). Genetic basis for specific language impairment: Evidence from a twin study. *Developmental Medicine and Child Neurology, 37,* 56–71.

Bishop, D. V. M., North, T., & Donlan, C. (1996). Nonword repetition as a behavioral marker for inherited language impairment: Evidence from a twin study. *Journal of Child Psychology and Psychiatry, 37*, 391–403.

Bishop, D. V. M., & Rosenbloom, L. (1987). Classification of childhood language disorders. In W. Yule & M. Rutter (Eds.), *Language development and disorders. Clinics and developmental medicine* (pp. 16–41). London: MacKeith Press.

Bolton, P., Macdonald, H., Pickles, A., Rios, P., Goode, S., Crowson, M., Bailey, A., & Rutter, M. (1994). A case-control family history study of autism. *Journal of Child Psychology and Psychiatry, 35*, 877–900.

Brook, S. L., & Bowler, D. (1992). Autism by another name? Semantic and pragmatic impairments in children. *Journal of Autism and Developmental Disorders, 22*, 61–81.

Cantwell, D., Baker, L., Rutter, M., & Mawhood, L. (1989). Infantile autism and developmental receptive dysphasia: A comparative follow-up into middle childhood. *Journal of Autism and Developmental Disorders, 19*, 19–31.

Caviness, V. S., Jr., Meyer, J. W., Makris, N., & Kennedy, D. N. (1996). MRI-based topographic parcellation of the human neocortex: An anatomically specified method with estimate of reliability. *Journal of Cognitive Neuroscience, 8*, 566–587.

Churchill, D. W. (1972). The relation of infantile autism and early childhood schizophrenia to developmental language disorders of childhood. *Journal of Autism and Childhood Schizophrenia, 2*, 182–197.

Collaborative Linkage Study of Autism. (1999). An autosomal genomic screen for autism. Collaborative linkage study of autism. *American Journal of Medical Genetics, 88*, 609–615.

Collaborative Linkage Study of Autism. (2001). Incorporating language phenotypes strengthens evidence of linkage to autism. *American Journal of Medical Genetics, 105*, 539–547.

Condouris, K., Evancie, L., & Tager-Flusberg, H. (2002, November). *Tense error patterns in children with autism and children with SLI.* International Meeting for Autism Research, Orlando, FL.

Condouris, K., Smith, J. L., Arin, D., & Tager-Flusberg, H. (2001, November). *Children with autism's performance on a nonword repetition task: Evidence of an SLI subgroup.* American Speech and Hearing Association meeting, New Orleans, LA.

Conti-Ramsden, G., & Botting, N. (1999). Classification of children with specific language impairment: Longitudinal considerations. *Journal of Speech, Language, and Hearing Research, 42*, 1195–1204.

Conti-Ramsden, G., Botting, N., & Faragher, B. (2001). Psycholinguistic markers for specific language impairment (SLI). *Journal of Child Psychology and Psychiatry, 42*, 741–748.

Craig, H., & Evans, J. (1993). Pragmatics and SLI: Within-group variations in discourse behaviors. *Journal of Speech Language and Hearing Research, 42*, 1195–1204.

Dawson, G., Webb, S., Schellenberg, G., Dager, S., Friedman, S., Aylward, E., & Richards, T. (2002). Defining the broader phenotype of autism: Genetic, brain, and behavioral perspectives. *Development and Psychopathology, 14*, 581–611.

De Fossé, L., Harris, G., Hodge, S., Makris, N., Kennedy, D., Caviness, V., McGrath, L., Steele, S., & Tager-Flusberg, H. (2002, November). *An abnormal cortical volumetric asymmetry pattern in language-cortext in children with autism and children with specific language impairment.* International Meeting for Autism Research, Orlando, FL.

Dollaghan, C., & Campbell, T. F. (1998). Nonword repetition and child language impairment. *Journal of Speech, Language, and Hearing Research, 41*, 1136–1146.

Edwards, J., & Lahey, M. (1998). Nonword repetitions of children with specific language impairment: Exploration of some explanations for their inaccuracies. *Applied Psycholinguistics, 19*, 279–309.

Evancie, L., Condouris, K., McGrath, L., Joseph, R. M., & Tager-Flusberg, H. (2002, November). *Verbal fluency in autism and language impairment.* International Meeting for Autism Research, Orlando, FL.

Falzi, G., Perrone, P., & Vignolo, L. A. (1982). Right-left asymmetry in anterior speech region. *Archives of Neurology, 39,* 239–240.

Fisher, S. E., Lai, C., & Monaco, A. (2003). Deciphering the genetic basis of speech and language disorders. *Annual Reviews in Neuroscience, 26,* 57–80.

Fisher, S. E., Vargha-Khadem, F., Watkins, K. E., Monaco, A. P., & Pembrey, M. E. (1998). Localisation of a gene implicated in severe speech and language. *Nature Genetics, 18,* 168–170.

Folstein, S., & Rutter, M. (1977). Infantile autism: A genetic study of 21 twin pairs. *Journal of Child Psychology and Psychiatry, 18,* 297–321.

Fombonne, E., Bolton, P., Prior, J., Jordan, H., & Rutter, M. (1997). A family study of autism: Cognitive patterns and levels in parents and siblings. *Journal of Child Psychology and Psychiatry, 38,* 667–684.

Foundas, A. L., Eure, K. F., Luevano, L. F., & Weinberger, D. R. (1998). MRI asymmetries of Broca's area: The pars triangularis and pars opercularis. *Brain and Language, 64,* 282–296.

Foundas, A. L., Leonard, C. M., & Heilman, K. M. (1995). Morphologic cerebral asymmetries and handedness: The pars triangularis and planum temporale. *Archives of Neurology, 52,* 501–508.

Galaburda, A. M., Corsiglia, J., Rosen, G. D., & Sherman, G. F. (1987). Planum temporale asymmetry, reappraisal since Geschwind and Levitsky. *Neuropsychologia, 25,* 853–868.

Gathercole, S. E., & Baddeley, A. D. (1990). Phonological memory deficits in language disordered children: Is there a causal connection? *Journal of Memory and Language, 29,* 336–360.

Gauger, L. M., Lombardino, L. J., & Leonard, C. M. (1997). Brain morphology in children with specific language impairment. *Journal of Speech, Language and Hearing Research, 36,* 1272–1284.

Hadley, P., & Rice, M. (1991). Conversational responsiveness of speech and language impaired preschoolers. *Journal of Speech and Hearing Research, 34,* 1308–1317.

Happé, F. (1994). An advanced test of theory of mind: Understanding of story characters' thoughts and feelings by able autistic, mentally handicapped, and normal children and adults. *Journal of Autism and Developmental Disorders, 24,* 129–154.

Herbert, M. R., Harris, G. J., Adrien, K. T., Ziegler, D. A., Makris, N., Kennedy, D. N., Lange, N. T., Chabris, C. F., Bakardjiev, A., Hodsgon, J., Takeoka, M., Tager-Flusberg, H., & Caviness, V. S., Jr. (2002). Abnormal asymmetry in language association cortex in autism. *Annals of Neurology, 52,* 588–596.

International Molecular Genetic Study of Autism Consortium. (1998). A full genome screen for autism with evidence for linkage to a region on chromosome 7q. *Human Molecular Genetics, 7,* 571–578.

Jones, M., Weismer, S. E., & Schumacher, K. (2000, June). *Grammatical morphology in school-age children with and without language impairment: Discriminant function analysis.* Poster presented at the Symposium on Research in Child Language Disorders, Madison, WI.

Kanner, L. (1943). Autistic disturbances of affective contact. *Nervous Child, 2,* 217–250.

Kjelgaard, M., & Tager-Flusberg, H. (2001). An investigation of language impairment in autism: Implications for genetic subgroups. *Language and Cognitive Processes, 16,* 287–308.

Kulynych, J. J., Vladar, K., Jones, D. W., & Weinberger, D. R. (1993). Three-dimensional surface rendering in MRI Morphometry: A study of the planum temporale. *Journal of Computer Assisted Tomography, 17,* 529–535.

Kurita, H. (1985). Infantile autism with speech loss before the age of 30 months. *Journal of the American Academy of Child Psychiatry, 24,* 191–196.

Lai, C., Fisher, S., Hurst, J., Vargha-Khadem, F., & Monaco, A. (2001). A forkhead-domain gene is mutated in a severe speech and language disorder. *Nature, 413,* 465–466.

Le Couteur, A., Bailey, A., Goode, S., Pickles, A., Robertson, S., Gottesman, I., & Rutter, M. (1996). A broader phenotype of autism: The clinical spectrum in twins. *Journal of Child Psychology and Psychiatry, 37,* 785–801.

Leonard, L. B. (1998). *Children with specific language impairment.* Cambridge, MA: The MIT Press.

Leonard, L. B., Miller, C., & Gerber, E. (1999). Grammatical morphology and the lexicon in children with specific language impairment. *Journal of Speech, Language, and Hearing Research, 42,* 678–689.

Lewis, B., & Thompson, L. (1992). A study of developmental speech and language disorders in twins. *Journal of Speech and Hearing Research, 35,* 1086–1094.

Lord, C., & Paul, R. (1997). Language and communication in autism. In D. J. Cohen & F. R. Volkmar (Eds.), *Handbook of autism and pervasive development disorders* (2nd ed.). New York: Wiley.

Lord, C., Risi, S., Lambrecht, L., Cook, E. H., Lenventhal, B. L., DiLavore, P. S., Pickles, A., & Rutter, M. (2000). The Autism Diagnostic Observation Schedule–Generic: A standard measure of social and communication deficits associated with the spectrum of autism. *Journal of Autism and Developmental Disorders, 30,* 205–223.

Lord, C., Rutter, M., & LeCouteur, A. (1994). Autism Diagnostic Interview–Revised: A revised version of a diagnostic interview for caregivers of individuals with possible pervasive developmental disorders. *Journal of Autism and Developmental Disorders, 24,* 659–685.

Loveland, K., Landry, S., Hughes, S., Hall, S., & McEvoy, R. (1988). Speech acts and the pragmatic deficits of autism. *Journal of Speech and Hearing Research, 31,* 593–604.

Loveland, K., & Tunali, B. (1993). Narrative language in autism and the theory of mind hypothesis: A wider perspective. In S. Baron-Cohen, H. Tager-Flusberg, & D. J. Cohen (Eds.), *Understanding other minds: Perspectives from autism* (pp. 247–266). Oxford: Oxford University Press.

Marchman, V. A., Wulfeck, B., & Weismer, S. E. (1999). Morphological productivity in children with normal language and SLI: A study of the English past tense. *Journal of Speech Language and Hearing Research, 42,* 206–219.

Meaburn, E., Dale, P., Craig, I., & Plomin, R. (2002). Language-impaired children: No sign of the FOXP2 mutation. *Neuroreport, 13,* 1075–1077.

Miller, J. (2001). *Systematic Analysis of Language Transcripts (SALT).* [Computer software, SALT for Windows, Research version 7.0]. Madison, WI: University of Wisconsin, Language Analysis Lab.

Montgomery, J. W. (1995). Examination of phonological working memory in specifically language-impaired children. *Applied Psycholinguistics, 16,* 355–378.

Newbury, D., Bonora, E., Lamb, J., Fisher, S., Lai, C., Baird, G., Jannoun, L., Slonims, V., Stott, C., Merricks, M., Bolton, P., Bailey, A., & Monaco, A. (2002). FOXP2 is not a major susceptibility gene for autism or specific language impairment. *American Journal of Human Genetics, 70,* 1318–1327.

O'Brien, E., Zhang, X., Nishimura, C., Tomblin, J. B., & Murray, J. (2003). Association of specific language impairment (SLI) to the region of 7q31. *American Journal of Human Genetics, 72,* 1536–1543.

Oetting, J. B., & McDonald, J. L. (2001). Nonmainstream dialect use and specific language impairment. *Journal of Speech, Language and Hearing Research, 44,* 207–223.

Paul, R., & Cohen, D. J. (1984). Responses to contingent queries in adults with mental retardation and pervasive developmental disorders. *Applied Psycholinguistics, 5,* 349–357.

Pinker, S. (1994). *The language instinct.* New York: William Morrow.

Piven, J., Palmer, P., Landa, R., Santangelo, S., Jacobi, D., & Childress, D. (1997). Personality and language characteristics in parents from multiple-incidence autism families. *American Journal of Medical Genetics, 74,* 398–411.

Plante, E., Swisher, L., Vance, R., & Rapcsak, S. (1991). MRI findings in boys with specific language impairment. *Brain and Language, 41,* 52–66.

Rademacher, J., Galaburda, A. M., Kennedy, D. N., Filipek, P. A., & Caviness, V. S. (1992). Human cerebral cortex: Localization, parcellation, and morphometry with magnetic resonance imaging. *Journal of Cognitive Neuroscience, 4,* 352–374.

Rapin, I. (Ed.). (1996). *Preschool children with inadequate communication* (Clinics in Developmental Medicine, No. 139). London: MacKeith Press.

Rapin, I., & Dunn, M. (2003). Update on the language disorders of individuals on the autistic spectrum. *Brain and Development, 25,* 166–172.

Rice, M. L. (1999). Specific grammatical limitations in children with specific language impairment. In H. Tager-Flusberg (Ed.), *Neurodevelopmental disorders* (pp. 331–359). Cambridge, MA: MIT Press.

Rice, M. L., Haney, K. R., & Wexler, K. (1998). Family histories of children with SLI who show extended optional infinitives. *Journal of Speech, Language, and Hearing Research, 41,* 419–432.

Rice, M. L., & Wexler, K. (1996). Toward tense as a clinical marker of specific language impairment in English-speaking children. *Journal of Speech and Hearing Research, 39,* 1239–1257.

Rice, M. L., Wexler, K., & Cleave, P. L. (1995). Specific language impairment as a period of extended optional infinitive. *Journal of Speech, Language, and Hearing Research, 38,* 850–863.

Roberts, J., Rice, M., & Tager-Flusberg, H. (2000, June). *Tense marking in children with autism: Further evidence for overlap between autism and SLI.* Symposium on Research in Child Language Disorders, Madison, WI.

Rutter, M. (1965). The influence of organic and emotional factors on the origins, nature, and outcome of childhood psychosis. *Developmental Medicine and Child Neurology, 7,* 518–528.

Santangelo, S. L., & Folstein, S. E. (1999). Autism: A genetic perspective. In H. Tager-Flusberg (Ed.), *Neurodevelopmental disorders* (pp. 431–447). Cambridge, MA: MIT Press.

Shields, J., Varley, R., Broks, P., & Simpson, A. (1996). Social cognition in developmental language disorders and high-level autism. *Developmental Medicine and Child Neurology, 38,* 487–495.

Steffenburg, S., Gillberg, C., & Hellgren, L. (1989). A twin study of autism in Denmark, Finland, Iceland, Norway, & Sweden. *Journal of Child Psychology and Psychiatry, 30,* 405–416.

Stothard, S. E., Snowling, J., Bishop, D. V. M., Chipcase, B., & Kaplan, C. S. (1998). Language-impaired preschoolers: A follow-up into adolescence. *Journal of Speech, Language, and Hearing Research, 41,* 407–418.

Tager-Flusberg, H. (1996). Current theory and research on language and communication in autism. *Journal of Autism and Developmental Disorders, 26,* 169–172.

Tager-Flusberg, H. (1999). A psychological approach to understanding the social and language impairments in autism. *International Review of Psychiatry, 11,* 325–334.

Tager-Flusberg, H., & Anderson, M. (1991). The development of contingent discourse ability in autistic children. *Journal of Child Psychology and Psychiatry, 32,* 1123–1134.

Tager-Flusberg, H., & Cooper, J. (1999). Present and future possibilities for defining a phenotype for specific language impairment. *Journal of Speech, Language, and Hearing Research, 42,* 1275–1278.

Tager-Flusberg, H., & Joseph, R. M. (2003). Identifying neurocognitive phenotypes in autism. *Philosophical Transactions of the Royal Society, Series B, 358,* 303–314.

Tager-Flusberg, H., & Sullivan, K. (1995). Attributing mental states to story characters: A comparison of narratives produced by autistic and mentally retarded individuals. *Applied Psycholinguistics, 16,* 241–256.

Tomblin, J. B. (1996). Genetic and environmental contributions to the risk for specific language impairment. In M. Rice (Ed.), *Toward a genetics of language* (pp. 191–210). Mahwah, NJ: Lawrence Erlbaum Associates.

Tomblin, J. B., & Buckwalter, P. (1998). Heritability of poor language achievement among twins. *Journal of Speech, Language, and Hearing Research, 41,* 188–199.

Tomblin, J. B., Hafeman, L., & O'Brien, M. (2003). Autism and autism risk in siblings of children with specific language impairment. *International Journal of Language and Communication Disorders, 38,* 235–250.

Tomblin, J. B., & Zhang, X. (1999). Language patterns and etiology in children with specific language impairment. In H. Tager-Flusberg (Ed.), *Neurodevelopmental Disorders* (pp. 361–382). Cambridge, MA: MIT Press/Bradford Books.

Warburton, P., Baird, G., Chen, W., Morris, K., Jacobs, W. B., Hodgson, S., & Docherty, Z. (2000). Support for linkage of autism and specific language impairment to 7q3 from two chromosome rearrangements involving band 7q31. *American Journal of Medical Genetics (Neuropsychiatric Genetics), 96,* 228–234.

Wagner, R., Torgesen, J., & Rashotte, C. (1999). *The comprehensive test of phonological processing.* Austin, TX: Pro-Ed.

Wassink, T., Piven, J., Vieland, V., Pietila, J., Goedken, R., Folstein, S., & Sheffield, V. (2002). Evaluation of FOXP2 as an autism susceptibility gene. *American Journal of Medical Genetics, 114,* 566–569.

Watkins, K. E., Paus, T., Lerch, J. P., Zijdenbos, A., Collins, D. L., Neelin, P., Taylor, J., Worsley, K. J., & Evans, A. C. (2001). Structural asymmetries in the human brain: A voxel based statistical analysis of 142 MRI scans. *Cerebral Cortex, 11,* 868–877.

Watkins, K. E., Vargha-Khadem, F., Ashburner, J., Passingham, R. E., Connelly, A., Friston, K. J., Frackowiak, R. S. J., Mishkin, M., & Gadian, D. G. (2002). MRI analysis of an inherited speech and language disorder: Structural brain abnormalities. *Brain, 125,* 465–478.

Weismer, S. E., Tomblin, J. B., Zhang, X., Buckwalter, P., Chynoweth, J. G., & Jones, M. (2000). Nonword repetition performance in school-age children with and without language impairment. *Journal of Speech, Language, and Hearing Research, 43,* 865–878.

Wetherby, A. (1986). Ontogeny of communication functions in autism. *Journal of Autism and Developmental Disorders, 16,* 295–316.

Zetzsche, T., Meisenzahl, E. M., Preuss, U. W., Kathmann, N., Leinsinger, G., Hahn, K., Hegerl, U., & Moller, H.-J. (2000). In-vivo analysis of the human planum temporale (PT): Does the definition of PT borders influence the results with regard to cerebral asymmetry and correlation with handedness? *Psychiatry Research: Neuroimaging Section, 107,* 99–115.

4

Dimensions of Individual Differences in Communication Skills Among Primary Grade Children

J. Bruce Tomblin
Xuyang Zhang
Amy Weiss
University of Iowa

Hugh Catts
University of Kansas

Susan Ellis Weismer
University of Wisconsin–Madison

The study of language disorders is conducted within many contexts that provide motivation for this research. One of these contexts is concerned with descriptive and explanatory accounts of individual differences in the development of communication skills. In this respect, the study of developmental language disorders (DLD) is part of a more general area of inquiry concerning the ways in which children differ with respect to communication development. As Revelle (2000) noted, there is an infinite number of ways in which individuals may differ from each other. However, psychological accounts attempt to reduce this number to a small set of latent traits that may account for a substantial amount of this variation. Once these latent dimensions of individual differences can be identified, we are then able to pose and test reasonable hypotheses that aim to explain these differences.

When viewed in the context of individual differences, cases of language impairment may be seen as representing extreme cases of normal variation, or, alternatively, language impairment may be viewed as qualitatively different from the variation found in normal language users. In the former view, explanations for normal variation should be sufficient to account for language impairment as well, whereas in the latter case, explanations for individual differences in the form of language impairment require additional factors. These are not questions that will yield to one method of investigation or one study.

In this chapter, we examine some data that may, in conjunction with past work, provide some progress toward answering these questions. We discuss some of the existing data concerning individual differences in language development in both typical and atypical learners. Then we present some of our data from a longitudinal study of children with a range of language skills.

INDIVIDUAL DIFFERENCES AMONG CHILDREN WITH DEVELOPMENTAL LANGUAGE DISORDERS

The children who enter our clinical service centers because of limitations in spoken communication have challenged us for decades with respect to ways to appropriately assess and characterize them. Our textbooks and research papers often begin by a claim that these children represent a heterogeneous group—where heterogeneity may refer to etiologies and/or behavioral characteristics. Despite this assumption, we remain uncertain as to the extent or nature of this heterogeneity.

Aram and Nation (1975) provided one of the first empirical attempts at addressing this issue. They studied 47 children who were receiving clinical services. These children were administered a battery of receptive, expressive, and imitative measures of semantics, syntax, and phonology performance. Using a factor analytic method, they concluded that there were six subgroups of children derived from three factors. Factor 1 (repetition ability) contained children with either high or low repetition ability. Factor 2 (severity) consisted of children with general deficits in all areas of semantics, syntax, and phonology or children with deficits limited to only phonology. Finally, Factor 3 (modality) represented children with deficits in either comprehension or production.

Certain features of this early attempt at the resolution of heterogeneity were later shown in a study by Bishop and Edmundson (1987), who found that most of the 83 preschool children who were receiving clinical services fit into one of four types characterized by a progression of language involvement, beginning with phonological impairments and then incorporating expressive semantics and syntax as well as phonology and, finally, expressive and receptive impairments. This single dimension appears to be similar to the severity dimension found by the Aram and Nation study. In each case, phonological impairments were able to stand in isolation, but semantics and syntax also implicated phonological impairments.

Shortly after Aram and Nation presented their results, Rapin and Allen (1983) presented a taxonomy for subtypes of DLD. This model was constructed from longitudinal observations of clinically served children and represented what may be viewed as a clinically informed theoretical model. This system provided for four major subtypes of DLD: verbal auditory agnosia, semantic pragmatic syndrome, autism, and syntactic-phonologic syndrome. More recent accounts of their diagnostic taxonomy no longer included autism within the diagnosis of DLD and also added syndromes that concerned poor word retrieval and sentence comprehension (lexical-syntactic deficit), verbal dyspraxia, and isolated phonological production (Rapin, 1998). Despite removing autism from this taxonomy, Rapin and Allen maintained that these same subtypes of DLD can be found within children with autism (Rapin, Allen, & Dunn, 1992).

In an effort to empirically test this taxonomic system, Rapin and colleagues (Rapin et al., 1996) examined a large sample of children with DLD and submitted these results to a taxometric analysis. This analysis sought to determine whether assessment profiles of children fit the subtypes proposed by the model. This analysis failed to show a fit of the data to the proposed taxonomy. Evidence was found for a separate subgroup of children with specific speech sound disorders. Evidence for two groups of children with DLD formed by either expressive only or expressive-receptive deficits was also not strongly supported. This analysis did, however, support the distinction between autism and DLD. Contrary to these negative findings, Conti-Ramsden et al. (Conti-Ramsden, Crutchley, & Botting, 2003) reported evidence of distinct subcategories that were formed on the basis of psychometric testing and teacher interview. These authors concluded that the resulting clusters corresponded to those of Rapin and Allen consisting of a phonological deficits syndrome, phonological-syntactic deficit syndrome, lexical-syntactic deficit syndrome, semantic-pragmatic deficit syndrome, and a verbal auditory agnosia syndrome.

The inclusion of a phonologic-syntactic syndrome in the Rapin and Allen and Conti-Ramsden's system was consistent with the Bishop and Edmundson notion of there being a unified disorder in which grammar and phonology are impaired. In their more recent versions of this system, Rapin and Allen distinguished between isolated phonological disorders and those that were associated with syntactic impairments. The empirical findings of Rapin et al. (1996) supporting this distinction are consistent with results we have reported, where phonological impairments appeared to be independent of semantic and syntactic impairments (Tomblin & Zhang, 1999).

The Rapin and Allen system also predicted that syntactic and phonological aspects of language could be differentially impaired relative to vocabulary and pragmatics as evidenced by the semantic pragmatic disorder. The notion that semantics and pragmatics can form a different dimension within DLDs has also been addressed by Bishop and her colleagues (Adams & Bishop, 1989; Bishop, 2000; Bishop & Adams, 1989). These authors described these children as having excessive speech output, socially inappropriate conversational responses, and difficulties understanding and producing connected discourse. Despite the similarity of these children to children with autism, Bishop and Norbury (2002) provided evidence that many children with these characteristics did not meet the criteria for autism diagnoses or pervasive developmental disorder not otherwise specified (PPNOS). Because these children were not impaired with respect to vocabulary, Bishop dropped the reference to semantics and refers to this condition as pragmatic language impairment (PLI). The profile of communication impairment in these children does not involve phonological or syntactic deficits, but does involve pragmatic deficits. Therefore, this subtype of DLD contrasts with the profile of SLI, wherein the deficits are predominantly phonological and syntactic. As a result of this contrast, Bishop proposed a two-dimensional scheme depicted in Fig. 4.1 within which patterns of individual differences among children with language impairment might be represented.

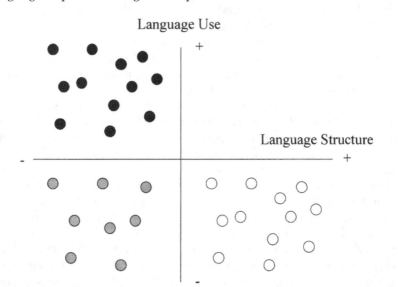

FIG. 4.1.   A model depicting the dimensionality of language impairment in children proposed by Bishop (Bishop, 2000). Two dimensions of language use and language structure provide for a group of children with pragmatic language impairment (PLI, open circles) and a group with impairments of phonology and syntax (SLI, black-filled circles). A third group of children with impairments in both is also represented (grey circles).

Following from Aram and Nation's and Rapin and Allen's work was that of Wilson and Risucci (1986). These authors constructed a theoretical system for characterizing subtypes of children with language disorders. This system was then tested by asking clinical psychologists using a panel consensus to sort children into groups based on test performance. None of these tests was concerned with pragmatics, but rather were traditional neuropsychological tests. The authors then collapsed the resulting 11 groups into 5 subtypes: receptive, expressive, global, memory and retrieval, and no deficits. Cluster analyses were then performed using some of the tests used by the clinicians. The authors concluded that these analyses supported the existence of these five groups. The presence of a receptive-expressive contrast in this system is consistent with Aram and Nation's Factor 3 that involved impairments of either reception or expression. The fact that isolated receptive and expressive impairments were found was not consistent with Bishop and Edmundson's model. Additionally, neither Tomblin and Zhang (1999) nor Rapin and her colleagues (Rapin et al., 1996) found support for the notion that subtypes are formed according to the modality of language use. Instead their data suggested that deficits in one modality were usually associated with deficits in the other.

The schemes for characterizing the patterns of individual differences among children with DLD described earlier are similar with respect to the fact that they organize their subtypes around communication behaviors. Thus, all the dimensions or contrasts that form the subtypes of DLD refer to such things as receptive or expressive language, phonology, semantics, or syntax. One of the most common schemes for subtyping children with DLD has been based on the contrast of language and nonlanguage abilities resulting in a group of children with apparently normal nonverbal development and poor language development. In recent years, these children have been referred to as having specific language impairment (SLI; Leonard, 1998). One of the first explicit conceptualizations of SLI was provided by Stark and Tallal (1981). Within this account, children with SLI could not have other sensory or neurodevelopmental disorders and, most important, were required to have nonverbal IQs above 85. Additionally, these children were required to have at least a 12-month discrepancy between expressive language and nonlanguage developmental levels. The requirement of normal nonverbal IQ in the context of poor spoken language development results in a pattern of language–nonlanguage dissociation. The formation of a subtype of DLD consisting of children with a discrepancy between language and nonlanguage skills by default forms a second group of children who have poor language and poor nonlanguage skills. We have been referring to these children without discrepancies as nonspecific language impaired (NLI). In recent years, several authors (Cole, Dale, & Mills, 1990; Lahey, 1990; Plante, 1998) have argued that the distinction between SLI and NLI is neither conceptually well founded nor supported by empirical data. We (Tomblin & Zhang, 1999) recently compared the language profiles of kindergarten children with SLI and NLI and found that the children with NLI had poorer language skills than the children with SLI, but no differences in the shapes of these profiles were observed. The differences in severity of language deficits for the two groups could be explained by the fact that nonverbal IQs and language scores of these children were correlated. Thus, selecting children with normal IQs naturally constrained the range of language scores in the children with SLI to have higher scores than the children with NLI. Thus, these results point to a quantitative, but not qualitative, difference between children with SLI and NLI. Recently, a panel of experts convened by the NIDCD proposed that the use of performance IQ as a part of the diagnosis of SLI be examined to determine whether this standard should be retained (Tager-Flusberg & Cooper, 1999). Thus, the validity of a distinction between SLI and NLI subtypes remains an open question.

This overview of various efforts to resolve the heterogeneity of children with DLD has shown that no single scheme has received consistent empirical support. Among these systems, we see the possibility that children with DLD differ systematically with respect to a modality dimension having to do with relative strengths and weaknesses in receptive or expressive language use. Additionally, subgroups may be formed with respect to differential abilities in phonology, semantics, syntax, and pragmatics. Finally, the contrast between language and nonlanguage abilities has served as an additional dimension around which this heterogeneity may be organized. Thus, there is a number of potential dimensions of communication and nonverbal performance on which children with DLD can and often do vary.

INDIVIDUAL DIFFERENCES IN TYPICALLY
DEVELOPING CHILDREN

As noted earlier, the study of atypical children is clearly a form of research on individual differences. Thus, it is not surprising to find a modest literature in the study of DLD that concerns the basis of these individual differences in these children. When one examines this literature, however, one finds little consideration of whether the nature of these individual differences in children with DLD is distinct from children who are typically developing. This is not to say, however, that this issue has not been addressed. Leonard (1987) concluded that at least within children with SLI, the empirical evidence suggested that these children represented the low end of the normal distribution of language ability, and these views were echoed by Dale and Cole (1991). Others have argued that distinctive profiles differentiate children with subtypes of DLD from normal learners (Aram, 1991; Johnston, 1988; Rice, Wexler, & Cleave, 1995). A key challenge to our ability to resolve this question lies in the fact that there are few studies of patterns of individual differences in typically developing older preschool and school-age children, which is the stage of development reached by most of the DLD children used for research.

A prevalent view of language development has been that there is a single course followed by all children. Thus, the dimensionality of individual differences among typical learners consists solely of the rate of language development. Despite the prominence of this view, there have been several studies demonstrating contrastive patterns of language development in young children. Perhaps the first of these was Bloom's (1970) nominal versus pronominal style followed closely by Nelson's (1973) work suggesting two styles of lexical learners: referential and expressive. Subsequently, Peters (1978) described analytic and gestalt styles of development based on the use of formulaic utterances or analyzed forms. These patterns of individual differences observed within small samples of toddlers within a period of development were also found to hold across a longer period of development by Bates and colleagues (1988). Shore's (1995) summary of this work provided evidence of two patterns of acquisition that extend through the early stages of language learning. One of these was the referential-analytic and the other the expressive-gestalt style. Shore emphasized that neither of these represented types of children as much as dimensions along which language learners could vary. Shore also noted that little work had been done to determine whether these patterns of individual differences extended past 3 years of age.

One recent study concerning individual differences in 4-year-old children was conducted by Colledge and colleagues (2002). In this study, the factor structure of several measures of language, articulation performance, and nonverbal IQ was examined in a group of 310 pairs of twins. An examination of the eigen values generated from the principal components suggested three factors. An oblique rotation of these three factors revealed that: the language measures loaded on one common factor, the nonverbal IQ measures loaded on a second measure, and the articulation and nonword repetition tasks loaded on a third.

This factor structure was similar to the results of a factor analysis of a similar set of language, nonverbal IQ measures, and articulation measures that we reported recently (Tomblin & Zhang, 1999). This analysis was performed on a set of 1,929 kindergarten children who had participated in an epidemiologic study and represented children with a wide range of communication ability. In this study, all receptive and expressive language measures loaded on a single factor. Articulation, however, was found to form a separate factor and performance IQ a third factor. We also subjected the data to a cluster analysis to determine whether subgroups of children could be identified based on these measures. Although several subgroups were formed, each subgroup had a similar profile. Differences between the cluster groups were largely due to different levels of language proficiency. The sampling methods in this study intentionally oversampled children with poor language abilities, and therefore these children were overrepresented. Despite this fact, the cluster analysis did not yield strong evidence of heterogeneity among these children with poor language abilities other than variation in severity. Additionally, there was no evidence that the patterns of performance in the children with poor language were different from those of the typically developing children.

SUMMARY

There is a general belief that children with language impairment represent a heterogeneous group, and that this heterogeneity can be described as being organized by patterns of strengths and weaknesses in (a) receptive and expressive language; (b) phonological, syntactic, semantic, and pragmatic aspects of language use; and/or (c) language versus nonverbal performance. Interestingly, the majority of the work on individual differences in the language development of typically developing children has revealed a different scheme for describing individual differences in these children. This scheme suggests the possibility of two styles of language development that have been described as analytic or holistic, which may represent alternative approaches children use to process linguistic input and employ language for communication. As noted earlier, most of the research concerning individual differences of typically developing children has been limited to children under 3 years of age, whereas the work on individual differences of children with language impairment has focused on older children. Additionally, these studies have rarely contained any or at best few typically developing children. The one study (Tomblin & Zhang, 1999) that we conducted that did contain both typically developing and poor language learners did not show much evidence of dimensionality within language nor did it show evidence of qualitative subtypes of children with language impairment.

However, we have continued to pursue this question in a study of 604 children who were age eligible to be in second grade (7–8 years old) and had been participants in the earlier study of kindergartners. In this case, we have been able to obtain data concerning these children's use of language in social communication settings that extend our measures of their communication beyond the traditional measures of language often obtained in more standardized testing settings. Our inclusion of this information was motivated by Bishop's (2000) claim that pragmatics represents a different dimension from semantic/syntactic functions, and that the two-dimensional space formed by these two aspects of communication can provide a means of describing the individual differences of children with poor communication skills.

DIMENSIONS OF INDIVIDUAL DIFFERENCES
IN TYPICAL AND POOR LANGUAGE LEARNERS

Ten years ago, we initiated a study of the epidemiology of children with SLI. This study required that we obtain a large representative sample of kindergarten children from which prevalence and risk factors for SLI could be estimated. This cross-sectional sample provided the opportunity to study the communication skills of children with language impairment drawn from a population sampling method rather than relying on clinical referral. Additionally, the children with language impairment were part of a larger sample of children with the full spectrum of language skills. Because this sample represented a relatively rare opportunity to study typical and atypical language, we designed and conducted a longitudinal study of a subsample of these children.

The subsample of children in our longitudinal study consisted of 604 of these children. The sampling for the longitudinal study occurred 2 years after these children participated as kindergartners. More than half (379) of these children had been found to have normal language status as kindergartners and were sampled to form a representative group of all of the typically developing children in the kindergarten study. The remaining 225 were children who had poor language skills in kindergarten. This group was subdivided into those who had SLI because of performance IQ scores above 85 and those with nonspecific language impairment (NLI) due to performance IQ scores of 85 or below.

Each of these children was examined on average 2 years after their initial participation as a kindergartner. This examination consisted of several standardized language measures including those listed in Table 4.1. As can be seen, these measures provided information on the children's expressive and receptive vocabulary and sentence use. Also two measures of phonological performance were obtained. Neither of these tasks was a measure of speech sound production skills, but rather addressed the children's ability to perform manipulations of phonological content of words (deletion) or store and produce increasingly lengthy phonological strings that formed novel words (nonword). A traditional measure of articulation

TABLE 4.1
Measures of Language Administered to All Participants

Language Domain	Language Test	Modality
Vocabulary	Peabody Picture Vocabulary Test–R (Dunn, 1981)	Receptive
	Comprehensive Receptive Expressive Vocabulary Test: Expressive Subtest (Wallace & Hammill, 1994)	Expressive
Sentence use	Clinical Evaluation of Language Fundamentals–III: Sentence structures, Concepts & Directions (Wiig, Secord, & Semel, 1992)	Receptive
	Clinical Evaluation of Language Fundamentals–III: Word Structure, Recalling Sentences (Wiig et al., 1992)	Expressive
Phonological processing	Deletion Task (Catts, 1993)	
	Nonword Repetition (Dollaghan, Biber, & Campbell, 1995)	

performance was not included because few children at this age produce articulation errors, and therefore this task would not provide much information on individual differences. Colledge et al. (2002) showed that their measure of phonological memory loaded on the same factor as articulation, thus the nonword repetition task should provide information about this potential dimension of language function.

Given our interest in exploring the potential dimensionality of individual differences created by the intersection of phonology, semantics, and syntax with pragmatics, it is clear that the measures shown in Table 4.1 are lacking information on pragmatics. The assessment of pragmatic performance requires that one obtain information regarding communication behaviors in various social contexts. Thus, although tasks can be constructed to observe these skills in naturalistic research environments, as exemplified by the *Communication and Symbolic Behavior Scales Developmental Profile* (Wetherby & Prizant, 2001), this can be quite challenging particularly if large numbers of children require evaluation. An alternative to this is the use of parent or teacher questionnaires. Recently, Bishop (1998) developed a questionnaire entitled Children's Communication Checklist (CCC), which she has shown to be sensitive to the identification of pragmatic disorders in children. At the time we observed these children, we did not have the CCC available. However, we did employ two questionnaires that contained questions directed to the child's teacher concerning the child's social communication performance. Some of these items were contained in the *Social Skills Rating System* (Gresham & Elliott, 1990), whereas others were developed as part of a teacher questionnaire. Table 4.2 lists each of the questions asked of the teachers that concerned some aspect of social communication behavior. These questions covered a range of social communication skills having to do with the amount of communication engagement ob-

TABLE 4.2

Questions Posed to Teachers Concerning the Social Communication
Performance of the Participants Along With the Response Choices
Teachers Could Provide and the Factor Loadings of These
Items Derived From a Factor Analysis of These Items

Questionnaire Item	Rating Choices Provided	Factor 1	Factor 2
Interrupts or intrudes on others	Never, sometimes, very often	0.9	0.16
Interrupts conversations of others	Never, sometimes, very often	0.492	0.12
Interrupts others who are talking	Never, sometimes, very often	0.95	0.04
Blurts out answers before questions have been completed	Yes, No	0.90	0.10
Talks while others are talking	Never, sometimes, very often	0.91	0.05
Often talks excessively	Never, sometimes, very often	0.91	0.05
Maintains the topic of the conversation	Never, sometimes, very often	.23	.73
Answers conversational questions appropriately	Never, sometimes, very often	0.25	0.67
Initiates conversations with peers	Never, sometimes, very often	−.20	0.72
Appropriately questions rules that may be unfair	Never, sometimes, very often	0.22	0.63
Invites others to join activities	Never, sometimes, very often	0.04	0.75
Appropriately tells you when he or she thinks you have treated him or her unfairly	Never, sometimes, very often	0.19	0.62
Gives compliments to peers	Never, sometimes, very often	0.18	0.72
Says nice things about him or herself when appropriate	Never, sometimes, very often	0.04	0.62
Introduces topics	Never, sometimes, very often	0.12	0.70
Talks too little	Yes/No		
Talks too much		0.80	0.35
Participates in conversations where partners share equally in the responsibilities of listening and communicating	Yes/No	0.35	0.70
Introduces her or himself to new people without being told	Never, sometimes, very often	0.07	0.68

served by the teacher, the manner in which the child participated in conversations, and the child's use of certain forms of polite communication conventions. For most of these questions, the teacher was asked to rate the child's performance on a three-point scale as shown in the table. In a few cases, the question was posed in a binary form. Two of these binary questions asked whether the child talked too much or too little. As expected there were no children who received positive endorsements on both of these, although some were perceived as doing neither. Thus, these two items were combined such that talking too little was assigned a negative 1 and talking too much was assigned a value of positive 1.

It is clear from looking at the content of the questions posed to the teachers that these items could be measuring more than one property of communication performance. To determine whether these questions were measuring a single property or multiple aspects of communication, we examined the factor structure underlying these individual items. The 18 items were submitted to the factor analysis routine in SAS, that revealed two prominent factors with eigen values of 6.6 and 5.1. The next factor had an eigen value of 1.5, and thus the first two factors were rotated using the varimax method to produce orthogonal factors. The loading of each question on these two factors is shown in Table 4.2. The interpretation of these two factors is fairly straightforward. The first factor contains items that concerned the child's conversational activity level. Items concerned with the amount the child talked loaded on this factor. In this case, excessive conversational activity was associated with high scores and these high values convey a negative feature to those children with such scores. The second factor was more concerned with the social politeness of the child's communication and in particular the child's appropriate accomplishment of conversational participation. We will refer to this as prosocial communication. High scores on this scale are generally desirable.

The questions that we posed to the teachers concerning communication behavior were certainly not exhaustive. However, they do appear to be sufficient to provide a reasonable amount of information concerning two principal dimensions of the pragmatics of communication. The factor analysis suggested that we could combine the items loading on conversational activity together, and that, likewise, we could combine the items loading on prosocial communication together. Thus, these two scales of pragmatics could be combined with the set of language, phonological processing measures described in Table 4.1 and with the Performance IQ subtest from the *Wechsler Intelligence Scales for Children–Third Edition* (*WISC–III*; Wechsler, 1989). These tests provided 12 different test scores for each of our 604 second-grade children. To what extent do we find distinctive dimensions across these scores? It would be within this dimensionality that we should find individual differences across our typical and atypical language users.

To determine this, we again used factor analysis. The principal components analysis yielded a solution containing one dominant component with an eigen value of 5.45. The next factor had an eigen value of 1.09, and then there followed three factors with similar eigen values between .88 and .77. After these five factors, the eigen values dropped considerably in value, thus the five-factor solution was selected. These five factors were submitted to a varimax rotation for factor analysis. Table 4.3 contains the results of this analysis.

The pattern of factor loading again was quite interpretable. The first factor contained all but one of the language measures concerning vocabu-

TABLE 4.3

Factor Loadings of 12 Measures of Language and Communication
Using Scores Obtained From Children With and Without
Language Impairment at Seven Years of Age

			Factor		
Measure	1	2	3	4	5
CREVT	0.80	0.03	0.17	0.18	0.09
PPVT–III	0.73	0.17	0.31	0.13	−0.01
CELF–III: Word Structure	0.69	0.32	0.38	0.06	0.04
CELF–III: Recalling Sentences	0.67	0.51	0.18	0.05	0.01
CELF–III: Concepts and Directions	0.61	0.37	0.38	0.12	0.13
Nonword Repetition	0.47	0.69	−.15	0.02	−0.17
Deletion	0.40	0.57	0.31	0.01	−0.07
Rapid Automatized Naming	0.0	−0.75	−0.37	−0.20	−0.13
CELF–III: Sentence Structure	0.29	0.15	0.78	−0.01	−0.2
WISC–III: Performance IQ	0.32	0.16	0.71	0.23	0.07
Prosocial Communication	0.20	0.12	0.11	0.94	0.03
Conversational Activity	0.07	0.03	0.03	0.03	0.98

lary and sentence use, thus this factor may be described as a semantic/
syntactic factor. The Sentence Structure subtest of the CELF–III, which is a
sentence comprehension test, did not load on this factor, but rather loaded
on Factor 3. We provide our explanation for this pattern later. We also see
that, although Recalling Sentences did have its greatest loading on Factor
1, it also loaded on Factor 2 fairly heavily. This is not too surprising because we see that Factor 2 seems to be a phonological processing factor
that contains a measure of working memory, which is likely to be involved in a sentence repetition task such as Recalling Sentences.

Note that we did not find a separate dimension for receptive and expressive tests. We also did not find that the vocabulary tests loaded separately from the sentence tasks. It is important at this point, however, to remember that our failure to find these dimensions may be due to the
measures used. Some of the tasks that were assigned to the expressive modality, such as the Word Structure test and the Recalling Sentences test,
also required that the child listen to utterances before the expression task.
Likewise, all of the sentence use tasks also required a degree of lexical
knowledge. Having said this, we also must recognize that these measures
are typically used to assess language. If we are unable to reveal
dimensionality along the lines of modality or domains of language with
these measures, then at least within our current measures we are not
likely to find individual differences.

The second factor in this analysis consisted of three measures: the deletion task, the nonword repetition task, and the naming speed on the Rapid

Automatized Naming Task. These are all tasks that in one way or another may involve phonological processing or verbal short-term memory. In fact analogues of these tasks can be found on the Comprehensive Test of Phonological Processing (CTOPP), and recently Schatschneider Francis, Foorman, Fletcher, and Mehta (1999) showed that the subtests of this battery are all associated with a single latent variable. Current results are consistent with these findings and furthermore suggest that this latent variable may be distinct from the latent variable of semantics and syntax that we presume characterizes Factor 1. The independence of the semantics and syntax from phonological processing does not mean, however, that measures loading on Factor 1 do not involve phonological processing/ working memory systems. We can see from Table 4.3 that the measures that required sentence use, and particularly sentence repetition, were also associated with Factor 2.

The third factor contained two items. One item was the Sentence Structure subtest of the CELF–III, and the other was the Performance IQ subscale of the *WISC–III*. This factor is somewhat puzzling in that it appears to represent nonverbal cognitive skills although the Sentence Structure test is clearly a verbal task. Our only explanation is that the Sentence Structure test for children of this age is generally fairly easy, and many children were near ceiling on this test. Most of the children with poor Sentence Structure scores were also children with low nonverbal IQ scores, and thus the variance on this test was associated with nonverbal IQ. Thus, we view this factor as representing nonverbal IQ. The fact that nonverbal IQ may represent a separate dimension from the semantic/syntactic trait of Factor 2 indicates that there is the potential for individual differences to form with regard to discrepancies in children's trait status on these. Consequently, there is the potential to differentiate between children with SLI and NLI.

Factors 4 and 5 represent the two social communication traits that had been found in the prior analysis of the teacher questionnaires that concerned social use of language. In this case, Factor 4 consisted of the prosocial social score derived from those items that loaded on this factor on the initial analysis, and Factor 5 represents the conversational activity or talkativeness trait revealed in the prior analysis. The fact that these two scores loaded on separate factors representing two domains of social communication is not surprising given that they had been constructed from items that had been found to be loading on separate dimensions in the prior analysis. However, in this current analysis, there was no reason to expect that these scores would continue to remain independent factors rather than joining some of the other communication variables to form more generalized communication competence traits. It is somewhat surprising to see how specific these two factors indeed were. They showed little tendency to load on any other factors.

The results of this factor analysis provided evidence for a five-dimensional space within which children were relatively free to vary with regard to relative strengths and weaknesses. We need to emphasize that this space was generated using data from children at one point in development, but who also had a wide range of abilities. Thus, this space represents variation in children with typical and atypical development at least with respect to language and nonverbal development. The sample was constrained to some degree by having excluded children with known developmental disabilities, including mental retardation and autism. Thus, we need to acknowledge that our exploration into the nature of individual differences is constrained by the population from which the individuals are sampled, both with regard to their developmental level and the range of atypical cases included in the sample. An additional constraint concerns the measures that were employed. As we noted earlier, our results cannot be used to claim that these dimensions in language performance do not exist, but only that commonly used measures do not reveal them.

PATTERNS OF INDIVIDUAL DIFFERENCES WITHIN THE FIVE-DIMENSIONAL FACTOR SPACE

As noted before, the five dimensions provided by the 12 measures used in this study create a theoretical space within which children can differ from each other. We can think of this as a universe with five dimensions. To continue with the metaphor, we can then ask whether children are randomly placed in this universe or are arranged in some patterns that deviate from randomness. That is, do we find constellations in our universe? If so, what are the characteristics of these patterns? In particular, how do children with language impairment fit within this universe? Clearly they should occupy one region that represents poor syntactic/semantic performance, but are they otherwise randomly distributed? That is, do we find them in a particular constellation or spread across constellations, should they exist?

There are several methods that might reveal patterns. One method is cluster analysis, which is what we employed in our earlier work with the data from the children who participated in our kindergarten study. In that cluster analysis, several cluster groups were found across the measures of vocabulary and sentences use. However, with the exception of one small group, all the cluster groups had similar profiles. The differences among clusters could be attributed to that of severity. Thus, although some degree of deviation from randomness was found, this might be viewed as local stratification in data that did not represent a coherent complex organizing system. To control for the occurrence of this local variation due to severity, it is best to compute profile scores across measures such that each child's score on each test is subtracted from the child's overall mean. In this way, the data being analyzed reflect the child's relative performance on each test. That is, the scores provide information about intra-individual variation across areas of assessment that is independent of the child's general relative standing among peers. Such scores are referred to as *ipsative scores*. By examining these ipsative scores, we can ask whether there are individual differences in profiles independent of severity.

Five ipsative scores were obtained by first computing a mean z score for each of the five factor domains found in the previous factor analysis. All five scores in the semantic/syntactic area were combined and averaged, as were the three scores concerned with phonology, as well as the sentence structure and performance IQ scores that we are assuming represent performance IQ. We should note that the reaction time score for the RAN task was in the opposite direction to the rest of the tasks in that poor performance (slow response) was represented with larger values. Thus, before being combined with the other phonology measures, the reaction time score was transformed into the complement of the z score of the log transformation of the reaction time score (the log transformation was to reduce the skewness of the variable—reaction time is usually skewed). Likewise, the conversational activity scale was inverted so that low scores would represent excessive and intrusive behaviors.

As mentioned earlier, the individual differences due to overall severity were then removed by subtracting each child's mean of z scores on these five subtests from each of the child's five z scores. Thus, the overall level of the profile for each child was removed from the analysis because all children had a mean of zero. The information retained was the child's profile shape. These ipsative scores were submitted to the Mplus program (Muthen & Muthen, 2001) parameterized to do an analysis of latent class of profiles. The latent class analysis program fitted profile mixture models to the data and provided the log likelihood for each model. Tests were then performed to determine whether models with one, two, or more classes provided better accounts of the data. The purpose of the model fitting was to identify the simplest model that could fit the data satisfactorily. Also just as we did with our factor analysis, the data were weighted such that the language-impaired children, who were oversampled, were given lower weights.

This analysis resulted in a two-class model as shown in Fig. 4.2. We can see that there are two complementary profiles characterizing these two latent classes. These two classes appear to be formed by two sets of measures. One set consists of the semantic/syntactic measures along with the phonological and working memory measures, and the other set consisted of the two measures of pragmatics particularly the prosocial communica-

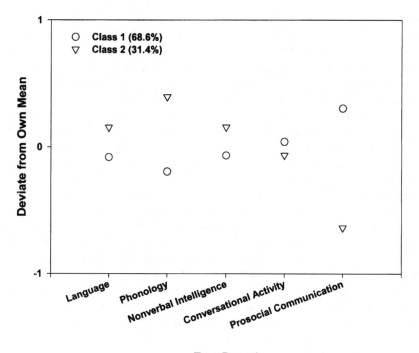

Test Domain

FIG. 4.2. Average ipsative scores on each of five communication and cognitive domains for children in each of the two groups formed by the Mplus profile analysis of each child's score, normalized around his or her grand mean to form an ipsative score.

tion measures. Thus, despite the potential for a large number of subgroups generated by different contrasts within the five latent traits underlying these measures, there seemed to be two dominant groups of these children within this space. That is, there appeared to be two constellations in our universe formed principally by their relative strength and weaknesses in semantics and syntax versus social communication.

Class 1 contained 68.6% of the children in the sample who were characterized by their relatively higher scores in the social communication measures and relatively lower scores in the phonological processing measures. This group also had somewhat lower relative scores in language. In contrast, 31.4% of the children had the opposite profile. It is important to emphasize that these groups were formed based on scores that were normalized around the child's mean score. Thus, some of the children in Class 1 who had phonological processing scores lower than their social communication scores actually had good phonological and semantic/syntactic skills relative to the group expectations. Consequently, the membership of these two groups was open to children with phonological, semantic/syntactic, or pragmatic skills relative to other children (norm referenced) rather than ipsative referenced profiles. Thus, we need to examine the characteristics of the children in each of these groups with respect to their norm-referenced language status either in the form of our clinical categories or continuously with respect to norm-referenced standard scores.

Figure 4.3 shows the composition of the two groups of children with respect to their diagnostic language status (SLI, NLI, Normal) as established when these children were in kindergarten. The distribution of children with typical language skills within these two profile classes was different from the children with atypical language skills. Class 1 contained 71% of the typically developing children. In contrast, 54% and 57% of the NLI and SLI children were members of Class 1. In contrast, Class 2 contained proportionately more of the children in the NLI and SLI groups. These results are not altogether surprising. The profile that provides for relative weakness in language ability also provides for the group that contains most of the poor language learners. However, Class 1 is not solely comprised of children with language impairment because 76% of the children in this class had normal language status. Thus, although the latent class program was provided with profile shapes and not severity information directly,

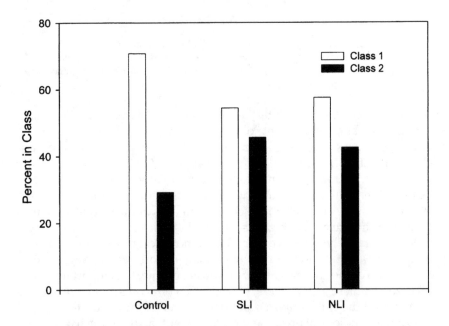

FIG. 4.3. Proportion of children who were categorized in Groups 1 and 2 within the diagnostic groups of normal language, specific language impairment (SLI), and nonspecific language impairment (NLI).

the resulting classification absorbed a disproportionate number of children with poor language skills.

Figure 4.4 provides an alternative way to look at the children in the two classes. In this case, the norm-referenced z score values of the measures used to generate the two classes can be seen for each class. This plot is similar to that of Fig. 4.2. However, in Fig. 4.2, the test scores are referenced to the group average of age mates for each of the measures and are, therefore, norm referenced rather than referenced to each child's mean performance across measures, as is provided in Fig. 4.2. What is clear in Fig. 4.4 is that the two groups differ most with respect to their prosocial abilities and yet are rather comparable with respect to their other skills. The view provided by these norm-referenced scores shows that, in fact, the children in Class 2 may be described, relative to their peers, as children with poor social communication skills. The Class 1 group had semantic and syntactic skills that were average for peers, but slightly above average pragmatic skills. When viewed from this perspective, pragmatics served

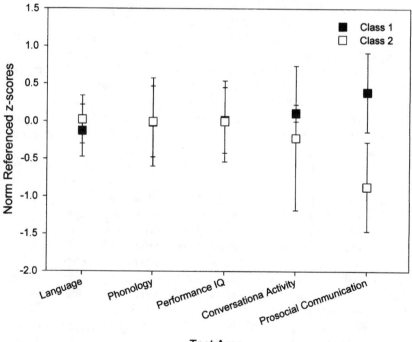

FIG. 4.4.   Average norm-referenced scores on each of five communication and cognitive domains for children in each of two groups formed by a profile analysis of each child's ipsative score.

as a performance domain around which semantic/syntactic skills, phonology, and performance IQ became differentiated in the two groups.
Thus, it would seem that systematic variations among these children's
language, phonology, and performance IQ achievement were sufficiently
independent of their pragmatic abilities to allow two groups to emerge.

IMPLICATIONS OF PATTERNS OF INDIVIDUAL
DIFFERENCES

These results permit us to address some of the issues that were raised in
the introduction. First, to what extent do we find that subtypes of language impairment represent extensions of patterns of individual differences found in typically developing children? Second, is there evidence
supporting particular taxonomic systems that have been proposed?

   With regard to the first issue, these data seem to suggest that language
impairment, as represented by the SLI and NLI groups, is associated with
the patterns of individual differences found across children with typical
and atypical development. The latent class analysis did not result in
groups that were either normal or language impaired at least as we have
defined these. Both groups were formed and, in fact, primarily comprised
of children who are viewed as typical learners. Thus, at least with respect
to this analysis, there was no strong support for a clear distinction between language impairment and normal ranges of language function.
However, the results did show that children with typical language development appear to systematically assort themselves into predominantly
one group structure (Class 1) that accounts for both typical and atypical
communication function. The common feature of this group is the relative
strength in pragmatics against a relative weakness in phonology and semantics and syntax. The most straightforward explanation for this is that
the measures of pragmatics are sufficiently independent of semantics and
syntax to serve as a reference point in the profiles of these children, such
that two groups were formed with regard to whether the child's phonological skills and language skills were better or poorer than their pragmatics ratings. In this respect, it would not be too surprising to find children with poor phonology and semantics and syntax usually having
relatively better pragmatics. That is, so long as pragmatics is an area of
function that is free to vary from semantics and syntax, children who are
poor in these domains would often be expected to have relative strengths
in pragmatics. This would mean that, although two groups were formed,
the contrast between them appears to exist along a continuum of pragmatic versus semantic/syntactic and phonological proficiency.

What are the implications of these findings with regard to subtypes of language impairment? First, it is of particular interest to the topic of this chapter that the children with SLI and NLI did not assort themselves into two different classes. As we have found in our other work (Tomblin & Zhang, 1999; Tomblin et al., 2002), children with SLI and NLI did not appear to be members of separate natural classes, but both assorted themselves into the two classes in a similar fashion. As already noted, most of the dimensions contained in the existing taxonomies that emphasized contrasts on modality or lexical/syntactic contrasts did not emerge from the initial factor analyses. The latent class analysis presented here collapsed these domains. Of the existing taxonomies for language impairment, our results are most consistent with one that allows for independent domains of pragmatics and semantics/syntax. Thus, these results are most compatible with the model proposed by Bishop (2000) and displayed in Fig. 4.1. This model allows for an independence of pragmatics and the domains of phonology and syntax. The latent class analysis suggested that profiles of strengths or weaknesses in semantics/syntax were associated with similar patterns in phonology and were independent of pragmatics. The fact that individual differences in pragmatics appear to be independent of those in semantics/syntax provides the opportunity for there to be a group of children with poor pragmatic skills despite relatively sound syntax/semantics as proposed by Bishop and her colleagues for children with PLI. At this point, the results of this analysis provide motivation for additional work examining the possibilities of these two forms of communication disorder.

SUMMARY

We began by noting that research on DLDs may be aided by placing this work within the context of research methods on individual differences. Several schemes for describing subtypes or subgroups of children with language impairment were described. These systems provide for several potential dimensions around which these subtypes might be formed. Existing research, however, has not provided a strong consensus about which dimension serves as a basis for subtypes of children with language impairment. It has also remained unclear as to whether patterns of individual differences among children with language impairment are similar to those found among typically developing children. In this chapter, we examined patterns of language and communication in a sample containing both children with and without language impairment. Evidence for two subgroups of children with different profiles of communication emerged. One group had relative strengths in social communication and relative weaknesses in the semantic/syntactic aspects of communication, whereas the other group had the opposite profile. Each group contained children with a wide range of absolute skill levels. However, most of the children with SLI and NLI were found in the first group. These results suggest that the patterns of individual differences that underlie normal levels of communication development may extend into the domain of atypical development. Additionally, these results allow for the existence of a group of children similar to those described as pragmatically impaired by Bishop.

REFERENCES

Adams, C., & Bishop, D. V. M. (1989). Conversational characteristics of children with semantic–pragmatic disorder .1. Exchange structure, turntaking, repairs and cohesion. *British Journal of Disorders of Communication, 24*, 211–239.

Aram, D. M. (1991). Comments on specific language impairment as a clinical category. *Language, Speech, and Hearing Services in Schools, 22*, 84–87.

Aram, D. M., & Nation, J. (1975). Patterns of language behavior in children with developmental language disorders. *Journal of Speech and Hearing Research, 18*, 229–241.

Bates, E., Bretherton, I., Snyder, L., Beeghly, M., Shore, C., & McNew, S. (1988). *From first words to grammar: Individual differences and dissociable mechanisms.* New York: Cambridge University Press.

Bishop, D. (2000). Pragmatic language impairment: A correlate of SLI, a distinct subgroup, or part of the autistic continuum? In D. V. M. Bishop & L. B. Leonard (Eds.), *Speech and language impairments in children: Causes, characteristics, intervention, and outcome* (pp. 99–113). East Sussex, England: Psychology Press.

Bishop, D. V. M. (1998). Development of the Children's Communication Checklist (CCC): A method for assessing qualitative aspects of communicative impairment in children. *Journal of Child Psychology and Psychiatry and Allied Disciplines, 39*, 879–891.

Bishop, D. V. M., & Adams, C. (1989). Conversational characteristics of children with semantic–pragmatic disorder .2. What features lead to a judgment of inappropriacy. *British Journal of Disorders of Communication, 24*, 241–263.

Bishop, D. V. M., & Edmundson, A. (1987). Language-impaired 4-year-olds—Distinguishing transient from persistent impairment. *Journal of Speech and Hearing Disorders, 52*, 156–173.

Bishop, D., & Norbury, C. F. (2002). Exploring the borderlands of autistic disorder and specific language impairment: A study using standardized diagnostic instruments. *Journal of Child Psychology & Psychiatry & Allied Disciplines, 43*, 917–929.

Bloom, L. (1970). *Language development.* Cambridge MA: MIT Press.

Catts, H. W. (1993). The relationship between speech-language impairments and reading disabilities. *Journal of Speech & Hearing Research, 36*, 948–958.

Cole, K. N., Dale, P. S., & Mills, P. E. (1990). Defining language delay in young children by cognitive referencing: Are we saying more than we know? *Applied Psycholinguistics, 11*, 291–302.

Colledge, E., Bishop, D. V. M., Koeppen-Schomerus, G., Price, T. S., Happe, F. G. E., Eley, T. C., Dale, P. S., & Plomin, R. (2002). The structure of language abilities at 4 years: A twin study. *Developmental Psychology, 38*, 749–757.

Conti-Ramsden, G., Crutchley, A., & Botting, N. (2003). The extent to which psychometric tests differentiate subgroups of children with SLI. *Journal of Speech, Language, and Hearing Research, 40,* 765–777.

Dale, P. S., & Cole, K. N. (1991). What's normal? Specific language impairment in an individual differences perspective. *Language, Speech, and Hearing Services in Schools, 22,* 80–83.

Dollaghan, C. A., Biber, M. E., & Campbell, T. F. (1995). Lexical influences on nonword repetition. *Applied Psycholinguistics, 16,* 211–222.

Dunn, L. M. (1981). *Peabody Picture Vocabulary Test–Revised.* Circle Pines, MN: American Guidance Service.

Gresham, F., & Elliott, S. (1990). *Social Skills Rating System.* Circle Pines, MN: American Guidance Service.

Johnston, J. R. (1988). Specific language disorders in the child. In N. J. Lass, L. McReynolds, J. Northern, & D. Yoder (Eds.), *Handbook of speech-language pathology and audiology* (pp. 685–715). Philadelphia: B. C. Decker.

Lahey, M. (1990). Who shall be called language disordered? Some reflections and one perspective. *Journal of Speech and Hearing Disorders, 55,* 612–620.

Leonard, L. (1987). Is specific language impairment a useful construct? In S. Rosenberg (Ed.), *Advances in applied psycholinguistics: Volume 1. Disorders of first-language development* (pp. 1–39). New York: Cambridge University Press.

Leonard, L. (1998). *Children with specific language impairment.* Cambridge, MA: MIT Press.

Muthen, L. K., & Muthen, B. O. (2001). *Mplus User's Guide.* Los Angeles: Muthen & Muthen.

Nelson, K. (1973). The structure and strategy in learning to talk. *Monographs of the Society for Research in Child Development, 38,* (1–2, Serial No. 149).

Peters, A. (1978). Language learning strategies: Does the whole equal the sum of the parts? *Language, 53,* 560–573.

Plante, E. (1998). Criteria for SLI: The Stark and Tallal legacy and beyond. *Journal of Speech, Language, and Hearing Research, 41,* 951–957.

Rapin, I. (1998). Understanding childhood language disorders. *Current Opinion in Pediatrics, 10,* 561–566.

Rapin, I., & Allen, D. (1983). Developmental language disorders: Nosologic considerations. In U. Kirk (Ed.), *Neuropsychology of language, reading and spelling* (pp. 155–184). New York: Academic Press.

Rapin, I., Allen, D. A., Aram, D., Dunn, D., Fein, D., Morris, R., & Waterhouse, L. (1996). Classification issues. In I. Rapin (Ed.), *Preschool children with inadequate communication* (pp. 190–228). London: MacKeith.

Rapin, I., Allen, D., & Dunn, M. (1992). Developmental language disorders. In S. Segalowitz & I. Rapin (Eds.), *Handbook of neuropsychology* (pp. 111–137). Amsterdam: Elsevier Science.

Revelle, W. (2000). Individual differences. In A. Kazdin (Ed.), *Encyclopedia of psychology* (pp. 249–252). Oxford: Oxford University Press.

Rice, M. L., Wexler, K., & Cleave, P. L. (1995). Specific language impairment as a period of extended optional infinitive. *Journal of Speech and Hearing Research, 38,* 850–863.

Schatschneider, C., Francis, D. J., Foorman, B. R., Fletcher, J. M., & Mehta, P. (1999). The dimensionality of phonological awareness: An application of item response theory. *Journal of Educational Psychology, 91,* 439–449.

Shore, C. (1995). *Individual differences in language development.* Thousand Oaks, CA: Sage.

Stark, R., & Tallal, P. (1981). Selection of children with specific language deficits. *Journal of Speech and Hearing Disorders, 46,* 114–122.

Tager-Flusberg, H., & Cooper, J. (1999). Present and future possibilities for defining a phenotype for specific language impairment. *Journal of Speech, Language, and Hearing Research, 42,* 1275–1278.

Tomblin, J. B., Rice, M., Miller, C., Weismer, S., Leonard, L., & Catts, H. (2002). *Language-nonverbal IQ discrepancies in children with SLI.* Symposium presented at the Joint Conference of the IX International Congress for the Study of Child Language and the Symposium on Research in Child Language Disorders Madison, WI.

Tomblin, J. B., & Zhang, X. (1999). Are children with SLI a unique group of language learners? In H. Tager-Flusberg (Ed.), *Neurodevelopmental disorders: Contributions to a new framework from the cognitive neurosciences* (pp. 361–382). Cambridge, MA: MIT Press.

Wallace, G., & Hammill, D. (1994). *Comprehensive Receptive And Expressive Vocabulary Test.* Austin, TX: Pro-Ed.

Wechsler, D. (1989). *Wechsler Intelligence Scale For Children–Third Edition.* San Antonio, TX: The Psychological Corporation.

Wetherby, A., & Prizant, B. M. (2001). *Communication and Symbolic Behavior Scales Developmental Profile.* Baltimore: Brookes.

Wiig, E., Secord, W., & Semel, E. (1992). *Clinical evaluation of language fundamentals–preschool.* San Antonio, TX: The Psychological Corporation.

Wilson, B. C., & Risucci, D. (1986). A model for clinical-quantitative classification: Generation I. Application to language-disordered preschool children. *Brain and Language, 27,* 281–309.

Language, Social Cognition, Maladaptive Behavior, and Communication in Down Syndrome and Fragile X Syndrome

Leonard Abbeduto
Melissa M. Murphy
University of Wisconsin–Madison

Down syndrome and fragile X syndrome are the two most common genetic causes of mental retardation (Dykens, Hodapp, & Finucane, 2000). Each syndrome is associated with pervasive impairments in many domains of psychological and behavioral functioning (Chapman & Hesketh, 2000; Hagerman, 1999; Mazzocco, 2000; Rozien, 1997). The program of research described in this chapter is designed to further specify the similarities and differences in the behavioral phenotypes of the two syndromes, with special attention given to language learning and use and the domains of functioning that support language (e.g., cognition, theory of mind). Such cross-syndrome comparisons provide clinically useful information about areas of relative strength and weakness and, thus, the appropriateness of syndrome-specific programs of assessment and intervention. These comparisons also can be theoretically interesting because they help to specify the behavioral consequences of particular genetic variations. They also help to identify relationships between the various dimensions of language learning and use and other dimensions of psychological and behavioral functioning. In this chapter, we present some of our preliminary findings and discuss some of their implications for theory and practice. We also discuss some of the strengths and limitations of the approach we have taken.

LIMITATIONS OF PREVIOUS RESEARCH

Previous research on the language problems associated with these two syndromes has been limited in at least three ways (Murphy & Abbeduto, 2003). First, it has often been based on a rather narrow view of language. For example, considerable effort has gone into studying the ways in which knowledge about syntactic forms is acquired, whereas equally important questions about how such syntactic knowledge is used (or not used) to meet the demands of everyday social interaction have been less well studied (Abbeduto & Hesketh, 1997). Second, previous research has been limited by an emphasis on dissociations between language and cognition and between various components within the linguistic system. For example, researchers have been intensely interested in whether one can have a relative sparing of syntax in the face of substantially impaired nonlinguistic cognitive capabilities (Abbeduto, Evans, & Dolan, 2001). No less important, however, are questions about how relative strengths and weaknesses in different domains combine to produce the behaviors seen in real-life social interactions (Abbeduto & Short-Meyerson, 2002). Third, previous research has attempted to understand the relationship between language and other domains of functioning by focusing largely on cognitive contributions to language. Researchers, for example, have sought to understand the role of auditory memory and other cognitive functions in the acquisition of various aspects of lexical and syntactic knowledge (Chapman & Hesketh, 2000). Language problems, especially problems in using language to interact with others, however, are likely to be shaped by the full behavioral phenotype associated with a syndrome, including the socioemotional dimensions of the phenotype (Abbeduto et al., 2001).

In our program of research, we have attempted to overcome these limitations. Thus, we have focused on (a) how knowledge of the forms and contents of language are acquired, as well as on how that knowledge is used in social interaction; (b) the dissociations between different domains of skill, as well as on how those domains combine to create complex, socially oriented language behavior; and (c) cognitive contributions to language, as well as on the impact of the social and emotional dimensions of the phenotype. In addressing each of these limitations, our goal has been to identify the strengths and weaknesses that differ between syndromes as well as those that are common to both.

BACKGROUND INFORMATION ON DOWN SYNDROME AND FRAGILE X SYNDROME

Down syndrome is the most common genetic cause of mental retardation, with a prevalence of 1 in 700 to 1,000 (Rozien, 1997). Most cases are caused by nondisjunction during meiosis that results in trisomy of the entire

Chromosome 21 or a critical region of it. The phenotype is defined by a number of physical and behavioral sequelae, including a characteristic facial appearance and frequent heart and respiratory problems. Most individuals with Down syndrome function in the mild to moderate range of mental retardation, displaying IQs between approximately 35 and 70 (Chapman & Hesketh, 2000). Their cognitive profile, however, is typically characterized by "unevenness" (i.e., areas of relative strength and weakness). Most notable perhaps is a weakness in auditory short-term memory relative to visual short-term memory and other aspects of cognition (Chapman, 2003; Merrill, Lookadoo, & Rilea, 2003). Although delayed relative to typically developing chronological age peers in virtually all domains of social and emotional functioning, individuals with Down syndrome as a group are highly sociable (Kasari & Bauminger, 1998) and display lower rates of maladaptive behavior compared with individuals with other etiologies (Dykens et al., 2000; Pueschel, 1996). As is discussed subsequently, acquiring the forms and contents of language is an especially challenging task for individuals with Down syndrome. The extent of the challenge, however, often varies depending on the domain of language (e.g., vocabulary or syntax) and modality (i.e., receptive or expressive).

Fragile X syndrome is second only to Down syndrome as a genetic cause of mental retardation, and it accounts for 40% of all X-linked mental retardation (Hagerman, 1999). Fragile X syndrome results from the mutation of a single gene (FMR1) on the X chromosome at Xq27.3 (Brown, 2002), which reduces or completely eliminates the production of its typical protein (Oostra, 1996). This protein, FMRP, has been shown in both animal and human research to be critical for neural development, affecting both the maturation of synapses and the pruning of synaptic connections (Churchill, Beckel-Mitchener, Weiler, & Greenough, 2002; Greenough, Klinsova, Irwin, Galves, Bates, & Weiler, 2001). Fragile X syndrome is associated with a variety of physical and behavioral impairments, although there is substantial within-syndrome variability (Bailey, Hatton, Tassone, Skinner, & Taylor, 2001; Hagerman, 1999; Keysor & Mazzocco, 2002; Mazzocco, 2000).

Much of the variability in the fragile X syndrome phenotype is related to the sex of the affected individual. As in other X-linked disorders, males are more likely to be affected and to be affected more severely than females (Hagerman, 1999; Keysor & Mazzocco, 2002). This sex difference is a consequence of the fact that females with the syndrome possess a second X chromosome that contains the healthy allele of the FMR1 gene, which serves to buffer them from some of the deleterious effects of the mutation (Brown, 2002).

The prevalence of affected males and females is 1 in 4,000 and 1 in 8,000, respectively (Sherman, 1996). Nearly all males with the full mutation meet criteria for mental retardation, with the range of IQs similar to that seen for Down syndrome (Dykens et al., 2000). About half of all females with the full mutation have mental retardation, whereas the remainder are characterized by learning disabilities or social adjustment difficulties without substantial cognitive effects (Keysor & Mazzocco, 2002). The behavioral profile of fragile X syndrome, like that of Down syndrome, also includes areas of relative strength and weakness. Maladaptive behaviors, particularly those reflective of social anxiety and attentional problems, are more frequent in individuals with fragile X syndrome compared with individuals with other forms of mental retardation (Dykens et al., 2000; Keysor & Mazzocco, 2002; Wisbeck, Huffman, Freund, Gunnar, Davis, & Reiss, 2000).

UTILITY OF THE COMPARISON BETWEEN DOWN SYNDROME AND FRAGILE X SYNDROME

Comparison of the behavioral phenotypes of Down syndrome and fragile X syndrome, especially their linguistic dimensions, is useful for at least three reasons. First, there has been considerable research on language development in Down syndrome. As a result, we know that, for Down syndrome, there are interesting asynchronies in development across different domains of language and across many of the behavioral and psychological domains that support language learning and use. Our knowledge of these asynchronies can guide our comparisons with fragile X syndrome, which has been less well studied from the perspective of language. Second, these syndromes account for a large proportion of the students encountered by special education teachers, speech-language clinicians, and other professionals who work with persons with mental retardation. Information about likely similarities and differences between the syndromes can guide the development of an affected individual's assessment and treatment plan. Third, comparison of the behavioral phenotypes of these two syndromes addresses issues of syndrome specificity in ways that are not possible through comparison of a single syndrome to a group of people with mental retardation who are heterogeneous as regards etiology or a group defined as having nonspecific mental retardation. Indeed the latter two comparison groups are problematic because they are likely to (a) include subgroups displaying different behavioral phenotypes, and (b) differ in their composition across studies and over time. As a result, differences between the syndrome and these comparison groups can be difficult to interpret.

DESIGN AND PARTICIPANTS

In all of the studies described in this chapter, the design involved comparisons on various measures of behavior between individuals with Down syndrome and individuals with fragile X syndrome who were matched groupwise on chronological age (CA) and a nonverbal measure of IQ. Matching in this way is important because it allows us to attribute group differences on our other behavioral measures to syndrome rather than IQ or CA. We also included a typically developing comparison group consisting of 3- to 6-year-old children.

The three groups—Down syndrome, fragile X syndrome, and typically developing—were matched groupwise on nonverbal mental age (MA). Matching on nonverbal MA is important because it allows us to use cognitive level as an anchor, or benchmark, for interpreting group differences in other areas of behavior. Inclusion of these three nonverbal MA-matched groups makes it possible to decide whether a difference observed between the syndrome groups on the dependent measure reflects a strength relative to cognition for the higher scoring syndrome group or a weakness relative to cognition for the lower scoring syndrome group.

In the studies described in this chapter, the sample size varied between 16 and 25 individuals per group.[1] The participants with Down syndrome or fragile X syndrome were adolescents and young adults who ranged in age from 11 to 24 years, with a mean near 16 years. Nearly all of the participants included in the analyses had received a formal diagnosis of mental retardation from a professional (e.g., clinical psychologist), and none had a nonverbal IQ above 70. The mean nonverbal IQ across the studies was approximately 40, which places our participants in the mild to moderate range of mental retardation. In most studies, the mean nonverbal MA of the participants ranged from 3 to 7 years, with a mean just under 5 years. At the time of enrollment, all of our participants were reported to use oral language as their primary means of communication and were capable of speaking in phrases and sentences.

There is considerable evidence of a relatively high co-morbidity between fragile X syndrome and autism (Bailey, Hatton, & Skinner, 1998; Feinstein & Reiss, 2001). Although appropriate epidemiological studies remain to be conducted, it has been estimated that 10% to 35% of individuals with fragile X syndrome also meet diagnostic criteria for autism

---

[1]There is overlap in the samples across studies. In some cases, different studies represent analyses of different data collected contemporaneously on the same participants. In other cases, different studies involve samples recruited at different times, with minimal overlap in participants.

(Feinstein & Reiss, 2001). Additionally, there is evidence from at least one study that those individuals with fragile X syndrome who meet diagnostic criteria for autism are qualitatively different from those with fragile X syndrome who do not meet criteria (Rogers, Wehner, & Hagerman, 2001). Additionally, the language problems of individuals with autism have been well documented and, by definition, would be expected to be especially serious in the domain of language use. In the studies described in this chapter, therefore, we have excluded from our samples any individual who also met diagnostic criteria for autism. Consequently, it is important to keep in mind that generalization of our results to those individuals with both fragile X syndrome and autism is not warranted.[2]

It is important to point out that the tradition in behavioral research on fragile X syndrome has been to study males and females separately (Murphy & Abbeduto, 2003). Although a consideration of the reasons for this tradition are beyond the scope of the present chapter, it is worth noting that the result has been to make difficult the integration of these parallel research tracks into a coherent picture of the fragile X syndrome phenotype (Murphy & Abbeduto, 2003). Different tasks or measurement conditions are often used for males and females even across studies purportedly studying the same dimension of behavior. In contrast to the traditional approach, we have included both males and females in all groups in the studies described in this chapter. We have ignored gender when making group comparisons, but then followed up with gender comparisons within the fragile X sample when possible. In the present chapter, we focus only on our diagnostic groups comparisons. It is important to note that to make our diagnostic groups comparable in terms of IQ, MA, and CA, we have included only lower functioning females with fragile X. Thus, our results should be seen as representative of the full range of affectedness for males with fragile X syndrome, but as applicable only to the most severely affected females with the syndrome.

STUDIES ON LANGUAGE, SOCIAL COGNITION, MALADAPTIVE BEHAVIOR, AND COMMUNICATION

Mastery of Language Forms and Contents

We began our studies by examining the extent to which individuals with Down syndrome or fragile X syndrome are delayed in achieving mastery

---

[2]In fact we have collected data on a sample of individuals with fragile X syndrome who also meet criteria for autism. However, the sample is too small at this writing to make any comparison with the results presented in this chapter.

of the basic forms and contents of language. Delays in this mastery are of interest for a number of reasons, not the least of which is that they often limit the individual's ability to communicate with other people. Thus, we addressed the following question with respect to our adolescent and young adult participants with Down syndrome or fragile X: Is language more delayed than nonverbal cognition?

This question was motivated by a considerable amount of previous research on Down syndrome, which has shown that, as a group, individuals with Down syndrome are slower to acquire mastery of basic language forms and contents than would be expected based on their developmental progress in (nonlinguistic) cognitive domains (Chapman & Hesketh, 2000). The gap between the rates of linguistic and cognitive achievements for Down syndrome are evident early in development and by adolescence are characteristic of both the receptive and expressive modalities (Chapman, Schwartz, & Kay-Raining Bird, 1991; Chapman, Seung, Schwartz, & Kay-Raining Bird, 1998; Rosin, Swift, Bless, & Vetter, 1988). Even within the domain of language form and content, however, individuals with Down syndrome display variable delays across different facets of the linguistic system. For example, vocabulary is often at or above nonverbal MA levels, whereas syntax lags behind both vocabulary and nonverbal cognition throughout development (Chapman et al., 1991). We sought to replicate the findings for Down syndrome and determine whether the same profile characterized fragile X syndrome.

We focused first on receptive language (see Abbeduto et al., 2003, for more details). The Test for Auditory Comprehension of Language–Revised (TACL–R; Carrow-Woolfolk, 1985) was administered to all three groups of participants. In this standardized test, the participant responds by pointing to the one drawing of three that matches the meaning of a word, phrase, or sentence spoken by the examiner. The 120 items are organized into three subtests: *Word Classes & Relations*, which measures vocabulary comprehension, and *Grammatical Morphemes* and *Elaborated Sentences*, which are both syntactically oriented. The Grammatical Morphemes subtest measures comprehension of inflectional and derivational morphology (e.g., the plural -s and past tense -ed). The Elaborated Sentences subtest measures comprehension of basic clause and multiclause patterns (e.g., passive sentences such as *The boy is chased by the girl*).

We found a different pattern of performance across the subtests for the two syndrome groups. Based on previous research (e.g., Chapman et al., 1991), we expected that the participants with Down syndrome would do more poorly overall on the TACL–R than expected for their MAs. We also expected them to do more poorly on the syntactically oriented subtests (i.e., Grammatical Morphemes and Elaborated Sentences) than on the vocabulary subtest (i.e., Word Classes & Relations). For the Down syndrome group the results are consistent with this expectation: (a) They achieved age-equivalent total scores for the TACL–R that were lower, on average, than those of the other groups; and (b) the mean age-equivalent score for the vocabulary subtest was significantly higher than the scores for the syntactic subtests, which did not differ. In contrast, the participants with fragile X syndrome displayed a synchronous pattern of development across the domains of behavior examined: (a) Their mean age-equivalent score for the total TACL–R was higher than that for the participants with Down syndrome, but no different than for the typically developing comparison children; and (b) their mean age-equivalent scores did not differ across the three subtests.

We also examined the correlations among the TACL–R subtests and between each subtest and nonverbal MA. After controlling for the contribution of nonverbal MA, we found that none of the subtests was correlated with each other for the participants with Down syndrome, suggesting that they had not organized these components into a single, coherent system of knowledge. For the participants with fragile X syndrome, some of the subtests were intercorrelated, but not as many as was true for the typically developing children. This finding suggests that despite achieving mastery over the same forms and contents as the typically developing, MA-matched comparison group, adolescents and young adults with fragile X syndrome have represented that knowledge in a less integrated manner. Interestingly, all three groups displayed significant correlations between nonverbal MA and virtually all of the TACL–R subtests, which is consistent with theoretical perspectives that place a heavy emphasis on cognitive contributions to language learning (Abbeduto et al., 2001).

In addition to receptive language, we examined expressive language. In doing so, we expanded our scope beyond the lexical and syntactic components of language to include the planning and production of speech. Samples of expressive language were audiotaped for participants in each of the three diagnostic groups. Each sample was transcribed and segmented into C-units, with a *C-unit* defined as an independent clause and any of its modifiers, which can include dependent clauses (Loban, 1976). The C-unit has a number of desirable properties for analyzing the speech of children beyond the age of 3 or 4 (see Abbeduto, Benson, Short, & Dolish, 1995). Four of the measures computed are relevant here: (a) the number of different words used in a sample of 50 C-units, which measured the breadth of vocabulary; (b) mean length of C-unit in morphemes, which provided a measure of syntactic maturity; (c) percentage of C-units that were fully intelligible to the transcriber, which provided a measure of speech articulation skills; and (d) percentage of C-units that contained one or more mazes (i.e., vocal dysfluencies, such as "er" and "um," or repetitions of all or part of a C-unit), which provided a measure of the fluency of speech.

We collected the language samples in two contexts: conversation (with an adult examiner) and narration (of a wordless picture book).[3] A standardized protocol was used for collecting each type of sample (see Abbeduto et al., 1995, for details). The standardization was designed to ensure that the materials and especially the examiner's behavior are reasonably consistent across participants. This consistency is necessary to make meaningful comparisons across participant groups. Unfortunately, standardized procedures for eliciting language samples have not been used in much of the language research on fragile X syndrome, which makes many of the findings difficult to interpret (Murphy & Abbeduto, 2003).

Preliminary analyses of the data yielded two differences between the groups on our measures of expressive language. The first difference was on speech intelligibility: Individuals with Down syndrome produced a higher rate of unintelligible utterances than did the other two groups. This finding is not surprising given that speech articulation problems among those with Down syndrome have been noted by both clinicians and researchers for virtually all points during language development (Chapman & Hesketh, 2000; Kumin, 1996). Poor intelligibility no doubt reflects anatomical differences between persons with Down syndrome and their typically developing peers, as well as the possible contribution of the otitis media that is so frequent in Down syndrome (Chapman & Hesketh, 2000). It is also possible, however, that problems in the construction of phonological representations of words are involved. In contrast to Down syndrome, the participants with fragile X syndrome did not differ from the typically developing comparison children on the measure of intelligibility. This result is surprising because problems with articulation, including harshness of voice and a rapid and variable rate of speech, are frequently noted for this population during clinical observations (Hagerman, 1999). Our results suggest that these problems may resolve by adolescence or young adulthood for individuals with fragile X syndrome. It is also possible, however, that our measure of intelligibility was too gross to capture more subtle, lingering problems in articulation.

The second group difference was on MLU, our measure of syntactic maturity: In the narrative context, the participants with Down syndrome produced speech that was less syntactically complex than did the partici-

---

[3]We collected only narrative samples from the typically developing children because of concerns about their ability to complete our entire protocol given the length of time required. In addition, we felt it would be difficult to arrive at a standardized set of topics that was sensible both for the adolescents and young adults with Down syndrome or fragile X and the typically developing preschoolers.

pants with fragile X syndrome or the typically developing children. There was no difference between the groups, however, in their MLUs in the conversational context. It is important to note that we have found this effect of context in previous studies with different populations: Narration tends to elicit more syntactically complex language in atypical as well as typical populations. As a result, diagnostic group differences in syntactic maturity, if they exist, are most apparent in narration (Abbeduto et al., 1995). Therefore, the findings for MLU are consistent with those for the previously described study of receptive language in suggesting an especially serious delay in acquiring syntax for individuals with Down syndrome, but a pace of syntactic acquisitions in fragile X syndrome that is appropriate to cognitive level expectations.

Social Cognition

In addition to our concern with language, we have been interested in social cognition because we believe that one's level of understanding and reasoning about the social world is likely to have an important impact on language use in social interaction. In examining social cognition, we have thus far focused our attention on the domain of "theory of mind" (Baron-Cohen, Tager-Flusberg, & Cohen, 1993). Theory of mind is the coherent body of knowledge about the human mind that we use to predict and explain our own behavior and that of others (Tager-Flusberg, 2001). We rely on a theory of mind whenever we reason about psychological states such as beliefs, emotions, and intentions. In addition, theory of mind provides the foundation for many important social tasks, including narration and other forms of social discourse (Ninio & Snow, 1996).

Typically, children construct a theory of mind through experience in the social world. It is thought that this experience interacts with neurological mechanisms that are well designed for processing social information, although the extent and nature of this biological preparedness is a matter of considerable debate and speculation (Tager-Flusberg, 2001). Regardless, having a theory of mind is not a unitary ability such that one either has or does not have such a theory. Rather it is multidimensional and encompasses a variety of skills and knowledge that emerge gradually. There are, however, some achievements in theory of mind that are foundational—for example, the recognition that the mind does not copy the world, but instead represents and interprets the world (Tager-Flusberg, 2001). Many theorists argue that the first reliable sign of this recognition is the ability to understand that people can hold false beliefs about the world (e.g., Perner, 1988). Although typically developing children come to recognize the possibility of false beliefs in a rudimentary way near the age of

4 (Tager-Flusberg, 2001), it takes years to fully work out the more nuanced aspects of reasoning about false beliefs (Tager-Flusberg & Sullivan, 1994).

Previous research has documented delays (relative to CA expectations) in achieving this basic recognition about the nature of the mind's activity in both individuals with Down syndrome (Yirmiya, Erel, Shaked, & Solomonica-Levi, 1998; Zelazo, Burack, Benedetto, & Frye, 1996) and individuals with fragile X syndrome (Garner, Callias, & Turk, 1999). Many previous studies, however, were not designed to determine whether theory of mind was more or less challenging than other domains of psychological functioning and behavior for these populations. Moreover, no previous studies have involved a comparison of the relative facility in theory of mind across these two syndromes. Thus, as a prelude to understanding the role that limitations in theory of mind might have on learning and using language in individuals with Down syndrome or fragile X syndrome, we sought to answer the following question: Are achievements in the domain of theory of mind more delayed than those in nonverbal cognition?

In our project, we have developed a task designed to assess the participants' ability to recognize false beliefs. It is similar to those widely used in previous research on typical and atypical populations, although it is modeled most closely on the work of Tager-Flusberg and Sullivan (1994). In this task, which is administered individually, the examiner narrates and enacts for the participant a story using some small props. In the story, an object changes location several times. Some characters in the story, however, do not witness the changes. These characters, therefore, hold a false belief; they think the object is in one location when it is actually in another. Our participants, however, always know the true location of the objects. We ask the participants two kinds of questions: (a) test questions, which assess their recognition of the characters' false beliefs; and (b) control questions, which assess their knowledge of critical events and their ability to handle the linguistic structure of the test questions.

The story and test questions are designed to assess two types or levels of false belief reasoning. First-order reasoning requires that the participants recognize that a story character holds a false belief about the world. In one question, for example, the participants are asked to respond directly to the question, "Where would Tiger look for the M&Ms right now?" Second-order reasoning is conceptually more difficult than first-order reasoning: The participant must recognize that a story character holds a false belief about what yet another story character believes about the world. In assessing second-order reasoning, we ask the participant to respond to the question, "Where would Tiger look for the M&Ms right now?" from the perspective of a story character who holds a false belief about Tiger's knowledge (e.g., "What would frog say [about where Tiger would look]?"). Although typically developing children answer first-order false belief questions correctly near age 4, they do not answer many second-order questions correctly until age 5 to 7 years (Tager-Flusberg & Sullivan, 1994).

In a preliminary analysis of the data for the participants tested to date, we found that the two syndrome groups achieved different levels of performance on the test questions. The participants with fragile X syndrome did as well as their typically developing, MA-matched peers in answering the test questions. In contrast, the participants with Down syndrome answered proportionally fewer test questions correctly than did either of the other groups.

It is important to point out that the poor performance of the participants with Down syndrome on the test questions was not simply a reflection of an inability to deal with the linguistic demands of the task. This is suggested by the fact that they answered the vast majority of the control questions correctly and did not differ from their peers with fragile X syndrome in this regard. Moreover, the difference between groups is still apparent even if we limit our analysis to only those participants who answered every control question correctly.

The especially poor performance of the participants with Down syndrome on the false belief task, therefore, appears to reflect a delay in acquiring a foundational concept that is greater than the delays seen in other aspects of their cognitive functioning. At first glance, this seems at odds with the popular and empirically supported view of the individual with Down syndrome as highly sociable (Kasari & Bauminger, 1998). As Kasari and Bauminger pointed out, however, sociability (i.e., an interest in and enjoyment of social interaction) is not necessarily indicative of social competence. Thus, our results suggest that, although as a group adolescents and young adults with Down syndrome embrace social interaction, they may do so with a decidedly immature conceptual framework.

Interestingly, for the group with fragile X syndrome, the relative competence of adolescents and young adults in the domain of false belief reasoning stands in stark contrast to their well-documented social anxiety and aversion to social interaction (Hagerman, 1999). Thus, they are uncomfortable in social interaction despite having a more advanced social-cognitive framework than their more sociable peers with Down syndrome. As our research continues, we seek to replicate these findings and establish their consequences for language learning and use.

Maladaptive Behavior

We have also been interested in the extent to which maladaptive behavior (i.e., behavior reflective of psychopathology) impacts the learning and use of language in social interaction. Included here are such potentially challenging conditions and behaviors as anxiety, inattentiveness, hyperactivity, depression, and aggression. Based on previous research, we would expect psychopathology and maladaptive behavior to be more prevalent among individuals with fragile X syndrome than among individuals with Down syndrome (Dykens et al., 2000), although such behavior does increase in frequency even for individuals with Down syndrome during the adolescent years (Pueschel, 1996). Before examining the contribution of maladaptive behavior to language, we sought to replicate previous findings of a syndrome difference in this regard. This replication allowed us to establish the reliability of our measurement tool and the representativeness of our samples of participants.

We measured maladaptive behavior by asking parents of our two syndrome groups to complete the Child Behavior Checklist/4–18 (CBCL; Achenbach, 1991).[4] The CBCL consists of a list of problem behaviors (e.g., aggression). For each behavior listed, the informant indicates whether the behavior is characteristic of the target individual. The responses are summed to yield a total score as well as various domain-specific scores. Across our studies and samples, we have generally found higher rates of parent-reported problems for adolescents and young adults with fragile X syndrome than for those with Down syndrome. In particular, attentional problems, problems with anxiety, and problems with social withdrawal tend to distinguish the two syndrome groups, with elevated levels of these problems in the group with fragile X syndrome. These findings replicate those from previous studies, suggesting that (a) use of the CBCL with these populations is appropriate, and (b) our samples are similar to those studied by previous researchers. More important, we have begun to garner evidence suggesting these maladaptive behaviors may have consequences for the use of language in social interaction.

Communication: Using Language in Social Interaction

In examining the ways in which adolescents and young adults with Down syndrome or fragile X syndrome use language in social interaction, we broadly conceptualized communication in terms of a framework developed by Clark (1996). In this *Collaborative Model*, the social use of language is thought to entail collaboration between people as they work toward shared goals. This contrasts with a traditional model of communication, in which the participants in an interaction are believed to be guided largely by a desire to adhere to principles of internal coherence that dictate what constitutes a good or bad conversation (e.g., "each utterance should be on

---

[4]Parents of the typically developing children did not complete the checklist because we expected very low rates of such behavior among the children.

topic"; Abbeduto, 2003). The Collaborative Model requires studying extended sequences of talk to identify the behaviors that speakers and listeners use to help each other achieve their goals.

In studying language use in social interaction by adolescents and young adults with Down syndrome or fragile X syndrome, we have addressed two questions: (a) Is collaborative behavior more impaired than nonverbal cognition? and (b) How is collaborative behavior shaped by other aspects of the behavioral phenotype? In addressing the first question, we have compared the performance of our three diagnostic groups—Down syndrome, fragile X syndrome, and typically developing—in laboratory-based verbal communication tasks designed to require specific types of collaborative behaviors. In addressing the second question, we have examined correlations between measures of these collaborative behaviors and the measures of language, social cognition, and maladaptive behavior described in the previous sections of this chapter.

The first study we conducted to address these questions focused on the process of making clear the referents of one's talk. We chose to focus first on referential talk because we see it as the foundation for all forms of social discourse (Graesser, Mills, & Zwaan, 1997). To study referential talk, we used a variant of the well-known *barrier task* (Glucksberg, Krauss, & Higgins, 1975). In our task, the participant played the role of speaker; a researcher, whose behavior was highly scripted, played the role of listener. The participant and listener each had the same set of four novel shapes. The participant's task was to produce a description of a shape (i.e., the target) on each trial so that the listener could select that same shape from his or her set. The participant and listener could not see each other or each other's shapes, thereby eliminating the use of nonverbal cues as a means of communication. None of the shapes had a ready, universally agreed on description. Thus, verbal collaboration was encouraged. Additionally, each shape recurred several times across trials, making it possible to examine the ways in which the talk changed or did not change as shared knowledge accrued.

Preliminary analyses of the referential talk generated during the task suggested that some aspects of the task were more challenging than others for the adolescents and young adults with Down syndrome or fragile X syndrome. In one analysis, for example, we focused on whether the participants created unique (i.e., one-to-one) mappings between their descriptions and the shapes. The alternative to unique mappings would be the indiscriminate use of descriptions, such that the same description was extended to multiple shapes (e.g., using *star* to describe two different shapes), an approach that reflects a failure to consider the listener's needs. The participants with Down syndrome and the participants with fragile X syndrome were proportionally less likely than the typically developing children to rely on unique mappings. This result suggests that both syndrome groups failed to fully take into account the informational needs of the listener.

In contrast to the results for unique mappings, there were other aspects of referential talk that did not distinguish the three groups. For example, we examined the extent to which the participants shifted from indefinite descriptions (e.g., "a house") on early trials to definite descriptions (e.g., "the house") on later trials. This measure reflects the extent to which the participants recognized that shared knowledge increased as the interaction progressed. Group differences were not found, which suggests that adolescents and young adults with Down syndrome or fragile X syndrome have a developmental level-appropriate appreciation of the fact that the accumulation of shared knowledge has consequences for language.

In still other aspects of referential talk, we found differences between the two syndrome groups. In one analysis, we focused on whether the same description was used for a shape each and every time it occurred. The alternative to such consistency would be use of a new description each time a particular shape was talked about, which would greatly increase the listener's processing burden. We found that the participants with fragile X syndrome were proportionally less likely than the participants in either the Down syndrome or the typically developing group to use consistent descriptions as a shape recurred. This finding suggests a failure to fully appreciate the listener's informational needs. Interestingly, the proportional use of consistent descriptions was negatively correlated with parent-reported attentional problems for the participants with fragile X syndrome. One interpretation of this finding is that an inability to control attention might be causing them to unnecessarily change their referential descriptions from trial to trial. In any case, this finding demonstrates that understanding communication challenges requires consideration of the profile of strengths and weaknesses that define the full behavioral phenotype of the syndrome.

In another analysis, we examined the extent to which the participants used what we termed a *referential frame* to qualify a description and thereby guide or scaffold the listener's comprehension. For example, a speaker would be using a referential frame if he or she said, "it's kind of like an ice cream cone," rather than "it is an ice cream cone." In our task, a higher proportion of referential frames reflected greater skill in collaboration. It was found that the participants with Down syndrome produced proportionally fewer referential frames than did either of the other groups, which did not differ. This finding suggests that the participants with Down syndrome were less inclined to, or adept at, providing scaffolding for their listeners. Moreover, our language measures, especially the expressive measures, were correlated with the proportional use of referential frames by the participants with Down syndrome. Thus, here again we see the influence on communication of the broader behavioral phenotype of the syndrome.

The second study we conducted was focused on noncomprehension signaling, or indicating to the speaker that his or her message has not been understood (e.g., by saying, "Which one?"). Noncomprehension signaling entails monitoring one's own comprehension, determining the source of any problem, and formulating a linguistic response to solicit the information needed for clarification. Failure to signal noncomprehension can seriously disrupt an interaction especially because early misunderstandings can have a snowball effect. In studying this aspect of collaboration, we used a task in which the participant was the listener and responded to simple directions from an adult speaker. The directions required moving one of several potential referents into a scene in a book. The challenge for the participant arose from the fact that some directions were designed to create noncomprehension. For example, the speaker said, "Put the red balloon in the sky," when the referents consisted of only a yellow balloon and a green balloon.

Preliminary analyses of the data suggest that noncomprehension signaling is an especially challenging facet of collaboration for the syndrome groups. Both the participants with Down syndrome and the participants with fragile X syndrome were less likely to signal noncomprehension than were their typically developing, MA-matched peers. Additionally, the participants with Down syndrome signaled noncomprehension less often than did the participants with fragile X syndrome. These results suggest that the development of the collaborative behaviors entailed in noncomprehension signaling is severely delayed in individuals with fragile X syndrome but even more so in individuals with Down syndrome. Interestingly, the appropriate use of noncomprehension signals was related to our measure of theory of mind for the participants with fragile X syndrome, suggesting that the recognition that people can represent the world differently may facilitate the development of noncomprehension signaling. This finding again demonstrates the need to consider the relations among impairments across domains when defining the behavioral phenotype of the syndrome.

CONCLUSIONS

The research reported in this chapter provides new insights into the behavioral phenotypes of Down syndrome and fragile X syndrome. With regard to Down syndrome, our research replicates previous findings demonstrating that affected individuals have especially serious delays (i.e., display below MA performance) in receptive and expressive syntax and in speech intelligibility (Kumin, 1996; Chapman et al., 1991, 1998). Adolescents and young adults with Down syndrome also display excessive delays in the domain of theory of mind, or at least in the achievements tapped by false belief reasoning. Although previous work in this area has often led to the conclusion that social cognition is a strength for individuals with Down syndrome, such conclusions have often failed to distinguish sociability from social-cognitive competence. Our findings are consistent with those of Zelazo et al. (1998), who have also reported a serious delay in false belief reasoning in this population. However, these findings differ from other studies that have not found this delay (Yirmiya et al., 1998). There is a need, therefore, to replicate our findings and better understand the nature of the deficit implied by errors in false belief reasoning and the role of task factors in those errors.

In the case of fragile X syndrome, language and theory of mind are delayed in their development, but no more so than expected from the rate of nonverbal cognitive development. In contrast, maladaptive behaviors—particularly those reflective of anxiety and depression, social withdrawal, and attentional limitations—occur at much higher rates in fragile X syndrome than in Down syndrome. These findings are consistent with a considerable body of previous research (Dykens et al., 2000) and highlight the importance of considering the impact of the full behavioral phenotype on language.

We also found that adolescents or young adults with Down syndrome or fragile X syndrome have especially serious problems in using language for social interaction, with some differences in the dimensions of language use they find most problematic. These syndrome differences in language use may reflect the influence of the broader behavioral phenotype of each syndrome, with expressive language limitations playing an especially important role in the case of Down syndrome and attentional limitations and achievements in theory of mind playing an important role in the case of fragile X syndrome. Evaluating the causal nature of these relationships will require longitudinal study, which we plan to do in the near future.

We conclude with two final points. First, we believe it is important to study problems in language learning and use because studying such problems will help us understand the indirect effects of genes on development (Hodapp, 1997). In other words, it is likely that the ways in which an individual who has Down syndrome or fragile X syndrome uses language in social interaction will shape environmental responses to him or her. These environmental responses will, in turn, set the individual on a cycle of development that will increasingly diverge from that of the typical individual over time. In this way, initial, genetically conditioned behavioral differences between individuals with different syndromes or between individuals with a syndrome and typically developing individuals will be magnified over time. Moreover, these indirect effects may be seen not only on subsequent language development, but also on developments in other domains of psychological and behavioral functioning because language is so often the system that mediates an individual's interactions with his or her world.

Second, it is important to place behavioral differences between syndromes, such as described in this chapter, in proper perspective. One interpretation of syndrome differences on some dimension(s) of behavior is that such differences are evidence of a need to create new, syndrome-specific interventions or educational environments for individuals with a given syndrome. This interpretation, however, does not take into account that there are far more commonalities than differences between most genetic syndromes associated with mental retardation, at least at the level of behavior. Thus, it is probably more appropriate to use data on syndrome differences to customize existing programs, interventions, and strategies rather than creating them anew according to a syndrome-specific profile.

ACKNOWLEDGMENTS

The research reported in this chapter was supported by NIH grant R01 HD24356 awarded to the first author, fellowships awarded to the second author through the John H. Merck Scholars II program and the Jeanette Anderson Hoffman Memorial Wisconsin Distinguished Graduate Fellowship, and NIH grant P30 HD03352 awarded to the Waisman Center. We gratefully acknowledge the contributions of the following colleagues to the research reported in this chapter: Adrienne Amman, Patti Beth, Lori Bruno, Stephanie Cawthon, Ingrid Curcio, Nancy Giles, Patti Johnstone, Selma Karadottir, Susan Kirkpatrick, Doris Kistler, Pamela Lewis, Robert Nellis, Erica Kesin Richmond, Shannon Theis Romanski, Jillyn Roxberg, Susen Schroeder, Susan Vial, Katey Verberkmoes, Elizabeth Wall, and Michelle Weissman. We are indebted to the families who participated in the research so enthusiastically and patiently.

REFERENCES

Abbeduto, L. (2003). Speaking and listening. In L. Nadel (Ed.), *Encyclopedia of cognitive science*. London: Macmillan.

Abbeduto, L., Benson, G., Short, K., & Dolish, J. (1995). Effects of sampling context on the expressive language of children and adolescents with mental retardation. *Mental Retardation, 33*, 279–288.

Abbeduto, L., Evans, J., & Dolan, T. (2001). Theoretical perspectives on language and communication problems in mental retardation and developmental disabilities. *Mental Retardation and Developmental Disabilities Research Reviews, 7*, 45–55.

Abbeduto, L., & Hesketh, L. J. (1997). Pragmatic development in individuals with mental retardation: Learning to use language in social interactions. *Mental Retardation and Developmental Disabilities Research Reviews, 3*, 323–334.

Abbeduto, L., Murphy, M. M., Cawthon, S. W., Richmond, E. K., Weissman, M. D., Karadottir, S., & O'Brien, A. (2003). Receptive language skills of adolescents and young adults with Down syndrome or fragile X syndrome. *American Journal on Mental Retardation, 108*, 149–160.

Abbeduto, L., Pavetto, M., Kesin, E., Weissman, M. D., Karadottir, S., O'Brien, A., & Cawthon, S. (2001). The linguistic and cognitive profile of Down syndrome: Evidence from a comparison with fragile X syndrome. *Down Syndrome Research and Practice, 7*, 9–15.

Abbeduto, L., & Short-Meyerson, K. (2002). Linguistic influences on social interaction. In H. Goldstein, L. Kaczmarek, & K. M. English (Eds.), *Promoting social communication in children and youth with developmental disabilities* (pp. 27–54). Baltimore: Brookes.

Achenbach, T. M. (1991). *Manual for the Child Behavior Checklist/4-18*. Burling, VT: University of Vermont Press.

Bailey, D. B., Hatton, D. D., & Skinner, M. (1998). Early developmental trajectories of males with fragile X syndrome. *American Journal on Mental Retardation, 103*, 29–39.

Bailey, D. B., Hatton, D. D., Tassone, F., Skinner, M., & Taylor, A. K. (2001). Variability in FMRP and early development in males with fragile X syndrome. *American Journal on Mental Retardation, 106*, 16–27.

Baron-Cohen, S., Tager-Flusberg, H., & Cohen, D. (Eds.). (1993). *Understanding other minds: Perspectives from autism*. Oxford: Oxford University Press.

Brown, W. T. (2002). The molecular biology of the fragile X mutation. In R. J. Hagerman & P. J. Hagerman (Eds.), *Fragile X syndrome: Diagnosis, treatment and research* (3rd ed., pp. 110–135). Baltimore: Johns Hopkins University Press.

Carrow-Woolfolk, E. (1985). *Test for Auditory Comprehension of Language–Revised*. Allen, TX: DLM Teaching Resources.

Chapman, R. S. (2003). Language and communication in individuals with Down syndrome. In L. Abbeduto (Ed.), *International review of research in mental retardation, Vol. 27* (pp. 1–34). New York: Academic Press.

Chapman, R. S., & Hesketh, L. J. (2000). The behavioral phenotype of individuals with Down syndrome. *Mental Retardation and Developmental Disabilities Research Reviews, 6*, 84–95.

Chapman, R. S., Schwartz, S. E., & Kay-Raining Bird, E. (1991). Language skills of children and adolescents with Down syndrome: I. Comprehension. *Journal of Speech and Hearing Research, 34*, 1106–1120.

Chapman, R. S., Seung, H.-K., Schwartz, S. E., & Kay-Raining Bird, E. (1998). Language skills of children and adolescents with Down syndrome: II. Production deficits. *Journal of Speech, Language, and Hearing Research, 41*, 861–873.

Churchill, J. D., Beckel-Mitchener, A., Weiler, I. J., & Greenough, W. T. (2002). Effects of fragile X syndrome and an FMR1 knockout mouse model on forebrain neuronal cell biology. *Microscopy Research & Technique, 57*, 156–158.

Clark, H. H. (1996). *Using language*. New York: Cambridge University Press.

Dykens, E. M., Hodapp, R. M., & Finucane, B. M. (2000). *Genetics and mental retardation syndromes: A new look at behavior and interventions*. Baltimore: Brookes.

Feinstein, C., & Reiss, A. L. (2001). Autism: The point of view from fragile X studies. *Journal of Autism and Developmental Disorders, 28*, 393–405.

Garner, C., Callias, M., & Turk, J. (1999). Executive function and theory of mind performance of boys with fragile X syndrome. *Journal of Intellectual Disability Research, 43*, 466–474.

Glucksberg, S., Krauss, R., & Higgins, E. T. (1975). The development of referential communication skills. In F. D. Horowitz (Ed.), *Review of child development research* (Vol. 4, pp. 305–346). Chicago: University of Chicago Press.

Graesser, A. C., Mills, K. K., & Zwaan, R. A. (1997). Discourse comprehension. In J. T. Spence, J. M. Darley, & D. J. Foss (Eds.), *Annual review of psychology* (pp. 163–189). Palo Alto, CA: The Annual Reviews.

Greenough, W. T., Klinsova, A. Y., Irwin, S. A., Galves, R., Bates, K. E., & Weiler, I. J. (2001). Synaptic regulation of protein synthesis and the fragile X protein. *Proceedings of the National Academy of Sciences of the United States of America, 98,* 7101–7106.

Hagerman, R. J. (1999). Fragile X syndrome. In R. J. Hagerman (Ed.), *Neurodevelopmental disorders* (pp. 61–132). Oxford: Oxford University Press.

Hodapp, R. M. (1997). Direct and indirect behavioral effects of different genetic disorders of mental retardation. *American Journal on Mental Retardation, 102,* 67–80.

Kasari, C., & Bauminger, N. (1998). Social and emotional development in children with mental retardation. In J. A. Burack, R. M. Hodapp, & E. Zigler (Eds.), *Handbook of mental retardation and development* (pp. 411–433). New York: Cambridge University Press.

Keysor, C. S., & Mazzocco, M. M. M. (2002). A developmental approach to understanding fragile X syndrome in females. *Microscopy Research and Technique, 57,* 179–186.

Kumin, L. (1996). Speech and language skills in children with Down syndrome. *Mental Retardation and Developmental Disabilities Research Reviews, 2,* 109–115.

Loban, W. (1976). *Language development: Kindergarten through grade twelve* (Res. Rep. No. 18). Urbana, IL: National Council of Teachers of English.

Mazzocco, M. M. M. (2000). Advances in research on the fragile X syndrome. *Mental Retardation and Developmental Disabilities Research Reviews, 6,* 96–106.

Merrill, E. C., Lookadoo, R., & Rilea, S. (2003). Memory, language comprehension, and mental retardation. In L. Abbeduto (Ed.), *International Review of Research in Mental Retardation, Vol. 27* (pp. 151–189). New York: Academic Press.

Murphy, M. M., & Abbeduto, L. (2003). Language and communication in fragile X syndrome. In L. Abbeduto (Ed.), *International Review of Research in Mental Retardation, Vol. 27* (pp. 83–119). New York: Academic Press.

Ninio, A., & Snow, C. E. (1996). *Pragmatic development.* Boulder, CO: Westview.

Oostra, B. A. (1996). FMR1 protein studies and animal model for fragile X syndrome. In R. J. Hagerman & A. C. Cronister (Eds.), *Fragile X syndrome: Diagnosis, treatment, and research* (2nd ed., pp. 193–209). Baltimore: Johns Hopkins University Press.

Perner, J. (1988). Higher-order beliefs and intentions in children's understanding of social interaction. In J. W. Astington, P. L. Harris, & D. R. Olson (Eds.), *Developing theories of mind* (pp. 271–294). New York: Cambridge University Press.

Pueschel, S. M. (1996). Young people with Down syndrome: Transition from childhood to adulthood. *Mental Retardation and Developmental Disabilities Research Reviews, 2,* 90–95.

Rogers, S. J., Wehner, D. E., & Hagerman, R. (2001). The behavioral phenotype in fragile X: Symptoms of autism in very young children with fragile X syndrome, idiopathic autism, and other developmental disorders. *Journal of Developmental & Behavioral Pediatrics, 22,* 409–417.

Rosin, M., Swift, E., Bless, D., & Vetter, D. (1988). Communication profiles of adolescents with Down syndrome. *Journal of Childhood Communication Disorders, 12,* 789–798.

Rozien, N. J. (1997). Down syndrome. In M. L. Batshaw (Ed.), *Children with disabilities* (4th ed., pp. 361–376). Baltimore: Brookes.

Sherman, S. (1996). Epidemiology. In R. J. Hagerman & A. Cronister (Eds.), *Fragile X syndrome: Diagnosis, treatment, and research* (pp. 165–192). Baltimore: Johns Hopkins University Press.

Tager-Flusberg, H. (2001). A reexamination of the theory of mind hypothesis of autism. In J. A. Burack, T. Charman, N. Yirmiya, & P. R. Zelazo (Eds.), *The development of autism: Per-*

spectives from theory and research (pp. 173–193). Mahwah, NJ: Lawrence Erlbaum Associates.

Tager-Flusberg, H., & Sullivan, K. (1994). A second look at second-order belief attribution in autism. *Journal of Autism and Developmental Disorders, 24,* 577–586.

Wisbeck, J. M., Huffman, L. C., Freund, L., Gunnar, M. P., Davis, E. P., & Reiss, A. L. (2000). Cortisol and social stressors in children with fragile X: A pilot study. *Developmental and Behavioral Pediatrics, 21,* 278–282.

Yirmiya, N., Erel, O., Shaked, M., & Solomonica-Levi, D. (1998). Meta-analyses comparing theory of mind abilities of individuals with autism, individuals with mental retardation, and normally developing individuals. *Psychological Bulletin, 124,* 283–307.

Zelazo, P. D., Burack, J. A., Benedetto, E., & Frye, D. (1996). Theory of mind and rule use in individuals with Down's syndrome: A test of the uniqueness and specificity claims. *Journal of Child Psychology and Psychiatry, 37,* 479–484.

6

Investigating Knowledge of Complex Syntax: Insights From Experimental Studies of Williams Syndrome

Andrea Zukowski
University of Maryland

DIFFICULT QUESTIONS IN LANGUAGE EVALUATION

It is relatively easy to quantify performance on tests of language. A more difficult task is translating a pattern of performance into conclusions regarding the linguistic abilities/mechanisms that underlie that performance. For example, poor performance can be caused by many things: deviant or missing knowledge, parsing difficulty, memory overload, and so on. In the adult processing literature, it is taken for granted that adults who are unable to interpret triple-embedded clauses or who misinterpret relative clauses of some types in speeded tasks do not do so because of impaired grammatical knowledge. However, when some population of interest has a cognitive or linguistic disorder, they cannot be granted the same benefit of the doubt because the integrity of their linguistic knowledge may itself be the object of study.

Despite the difficulty of translating performance on language measures into conclusions regarding grammatical knowledge, there are good reasons to at least try. One reason is that poor performance by disordered groups is sometimes equated with impaired competence, and premature conclusions are drawn about the relevance of those disorders to theories of language acquisition. Another important reason to try to understand the causes of poor performance is that a deeper understanding may elucidate cross-etiology comparisons. For example, at the level of performance, a particular structure may be difficult across many disorders, but this does not necessarily mean that the structure is difficult in the same way for everyone (just as two groups who share visuomotor integration problems may not share a common cause for those problems). One group may lack knowledge of the structure entirely, whereas another may have the requisite knowledge, but have difficulty deploying that knowledge for any number of reasons. To help investigate grammatical knowledge, especially with cognitively impaired groups, it is useful to draw on techniques that have been successfully used to evaluate linguistic knowledge in young typically developing children.

In this chapter, I review two recent studies that address claims of impaired or deviant language in Williams syndrome (WS). One study investigates the possibility that people with WS perform poorly in comprehension tests with items containing relative clauses because their grammars simply do not generate these structures. The main finding of this study is that the grammars of people with WS do generate these structures, suggesting that the requisite syntactic knowledge is intact. However, two additional findings corroborate the fact that people with WS do have problems with relative clauses at the level of performance. First, some relative clauses are much more rare in elicited speech than others, suggesting that they are more difficult to produce. Second, a consistent error of meaning/ form correspondence is observed in the production of the "difficult" type of relative clause. These results highlight the fact that having knowledge of a structure is not enough to guarantee consistently good performance. A second study investigates whether people with WS produce developmentally normal errors in the syntax of question formation. These errors are typically not observable without experimentation because they occur in question types that are infrequent in spontaneous speech. The finding is that WS children and adolescents do produce these developmentally normal syntactic errors even though the errors are not attested in the input. This provides evidence that syntactic development is driven by the same mechanisms in WS as it is in unimpaired children. The errors are not accounted for by theories that suggest that deviant or shallow mechanisms such as auditory rote memory drive language development in WS.

Both studies reviewed here use the technique of elicited production, which involves placing participants in communicative situations that are specifically designed so that the particular structure that the experimenter is interested in is the most natural response. In the ideal case, the target structure would be uniquely appropriate to the situation, but this ideal is difficult to attain in practice. For groups of people with reasonably good expressive language, elicited production is particularly well suited as a method for investigating knowledge of specific structures of interest. For example, this technique has proved successful in demonstrating competence in particular language domains in young unimpaired children who perform worse in these domains when tested by other means (many examples of this are summarized in Crain & Thornton, 1998).

Elicited production offers another important benefit as well. It allows the experimenter to examine knowledge of structures that tend to be rare in spontaneous speech. If a group of interest fails to produce any examples of a rare target structure in spontaneous speech, it is difficult to know what to conclude. However, if they fail to produce any examples of a structure, even with increased contextual pressure to do so (and with proof that this manipulation does increase attempts at the structure in other groups), this absence is more meaningful. It strengthens the possibility that the structure is simply beyond the grammatical capabilities of the group being tested. Alternatively, if a group of interest succeeds in producing unmodeled examples of a given structure, this provides compelling evidence of knowledge of that structure. Furthermore, the fidelity of the information provided by the attempted production of a given structure is often greater than that available from other sources. For example, in comprehension tests that require participants to pick out the correct picture that matches a spoken sentence from an array with several distractors, it is possible to do well even while lacking some grammatical knowledge because it is impractical to include the number of distractor items that would be required to violate every grammatical detail. By contrast, when producing a complex structure with no immediate model, every grammatical detail provides room for error so it is nearly impossible to accidentally produce a fully grammatical example of a complex syntactic structure. For similar reasons, overt errors in speech production also tend to be more informative than errors made in comprehension tests. Overt production errors provide more detailed information about exactly what aspect of the target structure is problematic. The elicitation studies are reviewed after a brief overview of WS.

WILLIAMS SYNDROME

WS is a neurodevelopmental disorder with an incidence of about 1/20,000 live births. It is caused by a hemizygous microdeletion on the long arm of Chromosome 7, which affects at least 17 genes (Osborne, et al., 2001). The deletion affects multiple physical and cognitive systems. Some of the prominent features include a distinctive combination of facial features, a hoarse voice, heart valve defects, kidney problems, hypersensitivity to sound, joint abnormalities, a unique personality profile, and mild to moderate mental retardation (see Morris & Mervis, 1999, for a detailed description of the full range of features). Cognitively, visuospatial constructive cognition is disproportionately weak relative to overall cognitive level, and this pattern has been identified by Mervis and colleagues as part of the clinical cognitive profile of WS (see Mervis, chap. 8, this volume, for further details regarding the profile).

In terms of language development, first words and first productive word combinations are usually delayed in WS relative to typically developing children (Mervis, Robinson, Rowe, Becerra, & Klein-Tasman, in press). The delay can be quite substantial. For example, in one longitudinal study of seven WS children, first novel word combinations varied from 26 months to 50 months (Mervis et al., 1995). The emergence of complex syntactic structures in spontaneous speech continues to be delayed throughout childhood (Klein, 1995). However, the complexity of the structures that people with WS produce is developmentally appropriate for the length of their utterances, and the structures seem to emerge in a developmentally normal sequence (Klein, 1995). By adolescence, if not before, the expressive language of people with WS is typically very good, and spontaneous speech may contain examples of full passives, relative clauses, and other types of multiclausal embedding (Bellugi, Marks, Bihrle, & Sabo, 1988). The emergence of grammatical morphology is also delayed in WS, although once it begins to emerge spontaneously, further morphological development proceeds at a normal pace (Mervis et al., 1995). By adolescence, if not before, grammatical morphology is usually very good in English-speaking people with WS (Bellugi et al., 1988), with near-ceiling use of grammatical morphemes in obligatory contexts (Clahsen & Almazan, 1998). There is evidence that grammatical morphology is less uniformly good for people with WS who speak morphologically richer languages, such as French, Italian, and Hebrew (Karmiloff-Smith et al., 1997; Levy & Hermon, 2003; Volterra, Capirci, & Caselli, 2001). Some have argued that the difficult aspects of grammatical morphology are restricted to things that must be memorized in the lexicon (Clahsen & Almazan, 1998, 2001; Clahsen & Temple, 2003). Syntactic binding has been examined in one small group of WS adolescents (Clahsen & Almazan, 1998); their interpretation of the referents of pronouns (e.g., *him*) and reflexives (e.g., *himself*) demonstrated perfect knowledge of binding constraints. Further details regarding relative clause syntax in WS are provided in the next section.

A STUDY OF RELATIVE CLAUSE SYNTAX IN WILLIAMS SYNDROME

Many studies have demonstrated that the comprehension of sentences containing relative clauses is difficult for both children and adults with WS as assessed by commonly used comprehension tests such as Bishop's

(1983) Test for Reception of Grammar (TROG; Karmiloff-Smith et al., 1997; Mervis et al., 1999; Volterra, Capirci, Pezzini, Sabbadini, & Vicari, 1996). When further details are provided, these studies also demonstrate that the degree of difficulty varies among different types of relative clauses, but it varies in the same way from study to study. These results for people with WS should not be at all surprising because the same structures that cause difficulty for people with WS also cause difficulty for people with no evidence of frank cognitive or language impairments, including typically developing children (Goodluck & Tavakolian, 1982; Volterra et al., 1996), elderly people (Karmiloff-Smith et al., 1998; Zurif et al., 1995), and even unimpaired adults (see Bishop, 1998, for a discussion of difficulty on the TROG; see Gibson, 1998, for references to the comparative difficulty of different types of relative clauses in studies utilizing phoneme-monitoring, reading times, response-accuracy to probe questions, and hemodynamic measures).

The difficulty in relative clause comprehension among people with WS has been cited as evidence that WS language is not intact (Karmiloff-Smith et al., 1997). If what is meant by this claim is that people with WS have difficulty with normally difficult aspects of language, then this is undeniably true. A stronger version of the claim, which would have deeper theoretical ramifications, is that the grammatical competence of people with WS is not intact.

The question that I address here is what people with WS know about the syntax of relative clauses and sentential embedding. Specifically, I would like to know whether these structures are simply absent from WS grammars. If the grammars of people with WS do not generate relative clauses and/or have no mechanism for allowing sentential embedding, there is no way to interpret these structures in the speech of others except by resorting to extralinguistic strategies. This would provide a straightforward explanation for poor comprehension test results. The alternative possibility is that people with WS do have some or all of the grammatical knowledge required to generate and evaluate these structures, but that other factors are responsible for the poor comprehension test results—perhaps the same factors that make these structures difficult for unimpaired groups.

In a recent study, I investigated knowledge of relative clauses and sentential embedding in WS using an elicited production test (see Zukowski, 2001a, for full details). Participants included 10 WS children and adolescents (ages 10;0–16;3) and 10 typically developing child controls (ages 4;6–7;6). Children were matched individual by individual according to similar raw scores on both the Vocabulary and Matrices subtests of the Kaufman Brief Intelligence Test (KBIT; Kaufman & Kaufman, 1990). Pooled t tests showed that the two groups did not differ on either subtest (for Matrices, $p = .80$; for Vocabulary, $p = .53$). Standard scores from these tests demonstrated mild to moderate levels of mental retardation in the WS group. Standard scores for the WS group for the Vocabulary subtest ranged from 40 to 90 ($M = 64.5$), and for the Matrices subtest they ranged from 40 to 87 ($M = 64.9$).

Methods

The TROG (Bishop, 1983) was first administered to both the WS group and the control children. The results demonstrate that both groups of children displayed the typical pattern of difficulty across different relative clause types, although the control group scored slightly higher than the WS group. Rates of errors by the WS group averaged from 40% for the easiest structures (subject gap relatives embedded in right-branching positions) to 75% for the most difficult structures (object gap relatives in center-embedded positions; see Table 6.1 for examples of these structures). The elicited production test was then administered. A widely used technique for making relative clauses particularly felicitous is to introduce two identical characters and then distinguish them by having one of them, but not the other, participate in some event (Hamburger & Crain, 1982; McKee, McDaniel, & Snedeker, 1998). When 3-year-olds are asked to tell a blind-folded adult which character the experimenter is pointing to, they are likely in this context to produce a noun phrase (NP) response containing a relative clause, such as *the horse that the boy is chasing*. However, these responses cannot be directly compared to the items used in comprehension tests because the latter typically consist of relative clauses embedded in full sentences (e.g., *the horse that the boy is chasing is fat*). To make the production results more comparable to the comprehension results, it was necessary to develop a new elicitation technique. The technique builds on the insight of the original design. In the new technique, two identical characters are introduced, which are distinguishable by their participation in dif-

TABLE 6.1
Sample Target Structures for Relative Clause Study

	Relative Clause Targets	
Embedding Context	Subject Gap	Object Gap
NP (noun phrase)	The girl who's pointing at the cow.	The man who the girl is jumping over.
Center embedded	The girl who's pointing at the cow turned pink.	The man who the girl is jumping over turned pink.
Right branching	Max is looking at the girl who's pointing at the cow.	Max is looking at the man who the girl is jumping over.

ferent events (e.g., a boy who is pointing an arrow at his finger vs. a boy who is pointing an arrow at his elbow). Both characters then undergo a change (e.g., one boy turns blue and the other turns purple), and children are asked a double question about the change (e.g., "Which boy turned purple and which boy turned blue?"). Note that a double question like this cannot be answered with two conjoined relative clauses inside NPs (e.g., *The one who's pointing to his elbow and the one who's pointing to his finger*). Thus, the simultaneous posing of both questions created the critical context requiring children to embed each relative clause inside a full matrix clause (e.g., *The boy who's pointing to his elbow turned purple, and the boy who's pointing to his finger turned green*). Participants examined pictures on a computer screen, observed the changes that occurred, and were then asked to tell a naive helper which character or characters the changes had happened to.

The types of relative clauses that were targeted included subject gap (SG) relatives, such as *the girl who's pointing at the cow*, and object gap (OG) relatives, such as *the man who the girl is jumping over*. One third of the SG trials were designed to elicit NP-only responses, one third were designed to elicit center-embedded relative clauses, and one third were designed to elicit right-branching relative clauses. The same three embedding contexts were targeted for the OG trials. Examples of all of these target structures can be seen in Table 6.1. Sixty-four trials created 48 opportunities to produce an SG relative clause, 48 opportunities to produce an OG relative clause, 32 opportunities to center-embed a relative clause, and 32 opportunities to embed a relative clause in a right-branching position for each child.

Results

The elicitation technique proved extremely successful at eliciting attempts at relative clauses. The test resulted in a corpus of over 600 relative-clause-containing responses for each group, and most responses to the double-question trials consisted of relative clauses embedded in full sentences. Table 6.2 provides examples of some of the WS responses. Table 6.3 provides a count of the total number of responses that contained SG and OG relative clauses separated by group (WS vs. control) and target relative type (SG vs. OG). Responses that did not contain relative clauses are not included in this summary, but alternative responses were almost always grammatically correct and semantically appropriate to the scenes described (see Zukowski, 2001a, for discussion of the full range of responses).

The first analysis is an examination of which basic structures each participant was capable of producing. The results demonstrate that all of the WS children (10/10) were able to produce SG relative clauses, 9/10 were

TABLE 6.2
Sample Responses From WS Participants

Participant Characteristics	Elicited Response
Female, age 10;5	Bill is looking at the, the horse that the other kid is sitting on.
Male, age 10;7	Max is looking at the boy that's waving his hand.
Female, age 11;5	Bill is looking at the boy who's pointing to his elbow.
Male, age 12;10	Max is looking at the cow who um the boy's pointing to.
Female, age 14;3	The one girl's pointing to.
Male, age 16;5	Bill is looking at the cat that the girl's chasing.

TABLE 6.3
Total Counts of Responses Containing Relative Clauses

Response		SG Target	OG Target
SG	WS	368	225
	Control	395	110
OG	WS	2	51
	Control	15	245

able to produce OG relatives, and 9/10 were able to embed relative clauses in both right-branching and center-embedded positions (for the control group, these figures were 10/10, 9/10, and 10/10, respectively). The second analysis is an examination of the grammatical details of the responses. Excluding the results of one child with WS and one control child who had slightly higher rates of errors, the grammatical details of these complex relative clauses were correct 95% of the time. These results clearly demonstrate that people with WS have the syntactic and morphological knowledge necessary to generate relative clauses and to do sentential embedding. Therefore, poor comprehension of sentences with these structures cannot be due to an inability of WS grammars to generate these structures. The explanation for the difficulty must lie elsewhere.

Despite the impressive knowledge of the syntax of relative clauses that these results demonstrate, two areas of difficulty for both groups of children were revealed by subsequent analyses, both of which may eventually inform proposals regarding the source of comprehension test difficulties. First, despite equal numbers of target opportunities for SG and OG relative clauses, both groups produced OG relatives much less frequently than SG relatives. This pattern was exaggerated in the WS group due to extremely low rates of production of OG relatives. Both of these patterns can be seen in Table 6.3.

A second area of difficulty is suggested by another pattern in Table 6.3. Many responses to OG target trials contained not OG relatives, but SG relatives (225 for the WS group and 110 for the control group). Some of these responses accurately described the scenes, but the majority of them did not. Rather, most of these responses consisted of novel errors that I call *mapping errors*. To illustrate, in a context designed to elicit the OG target "The truck that the girl is jumping over turned red," children often produced instead an SG response such as "The girl who's jumping over the truck turned red." Such mapping errors are not syntactically ill formed, but they do not express the child's intended meaning. Hence, they represent errors in mapping from meaning to structure. Mapping errors were made while viewing the pictures with the color changes, so they are not due to confusion about which object or person changed color. These errors were robustly present in responses from both groups, but were over two and a half times as frequent among the WS group (173 mapping errors in the WS group, 65 in the control group). Mapping errors were also confined almost exclusively to contexts where the intended target structure was an OG relative, and they occurred irrespective of the embedding context of the relative (right-branching, center-embedded, or NP only). This pattern was observed in both groups of children. This distribution of the errors suggests that the difficulty of OG relatives is independent of any difficulties that might be associated with embedding generally or with center embedding specifically.

Another distributional similarity between the groups regarding the occurrence of mapping errors was evident in an analysis of individual trials. Rates of mapping errors varied considerably from trial to trial among the eight trials designed to elicit OG relatives, and the pattern of intertrial variation was strikingly similar for the two groups of children. This variation in rates of mapping errors among OG trials suggests that differences among the events depicted in the trials were at least partially responsible for the commission of these errors. Post-hoc examination of the events suggested that mapping errors were most frequent when the targeted head of the relative was an inanimate object being acted on by a person (e.g., target: *the truck that the girl is jumping over*). Mapping errors were least frequent in the one event that had no animates at all (e.g., target: *the house that the helicopter is flying over*) and in the one event where the targeted head of the relative was a person (e.g., target: *the man who the girl is jumping over*).

The pattern of mapping errors observed in this study suggests that these errors occur, in part, because of a bias to view events from the perspective of human and/or agentive participants. It is known that such a bias influences adults' simple descriptions of events that consist of an agent doing something to a patient (Sridhar, 1988). Adults prefer to describe such events as an agent doing something to a patient, rather than as a patient having something done to it. For example, when viewing a scene with a girl jumping over a truck, adults would be much more likely to say that a girl is doing something, rather than that a truck is having something done to it. This bias may have influenced relative clause production in the relative clause task because the task required participants to incorporate descriptions of these kinds of events into their relative clause responses. In a relative clause structure, the event is expressed from the perspective of the head of the relative clause. That is, in the expression "The girl who is jumping over the truck," the jumping event is expressed from the perspective of the girl. By contrast, in the expression "The truck that the girl jumped over," the jumping event is expressed from the perspective of the truck. In experimental trials designed to elicit object gap relatives, participants may experience multiple competing pressures that bias them to express an answer from different perspectives. For example, in one scene, a truck that a girl is jumping over turns red. In this trial, participants are asked, "Which truck turned red?" The prompt question exerts pressure to respond from the perspective of the truck. But competing with this pressure is a natural bias to view the jumping event from the perspective of the girl. By hypothesis, the child's response will be dependent on the strength of these competing pressures, which will vary from trial to trial, as the cognitive bias varies from one event to another. This analysis of mapping errors is currently being tested via experimental manipulation. If accurate, it will provide evidence that underlying knowledge of both the syntactic form of SG and OG relatives, and their corresponding semantic interpretation, is intact in WS, but that implementation of this knowledge may be disrupted in the real-time process of language production in just the same way that it is in unimpaired children. It remains an open and interesting question why people with WS would be more prone to disruption from these proposed factors than others.

A STUDY OF QUESTION SYNTAX
IN WILLIAMS SYNDROME

The relative clause study documented a novel error that children make when attempting to produce certain kinds of relative clauses. Errors that are not simply a reflection of the input are tangible products of children's internal grammars and/or their language production systems. Thus, just as fully grammatical utterances exemplifying complex syntactic constructions can tell us something about these internal systems, consistent errors may provide another source of information about the properties of these systems. A second study, which I review next, probed for the existence of errors that typically developing children are known to make.

Yes/no and wh-questions are complex syntactic structures that until recently had not been systematically studied in WS. It was originally observed by Bellugi (1965) that typically developing 4- and 5-year-old children show a striking pattern in their question production of excellent performance with affirmative questions, but poor performance with otherwise similar negative questions. This asymmetry was explored in depth in elicited production studies by Thornton and colleagues (Guasti, Thornton, & Wexler, 1995; Thornton, 1993). These studies demonstrated that children make a variety of characteristic errors when producing negative questions that they never make in closely corresponding affirmative questions. For example, in a context designed to elicit questions like (1), they might instead produce questions like (2) or (3).

1. *Where can't your dogs sleep?* (target)
2. *Where can your dogs can't sleep?* (auxiliary doubling error)
3. *Where your dogs can't sleep?* (lack of subject/auxiliary inversion)

Such questions incorrectly double the auxiliary or leave it uninverted with respect to the subject. The affirmative counterparts of these errors, shown in (4) and (5), almost never occur by age 4.

4. *Where can your dogs can sleep?* (auxiliary doubling error)
5. *Where your dogs can sleep?* (lack of subject/auxiliary inversion)

Errors like (2) and (3) regularly go unnoticed in most children because opportunities to produce negative questions—and hence opportunities to produce negative question errors—occur very infrequently in naturalistic contexts (Zukowski, 2001b). Thornton's work additionally showed that even when children produce well-formed negative questions, they often prefer to leave the negative word in its unraised position, following the subject of the sentence, as in (6), instead of raising it with the auxiliary, as in (1).

6. *Where can your dogs not sleep?* (grammatical alternative with unraised negation)

Unpublished work that I have done has shown that unimpaired adults typically prefer the structure in (1) for negative questions, rather than the structure in (6). Thornton noted that the common thread to all of the nonadultlike patterns with negative questions (shown in Questions 2, 3, and 6) is that children prefer to leave negation in its unraised position, rather than raise it with the auxiliary.

The finding that typically developing children frequently make auxiliary doubling errors and errors of auxiliary inversion in negative questions, but almost never make these errors in corresponding affirmative questions, suggests several things about their grammars and/or language production systems. First, the highly specific distribution of the errors suggests that the errors are not haphazard, but rather are systematic products of their grammars and/or production systems. Second, although the explanation for this problem is not yet understood, adult English grammars allow negation to raise in questions, and adults do not produce negative question errors in either child- or adult-directed speech (Zukowski, 2001b). Thus, neither the presence of errors in child speech nor the features of child grammars that are suggested by the errors are copied from adult models. The fact that the same pattern of errors that has no basis in the input is observed in many children provides evidence for common internal mechanisms of acquisition and/or common weaknesses in child production systems.

In recent work, Karmiloff-Smith and colleagues have suggested that WS language is acquired via deviant mechanisms (Karmiloff-Smith, 1997). One specific proposal is that auditory rote memory masks deficiencies in the grammars of people with WS: "It has become increasingly clear . . . that the superficially impressive language skills of individuals with WS may be due to good auditory memory rather than an intact grammar module" (Karmiloff & Karmiloff-Smith, 2001, pp. 202–203). Although good auditory memory might allow one to acquire a vocabulary that is only superficially good, it is much more challenging for a memory-based explanation to account for successful unmodeled production of sentences with complex syntactic structures such as relative clauses. The plausibility of any memory-based explanation for the production of complex syntax in WS would be further strained if people with WS were found to produce developmentally normal errors, such as negative question errors, that are not modeled in the input.

In a recent study reported in full elsewhere (Zukowski, 2001a), I compared the well-articulated pattern of ease and difficulty in question syntax observed in typically developing children to the pattern exhibited by 11 WS children (ages 8;6–16;3) using an adaptation of Thornton's elicited production procedure. Eleven unimpaired younger children (ages 4;2–7;6) served as controls. Again WS participants and controls were matched individual by individual according to similar raw scores on both the vocabulary and matrices subtests of the KBIT. Pooled t tests showed that the two groups did not differ on either subtest (for matrices, $p = .76$; for vocabulary, $p = .60$).

Methods

In Thornton's procedure, participants addressed questions to a puppet who was said to be too shy to talk to grown-ups. Because the oldest participants who I examined were 16, the method had to be altered to make the task engaging and fun for them as well as for 4-year-olds. A method that seemed to fulfill this purpose was a mock telephone interview, in which participants phoned an accomplice who pretended to be a celebrity. Participants knew this was a game and were encouraged to choose for themselves who the accomplice should pretend to be (choices ranged from Britney Spears to George Washington). The experimenter pretended to be a reporter for the *New York Times* and whispered question prompts to the participant. The participant conducted the whole interview by following the experimenter's lead-ins and addressing the corresponding questions to the celebrity over the telephone. The experimenter and accomplice both took special care to avoid producing questions that model auxiliary inversion in their own speech to the participants. The techniques used to avoid auxiliary inversion in the experimenter prompts were developed by Thornton. One technique involves using an embedded question such as, "Ask her if she forgot something." Note that embedded questions neither require nor permit subject auxiliary inversion. That is, one cannot say, "Ask her if did she forget something." The other technique involves the "sluicing" of material following the wh-word, as in, "I wonder where her tarantula sleeps. Ask her where." The advantage of sluicing is that the experimenter prompt ends with the wh-word, which helps the child remember which question to ask.

Sample prompts for different target question types are given in Table 6.4. There were 50 trials, with 10 designed to elicit each of the five question types in Table 6.4.

The challenge for this study was designing the protocols intended to elicit negative questions. The problem is that the conditions that make negative questions particularly appropriate are quite subtle. For example, to elicit a question like "Where don't you ride your bike," the context that has to be established is one where it is presupposed that there are places that the listener does ride her bike and there are places that she does not. The fact that negative questions are quite rare in spontaneous speech suggests that these conditions do not naturally co-occur very often. Techniques used by Thornton (1993) suggested ideas about how to achieve the appropriate context. One technique involved using contrastive focus. For example, in one case, the "celebrity" told the child that during her vacation she visited her cousins. When the child repeated this to the experimenter, the next prompt was, "Hey, I heard that there's *one cousin* that she doesn't like. Ask her which one." This prompt simultaneously asserts the necessary negative proposition (she doesn't like one

TABLE 6.4
Sample Prompts and Target Questions for Question Study

Question Type	Experimenter Prompt	Target Question
Affirmative yes/no question	I wonder if she likes hamburgers. Ask her for me.	Do you like hamburgers?
Affirmative wh-object question	I don't know what kind of pets she has. Ask her (what kind).	What kind of pets do you have?
Affirmative wh-adjunct question	I wonder where her tarantula sleeps. Ask her where.	Where does your tarantula sleep?
Negative wh-object question	She doesn't like one of those flavors. Ask her what flavor.	What flavor of ice cream don't you like?
Negative wh-adjunct question	I heard that there's one place she doesn't want to live. Ask her where.	Where don't you want to live?

cousin) and implicates the necessary contrasting affirmative proposition (she *does* like some cousins).

Results

Table 6.5 presents the percentage of different question types produced by each group (collapsed across individuals) for all affirmative questions compared to all negative questions. The WS participants showed a strikingly similar pattern of results to the pattern observed in typically developing children, including those examined here. Nearly all of the affirmative questions (90%) produced by the WS group were perfect, showing subject/auxiliary inversion and correctly having just a single copy of the auxiliary verb. In fact the majority of WS participants (8/11) produced

TABLE 6.5
Percent of Different Questions Structures Produced

Variable	Affirmative Question Trials		Negative Question Trials	
Response Type	WS (287)	Controls (292)	WS (176)	Controls (184)
Target Question	90%	99%	49%	49%
No Auxiliary Raising	10%	1%	26%	7%
Doubled Auxiliary	0%	0%	9%	18%
Unraised "not"	—	—	14%	23%

Note. The total number of questions that the percentages are based on is shown in parentheses at the top of each column.

100% target responses for their affirmative questions (2 individuals accounted for 97% of the affirmative question errors made by the WS group). In contrast to these excellent results for affirmative questions, only half (49%) of the WS responses to negative questions matched the target structures. The control group achieved the same low rate of target structures for negative questions (49%). The types of alternative negative questions structures that the WS group produced were identical to the types produced by the control group, and included the same two types of ungrammatical questions that have been observed in previous studies as well as the grammatical structure containing an unraised "not." Summing together both the ungrammatical questions (which all fail to exhibit negative raising) and the grammatical questions that contain *not* in its unraised position, both groups left negation in its unraised position about half of the time in their negative questions. By contrast, in unpublished work with a group of 12 typically developing adult college students, I found that adults raise negation (produce target questions) 89% of the time, on average, in the context of the celebrity interview task, and none of their alternative responses are ungrammatical.

An additional finding in the question syntax study was that the WS group was similar to the child controls not just in what they did say, but also in what they did not say. Specifically, they did not produce any developmentally abnormal errors. It is easy to fail to appreciate the absence of abnormal errors because candidates for developmentally abnormal errors do not readily come to mind. But some possible errors can be imagined by extrapolating from the errors that the children did produce. For example, the WS group, like the controls, doubled the auxiliary in negative questions. What they never did was double the wh-phrase, in either affirmative or negative questions, as in "Who did/didn't you invite who to the party?"

The basic normality of the WS pattern in the production of questions provides strong evidence that WS syntax develops in a fundamentally normal manner. The difference, however, is that unimpaired children eventually move beyond this stage. That is, unimpaired adults do not make these errors in either the interview task or their spontaneous speech (Zukowski, 2001b). However, ongoing work with WS adults suggests that this developmentally normal stage may never be outgrown in this population. The appropriate interpretation of this developmental "stalling" (in at least some WS individuals) depends on the cause of this developmental stage in typically developing children, and on what mechanisms are normally responsible for the eventual elimination of negative question errors in child speech. There is suggestive evidence that negative question errors in typically developing children reflect a problem with the production system rather than with underlying knowledge of structure.

This evidence comes from work by Hiramatsu and Lillo-Martin (1997), who found that two thirds of a group of typically developing children who produce ungrammatical negative questions are nevertheless able to judge such questions to be ungrammatical in a grammaticality judgment test. This suggests that underlying knowledge of negative question syntax is adultlike in these children despite the evidence from their own elicited speech. In ongoing work, I am investigating whether WS children and/or adults show a similar production/judgment asymmetry.

SUMMARY AND IMPLICATIONS

The goal of this chapter was to demonstrate that carefully designed language experiments may play a critical role in evaluating the grammars of people with developmental disorders. If the question of interest is about underlying knowledge of syntactic structures, a finding of poor performance in some group of interest is really just the beginning of investigation because poor performance may be caused by many different things: deviant or missing knowledge, computational overload, lack of attention, and so on. The focus of the particular studies reviewed here was on people with WS, but the lessons to be learned from such studies extend to investigations of grammatical knowledge in other disorders.

One study reviewed here tested the possibility that people with WS do not know the syntax of relative clauses. This was one possible cause of poor performance in comprehension tests with these structures. Elicited production was used because successful production or lack of production of targeted structures provides convincing evidence of knowledge or lack of knowledge, and flawed production specifies precisely which details cause difficulty. The results demonstrate that a group of children and adolescents with WS were capable of generating both subject gap (SG) and object gap (OG) relative clauses in the absence of immediate models in the input. Yet in comprehension tests with items containing relative clauses and embedded clauses, the same group showed the typical degree and pattern of difficulty observed in other WS groups. This suggests that poor comprehension of sentences with these structures by people with WS is most likely not due to an inability of their grammars to generate these structures. Nevertheless, the results also demonstrate that knowledge of particular syntactic structures does not guarantee ease of production, and the elicited production procedure allowed us to observe and quantify two specific manifestations of difficulty with OG relatives: small numbers of OG responses relative to SG responses, and large numbers of errors where an intended message that should have been mapped onto an OG relative structure was inappropriately mapped onto an SG relative structure (mapping errors). Both of these patterns were observed in control children too, but the difficulty was more pronounced for the WS group. Although much remains to be understood about why OG relatives are particularly susceptible to difficulty, these results can already be factored into hypotheses about language production in people with WS as well as typically developing children.

A second study reviewed here demonstrated that experiments can also be used to test claims about mechanisms of language acquisition in disordered groups. This study investigated whether people with WS exhibit a stage of development that typically developing children exhibit, during which specific types of errors are made in negative questions, but not in otherwise similar affirmative questions. Experimentation was called for because negative questions are extremely rare in spontaneous speech, and thus negative question errors are not normally observable. This study was well suited to evaluating the claim that WS language is based on auditory rote memory because it is likely that few, if any, WS children will have ever heard negative question errors from other children. Thus, if WS children and adolescents produce negative question errors, this would provide evidence that they are following the same internally guided developmental path toward the adult grammar. The results show that every individual in a group of 11 WS children and adolescents did produce ungrammatical negative questions that are identical to errors produced by younger unimpaired children (questions with auxiliary doubling and lack of subject–auxiliary inversion). This finding suggests that people with WS do not just passively reproduce what they encounter in the input. Rather, their utterances (both grammatical and ungrammatical) seem to reflect the working of an internal system. In fact the full pattern of results in the question elicitation study supports a stronger conclusion. The WS and control groups were similar not just in the types of errors they produced, but also in the contexts in which they made these errors (in negative questions, but not in affirmative questions) and in the types of errors they did *not* make (no doubling of the wh-word). These results suggest that question syntax develops in a completely normal way in people with WS.

Having discussed some of the particular advantages of using elicited production tests to ask questions about underlying linguistic knowledge and mechanisms of syntactic development in children with WS, I would like to clarify that I do not think elicited production is the preferred experimental method for evaluating knowledge of every aspect of language. Elicited production is most likely to be helpful when it is possible to create a pragmatic context where the most natural response is the structure of interest. Thus, elicited production works well for studying restrictive relative clauses because it is easy to create a situation where one object must be distinguished from a similar object, but where the objects differ only in terms of different events in which they are participating. Similarly, elicited production works well for eliciting wh-questions because it is easy to create a situation where there is missing information about an event (somebody was not invited to the party; who was it?) or a state of affairs (Mary has three pets; what kind are they?).

By contrast, in some cases, elicited production is not the best choice because it is too difficult to create an appropriate pragmatic context. For example, consider the difficulty of eliciting negative yes/no questions such as "don't you like apples?" The context in which a question like this is most likely to occur is when the speaker has a suspicion that the listener does not like apples, but she finds it hard to believe. To experimentally create this kind of context, one would have to manipulate the speaker's attitude, which is extremely difficult to do. A better choice for negative yes/no questions would be grammaticality judgment. Extrapolating from the kinds of errors observed in the question study, one could create corresponding examples of negative yes/no questions (e.g., *Do you don't like Marmite?*). In this particular case, because negative yes/no questions are naturally related to other types of questions, if one wanted to examine the full set of affirmative and negative yes/no and wh-questions, the same method would have to be used to assess all of them, and thus some compromise in methodology would have to be made. One possibility would be to test all of these types of questions in a judgment format. An alternative would be to use elicited production, but to accommodate to the fact that the rate of attempts at negative yes/no questions will likely be lower than that for other questions by including more trials designed to elicit these questions.

Elicited production is also not the most sensitive method to use for assessing any kind of negative linguistic knowledge—that is, knowledge of what things are not possible. For example, "negative polarity items" are expressions such as the English word *any*, whose occurrence must be licensed by one of a finite number of licensors. In the absence of a licensor, the *any* cannot appear. Negation is one licensor of *any*, and thus it is natural to say *Nicole didn't buy any books*. But the identical sentence minus negation is not possible: *Nicole bought any books*. Knowledge of what is *not* possible is as much a part of our linguistic competence as knowledge of what is possible. The best one could do with elicited production in this case would be to try to elicit sentences with an unlicensed *any* and to interpret nonproduction of such examples as evidence of the ungrammaticality of these structures. Clearly, this would not provide the strongest evidence one might hope for in this domain. Stronger evidence could be achieved with a grammaticality judgment test, where people are asked to consider particular ungrammatical sentences and explicitly say whether they sound right or wrong (the results of one such study are reported in Zukowski, 2001a).

Elicited production is also not necessarily the best method for evaluating language in every disorder. It is most appropriate for groups of people who have reasonably good expressive language and are sensitive to pragmatic information that must be gleaned from context. Elicited production worked well in the studies reviewed here because these features accurately describe most people with WS. It would work less well with children with autism or Klinefelter's Syndrome.

Particular elicited production tasks may place additional constraints on which populations the test is best suited for. For example, in the relative clause study, subjects were asked to say which character changed color so that a parent who could not see the color change would know what had happened. This required the subjects to have *theory of mind*. One young WS child (age 8;6) who was examined was unable to perform the task because she did not understand why it was not sufficient for her to simply point to the character that had changed color and say (very emphatically) "*this* one." That is, she behaved as if her mother could see what she was pointing to even though she knew this was not the case. Theory of mind understanding is usually achieved in WS (Karmiloff-Smith, Klima, Bellugi, Grant, & Baron-Cohen, 1995), although it may be considerably delayed (Tager-Flusberg & Sullivan, 2000). By late childhood or early adolescence, the relative clause task is appropriate for the majority of people with WS. However, the task would not be appropriate for populations in which theory of mind is chronically deficient, such as autism (Baron-Cohen, Leslie, & Frith, 1985).

The crucial point is that we, as researchers, need to remain flexible and responsive in two important ways. First, we need to let the function and features of particular structures of interest, and their natural contexts of use, suggest the types of methods most appropriate to the assessment of knowledge of those structures. Second, if we want to give our participants a fighting chance to demonstrate what they do know, we need to let the cognitive, social, and linguistic strengths and weaknesses of their disorders suggest the most appropriate methods of assessment for those disorders. Unfortunately, there will be some kinds of linguistic knowledge that simply cannot be fairly tested for a given disorder because of collateral weaknesses associated with the disorder. I hope to have shown that, by carefully choosing a method that fits both the structure of interest and the disorder of interest, we can investigate questions about the integrity of grammatical knowledge and the causes of poor performance in people with disorders.

ACKNOWLEDGMENTS

This work was supported in part by NIH grant R03-HD-043113 and three grants to Barbara Landau (NSF SBR-9808585, March of Dimes FY98-0194, FY99-0670). My sincerest thanks go to the families and individuals who participated in these studies, to Nicole Kurz for her help in testing children, and to all of the "celebrities" who agreed to be interviewed for the question study (especially Elvis). Colin Phillips provided helpful comments on several drafts of this chapter, and, as always, the advice was much appreciated.

REFERENCES

Baron-Cohen, S., Leslie, A., & Frith, U. (1985). Does the autistic child have a "theory of mind"? *Cognition, 21,* 37–46.

Bellugi, U. (1965). *The acquisition of the system of negation in children's speech.* Unpublished doctoral dissertation, Harvard University, Cambridge, MA.

Bellugi, U., Marks, S., Bihrle, A., & Sabo, H. (1988). Dissociation between language and cognitive functions in Williams syndrome. In D. Bishop & K. Mogford (Eds.), *Language development in exceptional circumstances* (pp. 177–189). Hillsdale, NJ: Lawrence Erlbaum Associates.

Bishop, C. (1983). *Test for reception of grammar.* United Kingdom: Medical Research Council.

Bishop, D. (1998). *Uncommon understanding.* East Sussex, United Kingdom: Psychological Press.

Clahsen, H., & Almazan, M. (1998). Syntax and morphology in Williams syndrome. *Cognition, 68,* 167–198.

Clahsen, H., & Almazan, M. (2001). Compounding and inflection in language impairment: Evidence from Williams syndrome (and SLI). *Lingua, 111,* 729–757.

Clahsen, H., & Temple, C. (2003). Words and rules in children with Williams syndrome. In Y. Levy & J. Schaeffer (Eds.), *Language competence across populations* (pp. 323–352). Hillsdale, NJ: Lawrence Erlbaum Associates.

Crain, S., & Thornton, R. (1998). *Investigations in universal grammar.* Cambridge, MA: MIT Press.

Gibson, T. (1998). Linguistic complexity: Locality of syntactic dependencies. *Cognition, 68,* 1–76.

Goodluck, H., & Tavakolian, S. (1982). Competence and processing in children's grammar of relative clauses. *Cognition, 11,* 1–27.

Guasti, M., Thornton, R., & Wexler, K. (1995). *Negation in children's questions: The case of English.* Paper presented at the Boston University Conference on Language Development, Boston, MA.

Hamburger, H., & Crain, S. (1982). Relative acquisition. In S. Kuczaj (Ed.), *Language development: Vol. 1. Syntax and semantics.* Hillsdale, NJ: Lawrence Erlbaum Associates.

Hiramatsu, K., & Lillo-Martin, D. (1997). *Children who judge ungrammatical what they produce.* Paper presented at the Boston University Conference on Language Development, Boston, MA.

Karmiloff, K., & Karmiloff-Smith, A. (2001). *Pathways to language.* Cambridge, MA: Harvard University Press.

Karmiloff-Smith, A. (1997). Crucial differences between developmental cognitive neuroscience and adult neuropsychology. *Developmental Neuropsychology, 13*(4), 513–524.

Karmiloff-Smith, A., Grant, J., Berthoud, I., Davies, M., Howlin, P., & Udwin, O. (1997). Language and Williams syndrome: How intact is "intact"? *Child Development, 68*(2), 246–262.

Karmiloff-Smith, A., Klima, E., Bellugi, U., Grant, J., & Baron-Cohen, S. (1995). Is there a social module? Language, face, processing, and theory of mind in individuals with Williams syndrome. *Journal of Cognitive Neuroscience, 7*(2), 196–208.

Karmiloff-Smith, A., Tyler, L. K., Voice, K., Sims, K., Udwin, O., Howlin, P., & Davies, M. (1998). Linguistic dissociations in Williams syndrome: Evaluating receptive syntax in online and off-line tasks. *Neuropsychologia, 36*(4), 343–351.

Kaufman, A. S., & Kaufman, N. L. (1990). *Kaufman Brief Intelligence Test.* Circle Pines, MN: American Guidance Service.

Klein, B. P. (1995). *Grammatical abilities of children with Williams syndrome.* Unpublished MA thesis, Emory University, Atlanta, Georgia.

Levy, Y., & Hermon, S. (2003). Morphology in Hebrew speaking adolescents with Williams syndrome. *Developmental Neuropsychology, 23*(1&2), 59–83.

McKee, C., McDaniel, D., & Snedeker, J. (1998). Relatives children say. *Journal of Psycholinguistic Research, 27*(5), 573–596.

Mervis, C. B., Bertrand, J., Robinson, B. F., Klein, B. P., Armstrong, S. C., Baker, D. E., Turner, N. D., & Reinberg, J. (1995, March). *Early language development of children with Williams syndrome.* Paper presented at the biennial meeting of the Society for Research in Child Development, Indianapolis, IN.

Mervis, C. B., Morris, C. A., Bertrand, J., & Robinson, B. F. (1999). Williams syndrome: Findings from an integrated program of research. In H. Tager-Flusberg (Ed.), *Neurodevelopmental disorders: Contributions to a new framework from the cognitive neurosciences.* Cambridge, MA: MIT Press.

Mervis, C. B., Robinson, B., Rowe, M., Becerra, A., & Klein-Tasman, B. (in press). Language abilities of individuals with Williams syndrome. In L. Abbeduto (Ed.), *International Review of Research in Mental Retardation* (Vol. 27). Orlando, FL: Academic Press.

Morris, C., & Mervis, C. (1999). Williams syndrome. In S. Goldstein & C. Reynolds (Eds.), *Handbook of neurodevelopmental and genetic disorders in children* (pp. 591–590). New York: Guilford.

Osborne, L., Li, M., Pober, B., Chitayat, D., Bodurtha, J., Mandel, A., Costa, T., Grebe, T., Cox, S., Tsui, L. C., & Scherer, S. W. (2001). A 1.5 million-base pair inversion polymorphism in families with Williams–Beuren syndrome. *Nature Genetics, 29,* 321–325.

Sridhar, S. N. (1988). *Cognition and sentence production.* New York: Springer-Verlag.

Tager-Flusberg, H., & Sullivan, K. (2000). A componential view of theory of mind: Evidence from Williams syndrome. *Cognition, 76,* 59–89.

Thornton, R. (1993, January). *Children who don't raise the negative.* Paper presented at the LSA, Los Angeles.

Volterra, V., Capirci, O., & Caselli, M. C. (2001). What atypical populations can reveal about language development: The contrast between deafness and Williams syndrome. *Language and Cognitive Processes, 16*(2/3), 219–239.

Volterra, V., Capirci, O., Pezzini, G., Sabbadini, L., & Vicari, S. (1996). Linguistic abilities in Italian children with Williams syndrome. *Cortex, 32,* 663–677.

Zukowski, A. (2001a). *Uncovering grammatical competence in children with Williams syndrome.* Unpublished doctoral dissertation, Boston University.

Zukowski, A. (2001b, August). *Grammatical knowledge and language production in Williams syndrome.* Paper presented at the workshop Separability of Cognitive Functions: What Can be Learned from Williams Syndrome, University of Massachusetts.

Zurif, E., Swinney, D., Prather, P., Wingfield, A., & Brownell, H. (1995). The allocation of memory resources during sentences comprehension: Evidence from the elderly. *Journal of Psycholinguistic Research, 24*(3), 165–182.

Research on Fragile X Syndrome and Autism: Implications for the Study of Genes, Environments, and Developmental Language Disorders

Donald B. Bailey, Jr.
Jane E. Roberts
Stephen R. Hooper
Deborah D. Hatton
Penny L. Mirrett
Joanne E. Roberts
Jennifer M. Schaaf
University of North Carolina at Chapel Hill

Developmental language disorders almost certainly are influenced by both genetic and environmental factors. Sameroff and colleagues (e.g., Sameroff & Fiese, 2000) have argued for years that genotype, phenotype, and "environtype" interact over time in reciprocal and mutually influential transactions to shape developmental outcomes for children and adults. Understanding the relative contributions of each and discovering the mechanisms and directions of influence are goals that lie at the heart of understanding developmental phenomena, including developmental language disorders, and ultimately could lead to new insights into the nature and timing of events or experiences most likely to influence developmental outcomes (Reiss & Neiderhiser, 2000).

Many approaches can be used to study how genes, environments, and developmental language disorders (DLDs) interact. Historically, this research has been complicated by the lack of data documenting specific genetic causes of DLDs. Although recent research provides strong evidence for a genetic component of developmental disorders such as autism (Cook, 1998) and specific reading disability (DeFries & Alarcon, 1996), the identification of specific genes and an understanding of the biological mechanisms by which they influence language development are still unknown.

121

It is likely, however, that we will ultimately discover a genetic basis for many developmental disorders. This will probably involve multiple genes interacting in a complex way to affect language and other developmental outcomes. Until the various genetic bases of DLDs are understood, studying the influence of environmental mechanisms, which are complex constructs that are constantly changing, as they relate to genetic disorders can be difficult, and thus a real understanding of gene–environment interactions remains elusive. DLDs fall within this group of disorders where a genetic component is strongly suspected. There have been a number of family linkage studies where language deficits run in families (e.g., Gopnik & Crago, 1991; Plante et al., 1991; Tallal et al., 1991; van der Lely & Stollwerck, 1996), and twin studies have produced convincing evidence for a genetic basis as well (e.g., Bishop, 1997). For example, van der Lely and Stollwerck (1996) found a higher incidence of a history of language deficits in the parents and siblings of the children with specific language impairment (SLI) than in parents and siblings of control subjects. With about 78% of the families of children with language impairment having specific language problems, this was nearly three times the rate for control families. Despite these relatively strong findings reflecting a genetic basis for DLDs, the exact gene or, more likely, combination of genes has not been identified to date.

When the genetic bases of specific developmental disorders are identified, they become strong potential candidates for studying gene–environment interactions. Of relevance to this text are genetic disorders that have clear consequences for language development or secondary associations with DLDs. Given these criteria, fragile X syndrome (FXS) emerges as a disorder of interest because of its known genetic properties, the language deficits that occur as a result of this disorder, and its high degree of association with autism—a disorder known for its developmental language impairment. In this chapter, we provide a brief overview of FXS, describe what is known about its association with autism, and discuss several hypotheses for how these disorders can inform what we know about DLDs and their management.

FRAGILE X OVERVIEW

Genotypic Features of FXS

Fragile X syndrome is the most common known inherited cause of neurodevelopmental disability, with current prevalence rates of approximately 1:4,000 males and 1:8,000 females (Crawford, Acuna, & Sherman, 2001). FXS arises from the disruption in expression of protein from the fragile X mental retardation gene 1 (*FMR1*), most commonly caused by amplification of a CGG repeat in the 5' untranslated region.

Identification of the FMR1 gene (Verkerk et al., 1991) led to the discovery that FXS results from a trinucleotide (CGG) repeat expansion on the X chromosome at Xq27.3. In individuals without an FMR1 mutation, the repeat sequence ranges from 5 to approximately 45 to 55 CGG repeats. Individuals with 55 to 200 repeats are referred to as *premutation carriers* and have an expanded risk of having a child with the full mutation. Although premutation carriers have generally been described as unaffected, recent evidence suggests that cognitive, behavioral, and molecular symptoms may be present in a subset of these individuals. Individuals with the *full mutation* (>200 repeats) have hypermethlyation of the promoter region of FMR1 (Oberle et al., 1991), leading to transcriptional silencing and a number of characteristic physical, cognitive, and behavioral features.

The protein produced by FMR1 has been termed the *fragile X mental retardation protein* (FMRP). FMRP has been found in a number of adult and fetal tissues (Agulhon et al., 1999; Khandjian et al., 1995), and its presence is associated with normal brain function (Imbert, Feng, Nelson, Warren, & Mandel, 1998; Oostra, 1996). FMRP can bind to RNA transcripts, as well as with the ribosomal subunit involved in the translation of messages into proteins (Corbin et al., 1997). FMR1 mRNA levels are elevated in individuals with small (55–100) and large (100–200) premutations and with unmethylated full mutation alleles despite reduced levels of FMRP (Tassone, Hagerman, Chamberlain, & Hagerman, 2000; Tassone, Hagerman, Taylor, Gane, Godfrey, & Hagerman, 2000). This suggests that elevation in mRNA may represent increased transcriptional activity perhaps in response to decreased efficiency of translation (Tassone, Hagerman, Loesch, Lachiewicz, Taylor, & Hagerman, 2000).

The role of FMRP in the brain is critical. FMRP has both nuclear and cytoplasmic localization within neurons, including dendrites and dendritic spines (Feng, Gutekunst, Eberhart, Yi, Warren, & Hersch, 1997; Weiler & Greenough, 1999). As a result, transcriptional silencing of FMR1 and resultant loss of FMRP results in aberrant brain development and function (Devys, Lutz, Rouyer, Bellocq, & Mandel, 1993; Tamanini et al., 1997). When expression of FMRP is reduced, as occurs in human FXS or the mouse knockout model (Bakker et al., 1994; Kooy et al., 1996), abnormal morphology of cortical dendritic processes are observed, suggesting that FMRP is involved in synapse maturation and elimination (Weiler & Greenough, 1999). This indicates that FMRP most likely plays an important role in activity-dependent synaptic function, maturation, and plasticity during development.

Individuals with the full mutation FXS vary in the amount of FMRP produced, in part a function of gender and in part a function of mosaicism. Females with FXS have two X chromosomes in each cell, one is usually normal and one fragile X. Through the process of X inactivation, however, only one X is functional in each cell. Because this process is assumed to be random, the average female with FXS will have 50% cells expressing FMRP, although obviously there is considerable range around this number. In full mutation males who only have one X chromosome, all cells are affected; however, mosaicism, in which some cells with the premutation express FMRP and some with the full mutation, often occurs. Other individuals will have a partially methylated full mutation, with the gene methylated in some cells and unmethylated in others (Kaufman, Abrams, Chen, & Reiss, 1999; Tassone, Hagerman, Ikle et al., 1999).

Research to date supports the hypothesized relationship between levels of FMRP and severity of disability in FXS. For example, Merenstein, Sobesky, Taylor, Riddle, Tran, and Hagerman (1996) found that males with a fully methylated full mutation (associated with reduced FMRP) have lower average IQs and more physical features of FXS than mosaic males or those with the partially methylated full mutation. Similar findings were reported by Tassone et al. (1999), who reported decreased levels of FMRP were associated with lower IQs and increased physical features in males and females with FXS. Miller et al. (1999) found decreased levels of FMRP correlated with heightened sensory reactivity of males and females with FXS. Bailey, Hatton, Tassone, Skinner, and Taylor (2001) found that FMRP expression accounted for a small but significant amount of variance in level (but not rate) of cognitive, social, adaptive, language, and motor development.

Phenotypic Features of FXS

Extensive research over the past decade has documented the human consequences of FXS (Bailey & Nelson, 1995; Mazzocco, 2000). A number of physical features are associated with FXS including macroorchidism, elongated face, large ears, prominent jaw, increased head circumference, and mitral valve prolapse (Hagerman, 2002). Full mutation males typically exhibit moderate to severe mental retardation (Hagerman, 2002; Hooper, Hatton, Baranek, Roberts, & Bailey, 2000). However, a range of intellectual function is evident, and as many as 10% to 12% may not have retardation. Full mutation females generally display IQ scores in the mildly retarded to average range, although a wide range of functioning is also evident (Cronister, Hagerman, Wittenberger, & Amiri, 1991). Research on specific cognitive domains suggests a wide range of effects in attention, memory, executive function, and visuospatial abilities (Cornish, Munir, & Cross, 2001; Hooper et al., 2000; Munir, Cornish, & Wilding, 2000). In addition to general speech and language delay (Roberts, Mirrett,

Anderson, Burchinal, & Neebe, 2002; Roberts, Mirrett, & Burchinal, 2001), individuals with FXS appear to exhibit an etiology-specific tendency for tangential language (Sudhalter & Belser, 2001), repetitive speech (Belser & Sudhalter, 2001), and unintelligible speech (Paul, Dykens, Leckman, Watson, Bregman, & Cohen, 1987; Spinelli, Rocha, Giacheti, & Richieri-Costa, 1995).

Social and behavioral difficulties are prevalent in males (Hatton, Bailey, Hargett-Beck, Skinner, & Clark, 1999; Hatton, Hooper, Bailey, Skinner, Sullivan, & Wheeler, 2002). Despite relatively more intact neurocognitive functioning, such problems occur in females as well (Keysor & Mazzocco, 2002). Autistic spectrum behaviors are seen in up to 90% of males with FXS, including perseveration, self-injury, hand flapping, poor eye contact, and social anxiety (Merenstein et al., 1996). Approximately 25% to 30% of individuals with FXS meet the diagnostic criteria for autism (Bailey, Mesibov, Hatton, Clark, Roberts, & Mayhew, 1998; Rogers, Wehner, & Hagerman, 2001). Males have been described as impulsive, hyperactive, inattentive, and hypersensitive to a variety of sensory stimuli (Belser & Sudhalter, 1995; Hagerman, 2002), and females are described as shy and socially anxious (Freund, 1995; Hagerman, 2002). Freund, Reiss, and Abrams (1993) noted that nearly two thirds of their sample of females had a psychiatric diagnosis of Avoidant Disorder.

Many individuals with FXS appear to have difficulty regulating arousal (Cohen, 1995a), which appears to result in social anxiety, sensory defensiveness, temper tantrums, and problems with transitions. A number of studies utilizing varying physiological measures provide evidence that individuals with FXS have high levels of arousal and difficulties modulating arousal. In a preliminary study, Belser and Sudhalter (1995) provided evidence that males with FXS displayed significantly greater skin conductance levels than controls during conditions associated with high social stress (e.g., eye contact). Similarly, Miller et al. (1999) found that individuals with FXS exhibited greater magnitude, more responses per stimulation, and lower rates of habituation in electrodermal responses (EDR) than controls across multiple sensory conditions. Using heart activity as a physiological marker, Roberts, Boccia, Bailey, Hatton, and Skinner (2001) found that boys with FXS had higher baseline levels, atypical reactivity to cognitive challenge, and poorly coordinated sympathetic and parasympathetic/vagal systems. These differences in heart activity were due to increased sympathetic activity and reduced parasympathetic/vagal activity. Finally, Hessl et al. (2002) found elevated levels of salivary cortisol, a hormone associated with stress, in boys with FXS. Increased cortisol levels were associated with behavior problems, as measured by the Child Behavior Checklist, in boys and girls with FXS.

FRAGILE X SYNDROME AND AUTISM

Association Between FXS and Autism

A consistent clinical finding is that the behavior of children with FXS shares several characteristics with behavior seen in children with autism. However, the strength of existing research is limited by methodological factors such as small sample sizes, imprecise measurement of autism and development, failure to control for confounding demographic factors (e.g., age, gender, and IQ), and failure to examine this association in a developmental context with longitudinal studies.

One question is the extent to which FXS is a significant etiology for autism spectrum disorders. Although an early article suggested that a substantial proportion of autism cases might be due to FXS (Brown et al., 1982), subsequent research has not supported this assumption. Fisch (1992), summarizing existing studies related to this question, concluded that 4% to 5% of the cases of autism spectrum disorders are due to FXS, a figure that is still accepted today. Although accounting for only a small proportion of the cases of autism, FXS is the most common *known* genetic cause of autism.

A second question is the extent to which autistic behavior and autism diagnoses are present in individuals with the full mutation FXS. In a review by Dykens and Volkmar (1997), the authors noted a wide range of findings for the prevalence of categorically defined autism within FXS, ranging from 5% to 60%. Seven studies have reported a prevalence of 20% or greater, with more recent studies converging on an estimate of at least 25% (Bailey et al., 1998; Rogers et al., 2001; Turk & Graham, 1997). The significant percentage of cases of autism in FXS, paired with the considerable range of reported prevalence, suggests that there may be moderating factors for autistic behavior in FXS. These may include genetic factors such as the degree of FMR1 mutation; demographic factors like age, gender, and IQ; or other mechanisms including arousal, social anxiety, or neuropsychological deficits.

Cognitive status also appears to be significantly related to the expression of autistic features. In nonspecific mental retardation, a negative relationship appears to exist between IQ and the occurrence of both autistic features and a diagnosis of autism (Freeman et al., 1981; Rutter & Schopler, 1987). In FXS, research has suggested that autistic behavior may be associated with a greater degree of impairment in cognitive development (Cohen, 1995b; Hagerman, Jackson, Levitas, Rimland, & Braden, 1986; Turk & Graham, 1997). Our own research using both cross-sectional and longitudinal analyses has shown that children with both FXS and autism have lower levels and lower rates of development than do children with

FXS without autism (Bailey, Hatton, Mesibov, & Ament, 2000; Bailey, Hatton, Skinner, & Mesibov, 2001; Roberts, Mirrett et al., 2001).

Given that FXS is typically associated with mental retardation, the question arises as to whether the association between FXS and autism is secondary to the relationship between FXS and mental retardation. If the association between autism and FXS is not specific, but mediated through the common association of both autism and FXS with mental retardation, then further study of autistic features in FXS will provide an etiologically homogeneous model for teasing apart the nature of this relationship (i.e., perhaps some aspects of the pattern of autistic behaviors are more influenced by IQ, whereas others are not). Given the high rate of mental retardation in autistic individuals, understanding this relationship will be important. However, if the association between FXS and autism is not mediated by IQ, then the argument for shared genetic mechanisms between FXS and at least a subgroup of persons with autism is considerably strengthened. In this case, further study of FMR1 and other genes that may be regulated by FMR1 could provide important insights into the genetic basis of autism by providing additional candidate genes to be used in autism linkage studies.

Few studies have examined repetitive behavior in persons with FXS in comparison with persons with non-FXS autistic disorders, and findings to date suggest that repetitive behaviors occur at a lower rate in persons with FXS than is typically found for autism. Baumgardner, Reiss, Freund, and Abrams (1995) found that 30% of males with FXS (mean age = 8 years) exhibited stereotyped behavior, whereas studies of stereotyped behavior in autism typically find rates of 90% to 100% for this behavior (Bodfish, Symons, Parker, & Lewis, 2000; Campbell et al., 1990; Freeman et al., 1981). Also, Kau, Reider, Meyer, and Freund (2000) found no differences between FXS and an IQ-matched nonspecific developmental disability sample in terms of behavioral rigidity/insistence on sameness, whereas most if not all persons with autism exhibit this characteristic (Prior & MacMillan, 1973; Tager-Flusberg, 1999; Turner, 1999).

In contrast to individuals with non-FX autism, in which the symptoms of autism appear to either remain stable over time (Rumsey, Rapoport, & Sceery, 1985) or gradually improve with age (Piven, Harper, Palmer, & Ardnt, 1996), there is evidence that autistic behaviors in individuals with FX may change over time. Age-related decreases have also been found in the rate of adaptive behavior (Cohen, 1995b; Dykens et al., 1996) and cognitive skill development (Lachiewicz, Gullion, Spiridigliozzi, & Aylsworth, 1987) in FXS, which is not characteristic of autism. In addition, preliminary evidence suggests that the severity of abnormal behaviors such as social avoidance (Cohen et al., 1988; Merenstein et al., 1996), hyperactivity, and poor attention span (Kau et al., 2000; Merenstein et al., 1996) increases with age in FXS. Thus, given that there are age-related changes in many features of FXS, there is a strong rationale for investigating such changes in autistic behavior. Although there has been some work in this area, some studies have shown increased symptoms of autism at young ages (Borghgraef, Fryns, Dielkens, Pyck, & van Den Berghe, 1987; Reiss & Freund, 1992), whereas other studies have not (Bailey, Mesibov et al., 1998). Thus, the developmental trajectory for autistic features in persons with FXS remains unknown.

A recent methodological advance has come in the form of more rigorous methods for assessing and diagnosing autism (e.g., the ADI–R and ADOS), but these measures have thus far only been used in one study. Rogers et al. (2001), in a sample of 24 children with FXS ranging in age from 21 to 48 months, found that 33% of the children met ADI–R, ADOS, and *DSM–IV* criteria for autism. Our group has found preliminary evidence that discordant diagnostic results can occur when different assessment methods are used to identify autistic disorder in persons with FXS, and use of the ADOS typically results in a higher rate of autism diagnosis in persons with FXS compared with previous findings. Further research is needed to examine the way autism is expressed in an FXS population. One way to address this question is to more rigorously measure autistic symptoms in persons with FXS using these newer autism diagnostic techniques.

Autism Profiles in FXS

What do we know about the extent to which individuals with autism and individuals with both FXS and autism show similar or different profiles on measures of autistic behavior? Two studies have addressed this issue. Bailey et al. (1998) used the Childhood Autism Rating Scale to compare profiles of males with FXS and autism to those with autism only, and Rogers et al. (2001) used the ADI–R and ADOS in a similar fashion. Neither study was able to document a unique fragile X profile because the two groups were virtually indistinguishable on all of the autism measures.

Neurocognition in FXS and Autism

Research suggests that individuals with FXS exhibit profiles of cognitive strengths and weaknesses that tend to differ in ways from those exhibited by individuals with autism. The cognitive profile of FXS includes relative strengths in verbal-based cognitive skills coupled with relative weaknesses in visuospatial-based skills including visual memory and perception, mental manipulation of visuospatial relationships among objects, visuomotor coordination, and processing of sequential information

(Baumgardner et al., 1995; Hagerman, 2002; Mazzocco, Pennington, & Hagerman, 1993; Reiss & Freund, 1992). The pattern of cognitive strengths and weaknesses appears to be the same for both genders. In terms of overall level of cognitive development, males with FXS tend to function in the moderate to severe range of mental retardation, whereas females typically function at higher overall cognitive levels.

Numerous studies suggest that children with FXS demonstrate an abnormal trajectory of cognitive and behavioral development. In general, IQ stability is observed in typically developing children, most groups of individuals with mental retardation of mixed etiologies, and those with autism. However, several cross-sectional and longitudinal investigations of children with FXS indicate that development of cognitive abilities and adaptive behavioral skills may follow an abnormal trajectory. Slowing or early plateauing of development (as opposed to a loss of skills) leads to declining standardized scores in young children with FXS, perhaps beginning as young as 5 years of age (Dykens et al., 1996; Freund & Reiss, 1991; Lachiewicz et al., 1987). Although there is general agreement that declines in IQ and, to a lessor extent, adaptive behavior scores occur in young children with FXS, the precise timing and neurobiological basis of this pattern remain unknown.

Both the cognitive profile and the trajectory of cognitive development that has been found to be characteristic of FXS appear to differ from that seen in children with autism. For example, individuals with autism are hypothesized to show a processing bias in favor of featural information at the expense of configural information (e.g., they focus on the trees and not the forest) and to perform poorly on measures that require processing of contextual information (Happe, 1997). This has been demonstrated across visual tasks such as segmented versus unsegmented block designs and verbal tasks such as extracting sentence meaning from various degrees of contextualized verbal information (Shah & Frith, 1983, 1993). In contrast, individuals with FXS are reported to perform poorly on measures of sequential or featural information such as the Wechsler Block Design subtest (Kemper, Hagerman, & Altshul-Stark, 1988) and the Sequential Processing Composite of the Kaufman Assessment Battery for Children (Dykens, Hodapp, & Leckman, 1987) and to display strengths in processing meaningful and contextually bound information (Bennetto & Pennington, 2002). Although the cognitive profiles of individuals with FXS and autism suggest some general and distinct patterns of abilities, there is a tremendous amount of variability within the FXS and autism groups, and not all individuals display the same profile of skills. These differences suggest that examination of similarities and differences across the cognitive aspects of the autism and FXS phenotypes might elucidate a meaningful cluster of characteristics in autistic individuals.

Social Behavior and Language Skills in FXS and Autism

Previous studies have found a core set of behavioral and communication characteristics that appear to be part of the FXS phenotype. Some of these features co-occur in autism, whereas others may help to discriminate between autism and FXS. Reiss and Freund (1992) found that, when compared with age- and IQ-matched controls, males with FXS were more likely to display deficits in peer social play, nonverbal communication deficits, and repetitive motor behaviors. Moreover, they observed that the social dysfunction in FXS is most evident when social participation demands the processing of more complex, unstructured social information. This appears to contrast with autism, where a more generalized deficit in social reciprocity is typically found.

Several studies have identified significant deficits in discrete social behaviors such as social gaze and social avoidance in persons with FXS (Cohen et al., 1988, 1989; Sudhalter, Cohen, Silverman, & Wolf-Schein, 1990). Although deficient in several aspects of social gaze, persons with FXS are not significantly different from controls in terms of the social withdrawal/ social isolation behaviors that are pathognomonic for autism (Baumgardner et al., 1995). Further significant abnormalities in specific social behaviors, such as social gaze, have been found in boys with FXS who do not meet diagnostic criteria for autism (Cohen et al., 1988), and qualitative differences in patterns of social avoidance behavior have been found between FXS and non-FXS autistic samples (Cohen et al., 1988; Sudhalter et al., 1990).

We compared the social behavior, developmental status, and temperament of 31 boys with FXS who did not have autism, matched on age, gender, and race, with 31 boys with autism but no FXS (Bailey et al., 2000). Children with autism exhibited a more variable profile of development in comparison with a relatively flat profile for children with FXS. Children with autism were significantly more delayed in social skills and were rated by observers as exhibiting a greater degree of impairment in cognitive, communication, and social skills. On temperament ratings, both groups were slower to adapt, less persistent, and more withdrawing than the reference group of normal children. Boys with FXS were rated as more active than the referent group, whereas boys with autism were rated as less intense, more distractible, having a higher threshold for response, and less rhythmic than the reference group. A smaller three-group analysis compared boys with FXS, boys with autism, and boys with both FXS and autism. Children with both FXS and autism were substantially more delayed than children with autism or FXS alone, and they exhibited a pattern of deficits similar to that of children with autism alone (greater delays in language and social skills).

With respect to communication, speech and language delays are prevalent in persons with FXS (Levitas, Hagerman, Braden, Rimland, McBogg, & Matus, 1983; Roberts, Mirrett et al., 2001), another apparent similarity to autistic disorders. Research examining discrete types of language skills has revealed differences in the pattern of atypical language between persons with FXS and persons with autism (non-FXS). For example, tangential language is more prevalent in FXS, whereas echolalia is more prevalent in autism (Sudhalter & Belser, 2001; Sudhalter et al., 1990). Although significant variability is observed in the functional communication skills demonstrated by children with both autism and FXS, children with FXS tend to exhibit significant difficulties with form (i.e., grammar and vocabulary) as well as function, such as the use of language in regulatory and social contexts (Abbeduto & Hagerman, 1997). Children with autism tend to display intact language forms and significant deficits in language use for social interaction and communication (Wetherby, Prizant, & Hutchinson, 1998; Wilkinson, 1998). In addition, the majority of children with FXS present with persistent articulation difficulties (Abbeduto & Hagerman, 1997), whereas verbal children with autism were noted to have intact articulation skills (Kjelgaard & Tager-Flusberg, 2000).

We have found that profiles of communication and symbolic behavior in young males with FXS who did not have co-occurring autism differed from those reported in children with autism (Roberts et al., 2002). We examined the communication and symbolic behavior profiles of 22 males with FXS ranging in age from 21 to 77 months who were developmentally younger than 28 months. The males with FXS showed relative strengths in verbal and vocal communication and relative weaknesses in gestures, reciprocity, and symbolic play. They did not show deficits relative to other skills in social communication areas of joint attention and social-affective signaling, although relative difficulties with repair strategies were evident, indicating some possible social communicative difficulties. In comparison, children with autism show pervasive deficits in joint attention, social-affective signaling, and sociability of communication (Mundy, Sigman, & Kasari, 1994; Sigman & Ruskin, 1999; Wetherby et al., 1998). Thus, we found that the social communication deficits in young males with FXS differed from those reported for young children with autism of the same developmental age.

Other similarities and differences in the language profiles in FXS and autism become apparent as we learn more about the communication skills of individuals with FXS. Unlike the well-defined communication phenotype of autism, the communication phenotype in FXS is not well characterized. Markedly lacking are empirical studies of specific aspects of syntax, vocabulary, and pragmatic skills and their development, particularly in children.

MECHANISMS THAT UNDERLIE AUTISTIC
BEHAVIOR IN FXS

Evidence for similarities and differences in the profile of atypical social, language, and behavioral characteristics in FXS and autism suggests that a comparison of these groups on tasks that measure putative mechanisms for these features may prove enlightening. To date, little research has been conducted that has involved a direct comparison with individuals with autism, FXS, and autism/FXS. We propose three hypotheses that could be fruitful in examining the underlying mechanisms of autistic behavior in FXS.

Arousal

Although abnormal levels and modulation of arousal has been postulated as one theory underlying autism (Dawson & Lewy, 1989), it has not been one of the primary hypotheses examined in this population. In general, there has been little work examining the arousal hypothesis in autism, and findings have been inconclusive, with some studies reporting evidence of hyperarousal (Cohen & Johnson, 1977; Kootz, Marinelli, & Cohen, 1982; Ratey et al., 1987; Tordjman et al., 1997) and other work not supporting this finding (Corona, Dissanayake, Arbelle, Wellington, & Sigman, 1998). For example, a recent study reported that the majority of their sample of children with autism exhibited a hyperresponsive activation of the sympathetic system (as displayed in elevated electrodermal responses) in everyday behaviors. Yet a small percentage demonstrated a hyporesponsive pattern (Hirstein, Iversen, & Ramachandran, 2001). These authors hypothesized that many of the behaviors observed in individuals with autism may serve in a regulatory capacity to compensate for a malfunctioning autonomic nervous system (Hirstein et al., 2001). In light of the lack of systematic study and contradictory findings, it is unclear whether an arousal hypothesis is supported as a primary mechanism in autism. Given the heterogeneity observed in autism, it could be that hyperarousal is not a universal pattern, but that it affects a subset of individuals with autism. Indeed, hyperarousal could be a defining feature of the overlap between autism and FXS (Roberts, Boccia et al., 2001).

In contrast to autism, hyperarousal has been postulated to be a core feature of FXS and an underlying mechanism associated with aberrant behavior in general and autistic behavior in particular within FXS. In the one study that directly tested this hypothesis, Roberts, Boccia et al. (2001) reported elevated levels of heart activity (decreased vagal tone and increased sympathetic tone) for four boys with FXS and autism compared with four boys with FXS (nonautistic) and four typically developing boys matched on chronological age. Although these data are preliminary, they are in accordance with findings from Cohen (1995a), which indicate that males with FXS and autism show more disturbance in mood and physiological regulation than males with autism or FXS alone.

Additional support for the arousal hypothesis comes from physiological studies examining features in FXS that are associated with autism. For example, behaviors characteristic of impaired sensory modulation (e.g., unusual responses to sensory stimuli, tactile defensiveness) co-occur in both FXS and autism, and elevated levels of arousal (via galvanic skin responsivity) have been correlated with sensory reactivity in FXS (Miller et al., 1999). Repetitive language is also prevalent in both autism and FXS (Sudhalter & Belser, 2001), and it has been associated with hyperarousal (via electrodermal responsivity) in males with FXS (Belser & Sudhalter, 1995). Problem behavior is common to both autism and FXS, and recent studies investigating the nature of problem behaviors in FXS suggests that females with FXS have elevated baseline levels of arousal (Keysor, Mazzocco, McLeod, & Hoehn-Saric, 2002) as do males with FXS (Hessl et al., 2002). In the Hessl et al. (2002) study, increased arousal (reflected in salivary cortisol) was associated with greater severity of problems, particularly withdrawn behavior.

Social Anxiety

Persons with autism are characterized by disturbances in social functioning typically expressed as a lack of social awareness or reciprocity. Dawson, Meltzoff, Osterling, Rinaldi, and Brown (1998) found that children with autism more frequently failed to orient to both social and nonsocial stimuli in comparison with Down syndrome and typical controls. However, their failure to orient to social stimuli was much more extreme. In general, social aloofness and lack of social discrimination, rather than social anxiety, are hallmark features of autism (Adolphs, Sears, & Piven, 2001; Baron-Cohen, 1995; Klin, 2000).

In contrast to findings in autism, individuals with FXS are described as socially anxious and not socially aloof (Cohen, Sudhalter, Pfadt, Jenkins, Brown, & Vietze, 1991; Hagerman, 2002). In general, persons with FXS are interested in social interactions, and they are sensitive to the facial emotional cues shown by others (Simon & Finucane, 1996; Turk & Cornish, 1998). However, many persons with FXS appear to be anxious particularly in social situations. Anxiety is reported in 81% of postpubertal females with the full mutation, in 61% of postpubertal males with the full mutation, and in 91% of postpubertal males who are mosaic (Merenstein et al., 1996). Cohen and colleagues argued that social avoidance is more strongly associated with FXS than autism (Cohen et al., 1991) and that social anxiety may be the core of many autistic behaviors observed in FXS. In the only study to directly test this hypothesis, Mazzocco, Kates, Baumgardner, Freund, and Reiss (1997) found that more severe anxiety was associated with increased autistic features in 30 females with FXS.

Sudhalter et al. (1990) proposed that the language and social communication deficits seen in FXS are related to a combination of hyperarousal, inhibitory processing deficits, and social anxiety. They noted that persons with FXS can be very social (unlike persons with autism). However, due to an inability to modulate sensory input, they may become hyperaroused and overstimulated—a negative emotional state that could eventually lead to socially avoidant behavior (e.g., gaze aversion) and atypical communication. In their work, they found that the production of deviant language (e.g., tangential errors and perseveration) was highly correlated with the presence of eye contact and high arousal (Belser & Sudhalter, 1995). Although autism has been shown to be associated with a general deficit in inhibitory control of prepotent stimuli (Joseph, 1999; Ozonoff, 1997), FXS may involve an additional deficit associated with hyperarousal and related social anxiety, which may account for the tangential speech that persons with FXS exhibit in social contexts. Similar explanations have been proposed for language abnormalities in schizophrenia and ADHD—conditions that are associated with both deficient inhibitory control of behavior and specific patterns of tangential speech (Barkley, 1997; Frith, 1981; Sudhalter & Belser, 2001).

Neuropsychological Factors

Evidence exists for the presence of a number of neuropsychological deficits in autistic individuals. Baron-Cohen (1995) and others (Leslie, 1987) have argued that the impairments seen in autism result from an inability to use a "theory of mind" mechanism (i.e., to have an intuitive understanding of the mental states of others including their false beliefs, intentions, desires, and feelings). Poor central coherence, or the inability to integrate details into a context, have been proposed by Frith, Happe, and others (reviewed in Happe, 1999). Finally, executive function deficits that are associated with the ability to plan, inhibit prepotent responses, and shift mental sets are often observed in persons with autism (Ozonoff & Strayer, 1997; Rumsey et al., 1985). A number of neuropsychological deficits in autism have been linked to specific nuclei associated with these cognitive processes. For example, imaging studies have linked neuropsychological deficits in persons with autism with abnormalities of the prefrontal cortex (Ring et al., 1999), superior temporal gyrus (Baron-Cohen et al., 1999), amygdala, and cerebellum (Baron-Cohen et al., 1999; Critchley et al., 2000).

Although emergent evidence demonstrates the central role of neuro-psychological deficits in persons with autism, these processes have not been well studied in FXS. In one of the few studies of social cognition in FXS, Garner, Callias, and Turk (1999) found that boys with FXS (n = 8) performed more poorly on a first-order theory of mind task in comparison with a nonautistic group matched on vocabulary and age. As mentioned earlier, preliminary evidence suggests that individuals with FXS may have intact central coherence abilities as reflected by strong performance on measures of featural versus contextual information (Bennetto & Pennington, 2002; Dykens et al., 1987; Kemper et al., 1988). Executive functioning deficits have primarily been documented in adult females with FXS (Bennetto, Pennington, Porter, Taylor, & Hagerman, 2001). However, there is preliminary evidence that males and young children with FXS also show deficits in executive functioning (Kaufman et al., 1990; Munir et al., 2000). Taken together, the limited evidence of neuropsychological functioning in FXS suggests that persons with FXS may not have the same deficits in central coherence as those seen in autism. Yet both groups may have deficits in executive function, theory of mind, or broader social-cognition functions.

Structural brain imaging studies in FXS provide evidence that some of the neurobehavioral characteristics observed in FXS may be due to abnormal brain structure and function. This would certainly seem plausible given the evidence that lack of FMRP is associated with abnormal brain development in regions associated with these cognitive and behavioral processes. For example, there is evidence that males with FXS have larger caudate volumes (Eliez, Blasey, Freund, Hastie, & Reiss, 2001; Reiss, Abrams, Greenlaw, & Freund, 1995) relative to control samples, and the caudate nucleus comprises a portion of the frontal-subcortical circuit involved in executive functions in general and behavioral inhibition in particular. Thus, dysfunction of neuroanatomical circuits involving prefrontal-striatal connections would be consistent with some of the behavioral abnormalities observed in individuals with FXS. The hippocampus, associated with attention, learning, and memory, is also enlarged in FXS (Kates, Abrams, Kaufman, Breiter, & Reiss, 1997). In contrast, the superior temporal gyrus is described as being reduced in volume for FXS (Reiss, Lee, & Freund, 1994) and is part of the neuroanatomical system underlying language and language-related functions (Mesulam, 1985). Similarly, the cerebellar vermis appears to be smaller in FXS than controls (Mazzocco et al., 1997; Mostofsky, Mazzocco, Aakalu, Warsofsky, Denckla, & Reiss, 1998; Reiss, Aylward, Freund, Joshi, & Bryan, 1991; Reiss, Freund, Tseng, & Joshi, 1991). The cerebellar vermis is involved in processing sensory information and modulating attention, emotion, and movement, and may influence language development (Bobée, Mariette, Tremblay-Leveau, & Caston, 2000; Critchley, Corfield, Chandler, Mathias, & Dolan, 2000; Mostofsky et al., 1998; Parsons et al., 2000).

There are a number of neuroanatomical similarities that individuals with autism and FXS share. For example, larger brain size and weight, as well as increased volume in the caudate and lateral ventricular regions, are found in both FXS and autism (Piven et al., 1995; Sabaratnam, 2000). Direct associations between specific brain regions in persons with autism and persons with FXS with and without autism have been completed in two studies. First, Mazzocco and colleagues (1997) found a significant negative correlation between the volume of cerebellar vermi Lobules VI and VII and parental ratings of autistic behavior in females with FXS. Second, Kaufmann and colleagues (2003) studied males with FXS with and without autism and persons with Down syndrome with and without autism. Similar to Mazzocco and other studies, they found reduced posterior cerebellar vermi volume in Lobules VI and VII for individuals with autism, FXS, and Down syndrome. However, autism status was associated with reductions in the FX sample only (those with FX and autism showed larger volume) and not in the Down syndrome sample. These authors report that previous research has shown that most individuals with autism have reduced volume in these vermi. Yet a subset of individuals with autism has shown enlarged volumes. This suggests that volumetric differences in the posterior cerebellar vermi Lobules VI and VII may be important nuclei to study in determining common neurobiological pathways for the co-occurrence of autism in FXS.

ISSUES IN THE POTENTIAL RELATIONSHIP BETWEEN AUTISM AND FRAGILE X SYNDROME

The literature reviewed thus far demonstrates that children with FXS display a broad-ranging pattern of delays in multiple domains of development. This includes abnormal social behaviors, and delays in language use as well as atypical language patterns. Furthermore, it is clear that most children with FXS display a number of behaviors that resemble those of children with autism, and a significant portion of children—perhaps 25% to 40%—meets the diagnostic criteria for autism. However, this association has raised a fundamental question: Is it really autism, or does it just look like autism? This question has potential ramifications for our understanding of both autism and gene–environment interactions in the context of DLDs. The remainder of this chapter is devoted to an analysis of evidence related to this question and a discussion of implications for future research.

Distinctions Between FXS and Autism

First, we must make a clear distinction about known facts differentiating these disorders. Autism is a behaviorally defined syndrome that is diagnosed through observation and interview by a knowledgeable clinician. Lack of social responsivity, impaired relationships, and delayed language are key defining features used in conjunction with widely accepted measures and standards to make a diagnosis. Autism is known to have a genetic basis. However, the mechanisms of genetic transmission have not yet been determined. Findings from analyses of twin and family data are consistent with a model of three or more interacting loci (Pickles et al., 1995; Risch et al., 1999), with the understanding that a subset of different combinations of these genes may be present in affected individuals (Santangelo & Folstein, 2001). Fragile X syndrome, in contrast, is a single-gene disorder that is diagnosed using one of several genetic tests.

Both autism and FXS are developmental disorders that involve communication delays and impairments. However, the following distinction is essential for further discussion: Regardless of genetic background, you have autism if you meet clinical criteria based on observed behavior. Conversely, regardless of observed behavior, you have FXS if you have a specified number of CGG repeats at Xq27.3. Having made this distinction, we now proceed with a review of arguments on both sides of this issue.

Arguments in Favor of "It Just Looks Like Autism"

Several pieces of data support the argument that what appears to be autism in FXS may not be autism in its true expression. First is the argument that autistic-like behavior in FXS may be due primarily to hyperarousal or social anxiety. Studies of behavior and those using a variety of psychophysiological measures support the assumption that hyperarousal may be a defining feature present in many individuals with FXS. An innate tendency toward anxiety, hyperarousal, and the inability to modulate arousal effectively could mean that situations such as meeting strangers, changes in routines, unexpected events, or frustrating experiences may result in aberrant behavior, much of which may be topographically similar to behaviors evident in autism. Thus, an argument could be made that autism in FXS is really hyperarousal that results in autistic-like behavior that appears in many ways like autism, but in reality is not "true" autism.

A second piece of evidence in support of the "just looks like autism" hypothesis is clinical and involves family reports about the sociability of children with FXS. Many clinicians and family members describe children with FXS as being very socially aware and interested in social interactions. Sudhalter (1996) argued at one point that children with FXS want to be social, whereas children with autism appear not to desire social relationships with others. If this is indeed true, it would provide strong evidence in support of the hypothesis that what appears to be autism in FXS is fundamentally different from a true expression of autism because impaired social awareness and aloofness are essential defining features of autism (Tager-Flusberg, 1999). How these types of functions are expressed, and to what degree, in individuals manifesting both autism and FXS also may provide additional clues to better understanding this hypothesis.

A third area of evidence regards the comparative language research on children with FX and children with autism. This research is limited in that it has relied on small samples and typically has compared children with autism with children with FXS without reporting autism status in the FXS children or differentiating performance of FXS children with and without autism. Despite this limitation, at least two studies (Belser & Sudhalter, 2001; Sudhalter & Belser, 2001) have shown that, although children with autism and children with FXS both have language deficits, the way these deficits are expressed is different. In these studies, children with FXS were found to be more likely than children with autism to display tangential language (not related to the current topic) and repetitive speech in the context of tangential language. If replicated with larger samples of children with appropriate accounting for autism within the FXS samples, this finding provides additional evidence in support of the hypothesis that autism alone and autism in FXS are different clinical phenomena.

Finally, it could be argued that the apparently strong relationship between autism status and severity of delay is consistent with other research showing that severe mental retardation and autistic behavior are common co-occurrences across a broad range of causes of mental retardation and developmental disability. The limited communication, cognitive, and behavioral repertoire of individuals with severe cognitive delays could result in frustrations in the ability to communicate and the emergence of behaviors that, similar to the hyperarousal or social anxiety hypotheses, are topographically similar to those displayed in autism, but not similar in terms of etiology.

In summary, arguments in favor of the "just looks like autism" hypothesis rest heavily on the assumption that there is a fundamental mechanism underlying autism that in fact represents true autism. Of course this mechanism is not yet known. Nonetheless, these arguments assume that true autism stems not from arousal or retardation, as may be the case in FX, and cases that do stem from these causes are not really autism.

Arguments in Favor of "It Really Is Autism"

Several counterarguments could be posed to support an alternative hypothesis—namely, that the autistic behavior seen in FXS is a variant of true autism within the broad definition of autism spectrum disorders. One argument, although based on only two studies, draws on the finding that children with FX and autism and children with autism alone are virtually indistinguishable on measures of autism status. This finding has been reported using the Childhood Autism Rating Scale (Bailey et al., 1998) and the ADOS, ADI–R, and *DSM–IV* (Rogers et al., 2001). If children with autism and children with FXS showed significantly different profiles on measures of autism status that involve multiple items or multiple subscales, then it might be inferred that these differentiated patterns of autistic behavior could mean that we are dealing with two different disorders. The fact that differentiated patterns have not been found, especially when both of these studies used different measures of autism status, suggests that they may be similar in the way autistic behavior is expressed.

A second argument draws on findings that show comparable differentiated patterns across developmental domains consistent with the defining features of autism. Bailey et al. (2000) found that children with autism displayed a different profile of cross-domain development than children with FXS alone. Children with FXS (without autism) showed a relatively flat profile, whereas children with autism were relatively lower in language and social domains. When a third group of children with both FXS and autism were added, their overall levels of development were lower than either group, but the pattern was similar to that of the autism alone group (disproportionately lower communication and social scores). If replicated with a larger sample, this finding suggests that autism in FXS is not simply a matter of severe mental retardation, which theoretically should result in a flat profile across all developmental domains. The pattern of greater delays in language and social domains (and not in the cognitive domain) would suggest that this group exhibits a profile similar to that of children with autism alone.

Third is the possibility that arousal plays a role in a non-FXS spectrum of autistic disorders. Although a hyperarousal hypothesis has been posited to explain autism for many years (Dawson & Lewy, 1989; Rogers et al., 2001), there has been little work examining this hypothesis. In addition, findings regarding an arousal hypothesis in autism have been inconclusive, with some support for elevated levels of arousal (Cohen & Johnson, 1977; Ratey et al., 1987; Tordjman et al., 1997) that is not reported in other work (Corona et al., 1998). It could be that hyperarousal affects a subset of individuals with autism. Indeed it could be that hyperarousal explains some of the etiological differences within the autistic subgroups (Cohen et al., 1988; Roberts, Boccia et al., 2001).

Perhaps the most difficult argument to rebut, however, is the fact that autism is a clinical diagnosis based entirely on the observation and perception of behavior without regard to causative factors or underlying mechanisms. Thus, if it looks like autism, and multiple observers using various diagnostic methods agree that it looks like autism, what other choice is there but to label it autism?

Mechanistic Implications of Competing Theories

Research on FXS and autism has led to some interesting findings and associated controversies. How these controversies get resolved could have an important bearing on future research, practice, and theory. If autism in FXS is "really autism," then perhaps FXS is one of several events or processes that trigger one of the mechanisms that is at the root of autism. If this is true, studies of the basic genetics of FXS and "downstream" effects, especially in the regulation of other genes, could possibly lead to dramatic insights into the fundamental nature of autism and other multigene disorders, including DLDs.

However, if we conclude that "it just looks like autism," this will likely force a reexamination of the definition of *autism* and the criteria by which it is diagnosed. Something about the definition or diagnostic process will have to change, and this will pose a tremendous challenge to the field of autism. What will happen in the future if, as new disorders are discovered for which autism is a component, they become removed from the spectrum of autism disorders? Will what is left then be "true autism" or will it simply be cases for which an etiology is not known? If all etiologies become known, will any entity called autism remain? These are provocative questions particularly for proponents of the classic autism phenotype, but single-gene disorders such as FXS evoke such issues, and their resolution will only come from further systematic inquiry.

Developmental language disorders will likely be subject to this same set of issues. Like autism, DLDs cover a spectrum of expression with certain common core features. It can manifest as a single disorder, likely spread across heterogeneous manifestations, or it can co-occur as part of another disorder. It is this latter occurrence that is of interest in this chapter. Multiple genes likely cause both autism and DLDs, and it is probably the combination(s) of these genes that results in the delays and behavioral abnormalities noted. In the meantime, single gene disorders like FXS can serve to help us begin to map various types of language problems. As the genetic basis for other developmental disorders and their linkages to various types of language dysfunctions are mapped, will new disorders be named? Will we retain a category for unknown causes of DLDs, and will they be treated in a different way from known etiologies? How will they be similar and different in terms of etiology, prognosis, and treatment? For example, is FXS now considered a DLD?

TREATMENT IMPLICATIONS

Educators, psychologists, speech-language pathologists, and medical practitioners typically assess and then treat behavior. A child with a speech disorder or delayed language usually receives standard psychosocial or therapeutic interventions regardless of the etiology of the communication disorder. Although many exceptions to this statement exist, it is a general truism that etiology is not typically the primary determinant of treatment.

As we learn more about the genetic basis of DLDs and identify conditions or characteristics associated with those disorders, approaches to treatment are likely to change in the coming years. Treatments will be increasingly individualized on the basis of etiology, and we will see an intense search for biomedical treatments, such as gene therapy, medications targeted toward basic brain functioning, or medications targeted toward associated behavioral features (e.g., social anxiety, attention) that may or may not be causative, but likely interfere with treatment efficacy. How these treatments complement, interact with, or interfere with psychoeducational and therapeutic treatments is unknown. Research on other diseases suggests that medication is usually but one component of a successful intervention. For example, medication to increase attention (e.g., Ritalin) will not be as effective if an individual is part of a chaotic, disorganized environment with multiple and competing stimuli. Environmental and behavioral treatments will remain essential, but they increasingly will need to be evaluated in conjunction with biomedical treatments.

Also basic biomedical research will continue to inform this debate, but it may make it more complicated rather than more straightforward. For example, the genetic mutation causing FXS is known to reduce FMRP. Yet what does this protein do? Synaptic function, lack of dendritic pruning, and possible downstream effects on other genes have all been implicated in recent literature. These alterations in human biological function result in a number of both direct and indirect behavioral and social consequences, one of which could be a communication disorder. However, in frequent co-occurrence with this disorder are hyperarousal, social anxiety, ADD or ADHD, changes in temperament, mental retardation, and autism.

Although we already have a number of educational and behavioral options for treating the associated language problems in FXS, these options will soon expand. The ultimate treatment may be gene therapy, the targeted insertion of a corrected gene that eliminates the cause of FXS. This treatment will be difficult to perfect, however, and it is likely to be many years before this is possible in a brain-based disorder. However, basic biomedical research on the mechanisms by which genetic disorders exert their influence may lead to targeted pharmacological treatments, and three alternative mechanisms may be possible in FXS. If FXS is indeed a problem of learning and synaptic function, there is a new class of medications becoming available known as cognitive enhancers. Indeed a clinical trial of CX516, an Ampakine compound known to enhance learning and memory, is currently underway in FXS (Danysz, 2002). If FXS is primarily a problem of arousal or social anxiety, it may be that anxiety medications are effective for some individuals with FXS. If an attention deficit is the problem, then stimulant medication may be effective. Will the potential positive impact of any of these pharmacological agents, either by themselves or in selected combinations, have additional positive effects on language functions as well (e.g., will children with FXS have less tangential speech)?

Clinical experience suggests that each of these approaches to medication may be effective for some individuals with FXS, but rigorous clinical trials of medication efficacy are needed. In reality, it is likely that some medications will be effective for one group of individuals, whereas others will be effective for another group. One possible outcome of the Human Genome Project and related genetic and molecular biology research is a new field of pharmacogenetics, where genetic profiles can determine which individuals will respond to or have adverse reactions to certain medications based on their DNA (Collins, 1999; Collins & McKusick, 2001).

How autism and DLDs fit into this scenario depends on research on the genetics of these disorders. As their genetic underpinnings are elucidated, various pathways to biomedical treatment may appear. However, research on FXS suggests that even with a single gene disorder, the pathways and mechanisms quickly become complicated. Autism and DLDs almost certainly represent a combination of genes interacting with each other. If this turns out to be true, it is likely that the pathways will become even more complex.

CONCLUSION

Developmental language disorders are not caused by one gene, and language outcome is a product of the complexity of the human genome as well as the complexity of the environments in which we live. At the present time, the primary manipulable dimension is the environment. Thus, we need to continue to develop, evaluate, and apply well-documented educational, psychosocial, and therapeutic treatments. However, although there are many variations and causes of DLDs, there is likely a genetic component to almost all of them. At some point in the future, many of these genetic components will be known. Until then disorders such as FXS provide a fruitful area of research for helping us identify gene–environment–behavior relationships. We can explore ways to maximize treatment outcomes by incorporating new knowledge gained from a holistic and synergistic approach as we address DLDs.

REFERENCES

Abedutto, L., & Hagerman, R. J. (1997). Language and communication in fragile X syndrome. *Mental Retardation and Developmental Disabilities, 3*, 313–322.

Adolphs, R., Sears, L., & Piven, J. (2001). Abnormal processing of social information from faces in autism. *Journal of Cognitive Neuroscience, 13*, 1–8.

Agulhon, C., Blanchet, P., Kobetz, A., Marchant, D., Faucon, N., Sarda, P., Moraine, C., Sittler, A., Biancalana, V., Malafosse, A., & Abitbol, M. (1999). Expression of FMR1, FXR1, and FXR2 genes in human prenatal tissues. *Journal of Neuropathology and Experimental Neurology, 58*(8), 867–880.

Bailey, D. B., Hatton, D. D., Mesibov, G., & Ament, N. (2000). Early development, temperament, and functional impairment in autism and fragile X syndrome. *Journal of Autism and Developmental Disorders, 30*, 49–59.

Bailey, D. B., Hatton, D. D., Skinner, M., & Mesibov, G. (2001). Autistic behavior, FMR1 protein, and developmental trajectories in young males with fragile X syndrome. *Journal of Autism and Developmental Disorders, 31*, 165–174.

Bailey, D. B., Hatton, D. D., Tassone, F., Skinner, M., & Taylor, A. K. (2001). Variability in FMRP and early development in males with fragile X syndrome. *American Journal on Mental Retardation, 106*, 16–27.

Bailey, D. B., Mesibov, G. B., Hatton, D. D., Clark, R. D., Roberts, J. E., & Mayhew, L. (1998). Autistic behavior in young boys with fragile X syndrome. *Journal of Autism and Developmental Disorders, 28*, 499–508.

Bailey, D. B., & Nelson, D. (1995). The nature and consequences of fragile X syndrome. *Mental Retardation and Developmental Disabilities Research Reviews, 1*, 238–244.

Bakker, C. E., Verheij, C., Willemsen, R., Vanderhelm, R., Oerlemans, F., Vermey, M., Bygrave, A., Hoogeveen, A. T., Oostra, B. A., Reyniers, E., Deboulle, K., Dhooge, R., Cras, P., Van Velzen, D., Nagels, G., Martin, J. J., Dedeyn, P. P., Darby, J. K., & Willems, P. J. (1994). Fmr1 knockout mice: A model to study fragile X mental retardation. The Dutch-Belgian Fragile X Consortium. *Cell, 78*(1), 23–33.

Barkley, R. A. (1997). Behavioral inhibition, sustained attention, and executive functions: Constructing a unified theory of ADHD. *Psychological Bulletin, 121*, 65–94.

Baron-Cohen, S. (1995). *Mindblindness: An essay on autism and theory of mind.* Cambridge, MA: MIT Press.

Baron-Cohen, S., Ring, H. A., Wheelwright, S., Bullmore, E. T., Brammer, M. J., Simmons, A., & Williams, S. C. (1999). Social intelligence in the normal and autistic brain: An FMR1 study. *European Journal of Neuroscience, 11*(6), 1891–1898.

Baumgardner, T., Reiss, A., Freund, L., & Abrams, B. (1995). Specification of the neurobehavioral phenotype in males with fragile X syndrome. *Pediatrics, 45,* 744–752.

Belser, R. C., & Sudhalter, V. (1995). Arousal difficulties in males with fragile X syndrome: A preliminary report. *Developmental Brain Dysfunction, 8,* 270–279.

Belser, R. C., & Sudhalter, V. (2001). Conversational characteristics of children with fragile X syndrome: Repetitive speech. *American Journal on Mental Retardation, 106*(1), 28–38.

Bennetto, L., & Pennington, B. (2002). The neuropsychology of fragile X syndrome. In R. J. Hagerman (Eds.), *Fragile X syndrome: Diagnosis, treatment, and research* (3rd ed., pp. 206–248). Baltimore, MD: Johns Hopkins University Press.

Bennetto, L., Pennington, B. F., Porter, D., Taylor, A. K., & Hagerman, R. J. (2001). Profile of cognitive functioning in women with the fragile X mutation. *Neuropsychology, 15,* 290–299.

Bishop, D. V. M. (1997). Pre- and perinatal hazards and family background in children with specific language impairments: A study of twins. *Brain and Language, 56,* 1–26.

Bobée, S., Mariette, E., Tremblay-Leveau, H., & Caston, J. (2000). Effects of early midline cerebellar lesion on cognitive and emotional functions in the rat. *Behavioral Brain Research, 112,* 1–2, 107–117.

Bodfish, J. W., Symons, F. S., Parker, D. E., & Lewis, M. H. (2000). Varieties of repetitive behavior in autism: Comparisons to mental retardation. *Journal of Autism and Developmental Disorders, 30,* 237–243.

Borghgraef, M., Fryns, J., Dielkens, A., Pyck, K., & van Den Berghe, H. (1987). Fragile (X) syndrome: A study of the psychological profile in 23 prepubertal patients. *Clinical Genetics, 32,* 179–186.

Brown, W., Jenkins, E., Friedman, E., Brooks, J., Wisniewski, K., Raguthu, S., & French, J. (1982). Autism is associated with the fragile X syndrome. *Journal of Autism and Developmental Disorders, 12,* 303–307.

Campbell, M., Locascio, J. J., & Choroco, M. C., Spencer, E. K., Malone, R. P., Kafantaris, V., & Overall, J. E. (1990). Stereotypies and tardive dyskinesia: Abnormal movements in autistic children. *Psychopharmacology Bulletin, 26*(2), 260–266.

Cohen, D., & Johnson, W. (1977). Cardiovascular correlates of attention in normal and psychiatrically disturbed children. *Archives of General Psychiatry, 34,* 561–567.

Cohen, I. L. (1995a). A theoretical analysis of the role of hyperarousal in the learning and behavior of fragile X males. *Mental Retardation and Developmental Disabilities Research Reviews, 1,* 286–291.

Cohen, I. L. (1995b). Behavioral profiles of autistic and nonautistic fragile X males. *Developmental Brain Dysfunction, 8,* 252–269.

Cohen, I., Fisch, G., Sudhalter, V., Wolf-Schein, E., Hanson, D., Hagerman, R., Jenkins, E., & Brown, W. (1988). Social gaze, social avoidance, and repetitive behavior in fragile X males: A controlled study. *American Journal of Mental Retardation, 92*(5), 436–446.

Cohen, I. L., Sudhalter, V., Pfadt, A., Jenkins, E. C., Brown, W. T., & Vietze, P. M. (1991). Why are autism and the fragile-X syndrome associated? Conceptual and methodological issues. *American Journal of Human Genetics, 48,* 195–202.

Cohen, I. L., Vietze, P. M., Sudhalter, V., Jenkins, E. C., & Brown, W. T. (1989). Parent-child dyadic gaze patterns in fragile X males and in non-fragile X males with autistic disorder. *Journal of Child Psychology and Psychiatry, 30*(6), 845–856.

Collins, F. S. (1999). Medical and societal consequences of the Human Genome Project. *New England Journal of Medicine, 341,* 28–37.

Collins, F. S., & McKusick, V. A. (2001). Implications of the Human Genome Project for medical sciences. *Journal of the American Medical Association, 285,* 540–544.

Cook, E. H. (1998). Genetics of autism. *Mental Retardation and Developmental Disabilities Research Reviews, 4,* 113–120.

Corbin, F., Bouillon, M., Fortin, A., Morin, S., Rousseau, F., & Khandjian, E. W. (1997). The fragile X mental retardation protein is associated with poly(A)+mRNA in actively translating polyribosomes. *Human Molecular Genetics, 6*, 1465–1472.

Cornish, K. M., Munir, F., & Cross, G. (2001). Differential impact of the FMR-1 full mutation on memory and attention functioning: A neuropsychological perspective. *Journal of Cognitive Neuroscience, 13*, 144–150.

Corona, R., Dissanayake, C., Arbelle, S., Wellington, P., & Sigman, M. (1998). Is affect aversive to young children with autism? Behavioral and cardiac responses to experimenter distress. *Child Development, 69*(6), 1494–1502.

Crawford, D. C., Acuna, J. M., & Sherman, S. L. (2001). FMR1 and the fragile X syndrome: Human genome epidemiology review. *Genetics Medicine, 3*(5), 359–371.

Critchley, H. D., Corfield, D. R., Chandler, M. P., Mathias, C. J., & Dolan, R. J. (2000). Cerebral correlates of autonomic cardiovascular arousal: A functional neuroimaging investigation in humans. *Journal of Physiology, 523*, 259–270.

Cronister, A., Hagerman, R. J., Wittenberger, M., & Amiri, K. (1991). Mental impairment in cytogenetically positive fragile X females. *American Journal of Medical Genetics, 38*, 503–504.

Danysz, W. (2002). CX0516 cortex pharmaceuticals. *Current Opinion in Investigational Drugs, 7*, 1081–1088.

Dawson, G., & Lewy, A. (1989). Arousal, attention, and the socioemotional impairments of individuals with autism. In G. Dawson (Ed.), *Autism: Nature, diagnosis, and treatment* (pp. 49–74). New York: Guilford.

Dawson, G., Meltzoff, A. N., Osterling, J., Rinaldi, J., & Brown, E. (1998). Children with autism fail to orient to naturally occurring social stimuli. *Journal of Autism and Developmental Disorders, 28*(6), 479–485.

DeFries, J. C., & Alarcon, M. (1996). Genetics of specific reading disability. *Mental Retardation and Developmental Disabilities Research Reviews, 2*, 39–47.

Devys, D., Lutz, N., Rouyer, J., Bellocq, J. P., & Mandel, J. (1993). The FMR-1 protein is cytoplasmic, most abundant in neurons and appears normal in carriers of a fragile X premutation. *Nature Genetics, 4*, 335–340.

Dykens, E., Hodapp, R., & Leckman, J. (1987). Strengths and weaknesses in the intellectual functioning of males with fragile X syndrome. *American Journal of Mental Deficiency, 92*, 234–236.

Dykens, E., Ort, S., Cohen, I., Finucane, B., Spiridigliozzi, G., Lanchiewicz, A., Reiss, A., Freund, L., Hagerman, R., & O'Connor, R. (1996). Trajectories and profiles of adaptive behavior in males with fragile X syndrome: Multicenter studies. *Journal of Autism and Developmental Disorders, 26*(3), 287–300.

Dykens, E., & Volkmar, F. (1997). Medical conditions associated with autism. In D. Cohen & F. Volkmar (Eds.), *Handbook of autism and pervasive developmental disorders* (2nd ed., pp. 388–410). New York: Wiley.

Eliez, S., Blasey, C. M., Freund, L. S., Hastie, T., & Reiss, A. L. (2001). Brain anatomy, gender and IQ in children and adolescents with fragile X syndrome. *Brain, 124*, 1610–1618.

Feng, Y., Gutekunst, C., Eberhart, D., Yi, H., Warren, S., & Hersch, S. (1997). Fragile X mental retardation protein: Nucleocytoplasmic shuttling and association with somatodendritic ribosomes. *Journal of Neuroscience, 17*, 1539–1547.

Fisch, G. S. (1992). Is autism associated with the fragile X syndrome? *American Journal of Medical Genetics, 43*, 47–55.

Freeman, B., Ritvo, E., Schroth, P., Tonick, I., Guthrie, D., & Wake, L. (1981). Behavioral characteristics of high and low IQ autistic children. *American Journal of Psychiatry, 138*, 25–91.

Freund, L. (1995). Addressing the social developmental needs of girls with fragile X. *National Fragile X Advocate, 1*, 4–6.

Freund, L., & Reiss, A. (1991). Cognitive profiles associated with fra(X) syndrome in males and females. *American Journal of Medical Genetics, 38*(4), 542–547.

Freund, L. S., Reiss, A. L., & Abrams, M. T. (1993). Psychiatric disorders associated with fragile X in the young female. *Pediatrics, 91,* 321–329.

Frith, C. D. (1981). Schizophrenia: An abnormality of consciousness. In G. Underwood & R. Stevens (Eds.), *Aspects of consciousness* (pp. 437–443). New York: Academic Press.

Garner, C., Callias, M., & Turk, J. (1999). Executive function and theory of mind performance of boys with fragile-X syndrome. *Journal of Intellectual Disability Research, 43*(6), 466–474.

Gopnik, M., & Crago, M. G. (1991). Familial aggregation of a developmental language disorder. *Cognition, 39,* 1–50.

Hagerman, R. (2002). The physical and behavioral phenotype. In R. J. Hagerman & P. J. Hagerman (Eds.), *Fragile X syndrome: Diagnosis, treatment, and research* (3rd ed., pp. 1–109). Baltimore, MD: Johns Hopkins University Press.

Hagerman, R. J., Jackson, A. W., Levitas, A., Rimland, B., & Braden, M. (1986). An analysis of autism in fifty males with the fragile X syndrome. *American Journal of Medical Genetics, 64,* 356–361.

Happe, F. (1997). Central coherence and theory of mind in autism: Reading homographs in context. *British Journal of Developmental Psychology, 15,* 1–12.

Happe, F. (1999). Autism: Cognitive deficit or cognitive style? *Trends in Cognitive Sciences, 3,* 216–222.

Hatton, D. D., Bailey, D. B., Hargett-Beck, M. Q., Skinner, M., & Clark, R. D. (1999). Behavioral style of young boys with fragile X syndrome. *Developmental Medicine and Child Neurology, 41,* 625–632.

Hatton, D. D., Hooper, S. R., Bailey, D. B., Skinner, M., Sullivan, K., & Wheeler, A. (2002). Problem behavior in boys with fragile X syndrome. *American Journal of Medical Genetics, 108,* 105–116.

Hessl, D., Glaser, B., Dyer-Friedman, J., Blasey, C., Hastie, T., Gunnar, M., & Reiss, A. L. (2002). Cortisol and behavior in fragile X syndrome. *Psychoneuroendocrinology, 27*(7), 855–873.

Hirstein, W., Iversen, P., & Ramachandran, V. S. (2001). Autonomic responses of autistic children to people and objects. *Proceedings of the Royal Society of London Biological Sciences, 268*(1479), 1883–1888.

Hooper, S. R., Hatton, D. D., Baranek, G. T., Roberts, J. P., & Bailey, D. B. (2000). Nonverbal assessment of cognitive abilities in children with fragile X syndrome: The utility of the Leiter International Performance Scale–Revised. *Journal of Psychoeducational Assessment, 18,* 255–267.

Imbert, G., Feng, W., Nelson, D. L., Warren, S. T., & Mandel, J. L. (1998). FMR1 and mutations in fragile X syndrome: Molecular biology, biochemistry and genetics. In R. D. Wells & S. T. Warren (Eds.), *Genetic instability and hereditary neurobiological diseases* (pp. 27–53). New York: Academic Press.

Joseph, R. M. (1999). Neuropsychological frameworks for understanding autism. *International Review of Psychiatry, 11,* 309–325.

Kates, W. R., Abrams, M. T., Kaufman, W. E., Breiter, S. N., & Reiss, A. L. (1997). Reliability and validity of MRI measurement of the amygdala and hippocampus in children with fragile X syndrome. *Psychiatry Research: Neuroimaging Section, 75,* 31–48.

Kau, A. S., Reider, E. E., Meyer, W. A., & Freund, L. (2000). Early behavior signs of psychiatric phenotypes in fragile X syndrome. *American Journal of Mental Retardation, 105*(4), 286–299.

Kaufman, P., Leckman, J., Dykens, E., Sparrow, S., Zelinsky, D., & Ort, S. (1990). Delayed response performance in males with fragile X syndrome. *Journal of Clinical Experimental Neuropsychology, 12,* 69.

Kaufmann, W. E., Abrams, M. T., Chen, W., & Reiss, A. L. (1999). Genotype, molecular phenotype, and cognitive phenotype: Correlations in fragile X syndrome. *American Journal on Medical Genetics, 83*, 286–295.

Kemper, M. B., Hagerman, R. J., & Altshul-Stark, D. (1988). Cognitive profiles of boys with the fragile X syndrome. *American Journal of Medical Genetics, 30*, 191–200.

Keysor, C., & Mazzocco, M. M. (2002). A developmental approach to understanding fragile X syndrome in females. *Microscopy Research and Technique, 57*, 179–186.

Keysor, C. S., Mazzocco, M. M. M., McLeod, D. R., & Hoehn-Saric, R. (2002). Physiological arousal in females with fragile X or Turner Syndrome. *Developmental Psychobiology, 41*, 133–146.

Khandjian, E. W., Fortin, A., Thibodeau, A., Tremblay, S., Cote, F., Devys, D., Mandel, J. L., & Rousseau, F. (1995). A heterogeneous set of FMR1 proteins is widely distributed in mouse tissues and is modulated in cell culture. *Human Molecular Genetics, 4*(5), 783–789.

Kjelgaard, M., & Tager-Flusberg, H. (2000). An investigation of language profiles in autism: Implications for genetic subgroups. *Language and Cognitive Processes, 15*, 1–22.

Klin, A. (2000). Attributing social meaning to ambiguous visual stimuli in higher-functioning autism and Asperger syndrome: The social attribution task. *Journal of Child Psychology and Psychiatry, 7*, 831–846.

Kootz, J., Marinelli, B., & Cohen, D. (1982). Modulation of response to environmental stimulation in autistic children. *Journal of Autism and Developmental Disorders, 12*(2), 185–193.

Kooy, R. F., D'Hooge, R., Reyniers, E., Bakker, C. E., Nagels, G., Deboulle, K., Storm, K., Clincke, G., Dedeyn, P. P., Oostra, B. A., & Willems, P. J. (1996). Transgenic mouse model for the fragile X syndrome. *American Journal of Medical Genetics, 64*, 241–245.

Lachiewicz, A., Gullion, C., Spiridigliozzi, G., & Aylsworth, A. (1987). Declining IQs of males with the fragile X syndrome. *American Journal of Mental Retardation, 92*(3), 272–278.

Leslie, A. (1987). Pretense and representation: The origins of "theory of mind." *Psychological Review, 94*, 412–426.

Levitas, A., Hagerman, R., Braden, M., Rimland, B., McBogg, P., & Matus, I. (1983). Autism and the fragile X syndrome. *Journal of Developmental and Behavioral Pediatrics, 4*(3), 151–158.

Mazzocco, M. M. M. (2000). Advances in research on the fragile X syndrome. *Mental Retardation and Developmental Disabilities Research Reviews, 6*, 96–106.

Mazzocco, M. M. M., Kates, W., Baumgardner, T. L., Freund, L. S., & Reiss, A. L. (1997). Autistic behavior among girls with fragile X syndrome. *Journal of Autism and Developmental Disorders, 27*, 415–435.

Mazzocco, M. M., Pennington, B. F., & Hagerman, R. J. (1993). The neurocognitive phenotype of female carriers of fragile X: Additional evidence for specificity. *Journal of Developmental and Behavioral Pediatrics, 14*, 328–335.

Merenstein, S. A., Sobesky, W. E., Taylor, A. K., Riddle, J. E., Tran, H. X., & Hagerman, R. J. (1996). Molecular-clinical correlations in males with an expanded FMR1 mutation. *American Journal of Medical Genetics, 64*, 388–394.

Mesulam, M. M. (1985). Patterns in behavioral neuroanatomy: Association areas, the limbic system, and hemispheric specialization. In M. M. Mesulam (Ed.), *Principles of behavioral neurology* (pp. 1–70). Philadelphia, PA: F. A. Davis Company.

Miller, L., McIntosh, D., McGrath, J., Shyu, V., Lampe, M., Taylor, A., Tassone, F., Neitzel, K., Stackhouse, T., & Hagerman, R. (1999). Electrodermal responses to sensory stimuli in individuals with fragile X syndrome: A preliminary project. *American Journal of Medical Genetics, 83*(4), 268–279.

Mostofsky, S. H., Mazzocco, M. M. M., Aakalu, G., Warsofsky, I. S., Denckla, M. B., & Reiss, A. L. (1998). Decreased cerebellar posterior vermis size in fragile X syndrome—Correlation with neurocognitive performance. *Neurology, 50*(1), 121–130.

Mundy, P., Sigman, M., & Kasari, C. (1994). Joint attention, developmental level and symptom presentation in autism. *Development and Psychopathology, 6,* 389–401.

Munir, F., Cornish, K. M., & Wilding, J. (2000). A neuropsychological profile of attention deficits in young males with fragile X syndrome. *Neuropsychologia, 38,* 1261–1270.

Oberle, I., Rousseau, F., Heitz, D., Kretz, C., Devys, D., Hanauer, A., Boue, J., Bertheas, M. F., & Mandel, J. L. (1991). Instability of a 550-base pair DNA segment and abnormal methylation in fragile X syndrome. *Science, 252,* 1097–1102.

Oostra, B. (1996). Fragile X syndrome in humans and mice. *Acta Genet Med Gemellol (Roma), 45,* 93–108.

Ozonoff, S. (1997). Causal mechanisms of autism: Unifying perspectives from an information processing framework. In D. J. Cohen & F. R. Volkmar (Eds.), *Handbook of autism and pervasive developmental disorders* (2nd ed., pp. 868–879). New York: Wiley.

Ozonoff, S., & Strayer, D. L. (1997). Inhibitory function in nonretarded children with autism. *Journal of Autism and Developmental Disorders, 27,* 59–77.

Parsons, L. M., Denton, D., Egan, G., McKinley, M., Shade, R., Lancaster, J., & Fox, P. T. (2000). Neuroimaging evidence implicating cerebellum in support of sensory/cognitive processes associated with thirst. *Proceedings of the National Academy of Sciences, U.S.A. 97,* 2332–2336.

Paul, R., Dykens, E., Leckman, J. F., Watson, M., Bregman, W. R., & Cohen, D. J. (1987). A comparison of language characteristics of mentally retarded adults with fragile X syndrome and those with nonspecific mental retardation and autism. *Journal of Autism and Developmental Disorders, 17,* 457–468.

Pickles, A., Bolton, P., Macdonald, H., Bailey, A., Le Couteur, A., Sim, C. H., & Rutter, M. (1995). Latent-class analysis of recurrence risks for complex phenotypes with selection and measurement error: A twin and family history study of autism. *American Journal of Human Genetics, 57*(3), 717–726.

Piven, J., Arndt, S., Bailey, J., Havercamp, S., Andreasen, N. C., & Palmer, P. (1995). An MRI study of brain size in autism. *American Journal of Psychiatry, 152*(8), 1145–1149.

Piven, J., Harper, J., Palmer, P., & Ardnt, S. (1996). Course of behavioral change in autism: A retrospective study of high-IQ adolescents and adults. *Journal of American Academy of Child and Adolescent Psychiatry, 35,* 523–529.

Plante, E., Swisher, L., Vance, R., & Rapcsak, S. (1991). MRI findings in boys with specific language impairment. *Brain and Language, 41*(1), 52–66.

Prior, M., & MacMillan, M. (1973). Maintenance of sameness in children with Kanner's syndrome. *Journal of Autism and Childhood Schizophrenia, 3,* 154–167.

Ratey, J. J, Mikkelsen, E., Sorgi, P., Zuckerman, H. S., Polakoff, S., Bemporad, J., Bick, P., & Kadish, W. (1987). Autism: The treatment of aggressive behaviors. *Journal of Clinical Pharmacology, 7*(1), 35–41.

Reiss, A. L., Abrams, M., Greenlaw, R., & Freund, L. (1995). Neurodevelopmental effects of the FMR-1 full mutation in humans. *Natural Medicine, 1*(2), 159–167.

Reiss, A. L., Aylward, E., Freund, L. S., Joshi, P. K., & Bryan, R. N. (1991). Neuroanatomy of fragile X syndrome: The posterior fossa. *Annals of Neurology, 29*(1), 26–32.

Reiss, A. L., & Freund, L. (1992). Behavioral phenotype of fragile X syndrome: *DSM–III–R* autistic behavior in male children. *American Journal of Medical Genetics, 43,* 35–46.

Reiss, A. L., Freund, L., Tseng, J. E., & Joshi, P. K. (1991). Neuroanatomy in fragile X females: The posterior fossa. *American Journal of Human Genetics, 49*(2), 279–288.

Reiss, A. L., Lee, J., & Freund, L. (1994). Neuroanatomy of fragile X syndrome. The temporal lobe. *Neurology, 44*(7), 1317–1324.

Reiss, D., & Neiderhiser, J. M. (2000). The interplay of genetic influences and social processes in developmental theory: Specific mechanisms are coming into view. *Development and Psychopathology, 12,* 357–374.

Ring, H. A., Baron-Cohen, S., Wheelwright, S., Williams, S. C, Brammer, M., Andrew, C., & Bullmore, E. T. (1999). Cerebral correlates of preserved cognitive skills in autism: A functional MRI study of embedded figures task performance. *Brain, 122*(Pt. 7), 1305–1315.

Risch, N., Spiker, D., & Lotspeich, L., Nouri, N., Hinds, D., Hallmayer, J., Kalaydjieva, L., McCague, P., Dimiceli, S., Pitts, T., Nguyen, L., Yang, J., Harper, C., Thorpe, D., Vermeer, S., Young, H., Hebert, J., Lin, A., Ferguson, J., Chiotti, C., Wiese-Slater, S., Rogers, T., Salmon, B., Nicholas, P., Petersen, B. P., Pingree, C., McMahon, W., Wong, D. L., Cavalli-Sforza, L. L., Kraemer, H. C., & Myers, R. M. (1999). A genomic screen of autism: Evidence for a multilocus etiology. *American Journal of Human Genetics, 65*(2), 493–507.

Roberts, J. E., Boccia, M. L., Bailey, D. B., Hatton, D. D., & Skinner, M. (2001). Cardiovascular indicators of arousal in boys affected by fragile X syndrome. *Developmental Psychobiology, 39*(2), 107–123.

Roberts, J. E., Mirrett, P., Anderson, K., Burchinal, M., & Neebe, E. (2002). Early communication, symbolic behavior, and social profiles of young males with fragile X syndrome. *American Journal of Speech Language Pathology, 11*, 295–304.

Roberts, J. E., Mirrett, P., & Burchinal, M. (2001). Receptive and expressive communication development of young males with fragile X syndrome. *American Journal of Mental Retardation, 106*(3), 216–230.

Rogers, S. J., Wehner, E. A., & Hagerman, R. J. (2001). The behavioral phenotype in fragile X: Symptoms of autism in very young children with fragile X syndrome, idiopathic autism, and other developmental disorders. *Journal of Developmental and Behavioral Pediatrics, 22*, 409–417.

Rumsey, J. M., Rapoport, J. L., & Sceery, W. R. (1985). Autistic children as adults: Psychiatric, social, and behavioral outcomes. *Journal of American Academy of Child Psychiatry, 24*, 465–473.

Rutter, M., & Schopler, E. (1987). Autism and pervasive developmental disorders: Concepts and diagnostic issues. *Journal of Autism and Developmental Disorders, 17*, 159–186.

Sabaratnam, M. (2000). Pathological and neuropathological findings in two males with fragile X syndrome. *Journal of Intellectual Disability Research, 44*, 81–85.

Sameroff, A. J., & Fiese, B. H. (2000). Transactional regulation: The developmental ecology of early intervention. In J. P. Shonkoff & S. J. Meisels (Eds.), *Handbook of early childhood intervention* (2nd ed., pp. 135–159). Cambridge: Cambridge University Press.

Santangelo, S., & Folstein, S. (2001). Autism: A genetic perspective. In H. Tager-Flusberg (Ed.), *Neurodevelopmental disorders: Contributions to a new framework from the cognitive neurosciences* (pp. 33–59). Boston: MIT Press.

Shah, A., & Frith, U. (1983). An islet of ability in autistic children: A research note. *Journal of Child Psychology and Psychiatry, 24*, 613–620.

Shah, A., & Frith, U. (1993). Why do autistic individuals show superior performance on the block design task? *Journal of Child Psychology and Psychiatry, 34*, 1351–1364.

Sigman, M., & Ruskin, E. (1999). Continuity and change in the social competence of children with autism, Down syndrome, and developmental delays. *Monographs of the Society for Research in Child Development, 64*(1), Serial No. 256.

Simon, E. W., & Finucane, B. M. (1996). Facial emotion identification in males with fragile X syndrome. *American Journal of Medical Genetics, 67*, 77–80.

Spinelli, M., Rocha, A., Giacheti, C., & Richieri-Costa, A. (1995). Word-finding difficulties, verbal paraphasias, and verbal dyspraxia in ten individuals with fragile X syndrome. *American Journal of Medical Genetics, 60*, 39–43.

Sudhalter, V. (1996, June). *Language and communication.* Paper presented on the Meeting on Fragile X Syndrome, London.

Sudhalter, V., & Belser, R. C. (2001). Conversational characteristics of children with fragile x syndrome: Tangential language. *American Journal of Mental Retardation, 106*(5), 389–400.

Sudhalter, V., Cohen, I. L., Silverman, W., & Wolf-Schein, E. G. (1990). Conversational analyses of males with fragile X, Down syndrome, and autism: Comparison of the emergence of deviant language. *American Journal on Mental Retardation, 94*(4), 431–441.

Tager-Flusberg, H. (1999). A psychological approach to understanding the social and language impairments in autism. *International Review of Psychiatry, 11*, 325–334.

Tallal, P., Townsend, J., Curtiss, S., & Wulfeck, B. (1991). Phenotypic profiles of language-impaired children based on genetic/family history. *Brain and Language, 41*(1), 81–95.

Tamanini, F., Willemsen, R., Van Unen, L., Bontekoe, C., Galjaard, H., Oostra, B. A., & Hoogeveen, A. T. (1997). Differential expression of FMR1, FXR1, and FXR2 proteins in human brain and testis. *Human Molecular Genetics, 6*(8), 1315–1322.

Tassone, F., Hagerman, R. J., Chamberlain, W. D., & Hagerman, P. J. (2000). Transcription of the FMR1 gene in individuals with fragile X syndrome. *American Journal of Medical Genetics, 97*, 195–203.

Tassone, F., Hagerman, R. J., Ikle, D. N., Dyer, P. N., Lampe, M., Willemsen, R., Oostra, B. A., & Taylor, A. K. (1999). FMRP expression as a potential prognostic indicator in fragile X syndrome. *American Journal of Medical Genetics, 84*, 250–261.

Tassone, F., Hagerman, R. J., Loesch, D. Z., Lachiewicz, A., Taylor, A. K., & Hagerman, P. J. (2000). Fragile X males with unmethylated, full mutation trinucleotide repeat expansions have elevated levels of FMR1 messenger RNA. *American Journal of Medical Genetics, 94*, 232–236.

Tassone, F., Hagerman, R. J., Taylor, A. K., Gane, L. W., Godfrey, T. E., & Hagerman, P. J. (2000). Elevated levels of FMR1 mRNA in carrier males: A new mechanism of involvement in the fragile-X syndrome. *American Journal of Human Genetics, 66*, 6–15.

Tordjman, S., Anderson, G. M, McBride, P. A., Hertzig, M. E., Snow, M. E., Hall, L. M., Thompson, S. M., Ferrari, P., & Cohen, D. J. (1997). Plasma beta-endorphin, adrenocorticotropin hormone, and cortisol in autism. *Journal of Child Psychology and Psychiatry, 38*(6), 705–715.

Turk, J., & Cornish, K. M. (1998). Face recognition and emotion perception in boys with fragile X syndrome. *Journal of Intellectual Disability Research, 42*, 490–499.

Turk, J., & Graham, P. (1997). Fragile X syndrome, autism, and autistic features. *Autism, 1*, 175–197.

Turner, M. (1999). Repetitive behavior in autism: A review of psychological research. *Journal of Child Psychology and Psychiatry, 40*, 839–849.

van der Lely, H. K. J., & Stollwerck, L. (1996). A grammatical specific language impairment in children: An autosomal dominant inheritance? *Brain and Language, 52*, 484–504.

Verkerk, A., Pieretti, M., Sutcliffe, J. S., Fu, Y., Kuhl, D., Pizzuti, A., Reiner, O., Richards, S., Victoria, M., Zhang, F., Eussen, B., van Ommen, G., Blonden, L., Riggins, G., Chastain, J., Kunst, C., Galjaard, H., Caskey, C. T., Nelson, D., Oostra, B., & Warren, S. (1991). Identification of a gene (FMR-1) containing a CGG repeat coincident with a breakpoint cluster region exhibiting length variation in fragile X syndrome. *Cell, 65*, 905–914.

Weiler, I. J., & Greenough, W. T. (1999). Synaptic synthesis of the fragile X protein: Possible involvement in synapse maturation and elimination. *American Journal of Medical Genetics, 83*(4), 248–252.

Wetherby, A. M., Prizant, B. M., & Hutchinson, T. A. (1998). Communicative, social/affective, and symbolic profiles of young children with autism and pervasive developmental disorders. *American Journal of Speech-Language Pathology, 7*(2), 79–91.

Wilkinson, K. (1998). Profiles of language and communication skills in autism. *Mental Retardation and Developmental Disabilities Research Reviews, 7*, 73–79.

_II_

INVESTIGATING LANGUAGE IMPAIRMENTS ACROSS DIAGNOSTIC CATEGORIES

8

Cross-Etiology Comparisons of Cognitive and Language Development

Carolyn B. Mervis
University of Louisville

CROSS-ETIOLOGY COMPARISONS OF COGNITIVE AND LANGUAGE DEVELOPMENT

Researchers interested in a particular syndrome or developmental disorder often wish to elucidate the cognitive and language characteristics associated with that group, with the goal to determine characteristics that are universal within and specific to the target group. To this end, researchers typically compare a group with the target disorder to contrast groups matched for certain variables (CA, IQ, and MA are common choices). If the target group performs significantly worse than both normally developing and delayed contrast groups on the dependent variable(s), it is commonly concluded that the target group evidences a universal deficit on the dependent variable and that the deficit is specific to that group. For example, suppose that a group of children with autism responds significantly less often to an experimenter's bids for joint attention than either a language-matched group of children with other forms of developmental delay or a language-matched group of children who are developing normally. Given this pattern of results, researchers typically would conclude (as Sigman & Ruskin [1999] did) that deficits in responding to bids for joint attention were universal and specific to children with autism. Sometimes such conclusions are based on comparisons of only two syndrome groups. As another example, suppose a group of adolescents with Williams syndrome performed very well on a series of syntactic measures and significantly better than a CA- and IQ-matched group of adolescents with Down syndrome. Given this pattern of results, the conclusion drawn by Bellugi and her colleagues (e.g., Bellugi, Marks, Bihrle, & Sabo, 1988; Bellugi, Wang, & Jernigan, 1994) as well as many other language researchers (e.g., Jackendoff, 1994; Pinker, 1999) was that the language ability of individuals with Williams syndrome was both much higher than expected for their level of mental retardation and essentially normal.

Until recently, claims that certain characteristics or patterns of characteristics were universal to and specific for a particular syndrome or developmental disorder were important primarily either for theoretical reasons or as a basis for more targeted cognitive or linguistic intervention. However, as the genetic basis for more syndromes becomes known, these claims serve another important purpose as phenotypes that occur due to particular genetic characteristics (e.g., gene deletions, duplications, or mutations) in transaction with other genes and the environment. For sets of behavioral characteristics to be effectively used in genotype/phenotype research, it is critical that they be characteristic of the vast majority of people expected to have the same genotype and not characteristic of most people who are expected not to have the target genotype. In this chapter, I argue that comparison of mean differences between groups is not the most fruitful approach to producing a cognitive-linguistic description (henceforth, profile) that is characteristic of a particular syndrome and largely limited to that syndrome, and thus is not the approach best suited to genotype/phenotype research. I argue that a profiling method that focuses on the performance of individuals across multiple measures, but allows the performance of these individuals to be aggregated by disability (or any other variable of interest), is more appropriate. Once a specific profile of performance is proposed, signal detection theory can be used to determine the extent to which that profile is characteristic of and/or specific to that disability. Profiles that have high sensitivity and specificity are particularly useful for genotype/phenotype research. Although studies focused on mean differences between matched groups are not ideal for identifying genotype/phenotype correlations, such studies may play an important role in identifying characteristics that could be included in profiling studies. For this reason, in the second part of the chapter, suggestions for maximizing the methodological strength of studies using group-matching designs are presented.

COGNITIVE-LINGUISTIC PROFILES

Statistical comparisons of a group with a particular developmental disability to one or more contrast groups for mean level of performance on measures of cognition or language frequently yield very low p values (e.g., $p < .001$ or even $p < .0001$), indicating highly significant differences between the target group and the contrast groups on the dependent variables. Given such a very low p value, why shouldn't the conclusion that the lower performing group has a universal and specific deficit on the characteristic measured by the dependent variable follow automatically? The problem is that the conclusion that a particular characteristic is universal and specific to a syndrome requires an examination of the distribution of scores on the dependent variable, rather than consideration of the magnitude or significance of the mean difference. If the distributions are nonoverlapping or evidence very little overlap, then the conclusion that poor performance on the dependent variable is universal and specific to the target group may be warranted. (The appropriateness of such a conclusion is also dependent on the determination that the contrast groups are well matched on the control variables; issues related to group matching are discussed in the second section of this chapter.)

However, it is quite possible that despite an extremely low p value, the distributions of scores on the dependent variable may overlap a great deal. An example of this situation, which is very common in research on cognition and language, is illustrated in Fig. 8.1. The distributions in this figure were drawn based on the means and standard deviations reported by Sigman and Ruskin (1999) for the percentage of trials on which a child

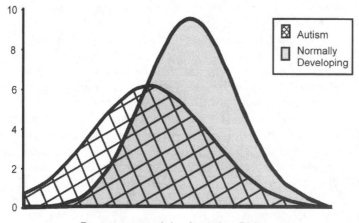

Responses to Joint Attention Bids

FIG. 8.1. Distributions of percentage of bids for joint attention responded to by children with autism and children who are developing normally, based on means and standard deviations from Sigman and Ruskin (1999). Note the extensive overlap between the two distributions despite a significant between-group difference at the $p < .00001$ level. Groups were matched for language age at the $p > .17$ level. Adapted from Mervis and Robinson (2003).

responded to the experimenter's bids for joint attention. The difference in mean percent responses between the autism group and the language-matched normally developing group was significant at the $p < .00001$ level. Despite this highly significant difference, the two distributions evidence a large amount of overlap. The mean for the autism group is less than 1 standard deviation below the mean for the normally developing group, suggesting that if the distributions are not skewed, more than 20% of the children with autism responded to the experimenter's bids more frequently than the average, normally developing child.

This result suggests that only a relatively small subset of children with autism evidences a significant deficit in joint attention relative to levels expected for language age. Note that because autism is expected to have multiple genetic and/or environmental etiologies, it would not be surprising to find that only a subset of these etiologies is associated with deficits in joint attention relative to language level. Yet the critical conclusion here is that extremely low p values cannot be taken as equivalent to the nonoverlapping or minimally overlapping distributions that are needed to conclude that a characteristic is true of most members of the target group and not true of most members of the contrast group (Fig. 8.1).

In the remainder of this section, I describe a two-step method for determining whether a particular pattern of language and/or cognitive strengths or weaknesses is characteristic of and relatively unique to a particular group. The first step involves determining whether a particular profile is characteristic of a particular individual. The second step involves determining how characteristic that profile is of the other participants in the individual's group (the proportion of people in the target group who fit the profile) and how uncharacteristic that profile is of the individuals who are not in the target group (the proportion of people in the contrast group who do not fit the profile). This approach provides a methodological parallel to the idea that a particular characteristic is a quality of an individual, not a group of individuals. Rather than a group approach, I suggest that specific deficits (weaknesses) be defined as abilities that are below the level expected given an individual's other skill levels, and that specific strengths be defined as abilities that are above the level expected given an individual's other skill levels, regardless of the syndrome group to which he or she belongs. This is achieved by assessing a number of skills for all participants and, instead of comparing group means, examining the profile of each individual. For instance, one could measure language variables (e.g., receptive vocabulary, expressive vocabulary), nonverbal skills (e.g., performance on matrices, drawing ability), and joint attention. If a particular child's joint attention skills are worse than would be predicted based on the other abilities that were measured, then joint attention is a likely candidate for a specific deficit for that particular individual (Step 1). If this same pattern is shown by a large proportion of the children with autism and is not shown by most of the children who do not have autism, then joint attention may be argued to be a specific deficit for autism (Step 2). Signal detection analysis (Siegel, Vukicevic, Elliott, & Kraemer, 1989) may be used to quantify the strength of a potential pattern for a particular target group. In particular, *sensitivity* (*Se*) is defined as the percentage of individuals in the target group that fit the predicted pattern (profile). Specificity (*Sp*) is defined as the percentage of individuals in the contrast group who do not fit the profile.

Ideally, profiles are developed based on a single well-standardized measure or multiple well-standardized measures that were normed on the same group. For example, the profile could be based on relative performance on subtests of a single well-standardized assessment such as the Differential Ability Scales (Elliott, 1990) or one of the Wechsler intelligence tests (e.g., *WISC–IV*; Wechsler, 2003). If necessary, multiple well-standardized assessments that were normed at about the same time could be included in a single profile. Another possibility is for the investigator to gather norms for the particular experimental measures that he or she wishes to include in the profile. These norms could be restricted to the CA range of the participants in the profiling study. In this case, it is important to ensure that the "normal" group used to derive the norms has a mean IQ of ~100. For reasons to be addressed in the second section of this chapter, it is important that profiles be based on standard scores rather than age equivalents.

In most cases, profiles are proposed to differentiate a particular syndrome or developmental disorder group from other groups. Such profiles, if found to be highly characteristic of the target group and much less likely to be characteristic of other groups, have the potential to be particularly helpful in genotype/phenotype correlation studies. The Williams Syndrome Cognitive Profile (Mervis et al., 2000) is presented as an example of this type of profile. Alternatively, profiles may be defined to differentiate other types of groups that share particular patterns of cognitive-linguistic levels of functioning that are expected to cross syndrome lines. The Nonlinear Vocabulary Growth Cognitive-Linguistic Profile is presented as an example of this type of profile. In this case, 4-year-olds are expected to fit this profile, regardless of syndrome, if their expressive vocabulary growth has been nonlinear, but they are expected not to fit this profile if their vocabulary growth has been linear.

The Williams Syndrome Cognitive Profile

The Williams Syndrome Cognitive Profile (WSCP) is an example of the two-step profiling method. This profile is based on individual participants' performance on the Differential Ability Scales (DAS; Elliott, 1990), a full-scale assessment that includes measures of verbal ability, nonverbal reasoning, visuospatial construction, and verbal short-term memory. The WSCP was developed to quantify the pattern of cognitive strengths and weaknesses of individuals with Williams syndrome relative to overall intellectual ability. This pattern involves three characteristics: (a) relative strength in verbal short-term memory, (b) (limited) strength in language, and (c) extreme weakness in visuospatial construction. All components of the WSCP are measured using the DAS. These characteristics were operationalized as four criteria:

1. T score for Recall of Digits, Naming/Definitions, or Similarities subtest > 1st percentile
2. Pattern Construction T score < 20th percentile
3. Pattern Construction T score < Mean T score for the core subtests
4. Pattern Construction T score < Recall of Digits T score

The basis for the choice of these particular criteria is described in Mervis et al. (2000). A person was considered to fit the WSCP only if he or she fit all four criteria.

To test the effectiveness of the WSCP in differentiating individuals with Williams syndrome from individuals with other forms of mental retardation or borderline normal intelligence, Mervis et al. (2000) considered the performance of 84 individuals with Williams syndrome and 56 individuals who had mental retardation or borderline normal intelligence of other etiologies. Step 1 of the two-step profiling method involves determining the fit of each of the 130 individuals to the WSCP. As indicated in Table 8.1, 74 of the 84 individuals with Williams syndrome fit all four of the WSCP criteria and thus were considered to fit the WSCP. In contrast, only 4 of the 56 individuals who did not have Williams syndrome fit all four WSCP criteria. Step 2 of the two-step profiling method involves determining the Se and Sp of the WSCP. As indicated in Table 8.1, $Se = .88$ and $Sp = .93$, indicating that the WSCP is effective at differentiating individuals with Williams syndrome from individuals with other etiologies of developmental disability.

TABLE 8.1
Number and Proportion of Individuals With Williams Syndrome and Individuals Who Do Not Have Williams Syndrome Who Fit the WSCP

Group	Fit WSCP	Do Not Fit WSCP	Sensitivity	Specificity
Williams syndrome	74	10	.88	.93
Mixed etiology	4	52		

Note that Sp for a profile is highly dependent on the composition of the contrast group. For example, Sp for the WSCP would be considerably higher if the contrast group were composed primarily of individuals who had average intelligence (making it much less likely that Criterion 3 would be satisfied). Similarly, a contrast group composed primarily of individuals with moderate to severe mental retardation (making it much less likely that Criterion 1 would be satisfied) or individuals with Down syndrome (making it considerably less likely that Criterion 4 would be satisfied and somewhat less likely that Criterion 1 would be satisfied) would yield a very high Sp. However, a contrast group composed primarily of individuals with nonverbal learning disability who had borderline normal intelligence would yield a lower Sp. Thus, careful selection of the contrast group to ensure that the target group is compared to groups that are appropriate for addressing the theoretical or practical purposes for which the profile was proposed is critical.

Williams syndrome is now defined genetically; only individuals who have a particular microdeletion of Chromosome 7q11.23 are considered to have this syndrome (Morris & Mervis, 2000; Morris et al., 2003). There are, however, a number of individuals who received a clinical diagnosis of Williams syndrome, but were later found not to have a deletion. From the perspective of Sp, the fit of this group of individuals to the WSCP is particularly important. The contrast group included in Mervis et al. (2000) contained 18 such individuals. As indicated in Table 8.2, only two of these participants fit the WSCP, yielding a Sp of .89 even for a contrast group that would be expected to be highly similar to individuals with Williams syndrome.

The genetic deletion involved in Williams syndrome includes at least 19 genes (Hillier et al., 2003; Osborne et al., 2001). Because so many genes are deleted, studies of individuals who have Williams syndrome are unlikely to be useful in identifying specific deleted genes associated with either the extreme difficulty with visuospatial construction or the mental retardation or borderline normal intelligence associated with the syndrome. However, there are individuals who have smaller deletions within the

TABLE 8.2
Number and Proportion of Individuals With Williams Syndrome
and Individuals With a Clinical Diagnosis of Williams Syndrome
Who Do Not Have a Deletion Who Fit the WSCP

Group	Fit WSCP	Do Not Fit WSCP	Sensitivity	Specificity
Williams syndrome Del7q11.23	74	10	.88	.89
"Williams syndrome" No Deletion	2	16		

Williams syndrome region who are not considered to have Williams syndrome because they do not have the facial appearance associated with this syndrome (Morris et al., 2003). In many cases, these individuals have children who also have the deletion, resulting in multigeneration kindreds with the same deletion. Use of the WSCP to assess members of the small-deletion kindreds would be expected to be helpful in narrowing down the set of genes likely to be involved in the particular difficulty with visuospatial construction found in Williams syndrome.

Our research group has assessed five small-deletion kindreds for the WSCP (Frangiskakis et al., 1996; Morris et al., 2003; Morris, chap. 4, this volume, provides an extensive discussion of genotype/phenotype research methodology). The smallest deletion involved only two genes: *elastin* and *LIM-kinase 1*. We were able to test eight individuals with deletions from this kindred using the DAS. Seven of these individuals fit the WSCP, yielding a *Se* of .88. We also tested 10 individuals with deletions from the other four kindreds; all 10 fit the WSCP. Of the kindred members who did not have deletions and were tested for the WSCP, none fit the profile. Furthermore, on an assessment of intelligence that did not include visuospatial construction (Kaufman Brief Intelligence Test; Kaufman & Kaufman, 1990), kindred members with deletions earned IQs similar to unaffected members ($p = .48$), but scored significantly lower on DAS Pattern Construction ($p < .006$) and showed a significantly larger discrepancy between DAS Pattern Construction and DAS Recall of Digits *T* scores ($p < .001$; Morris et al., 2003). This pattern suggests that hemizygous deletion of either *elastin* or *LIM-kinase 1* (the two genes deleted in the smallest deletion), in transaction with other genes and the environment at all levels, leads to the weakness in visuospatial construction associated with Williams syndrome and reflected in the pattern of performance characterized by the WSCP. *Elastin* is responsible for the heart disease and other connective tissue disorders associated with Williams syndrome. However, this gene is unlikely to play a role in cognitive aspects of Williams syndrome for at least two reasons. First, *elastin* has very limited expression in the brain. Second, individuals who have mutations of *elastin* resulting in the same heart disease and connective tissue problems as Williams syndrome have normal intelligence and do not fit the WSCP (Frangiskakis et al., 1996). *LIM-kinase 1*, in contrast, is much more likely to be involved in cognition. This gene encodes a protein kinase that is strongly expressed in the developing brain, especially in the cerebral cortex. This protein interacts with the transmembrane receptor neuregulin (Wang et al., 1998) and also phosphorylates cofilin, a regulator of the actin cytoskeleton important in cell movement and axonal growth of neurons (Arber et al., 1998; Yang et al., 1998). The finding that kindred members with deletions fit the WSCP, but do not otherwise evidence cognitive impairments relative to kindred members who do not have deletions, implicates hemizygous deletion of *LIM-kinase 1* as a contributor, in transaction with other genes and the environment, to the weakness in visuospatial construction associated with Williams syndrome.

The Mullen WSCP

Although the DAS is normed for children as young as 2½ years old, it is not useful for assessing the WSCP until at least age 4 for several reasons. First, the early items on the Block Building subtest (which is administered in place of Pattern Construction until age 3½) involve stacking blocks. Because block stacking is routinely included as a goal in the Infant-Family Service Plans (IFSPs) of young children with Williams syndrome, these children receive extensive instruction on this skill, invalidating their Block Building score. Second, until age 4, it is possible to obtain a relatively good score on Pattern Construction by chance arrangement of the rubber blocks. Thus, demonstration that the pattern of cognitive strengths and weaknesses associated with Williams syndrome is evident prior to age 4 years requires a different assessment measure.

Mervis and Bertrand (1997) found that all the toddlers with Williams syndrome who were tested on the Mental Scale of the Bayley Scales of Mental Development (Bayley, 1969) passed a larger proportion of language items than nonlanguage items in the critical range (10 items before the first item failed through the last item passed). In contrast, almost all the toddlers with Down syndrome passed a larger proportion of nonlanguage items than language items, and the toddlers who were developing normally passed about the same proportions of language items as nonlanguage items. The second edition of the Bayley (Bayley, 1993) is designed quite differently from the first edition, both with regard to basal and ceiling rules (yielding a very different critical range of items) and the types of items included. In the revision, there are many more items that straddle the line between language and nonlanguage items. Thus, the second edition is not appropriate for assessing the WSCP. Furthermore, although passing a larger proportion of language items than nonlanguage items on the first edition is consistent with the WSCP, it is not nearly as specific as the WSCP and therefore would be expected to yield a much lower Sp, although Se would likely be high. A further difficulty with using the Bayley to measure the WSCP is that the Mental Scale of the Bayley only yields a single standard score (DQ); separate standard scores cannot be computed for verbal and nonverbal items.

The Mullen Scales of Early Learning (Mullen, 1995) addresses many of these problems. This measure, which is normed for ages 1 to 68 months, is designed to provide a comprehensive assessment of young children's cognitive and language abilities. Four subtests are included: Visual Reception (measuring visual perceptual and conceptual ability, including matching, discrimination, and memory), Fine Motor (measuring primarily visuo-spatial construction), Receptive Language, and Expressive Language (measuring expressive language and verbal short-term memory). Thus, the Mullen measures all the components of the WSCP. However, because verbal short-term memory is not assessed in a separate subtest, it is not possible to directly translate the WSCP criteria to the Mullen. The Mullen WSCP was initially defined as:

1. Fine Motor T score $< T$ score for any other subtest
2. Fine Motor $T < 20$th percentile

To fit the Mullen WSCP, a child's performance had to meet both criteria.

The Mullen WSCP was initially tested on 34 children with Williams syndrome ages 2 to 5 years, 10 children in the same CA range who had other forms of developmental delay, and 20 same-CA children who were developing normally. As indicated in Table 8.3, the Mullen WSCP had very high Se; almost all the children with Williams syndrome fit the profile. Thus, this profile accurately captures the pattern of performance of young children with Williams syndrome and suggests that it is similar to that of older children and adults. The Sp value expected by chance would be .95 for children with normal intelligence: 25% would be expected to earn their lowest T score on the Fine Motor subtest (because it is one of four subtests), and approximately 20% of these children would be expected to score below the 20th percentile for the Fine Motor subtest, yielding approximately 5% who fit the Mullen WSCP, for an Sp of .95. This is in fact the rate that was found for the normally developing contrast group.

For children with developmental delay, a lower Sp would be expected. Once again, 25% would be expected to earn their lowest T score on the Fine Motor subtest. This time, however, most of these children would be expected to score below the 20th percentile on this subtest (as well as on the other three), yielding a predicted Sp of slightly higher than .75. The calculation of Sp for the developmentally delayed contrast group is indicated in Table 8.4. The obtained Sp of .80 is consistent with the expected value.

TABLE 8.3
Number and Proportion of Children With Williams Syndrome and
Children Who Are Developing Normally Who Fit the Mullen WSCP

Group	Fit WSCP	Do Not Fit WSCP	Sensitivity	Specificity
Williams syndrome	32	2	.95	.95
Normally developing	1	19		

TABLE 8.4
Number and Proportion of Children With Williams Syndrome
and Children With Developmental Delay Due to Other
Causes Who Fit the Mullen WSCP

Group	Fit WSCP	Do Not Fit WSCP	Sensitivity	Specificity
Williams syndrome	32	2	.95	.80
Mixed etiology	2	8		

Thus, the initial version of the Mullen profile had both high *Se* and high *Sp*. However, children who had any syndrome associated with developmental delay combined with weakness in visuospatial construction would likely fit the profile. To make the profile more specific to Williams syndrome, an additional criterion was added that reflected the prior finding that individuals with Williams syndrome only rarely demonstrate significant expressive language delay relative to receptive language ability:

3. Receptive Language T < Expressive Language $T + 8$

Based on the original sample of participants, the modified Mullen WSCP yielded a *Se* of .95 (same as the original version) and a *Sp* of .90 (9 out of 10 children in the contrast group did not fit the profile). The modified profile was also tested on an additional group of nine children with Williams syndrome and four children with other forms of developmental delay. Of the nine children with Williams syndrome, eight fit the modified profile. The child who did not would not have fit the original profile either; his weakest abilities were in the language domain. This child has an older sibling who is intellectually gifted, but had significant language delay, raising the possibility that the child with Williams syndrome may have a co-morbid language disorder. The four children in the contrast group included one child who had a clinical diagnosis of Williams syndrome, but did not have a deletion of Chromosome 7q11.23, and three children with Kabuki syndrome, a rare syndrome associated with developmental delay, relative weakness in visuospatial construction, and at least during early childhood considerably stronger receptive than expressive language (Mervis, Becerra, Rowe, Hersh, & Morris, in press). None of the four children fit the modified Mullen WSCP; two of the children with Kabuki syndrome would have fit the original Mullen WSCP.

In summary, two quantitative descriptions of the Williams syndrome cognitive profile—the WSCP for children ages 4 years and older and the modified Mullen WSCP for children ages 2 to 5 years—have been shown to have high *Se* and *Sp*, indicating that the cognitive profile associated with Williams syndrome is highly characteristic of individuals who have this syndrome and rare among individuals who do not have this syndrome. Williams syndrome has a single genetic etiology—a microdeletion of Chromosome 7q11.23. Thus, a genetic basis for the cognitive profile would be expected. As described in this chapter and in Morris' chapter (chap. 14, this volume; see also Morris et al., 2003), so far two genes (in transaction with other as yet unidentified genes and the environment at all levels) have been associated with particular cognitive characteristics of Williams syndrome: *LIM-kinase 1* with impaired visuospatial construction and *GTF2I* with lowered overall intelligence.

Nonlinear Vocabulary Growth Cognitive-Linguistic Profile

The profiles described in the previous section were designed to differentiate individuals who had a particular genetic syndrome from individuals who did not have this syndrome. Profiles need not be restricted to this purpose, however. Instead they could be designed to characterize a group of interest that included some but not all individuals with a particular syndrome while including some but not all members of other syndromes. The Nonlinear Vocabulary Growth Cognitive-Linguistic Profile (NVGP) is presented as an example of this type of profile. In this case, young 4-year-olds whose expressive vocabulary growth has been nonlinear are predicted to fit this profile regardless of syndrome. In contrast, young 4-year-olds whose expressive vocabulary growth has been linear are predicted not to fit this profile again regardless of syndrome. The NVGP is based on the premise that a child's pattern of expressive vocabulary growth is closely linked to other aspects of his or her language acquisition and verbal memory and also to nonverbal cognitive development.

The criteria for the NVGP are:

1. At age 4, DAS Verbal Cluster standard score > floor
2. At age 4, DAS Nonverbal Cluster standard score > floor
3. At age 4, digit span > = 1
4. At age 4, child's expressive language includes some productive word combinations

To be considered to fit the NVGP, a child had to meet all four criteria.

Data from 17 young 4-year-olds with Williams syndrome and 6 young 4-year-olds with Down syndrome were available to provide a preliminary test of this profile. Expressive vocabulary growth pattern was determined based on longitudinal records of productive vocabulary from the 680-word vocabulary checklist on the Words and Sentences form of the MacArthur Communicative Development Inventory (CDI; Fenson et al.,

1993). Fifteen of the children with Williams syndrome and 4 of the children with Down syndrome evidenced nonlinear vocabulary growth. In most cases, this growth was best characterized as logistic due to the children reaching the ceiling on the CDI. Examples of linear and nonlinear growth curves are provided in Fig. 8.2 for children with Williams syndrome and Fig. 8.3 for children with Down syndrome.

Examination of the performance of the 19 children with nonlinear vocabulary growth indicated that 18 scored above floor on the DAS Verbal Cluster; the child who did not had Williams syndrome. All 19 scored above floor on the DAS Nonverbal Cluster, were able to repeat at least 1 digit, and produced spontaneous productive (nonrote) word combinations. Thus, as indicated in Table 8.5, 18 of 19 children fit the NVGP, yielding a *Se* of .95. None of the four children who had linear vocabulary growth met any of the four NVGP criteria; all scored at floor on both DAS clusters, were unable to repeat one digit, and had not yet produced spontaneous nonrote word combinations. Thus, the *Sp* of the NVGP for this small contrast group was 1.00.

Based on general perceptions of Williams syndrome as associated with excellent language and Down syndrome with poor language, one might have expected that children with Williams syndrome would be expected to fit the NVGP and children with Down syndrome would be expected not to fit the NVGP. To consider this possibility, the *Se* and *Sp* of the NVGP for Williams syndrome and the *Se* and *Sp* of the opposite profile for Down syndrome were calculated. *Se* for the NVGP was .82 (14/17) for

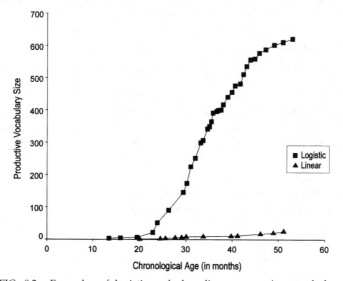

FIG. 8.2. Examples of logistic and slow linear expressive vocabulary growth curves for young children with Williams syndrome.

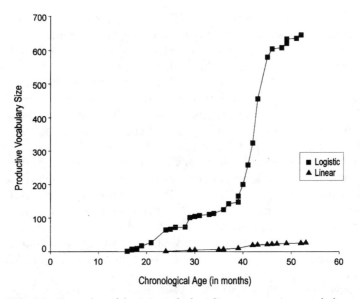

FIG. 8.3. Examples of logistic and slow linear expressive vocabulary growth curves for young children with Down syndrome.

Williams syndrome, which is lower than *Se* for the nonlinear cross-syndrome group (.95). *Sp* was quite poor (2/6 or .33), reflecting the fact that the children with Down syndrome with nonlinear vocabulary growth actually fit the NVGP. *Se* for the opposite profile for Down syndrome was very low (2/6 or .33), although *Sp* was relatively high (14/17 or .82). Thus, the NVGP is best thought of as characterizing younger 4-year-olds with nonlinear vocabulary growth independent of syndrome.

In summary, two types of profiles were considered: profiles designed to characterize the cognitive strengths and weaknesses of individuals who have a particular syndrome and profiles designed instead to cross syndrome lines to characterize the cognitive and linguistic patterns of individuals who have a particular pattern of early expressive vocabulary development. Both types of profiles evidenced high *Se* and *Sp*. Evidence of

TABLE 8.5
Number and Proportion of Children With Nonlinear and Linear
Expressive Vocabulary Growth Curves Who Fit the Nonlinear
Vocabulary Growth Cognitive/Linguistic Profile

Group	Fit Profile	Do Not Fit Profile	Sensitivity	Specificity
Nonlinear	18	1	.95	1.00
Linear	0	4		

high *Se* and *Sp* provides considerably stronger evidence that a particular characteristic or pattern of characteristics is strongly associated with the syndrome or target group than a finding that mean performance of a target group is significantly different from that of the contrast groups and thus is more useful for directly addressing genotype/phenotype relations.

MAXIMIZING THE METHODOLOGICAL STRENGTH OF STUDIES USING GROUP-MATCHING DESIGNS

As of yet, researchers investigating the cognitive and language characteristics of children with specific types of developmental disabilities rarely focus on the *Se* and *Sp* of these characteristics. Instead the primary strategy used is to compare the performance of a group that has the target syndrome or disability to the performance of one or more groups that do not after matching the groups on one or more control variables. The validity of any conclusions drawn from statistical tests comparing the performance of the two groups on the dependent measures rests critically on at least two factors: How closely were the groups matched on the control variables? What are the measurement characteristics of the scores used to compare the groups, whether on the control variables or the target variables? In this section of the chapter, I consider these questions and suggest ways to maximize the value of these types of studies both for understanding cognitive and linguistic aspects of the groups included and identifying clusters of characteristics (profiles) that could later be used in genotype/phenotype research using the two-step method outlined in the first section of this chapter.

Determining Whether Groups Are Matched: Accepting the Null Hypothesis

Most researchers are well aware that if the groups included in a study are not matched on the control variables, then any "significant" differences found on the target variables are uninterpretable because the contribution of the control variable cannot be ruled out. That is, they know that the logic underlying group-matching designs requires that the two (or more) groups not differ on the control variable(s). Determination that the groups do not differ is usually made based on the results of a test of the difference between group means on the control variable (e.g., a *t* test). If the null hypothesis of no group differences on the control variables cannot be rejected (typically because $p > .05$), researchers often automatically respond by tacitly accepting the null hypothesis and assuming that the groups are equivalent. However, as is stressed in undergraduate statistics books, this should not be an automatic response; *rejecting* the null hypothesis because it is improbable under the theoretical sampling distribution should be a very different decision from *accepting* the null hypothesis because it is likely to be true.

As Cohen (1990) pointed out, the null hypothesis is almost never literally true. Therefore, researchers must consider this question: How close to true is close enough? That is, researchers must determine how to index the equivalence of the two groups on the control variable. Usually the decision is to set α to the traditional .05 level. Thus, in the case of the matching design, if the probability that the groups differ on that variable is >.05, then the groups are considered to be matched. In most studies, the actual p value for the test for the control variable is not reported; it is simply stated as ">.05." If the means and standard deviations for the control variable for the two groups are reported, however, the p value may be determined by the reader. In many studies, p values for comparisons involving control variables are only slightly higher than .05. Nevertheless, these values are accepted by the authors (and reviewers) as evidence that the groups are appropriately matched. For example, in a study comparing receptive vocabulary ability of a Williams syndrome group and a Down syndrome group (Paterson, 2001), the two groups were considered to be matched on cognitive ability based on the results of a t test with a significance value of $p < .07$. Sigman and Ruskin (1999) used the slightly more stringent standard of $p > .10$ as their criterion for considering groups to be matched on the control variables. Harcum (1990) described the acceptance of such p values as evidence that groups are matched as "casual acceptance of the null hypothesis" (p. 404).

In terms of the matching design, it is not so much the α level, but rather the probability of making a type II error (accepting the hypothesis that the groups do not differ even though they do) that is of primary concern. For practical purposes, it can be difficult to estimate accurately the probability of making a type II error. However, it is known that the larger the α level, the less likely the researcher is to make a type II error. The question then becomes, how high should α be for the researcher to accept the null hypothesis that the groups do not differ on the matching variable? Frick (1995) proposed the following guidelines: Any p value less than .20 is too low to accept the null hypothesis. A p value greater than .50 is large enough to accept the null hypothesis. Finally, p values between .20 and .50 are ambiguous. Thus, Mervis and Robinson (2003) suggested that, at a minimum, p values of at least .50 be obtained before the groups are considered matched.

An example drawn from actual data may be used to illustrate the consequences of accepting the null hypothesis when the p value for the test of mean differences for the control variable is low. As part of a study examining intellectual strengths and weaknesses of 9- and 10-year-olds with Williams syndrome or Down syndrome, Klein and Mervis (1999) tested a cohort of 18 children with Williams syndrome and 23 children with Down syndrome on the McCarthy Scales of Children's Abilities (McCarthy, 1972) and the Peabody Picture Vocabulary Test–Revised (PPVT–R; Dunn & Dunn, 1981). The two groups were well matched on CA ($p = .502$). Mervis and Robinson (2003) used these samples to address the question of whether children with Williams syndrome have significantly larger receptive vocabularies than children with Down syndrome even when the groups are matched for overall level of cognitive ability (in this case, raw score on the McCarthy).

As shown in Table 8.6, when the full sample was compared, the Williams syndrome group earned a significantly higher standard score than the Down syndrome group on the PPVT–R. Given that the two groups were well matched on CA, the significant difference on the PPVT–R can appropriately be interpreted as indicating that, in the CA range studied, children with Williams syndrome on average have significantly better receptive vocabularies than children with Down syndrome. However, the two groups also differed substantially and significantly in raw score on the McCarthy; the Williams syndrome group on average had much higher intellectual ability than the Down syndrome group. Because the two groups were not matched on this control variable, there is a reasonable possibility that the apparent weakness of the Down syndrome group on receptive vocabulary reflected a general weakness in overall cognitive ability rather than a specific difficulty with receptive vocabulary. To begin to equate the two groups on overall intellectual ability, Mervis and Robinson (2003) followed the standard policy (e.g., Sigman & Ruskin, 1999) of removing the children with the lowest McCarthy scores from the Down syndrome group and the children with the highest McCarthy scores from the Williams syndrome group until the two groups no longer differed significantly on this variable. As indicated in Table 8.6, the two groups still differed significantly on PPVT–R standard score. The p level for the con-

TABLE 8.6
Impact of Group-Match p Level for Cognitive Performance on the
Significance of Between-Group Differences on the PPVT–R

p Level for Cognitive Match	Frick's Category	p Level for PPVT–R Comparison
<.001 (full sample)	Not matched	<.001 (significant)
.106	Not matched (but commonly used)	<.030 (significant)
.254	Unclear if matched	.074 (not significant)
.650	Definitely matched	.204 (not significant)

trol variable comparison ($p = .106$), although at a level commonly seen in published studies, is still within the range that Frick (1995) considered to indicate that the groups are definitely not matched for overall intellectual ability. As indicated in Table 8.6, once Mervis and Robinson removed enough additional participants to obtain a p value for the control variable that was within Frick's ambiguous range ($p = .254$), the Williams syndrome and Down syndrome groups no longer differed significantly on PPVT–R standard score. When enough participants were removed from the two groups to yield a p value for the control variable that was clearly within Frick's matched range ($p = .650$), the p value for the PPVT–R comparison increased to $p = .204$.

This exercise clearly demonstrates the potential impact of the quality of the match on the control variable(s) to the determination of whether two groups differ significantly on the target variable. Note that although following Frick's guidelines reduces the likelihood of Type II errors (deciding that the two groups are equivalent on the control variable when in fact they are not), and therefore reduces the likelihood of finding (spurious) differences between groups on the target variables, this procedure by no means precludes finding significant between-group differences. For example, Klein and Mervis (1999), despite matching the Williams syndrome and Down syndrome groups very tightly on the control variables of both CA and raw score on the McCarthy, found that the groups differed significantly on both their performance on the verbal memory subtests of the McCarthy (with the difference favoring the Williams syndrome group) and on the visuospatial construction subtests (with the difference favoring the Down syndrome group). It is also important to note that, as described in Mervis and Robinson (1999, 2003), Frick's p levels are only guidelines; hard-and-fast rules on acceptable p levels for matching will depend on the correlation between the control and target variables, with higher correlations requiring higher p levels for the groups to be considered matched. Simulation studies are now underway to provide more specific guidelines. In the meantime, researchers can reduce the likelihood of making invalid inferences from the matching design by accepting two groups as matched on the control variable only if α is set at Frick's acceptable (matched) level.

Measurement Characteristics of Scores
for Control and Target Variables

Comparisons using the group-matching design necessarily require measuring both control and target variables. In some cases, the only control variable is CA. For example, in the sequence of comparisons from Mervis and Robinson (2003) described previously, the initial comparison of the receptive vocabulary ability of the Williams syndrome and Down syndrome groups involved matching only for CA. In other cases, the performance of a group with a developmental disability such as SLI might be compared to the performance of a group of typically developing children of the same CA.

In most cases, however, group-matching designs include a control variable that is measured by performance on a standardized assessment. Standardized assessments are sometimes used to measure target variables even in cases when they are not used to match the groups. Standardized assessments typically offer several different types of scores: standard scores (e.g., scaled scores, T scores), raw scores, percentiles, and age equivalents. These scores differ in their level of measurement: Standard scores and raw scores are based on an interval scale, whereas percentiles and age equivalents are based on an ordinal scale. As described later, these differences have important implications for the appropriateness of between-group statistical comparisons.

Ideally, in addition to being matched for performance on a control variable derived from a standardized assessment, groups are also closely matched for CA, with each group including only a narrow CA range. For example, as in the Klein and Mervis (1999) study described before, two syndrome groups closely matched for both overall intellectual ability and CA and including only a narrow CA range may be compared. In many cases, however, although groups are matched for a control variable such as language ability, they either are not matched for CA and/or the CA range in each group is very broad. It also is not uncommon for a single study to include both groups matched for CA and groups not matched for CA. For example, a three-group study might include two syndrome groups matched for CA and language ability and a third younger group of typically developing children matched for language ability. The use of groups that are not matched for CA introduces additional complications into both the matching procedure and the interpretation of results on the target variable. The type of standardized test score used to measure the control variable is critical in determining the validity of the matching procedure even in cases in which Frick's (1995) acceptable p level has been met. Next I consider the choice of score type for both control and target variables, first for the case in which groups are matched for CA and only a narrow CA range is included and then the case in which groups are not matched for CA.

The Case of CA-Matched Narrow CA-Range Groups: Measurement Choice for Control Variable(s). When groups are closely matched for CA, only a narrow range of CA is included, and this range is within the norming range for the assessment being used as the control variable, then under most circumstances standard scores should be used to match the groups on the control variable. A standard score is simply an individual's raw score relative to the distribution of raw scores for a group of similar-CA individuals in the norming sample. Standard scores are measured on an interval scale, which is critical for parametric statistical comparisons. Because standard scores are only as good as the norming sample from which they were drawn, it is important that the norming sample match the demographics of the population to which the research wishes to make comparisons (e.g., for researchers in the United States, the demographics of that country; see Mervis & Robinson, 2003).

In studies involving children with language delay, general developmental delay, or mental retardation, some children may earn the lowest possible standard score on the control variable. (Conversely, in studies involving gifted children, some may earn the highest possible standard score.) Careful attention needs to be paid to these individuals because the lowest (or highest) standard score often corresponds to a wide range of raw scores. In these cases, individuals who have the same standard score may in fact have very different levels of ability and therefore should not be considered to be matched. For example, at age 8;0 (8 years 0 months), a standard score of 40 on Peabody Picture Vocabulary Test–III (PPVT–III; Dunn & Dunn, 1997) is assigned to children whose raw scores range from 0 to 33. When the groups to be matched include children who earn extreme scores, these children should not be considered matched—even though they have identical standard scores—unless they also have similar raw scores. In cases in which a large proportion of children earn extreme standard scores on the control variable, the matching procedure should involve raw rather than standard scores. (Although on the surface this also appears to be a solution for groups differing in CA or for groups covering a wide CA range, in fact it is not for reasons to be described later.)

The use of raw scores as the basis for group matching may also be appropriate when the groups are well matched and include only a narrow CA range, but that range is older than the oldest group included in the norming sample (and therefore no standard scores are available). This situation is most likely to occur when many or most of the participants have mental retardation or developmental delay. For example, in the Klein and Mervis (1999) study of 9- and 10-year-olds described earlier, raw score on the McCarthy was used as the matching variable because the oldest CA for which this assessment was normed was 8;7. Use of a measure as a control variable when the participants are outside the CA range for which the measure was normed is appropriate only if the measure accurately captures the ability levels of the participants—that is, participants do not score at floor or at ceiling on the control variable (e.g., if matching for overall raw score, performance is above floor and below ceiling for overall raw score and each subtest included in the overall raw score).

Researchers often match groups on language age (LA) or other types of age equivalent (AE) scores rather than on standard or raw scores. The name *age equivalent* appears to offer face validity, which may encourage researchers to use these scores without considering their measurement characteristics, which are highly problematic. An AE score is simply the median CA at which a particular raw score was obtained. Thus, AE scores are not measured on an interval scale and, as is described next, therefore have multiple measurement characteristics that make them inappropriate for statistical comparisons. Recently, test authors have indicated concerns regarding the use of AE scores for clinical purposes as well (e.g., Semel, Wiig, & Secord, 2003). In some cases, researchers use AE scores because the measure chosen as the control variable does not provide standard scores. For example, the Sequenced Inventory of Communicative Development–Revised (SICD–R; Hedrick, Prather, & Tobin, 1984) provides AE scores, but not standard scores. In other cases, the assessment provides standard scores, but only for younger children. In still other cases, standard scores are available for the participants' CA, but researchers choose to use AE scores instead.

A critical problem with AE scores is that they are not measured on an interval scale (and are not normally distributed). This is especially a problem in domains such as language or cognition, for which development is clearly nonlinear. Consider a real-world example: The 4-month difference in LA between 5;0 and 5;4 equates to small differences in actual language ability. In contrast, the same 4-month difference in LA between 1;4 and 1;8 corresponds to enormous differences in language ability. At age 1;4, children typically have small vocabularies and speak in single words. In contrast, at age 1;8, children typically are in the midst of a vocabulary spurt, and a large proportion of their utterances involves multiple words. However, statistical comparisons based on LA treat these two 4-month differences in LA as equivalent, making these comparisons clearly invalid.

These same types of problems occur when AE is based on standardized assessments. On measures such as the PPVT–III, which include large numbers of items, an increase of 1 item correct usually corresponds to a 1-month increase in AE. Thus, across much of the range, AE on this measure functions similarly to raw scores. Even on the PPVT–III, however, this correspondence falls apart for both very low and very high raw scores. (On Form A, raw scores from 0–22 correspond to an AE of "<1;9," and raw scores from 176–204 correspond to an AE of "22+".) Most measures do not include nearly as many items, with the result that AE scores on even well-normed measures such as the Clinical Evaluation of Language Fundamentals–4th edition (CELF–4; Semel et al., 2003) are unevenly distributed and an increase or decrease of one item may correspond to a change of several months AE. Alternatively, several raw scores may be associated with the same AE. For example, consider the correspondence among raw score, scaled score, and AE for the Word Structure subscale of the CELF–4 for raw scores between 0 and 14, as illustrated in Table 8.7. The 1-item increase between raw scores of 2 and 3 is associated with a 1-point change in scaled score but a >4 month increase in AE. At the same time, the 7-item increase between raw scores of 7 and 13 is associated with a 4-point change in scaled score but no change at all in AE; the AE for each of these raw scores is 4;6. A further difficulty with AE is that for ages younger than the youngest age in the norming sample, AE is based on statistical extrapolation rather than empirical data.

Concerns with AE are often noted in manuals for standardized assessments. For example, the CELF–4 manual (Semel et al., 2003) provides a thoughtful discussion of difficulties in interpreting AE scores. This discussion begins with the point that, unlike standard scores, AE does not reflect relative standing among same-CA peers, which is the critical question for determining whether a child's performance is at the level expected for his or her age. Another important point made by the authors is that AE scores substantially above or below CA may well be associated with performance in the average range. For example, for a child age 7;6, AE scores corresponding to average ability (+ or − 1 standard deviation of the CA mean) on the Recalling Sentences subtest cover more than a 5-year span

TABLE 8.7
Correspondence Among Raw Score, Scaled Score (for CA 5;0–5;5),
and Subtest Age Equivalent on the Word Structure Subtest
of the CELF–4 for Raw Scores Between 0 and 14

Raw Score	Scaled Score (CA 5;0–5;5)	Age Equivalent
0	1	<3;2
1	2	<3;2
2	2	<3;2
3	3	3;6
4	3	3;8
5	4	3;11
6	4	4;2
7	5	4;2
8	5	4;2
9	6	4;2
10	6	4;2
11	7	4;2
12	7	4;2
13	8	4;2
14	8	4;5

(from 5;9–10;11). A third point is that apparently substantial differences in AE between children of the same CA should not be interpreted as indicating how much more advanced the highest scoring children are than the lowest scoring children. For example, Semel and her colleagues (2003) noted that a 12-month difference in AE for two children age 5;4 does not indicate that the language skills of the child with the higher AE are 12 months more advanced than those of the child with the lower AE. Unfortunately, statistical analyses using AE as the dependent variable make precisely this assumption.

The Case of CA-Matched Narrow CA-Range Groups: Measurement Choice for Target Variables.   Target variables often involve performance on researcher-designed measures. In these cases, provided groups are closely matched for CA and any other control variable included by the researcher and each group covers only a narrow CA range, group comparison of raw scores is appropriate. For example, in a fast-mapping study, a researcher may provide nonsense word labels for several different novel objects and then test the child for comprehension of these labels. If the researcher wished to compare performance across tasks (e.g., fast mapping of object labels vs. action labels vs. descriptors), z-scores (a type of standard score) could be used.

In many cases, target variables are measured from standardized assessments. In such cases, the same guidelines apply as for control variables: Measurement on an interval scale is critical. Standard scores are appropriate both when the target variable is a single subtest and when there are multiple target variables (subtests) from the same assessment. (For a discussion regarding comparison of standard scores across measures that were not normed on the same sample, see Mervis & Robinson, 2003.) Raw scores are appropriate when the target variable is a single subtest, but not when comparing across subtests. AE scores are as problematic for measurement of target variables as for measurement of control variables. In many cases, use of AE scores would lead to erroneous conclusions as illustrated in the scenarios in the next two paragraphs.

Often researchers are interested in determining whether a particular syndrome is associated with specific strengths and weaknesses within the language domain. The appropriate dependent variable to address this question is standard score: A person who evidences the same standing relative to his or her CA peers on subtests measuring different abilities will earn the same standard score (within the measurement error of the test) on each of the subtests. These identical standard scores—indicating that the child has a flat profile—may be associated with differing AEs, however. This is especially likely to be true for children whose abilities are at the low or high end of the distribution. For example, an 8-year-old who earned a scaled score of 4 (2.00 standard deviations below the mean) on each of the Level 1 subtests of the CELF–4 would earn the following AEs: Concepts and Following Directions, 5;5–5;8; Word Structure, 5;7–5;9; Recalling Sentences, 4;9–5;2; Formulated Sentences, 5;11–6;00. Use of AE instead of scaled score would lead to the incorrect conclusion that the child showed a jagged profile with a strength in Formulated Sentences and a weakness in Recalling Sentences when in fact the child showed a flat profile. Now consider an 8-year-old who earned an AE of 5;7 on all four subtests. This pattern is often interpreted as indicating that the child has equivalent levels of ability for the skills measured by each of the four subtests. Examination of the standard scores corresponding to these AEs, however, contradicts this interpretation: This AE is associated with a scaled score of 4 for the Concepts and Following Directions subtest and the Word Structure subtest, a scaled score of 5 for Recalling Sentences, and the much lower scaled score of 1 for Formulated Sentences. Assuming the findings for these two children are representative of individuals with their syndrome, the use of scaled scores would indicate a flat profile for Syndrome A and a jagged profile for Syndrome B, whereas the use of AE scores would erroneously lead to exactly the opposite conclusion that Syndrome A is associated with a jagged profile and Syndrome B with a flat profile.

As another example, suppose a researcher hypothesized that Syndrome C was associated with equivalent levels of receptive and expressive vocabulary ability, whereas Syndrome D was associated with relative strength in receptive vocabulary and relative weakness in expressive vocabulary. A child with Syndrome C age 7;0 earned standard scores of 55 on both the PPVT–III and the Expressive Vocabulary Test (EVT; Williams, 1997); the corresponding AE scores are 3;0 for the PPVT–III and 4;1 for the EVT. (Comparison of standard scores across the PPVT–III and EVT is appropriate because both were normed on the same sample.) A child with Syndrome D of the same CA earned standard scores of 66 on the PPVT–III and 55 on the EVT; AE scores were 4;1 for both tests. Assuming these children were representative of their syndrome groups, the researcher's hypothesis would be supported based on analyses of standard scores, but would be rejected erroneously based on AE scores. In fact examination of AE scores suggests the opposite scenario—that Syndrome C is associated with a relative strength in expressive vocabulary, and Syndrome D is associated with equal receptive and expressive vocabulary ability.

The Case of Groups That Are Not Matched for CA: Measurement Choice for Control Variables.   AE scores are especially likely to be used as control variables when groups are not matched for CA. This situation most often occurs when a group of younger children who are developing normally is compared with one or more groups of older children with developmental disabilities. However, sometimes studies involve comparisons of different-CA groups of children with different types of developmental disabilities with or without a further control group of normally developing children. For example, Jarrold, Baddeley, and Phillips (2002) matched a group of adolescents with Down syndrome (mean CA 14;2) to a significantly younger group of adolescents with moderate learning difficulties (mean CA 11;0) and a still younger group of normally developing children (mean CA 5;4) for AE on the British Picture Vocabulary Scale (the British equivalent of the PPVT–R). As indicated earlier in this chapter, on the PPVT, AE approaches an interval scale except at extremes of the AE range, so use of AE was essentially equivalent to matching for raw score. As also described earlier, however, there are serious difficulties with the measurement characteristics of AE scores on most assessments. Thus, groups generally should be matched for raw score rather than AE.

Once groups are matched for AE (or raw score), they are generally compared for level of performance (AE or raw score) on the target variable. The assumption is that if the two groups show the same relation between control and target variables, they should not differ significantly on the target variable. If the groups do differ significantly on the target variable, the findings are interpreted as indicating a different pattern of relations between the control and target variables for the two groups. In designs comparing the performance of an older group with a disability to the performance of a younger group of normally developing children, significant differences on the target variable almost always favor the normally developing group and are interpreted as indicating that the disabled group has a "deficit" on the target variable.

There is a fundamental flaw in this logic, however: It is based on the assumption that rate of development is similar for the control and target variables. This assumption is often not correct. If development on the control and target variables proceeds at different rates, then differences in CA will confound the matching design because the differences in raw scores (and therefore the AE scores) will not be stable across CA. In such cases, one cannot predict that two groups with identical AEs on the control variable but different CAs should be expected to have similar scores on the target variable.

The situation in which two or more abilities are developing at different rates is not unusual. To illustrate this issue, the relations between AE scores on different subtests from the DAS were examined as a function of CA. Figure 8.4 shows the case in which children ranging in age from 5 to 17 years were matched for AE on the Matrices subtest at the 7;10 level (corresponding to an ability score—the DAS equivalent of a raw score—of 79) and then compared to the expected AEs for four other subtests based

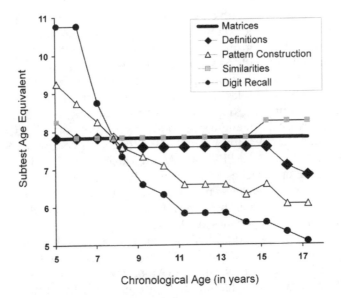

FIG. 8.4. Variability in expected AE on DAS verbal, verbal memory, and visuospatial construction subtests as a function of CA, given a constant AE of 7 years 10 months on the Matrices subtest and the assumption that the child has earned identical standard scores on all subtests.

on the DAS norms. Thus, Matrices AE was treated as the control variable and the AE scores for the other subtests as target variables. (The Matrices subtest measures nonverbal reasoning—an ability often selected as a matching variable in developmental research.) The graph represents the answer to this question: "If children have an AE of 7;10 on the Matrices subtest, and all of their abilities are at the same level relative to their CA peers (i.e., they earn the same standard score on each subtest), then what are their predicted AE scores for each of the target subtests?" As expected, for children age 7;10 who earned an AE of 7;10 on the Matrices subtest, their expected AE for all four target subtests was also 7;10. These hypothetical children would be performing at the median level for their CA on Matrices and would therefore be expected to perform at the median level for their CA on the other subtests as well, assuming they have equivalent abilities in each of the domains tested. Yet what happens if their performance on Matrices is either above or below the median for their CA? As illustrated in Fig. 8.4, the relation varies as a function of which subtest is the target variable. If the target variable was Similarities, then for much of the CA range the expected AE is the same. Therefore, the researcher could reasonably sample from a wide CA range without invalidating group comparisons. If the target variable was Definitions, there is a wide age range in which very similar AEs are expected, so comparisons could reasonably be made as long as the researcher is careful in interpreting significant but small differences. (A 3-month AE difference is expected across much of the CA range.) Comparisons that included 16- and 17-year-olds as well as younger children would be problematic, however. Comparisons with Matrices as the control variable and either Pattern Construction or Recall of Digits as the target variable would be highly problematic. Note that for these two subtests, there is actually a crossover in their relations with the target variable. For example, a 5- or 6-year-old who earned an AE of 7;10 on Matrices would be expected to earn the much higher AE of 10;10 on Recall of Digits. In contrast, 11-, 12-, and 13-year-olds who earned an AE of 7;10 for Matrices would be expected to earn an AE of only 5;10 for Recall of Digits, and 17-year-olds would be expected to earn an AE of only 5;1. Thus, significant differences between CA groups would be *predicted* for Recall of Digits assuming the groups had been well matched for AE on the Matrices subtest and the participants had the same level of ability (same standard score) for the constructs measured by the Matrices and Recall of Digits subtests.

The graph in Fig. 8.4 also suggests that verbal short-term memory develops at a very different rate not only from nonverbal reasoning, but also from language ability as measured by the Definitions or Similarities subtests. Examination of the CELF–4 norms with performance on Concepts and Following Directions (a measure of receptive relational vocabulary) as the control variable and Number Repetition Forward as the target variable shows the same pattern, suggesting that this pattern is likely to be correct. If so it is critical for studies of the relation between language and verbal short-term memory (a popular research topic) that either groups be matched for CA (if comparisons are to be based on raw scores) or if CA matching is not possible, then cross-CA comparisons be made based on a comparison of standard scores for language and verbal memory measures. Otherwise findings that the older of two groups matched for vocabulary AE had significantly worse performance (got significantly fewer items correct) than the younger group on a verbal memory test cannot automatically be interpreted to mean that the older group had a specific deficit in verbal memory. The result that would be noteworthy in this situation would be that the groups did not differ in verbal memory.

Even two relatively similar abilities may develop at different rates especially for children at the extremes of the distribution (who either are gifted or have developmental delay or mental retardation). Thus, children of the same CA who have identical standard scores on two measures normed on the same sample may still have different age-equivalent scores on these measures. As an example, consider performance on two language measures normed on the same extensive and carefully stratified sample. As mentioned earlier, a 7-year-old child with standard scores of 55 on both the PPVT–III (measuring receptive vocabulary) and the EVT (measuring expressive vocabulary) will have a receptive vocabulary AE of 3;0, but an expressive vocabulary AE of 4;1 more than a year higher. Examples such as this one illustrate the problem of using AE scores even when children are the same CA and the measures are normed on the same sample. These problems are due to the fact that AEs do not constitute an interval scale and are subject to distortion due to patterns of developmental trajectories, especially across measures or subtests within measures. (Note that standard scores are not susceptible to these problems.) Thus, the use of AE scores violates the standard assumptions underlying statistical analysis. Unfortunately, statistical comparisons often are made based on AE scores. Results of such comparisons are uninterpretable due to violations of the assumptions underlying the statistics used. Use of standard scores prevents these problems.

Measurement Choice for Studies of Possible Changes in Relations Between Abilities in Different Domains as a Function of CA. Another type of research question for which the use of AE scores is common is the question of whether there are changes in discrepancies between two types of abilities as a function of CA. For example, researchers (e.g., Bellugi, Lichtenberger, Jones, Lai, & St. George, 2000) recently suggested that differences between verbal and visuospatial construction abilities increase with CA for individuals with Williams syndrome. These claims typically are supported by comparisons of AE scores for the abilities being studied for younger and older groups; designs may be cross-sectional (e.g., Bellugi et al., 2000) or longitudinal (e.g., Jarrold, Baddeley, Hewes, & Phillips, 2001). If the difference in AE is significantly larger for the older group, the trajectories are claimed to diverge. However, because AE is nonlinear and is affected by the underlying rate of development for each of the abilities measured, this type of comparison is not appropriate. Apparently significant changes in developmental trajectory as indicated by diverging AE scores may be associated with a constant relation between standard scores as illustrated in Fig. 8.5, which plots AE scores for performance on the PPVT–III and VMI 3rd revision (Beery, 1989) for CAs ranging from 6 to 18 years, with a constant standard score of 78 on the PPVT–III and 57 on the VMI (the mean standard scores for the participants in my Williams syndrome sample).

A more accurate way to address the question of diverging trajectories is to compare standard scores (rather than AE scores) at different CAs. Significant changes in standard scores over time on a particular assessment or subtest of a larger assessment indicate that a participant's (or group's)

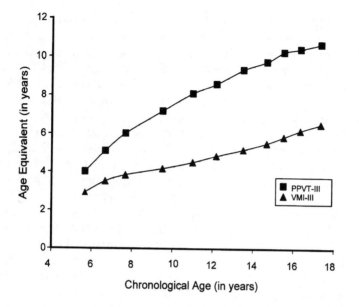

FIG. 8.5. AE as a function of CA for the PPVT–III (standard score = 78) and the VMI 3rd rev. (standard score = 57). Although the two AE curves diverge, the relation between the abilities measured by the PPVT–III and VMI remains consistent across CA as evidenced by constant standard scores.

developmental trajectory is either increasing or decreasing relative to the rate expected for same-CA peers. Developmental trajectories for different abilities measured by the same assessment (e.g., verbal abilities and visuospatial construction abilities) can easily be compared based on standard scores. Comparisons also could be made between standard scores on two different assessments over time for the same participant or group of participants provided the assessments were normed on the same or equivalent samples. Although longitudinal comparisons would be ideal, cross-sectional comparisons may provide valuable initial information regarding developmental trajectories.

SUMMARY AND CONCLUSION

Researchers concerned with language and cognitive development often have as a goal to demonstrate that characteristics or patterns of characteristics are universal to and specific for a particular syndrome or developmental disorder. Until recently these claims were important primarily either for theoretical reasons or to provide a basis for more targeted cognitive or language intervention. As the genetic basis for more syndromes or developmental disorders becomes known, however, these claims also serve another important purpose as phenotypes that are due to particular genetic characteristics in transaction with other genes and the environment. Phenotypes are most useful if they have very high Se and Sp—that is, if they accurately characterize most individuals in the target group and do not characterize most people who are not in the target group. Profiling methods, by considering first the pattern of performance of individuals and then aggregating across group members to determine Se and Sp, provide clear indications of the separability of the target group from contrast groups based on the pattern of performance operationalized in the profile. The WSCP demonstrates the value of phenotypes validated by the two-step profiling method for genotype/phenotype research: Studies using the WSCP as a cognitive phenotype in assessments of individuals who have small deletions in the Williams syndrome region (Frangiskakis et al., 1996; Morris et al., in press) have implicated the hemizygous deletion of *LIM-kinase 1*, in transaction with other as yet unspecified genes and the environment, in the particular difficulty individuals with Williams syndrome have in visuospatial construction.

Most research on syndromes or developmental disorders involves more traditional comparisons of mean differences between the target and contrast groups on the characteristic of interest. The value of this approach is highly dependent on careful research design. It is critical that the target group be tightly matched to the contrast group(s) on the control variables(s) and that comparisons be made based on variables measured on an interval scale (standard scores or raw scores). Because even closely related language or cognitive abilities usually develop at different rates and in a nonlinear manner, comparisons of AE scores are highly problematic. If at all possible, groups should be closely matched for CA, with only a narrow CA range included in each group. When this is not possible, special precautions are necessary. In interpreting the results of studies using traditional group designs, it is important to keep in mind that a highly significant mean difference simply indicates that the distributions of scores on the dependent variable are significantly different. In many cases, the distributions still have considerable overlap. Graphing the data provides a clear indication of the separability of the distributions. Characteristics on which groups differ significantly are most likely to be useful for genotype/phenotype research if the distributions are largely nonoverlapping. When these precautions are followed, research concerned with mean differences between groups provides an important first step in identifying promising characteristics to be included in profiles to be used in future genotype/phenotype research.

ACKNOWLEDGMENTS

This research was supported by Grant No. HD29957 from the National Institute of Child Health and Human Development and Grant No. NS35102 from the National Institute of Neurological Disorders and Stroke. I thank all of the participants and their families. I am grateful to the geneticists, cardiologists, and early intervention agencies who referred individuals with Williams syndrome or other developmental disorders to our research, as well as to Terry Monkaba, executive director of the National Williams Syndrome Association, who has encouraged and facilitated the conduct of research at regional and national meetings of the Williams Syndrome Association. I would like to thank Melissa Rowe, Angela Becerra, Jacquelyn Bertrand, and Sharon Armstrong for data collection and analysis; Joanie Robertson for database management and figure creation; and Byron Robinson and Bonnie Klein-Tasman for discussions regarding many of the methodological issues discussed in this chapter. Portions of this chapter are based on Mervis and Robinson (2003) and Mervis and Klein-Tasman (in press).

REFERENCES

Arber, S., Barbayannis, F. A., Hanser, H., Schneider, C., Stanyon, C. A., Bernard, O., & Caroni, P. (1998). Regulation of actin dynamics through phosphorylation of cofilin by LIM-kinase. *Nature, 393,* 805–809.

Bayley, N. (1969). *Bayley scales of infant development.* New York: Psychological Corporation.

Bayley, N. (1993). *Bayley scales of infant development* (2nd ed.). San Antonio, TX: Psychological Corporation.

Beery, K. E. (1989). *Developmental test of visual motor integration* (3rd rev.). Chicago, IL: Modern Curriculum Press.

Bellugi, U., Lichtenberger, L., Jones, W., Lai, Z., & St. George, M. (2000). The neurocognitive profile of Williams syndrome: A complex pattern of strengths and weaknesses. *Journal of Cognitive Neuroscience, 12*(Suppl. 1), 7–29.

Bellugi, U., Marks, S., Bihrle, A., & Sabo, H. (1988). Dissociation between language and cognitive functions in Williams syndrome. In D. Bishop & K. Mogford (Eds.), *Language development in exceptional circumstances* (pp. 177–189). Edinburgh: Churchill Livingstone.

Bellugi, U., Wang, P. P., & Jernigan, T. L. (1994). Williams syndrome: An unusual neuropsychological profile. In S. H. Broman & J. Grafman (Eds.), *Atypical cognitive deficits in developmental disorders: Implications for brain function* (pp. 23–56). Hillsdale, NJ: Lawrence Erlbaum Associates.

Cohen, J. (1990). Things I have learned (so far). *American Psychologist, 45,* 1304–1312.

Dunn, L. E., & Dunn, L. E. (1981). *Peabody Picture Vocabulary Test–Revised.* Circle Pines, MN: American Guidance Service.

Dunn, L. E., & Dunn, L. E. (1997). *Peabody Picture Vocabulary Test* (3rd ed.). Circle Pines, MN: American Guidance Service.

Elliott, C. D. (1990). *Differential ability scales.* San Diego: Harcourt Brace Jovanovich.

Fenson, L., Dale, P. S., Reznick, J. S., Thal, D., Bates, E., Hartung, J. P., Pethick, S., & Reilly, J. S. (1993). *MacArthur communicative development inventories: User's guide and technical manual*. San Diego, CA: Singular.

Frangiskakis, J. M., Ewart, A. K., Morris, C. A., Mervis, C. B., Bertrand, J., Robinson, B. F., Klein, B. P., Ensing, G. J., Everett, L. A., Green, E. D., Pröschel, C., Gutowski, N., Noble, M., Atkinson, D. L., Odelberg, S., & Keating, M. T. (1996). LIM-kinase 1 hemizygosity implicated in impaired visuospatial constructive cognition. *Cell, 86*, 59–69.

Frick, R. W. (1995). Accepting the null hypothesis. *Memory & Cognition, 23*, 132–138.

Harcum, E. R. (1990). Methodological vs. empirical literature: Two views on the acceptance of the null hypothesis. *American Psychologist, 45*, 404–405.

Hedrick, D., Prather, E., & Tobin, A. (1984). *Sequenced inventory of communication development–revised*. Seattle, WA: Washington University Press.

Hillier, L. W., Fulton, R. S., Fulton, L. A., Graves, T. A., Pepin, K. H., Wagner-McPherson, C. et al. (2003). The DNA sequence of chromosome 7. *Nature, 424*, 157–164.

Jackendoff, R. (1994). *Patterns in the mind: Language and human nature*. New York: Basic.

Jarrold, C., Baddeley, A. D., Hewes, A. K., & Phillips, C. (2001). A longitudinal assessment of diverging verbal and non-verbal abilities in the Williams syndrome phenotype. *Cortex, 37*, 423–431.

Jarrold, C., Baddeley, A. D., & Phillips, C. E. (2002). Verbal short-term memory in Down syndrome: A problem of memory, audition, or speech? *Journal of Speech, Language, & Hearing Research, 45*, 531–544.

Kaufman, A. S., & Kaufman, N. L. (1990). *Kaufman brief intelligence test*. Circle Pines, MN: American Guidance Service.

Klein, B. P., & Mervis, C. B. (1999). Cognitive strengths and weaknesses of 9- and 10-year-olds with Williams syndrome or Down syndrome. *Developmental Neuropsychology, 16*, 177–196.

McCarthy, D. (1972). *McCarthy scales of children's abilities*. New York: The Psychological Corporation.

Mervis, C. B., Becerra, A. M., Rowe, M. L., Hersh, J., & Morris, C. A. (in press). Intellectual abilities and adaptive behavior of children and adolescents with Kabuki syndrome: A preliminary study. *American Journal of Medical Genetics*.

Mervis, C. B., & Bertrand, J. (1997). Developmental relations between cognition and language: Evidence from Williams syndrome. In L. B. Adamson & M. A. Romski (Eds.), *Communication and language acquisition: Discoveries from atypical development* (pp. 75–106). New York: Brookes.

Mervis, C. B., & Klein-Tasman, B. P. (in press). Methodological issues in group-matching designs: α levels for control variable comparisons and measurement characteristics of control and target variables. *Journal of Autism and Developmental Disorders* (special issue on matching strategies).

Mervis, C. B., & Robinson, B. F. (1999). Methodological issues in cross-syndrome comparisons: Matching procedures, sensitivity (*Se*), and specificity (*Sp*). Commentary on M. Sigman & E. Ruskin, Continuity and change in the social competence of children with autism, Down syndrome, and developmental delays. *Monographs of the Society for Research in Child Development, 64*(Serial No. 256), 115–130.

Mervis, C. B., & Robinson, B. F. (2003). Methodological issues in cross-group comparisons of language and/or cognitive development. In Y. Levy & J. Schaeffer (Eds.), *Language competence across populations: Toward a definition of specific language impairment* (pp. 233–258). Mahwah, NJ: Lawrence Erlbaum Associates.

Mervis, C. B., Robinson, B. F., Bertrand, J., Morris, C. A., Klein-Tasman, B. P., & Armstrong, S. C. (2000). The Williams Syndrome Cognitive Profile. *Brain and Cognition, 44*, 604–628.

Mervis, C. B., Robinson, B. F., Rowe, M. L., Becerra, A. M., & Klein-Tasman, B. P. (in press). Language abilities of people with Williams syndrome. In L. Abbeduto (Ed.), *International Review of Research in Mental Retardation (vol. 27)*. Orlando, FL: Academic Press.

Morris, C. A. (2004). Genotype phenotype correlations: Lessons from Williams syndrome research. In M. L. Rice & S. Warren (Eds.), *Developmental language disorders: From phenotypes to etiologies*. Mahwah, NJ: Lawrence Erlbaum Associates.

Morris, C. A., & Mervis, C. B. (2000). Williams syndrome and related disorders. *Annual Review of Genomics and Human Genetics, 1*, 461–484.

Morris, C. A., Mervis, C. B., Hobart, H. H., Gregg, R. G., Bertrand, J., Ensing, G. J., Sommer, A., Moore, C. A., Hopkin, R. J., Spallone, P., Keating, M. T., Osborne, L., Kimberley, K. W., & Stock, A. D. (2004). *GTF2I* hemizygosity implicated in mental retardation in Williams syndrome: Genotype/phenotype analysis of 5 families with deletions in the Williams syndrome region. *American Journal of Medical Genetics, 123A*, 45–59.

Mullen, E. M. (1995). *Mullen scales of early learning*. Circle Pines, MN: American Guidance Service.

Osborne, L. R., Li, M., Pober, B., Chitayat, D., Bodurtha, J., Mandel, A., Costa, T., Grebe, T., Cox, S., Tsui, L. C., & Scherer, S. W. (2001). A 1.5 million-base pair inversion polymorphism in families with Williams-Beuren syndrome. *Nature Genetics, 29*, 321–325.

Paterson, S. (2001). Language and number in Down syndrome: The complex developmental trajectory from infancy to adulthood. *Down Syndrome Research and Practice, 7*, 79–86.

Pinker, S. (1999). *Words and rules*. New York: Basic.

Semel, E., Wiig, E. H., & Secord, W. A. (2003). *Clinical evaluation of language fundamentals* (4th ed.). San Antonio, TX: Psychological Corporation.

Siegel, B., Vukicevic, J., Elliott, G. R., & Kraemer, H. C. (1989). The use of signal detection theory to assess *DSM–III–R* criteria for autistic disorder. *Journal of the American Academy of Child & Adolescent Psychiatry, 28*, 542–548.

Sigman, M., & Ruskin, E. (1999). Continuity and change in the social competence of children with autism, Down syndrome, and developmental delays. *Monographs of the Society for Research in Child Development, 64*(Serial No. 256).

Wang, J. Y., Frenzel, K. E., Wen, D., & Falls, D. L. (1998). Transmembrane neuregulins interact with LIM kinase 1, a cytoplasmic protein kinase implicated in development of visuospatial cognition. *Journal of Biological Chemistry, 273*, 20525–20534.

Wechsler, D. (2003). *Wechsler Intelligence Scale for Children* (4th ed.). San Antonio, TX: Psychological Corporation.

Williams, K. T. (1997). *Expressive vocabulary test*. Circle Pines, MN: American Guidance Service.

Yang, N., Higuchi, O., Ohashi, K., Nagata, K., Wada, A., Kangawa, K., Nishida, E., & Mizuno, K. (1998). Cofilin phosphorylation by LIM-kinase 1 and its role in Rac-mediated actin reorganization. *Nature, 393*, 809–812.

9

Intervention as Experiment

Steven F. Warren
The University of Kansas

A *phenotype* is defined as "the manifest characteristics of an organism collectively, including anatomical and psychological traits, that result from both its heredity and its environment" (Neufeldt & Guralnik, 1988, p. 1013). The purpose of this chapter is to demonstrate the potential value of intervention research as a tool for understanding the nature of various behavioral phenotypes that are manifested at least in part by developmental language disorders. Because a phenotype by definition results from the interaction of heredity and environments, the first part of this chapter is devoted to the role of the environment in determining a phenotype and then the role of the phenotype in determining the environment. This discussion sets the stage for an examination of the central question: How can intervention research enhance our knowledge of specific phenotypes?

HOW CAN THE ENVIRONMENT
AFFECT A PHENOTYPE?

The genetic contribution to an individual phenotype is in part a collection of trait propensities. Traits are considered probabilistic in nature, not deterministic. However, the probability of some traits being manifested may be very high (e.g., eye color). Nevertheless, many phenotypic characteristics reflect some degree of gene–environment interaction over time. Consequently, changes in the environment may have an impact on the expression of phenotypic characteristics. This is true of even highly heritable characteristics (Rutter, 2002). Height, for example, is among the human traits most influenced by genetic heritage. Yet the environment, in the form of diet, can have a huge influence as well. The average height achieved by citizens in many countries around the world has increased by several inches over the past 60 years as the typical diet of children in those societies changed radically (Kuh, Power, & Rodgers, 1991).

What does it mean to have the Down syndrome phenotype? Is this phenotype highly stable across time? Some aspects of it are, whereas others are not. According to a study of the death records of 18,000 people with Down syndrome from 1983 to 1997 (Yang, Rasmussen, & Friedman, 2002), the life expectancy of individuals with Down syndrome in the United States nearly doubled in just 14 years—from an average of 25 years in 1983 to an average of 49 in 1997. Furthermore, during roughly this same time period, our phenotypic expectations of individuals with Down syndrome have gone from a prediction that such individuals will have severe mental retardation to an expectation of moderate and in some cases only mild retardation as well as the attainment of modest levels of literacy (Cohen, Nadel, & Madnick, 2002). What happened? These changes cannot be due to genetic mechanisms. Instead they surely reflect major changes in the environment. Individuals with Down syndrome went from lives spent in emotionally and environmentally impoverished institutional environments to living in their home communities, going to school with their peers, and in general experiencing an enhanced quality of life along many dimensions.

Many genetic propensities, whether they represent vulnerabilities or strengths, may only be manifested in the presence of an "environmental trigger." Research at the molecular genetics level has shown that positive and negative environments can alter gene expression (i.e., the rate at which the DNA is transcribed into RNA and subsequent protein synthesis, which can then alter the structure of the function of the brain; National Research Council and Institute of Medicine, 2000). Known environmental triggers for various problems include stress, poor diet, chronic sleep disorders, drugs, and harsh parenting (Reiss & Neiderhiser, 2000). On the positive side, stable, long-term, highly responsive parenting appears to set the parameters for enhanced learning, resulting in emotional, cognitive, and language development (Landry, Smith, Swank, Assel, & Vellet, 2001), just as a stable, healthy diet over time may influence both neurological and physical development. Positive environmental conditions may activate the transcription of RNA from dormant genes with subsequent production of new protein and alteration of key processes such as synaptic function (National Research Council and Institute of Medicine, 2000). Environmental effects, negatively or positively, appear to have maximal impact via cumulative experience across time. We explore this notion deeper by considering the cumulative impact of a stable style of maternal responsivity on child development.

What Are the Effects of Maternal Responsivity on Phenotype Development?

At the most general level, parental responsivity refers to a "healthy, growth-producing relationship consisting of such caregiver characteristics as warmth, nurturance, stability, predictability and contingent responsiveness" (Spiker, Boyce, & Boyce, 2002, p. 37). Responsivity can be defined and observed on a continuum that spans the molecular level of interaction to the molar. On the molecular level, it refers to "parental behavior that responds contingently to the child's cues, follows the child's lead, and provides input and suggestions that build on the child's focus of attention and activity" (Spiker et al., 2002). At this molecular level, directive statements such as imitation prompts and questions can be responsive if they follow the child's attentional lead. However, directive statements can be nonresponsive and potentially disruptive to learning if they redirect the child's attention (McCathren, Yoder, & Warren, 1995). At the somewhat more molar level, parental behavior can be defined as "responsive" when characterized by general qualities such as warmth and nurturing (Landry, Smith, Swank, & Miller-Loncar, 2000). Not surprisingly, a strong correlation has been shown between these general qualities of responsiveness and the more molecular definitions of contingent parental responsiveness to specific behaviors of the child (Landry et al., 2001). Finally, at the most molar level, parents might certainly be viewed as responsive if they actively seek out special services and activities and advocate for the child's needs in the community. However, parents could be responsive at this most general level, yet tend to be unresponsive and directive in their moment-to-moment interactions with their child. Likewise, a parent's affect toward her child might be characterized as "warm and responsive," yet at a more molecular level that same parent might engage in relatively few growth-enhancing contingent responses to her child's initiations (e.g., contingently respond to child initiations by compliance and linguistic mapping relative to her interest).

What Are the Effects of Maternal Responsivity on Development?

A substantial body of research has investigated the effects of maternal responsivity on child development. Viewed overall, this body of research strongly supports the contention that maternal responsivity can and often does play an important role in enhancing child development (Osofsky & Thompson, 2000). Children whose mothers display more responsive behavior during the first several years of life achieve language milestones earlier (Landry et al., 2001; Tamis-LeMonda, Bornstein, & Baumwell, 2001), score significantly higher on cognitive tests (Landry, Garner, Swank, & Baldwin, 1996; Landry et al., 2000), develop better social skills (Calkins, Smith, Gill, & Johnson, 1998; Kochanska, Forman, & Coy, 1999; Landry, Smith, Miller-Loncar, & Swank, 1997), and have fewer emotional and behavior problems (Goldberg, Lojkasek, Gartner, & Corter, 1989). Landry and her colleagues recently demonstrated in a longitudinal study of 282 young children (the sample included 103 full-term children, 102 low-risk preterm children, and 77 high-risk preterm children) that highly responsive parenting achieves its most substantial effects when it is sustained throughout the early childhood period (up to age 5). Children in her study who were exposed to highly responsive parenting early in development, but not later, or later but not earlier, scored substantially lower on measures of language, cognitive, and social development than children who experienced ongoing, consistent responsiveness as well as maternal warmth over a period of several years (Landry et al., 2001).

At the opposite end of the continuum from warm, highly responsive parenting is a style of unresponsive and/or harsh parenting. Unresponsive parenting has been associated with low maternal education level (Hooper, Burchinal, Erwick-Roberts, Zeisel, & Neebe, 1998), depression (Rutter & Quinton, 1984), substance abuse (Osofsky & Thompson, 2000), and mild mental retardation (Miller, Heysek, Whitman, & Borkowski, 1996). Just as highly responsive parenting has been associated with accelerated growth in language, cognition, and social behavior, unresponsive parenting has been associated with lower growth trajectories in these skills (Tomasello & Farrar, 1986; Tomasello & Todd, 1983). Harsh parenting, which sometimes co-occurs with unresponsive parenting, has been shown to have a markedly negative impact on child development and behavior (Dodge, Bates, & Pettit, 1990).

The degree of parental sensitivity and responsiveness has also been shown to be predictive of outcomes in children with disabilities. In a large-scale longitudinal study of the development of children with mental retardation and parent well-being, researchers found that when mental age was controlled, the quality and frequency of mother–child interaction was the only significant correlate of communication skills at age 3 years (Hauser-Cram, Warfield, Shonkoff, & Krauss, 2001). By 10 years of age, children with parents whose interaction scores were more positive had an advantage of approximately 10 months in communications skills on average. Conversely, Wasserman and colleagues (Waserman, Allen, & Solomon, 1985) found that infants with disabilities whose mothers ignored them for a proportion of a free play observation conducted when their children were 12 months of age had significantly lower intelligence scores at 24 months of age.

Yoder and Warren also demonstrated that young children with mental retardation who have highly responsive mothers achieve much greater gains in terms of later language development as a result of early prelinguistic communication intervention than do children with low responsive mothers (Yoder & Warren 1998, 2001a). A number of other studies have demonstrated correlational relationships between maternal responsivity and style and the development of children with mental retardation (Shapiro, Blacher, & Lopez, 1998). However, the extent to which maternal responsivity and style is an adaptive or maladaptive response to the behavior of the child with mental retardation has been more the subject of speculation than research (Marfo, Dedrick, & Barbour, 1998; Osofsky & Thompson, 2000).

How Can Highly Responsive Parenting Impact Cognitive and Language Development?

The transactional model of development provides a theoretical framework for understanding how highly responsive parenting may impact key aspects of phenotypic development such as cognition and language, and how low responsive parenting may also impact phenotypic expression (Sameroff & Chandler, 1975; Sameroff & Fiese, 2000). The model presumes that early communication and social/cognitive development are facilitated via bidirectional, reciprocal interactions between the child and his or her environment. For example, a change in the young child, such as the onset of intentional communication around 9 months of age, may trigger a change in the social environment, such as increased linguistic mapping by their caregivers (linguistic mapping is known to facilitate receptive and productive language development; Gallaway & Richards, 1994). These changes then support further development in the child (e.g., increased vocabulary) and subsequent changes by caregivers (e.g., more complex language interactions with the child). In this way, both the child and the environment change over time and affect and adapt to each other in reciprocal fashion as early achievements pave the way for subsequent development (Warren & Walker, in press). Maternal responsiveness, operating through the reciprocally adjusting mechanism of the transactional model, may enhance early cognitive development by directly supporting the child's active exploration and engagement in the environment (Landry et al., 2000).

A transactional model may be particularly well suited for understanding early cognitive and language development because caregiver–child interaction can play such a unique role during this period. During their first few years, children's relatively restricted behavior repertoire allows changes in their behavior to be more salient and easily observable to caregivers. This in turn may allow adults to be more specifically contingent with their responses to the child's developing interests and skills than is possible later in development after the child's behavioral repertoire has become far more expansive and complex. For example, consider the relative ease by which a responsive parent can note instances of new learning in an infant or toddler (e.g., specifically acknowledging new words and word attempts), and how unlikely it is that a parent can accurately account for instances of new learning just 2 years later (Sokolov & Snow, 1994).

To appreciate the true potential of transactional effects, it is necessary to consider the relentless manner by which cumulative advantages and disadvantages in experience can develop across the first few years of life. For example, an input difference in positive affect expressed by a parent toward his or her child of 10 events per day (a difference of less than 1 event per waking hour on average) would result in a cumulative difference of 10,950 such events over a 3-year period. If a child who experiences less positive affect also experiences more negative affect (e.g., "Stop that," "Get out of there," "Shut your mouth up," "You're a bad boy"), it becomes relatively easy to conceive of combinations of these qualitative and quantitative experiential differences contributing to deficits in exploratory behavior, self-concept, language, and social development (Hart & Risley, 1995; Warren & Walker, in press; Warren & Yoder, 2004). Furthermore, we have substantial evidence that such large cumulative deficits occur in typically developing young children and that these differences strongly correlate with important indicators of development later in childhood (e.g., vocabulary size, IQ, reading ability, school achievement; Gottfried, 1984; Hart & Risley, 1992; Walker, Greenwood, Hart, & Carta, 1994). In part because they often display low rates of initiation and responsiveness (Hauser-Cram et al., 2001; Yoder, Davies, & Bishop, 1994), young children with developmental delays such as those associated with fragile X syndrome (FXS) are also likely to experience relative deficits in various types of environmental input compared with typically developing children despite their caregivers' best intentions.

Summary

Maternal responsivity works its magic on the expression of a phenotype in a cumulative, stable, long-term fashion. As a general principle for understanding environment–gene interactions, it might be described as an example of stable, environmental characteristics evoking and supporting a stable pattern of child behavior and development. Furthermore, optimal maternal responsivity obviously only influences the outcome of some aspects of development. In fact a critical challenge is to separate out those components of a phenotype that are malleable and subject to certain types of environmental impact from those that are more resistant to change despite long-term exposure to stable environmental variables. Intervention research can be one tool for doing just this. However, we must first consider how phenotypic propensities may shape and impact the environment.

HOW CAN A PHENOTYPE AFFECT THE ENVIRONMENT?

Phenotypes evolve and develop over time through the process of genotype–environment interaction. At any given point in time, an individual phenotype is the collective manifestation of anatomical, neurological, and behavioral traits resulting from that phenotype's past history of interaction as well as the ongoing interaction of heredity and environment. In the case of child development, heritable characteristics of the child may evoke a stable pattern of particular parental responses that have a cumulative impact on the child's behavior and development over lengthy periods of time (Abbeduto, Evans, & Dolan, 2001; Collins, Maccoby, Steinberg, Hetherington, & Bornstein, 2000). In the case of fragile X syndrome or autism, it may be hypothesized that the high heritability of problematic behavior, including impaired social and cognitive engagement, may suppress parental warmth and responsiveness and over time evoke a pattern of parent directiveness, restrictiveness, and low responsivity. In a sense, the child's phenotype creates its own learning environment—one that may be adaptive but nevertheless far from optimal in terms of development. As Landry and her colleagues have shown with high-risk preterm infants (Landry et al., 2000; Smith, Landry, & Swank, 2000a, 2000b) and Hart and Risley (1992, 1995) with typically developing young children, it is the stable, cumulative nature of parental responsivity that matters most.

Maternal responsivity does not function independently of the child's own behavior and responsiveness. Either partner in the "dance" between parent and child is capable of disrupting the interaction and altering its nature (Kelly & Barnard, 2000). Initiating and maintaining a warm, responsive interaction style with a child with FXS, autism, or any of a number of other disorders can be highly challenging even for a parent with the best of intentions. For example, a number of phenotypic characteristics of FXS may be disruptive to parental responsivity alone or in combination with other characteristics. These include gaze avoidance or atypical eye gaze, hypersensitivity to sensory input, social anxiety and shyness, perseveration and repetitiousness, stereotypical behavior, unintelligible speech, and problems with conversational discourse (Abbeduto & Hager-man, 1997; Bailey, Hatton, & Skinner, 1998). In addition, a substantial number of children with FXS also fall within the autism spectrum and may display particularly severe forms of the behaviors noted earlier (Bailey, Hatton, Mesibov, Ament, & Skinner, 2000; Bailey, Hatton, Tas-sone, Skinner, & Taylor, 2001). These deficits may be in addition to prob-lems with social interaction, which may be associated primarily with de-velopmental delay and mental retardation.

The mother of a child with FXS may strive to be warm, nurturing, and highly responsive during the first few years of the child's life, but over time her behavior may be cumulatively shaped by the child and possibly affected by her own struggles with anxiety, stress, and depression and/or her own struggles with FXS (mothers are carriers of the disorder, and some of them manifest symptoms themselves; see Bailey et al., chap. 7, this volume). This may ultimately result in a cool, distant, and directive parenting style. However, the opposite may occur as well. That is, early on a young child may manifest various phenotypic characteristics of FXS that are met head on and cumulatively shaped by stable, adapted forms of pa-rental warmth and responsivity that impact more malleable aspects of the phenotype and eventually result in a relatively social and high-func-tioning individual despite various ongoing cognitive challenges and limi-tations. It is well established in the biology and psychology literature that either outcome is possible (Cicchetti & Cannon, 1999; Plomin, 1994; Reiss & Neiderhiser, 2000; Rutter, 2002; Sameroff & Fiese, 2000). However, we do not have direct evidence in support of either of these plausible out-comes with children with FXS.

Summary

Heritable aspects of a phenotype may shape a stable pattern of environ-mental response in a variety of ways. High heritability of problematic be-haviors may be due to the transmission of unpleasant traits, which evoke family hostility. High heritability of problematic social engagement and impaired attractiveness may suppress parental warmth and responsive-ness. Finally, children who are inherently passive and dispositionally less engaged will elicit less input across a variety of transactional dimensions relative to children who are dispositionally more active and engaged.

INTERVENTION AS EXPERIMENT

Experimental interventions are an important tool in determining the mal-leability of phenotypic characteristics and traits. Intervention studies can also reveal the existence of subgroups within a hypothesized group or phenotype. For example, they can reveal subgroups of individuals who respond positively to a new cancer treatment as well as those who have no response or even respond negatively. Interventions can function the same way with behavioral phenotypes associated with developmental impairments. One of the most important effects of the intensive early intervention studies carried out in the 1970s by Ivar Lovaas and his colleagues was its support for the existence of subgroups within the population of children diagnosed at that time with infantile autism (Lovaas, 1987). The identification of such subgroups can lead to more meaningful classification and more accurate knowledge of the traits and propensities that various phenotypes actually manifest.

Interventions may lead to the discovery of subgroups within a phenotype that may be the result of genetic variation, environmental variation, or an interaction. However, long-term interventions may also create either general or subgroup changes in a phenotype in part by their impact on gene expression. For example, deinstitutionalization eventually changed our definition of the general Down syndrome phenotype. It affected behavior and development at the observable level over relatively long periods of time, likely altering gene expression at the molecular level in a variety of ways (Reiss & Neiderhiser, 2000). Individuals with autism who respond positively to intensive intervention may do so in part because these interventions alter gene expression and/or activate dormant genes. New biotechnology developments in the form of DNA microarrays and gene chips will increasingly allow the monitoring of specific gene expression for thousands of genes over time. This may allow researchers to directly assess the impact of interventions of specific gene expression (Reiss & Neiderhiser, 2000) and ultimately tie these changes to alterations in behavior.

Interventions may reveal either how malleable a trait is or how resistant to change it is. For example, certain personality characteristics (e.g., perceptual style, basic temperament) may be highly resistant to change and indicate a dominant genetic effect and/or (in some cases) a long, stable history that is difficult to overcome (e.g., ease of attachment to others, basic trust of others, language skills, etc.). Malleability may indicate a trait has a larger environmental component in its origin or perhaps a shorter history.

Intervention as Experiments on Phenotypes: Two Examples

Two studies are discussed next as examples of how interventions may reveal important, functional information about phenotypes. The first example demonstrates how history can create propensities that could easily be mistaken for genetic propensities and, more important, can alter the effects of intervention. This example uses a mixed-etiology sample, an important control because this means that the effects obtained are likely the results of history rather than genetic endowment. The second example reports on how children with Down syndrome responded differently to an intervention than did children with mixed etiology who received the same intervention.

Example 1

Yoder and Warren (1998, 1999a, 1999b, 2001a, 2001b) conducted a longitudinal experimental study of the effects of prelinguistic communication intervention on the communication and language development of children with general developmental delays. This study represented an experimental analysis of the transactional model of social communication development.

Fifty-eight children between the ages of 17 and 32 months ($M = 23$; $SD = 4$) with developmental delays and their primary parent participated in the study. Fifty-two of the children had no productive words at the outset of the study; the remaining six children had between one and five productive words. All children scored below the 10th percentile on the expressive scale of the *Communication Development Inventory* (Fenson et al., 1991). All of the children fit the Tennessee definition of *developmental delay* (i.e., at least a 40% delay in at least one developmental domain, or at least a 25% delay in at least two developmental domains).

The children were randomly assigned to one of two treatment groups. Twenty-eight of the children received an intervention termed *prelinguistic milieu teaching* (PMT) for 20 minutes per day, three or four days per week, for 6 months. The other 30 children received an intervention termed *responsive small group* (RSG). PMT represented an adaptation of milieu language teaching (Kaiser, Yoder, & Keetz, 1992). It was based on following the child's attentional lead, building social play routines (e.g., turn-taking interactions like rolling a ball back and forth), and using prompts such as time delays (e.g., interrupting a turn-taking routine such as rolling the ball back and forth by not taking your turn until the child initiates a request for you to continue), as well as models and natural consequences to teach the form and functions of requesting and commenting at the prelinguistic level. RSG represented an adaptation of the responsive interaction approach. The adult played with the child in a highly responsive manner and commented on what the child was doing, but never attempted to directly elicit or prompt any communication function or form. These interventions are described in detail elsewhere (e.g., Warren & Yoder, 1998). Caregivers were kept naive as to the specific methods, measures, records of child progress, and child goals throughout the study. This allowed

Yoder and Warren to investigate how change in the children's behavior as a result of the interventions might affect the behavior of the primary caregiver and how this in turn might affect the child's development later in time. Data were collected at five points in time for each dyad: at pretreatment, at posttreatment, and 6, 12, and 18 months after the competition of the intervention.

Both interventions had generalized effects on intentional communication development. However, the treatment that was most effective depended on the pretreatment maternal interaction style and the mother's education level (Yoder & Warren, 1998, 2001b). Specifically, Yoder and Warren found that for children of highly responsive, relatively well-educated mothers, PMT was effective in fostering generalized intentional communication development. For children who already had a history of unresponsive parenting, RSG was relatively more successful in fostering generalized intentional communication development.

The two interventions differed along a few important dimensions that provide a plausible explanation for these effects. PMT uses a child-centered play context in which communication prompts for more advanced forms of communication are employed as well as social consequences for target responses such as specific acknowledgment and compliance. The RSG emphasized following the child's attentional lead and being highly responsive to child initiation while avoiding the use of direct prompts for communication. Children's history with different maternal interaction styles may have influenced which intervention was most beneficial because children may develop expectations concerning interactions with adults (including teachers and interventionists) based on their history of interaction with their primary caregiver. Thus, children with responsive parents may learn to persist in the face of communication breakdowns, such as might be occasioned by a direct prompt or time delay, because their history leads them to believe that their communication attempts will usually be successful. In contrast, children without this history may cease communicating when their initial attempt fails. Thus, children of responsive mothers in the PMT group persisted when prompted and learned effectively in this context, whereas children with unresponsive parents did not. Yet when provided with a highly responsive adult, who virtually never prompted them over a 6-month period, children of unresponsive mothers showed greater gains than children of responsive parents receiving the same treatment.

The effects of maternal responsivity as a mediator and moderator of intervention effects rippled throughout the longitudinal follow-up period. Yoder and Warren demonstrated that children in the PMT group with relatively responsive mothers received increased amounts of responsive input from their mothers in direct response to the children's increased intentional communication (Yoder & Warren, 2001a). Furthermore, the effects of the intervention were found on both requests and comments (Yoder & Warren, 1999b), became greater with time, and impacted expressive and receptive language development 6 and 12 months after intervention ceased (Yoder & Warren, 1999a, 2001a).

The research by Yoder and Warren represents a relatively rare experimental example of child influence on adults' use of behavior that in turn fosters the child's further development (Bell & Harper, 1977). Their study suggests how history can engender a trait such as "persistence in the face of directives and questions," which can interact with an intervention to generate differential outcomes. Such traits could easily be confused at any given point in time as a phenotypic characteristic related to genetic endowment, not history. At the same time, this demonstrates in part why mixed etiology studies (which the Yoder and Warren study was) can reveal little about specific gene–environment interactions related to genetic endowment. However, a second study by Yoder and Warren (2002) does just this.

Example 2

Yoder and Warren (2002) investigated the effects of facilitating prelinguistic communication on both parents' responsivity and children's communication and productive language development. Thirty-nine prelinguistic toddlers and their primary caregivers were randomly assigned to either a "prelinguistic milieu teaching plus responsive parenting training group" (RPMT) or a control group. As in the earlier Yoder and Warren study, various interaction effects were discovered. One of these interactions is of particular interest to this discussion. The effect of RPMT on the growth rate of child-initiated requests (the most common way for prelinguistic children to regulate the behavior of others) varied by presence or absence of Down syndrome (17 of the children in the study had Down syndrome—8 in the intervention group and 9 in the control group). That is, children with Down syndrome did not learn to request more often as a result of the intervention despite the fact that this was one of the primary goals.

Why would an extra 21st chromosome make it more difficult to learn to request? One possibility is that children with Down syndrome may find it more difficult to request due to hypotonicity and consequent passivity. Children with Down syndrome tend to exhibit more hypotonicity than other children with intellectual disabilities matched for developmental level (Favuto & Cocchi, 1992; Kumin & Bahr, 1999). Furthermore, many children with Down syndrome exhibit more passivity than other children with intellectual disabilities matched on developmental level (Gunn &

Cuskelly, 1991; Linn, Goodman, & Lender, 2000). However, no study has yet demonstrated an association among hypotonicity, passivity, and requesting.

During intervention sessions, it may have been that most of the forms children with Down syndrome used to comment (i.e., their rate of commenting did increase as a result of the intervention) required simpler motor skills than the forms they used to request. Within these sessions, interventionists typically prompted "gives," "reaches," and "points" by the children (all communication forms requiring a significant motor component). In contrast, comments by their very nature could not be directly prompted, but only modeled. Additionally, interventionists accepted gaze shifts coordinated with vocalizations by the children as comments. In short, comments may have been much easier for children with Down syndrome to do, whereas requests were more demanding and difficult for them to executive successfully. As a result, they may have resisted prompts to request. This hypothesis matches informal observations reported by individual interventionists (Yoder & Warren, 2002).

It is quite possible that the interaction effect between Down syndrome and the PMT intervention will not be replicated in future research (a replication effort is underway). However, at present it represents one of the first times that the specific etiology of an intellectual disability has been shown to explain the variance in children's response to an educational/behavioral treatment aimed at communication or language outcomes. Furthermore, it serves as an example of how diagnosis by treatment interactions of specific behavior differences or traits may be useful as a guide for future treatment adaptation and selection.

Challenges to Conducting Specific Etiology Intervention Research

A large number of small N intervention studies aimed at enhancing or modifying some aspect of communication and language development or use by individuals with intellectual disabilities has been reported over the past four decades (Yoder & Warren, 1993). These studies have formed part of the foundation for the development over time of a comprehensive model of communication and language intervention (Warren & Yoder, 1997). Single-subject studies have allowed researchers to develop specific techniques (e.g., time delay, mand-model, recasting) aimed at specific communication and language targets (e.g., expressive vocabulary, requests, comments, two-term semantic relations) or developmental markers (e.g., mean length of utterance above 2.0) relatively inexpensively. As a result, the development of procedures for enhancing and facilitating communication and language development has been substantial. In fact we have reached the point where innovations in terms of specific intervention techniques are becoming increasingly rare (Warren & Yoder, 1997).

Although single-subject designs have been useful in developing intervention techniques and conducting relatively short-term tests of their efficacy, they are inappropriate for systematically studying the interactions of interventions and specific etiologies. The ideal design for addressing questions of this nature is the longitudinal experimental design with random assignment to a treatment and control group or, alternatively (and increasingly), to one of two contrasting treatments. These designs allow direct comparisons of effects and also control for potential confounds in the samples. However, they do not necessarily control for development outside of intervention unless they include a true no-treatment control. They typically require at least 40 or more participants (the specific number of subjects should be determined by a statistical power analysis) randomly assigned to two or more conditions to ensure sufficient power to allow analyses for aptitude by treatment interactions as well as main effects. The results of a few well-executed longitudinal experiments have the potential to uncover important phenotypic traits and subgroups.

The difficulty in recruiting sufficient sample sizes is magnified in intervention research because of the necessity to directly work with participants for extended periods of time. This is probably another reason for the historic popularity of small N designs. Most intervention studies, whether they have used small N designs or longitudinal experimental designs with random assignment, have used mixed-etiology samples at similar developmental levels. The main exception to this has been in the area of autism. However, even intervention studies that include only participants with Down syndrome are rare, and no communication intervention study has yet been published with FXS participants despite the fact that it is the most common inherited cause of mental retardation. The logistical difficulty in recruiting subjects for even mixed-etiology studies has been further increased by the success of educational and social inclusion practices in early intervention and education in recent years. That is, centers or schools with lots of children with intellectual and developmental disabilities are now all but nonexistent at least in the United States and Canada. As a result, researchers must budget for substantial amounts of staff time and travel expense to reach participants in their homes or schools for screening, assessment, and intervention activities. This side effect of inclusion increases both the cost and complexity of conducting intervention research on anything but a small scale.

The problem of recruiting sufficient samples is greatly magnified when we choose to study intervention effects with specific etiologies other than the relatively frequent conditions of Down syndrome and autism. For example, although FXS is the most common inherited cause of intellectual disabilities (estimated prevalence ranges from 1 in 4,000 to 6,000 births; Mazzocco, 2000), it would be prohibitively expensive (i.e., we estimate that it would cost at least $1 million per year) to conduct just one longitudinal experimental behavioral intervention study with 40 or more children with FXS, and it would probably be a logistical nightmare as well (this would not be true for pharmacological interventions). Thus, it is difficult to imagine such a study being conducted in the near term at least if it requires frequent and sustained contact between interventionist and child, like most behavioral intervention studies do. Even a multiple baseline design across subjects presents formidable problems with logistics, although such a study is conceivable within a large metropolitan area. Given these constraints, how could the effects of an intervention that may be particularly well suited for the unique phenotypic characteristics of a disorder such as FXS be conducted using an adequate experimental design? Figure 9.1 depicts one possible option.

Figure 9.1 shows the hypothetical growth curves for a large number of young children with FXS. The development of most of these children was studied longitudinally over several years, and no systematic, experimental intervention was conducted with them. However, a small group of the children—those indicated by dark lines—received an intensive behavioral intervention for 1 year between the ages of 2 and 3. The growth curves of these 10 children are then compared to the growth curves of the much larger group of children who did not receive this intervention.

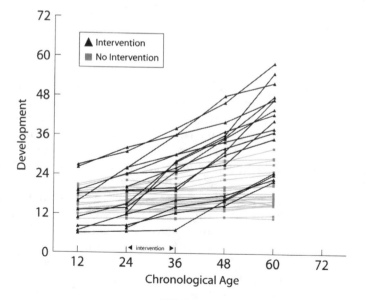

FIG. 9.1.

A study of this nature might be built over time. Random assignment might even be used with the proposed design assuming it is possible to recruit at least 20 children at a relatively early age—say 2 to 3 years. Ten of these 20 children would be selected at random to receive the experimental early intervention. The 10 additional children would be assigned to the nontreatment control group. For analytical purposes, this group of children could be expanded by additional participants identified later in development (say at age 3). These children could still be part of a longitudinal comparison in which their development would be compared with the intensive early intervention subjects and other control subjects at age 4, 5, and so on. This would allow questions such as the following to be asked: Do FXS children who receive an intensive intervention between ages 2 and 3 differ significantly at age 4 compared with other FXS children at age 4 who did not receive this intervention? Do FXS children with trait "P" respond differently than those without trait "P"? Are certain traits of children with FXS amenable to change via intervention and other traits less so?

It is unclear what the minimum number of subjects for the intervention condition needs to be for a design like this to provide reliable, valid data. In any case, designs like this may provide one of the few practical ways to study the effects of various intervention approaches with specific etiologies. Furthermore, such a design would still be expensive to apply in an absolute sense, but would likely be much less expensive and far more feasible than alternative designs.

CONCLUSION

Genetic influences are as changing and dynamic as environmental influences. Consequently, behavioral phenotypes must be viewed as a collection of propensities in which traits exist on a continuum of stability, oscillating as a result of gene-immediate environment–history interactions. From this perspective, the relative malleability of genetic propensities is of paramount interest. Discovering the conditions under which a genetic propensity can be meaningfully altered via intervention of one sort or another (pharmacological, behavioral, etc.) should be a central aim of clinical science. When properly conceptualized and designed, intervention research can become as much a tool of discovery as of clinical evaluation. Indeed intervention research so far has been an underutilized tool for ferreting out the functional similarities and differences of various phenotypes that appear to superficially share overlapping areas of variance (e.g., autism, FXS, specific language disorder). Because successful interventions may well alter mechanisms of genetic expression, the evolving biotechnological capability to track the expression of specific genes over time in various body locations can further enhance the role of intervention research.

REFERENCES

Abbeduto, L., Evans, J., & Dolan, T. (2001). Theoretical perspectives on language and communication problems in mental retardation and developmental disabilities. *Mental Retardation and Developmental Disabilities Research Reviews, 7*, 45–55.

Abbeduto, L., & Hagerman, R. (1997). Language and communication in fragile X syndrome. *Mental Retardation and Developmental Disabilities Research Review, 3*(4), 313–322.

Bailey, D. B., Hatton, D. D., Mesibov, G., Ament, N., & Skinner, M. (2000). Early development, temperament, and functional impairment in autism and fragile X syndrome. *Journal of Autism and Developmental Disorders, 30*(1), 49–59.

Bailey, D. B., Hatton, D. D., & Skinner, M. (1998). Early developmental trajectories of males with fragile X syndrome. *American Journal of Mental Retardation, 103*(1), 29–39.

Bailey, D. B., Hatton, D. D., Tassone, F., Skinner, M., & Taylor, A. K. (2001). Variability in FMRP and early development in males with fragile X syndrome. *American Journal of Mental Retardation, 106*(1), 16–27.

Bell, R., & Harper, L. (1977). *Child effects on adults.* Hillsdale, NJ: Lawrence Erlbaum Associates.

Calkins, S. D., Smith, C. L., Gill, K. L., & Johnson, M. C. (1998). Maternal interactive style across contexts: Relations to emotional, behavioral, and physiological regulation during toddlerhood. *Social Development, 7*(3), 350–369.

Cicchetti, D., & Cannon, T. D. (1999). Neurodevelopmental processes in the ontogenesis and epigenesis of psychopathology. *Development and Psychopathology, 11*, 374–393.

Cohen, W. I., Nadel, L., & Madnick, M. E. (Eds.). (2002). *Down syndrome: Vision for the 21st century.* New York: Wiley-Liss.

Collins, W., Maccoby, E., Steinberg, L., Hetherington, E., & Bornstein, M. H. (2000). Contemporary research on parenting: The case for nature and nurture. *American Psychologist, 55*(2), 218–232.

Dodge, K. A., Bates, J. E., & Pettit, G. S. (1990). Mechanisms in the cycle of violence. *Science, 250*(4988), 1678–1683.

Favuto, M., & Cocchi, R. (1992). Hypotonia in children with Down's syndrome: An epidemiological study. *Italian-Journal-of-Intellective-Impairment, 5*(1), 113–117.

Fenson, L., Dale, P., Reznick, S., Thal, D., Bates, E., Hartung, J., Pethick, S., & Reilly, J. (1991). *Technical manual for the MacArthur communicative development inventories.* San Diego, CA: San Diego State University.

Gallaway, C., & Richards, B. J. (1994). *Input and interaction in language acquisition.* New York: Cambridge University Press.

Goldberg, S., Lojkasek, M., Gartner, G., & Corter, C. (1989). Maternal responsiveness and social development in preterm infants. In M. H. Bornstein (Ed.), *Maternal responsiveness: Characteristics and consequences* (43rd ed., pp. 89–103). San Francisco, CA: Jossey-Bass/Pfeiffer.

Gottfried, A. W. (1984). Home environment and early cognitive development: Integration, meta-analyses, and conclusions. In A. W. Gottfried (Ed.), *Home environment and early cognitive development: Longitudinal research* (pp. 329–342). New York: Academic Press.

Gunn, P., & Cuskelly, M. (1991). Down syndrome temperament: The stereotype at middle childhood and adolescence. *International Journal of Disability, Development and Education, 38*(1), 59–70.

Hart, B., & Risley, T. (1992). American parenting of language-learning children: Persisting differences in family child interactions observed in natural home environments. *Developmental Psychology, 28*(6), 1096–1105.

Hart, B., & Risley, T. (1995). *Meaningful differences in the everyday experience of young American children.* Baltimore, MD: Paul H. Brookes.

Hauser-Cram, P., Warfield, M., Shonkoff, J., & Krauss, M. (2001). Children with disabilities: A longitudinal study of child development and parent well-being. *Monographs of the Society for Research in Child Development, 66*(3), 1–131.

Hooper, S., Burchinal, M., Erwick-Roberts, J., Zeisel, S., & Neebe, E. (1998). Social and family risk factors for infant development at one year: An application of the cumulative risk model. *Journal of Applied Developmental Psychology, 19*(1), 85–96.

Kaiser, A. P., Yoder, P. J., & Keetz, A. (1992). Evaluating milieu teaching. In S. F. Warren & J. Reichle (Eds.), *Causes and effects in communication and language intervention* (Vol. 1, pp. 9–46). Baltimore, MD: Paul H. Brookes.

Kelly, J. F., & Barnard, K. E. (2000). Assessment of parent–child interaction: Implications for early intervention. In J. Shonkoff & S. Meisels (Eds.), *Handbook of early childhood intervention* (2nd ed., pp. 258–289). New York: Cambridge University Press.

Kochanska, G., Forman, D. R., & Coy, K. (1999). Implications of the mother–child relationship in infancy socialization in the second year of life. *Infant Behavior and Development, 22*(2), 249–265.

Kuh, D. L., Power, C., & Rodgers, B. (1991). Secular trends in social class and sex differences in adult height. *International Journal of Epidemiology, 20,* 1001–1009.

Kumin, L., & Bahr, D. (1999). Patterns of feeding, eating, and drinking in young children with Down syndrome with oral motor concerns. *Down Syndrome Quarterly, 42,* 1–8.

Landry, S. H., Garner, P. W., Swank, P. R., & Baldwin, C. D. (1996). Effects of maternal scaffolding during joint toy play with preterm and full-term infants. *Merrill-Palmer Quarterly, 42*(2), 177–199.

Landry, S. H., Smith, K. E., Miller-Loncar, C. L., & Swank, P. R. (1997). Predicting cognitive-language and social growth curves from early maternal behaviors in children at varying degrees of biological risk. *Developmental Psychology, 33*(6), 1040–1053.

Landry, S. H., Smith, K. E., Swank, P. R., Assel, M. A., & Vellet, S. (2001). Does early responsive parenting have a special importance for children's development or is consistency across early childhood necessary? *Developmental Psychology, 37*(3), 387–403.

Landry, S. H., Smith, K. E., Swank, P. R., & Miller-Loncar, C. L. (2000). Early maternal and child influences on children's later independent cognitive and social functioning. *Child Development, 71*(2), 358–375.

Linn, M., Goodman, J., & Lender, W. (2000). Played out? Passive behavior by children with Down syndrome during unstructured play. *Journal of Early Intervention, 23*(4), 264–278.

Lovaas, O. I. (1987). Behavioral treatment and normal educational and intellectual functioning in young autistic children. *Journal of Consulting and Clinical Psychology, 55*(1), 3–9.

Marfo, K., Dedrick, C. F., & Barbour, N. (1998). Mother–child interactions and the development of children with mental retardation. In J. Burack, R. M. Hodapp, & E. Zigler (Eds.), *Handbook of mental retardation and development* (pp. 637–668). New York: Cambridge University Press.

Mazzocco, M. (2000). Advances in research on the fragile X syndrome. *Mental Retardation and Developmental Disabilities Research Reviews, 6*(2), 96–106.

McCathren, R. B., Yoder, P. J., & Warren, S. F. (1995). The role of directives in early language intervention. *Journal of Early Intervention, 19,* 91–101.

Miller, C. L., Heysek, P. J., Whitman, T. L., & Borkowski, J. G. (1996). Cognitive readiness to parent and intellectual emotional development in children of adolescent mothers. *Developmental Psychology, 32,* 533–541.

National Research Council and Institute of Medicine. (2000). *From neurons to neighborhoods: The science of early childhood development.* Washington, DC: National Academy Press.

Neufeldt, V., & Guralnik, D. (Eds.). (1988). *Webster's New World Dictionary of American English* (3rd College ed.). New York: Simon & Schuster.

Osofsky, J., & Thompson, M. (2000). Adaptive and maladaptive parenting: Perspectives on risk and protective factors. In J. Shonkoff & S. Meisels (Eds.), *Handbook of early childhood intervention* (2nd ed., pp. 54–75). New York: Cambridge University Press.

Plomin, R. (1994). *Genetics and experience. The interplay between nature and nurture.* Newbury Park, CA: Sage.

Reiss, D., & Neiderhiser, J. (2000). The interplay of genetic influences and social processes in developmental theory: Specific mechanisms are coming into view. *Development and Psychopathology, 12*(3), 357–374.

Rutter, M. (2002). Nature, nurture, and development: From evangelism through science toward policy and practice. *Child Development, 73*(1), 1–21.

Rutter, M., & Quinton, D. (1984). Long-term follow up of women institutionalized in childhood: Factors promoting good functioning in adult life. *British Journal of Developmental Psychology, 2*(3), 191–204.

Sameroff, A. J., & Chandler, M. J. (1975). Reproductive risk and the continuum of caretaking casualty. In F. D. Horowitz, E. Hetherington, S. Scarr-Salapatek, & G. Siegel (Eds.), *Review of child development research* (Vol. 4, pp. 187–244). Chicago, IL: University of Chicago Press.

Sameroff, A. J., & Fiese, B. H. (2000). Transactional regulation: The development ecology of early intervention. In J. Shonkoff & S. Meisels (Eds.), *Handbook of early childhood intervention* (2nd ed., pp. 135–159). Cambridge, United Kingdom: Cambridge University Press.

Shapiro, J., Blacher, J., & Lopez, S. R. (1998). Maternal reactions to children with mental retardation. In J. Burack, R. M. Hodapp, & E. Zigler (Eds.), *Handbook of mental retardation and development* (pp. 606–636). New York: Cambridge University Press.

Smith, K. E., Landry, S. H., & Swank, P. R. (2000a). Does the content of mothers' verbal stimulation explain differences in children's development of verbal and nonverbal cognitive skills? *Journal of School Psychology, 38*(1), 27–49.

Smith, K. E., Landry, S. H., & Swank, P. R. (2000b). The influence of early patterns of positive parenting on children's preschool outcomes. *Early Education and Development, 11*(2), 147–169.

Sokolov, J. L., & Snow, C. E. (1994). The changing role of negative evidence in theories of language development. In C. Gallaway & B. Richards (Eds.), *Input and interaction in language acquisition* (pp. 38–55). Cambridge, United Kingdom: Cambridge University Press.

Spiker, D., Boyce, G. C., & Boyce, L. K. (2002). Parent–child interactions when young children have disabilities. In L. Masters-Glidden (Ed.), *International review of research in mental retardation* (Vol. 25, pp. 35–70). San Diego, CA: Academic Press.

Tamis-LeMonda, C. S., Bornstein, M. H., & Baumwell, L. (2001). Maternal responsiveness and children's achievement of language milestones. *Child Development, 72*(3), 748–767.

Tomasello, M., & Farrar, M. J. (1986). Joint attention and early language. *Child Development, 57*, 1454–1463.

Tomasello, M., & Todd, J. (1983). Joint attention and lexical acquisition style. *First Language, 4*(12), 197–211.

Walker, D., Greenwood, C., Hart, B., & Carta, J. (1994). Prediction of school outcomes based on early language production and socioeconomic factors. *Child Development, 65*(2 Spec No), 606–621.

Warren, S. F., & Walker, D. (in press). Fostering early communication and language development. In D. M. Teti (Ed.), *Handbook of research methods in developmental psychology.* Oxford, United Kingdom: Blackwell.

Warren, S. F., & Yoder, P. J. (1997). A developmental model of early communication and language intervention. *Mental Retardation and Developmental Disabilities Research Review, 3*, 358–362.

Warren, S. F., & Yoder, P. J. (1998). Facilitating the transition from preintentional to intentional communication. In A. Wetherby, S. Warren, & J. Reichle (Eds.), *Transitions in prelinguistic communication* (pp. 365–385). Baltimore: Brookes.

Warren, S. F., & Yoder, P. J. (2004). The emerging model of intervention for young children with language impairments. In L. Verhoeven & H. v. Balkon (Eds.), *Classification of developmental language disorders: Theoretical issues and clinical implications* (pp. 367–381). Amsterdam: Lawrence Erlbaum Associates.

Waserman, G. A., Allen, R., & Solomon, C. (1985). At-risk toddlers and their mothers: The special case of physical handicap. *Child Development, 56*(1), 73–83.

Yang, Q., Rasmussen, S. A., & Friedman, J. M. (2002). Mortality associated with Down's syndrome in the USA from 1983 to 1997: A population-based study. *The Lancet, 359*, 1019–1025.

Yoder, P. J., Davies, B., & Bishop, K. (1994). Reciprocal sequential relations in conversations between parents and children with developmental delays. *Journal of Early Intervention, 18*(4), 362–379.

Yoder, P. J., & Warren, S. F. (1993). Can developmentally delayed children's language development be enhanced through prelinguistic intervention? In A. P. Kaiser (Ed.), *Enhancing children's communication: Research foundations for intervention communication and language intervention series* (Vol. 2, pp. 35–61). Baltimore, MD: Paul H. Brookes.

Yoder, P. J., & Warren, S. F. (1998). Maternal responsivity predicts the extent to which prelinguistic intervention facilitates generalized intentional communication. *Journal of Speech, Language, and Hearing Research, 41*(5), 1207–1219.

Yoder, P. J., & Warren, S. F. (1999a). Maternal responsivity mediates the relationship between prelinguistic intentional communication and later language. *Journal of Early Intervention, 22*, 126–136.

Yoder, P. J., & Warren, S. F. (1999b). Self-initiated proto-declaratives and proto-imperatives can be facilitated in prelinguistic children with developmental disabilities. *Journal of Early Intervention, 22*, 337–354.

Yoder, P. J., & Warren, S. F. (2001a). Intentional communication elicits language-facilitating maternal responses in dyads with children who have developmental disabilities. *American Journal of Mental Retardation, 106*(4), 327–335.

Yoder, P. J., & Warren, S. F. (2001b). Relative treatment effects of two prelinguistic communication interventions on language development in toddlers with developmental delays vary by maternal characteristics. *Journal of Speech, Language, and Hearing Research, 44*(1), 224–237.

Yoder, P. J., & Warren, S. F. (2002). Effects of prelinguistic milieu teaching and parent responsivity education on dyads involving children with intellectual disabilities. *Journal of Speech, Language, and Hearing Research, 45*(6), 1158–1174.

10

Growth Models of Developmental Language Disorders

Mabel L. Rice
University of Kansas

> *From cells to whole organisms, there is a time to grow and a time to prolifer-*
> *ate; a time to keep silent and a time to express; a time to change and a time to*
> *refrain from transformation. But where are the cellular and organismal time-*
> *pieces and how do they mark off time and keep the myriad physiological*
> *events in sync?*
>
> —Purnell (2003, p. 325)

The prior quote is from a recent issue of *Science* with a special section on the topic of developmental timing. The temporal events that guide development are key parts of the puzzle of contemporary molecular genetics. Genes are known to turn on at certain times in development; microRNAs show temporal- and tissue-specific patterns of gene expression (cf. Carrington & Ambros, 2003); and genes activate to trigger downstream developmental events removed in time from the triggering event (cf. Gehring & Ikeo, 1999; Marcus & Fisher, 2003). Timing mechanisms are fundamental to the way that inherited elements direct an individual's growth, whether at the cellular or organism level.

The fact that language acquisition is a developmental phenomenon that emerges in the early childhood period is a commonplace observation that is known to parents and scholars alike. The literature is full of debates about the extent to which growth in language early on is attributable to inborn, language-specialized mechanisms; inborn, generalized learning mechanisms that are heavily influenced by environmental input; or fundamental learning algorithms that are largely acquired by experience. As the contents of this volume attest, there is a growing consensus that language acquisition is guided by an exquisitely elegant interface of inherited individual aptitudes and personal experiences with other language-users. In other words, genetic influences are modulated by environmental influences. A parallel conclusion is that faulty genetic mechanisms are implicated in language impairments and characterized by breakdowns in the expected development of language.

At this early stage of formal investigation of the genetics of language (cf. Rice, 1996a), although the developmental dimension of language acquisition is so salient, there is surprisingly little in the literature about the developmental dimension of the phenotype and underlying timing mechanisms. Recently the first wave of studies established genetic influences on the basis of one-time, static classification of the phenotype, either as a categorical or quantitative phenotype. Given the current state of inquiry, this approach to phenotyping is of vital importance and is essential to progress in the identification of genotype/phenotype correlations. Current attention focuses on the need for greater precision in the language phenotype, for improved accuracy in the identification of affected children, and more precise description of the dimensions of affectedness.

In this chapter, I direct attention to the timing elements of language impairment as potentially of great import in moving us forward in our understanding of causal mechanisms and genotype/phenotype relationships. I draw on longitudinal outcomes in ongoing studies of children with specific language impairment (SLI) to demonstrate what appear to be powerful timing mechanisms at work in language impairment. Just as the developmental program of gene expression in the cells of plants and animals shows timing differences across structures and tissues, the developmental trajectory of language growth in children shows different timing mechanisms across various elements of the linguistic system. Although children with SLI can be identified on the basis of weaknesses within the linguistic system, at the same time their growth trajectories show strikingly robust parallels with the trajectories of unaffected children. It is as if the timing mechanisms are set to unfold in the same way once activated. Thus, there is a puzzling combination of developmental robustness in language acquisition coexisting with developmental weaknesses in the linguistic system for children affected with SLI. To make sense of the full picture, one must consider the following elements of linguistic growth: onset timing, configuration of the linguistic system with delineated subcomponents, acceleration rate, and points of change in the acceleration. Consideration of these elements will lead to further specificity of the language phenotype and to phenotypes that apply across different clinical conditions. It will also help with the investigation of possible etiologic subtypes attributable to genetically based timing mechanisms.

The conclusions of the chapter require some preliminary sections. First, to provide a background on language and language delays, and the design rationale for control groups, a nontechnical metaphor of language acquisition and impairments is provided. This is followed by a section describing the condition of SLI and the genetics of SLI to serve as background for the illustrative growth curves to follow and to establish the plausible relevance for genetics of language. The section on illustrative growth outcomes begins with a description of the groups of children who participated in the studies, as well as the design and interpretive rationale for observed group differences. The motivation for the language measures is laid out next, to establish a focus on finiteness and the expectation that in English-speaking children the acquisition of finiteness-marking is delayed, in the form of an Optional Infinitive period, and that this delayed period is even more extended in children with SLI (an Extended Optional Infinitive period), which leads to measures that serve as a "grammatical tense marker" that can differentiate affected from unaffected children. This section ends with a summary of what is known about the grammatical tense marker in children with autism, Down syndrome, and Williams syndrome. The core section on growth appears next, which reports on patterns of change over time in children with SLI compared with unaffected younger children. The picture that emerges is one of robust maturationally governed growth for the affected children as well as unaffected children. Yet the strengths, delays, and disruptions are referenced to linguistic distinctions, and the affected children may never reach fully adultlike competencies. A section then compares growth outcomes for children with language impairment above and below the 85 nonverbal IQ level. Although a lower IQ does not necessarily lead to low performance on the grammatical marker, in concert with language impairment it protracts growth for a longer time. Next is a discussion of timing and possible maturational mechanisms, followed by a summary of future directions for growth-focused research across clinical conditions. The chapter concludes with some implications for genetics of language impairments and future directions.

ELEMENTS OF LANGUAGE GROWTH: ONSET, CONFIGURATION OF THE LANGUAGE SYSTEM, ACCELERATION, AND RATE OF CHANGE

Just as a train has an expected configuration of engine, cars, and tracks, so does the language system. Lexical, syntactic, morphological, and computational elements must mesh together in a tightly synchronized way, roughly analogous to the alignment of cars, wheels, connections between cars, engine, drive shafts, and so on. These elements are constrained to follow a developmental trajectory, again roughly analogous to the tracks of the train that constrain the route of forward motion. As described by Phillips (chap. 11, this volume), linguists conclude that there is a common cognitive infrastructure available to children—an aptitude that enables them to acquire any of the world's languages during the early period of childhood. From this perspective, the configuration and constraints of the train's structure and path of acceleration can be thought of as this common infrastructure. The fundamental operating system and constraints are thought to be the same, although details of the train's configuration vary across languages.

Trains have an expected time of departure. This is when the acceleration mechanisms are activated. When the language train leaves on time, as in Panel A of Fig. 10.1, parents are pleased that their youngster is beginning to understand and use words; the language system is likely to emerge on the expected subsequent trajectory. For unknown reasons, however, the language train can be *delayed at departure*, as in Panel B of Fig. 10.1. Although the startup time is delayed, the train may follow the expected acceleration patterns afterward, in which case the youngster never catches up with the child whose train leaves on time. Another possibility is that the late-starting child has an unknown factor that resets the acceleration rate to catch up to the expected rate, with a subsequent deceleration to follow the expected rate. This popular model of "catch up" is in fact a complex model of growth with little known about the mechanisms that readjust rate. Intervention seems to adjust acceleration rates for at least some elements of language, as described by Warren (chap. 9, this volume), but it is not clear what the exact mechanisms would be or how or why the rates would subsequently stabilize at the normal rate following intervention.

Another scenario is shown in Panel C of Fig. 10.1, in which the language system is not only *delayed, but also disrupted* in the expected configuration. In this terminology, *disrupted* is the dictionary sense of "impeding the usual course or harmony of."[1] In this case, although the overall momentum of language growth is forward, certain elements are slowed, thereby disrupting the overall harmony. This can appear in localized elements of the language system, where perhaps coupling or computational relations between elements are not the same as the expected alignments. Such a language system could start late, and perhaps some elements might eventually catch up to those of unaffected children, or perhaps the

---

[1]In an earlier publication (Rice, 2003), I referred to this scenario as a "delay-within-a-delay" outcome. Here I adopt the *disruption* terminology as a way to encompass a broader range of phenomena that may hold beyond the classic SLI situation.

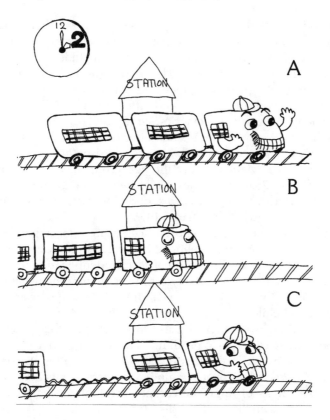

FIG. 10.1. A train metaphor of language acquisition, delays, and disruptions.

disrupted element is never fully resolved and remains out of sync for protracted periods, even into adulthood as is suggested by current evidence. In the *disrupted* scenario, it is essential to have the details about different elements of the linguistic system to capture where the system is robust, where it is delayed, and where it is disrupted. Whereas in the *delayed* system it is possible to predict one element of the linguistic system from other elements in the system according to the relationships evident in the unaffected language system, in the *disrupted* system this language-internal prediction may vary from the expected relationships.

Specific Language Impairment: Clinical Definitions

The condition of SLI is conventionally defined according to inclusionary and exclusionary criteria (cf. Leonard, 1998; also see de Villiers, 2003, for a thoughtful examination of the criteria). The inclusionary criteria establish that a child has a level of language growth that is lower than expected for his or her age. Typically, this is determined by performance on an omnibus measure of language performance, which includes a variety of language tasks, item selection by psychometric criteria (as opposed to linguistically motivated item sets), blocking of tasks by performance versus comprehension mode of response, and differentiation of tasks by major elements of language such as semantics, syntax, and/or narrative tasks. The dividing line between "normal" and "affected" is roughly at the 10th to 15th percentile of the chronological age comparison group, often defined as one standard deviation below the age group mean or a somewhat lower cutoff of −1.25 standard deviations below the age mean, which has been identified as a level that corresponds to practitioner clinical judgments (Tomblin, Records, & Zhang, 1996).

Recently, new instruments report outcomes in terms of sensitivity and specificity. Sensitivity is the likelihood of correct identification of affected children; specificity is the likelihood of correct identification of unaffected children. Sensitivity and specificity estimates require the usual reference group of a normative distribution of children of the same age and, in addition, a group of children of the same age who are identified as language impaired (cf. Rice & Wexler, 2001; see Mervis, chap. 8, this volume, for an extension of these concepts to profiling of relative cognitive strengths and weaknesses). The psychometric approach to assessment is also being supplemented by newer linguistically motivated instruments intended to target particular areas of linguistic competence that can be meaningfully compared to the adult linguistic system (cf. Rice & Wexler, 2001; Seymour, Roeper, & de Villiers, 2003; Zukowski, chap. 6, this volume). A strong advocacy for linguistically motivated instruments is put forth by de Villiers (2003), who argued for substantive advantages for defining children as affected on the basis of precisely defined linguistic deficits. All things considered, the inclusionary criteria are evolving so that we have more precise information to identify the phenotype of language impairment.

The exclusionary criteria have conventionally ruled out hearing loss, intellectual impairment, known neurological conditions, and the condition of autism. The precise purpose of the exclusionary criteria in research investigations is sometimes unclear for a particular investigation. In general, the criteria have served as a way to document the existence of language impairments in children for whom other developmental competencies are at levels thought to be sufficient for language acquisition, thereby establishing the existence of language impairment without obvious concomitant contributing conditions. Another research benefit of the exclusionary criteria is that the criteria help restrict unknown sources of error or variability within a given clinical sample, which enhances replicability and generalization of findings across studies. These exclusionary criteria are now under reexamination to determine whether there are areas of overlap between: SLI and autism, SLI and mild hearing impairment, or SLI and borderline levels of nonverbal intellectual impairment (Conti-Ramsden, Botting, & Faragher, 2001; McGuckian & Henry, 2003; Norbury, Bishop, & Briscoe, 2001; Plante, 1998; Rice et al., under review; Tager-Flusberg, chap. 3, this volume; Tager-Flusberg & Cooper, 1999).

Finally, another area of possible overlap in the clinical symptoms of SLI is the likelihood of speech impairments coexisting with language impairments. Although it was long assumed that problems with speech production and related unintelligibility of speech should be expected for children with language impairments, recent epidemiological findings establish that by 5 to 6 years of age, the estimated co-occurrence of speech and language impairments is less than 2%. For children with SLI, speech disorders were evident in approximately 5% to 8% of the children (Shriberg, Tomblin, & McSweeny, 1999; cf. Tager-Flusberg, chap. 3, this volume, for similar findings for children with autism).

Genetics of SLI

Putting aside the details of definitional issues, there is a growing body of evidence establishing a strong likelihood of genetic contributions to SLI. Case-control familial aggregation studies document aggregation for SLI probands (Rice, Haney, & Wexler, 1998; Tallal et al., 2001; Tallal, Ross, & Curtiss, 1989; Tomblin, 1989; van der Lely & Stollwerck, 1996). New findings provide explicit evidence of possible genetic influences on verb morphology deficits in 6-year-old twins. Using the experimental tasks for elicitation of third-person singular present tense -s and past tense developed by Rice and colleagues (described in further detail later), Adams and Bishop (2002) used the DeFries–Fulker analysis to investigate MZ and DZ twins. They found a shared genetic influence on these grammatical markers as predicted by Rice and Wexler (1996a), as well as evidence of heritability of nonword repetition, although the genetic influence on this trait was not shared with tense marking. In personal communication, Bishop cautioned that the bivariate analyses should be considered preliminary. The twin data join the recent identification of the *FOXP2* gene on Chromosome 7 for a large extended family in London known as "KE" (Lai, Fisher, Hurst, Vargha-Khadem, & Monaco, 2001). Although the *FOXP2* gene discovery is surely an important one, the phenotype of the affected individuals is complex, with severe oral dyspraxia, language impairments, and some individuals with limited nonverbal intelligence. Attempts to identify this gene as affected in individuals with SLI or autism have so far been unsuccessful (Meaburn, Dale, Craig, & Plomin, 2002; Newbury et al., 2002; SLI Consortium, 2002), although it is too early to rule out a possible role for *FOXP2*. A new study by O'Brien et al. (2003) reported positive association of SLI to the region of 7q31. Although no mutations were found in *FOXP2*, strong association was found on markers adjacent to *FOXP2* (one on the *CFTR* gene and one on 7q31, D7S3052). Sample sizes ranged from 58 to 164 family triads. The language phenotype was based on performance on standardized language tests at second grade, and the performance IQ level was broadened beyond the conventional level of 85 to include children at 70 or above. This raises the possibility that the inherited elements may involve the overlap of lowered IQ with language impairments. At the same time, inclusion of children with low nonverbal IQ may contribute confounding variance that obscures genetic contributions to language impairments (although Marcus & Fisher, 2003, argued this is not the case for the KE family). Meaburn et al. (2002) included low IQ children and found no connection to *FOXP2*, whereas the SLI Consortium (2002) and Newbury et al. (2002) excluded children whose nonverbal IQ was less than 80 and also found no connection.

In addition, Bartlett et al. (2002) reported a major susceptibility locus for SLI on 13q21 in a study of five Canadian pedigrees. They used three categorical phenotypic classifications: clinical diagnosis (via family history), language impairment (below normal range on a standardized omnibus language test), and reading discrepancy (nonverbal IQ minus reading level). The locus was identified using the reading phenotype, and the authors noted the difficulty in differentiating the possible role of the SLI language impairment in the reading phenotype. It is well known that there is an increased likelihood relative to controls for young children with SLI to subsequently encounter problems with reading (Catts, Fey, Tomblin, & Zhang, 2002).

At this early stage of inquiry, it continues to be important to aim for precise measurement of the phenotype for the identification of affected individuals (Smith, chap. 13, this volume). Family history methods can be inconsistent with current testing (cf. Tallal et al., 2001), language impairments that are outgrown can be missed in older children and adults, omnibus language assessments are broadly configured and may obscure important details of linguistic performance, and the current identification methods do not include developmental information.

Illustrative Growth: Description of the Child
Participants, Design, and Interpretive Rationale

The following illustrative growth data are drawn from an ongoing longitudinal study initiated in 1993 with funding from the National Institute of Deafness and Communicative Disorders (NIDCD, Award #R01 DC01803). This section provides a general description of the child participants, design, and interpretive rationale of the design. More detailed descriptions are available in Redmond and Rice (2001), Rice and Wexler (1996b), Rice, Wexler, and Cleave (1995), Rice, Wexler, and Hershberger (1998), Rice, Wexler, Marquis, and Hershberger (2000), Rice, Wexler, and Redmond (1999), Rice (2003), Rice (2000), and Rice (1997).

Child Participants.   The participants include children identified as SLI and typically developing comparison groups of children. The affected children were ascertained from clinical caseloads of speech/language pathologists. The children in the SLI group met the following exclusionary criteria at intake: no hearing loss, nonverbal IQ of 85 or above, no diagnosis of autism, no intelligibility problems with speech, a passing score on a screening test of word-final sounds used in grammatical morphology, and no known neurological impairments.

The inclusionary criteria identified children with receptive and expressive language impairments defined as follows: performance one standard deviation or more below the age group mean on the Peabody Picture Vocabulary Test–Revised (PPVT–R; Dunn & Dunn, 1981), on the Test of Language Development–Primary (TOLD–P:2; Newcomer & Hammill, 1988), and on the mean length of utterance (MLU) obtained from a spontaneous speech sample (Leadholm & Miller, 1992).

The figures reported here are from a longitudinal sample of 23 affected children followed for more than 10 years. The children were in the age range of 52 to 62 months (M = 56 months) at the initial assessment. An additional 60 children with SLI who meet the same criteria (and who do not differ from the original sample in mean levels of performance on the PPVT, TOLD–P:2, and Goldman–Fristoe Test of Articulation; Goldman & Fristoe, 1986) have subsequently been recruited and are followed longitudinally. The additional recruits to the longitudinal study have verified that the growth outcomes are characteristic of the full sample of 83 affected children, suggesting that the illustrative growth curves are likely to generalize to other groups of similarly defined children. Furthermore, the growth curves of the affected children are highly similar to those obtained from an epidemiologically ascertained group of 130 children with SLI recruited at kindergarten, which included children with only expressive or receptive disorders as well as those with expressive and receptive disorders (Rice et al., in press). Although definitive conclusions await more extensive data collection and analyses, the working conclusion here is that the illustrative growth curves of affected children (in Figs. 10.2– 10.5) are likely to be representative of many, if not most, of the children who meet a conventional definition of SLI.

Two groups of typically developing children were recruited as control groups: One was the same chronological age (age range of 52–67 months,

$M = 59$) at initial assessment, and the other was the same MLU (indexed by MLU in morphemes, although the same outcomes hold for MLU in words; range of 2.25–4.64 in the affected group, $M = 3.49$; 2.75–4.81 in the control group, $M = 3.66$). The MLU comparison group was selected on the basis of MLU, which yielded a mean age about 2 years younger than the affected group (with an age range of 30–44 months, $M = 35$ months).

A family study (Rice, Haney, & Wexler, 1998) found evidence of family aggregation in this sample. The rate of reported affectedness was higher in the SLI group (probands) than in the control children's families. About 22% of nuclear proband family members reported speech and/or language difficulties as compared with 7% of nuclear control family members; at the level of extended family (including aunts, uncles, cousins, and grandparents), the rate is 15% of proband family members versus 6% of control family members.

Design and Interpretations.   Following a widely used design in the study of SLI (cf. Leonard, 1998), the longitudinal study compared the growth of three groups: SLI, chronological age (CA) match, and language (MLU) match. The CA group allowed for documentation of: (a) the expected age-referenced growth in the target areas of language; (b) the lower level of performance of the affected group relative to age expectations on the experimental dependent outcome variables as well as the initial grouping variables; and (c) the age-referenced levels for possible catch-up for the affected group as growth occurs. To return to the train example, the CA group describes the outcome of Panel A, with a normally configured train following the usual acceleration mechanisms.

The MLU group allowed for evaluation of the train scenarios in Panels B and C. As noted earlier, if the affected group performed at levels of language similar to the younger children at the same general language levels, it is presumed that the group's performance is consistent with a *delay* in language acquisition. That is, the children have not yet overcome a late start in language acquisition, leaving them with a generally immature language system that does not show particular areas of deficit once the late start is taken into consideration (see Panel B).

In many ways, the generally immature system is the default expectation, consistent with the idea that the affected children are following the same mechanisms of language acquisition as other children, but they are slow in getting started. Under this model, the onset timing mechanisms are carrying the bulk of the interpretive weight. It is widely assumed that children with a late start will relatively quickly catch up to their age peers. About 75% of children whose first words appear later than expected— sometimes known as "late talkers"—recover from their initial delays by 6 years of age (cf. Paul, 1996; Rescorla, 1993, 2002), although the available evidence is limited to a few studies of small numbers of children, and long-term outcomes at ages 8 to 9 years are not robust. As noted earlier, such a recovery would involve a relatively complex pattern of developmental change that requires some resetting of the expected acceleration rates. The initial rate is slow, then it accelerates greater than usual, then it decelerates to the normal rate after the age-expected level is reached (otherwise the late talkers would shoot up into the range of verbally gifted, and that is not attested to by the outcome data). The timing mechanisms or environmental effects for accomplishing such adjustments in rate are not known.

The other possible scenario is depicted in Panel C of Fig. 10.1, in which some elements of language acquisition in the SLI group lag behind that of the younger MLU-equivalent group in a way that shows *disruption* of the expected language configuration. Three implications follow from this scenario. If some elements of language show even lower levels of performance than expected by a general delay, then those elements must correspond to some potential lines of cleavage in the linguistic system. Growth in unaffected children is so fast and well synchronized that it may obscure the different systems coming on-line and changing in tandem. Second, an element that lags behind other language components would be a good candidate for a clinical marker because the low levels of performance are less likely to overlap with the lower end of the normative range, allowing for clearer differentiation of affected and unaffected children (as indexed by sensitivity and specificity). Third, the genotype/phenotype correlation may be especially detectable in this element because the identification of affected individuals is more accurate.

Illustrative Growth: Grammatical Tense as a Clinical Marker

By the early 1990s, it was generally recognized that children with SLI have difficulties with morphology and verbal morphology, although morphology was widely viewed as a problem of lexical stem + affix, and surface characteristics of morphology, such as perceptual salience, were accorded a strong role in accounting for affected children's limitations (cf. Leonard, 1998). The Extended Optional Infinitive account (cf. Rice & Wexler, 1995; Rice, Wexler, & Cleave, 1995) was developed as an alternative interpretation based on developments in theoretical linguistics and the Optional Infinitive model of a stage of acquisition observed in young unaffected children (cf. Wexler, 1991, 1994, 2003). This model focuses on the grammatical features of tense and subject/verb agreement, which are involved in finiteness marking on verbs and the way these features are operative in clausal structures. Roughly speaking, each main clause in English (and many other languages) has functional projections for tense and agreement marking that are related to movement operations among clausal elements, hence the term *morphosyntax* (cf. Haegeman, 1994). In many languages, children show an acquisition period in which they produce infinitival forms of verbs where finite forms (i.e., those marked for tense and/or subject/verb agreement) are required in the adult grammar. At the same early period of word combinations, English-speaking children produce uninflected verbal forms such as "Papa have it," "Cromer wear glasses," and "Marie go." Wexler and others recognized that the uninflected verbal forms of English were the English variants of infinitives in other early child grammars, thereby unifying the observations across languages and relating the child grammars to the end-state adult grammar (cf. Guasti, 2002). Wexler referred to this period as *optional infinitive*; an alternative term is *root infinitive*. Both have come to be used descriptively without any theoretical differentiation between them. The fundamental notion is that, in some languages, young children go through a period in which they seem to treat finiteness marking as optional, although it is obligatory in the adult grammar, while they know many other properties of clausal construction. In the normative literature, the phenomenon of optional (root) infinitives has become an accepted general description of young children's grammars. It has spawned a rich and ongoing debate about the nature of the underlying linguistic representations, reasons this period is evident in some but not all languages, and the way in which finiteness is linked to other properties of clausal structure, such as null subjects and case marking (cf. Phillips, chap. 11, this volume).

The Extended Optional Infinitive (EOI) model hypothesized that the long delay in acquisition of verbal morphology by children with SLI is an extension of a phase that is part of younger children's grammatical development. It can be viewed as an enriched Extended Development Model (cf. Rice & Wexler, 1996b), which recognizes the many ways in which the language of children with SLI is similar to younger unaffected children, but with a greatly protracted period of incomplete acquisition of grammatical tense-marking. More recently, Rice (2003) reexamined the notion of language delay to note that the extended difficulties with finiteness-marking (the grammatical tense marker) have implications for explicating the nature of language impairment across clinical conditions. This in turn helps sort out the ways in which genetic and environmental etiological factors contribute to language impairments in children. In this chapter, these arguments are extended to the issue of timing mechanisms.

The EOI model focuses on a small set of morphemes in English that mark tense and agreement and are obligatory in clausal structure. They are: third-person singular present tense -*s* (e.g., *Patsy walks*); regular past tense -*ed* (e.g., *Patsy walked*); irregular past tense (e.g., *Patsy ran*); copular

BE (e.g., *Patsy is happy*); and auxiliary *BE* and *DO* (e.g., *Patsy is walking*; *Does Patsy walk?*). Note that the set of morphemes varies in that some are affixes and some are free-standing morphemes; some can move in questions (i.e., *BE* copula and auxiliary), but others cannot (i.e., third-person singular present tense; past tense) and one is uniquely inserted in questions (i.e., *DO* auxiliary). Although past tense has a salient semantic component, the other morphemes carry little or no apparent semantic weight in a clause. Instead the group of morphemes is thought to be part of a grammatical computational system that is more about grammatical well formedness than the expression of meaning.

A series of research reports from the longitudinal study documented that, as predicted individually and collectively, the finiteness-marking morphemes differentiated the performance of children with SLI from younger MLU-matched children in: spontaneous language samples, elicited production tasks, and grammaticality judgment tasks—across multiple times of measurement (cf. Redmond & Rice, 2001; Rice & Wexler, 1996b; Rice, Wexler, & Cleave, 1995; Rice, Wexler, & Hershberger, 1998; Rice, Wexler, Marquis, & Hershberger, 2000; Rice, Wexler, & Redmond, 1999). These outcomes support the theoretical assumption that this part of the grammar is to some extent a discrete component in the overall linguistic system.

These investigations are now part of a lively scientific dialogue about the EOI model and other models of SLI, children's acquisition of the set of target morphemes, and interpretation of the grammatical marker. In general, the basic finding replicated across labs is that, as a group, children with SLI perform less accurately than younger controls on morphemes associated with the grammatical marker of the EOI model, although the details vary depending on the ages of participants and the level of linguistic detail. Reports from other investigators include studies of the acquisition of copula and auxiliary *BE* and possible constraints on optionality (Grela & Leonard, 2000; Leonard, Eyer, Bedore, & Grela, 1997; Joseph, Serratrice, & Conti-Ramsden, 2002); past tense (Marchman, Wulfeck, & Ellis Weismer, 1999; Oetting & Horohov, 1997); and third-person singular present *-s* and past tense (Bedore & Leonard, 1998; Conti-Ramsden, Botting, & Faragher, 2001; Eadie, Fey, Douglas, & Parsons, 2002). Rescorla and Roberts (2002) reported that children with a history of late talking at 3 and 4 years of age show deficits relative to age controls on all four of the tense-marking morphemes they investigated in spontaneous speech samples (i.e., copula and auxiliary *BE*, auxiliary *DO*, and third-person singular present *-s*). Oetting and McDonald (2001) found that the grammatical marker is evident in children speaking various dialects of English.

These findings, and the newly available normative data from a nationally standardized assessment instrument (Rice & Wexler, 2001), demonstrate that the grammatical marker of the EOI model is evident in young children with SLI, and it appears as a delay even beyond that of a generally immature language system. As proposed early on (cf. Rice & Wexler, 1996a; Tager-Flusberg & Cooper, 1999), the grammatical marker of the EOI is shaping up as a solid clinical marker of language impairments in children with SLI and a good candidate for a phenotype as demonstrated by the findings of Adams and Bishop (2002).

Grammatical Tense Marker in Other Clinical Populations.   Studies of the grammatical tense marker in other clinical conditions show patterns of relative strength and limitations. Tager-Flusberg and colleagues explored the marker in children with autism and found that language-impaired children with autism performed below nonlanguage-impaired children with autism on the same elicitation tasks used in the Rice et al. studies for past tense and third-person singular -*s* (Roberts, Rice, & Tager-Flusberg, in press). In a comparison study of nonlanguage-impaired children with autism, language-impaired children with autism, and children with SLI matched for nonverbal IQ and MLU, they found that the two language-impaired groups were below normal levels on the third-person singular -*s* and not below normal on other morphemes (tense-marking and nontense-marking) although the children were as old as 13 years (Condouris, Evancie, & Tager-Flusberg, 2002).

Studies of children with Down syndrome have documented that these youngsters are likely to perform below mental age on general language tests and more poorly on the morphology and syntax subtests than on vocabulary subtests (cf. Abbeduto & Murphy, chap. 5, this volume). Eadie et al. (2002) examined the grammatical tense marker and control morphemes in spontaneous language samples in 10 children with Down syndrome, 10 children with SLI, and 10 normal controls matched for MLU. They concluded that the SLI profile is similar to that of children with Down syndrome. Unexpectedly, the performance on the tense-marking morphemes did not differ from the control morphemes for either group—an outcome attributable to somewhat anomalous findings for certain morphemes, which in turn are possibly attributable to problems of sampling validity in the spontaneous language samples. Although the study needs to be replicated, it is well motivated and points in the direction of appropriate future studies.

Children with Williams syndrome show a contrasting profile. Rice, Mervis, Klein, and Rice (1999; also reported in Rice, 2003) compared the grammatical marker in samples of children with Williams syndrome matched for MLU to the longitudinal SLI children and younger control children studied by Rice and colleagues as reported in the growth curves in this chapter. The samples were compared at the first time of measurement when the SLI children were 5 years of age, younger controls were 3 years, and the WMS group was a mean of 7.7 years. The outcomes show that the performance of the WMS group was at higher levels than the SLI and younger controls and, in fact, were at levels similar to the 5-year-old unaffected group—near ceiling. In short, the WMS group's mean level of performance on the grammatical marker was near adult levels of competence, although their MLU was like unaffected children 3 years of age.

Although comparison of performance on the grammatical tense marker across clinical conditions is at an early stage of investigation, these early findings clearly show that this part of the grammar can be selectively spared or impaired relative to other levels of language growth. Many details remain to be explored regarding the ways in which morphosyntax is acquired across different conditions of language impairment.

Illustrative Growth of Grammatical Tense Marking: Patterns of Change Over Time of Affected and Unaffected Younger Children

Let us begin the discussion of growth in the age range of 3 to 8 years, which corresponds to the time in which English-speaking children move from optional to obligatory when they use the morphemes of interest in the clinical grammatical marker as part of simple clauses, including the extended period for the children with SLI. In this age range, growth in the grammatical marker is essentially completed in unaffected English-speaking children by ages 4 to 4;6. Recall that the affected children and chronological age controls were ages 4;6 to 5;6 at the start of the study. Because the age control group was, as expected, at adultlike ceiling levels, no growth is apparent. Therefore, the groups of interest for growth are the affected group and the younger MLU-equivalent group.

Delays in Utterance Length and Vocabulary Growth. A delay model predicts that the affected children would track alongside the younger children in general indexes of language acquisition. This is apparent in the utterance length of spontaneous utterances and semantic development. Figure 10.2 shows a schematized rendering of the group means as a function of age. The semantic measure is a child's raw score on the PPVT–R (a measure of receptive vocabulary on a picture-pointing task), which was administered annually; the utterance length (MLU-morph) was measured in 6-month intervals (see Figs. 2.14 and 2.15 of Rice, 2003, for actual means and range of performance per group per time of measurement). In Fig. 10.2, there is no scale on the Y axis because the actual levels of performance on the two variables are in different ranges (mean PPVT-raw scores are from 25–90 in this time period, and mean MLU levels are 3.5–4.8). Two empirical generalizations are of interest here: (a) For both variables, the two groups start at equivalent levels and remain at equiva-

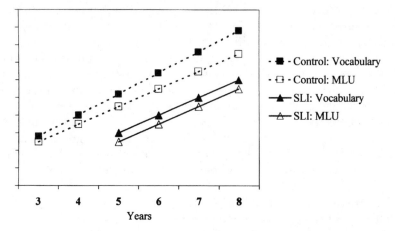

FIG. 10.2. Growth in receptive vocabulary and MLU for children with SLI and unaffected children.

lent levels throughout this 3-year period; and (b) the trajectories of growth for the two variables are highly similar and generally linear in nature.

With regard to the first generalization, recall that the MLU group was selected for equivalence to the affected group on the MLU measure, so it is not surprising that at the initial time of measurement the MLUs are in fact equivalent. The age of the younger group was not controlled beyond the constraint that children below 2;6 were not likely to complete the experimental tasks, thereby excluding very young children at equivalent MLUs. Empirically, the MLU-equivalent group turned out to be almost exactly 2 years younger than the SLI group—an outcome that is replicated repeatedly in my lab and in other investigators' studies.

There is controversy regarding the use of MLU as a matching variable because it is thought to be unstable (cf. Eisenberg, Fersko, & Lundgren, 2001). On the contrary, our outcome data show that it is in fact quite stable. As illustrated in Fig. 10.2, it remains at equivalent levels of performance with the affected group for years. Rice, Rice, and Redmond (2000) and Redmond, Rice, Haney, and Hoffman (under review) reported that at each time of measurement the group means do not differ statistically. Furthermore, the groups do not differ in growth trajectories. Redmond, Rice, Haney, and Hoffman (under review) reported neither group effects nor group interactions in the growth terms of individual growth curve modeling, which shows a strong linear component and a relatively weak quadratic component attributable to a slight leveling effect at the upper levels for the affected group.

Methodological diligence may have contributed to the documentation of stable growth in MLU (cf. Mervis, chap. 8, this volume). A relatively stringent equivalency criterion was used for grouping (i.e., a candidate child for the MLU group had to obtain MLU-morph within .10 of at least one child in the affected group). The same spontaneous sample elicitation contexts were maintained over time, involving interactive play with age-appropriate toy materials. Examiners were carefully trained to eliminate possible sources of error in data collection (such as too many yes/no questions on the part of examiners; cf. Johnston, 2001). Transcription and coding conventions were explicitly documented and maintained. Intercoder reliability was consistently monitored to minimize coding errors.

Overall, the MLU growth outcomes can be summarized as follows: The SLI group is 2 years behind the expected growth levels in utterance length and remains 2 years behind during the period of 5 to 8 years. Furthermore, although displaced by 2 years, the growth in the affected children follows the same generally linear trajectory as the younger unaffected children.

Turning our attention to semantic growth, another unplanned empirical outcome of the matching design is that the groups' performance on the PPVT–R raw scores at time of entry, as shown in Fig. 10.2, is equivalent and remains so at each time of measurement (Rice, Rice, & Redmond, 2000). Models of individual growth curves (Redmond, Rice, Haney, & Hoffman, under review) differ somewhat from the outcomes for MLU, with a group × linear interaction such that there is a slight tilt in the growth trajectory for the younger children; they start a bit lower and end a bit higher than the affected children. The major growth elements, however, are linear for both groups.

Taking into consideration the two variables, my working conclusions are: Utterance length and semantic development are in close alignment throughout this age period, and the SLI group is 2 years behind the expected growth levels and remains 2 years behind during the period of 5 to 8 years. Furthermore, although displaced by 2 years, growth in the affected children follows the same generally linear trajectory as the younger unaffected children (with a small adjustment in the slope of the receptive vocabulary growth to show slightly greater growth in the younger group). Thus, growth in the SLI group clearly follows a language delay trajectory in these two important indicators of language growth, with no indication of catch up during this period.

Growth Complexities in Morphosyntax and Morphology.   Consideration of other elements of language growth shows that more is involved than a simple delay of an inherently highly synchronized language system. Consider Fig. 10.3, which plots the growth in grammatical tense marking in simple clauses for the two groups in terms of percentage correct use and contrasts growth in tense marking with that in regular plural -*s* during the same time period. The regular plural affix (e.g., *hats*) has

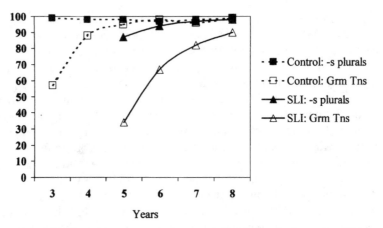

FIG. 10.3.   Growth in grammatical tense marking in simple clauses for children with SLI and unaffected children compared with -s plurals.

been of interest because it is phonetically similar to the third-person singular present tense -s, and presumably similar learning mechanisms
would be involved in acquisition (cf. Leonard, 1998). If growth in the two
morphemes followed similar trajectories, it would be consistent with the
idea that affected children had problems learning morphological rules for
affixation, in general, and/or they had selective difficulties with certain
morphemes that could be less salient such as -s. Although as an explanation there are many appealing elements of this interpretation, the empirical outcomes are not supportive.

As shown in Fig. 10.3, at the same time that the affected children have
mastered plural -s (at levels of 90% or above accuracy), they continue to
sometimes use finiteness markers in obligatory contexts in simple clauses
and sometimes omit them. The variable plotted for grammatical tense
marking is the proportion of finiteness markers collapsed across the full
set of morphemes that carry out this function (i.e., third-person singular
present tense -s, past-tense regular and irregular, BE and DO). The same
general growth curve holds for each of the individual morphemes (cf.
Rice, Wexler, & Hershberger, 1998), including third-person singular present tense -s.

It is clear that the growth of plural -s and third-person singular present
tense -s is not synchronized (although the morphemes marking finiteness
are correlated throughout this period). Of course it is possible that growth
of plural -s for the affected children follows a delay pattern linked with the
younger children at an earlier period of development; this delay is resolved by the observed age levels. As suggested by Leonard (1998), there
could be a semantic advantage for plural marking, which makes it conceptually useful or salient for a child to master. In this case, plural marking

might follow the general delay pattern associated with utterance length and early semantic development, although the delay would only be detectable at earlier ages. However, the most obvious elements that are shared by the two different -s affixes (i.e., similar phonology and learned patterns of affixation) do not account for the markedly different growth pattern for the grammatical tense marker.

It is clear from Fig. 10.3 that, as expected by the Extended Optional Infinitive account, growth of finiteness marking for unaffected English-speaking children is relatively delayed, and it is even more delayed in the SLI group. Of interest here is that the growth trajectories are strikingly similar for the two groups, involving relatively strong quadratic elements with shifts in acceleration.

At the same time, the grammatical marker's growth curve of the affected children lags below that of the younger children and traces lower levels of performance throughout (see Rice, Wexler, & Hershberger, 1998; Rice, Wexler, Marquis, & Hershberger, 2000, for detailed reports of Hierarchical Linear Modeling of Growth). The bends in the curve are not marked by chronological age, but by relative position in the growth curve. It is as if the train left the station late for the affected children, but a particular component was delayed even further; once activated, it followed the same plan for change as the younger children.

This is really quite amazing given that the affected children are considerably older and have experiences that are meaningfully different from the controls. All the affected children were enrolled in intervention at the initial time of measurement and had therefore been identified for special services. Presumably the intervention activities would have greatly enriched a child's language experiences even if the targeted morphemes were not explicit intervention goals. The children were enrolled in kindergarten to third grade during this time, when the younger children were in preschool experiences and lagging behind 2 years in the grades. Affected children are more likely to encounter social rejection from peers (Gertner, Rice, & Hadley, 1994), be somewhat introverted (Redmond & Rice, 2002) or somewhat aggressive (Tomblin, Zhang, Buckwalter, & Catts, 2000), and encounter difficulties learning to read (the mean levels of reading performance for this group of affected children also lag below that of their age comparison group throughout the elementary grades). The children in our study were not drawn from the same schools and attendance centers, but rather were distributed across a wide array of school settings. A wide range of socioeconomic circumstances is represented in the sample. All in all, there are no apparent experiential similarities that can account for the robust mirroring of the unaffected growth pattern in affected children. Instead there would be reason to think that the affected children would either catch up (as an unspecified default outcome) or labor along in a compensated learning approach to the problem presumably manifested in a mostly linear trajectory, one step at a time. Neither of those plausibly assumed outcomes proved to be true.

It would be misleading to conclude that the disrupted delay evident in growth toward obligatory use of finiteness markers means that the affected children have a generally weak understanding of morphosyntax. At the same time that they persist in omitting the targeted forms, it is rare that they make errors involving misuse of the forms. They are very unlikely to make mistakes like: "tomorrow I am going to walked my dog," "I walks home," "he do wants a cookie," "is he want a cookie?", "where is he want a cookie?", "does they happy?", or "he not is going." Laborious documentation of the children's errors reveals that although errors of this sort occasionally appear, such errors are rare (<1%) given the number of opportunities for error—a generalization that holds for both groups. Grammaticality judgment data provide further evidence of selective grammatical weakness combined with robustness. Although the affected children are likely to accept as okay the statement "he eat toast" (an utterance they are likely to produce), they are likely to reject "I drinks milk" (an utterance they are unlikely to produce; Rice, Wexler, & Redmond, 1999). Just as the train in the acquisition metaphor does not wander off on all possible trajectories, it is as if the children are constrained to a limited set of possibilities. As they are working out grammatical tense marking, their utterances conform to this set of constraints.

The list of linguistic constraints is surprisingly long and substantive. It includes word order, knowledge of finiteness constraints (such as one site per main clause with no more than one occupant of the site), relationships among functional elements (such as the constraint in English that will not allow a lexical verb to move forward to form a question in the way that copular and auxiliary *BE* can move from the clause internal position in a declarative, and instead *DO* must be inserted, but *DO* is not used in questions with predicate adjectives or with the progressive ending on the lexical verb), and knowledge of subject–verb agreement (such as knowing that third-person singular *-s* cannot be applied to subjects carrying first- or second-person or plurals, and the forms of *BE* and *DO* must conform to the person/number markings on the subject). The affected children seem to be as adept in avoiding these kinds of errors as are the unaffected children. It is difficult to measure this kind of growth, but there is obviously a great deal of growth in morphosyntax at the same time that the grammatical tense marker is apparent. To be complete, any proposed models of language impairment in children with SLI must account for not only the selectivity of grammatical tense marking, but also the apparent sparing of related fundamental properties of morphosyntax.

Growth Plateaus Beyond 8 Years. One possibility is that the affected children do eventually catch up to younger children, somewhere beyond 8 years of age. The tasks for the children younger than 8 years have focused on simple declaratives, such as "he is sleepy" or "a dentist fixes teeth." To explore later growth, we turned our attention to simple questions where finiteness marking appears in the *BE* and *DO* forms that precede the subject (Rice & Wexler, 2000). The EOI model predicts that just as the children regard the use of *BE* copula and auxiliary as optional in declaratives, they will also regard them as optional in questions, where there is the additional requirement of movement to the left of the subject. This prediction was evaluated in judgment tasks, with items such as "what do you like to eat/what you like to eat?" and "what is she saying?/ what she saying?" The outcomes are presented in Fig. 10.4 in terms of A' values, which are adjusted for a tendency of children to say "yes" and are roughly interpretable as percentage correct. It is apparent that well before 8 years almost all growth in this judgment has occurred for unaffected children, although the affected children are not at ceiling and instead level off in a plateau some 10 to 15 points lower than the control children—a gap that persists through 14 years of age.

Following the assumption that the question data are an upward extension of the earlier finiteness-marking growth curve, the picture suggests that the affected children may never reach fully robust competencies in this area of the grammar, although they now show many areas of linguistic competency and adherence to subtle linguistic constraints. It is as if the

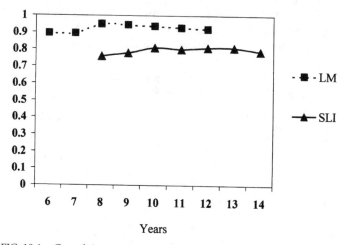

FIG. 10.4. Growth in grammatical tense marking in questions for children with SLI and unaffected language-matched children.

growth mechanisms are programmed to follow the expected track and rate, but the train never quite makes it to the destination.

Growth With Language Impairment Above and Below 85 Nonverbal IQ

As noted earlier, there is great interest in examining the ways in which the condition of SLI is manifest if the exclusionary criteria are relaxed to include children in the borderline level of nonverbal intelligence. Figure 10.5 illustrates data from a recent study by Rice et al. (in press), which followed children epidemiologically ascertained at kindergarten (Tomblin et al., 1997). The children were grouped into categories of: unaffected age controls ($N = 117$ at kindergarten; 24 in the longitudinal sample); SLI, defined as having receptive or expressive language deficits with a criterion of 1.25 standard deviations below the mean ($N = 130$ at kindergarten, 57 longitudinal); nonspecific language impairments (NLI), defined as language impaired with nonverbal intelligence levels below 85 (mostly in the 70–85 range with a few children below 70; $N = 100$ at kindergarten, 54 longitudinal); and low cognition (LC; $N = 73$ at kindergarten, 16 longitudinal), or children who performed below 85 nonverbal IQ but whose language performance was above the criteria for impairment.

The children were assessed annually for 5 years on two picture-elicitation tasks to estimate the grammatical tense marker—one for regular and irregular past tense and the other for third-person singular present tense -s. Figure 10.5 reports the composite of the tasks for each time of measurement. Several things are immediately clear. One is that the growth curve for the SLI group is similar to that of the Kansas sample of Fig. 10.3, suggesting that the pattern of growth is evident across modest

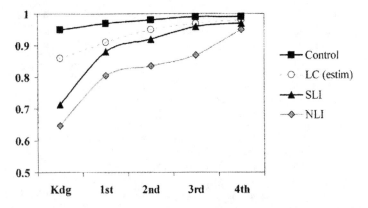

FIG. 10.5.   Growth in grammatical tense marking for control, SLI, NLI, and LC groups.

variations in definition of the grouping criteria. Second, as expected, the control group stays at ceiling levels throughout. Third, the NLI children, with lower levels of nonverbal IQ, follow a growth trajectory similar to that of the SLI group; growth curve modeling reveals linear, quadratic, and cubic elements for the composite score for both groups.[2] Finally, the LC group shows a much higher level of performance. Because so many of the LC children were at or near ceiling on the tasks in kindergarten, only the low-scoring members of the group were followed longitudinally. What is displayed in Fig. 10.5 is a best estimate of the full trajectory for the full group.

These group comparisons suggest that, just as the SLI group presumably starts later and lags below their age peers, the NLI group is even further behind. It is tempting to attribute the lower language performance to the lower nonverbal IQ levels of the NLI group, but the performance of the LC group provides counterevidence to that interpretation. The LC group demonstrates that some children with low nonverbal IQs nevertheless perform well on the grammatical tense marker. Thus, low IQ is neither necessary nor sufficient for language impairment or, more particularly, low performance on the grammatical tense marker (cf. Tager-Flusberg, chap. 3, this volume; Mervis, chap. 8, this volume; Zukowski, chap. 6, this volume). Instead it seems that deficits in grammatical tense marking and low nonverbal IQ are additive independent elements, such that if both are present growth is slower. The NLI group requires 2 years more than the SLI group to come to ceiling levels on the grammatical marker. Yet the way growth unfolds is remarkably similar, with the addition of an apparent acceleration burst around 9 to 10 years of age for the NLI group.

Timing and Possible Maturational Mechanisms

There is a strong impression of maturational mechanisms at work in these observed growth patterns for typical development and in nonsyndromic language impairment (i.e., SLI and NLI). In the age ranges observed, the timing mechanisms differ by linguistic subcomponents, with obvious differences between the general dimensions of growth in utterance length and semantic/vocabulary acquisition, and that of the grammatical marker in the morphosyntax domain. In these areas, timing patterns show invariance once activated, involving a change in acceleration leading to

---

[2]At the level of linguistic details, there are indications of differences between the SLI and NLI groups in growth for irregular past tense, with only a linear element for the NLI group and an additional small quadratic element for the SLI group. This suggests some qualitative differences may apply to certain elements of linguistic growth in the NLI group, particularly in the phonological learning needed to master exceptions to phonologically regular morphemes (see Rice et al., under review, for discussion).

relatively rapid growth, followed by a final phase of deceleration to arrive at asymptote. As noted earlier in the chapter, this story requires consideration of onset, configuration of the language system, acceleration, points of change, and slope (rate of change). A full account is not complete without considering the ways in which the linguistic system is robust, especially in the form of subtle but powerful morphosyntactic constraints that block errors and inform judgments.

There are precedents for maturational models of language acquisition, most notably that of Lenneberg (1967), a biological model ahead of its time. Wexler (2003) proposed a contemporary maturational model in which he argued that children are genetically prepared to acquire the configurational properties and associated principles of linguistic structure. He followed a slightly modified full competency model, in which children are presumed to have the same set of fundamental linguistic principles and constraints as adults. This assumption avoids the problem of how a child system later switches over to an adult system (cf. Phillips, chap. 11, this volume). Wexler's model also assumes learning components that are operative to allow a child to deduce properties of the input language at the level of parameters of possible cross-linguistic variation, and with regard to the phonological ways in which a given language represents words and morphemes. His assumptions, and those of other full competency theorists, account for the strong role of constraints in the acquisition of morphosyntax (and other elements of language).

Wexler (2003) proposed that the particular delay in finiteness marking is attributable to a discrete constraint that children follow, the Unique Checking Constraint (UCC), formulated within a generative framework of grammar (Chomsky, 1995). Essentially, the notion is that early in acquisition children employ a single computational operation where two operations are required. Under maturational control, the UCC withers away leaving the two-operation checking procedure of the adult grammar. The UCC and its associated theoretical framework accounts for a variety of linguistic phenomena related to finiteness marking and the ways that this system emerges differently across different languages.[3] The UCC model is the topic of lively discussion, debate, and challenge from counterproposals (cf. Borer & Rohrbacher, 2002; Guasti, 2002; Phillips, chap. 11, this volume).

---

[3]In languages such as French and Spanish, young unaffected children do not display the protracted period of acquisition that is evident in English, but it appears that French-speaking SLI children do follow a prolonged growth trajectory that makes their development even more behind that of their age peers than English-speaking SLI children (cf. Paradis, Crago, Genesee, & Rice, 2003; see de Villiers, 2003, for discussion of cross-linguistic issues).

Although many of the technical linguistic details are yet to be worked out, a maturational model of this sort accounts for the major findings in the growth curves presented here (i.e., why general elements of language acquisition can show a language delay in children with SLI, but some other elements shear off for a more protracted acquisition period). I have three observations in this regard. First, once activated, growth seems to be invariant in trajectory. Second, robust elements of morphosyntax are evident at the same time that other elements are greatly delayed. Third, a particular element of morphosyntax can be relatively robust in individuals with low levels of nonverbal IQ while it can be combined with a low level of nonverbal IQ to create a double burden in development. These observations align if we assume that children are equipped with powerful language insights that are comprised of differentiable linguistic elements, and such elements can play out according to different onset triggers and growth trajectories. This does not eliminate a role for environmental modulations or general learning mechanisms, but it does suggest that genetically guided language-specific onset and growth mechanisms play a powerful role.

Relevant maturational models also exist in the area of reading disabilities, where growth issues similar to those raised in this chapter have been addressed. A big issue has been whether poor readers eventually catch up in the form of a developmental lag or whether they demonstrate a deficit, which leads to a plateau level below age expectations from which they do not recover. Francis et al. (1996) studied this question with longitudinal reading outcomes data. With growth curves not greatly different from that of the grammatical tense marker illustrated earlier, they concluded that the developmental deficit model held, characterized by quadratic growth, to a plateau. They operationalized the difference between the two models as follows:

> the notion of developmental lag could be operationalized as a difference in the age at which two groups reach their final level of performance. In contrast, the notion of developmental deficit was operationalized as a difference in the final level of performance and may or may not be associated with any lag in development. (p. 14)

In analyses of individual growth curves assuming a start point of 8 years, they noted that there were no differences between the groups in the age at which scores reached a plateau thereby supporting the developmental deficit model. In contrast, the grammatical tense growth curves reported here show strong indications of developmental lag prior to 8 years, and probable developmental deficit beyond 8 years of age. Francis et al. (1996) called for the incorporation of longitudinal assessments into the diagnostic process for identifying children with poor reading skills—a suggestion I return to later.

Of course growth in reading and in the morphosyntax of language have obvious differences in that reading is explicitly taught in formal educational settings, whereas morphosyntax is spontaneously acquired by young children without explicit instruction. Reading impairments have known genetic contributions (cf. Smith, chap. 13, this volume), and reading impairments are also known to be closely associated with language impairments. As suggested by Bartlett et al. (2002), perhaps SLI and dyslexia share the same gene loci as indicated in the region of 13q (see Smith, chap. 13, this volume). If particular genes affect both phenotypes, perhaps these genes are also involved in the timing mechanisms that the phenotypes share.

GROWTH TRAJECTORIES FOR LANGUAGE IMPAIRMENTS ACROSS CLINICAL CONDITIONS: FUTURE DIRECTIONS FOR RESEARCH

These examples of language growth in children with SLI and NLI point toward possibly fruitful approaches to determine the ways in which language impairment can be manifest across a wide range of clinical conditions. What we should aim for is an enhanced understanding of the exact nature of language impairment, in the form of knowing about the elements of language growth that can be compromised, and the pattern of growth. As the chapters in this volume attest, there is no doubt that various elements of language can be spared while others are affected. What we need to know is the way the linguistic system comes on-line, the extent to which the "linguistic train" components are well synchronized, and the expected end state relative to the adult grammar.

The observations of developmental growth and linguistic issues raised in this chapter suggest a series of questions to be answered about the way that language impairment is manifest across different clinical conditions and if the symptoms hold across individuals within a particular diagnostic category. These questions lay out as follows:

1. Is onset delayed?
2. Is speech/phonology affected?
3. Is vocabulary growth in line with age expectations or at lower levels?
4. Do nonfiniteness-marking morphemes appear when expected, such as plurals and progressives?

5. Does the grammatical tense marker appear when expected?
6. Are there signs of disrupted grammatical systems, such as errors of word order, errors of subject–verb agreement, or errors of form choice (such as confusion of BE and DO)?
7. Is growth following the expected trajectory for given elements of the language system?
8. Does growth plateau before expected levels of acquisition?
9. Is growth synchronized across elements of language, or are there unexpected areas of growth delay or disruption?
10. Are the predictors of growth as expected?
11. Does intervention lead to a change in acceleration of growth in a given domain?

This list is not meant to be exhaustive, but answers to these questions allow us to:

1. Confirm that a delayed onset is characteristic of language impairment in general, although a delayed onset is not diagnostic of subsequent language impairment (as shown by the Late Talker outcomes). Of course it is important that measures of delayed onset are obtained at the time of the delay. As noted by Lord et al. (chap. 2, this volume), retrospective reports by parents are subject to error.

2. Determine the co-morbidity of language and speech impairments at the time that language emerges. This information is much needed for the early period, across clinical conditions, to further sort out the speech and language phenotypes (cf. the KE family and the work on FOXP2).

3. Determine whether a general language delay is the default condition for language impairments. This is at least a plausible first hypothesis that entails the assumption that the language acquisition mechanisms are robust in human children, but they can be slow in activation.

4. Determine whether there are particular weaknesses or strengths in vocabulary development, general morphology, and/or grammatical tense marking (or other linguistic properties). An EOI period could be characteristic of some, but not all, forms of language impairment, or it could be characteristic of relatively mild forms of language impairment such as SLI, in which the semantic and general morphological components of language are developing but the grammatical tense-marking system is much more delayed. At the same time, it is clearly the case that in some forms of language impairment, such as Williams syndrome, the morphosyntactic system is relatively robust.

5. Determine whether there is a disrupted grammatical system as manifest by unexpected grammatical errors. Such errors imply that the under-

lying linguistic constraints and principles are affected. Fundamental disruptions to grammatical systems are of considerable theoretical interest, although seldom documented (cf. van der Lely, 2003, and the diagnosis of a grammatical subtype of SLI characterized by a representational deficit for dependent relations in a selected sample of adolescents).

6. Determine whether linguistic growth is well synchronized and the pattern of growth for different elements of the linguistic system. If growth is flat or decelerating to earlier levels, this would be a red flag for serious concerns about neurocortical integrity because it is a profound violation of the powerful growth mechanisms at work in language acquisition (cf. Lord et al., chap. 2, this volume). Further study is needed to confirm the growth patterns reported in this chapter and the apparent differences in growth trajectories across the different linguistic domains. To echo the suggestion of Francis et al. (1996), growth indexes would be powerful identifiers of language impairment. We need to know whether children with a given clinical condition are likely to start late and then show a strong acceleration, as seems to be the case for children with Williams syndrome, or if they start late and instead follow a slow rate of change without subsequent changes in acceleration—a profile with a guarded prognosis for arriving at the adult grammar. We need to know what is triggering the points of change (i.e., the biochemical, neurocortical, or environmental events associated with these points of change). Without detailed longitudinal records we will not be able to identify these crucially important components of language impairment and possible ways to reset delayed or defective growth.

7. Determine the ways in which intervention leads to an acceleration of linguistic growth and optimal timing for targeted intervention. Knowledge of the expected growth trajectory in various areas of language are immensely helpful in planning for intervention. The fact that grammatical tense marking is a relatively late acquisition in English-speaking children, and is even more protracted in children with SLI, means that it is probably not an appropriate early goal for language intervention in young children with language impairments. A fruitful intervention strategy would be to look for maturational change points, the time at which the obligatory use begins to increase, and then build on this point of change to further enhance acquisition.

Implications for Genetics of Language Impairments

The chapter opened with reference to current studies of genetically controlled timing mechanisms at the cellular level as well as for organs such as eye structure and even entire organisms. Although the maturational mechanisms advocated by Lenneberg (1967) seemed rather far-fetched at the time, the existence of such mechanisms is now well attested by modern genetics. Marcus and Fisher (2003) discussed how the *FOXP2* gene regulates a wide range of cellular development and is one element of a complex pathway involving multiple genes that, among other things, controls the development of brain structures. They described a gene with pervasive developmental effects that is linked to a relatively specific phenotype of higher order cognitive functioning in the form of speech and language impairment. Marcus and Fisher speculated that the consequences of disruption to a gene are expressed in separate systems, and the gene provides "an entry-point into the relevant neural pathway (or pathways), by pointing to the downstream targets which it regulates or the proteins with which it interacts" (p. 262).

As shown by Bailey et al. (chap. 7, this volume), investigation of the genetics of some of the clinical conditions associated with language impairment, such as fragile X, is already focused on the proteomics of genetic expression. It is not at all far-fetched to imagine that within the foreseeable future more will be known about regulatory genes and protein expression in various conditions of language impairment.

Although specification of the phenotype is important in determining genetic effects—a specific phenotype does not entail a discrete gene/phenotype connection. Just as the genetic contributions to reading impairments are thought to be at the level of underlying neurocognitive structures essential for reading skill, so the genetic contributions to particular linguistic elements, such as grammatical tense marking, surely are at more abstract levels than a child's knowledge of when to say *walked* instead of *walk*. Instead the omitted finiteness markers are thought to indicate fundamental properties of underlying linguistic representations consistent with universal properties of linguistic structures and principles, which in turn are expressed in neurocognitive pathways (cf. Rice, 1996b; Wexler, 1996; Phillips, chap. 11, this volume).

Inclusion of growth indicators in the phenotype of language impairment, and evaluation of possible phenotype/genotype correlations for different growth patterns, would be useful for adding greater precision to estimates of genetic contributions and for inferring time-controlled gene expression that may operate across different elements of language in different ways. In turn, this would greatly enhance our understanding of environmental influences, the points in development when such influences might be most powerful, and how to design intervention programs to make maximal use of developmental trajectory. The search for this information will be greatly facilitated by cooperative study across the wide range of clinical conditions in which language impairments appear, just as the benefits of improved intervention strategies would be applicable to a wide range of affected children.

ACKNOWLEDGMENTS

Preparation of this chapter was supported by grants from the National Institute of Deafness and Communicative Disorders (R01 DC01803 and R01 DC05226). Appreciation goes to Allen Richman and Lesa Hoffman for assistance with data analyses and to Patsy Woods and Joy Simpson for assistance with manuscript preparation. I wish to thank the many families and children who have participated in the studies and the many practitioners and school systems who make data collection possible. Special appreciation goes to a great team of research staff, doctoral students, and assistants who have collected and coded data over the 10 years represented in the results reported here. Finally, I wish to express gratitude to Ken Wexler for his collaboration and unwavering advocacy for maturational mechanisms at work in language acquisition.

REFERENCES

Adams, C. V., & Bishop, D. V. M. (2002, July). *Genetic influences on verb morphology deficits in 6-year-old twins*. Poster presented at the joint conference of the International Association for the Study of Child Language and the Symposium for Research on Children with Language Disorders, Madison, WI.

Bartlett, C. W., Flax, J. F., Logue, M., Vieland, V. J., Bassett, A. S., Tallal, P., & Brzustowicz, L. M. (2002). A major susceptibility locus for specific language impairment is located on 13q21. *American Journal of Human Genetics, 71*, 45–55.

Bedore, L. M., & Leonard, L. B. (1998). Specific language impairment and grammatical morphology: A discrimination function analysis. *Journal of Speech, Language, and Hearing Research, 41*, 1185–1192.

Borer, H., & Rohrbacher, B. (2002). Minding the absent: Arguments for the full competence hypothesis. *Language Acquisition, 10*, 123–175.

Carrington, J. C., & Ambros, V. (2003). Role of MicroRNAs in plant and animal development. *Science, 301*, 336–338.

Catts, H. W., Fey, M. E., Tomblin, J. B., & Zhang, X. (2002). A longitudinal investigation of reading outcomes in children with language impairments. *Journal of Speech, Language, and Hearing Research, 45*, 1142–1157.

Chomsky, N. (1995). *The minimalist program*. Cambridge, MA: MIT Press.

Condouris, K., Evancie, L., & Tager-Flusberg, H. (2002, November). *Tense error patterns in children with autism and children with SLI*. International Meeting for Autism Research, Orlando, FL.

Conti-Ramsden, G., Botting, N., & Faragher, B. (2001). Psycholinguistic markers for specific language impairment (SLI). *Journal of Child Psychology and Psychiatry, 42*, 741–748.

de Villiers, J. (2003). Defining SLI: A linguistic perspective. In Y. Levy & J. Schaeffer (Eds.), *Language competence across populations: Toward a definition of specific language impairment* (pp. 425–447). Mahwah, NJ: Lawrence Erlbaum Associates.

Dunn, A., & Dunn, A. (1981). *Peabody Picture Vocabulary Test–Revised*. Circle Pines, MN: American Guidance Service.

Eadie, P. A., Fey, M. E., Douglas, J. M., & Parsons, C. L. (2002). Profiles of grammatical morphology and sentence imitation in children with specific language impairment and Down syndrome. *Journal of Speech, Language and Hearing Research, 45,* 720–732.

Eisenberg, S. L., Fersko, T. M., & Lundgren, C. (2001). The use of MLU for identifying language impairment in preschool children: A review. *American Journal of Speech-Language Pathology, 10,* 323–342.

Francis, D. J., Shaywitz, S. E., Stuebing, K. K., Shaywitz, B. A., & Fletcher, J. M. (1996). Developmental lag versus deficit models of reading disability: A longitudinal, individual growth curves analysis. *Journal of Educational Psychology, 88,* 3–17.

Gehring, W. J., & Ikeo, K. (1999). Pax 6: Mastering eye morphogenesis and eye evolution. *Trends in Genetics, 15,* 371–377.

Gertner, B. L., Rice, M. L., & Hadley, P. A. (1994). The influence of communicative competence on peer preferences in a preschool classroom. *Journal of Speech and Hearing Research, 37,* 913–923.

Goldman, R., & Fristoe, M. (1986). *The Goldman-Fristoe Test of Articulation.* Circle Pines, MN: American Guidance Service.

Grela, B. G., & Leonard, L. B. (2000). The influence of argument structure complexity on the use of auxiliary verbs by children with SLI. *Journal of Speech, Language and Hearing Research, 43,* 1115–1125.

Guasti, M. T. (2002). *Language acquisition: The growth of grammar.* Cambridge, MA: MIT Press.

Haegeman, L. (1994). *Introduction to government and binding theory.* Cambridge, MA: Blackwell.

Johnston, J. R. (2001). An alternate MLU calculation: Magnitude and variability of effects. *Journal of Speech, Language and Hearing Research, 44,* 156–164.

Joseph, K. L., Serratrice, L., & Conti-Ramsden, G. (2002). Development of copula and auxiliary BE in children with specific language impairment and younger unaffected controls. *First Language, 22,* 137–172.

Lai, C. S. L., Fisher, S. E., Hurst, J. A., Vargha-Khadem, F., & Monaco, A. P. (2001). A forkhead-domain gene is mutated in a severe speech and language disorder. *Nature, 413,* 519–523.

Leadholm, B., & Miller, J. (1992). *Language sample analysis: The Wisconsin guide.* Milwaukee: Wisconsin Department of Public Instruction.

Lenneberg, E. (1967). *Biological foundations of language.* New York: Wiley.

Leonard, L. B. (1998). *Children with specific language impairments.* Cambridge, MA: MIT Press.

Leonard, L. B., Eyer, J., Bedore, L., & Grela, B. (1997). Three accounts of the grammatical morpheme difficulties of English-speaking children with specific language impairment. *Journal of Speech and Hearing Research, 40,* 741–753.

Marchman, V. A., Wulfeck, B., & Ellis Weismer, S. (1999). Morphological productivity in children with normal language and SLI: A study of the English past tense. *Journal of Speech, Language, and Hearing Research, 42,* 206–219.

Marcus, G. F., & Fisher, S. E. (2003). FOXP2 in focus: What can genes tell us about speech and language? *Trends in Cognitive Sciences, 7,* 257–262.

McGuckian, M., & Henry, A. (2003). Grammatical morpheme omission in children with hearing impairment acquiring spoken English. In B. Beachley, A. Brown, & F. Conlin (Eds.), *Proceedings of the 27th Annual Boston University Conference on Language Development* (pp. 519–530). Somerville, MA: Cascadilla Press.

Meaburn, E., Dale, P. S., Craig, I. W., & Plomin, R. (2002). Language-impaired children: No sign of the FOXP2 mutation. *Cognitive Neuroscience and Neuropsychology, 13,* 1075–1077.

Newbury, D. G., Bonora, E., Lamb, J. A., Fisher, S. E., Lai, C. S. L., Baird, G., Jannoun, L., Slonims, V., Stott, C. M., Merricks, M. J., Bolton, P. F., Bailey, A. J., Monaco, A. P., and the International Molecular Genetic Study of Autism Consortium. (2002). FOXP2 is not a major susceptibility gene for autism or specific language impairment. *American Journal of Human Genetics, 70,* 1318–1327.

Newcomer, P. L., & Hammill, D. D. (1988). *Test of language development 2–primary* (2nd ed.). Austin, TX: Pro-Ed.

Norbury, C. F., Bishop, D. V. M., & Briscoe, J. (2001). Production of English finite verb morphology: A comparison of SLI and mild-moderate hearing impairment. *Journal of Speech, Language, and Hearing Research, 44,* 165–178.

O'Brien, E. K., Zhang, X., Nishimura, C., Tomblin, J. B., & Murray, J. C. (2003). Association of specific language impairment (SLI) to the region of 7q31. *American Journal of Human Genetics, 72*(6), 1536–1543.

Oetting, J. B., & Horohov, J. E. (1997). Past-tense marking by children with and without specific language impairment. *Journal of Speech, Language, and Hearing Research, 40,* 62–74.

Oetting, J. B., & McDonald, J. L. (2001). Nonmainstream dialect use and specific language impairment. *Journal of Speech, Language, and Hearing Research, 44,* 207–223.

Paradis, J., Crago, M., Genesee, F., & Rice, M. (2003). French-English bilingual children with SLI: How do they compare with their monolingual peers? *Journal of Speech, Language, and Hearing Research, 46,* 113–127.

Paul, R. (1996). Clinical implication of the natural history of slow expressive language development. *American Journal of Speech-Language Pathology, 5,* 5–21.

Plante, E. (1998). Criteria for SLI: The Stark and Tallal legacy and beyond. *Journal of Speech, Language, and Hearing Research, 41,* 951–957.

Purnell, B. (2003). To every thing there is a season. *Science, 301,* 325.

Redmond, S. M., & Rice, M. L. (2001). Detection of irregular verb violations by children with and without SLI. *Journal of Speech, Language, and Hearing Research, 44,* 655–669.

Redmond, S. M., & Rice, M. L. (2002). Stability of behavioral ratings of children with SLI. *Journal of Speech, Language, and Hearing Research, 45,* 190–201.

Redmond, S. M., Rice, M. L., Haney, K. R., & Hoffman, L. (under review). Stability and validity of MLU as a matching criteria for SLI.

Rescorla, L. (1993). Outcome for toddlers with specific expressive language delay (SELD) at ages 3, 4, 5, 6, 7, & 8. *Society for Research in Child Development Abstracts, 9,* 566.

Rescorla, L. (2002). Language and reading outcomes to age 9 in late-talking toddlers. *Journal of Speech, Language, and Hearing Research, 45,* 360–371.

Rescorla, L., & Roberts, J. (2002). Nominal versus verbal morpheme use in late talkers at ages 3 and 4. *Journal of Speech, Language and Hearing Research, 45,* 1219–1231.

Rice, M. L. (1996a). *Toward a genetics of language.* Mahwah, NJ: Lawrence Erlbaum Associates.

Rice, M. L. (1996b). Of language, phenotypes, and genetics: Building a cross-disciplinary platform for inquiry. In M. L. Rice (Ed.), *Toward a genetics of language* (Preface, pp. xi–xxv). Mahwah, NJ: Lawrence Erlbaum Associates.

Rice, M. L. (1997). Specific language impairments: In search of diagnostic markers and genetic contributions. *Mental Retardation & Developmental Disabilities Research Reviews, 3,* 350–357.

Rice, M. L. (2000). Grammatical symptoms of specific language impairment. In D. V. M. Bishop & L. B. Leonard (Eds.), *Speech and language impairments in children: Causes, characteristics, intervention and outcome* (pp. 17–34). East Sussex, UK: Psychology Press.

Rice, M. L. (2003). A unified model of specific and general language delay: Grammatical tense as a clinical marker of unexpected variation. In Y. Levy & J. Schaeffer (Eds.), *Language competence across populations: Toward a definition of specific language impairment* (pp. 63–95). Mahwah, NJ: Lawrence Erlbaum Associates.

Rice, M. L., Haney, K. R., & Wexler, K. (1998). Family histories of children with SLI who show extended optional infinitives. *Journal of Speech, Language, and Hearing Research, 41,* 419–432.

Rice, M. L., Mervis, C., Klein, B. P., & Rice, K. J. (1999, November). *Children with Williams syndrome do not show an EOI stage*. Paper presented at the Boston University Conference on Language Development, Boston.

Rice, M. L., Rice, K. F., & Redmond, S. (2000). *MLU outcomes for children with and without SLI: Support for MLU as a matching criterion*. Paper presented at the Society for Research in Child Language Disorders conference, Madison, WI.

Rice, M. L., Tomblin, J. B., Hoffman, L., Richman, W. A., & Marquis, J. (in press). Grammatical tense deficits in children with SLI and nonspecific language impairment: Relationships with nonverbal IQ over time. *Journal of Speech, Language, and Hearing Research*.

Rice, M. L., & Wexler, K. (1995). *Tense over time: The persistence of optional infinitives in English in children with SLI*. Paper presented at the 20th Annual Boston University Conference on Language Development, Boston, MA.

Rice, M. L., & Wexler, K. (1996a). A phenotype of specific language impairment: Extended optional infinitives. In M. L. Rice (Ed.), *Toward a genetics of language* (pp. 215–237). Mahwah, NJ: Lawrence Erlbaum Associates.

Rice, M. L., & Wexler, K. (1996b). Toward tense as a clinical marker of specific language impairment in English-speaking children. *Journal of Speech and Hearing Research, 39*, 850–863.

Rice, M. L., & Wexler, K. (2000, November). *What she saying? SLI children's judgments of questions*. Paper presented at the BU Conference on Language Development, Boston, MA.

Rice, M. L., & Wexler, K. (2001). *Rice/Wexler test of early grammatical impairment*. San Antonio, TX: The Psychological Corporation.

Rice, M. L., Wexler, K., & Cleave, P. L. (1995). Specific language impairment as a period of extended optional infinitive. *Journal of Speech, Language, and Hearing Research, 38*, 850–863.

Rice, M. L., Wexler, K., & Hershberger, S. (1998). Tense over time: The longitudinal course of tense acquisition in children with specific language impairment. *Journal of Speech, Language, and Hearing Research, 41*, 1412–1431.

Rice, M. L., Wexler, K., Marquis, J., & Hershberger, S. (2000). Acquisition of irregular past tense by children with SLI. *Journal of Speech, Language, and Hearing Research, 43*, 1126–1145.

Rice, M. L., Wexler, K., & Redmond, S. M. (1999). Grammaticality judgments of an extended optional infinitive grammar: Evidence from English-speaking children with specific language impairment. *Journal of Speech, Language, and Hearing Research, 42*, 943–961.

Roberts, J., Rice, M. L., & Tager-Flusberg, H. (in press). Tense marking in children with autism. *Applied Psycholinguistics*.

Seymour, H. N., Roeper, T. W., & de Villiers, J. (2003). *Diagnostic Evaluation of Language Variation (DELV)*. San Antonio, TX: The Psychological Corporation.

Shriberg, L. D., Tomblin, J. B., & McSweeny, J. L. (1999). Prevalence of speech delay in 6-year-old children and comorbidity with language impairment. *Journal of Speech, Language, and Hearing Research, 42*, 1461–1481.

SLI Consortium. (2002). A genomewide scan identifies two novel loci involved in specific language impairment. *American Journal of Human Genetics, 70*, 384–398.

Tager-Flusberg, H., & Cooper, J. (1999). Present and future possibilities for defining a phenotype for specific language impairment. *Journal of Speech, Language, and Hearing Research, 42*, 1275–1278.

Tallal, P., Hirsch, L. S., Raelpe-Bonilla, T., Miller, S., Brzustowicz, L. M., Bartlett, C., & Flax, J. F. (2001). Familial aggregation in specific language impairment. *Journal of Speech, Language, and Hearing Research, 44*, 1172–1182.

Tallal, P., Ross, R., & Curtiss, S. (1989). Familial aggregation in specific language deficits. *Journal of Speech and Hearing Research, 54*, 167–176.

Tomblin, J. B. (1989). Familial concentration of developmental language impairment. *Journal of Speech and Hearing Disorders, 54*, 287–295.

Tomblin, J. B., Records, N. L., Buckwalter, P., Zhang, Z., Smith, E., & O'Brien, M. (1997). The prevalence of specific language impairment in kindergarten children. *Journal of Speech and Hearing Research, 40,* 1245–1260.

Tomblin, J. B., Records, N. L., & Zhang, X. (1996). A system for the diagnosis of specific language impairment in kindergarten children. *Journal of Speech and Hearing Research, 39,* 1284–1294.

Tomblin, J. B., Zhang, X., Buckwalter, P., & Catts, H. (2000). The association of reading disability, behavioral disorders, and specific language impairment in second grade children. *Journal of Child Psychology and Psychiatry, 41,* 473–482.

van der Lely, H. K. J. (2003). Do heterogeneous deficits require heterogeneous theories? SLI subgroups and the RDDR hypothesis. In Y. Levy & J. Schaeffer (Eds.), *Language competence across populations: Toward a definition of specific language impairment* (pp. 111–133). Mahwah, NJ: Lawrence Erlbaum Associates.

van der Lely, H. K. J., & Stollwerck, L. (1996). A grammatical specific language impairment in children: An autosomal dominant inheritance? *Brain and Language, 52,* 484–504.

Wexler, K. (1991). On the argument from the poverty of the stimulus. In A. Kasher (Ed.), *The Chomskyan turn.* Cambridge, MA: Blackwell.

Wexler, K. (1994). Optional infinitives, head movement and the economy of derivations. In D. Lightfoot & N. Hornstein (Eds.), *Verb movement* (pp. 305–350). Cambridge, England: Cambridge University Press.

Wexler, K. (1996). The development of inflection in a biologically based theory of language acquisition. In M. L. Rice (Ed.), *Toward a genetics of language* (pp. 113–144). Mahwah, NJ: Lawrence Erlbaum Associates.

Wexler, K. (2003). Lenneberg's dream: Learning, normal language development and specific language impairment. In Y. Levy & J. Schaeffer (Eds.), *Language competence across populations: Towards a definition of specific language impairment* (pp. 11–61). Mahwah, NJ: Lawrence Erlbaum Associates.

11

Linguistics and Linking Problems

Colin Phillips
University of Maryland

LINKING GENES, BRAINS, AND BEHAVIOR

I am not an expert on language disorders. As a relative outsider at the meeting on which this volume is based, I was impressed by two general conclusions. First, I was impressed by the extreme specificity that is now possible in the descriptions of both genotypes and phenotypes for a number of different developmental disorders that affect language. Second, I was impressed by the gulf that lies at present between our understanding of the genetic causes and the behavioral outcomes of developmental disorders. Although we know a great deal in some instances about which genes are associated with which specific disorders, we have little idea about why those genes have the specific consequences that they have for language. The goal of this chapter is to outline two ways in which linguistics can be put to good use in helping to narrow this gap, particularly in relation to the search for brain-level models of language. In other words, my concern here is with the role of linguistics in the search for "linking hypotheses," for normal and disordered language alike.

I should make it clear at the outset that I do not mean to claim that linguistics has all of the answers. One of the main goals of the chapter is to argue that some basic changes are needed in fundamental assumptions about how linguistic knowledge is encoded to make linking hypotheses more tractable.

There are many good reasons to want to answer the question of how the human brain makes natural language possible. (This is the question of how specific patterns of activity in specific cells or cell assemblies give rise to language, not the question of which brain regions are associated with which general functions, which I take to be a first step toward addressing more interesting questions.) The search for an answer to this question should be interesting for purely scientific reasons.

If it were the case that individual genes control individual behavioral traits, it might be satisfying to know which genetic disruptions lead to disruptions in which behavioral traits while having little understanding of exactly how the genes give rise to specific traits in terms of protein synthesis, brain development, or whatever else might be involved. Correlations between genes and behavioral outcomes could reasonably be viewed as partial linking hypotheses, and it would not much matter whether we understood in detail how specific neuronal structures support language.

As we know, however, there is little plausibility to the notion that individual genes control individual behavioral traits. Genes play a far more complex role in regulating the synthesis of proteins, which, among many other things, give rise to specific events in neuronal growth, which in turn somehow give rise to a human brain, which is somehow equipped to learn and use human language. Besides there are simply not enough genes available for each gene to control an individual trait.

Therefore, the observation that specific genetic disruptions lead to specific cognitive and linguistic disorders becomes all the more puzzling. For example, if it is true that there are genetic disruptions that cause children to have special difficulty in the marking of tense morphology in their speech, and if we can be fairly confident that there is no gene that codes for tense morphology, it is all the more puzzling that specific areas of language turn out to be more vulnerable than others. In fact the puzzle is made even more interesting by the fact that *different* genetic disruptions appear to lead to similar areas of vulnerability in language (e.g., inflectional morphology, nonword repetition, noncanonical word order in syntax), as appears to be the case. If we are to understand these connections between genes and behavior, we have no choice but to understand the complex sequence of causes and effects that link genes with brain development and that link brain circuitry with language abilities. In other words, the search for linking hypotheses for language takes on far more than mere academic interest.

On the question of how to link genes and brain development, I must defer to the expertise of others. However, the question of how to link up our understanding of language with what we know about brain circuitry is one that has occupied me a great deal and one that is also relevant to the question of how we can gain a deeper understanding of language disorders. In this chapter, I discuss two ways in which linguistic research can make valuable contributions to our understanding of the causes of developmental language disorders (DLDs).

In the first section of the chapter, I present a number of examples that show that systematic patterns of errors in the course of normal language development can be better understood in light of a detailed understanding of cross-linguistic variation in adult languages. These findings fit with the common suggestion that constraints on language development reflect constraints on the range of possible adult languages. If the systematicity of errors in normal language development often reflects constraints on cross-language variation, and if it is true that many features of DLDs parallel difficulties observed in normal development, it is reasonable to expect a connection between the systematic nature of breakdown in language disorders and the scope of cross-language variation. In other words, this section shows how the tools of linguistic analysis can already be brought to bear on the problem of understanding language disorders.

In the second section of the chapter, I argue that the results of linguistic analysis can more usefully be brought to bear on linking hypotheses about brain and behavior if grammatical knowledge is viewed as a real-time system for constructing sentences. This contrasts with the standard view in linguistics and psycholinguistics, according to which knowledge of language is fractionated into separate time-independent and time-dependent systems (sometimes known as "competence systems" and "performance systems"). Therefore, an important part of my argument involves a critical review of arguments in favor of the standard view. I argue that today the grammar, parser, and producer appear much more similar than they once did, and that their unification can provide an important step toward developing linking hypotheses for normal and disordered language. If, on the other hand, we are forced to maintain the standard view that grammatical knowledge involves mental computations that are too elusive to be pinpointed in time, I believe that we have little hope of developing and testing viable linking hypotheses for linguistic knowledge.

Throughout the chapter, I focus on issues involving syntax—the study of sentence structure. This should not be taken to imply that syntax is more important or more central than other areas of language. It merely reflects that this is one area of language where enough of the pieces are in place to allow us to seriously consider how to address the linking problem.[1]

---

[1]For discussion of some specific linking proposals in the area of phonetic and phonological categories, see Phillips (2001).

Language Development and Cross-Language Variation

In research on developmental disorders, the finding that specific areas of language are more vulnerable than others is also seen in the literature on normal language development. Our understanding of the constraints on normal language development has been strongly informed by theoretical and descriptive linguistic research on cross-language diversity. In this section, I review a number of examples from our own work, where the study of cross-language variation has provided new insight into the question of why children make certain kinds of errors and do not make other kinds of errors. This typological approach leads to evidence of both language-internal and cross-linguistic constraints on development. I should point out that the studies described here were not conceived with the programmatic goal of showing that children's errors reflect constraints on possible adult languages. In some instances, we were pursuing an entirely different hypothesis. However, we were repeatedly led back to the same conclusion by our findings.

#1: Root Infinitives. Normally developing 2- to 3-year-olds show patterns of morphosyntactic errors in their spontaneous speech that are similar to errors that have been widely observed in developmental language disorders. Over the past 15 years, this has been one of the most fruitful domains of research in normal language development, due in large part to the fact that it has become possible to compare findings from a wide variety of languages. The point of this section is to outline some systematic differences in the distribution of these errors across languages, which may provide clues to the source of the errors.

Some of the studies of different languages have revealed striking cross-language similarities. For example, the reason that inflection omissions in English-speaking children are described as *root infinitives* is because the counterparts of these errors in many other languages appear as verb forms that are clearly marked as infinitives (1–3; Wexler, 1994). Even in languages where the relevant form is not an infinitive per se, such as Greek (Stephany, 1997; Varlokosta, Vainikka, & Rohrbacher, 1998), it is still the case that young children frequently replace correctly inflected forms with a morphologically unmarked default form (4).

(1) Eve sit floor.   [Eve, 1;7]   English

(2) Maman manger   [Daniel, 1;8]   French
     mom   eat.inf

(3) Ty   mame   pomogat'.   [Varvara, 2;0]   Russian
you.nom mommy.dat help.inf
"You to help mommy"

(4) Ego katiti   [Janna, 1;11]   Greek
I   sit.3per.perf.

Another consistent result of these studies is that children's infinitive forms are not randomly distributed across the different syntactic constructions that they use. Whereas some constructions, including run-of-the-mill declarative sentences, show large numbers of infinitive errors, other constructions show a striking absence of infinitive errors. For example, it is not uncommon for a 2-year-old child learning German, Dutch, or Swedish to produce infinitive verb forms in 20% to 30% of his declarative utterances, but this percentage drops to 0% to 2% when we look only at his questions (Clahsen, Kursawe, & Penke, 1996; Haegeman, 1995; Santelmann, 1994) or sentences in which a nonsubject is topicalized (Poeppel & Wexler, 1993).

(5) Dutch: Finiteness in declaratives and questions (Haegeman, 1995)

Hein, 2;4–3;1	+*finite*	–*finite*
All clauses	3,768 (84%)	721 (16%)
wh-questions	88 (98%)	2 (2%)

Total = 4,579, χ^2 = 12.71, p < .001

(6) German: Finiteness in declaratives and questions (Clahsen, Kursawe, & Penke, 1996)[2]

4 children, 1;10–3;8	+*finite*	–*finite*
wh-questions	306 (99.7%)	1 (0.3%)

Similarly, root infinitives are frequent in the speech of Dutch 2-year-olds, particularly in sentences where the child omits the subject of the sentence, but they are exceedingly rare in sentences in which the sentence begins with an overt subject NP (Haegeman, 1995; Krämer, 1993). A similar pattern is found among children learning Russian (Bar-Shalom, Snyder, & Boro, 1996) or German (Behrens, 1993).

---

[2]Although this study does not provide baseline rates of correct inflection from declarative clauses, root infinitives are a robust phenomenon in child German, typically occurring in 10% to 30% of declarative clauses in the speech of children at that stage.

(7) Dutch: Finiteness and null subjects (Krämer, 1993)

Thomas, 2;3–2;8	+finite	–finite
Overt subject	431 (95.4%)	21 (4.6%)
Null subject	165 (40.1%)	246 (59.9%)

Total = 863, χ^2 = 307.07, $p < .0001$

(8) Russian: Finiteness and null subjects (Bar-Shalom, Snyder, & Boro, 1996)

Varvara, 1;6–2;4	+finite	–finite
Overt subject	545 (99.1%)	5 (0.9%)
Null subject	451 (81.9%)	100 (18.1%)

Total = 1,101, $\chi^2 > 50$, $p < .0001$

(9) German: Finiteness and null subjects (Behrens, 1993)

Simone, 1;8–4;1	+finite	–finite
Overt subject	2,918 (91.3%)	278 (8.7%)
Null subject	781 (26.2%)	2,199 (73.8%)

Total = 6,176, χ^2 = 102.15, $p < .0001$

Both of these patterns are striking because they reveal better morphosyntactic performance in more complex sentences and worse performance in less complex sentences. Furthermore, it can be clearly shown that these results are not just artifacts of sampling from speech transcripts that cover a broad developmental time window. Patterns such as those shown in (5) to (9) provide a straightforward challenge to any attempt to explain the root infinitive phenomenon as a simple production overload effect because such an account would surely predict greater difficulty in more complex sentences.

However, a review of the cross-language literature reveals further selectivity in the distribution of root infinitives across languages. The two effects shown in (5) to (9) appear in some languages, but not in others. The selective appearance of these effects can shed light on the nature of root infinitives in individual languages.

As we have seen in (7) to (9), children in a number of languages produce few root infinitives in sentences with overt subjects, in contrast to their frequent use in sentences with null subjects. However, there are other languages where root infinitives remain frequent in sentences with overt subjects. Such languages include Danish, Icelandic, Faroese, and English (10–13).[3] This cross-language contrast can be explained once we consider the range of possible infinitival clauses in the corresponding adult languages. In the adult languages, of course, the infinitival clauses occur overwhelmingly as embedded clauses. English and the Scandinavian languages all allow embedded infinitival clauses with overt subjects as shown in (14) and (15). These constructions are known in the linguistics literature as *exceptional case marking* (ECM) constructions because the subject of the embedded clause appears with accusative case as if it were the direct object of the main clause verb. In contrast, German, Dutch, and Russian lack ECM constructions (16), although they do allow infinitival complement clauses with null subjects (17).[4]

(10) English: Finiteness and null subjects (Phillips, 1995b)

Adam, 2;3–3;0	+finite	–finite
Overt subject	79 (28.8%)	195 (71.2%)
Null subject	34 (42%)	47 (58%)

Total = 355, χ^2 = 4.98, p = .026

(11) Faroese: Finiteness and null subjects (Jonas, 1995)

Osvalt, 1;10	+finite	–finite
Overt subject	44 (31.9%)	94 (68.1%)
Null subject	8 (10.7%)	67 (89.3%)

Total = 213, χ^2 = 11.86, p < .001

---

[3]In the Scandinavian languages, it is still generally the case that rates of infinitive production are lower in sentences with overt subjects than in sentences with null subjects. This is probably also true in English, although there have been conflicting reports (cf. Phillips, 1995b; Schütze, 1997; Schütze & Wexler, 2000). However, it is probably a mistake to conflate a *reduction* in rates of root infinitive production with the *extreme rarity* of root infinitives following overt subjects in languages like Dutch and Russian.

[4]Although Dutch and German do not allow most of the types of ECM constructions available in English, they do allow ECM in the complements of perception verbs such as *see*. This may be related to the fact that in such contexts the embedded verb (*dance* in Example i) is raised from the embedded clause to form a complex predicate with the main verb. This has led some linguists to conclude that the apparent accusative-marked subject of the embedded clause is really a semantic argument of the main clause perception verb (e.g., Steinbach, 2002).

(i) dat Jan [haar.acc de tango] ziet dansen   [Dutch]
    that John her   the tango sees dance

(12) Icelandic: Finiteness and null subjects (Sigurjónsdóttir, 1999)

Birna, 2;0–2;6	+*finite*	–*finite*
Overt subject	689 (70.2%)	293 (29.8%)
Null subject	111 (34.2%)	214 (65.8%)

Total = 1,307, $\chi^2 > 50$, $p < .0001$

(13) Danish: Finiteness and null subjects (Hamann & Plunkett, 1998)[5]

Anne & Jens, 2;0–2;10	+*finite*	–*finite*
Overt subject	75%	40%
Null subject	25%	60%

(14) a. They consider [him to be a genius] English
    b. They want [him to leave]

(15) a. Eg tel hana hafa borðað epli.   Icelandic (Vikner, 1995)
       I believe her to.have eaten apple
    b. Jag anser   Peter att vara dum.   Swedish (Holmberg, 1986)
       I   consider Peter to be   stupid
    c. Vi anser honom (ha) kommit för sent. Norwegian (Julien, 2001)
       we consider him have come too late

(16) a. *Sie erwarten [ihn anzukommen]   German
       They expect him to.leave
    b. *Ja ozhidaju [jego prijehat' zavtra]   Russian
       I expect him arrive tomorrow

(17) a. Maria versprach, [das Büro zu pützen] German
       Maria promised the office to.clean
    b. Maria poobesh'ala [podmesti v ofise] Russian
       Maria promised   sweep.inf in office

A similar cross-linguistic contrast may be observed in children's questions. Whereas rates of root infinitive production fall close to zero in children's questions in German, Dutch, and Swedish, as illustrated in (5) and (6), we find high percentages of uninflected verb forms in early *wh*-ques-

---

[5]These percentages are estimates based on the graphs in Hamann and Plunkett (1998). Note that the percentages shown apply to the columns of the table, in contrast to the other tables in this section.

tions in English (18). We again find a related contrast when we look at infinitival clauses in the corresponding adult languages. English allows fronting of *wh*-phrases in infinitival clauses in indirect questions (19), but such constructions are impossible in adult German (20) and at best marginal in many dialects of Dutch.[6] The distribution of infinitives in questions has been documented in fewer languages than has the distribution of infinitives relative to null subjects for the simple reason that the relevant utterances are less common in transcripts of spontaneous speech. We need either large corpora or highly inquisitive children.

(18) English: Finiteness in declaratives and questions (Phillips, 1995b)

Adam, 2;3–3;1	*inflected V*	*uninflected V*	*% inflected*
Declaratives	134	203	40%
wh-questions	69	92	43%

Total = 498, χ^2 = 0.43, p = .51

(19) John knows which man to ask.   English

(20) *Hans weiss, welchen Mann zu fragen.   German
 Hans knows which.acc man to ask.inf

Similarly, child German shows low rates of root infinitives in sentences in which a nonsubject is moved to sentence-initial position by topicalization (21). The widespread availability of topicalization in German is a result of the verb-second property of German. Adult German disallows verb second (and hence also topicalization) in all embedded clauses (22).[7]

---

[6]There are certain circumstances where adult German allows infinitival *wh*-clauses as main clauses (Fries, 1983; Reis, 2002). However, these constructions are limited to root clauses and are described as "a comparatively rare species, even among RIs in German" (Reis, 2002, p. 288). An example is shown in (i):

(i) Wem noch trauen?
 Who still trust.inf.
 'Who can you trust anymore?'

[7]I illustrate this property with a finite embedded clause because the effects of topicalization are easier to see in a clause that contains an overt subject. Because German lacks ECM constructions, we must rely on finite embedded clauses to construct examples with an overt subject.

(21) German: Finiteness and topicalization (Poeppel & Wexler, 1993)

Andreas, 2;1	+finite	–finite
Subject initial	130	24
Nonsubject initial	50	0

Total = 204, χ^2 = 8.83, $p < .01$

(22) *Er sagt, daß diesen Film haben die Kinder gesehen.
    He says that this.acc film have the children.nom seen
    (Vikner, 1995, p. 66)

Taken together, these cross-language findings suggest an interesting language-internal constraint on the kinds of errors that normally developing children make. Despite that children's root infinitives are not possible adult utterances, their errors generally respect broad constraints on the possible forms of infinitival clauses in the target language. The rare appearance of overt subjects with root infinitives appears to be a property of child language only when the target language lacks overt subjects with infinitival clauses. Similarly, the disappearance of root infinitives in children's questions and topicalizations in some languages may be related to the absence of corresponding interrogative infinitival clauses in the target language.

The implication of this is that many of the root infinitive errors made by normally developing children are closer to the adult target language than one might suspect at first. The child's primary error is to allow an infinitival in the root clause, but beyond that the child produces the infinitival clause with syntax that is overwhelmingly appropriate for infinitival clauses in the ambient adult language. This conclusion lends support to the proposal by Weissenborn (1994) that children's early multiword utterances respect a "local well-formedness" condition and could also be viewed as an extreme version of Rizzi's (1994) widely discussed "clausal truncation" hypothesis. It has the advantage of explaining cross-language variation in the distribution of children's root infinitives that has not previously been explained.[8]

---

[8]In an earlier article (Phillips, 1995b), I offered an account of a subset of the cross-language facts reviewed here based on cross-language differences in verb placement and verb movement. However, that account faces difficulties when faced with the range of facts presented here. In particular, the facts about overt subjects of children's root infinitives in Scandinavian languages favor the current account based on ECM constructions in the corresponding adult languages. Icelandic and Mainland Scandinavian languages pattern together in allowing ECM constructions, but diverge with respect to independent verb movement. The distribution of overt subjects in children's root infinitives appears to be similar across all Scandinavian languages and different from German, Dutch, and Russian.

Note that this claim applies specifically to children's infinitival clauses. It is not intended as a general claim that children's root clauses can freely adopt embedded clause syntax. This is not supported by the facts. For example, in adult English indirect questions, subject–auxiliary inversion and *do*-support are not required (23), but children's questions do not show frequent noninversion (24a) or finite verbs without *do*-support (24b).[9]

(23) a. Bill understands what he has done.
     b. Bill understands what Sally does.

(24) a. *What he has done?
     b. *What Sally does?

Also the generalization about the syntax of children's infinitival clauses does not provide a general answer to the question of why children produce infinitival root clauses in the first place; it merely explains how these clauses are structured to conform maximally to the adult grammar.[10] Nevertheless, these remaining questions do not undermine the moral of this section, which is that the understanding of the specific properties of children's morphosyntactic errors depends on a detailed understanding of the structure of the relevant adult languages.

It remains to be seen whether the extended period of root infinitive production observed in Specific Language Impairment (SLI; Leonard, 2003; Rice, Wexler, & Cleave, 1995) shows the same specific syntactic properties as the root infinitives found in normally developing children. If SLI genuinely reflects selective language delay, we should expect to find the same distribution of facts discussed here in the speech of SLI children across languages. Alternatively, if SLI children do not show the same pattern of cross-language variation in root infinitives observed in normally developing children, then this is a challenge for the claim that SLI syntax is simply selectively delayed.

---

[9]Forms such as these do occur in child English, but with very low frequency. However, we cannot exclude the possibility that the presence of such forms in child English is masked by the independent fact of auxiliary omission at early stages of development (e.g., *What doing?*). For further discussion of questions in child English, see Roeper and Rohrbacher (2000).

[10]Note that my generalization about the syntax of root infinitives makes a prediction about the overt subjects of children's infinitives that is probably too strong. The overt subjects of infinitives in adult languages are typically accusative-marked ECM subjects. Although it is true that English-speaking children often produce sentences with accusative subject pronouns (e.g., "him go") and that these non-nominative subjects are mostly restricted to infinitival clauses (cf. Schütze, 1997; Wexler, Schütze, & Rice, 1998), there are also many instances of nominative subjects of infinitival clauses.

#2: *Universal Constraints I: Verb Argument Structure.* We also find cases where systematic patterns of errors in normally developing children reflect universal constraints on adult languages. Two examples serve to illustrate this point.

The first example, based on work conducted with Meesook Kim and Barbara Landau, concerns the argument structure of so-called *locative verbs*—verbs that describe the movement of an object, typically known as the "figure," to a location, typically known as the "ground." In English and many other languages, locative verbs allow their arguments to appear in two different configurations. In the *figure frame*, the figure is the direct object of the verb, and the ground is marked by an oblique phrase such as a PP. In the *ground frame*, the ground appears as the direct object, and the figure is marked by an oblique phrase. In English, verbs that describe a manner of motion, such as *pour, spill,* and *shake,* allow the figure frame (25). Verbs that describe a change of state, such as *fill, cover,* and *decorate,* allow the ground frame (26). Verbs that describe both a manner of motion and a change of state, such as *pile, load,* and *stuff,* allow both figure and ground frames and are known as *alternating verbs* (27).

(25) a. Jane poured the water into the glass.   *figure frame*
     b. *Jane poured the glass with water.   *ground frame*

(26) a. *Jane filled the water into the glass.   *figure frame*
     b. Jane filled the glass with water.   *ground frame*

(27) a. Jane stuffed the feathers into the pillow.   *figure frame*
     b. Jane stuffed the pillow with feathers.   *ground frame*

Because the structural frames that these verbs allow are determined by the semantics of the verbs, studies of the acquisition of these verbs have focused on demonstrating that children are able to use this syntax–semantics correspondence to constrain their choices of argument structure (Gropen et al., 1991a, 1991b; Pinker, 1989). Nevertheless, it has also been found that children make errors with locative verbs and produce argument structures that do not occur in adult English. Bowerman (1982) reported examples of the ground verbs *fill* and *cover* used in the figure frame in the spontaneous speech of 4- to 5-year-olds (e.g., **I'm going to cover a screen over me*). Bowerman characterized these examples as overgeneralizations to ground verbs of structures that the children had observed with figure verbs. Gropen et al. (1991b) replicated the errors with *fill* in an elicited production study, and Kim, Landau, and Phillips (1999) showed figure frame errors with *fill, cover,* and *decorate* in another elicited production study. In that study, the errors with *fill* were so frequent that children almost never used the correct ground frame. This in no way reflects the properties of the input to children—we also tested the children's own mothers, who made no errors at all. Importantly, however, the high frequency of errors with ground verbs stands in clear contrast to the children's high performance on figure verbs, such as *pour*, *spill*, and *stick*, where they never produced figure verbs in the ground frame. Therefore, this is another case of a speech production error in children that is syntactically highly specific.

In a survey of locative verb syntax in 20 different languages[11] drawn from a wide variety of language families, we found a contrast that resembles the pattern of errors observed in children. In every language in the sample, manner-of-motion verbs allow the figure frame, but do not allow the ground frame (28–30), exactly as in English. In contrast, change-of-state verbs show more cross-language variation. Many languages pattern with English in allowing only ground frames with change-of-state verbs, but there are many other languages that allow change-of-state verbs with both figure and ground frames (31–33).[12]

(28) a. Juan vertió agua en el vaso.   Spanish
     J. poured water in the glass
  b. *Juan vertió el vaso con agua.
     poured the glass with water

(29) a. Dani shafax mayim letox ha-kos   Hebrew
     D. poured water into the-glass
  b. *Dani shafax et ha-kos be-mayin
     D. poured acc.the-glass with-water

(30) a. Yumi-ka mwul-ul cep-ey pwu-ess-ta.   Korean
     Nom   water-Acc cup-Loc pour-Past-Dec
     "Yumi poured water into the cup."
  b. *Yumi-ka cep-ul   mwul-lo   pwu-ess-ta.
     Nom   cup-Acc water-with pour-Past-Dec
     "*Yumi poured the cup with water."

---

[11]The languages surveyed were English, French, Spanish (Castilian and Argentinian), Italian, Brazilian Portuguese, Polish, Russian, Mandarin Chinese, Japanese, Korean, Thai, Malay, Hindi, Hebrew, Arabic, Luganda, Yoruba, and Ewe. Thanks to Beth Rabbin for her help in conducting this survey. Detailed results of the survey are available on request.

[12]See Kim (1999) and Kim, Landau, and Phillips (1999) for an account of what determines this cross-language variation. The account is based on an additional syntactic property of the languages in which change-of-state verbs allow both figure and ground frames. All of these languages allow serial verb constructions (i.e., complex predicate constructions in which a single clause contains more than one lexical verb), whereas none of the other languages in the sample allows this.

(31) a. Yumi-ka mwul-ul   cep-ey   chaywu-ess-ta.   Korean
        Nom   water-Acc cup-Loc fill-Past-Dec
        "*Yumi filled water into the cup."
     b. Yumi-ka cep-ul   mwul-l   chaywu-ess-ta.
        Nom   cup-Acc water-with fill-Past-Dec
        "Yumi filled the cup with water."

(32) a. John bardag-a su-ylu   doldur-du.   Turkish
        John glass-Dat water-Acc filled-Past
        "*John filled water into the glass."
     b. John bardag-I su-yla   doldur-du.
        John glass-Acc water-with filled-Past
        "John filled the glass with water."

(33) a. Petero ya-jju a-mazzi   mu-gilaasi.   Luganda
        Petero filled the water into-glass
        "*Petero filled water into the glass."
     b. Petero ya-jjuza gilaasi na-mazzi.
        Petero filled   glass with-water
        "Petero filled the glass with water."

Therefore, the accuracy of English-speaking children with verbs like *pour* reflects a cross-language universal. The frequent errors that the same children make with verbs like *fill* are consistent with the variability observed in the languages of the world. The range of errors that children produce is constrained by the range of forms that are possible in adult languages. This typological observation does not answer the question of why children do not immediately converge on the target-language forms for the *fill*-class, but it provides important clues to why the children's errors are so selective.

#3: Universal Constraints II: Pronoun Interpretation.
A second example of the impact of cross-language universals comes from work with Nina Kazanina on children's interpretation of pronouns (Kazanina & Phillips, 2001), which shows that children distinguish universal and language-particular constraints even when the surface consequences of the two types of constraints are broadly similar in the target language.

A pronoun may (but need not) co-refer with another noun phrase in the same sentence. Importantly, the pronoun may either follow its antecedent ("forwards anaphora," 34a) or precede its antecedent ("backwards anaphora," 34b). Co-referring NPs are indicated by subscripting.

(34) a. John$_i$ thinks that Sue likes him$_i$.
     b. The man that he$_i$ met at the bus stop told John$_i$ that it would rain.

However, there are also a number of constraints on the possible configurations of pronouns and their antecedents. These constraints have been the subject of intensive investigation in linguistics. For example, a pronoun cannot co-refer with a noun phrase that is structurally within the scope of the pronoun (i.e., contained within the structural sister of the pronoun). This constraint, which in the syntax literature is known cryptically as *Condition C* (Chomsky, 1981), accounts for the fact that (35a) and (36a) allow co-reference, whereas (35b) and (36b) do not. In each of the examples in (35) and (36), the phrase that is the structural sister of the pronoun is italicized. The noun phrase *John* cannot serve as the antecedent of the pronoun when it appears within the italicized region. Corresponding structures are shown in (37a) and (37b).

(35) a. The woman that he$_i$ *met* likes John$_i$.
    b. *He$_i$ *likes John$_i$*.

(36) a. While he$_i$ *was reading the book*, John$_i$ ate an apple.
    (structure = 37a)
    b. *He$_i$ *ate an apple while John$_i$ was reading the book*.
    (structure = 37b)

(37) a.   b.

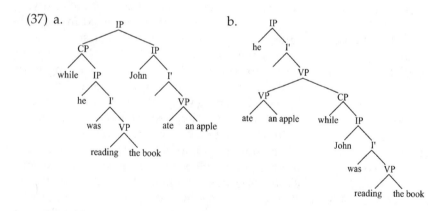

Cross-language research has shown that Condition C is a good candidate for a universal constraint on interpretation. Its effects have been found in a large number of typologically diverse languages, including even polysynthetic languages such as Mohawk, where the effects of Condition C are extremely difficult to observe (Baker, 1991). Consistent with the universal status of this constraint, language-acquisition studies have shown that children respect the constraint at an early age. In a pioneering study, Stephen Crain and Cecile McKee showed that English-speaking children as young as 3 years of age disallow a co-reference interpretation for sentences like (36b), which violate Condition C (Crain & McKee, 1985), while allowing co-reference of the type in (36a).

We have recently extended this line of language acquisition research to Russian, which provides an interesting additional twist to the story. Although there is a sharp contrast in the acceptability of co-reference in (36a) and (36b) in English, their Russian counterparts (38a–38b) are both reliably rated as unacceptable by Russian adults. Further, (38b) is ruled out by the universal Condition C constraint, whereas (38a) is ruled out by an additional constraint that is particular to Russian (Avrutin & Reuland, 2002; Kazanina & Phillips, 2001).[13]

(38) a. *Poka on$_i$ chital   knigu,   Pooh$_i$ s'el   yabloko.
        while he was reading.imp the book Pooh ate.perf the apple
     b. *On$_i$ s'el   yabloko, poka Pooh$_i$ chital   knigu.
        he   ate.perf the apple while Pooh was reading.imp the book

Using a similar truth-value judgment task to Crain and McKee's study, we investigated what pronoun interpretations are available to Russian 3- to 5-year-olds (Kazanina & Phillips, 2001). Children watched a set of stories in the company of an experimenter and a puppet; after each story, the puppet made a statement about something that happened in the story. The child's task was simply to judge whether the puppet's statement was true or false. We tested possible pronoun interpretations by asking children to judge the truth of sentences like (38a) and (38b) following stories in which the sentences would be *true*, if the co-reference interpretation were available, but *false* under a reading where the pronoun is taken to refer to another character (e.g., Eeyore). Therefore, if children judge that the puppet told the truth, it must be that they allow the co-reference interpretation; if they judge that the puppet did not tell the truth, then it must be that the co-reference interpretation is blocked by a constraint (see Crain & Thornton, 1998, for full details of this technique). We found that Russian 5- to 6-year-olds disallow co-reference in both (38a) and (38b), just like Russian adults. However, Russian 3-year-olds ($n = 9$) showed a clear contrast between (38a) and (38b) by rejecting co-reference in sentences like (38b) in 85% of trials, but rejecting co-reference in sentences like (38a) in only 13% of trials. These percentages of acceptance and rejection are almost identical to those obtained for the youngest group of children in Crain and McKee's study on Condition C in English. The Russian 4-year-

---

[13]It is not the case that Russian excludes (38a) simply because it disallows all backwards anaphora. The Russian counterparts of (35a) and (35b) show exactly the same contrast in acceptability as in English.

olds showed an intermediate pattern of judgments, overwhelmingly rejecting co-reference in (38b), but allowing co-reference in (38a) in 50% of trials.

Therefore, the Russian 3-year-olds show a contrast in pronoun interpretation possibilities that is present in child and adult English, but is not evident in the judgments of their own parents. They adhere to the universal constraint on co-reference that rules out (38b), but do not yet respect the Russian-specific constraint on co-reference that applies in minimally different sentences like (38a). This is a particularly striking example of a selective pattern of errors in children that reflects the operation of cross-language constraints. The information that leads young children to distinguish (38a) from (38b) is presumably not available in the speech input to Russian children. Even in the unlikely event that the two types of sentences were present in the input, with pronouns in the relevant positions, children would never receive explicit information on which pronoun interpretations are unavailable.

#4: Cross-Language Semantic Contrasts: Aspect. A fourth example of the connection between cross-language variation and selective errors in children comes from a series of recent studies with Nina Kazanina on children's understanding of the semantics of aspect (Kazanina & Phillips, 2003a, 2003b). In this case, we observe errors in young children that at first glance appear to reflect a general cognitive limitation, but that on closer inspection turn out to again reflect the structure of cross-language variation.

Grammatical aspect is a morphosyntactic category that encodes a speaker's perspective on an event. Intuitively, perfective aspect presents an "external" perspective on an event, whereas imperfective aspect presents an "internal" perspective on the event, viewing it as an ongoing process. These differences in perspective have important consequences for the semantic entailments of perfective and imperfective sentences. Consider the implications of the English simple past and past progressive sentences in (39a) and (39b).

(39) a. Sue drove from Washington to Boston.
    b. Sue was driving from Washington to Boston.

Both (39a) and (39b) refer to an event of driving from Washington to Boston. However, (39a) implies that the event reached completion (i.e., Sue did reach Boston), whereas (39b) is compatible with a situation in which Sue's car broke down in New York and she never made it to Boston. Although the event of driving to Boston does not reach completion, speakers understand that it is nevertheless appropriate to describe it using the predicate *driving from Washington to Boston* because this appropriately describes what Sue intended to do and what she was on the way to achieving. In fact, it even sounds misleading to describe what happened as *Sue was driving from Washington to New York*. Thus, whereas perfective predicates carry completion entailments, imperfective predicates lack completion entailments.[14] The fact that imperfectives do not entail the existence of the event to which they intuitively refer gives rise to what is sometimes known as the *Imperfective Paradox* (Dowty, 1979; Parsons, 1991).

It is well known that grammatical aspect is highly salient in Russian. Each verb has distinct perfective and imperfective roots (e.g., *pisat'* 'read.imp', *napisat'* 'read.perf'; *govorit'* 'say.imp', *skazat'*, 'say.perf'), and the morphological marking of tense and aspect is clearly distinct. Previous studies have shown that Russian 2-year-olds already use both perfective and imperfective forms frequently and overwhelmingly appropriately in their spontaneous speech, suggesting early mastery of grammatical aspect (Bar-Shalom, in press; Brun et al., 1999; Gvozdev, 1961). However, our experiments on Russian children's comprehension of the semantics of aspect reveal strikingly nonadultlike performance.

In a series of studies, we tested Russian 3- to 5-year-olds' understanding of the completion entailments of perfective and imperfective forms in the past tense. For example, we wanted to know whether children know that the perfective statement *Obez'yanka postroila dom* (The monkey built.perf a house) entails that a house was built to completion, whereas the imperfective statement *Obez'yanka stroila dom* (The monkey built.imperf. a house) does not entail the completion of the house-building event. In a first pair of studies, we investigated this by asking children questions about stories in which a toy animal took a journey down a road and performed a given action to varying degrees of completion at different landmarks along the road. At the end of each story, the child was asked questions like *Where did the monkey build the house?* using either perfective or imperfective verb forms. All children gave adultlike responses to perfective questions, naming only locations where the event reached completion. However, many children (including most of the 3-year-olds) gave nonadultlike answers to imperfective questions, consistently failing to choose the location where the event happened incompletely.[15] Older chil-

---

[14]The contrast in (39) between the English simple past and past progressive is presented for illustrative purposes only and is not intended as a genuine perfective/imperfective contrast. Although the imperfective and progressive are similar in many respects, there are also important differences (cf. Klein, 1995).

[15]We have run a number of control tasks that show that the failure to name the incomplete location is not a task-related artifact. First, the stories all contained interrupting events that took place at two different locations. All children successfully named both locations when asked where the interrupting events occurred. This shows that all children are able to

dren and adults performed exactly as predicted. We have observed the failures in younger children for a number of different predicate types, including creation predicates (e.g., *build a smurf*), change-of-state verbs (e.g., *color in a flower*), and motion predicates (e.g., *bike to the farm*).

The results of our first set of studies suggest that younger children fail the Imperfective Paradox and have not yet learned that imperfectives lack completion entailments. This error was not noticed in previous studies of aspectual development in Russian (e.g., Vinnitskaya & Wexler, 2001) due to the fact that children were tested on their ability to associate imperfectives with events that were in progress, rather than with events that specifically failed to reach completion. One might conclude from this that the younger Russian children are missing a fundamental piece of the semantics of the imperfective or that their failures reflect a conceptual problem, which prevents them from recognizing the relationship between partial and complete events or which forces them to consider only what the protagonist actually did, rather than what he intended to do. One might even suppose that the younger children have yet to learn that imperfectives and perfectives are semantically distinct. We were attracted by all of these possibilities and ran a series of follow-up studies to test possibilities such as these. In the end, however, none of these possible explanations turned out to be viable, and we were led back to an explanation that again links specific child errors to specific patterns of variation in the adult languages of the world.

The crucial follow-up studies were ones in which the children again judged perfective and imperfective statements, but now in the context of additional clauses that specified a temporal "frame-of-reference," as in (40).

(40) a. Poka malchik polival cvety, devochka vyterla stol.   *perfective*
while boy water.past.imp flowers girl clean.past.perf table
While the boy was watering flowers, the girl cleaned the table.
b. Poka malchik polival cvety, devochka vytirala stol.   *imperfective*
while boy water.past.imp flowers girl clean.past.imp table
While the boy was watering flowers, the girl was cleaning the table.

---

name multiple locations in their answers. Second, children in this study also gave truth-value judgments to statements made by a puppet, such as "The monkey built a house by the tree." The same children who rejected incomplete events in responding to imperfective *where*-questions also rejected imperfective statements about incomplete events in the truth-value judgment task. Third, we ran another study in which each protagonist carried out only one complete or incomplete event. Younger children still showed errors in associating imperfective statements with incomplete events. This shows that the children do not fail simply because they only choose the event that is the "best match" to the target statement and prefer complete events to incomplete events.

Children judged sentences like (40a) or (40b) in a truth-value judgment setting (Crain & Thornton, 1998) after watching stories in which the event described by the main clause extended beyond the time interval specified by the *while*-clause. In one study, the main clause event did ultimately reach completion. In another study, it did not reach completion and remained incomplete at the end of the story. This manipulation had no effect on the children's responses, which were overwhelmingly adultlike at all ages. When tested on perfective sentences like (40a), children consistently responded *No!* because the main clause event did not reach completion during the interval described by the *while*-clause. When tested on imperfective sentences like (40b), however, children consistently responded *Yes!* because the main clause event was occurring during the interval described by the *while*-clause. They also responded *Yes!* to imperfective sentences in situations where the main clause event failed to reach completion at some time following the frame of reference. Many of the children who showed consistent adultlike performance on these tasks were among the children who consistently gave nonadultlike answers in the earlier experiments when judging statements with no explicit frame of reference.

These results show that young Russian children do know about key differences between the semantics of perfective and imperfective aspect. More important, they know that the imperfective can be used to describe a part of an event and does not require that the event ultimately reach completion. Therefore, they do not fail the Imperfective Paradox after all. This is encouraging, but it also begs the question of why so many young children fail to match imperfectives to incomplete events when judging simple sentences. Interestingly, van der Feest and van Hout (2002) observed that the simple past in adult Dutch shows a similar semantics. Simple past carries completion entailments in the absence of a temporal frame of reference as in (41a). The completion entailments disappear when an explicit frame of reference is provided as in (41b). We have confirmed these judgments with a number of Dutch speakers.

(41) a. Maria maakte de tafel schoon. [completion entailment]
       "Maria cleaned the table."
     b. Terwijl Hans de bloemen aan het water geven was, maakte
        Maria de tafel schoon. [no completion entailment]
        "While the boy was watering the flowers, Maria cleaned the table."

Why does the presence of the frame of reference matter to the completion entailments of the imperfective? Recall from earlier that a function of imperfective aspect is to convey a specific perspective on an event. An internal perspective on a past event suspends completion entailments. We suggest that adult Dutch and child Russian require that this temporal perspective be explicitly provided by prior discourse, whereas adult Russian is more liberal and does not impose this constraint (see Kazanina & Phillips, 2003b, for a more detailed account). The Dutch system has the advantage of being a more restrictive semantics, and hence a young Russian child should be able to move from the initial "Dutch" semantics to the adult Russian semantics based on hearing examples of past imperfectives used with incomplete events in simple sentences.

This case provides a good example of how nonadultlike language performance in children can be either overlooked or misinterpreted. Earlier studies suggested that Russian children had mastered grammatical aspect by age 3 because they never tested whether children understand the completion entailments of perfective and imperfective. Our initial experiments suggested that younger children have a deviant semantics for the imperfective, but subsequent testing on more complex sentences revealed that children's semantics for imperfective is in fact very close to adultlike, and that their initial semantics for the imperfective is a good starting point from the perspective of cross-language learning considerations.

Implications and Questions

The four examples from normal language development reviewed in this section all reinforce the common observation that the errors that children make are highly specific. Some errors are quite robust, whereas other potential errors are not found at all. This specificity in error patterns matches the emerging picture in research on developmental language disorders, but it has been established in a far broader set of cases among normally developing children. In each of the four examples, we observed that children deviate from the language of their parents, but that their errors closely match forms that are possible in other languages or other parts of the grammar of their own language. Children's errors respect universal constraints on language.

It is important to note that it was only through detailed linguistic research that it was possible for us to notice connections between the children's errors and cross-language variation in adult languages. The relevant facts were not available in off-the-shelf reference works, and in all of the examples described earlier there are crucial cross-linguistic generalizations that were uncovered only as a result of questions arising from developmental investigations.

Therefore, amid the enthusiasm for investigating language development using sophisticated brain-imaging tools, we should not lose sight of the continuing value of low-tech cross-linguistic research, which continues to yield results that are clearly relevant to questions about the specificity of developmental errors and at a fraction of the cost of more high-tech approaches.

The examples from normal language development reviewed here also raise questions about developmental language impairments (DLIs). We have seen that normal language learning is guided by a number of constraints that lead to highly specific error patterns. It is important to establish whether children with developmental impairments are guided by the same constraints. Current indications suggest that language-impaired and normally developing children make similar kinds of errors in the area of morphosyntax, but it remains to be seen whether the parallels extend to other areas of language. It is important to know whether normal and DLI children are similarly constrained because this will help indicate whether the affected children are guided by the same language learning mechanisms as the general population. It is even possible that we will reach different conclusions in different areas of language. In the area of morphosyntax, the constraint that we observed comes primarily from the grammar of the adult language to which the child is exposed. For a DLI child to follow the same constraint, he or she must be able to successfully internalize the details of embedded clauses in his input. In the areas of argument structure and pronoun interpretation, however, the constraints we observed are not apparent in the particular language to which the child is exposed. Rather, they reflect universal constraints that the child brings to the learning task. In the area of grammatical aspect, the children's errors reflect constraints on possible adult tense/aspect systems. Before we can conclude that DLI children are guided by the same language learning mechanisms that guide normally developing children, it is necessary to demonstrate parallel constraints on the learners in multiple subareas of language.

REAL-TIME KNOWLEDGE OF LANGUAGE

In the first part of the chapter, I argued that detailed linguistic studies can provide valuable information about the causes of the specificity of linguistic deficits. This argument was based entirely on connections between developmental errors and standard theoretical and typological approaches to linguistics. The aim in this section is to argue that a basic change in how we normally think about linguistic knowledge can pave the way for more ambitious attempts to draw deep links between genetics and neuroscience, on the one hand, and specific developmental disorders, on the other hand.

Even if we were presented with a complete description of the phenotype of a developmental language disorder (DLD), together with an accurate description of the corresponding genotype, we would still have a long way to go to understand how specific genetic causes give rise to specific linguistic outcomes. The challenge is to make a seamless connection between our understanding at the level of genes and our understanding at the level of linguistic behavior. This connection involves a number of different levels of description.

It is certainly important to understand how specific genetic changes give rise to specific changes in brain development, but it would be foolish of me to speculate on what this might involve. Nevertheless, I think that the task of linking neuroscience with linguistic behavior presents some fairly well-defined challenges, which I believe we are now in a position to address. I argue that central among these challenges is the need to understand linguistic knowledge from the perspective of real-time computation.

The Need for a Real-Time Perspective

There are a couple of reasons why a real-time perspective is so important. The first involves a basic theoretical issue. The second involves more practical considerations.

Discrete Infinity Problem. Linguists often use the term *discrete infinity* to refer to the property of human language that allows generation of infinitely many different expressions using finitely many stored elements. This property has implications for the importance of time in understanding language. In light of speakers' facility with novel sentences, and given the infinitely large range of sentences that are possible in any natural language, it is clear that all but the most formulaic of utterances must be constructed in real time and cannot simply be retrieved from long-term memory. Therefore, a full account of speakers' knowledge of sentences must include an explanation of how sentence structures are assembled in time.

Granularity Problem. The second motivation for a detailed understanding of real-time structure-building processes is more practical. Put simply, the granularity of our theories must match the granularity of our tools. A variety of new brain-recording tools hold great promise for bridging the gap between brain and behavior, and it is likely that these tools will play an important role in linking phenotypes and genotypes for language disorders. Also it is certainly true that the millimeter precision of techniques such as PET and fMRI, or the millisecond precision of techniques such as EEG, MEG, and TMS (transcranial magnetic stimulation), will play an important role in the search to understand how the brain supports language. However, the high resolution in space and time that these tools offer is of limited value unless the theoretical models that we use to make sense of the brain recordings have similarly high resolution. To take full advantage of millisecond-accuracy data, we need millisecond-accuracy models of language. Our current models do not provide this resolution. Although it is sometimes assumed that we could make great strides in our understanding of language in the brain, if only we had more precise brain-recording tools, the mismatch in granularity between tools and theories suggests that we may currently be more limited by the precision of our hypotheses than by the precision of our tools.

The standard conception of linguistic knowledge is built around a core system for representing sentence structures that does not operate in real time. The standard assumption in linguistics and psycholinguistics for at least the past 30 years has been that each speaker has multiple different structure-building systems: the grammar, parser, and producer are all viewed as related, but independent, mental systems that each incorporates a structure-building mechanism of its own. The parser and producer are assumed to operate in real time and to somehow draw on the knowledge that is represented in the grammar, but the grammar itself is assumed to operate independently of real-time processing. It may be possible to specify the operations of the grammar as a sequence of well-defined structure-building actions—as, for example, in recent incarnations of transformational grammar (Chomsky, 1995)—but these are not assumed to be amenable to real-time investigation. Meanwhile, in nontransformational approaches to syntax (e.g., Bresnan, 2000; Brody, 1995; Pollard & Sag, 1994), the irrelevance of timing in the creation of structure is often argued to be a virtue.

However, this standard architecture creates significant obstacles for efforts to link phenotypes and genotypes, and for bridging brain and behavior, particularly with regard to grammatical knowledge. If knowledge of grammar consists of knowledge of a procedure for building sentences, and if this procedure operates on a time scale independent of speaking and understanding, it is going to be extremely difficult to ever pinpoint this process in time. This in turn will make it almost impossible to test or confirm detailed linking hypotheses about grammatical encoding in the brain.

In light of considerations such as these, a solution to the linking problem for linguistic knowledge would be more within reach if it could be shown that there is just a single structure-building system in the brain, which works across comprehension, production, and grammaticality judgments. The linking problem would be more tractable if it could also be shown that this system operates on a time course that closely tracks the word-by-word unfolding of sentences, both in comprehension and production. If this were true, it would become feasible to generate highly specific predictions about the nature and timing of structure-building operations, and therefore also more feasible to test and verify these predictions using a variety of behavioral, computational, and neuroscientific tools. In this way, it would be possible to identify the specific brain processes associated with individual structure-building operations. This would be a valuable starting point for efforts to pinpoint exactly which brain processes are disrupted in DLDs.

Of course it is already possible to make brain recordings of both normally developing children and children with language disorders during a variety of tasks, and to observe differences in these recordings. Yet there are clear limits to our ability to interpret such findings in the absence of theoretical and computational models that match the granularity of the brain recordings.

Of course these considerations do not guarantee that knowledge of sentence structure is a parsimonious real-time system. They only show that it would be convenient if true. However, the biological world is not always so kind. It is possible that linguistic knowledge may turn out to be the kind of cognitive system that is hard to pin down in terms of real-time computation. This is almost certainly true for a number of other cognitive abilities, particularly nonautomatic cognitive abilities such as reasoning and arithmetical knowledge. If language turns out to be like these other abilities and cannot be characterized in terms of consistent real-time computation, the task of linking linguistic behavior to neuroscience and genetics will be vastly more difficult. Therefore, the question of the real-time status of linguistic knowledge is of central importance for efforts to link linguistic abilities with brain-level models of language.

Nevertheless, the promise that the real-time perspective holds for the linking problem is of little consequence unless it can be shown that it is possible to characterize knowledge of sentence structure as a single structure-building procedure, and unless the classic arguments against this architecture can be answered. I sketch the outline of such an answer in what follows.

Challenges for the Simple Architecture

There are a number of arguments in favor of the standard view of linguistic knowledge as a set of distinct, task-specific systems, with a parser and producer that operate in real time and a grammar that operates more slowly, but is highly accurate. Many of these arguments go back 30 years or more to a period in the late 1960s and early 1970s when the question of the relation between "competence systems" and "performance systems" for language received a good deal of attention (see Fodor, Bever, & Garrett, 1974; Levelt, 1974; for more recent reviews, see also Phillips, 1996; Townsend & Bever, 2001). The list of arguments includes:

#1: Available grammars do not appear suitable for direct deployment in speaking and understanding.

#2: Available evidence on parsing and production suggests systems that lack the precision required of a grammar.

#3: Furthermore, grammars typically do not provide the tools needed to account for well-studied parsing phenomena such as garden-path sentences.

#4: The apparently slow and effortful nature of many grammaticality judgments suggests the existence of a system that operates on a different time scale from parsing and production.

#5: Speaking and understanding are clearly different processes that break down in different ways. This is unsurprising if they are the product of different systems.

#6: It is widely assumed that a famous set of studies from the 1960s (on the *Derivational Theory of Complexity*) confirmed the need for distinct grammars and parsers.

Each of these arguments appears compelling, and together they have been decisive in thinking about the architecture of linguistic knowledge in recent decades. However, I think that all of them can be overcome, and that it is worthwhile to pursue this possibility given the enormous potential benefit of a real-time architecture for linguistic knowledge.

#1: *Grammars Don't Look Like Parsers.*   Perhaps the most straightforward argument for separation of grammars and parsers has been that grammars tend not to look much like effective parsing devices. In particular, they do not build structure in a left-to-right fashion as parsing and production devices clearly must. This argument was developed quite clearly by Fodor, Bever, and Garrett (1974) and applies to a broad range of grammatical frameworks, not just to transformational grammars.

Therefore, the first piece of the argument for the unified architecture comes from evidence that grammars look more like real-time systems than previously thought. A number of pieces of evidence of this kind have appeared in recent years. In each case, the argument is that problems from within the traditional domain of syntax can be better understood if they are recast in an approach that more closely matches the incremental structure building found in speaking and understanding.

For example, I have argued that it is possible to make sense of a long-standing mystery about the constituent structure of sentences simply by viewing sentence construction from a real-time perspective (Phillips, 1996, 2003). The argument focuses on a long-standing puzzle about sentence structure.

A basic tool of syntactic research is a series of tests of constituency, which are used to diagnose the structural organization of sentences. These include tests based on coordination, deletion (ellipsis), movement of phrases, and co-reference possibilities (binding), to name but a few. Although the logic of the tests dictates that their results should converge, and in some cases they do, it is well known that there are many situations where different tests yield different results, sometimes even contradictory results. One simple example of this comes from coordination, which tends to be a rather liberal diagnostic of constituency. Sentences like (42a) show that it is possible to coordinate a subject–verb sequence to the exclusion of the direct object of the verb. This contradicts the general assumption that the verb and its object form a unit to the exclusion of the subject ("verb phrase"); it also contradicts the results of a number of other constituency diagnostics and even the result of the coordination in (42b).

(42) a. [Sarah chopped] and [Harry fried] the large pile of vegetables.
    b. Sarah [chopped the vegetables] and [fried the chicken].

However, if we make the assumption that sentences are assembled incrementally, from left to right, we can explain the conflicts. As a standard right-branching sentence structure is built up, there are sequences of words that are constituents at one stage, but are no longer constituents at a later point. This can be seen in the example of the hypothetical sequence ABC in (43). The string AB is a constituent at one stage (43a), but ceases to be a constituent at a later point, when the element C is added at the right (43b).

(43) a.

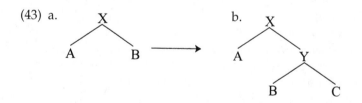

b.

This transient property of constituents in an incremental derivation of a sentence can explain why different constituency diagnostics yield different results. Diagnostics that are able to look at an early stage in the derivation may be able to see constituents that are not visible to diagnostics that only see later stages in the derivation. Coordination is a diagnostic that can see early, temporary constituents because it has the property that it applies to pairs of linearly adjacent phrases, and therefore can apply to a piece of structure before that structure is destroyed. This is why it can apply to subject–verb sequences, as in (42a), because they form a constituent at the point in the assembly of the structure before the direct object is added. In contrast, diagnostics that rely on between-sentence relations necessarily apply to later stages in the derivation, and therefore fail to see some constituents that were present at earlier stages. The logic of this argument is developed elsewhere in much more detail with many more examples (Phillips, 1996, 2003).

Related arguments for left-to-right structure building have been presented in the domains of *wh*-movement (Richards, 1999, 2002), prosodic phrasing (Guimaraes, 1999), and agreement processes (Legate, 1999; Schlenker, 1999). Meanwhile, a number of independent proposals have emerged from other grammatical frameworks that also allow for incremental derivations, and hence closer links with parsing systems (e.g., Kempson, Meyer-Viol, & Gabbay, 2001; Milward, 1994; Steedman, 2000). All of these approaches make it seem more feasible to view knowledge of sentence structure as knowledge of a real-time computational process, and hence remove one of the primary motivations for assuming multiple syntactic systems.

#2: Parsers Don't Look Like Grammars. The second argument for multiple syntactic systems is the mirror image of the first. A good deal of research on parsing and production has focused on errors that arise in speaking and understanding. The literature on sentence comprehension is dominated by studies of breakdown in "garden path" sentences and complexity-induced processing overload, such as occurs in multiply center-embedded sentences like *The dog the cat the mouse feared chased fled.* In work on sentence production, a good deal of attention has been paid to "slips of the tongue" and other dysfluencies. To the extent that the systems for comprehension and production are fallible and grammatically inaccurate, they do not look like good candidates to be the grammar, which is generally assumed to be robust and precise, if not particularly fast. The parser and the producer have sometimes been viewed as covering grammars, which perhaps imperfectly capture the detail of the true grammar (Ferreira, Bailey, & Ferraro, 2002; Townsend & Bever, 2001).

However, this argument is less convincing than it may first appear. To show that the parser lacks the precision of the grammar, it would need to be shown that it builds structures that are ungrammatical or systematically avoids building structures that are grammatical. Garden path and center-embedded sentences are cases where certain grammatical structures fail to be constructed, but in neither case can this be blamed on lack of grammatical detail. Garden path sentences arise in circumstances of structural ambiguity, where two or more possible grammatical analyses are available. If the parser makes the wrong choice and subsequently breaks down when it becomes clear that the choice was the wrong one, this reflects lack of telepathy, not lack of grammatical precision. Center-embedded sentences often lead to processing breakdown, but this more likely reflects resource limitations than specific grammatical details of the parser. Meanwhile, there is a good deal of evidence that the parser is highly grammatically accurate provided that it is operating within the bounds of available resources and is not misled by structural ambiguity. Many studies of comprehension have shown that the parser is grammatically precise in such domains as verb argument structure (e.g., Boland et al., 1995; Phillips, Edgar, & Kabak, 2000), co-reference relations (Nicol & Swinney, 1989; Sturt, 2003), and long-distance dependencies (Phillips, Rabbin, Pablos, & Wong, 2003; Stowe, 1986; Traxler & Pickering, 1996).

The most serious challenge to this conclusion in recent work comes from a series of studies by Ferreira and colleagues, which appear to show that speakers construct clearly ungrammatical sentence structures during parsing (Christianson, Hollingworth, Halliwell, & Ferreira, 2001; Ferreira, Christianson, & Hollingworth, 2001). The evidence comes from the inferences that speakers draw after reading garden path sentences like (44).

(44) While the man hunted the deer ran into the woods.

As is well known, in sentences like (44), speakers often initially misinterpret the subject NP of the main clause (*the deer*) as the object of the embedded clause verb (*hunted*). This gives rise to a garden path effect from which speakers must recover (Ferreira & Henderson, 1991; Frazier & Rayner, 1982; Sturt, Pickering, & Crocker, 1999). Ferreira and colleagues used comprehension questions to investigate what interpretations speakers arrive at by the end of the sentence. They found that even after recovery from the garden path, when the NP *the deer* is correctly analyzed as the main clause subject, many speakers continue to believe that the man hunted the deer—something that the sentence does not, in fact, assert. Ferreira and colleagues argued that these findings show that speakers construct "good enough" sentence structures that do not fully conform to the grammatical analysis of the input sentence.

If true, these findings present a serious challenge to the widespread assumption that the parser constructs only grammatically sanctioned representations, and would therefore also constitute a strong motivation for a parser–grammar distinction. However, I do not think that we are forced into this conclusion by these results. What these findings may instead show is that syntactic reanalysis is insufficient to cause the dismantling of previously constructed semantic analyses. In the case of sentences like (44), this would mean that, although the sentence undergoes correct syntactic reanalysis, such that *the deer* becomes the main clause subject and *hunted* becomes intransitive, this does not trigger corresponding retraction of prior semantic commitments.[16] Nevertheless, these examples are important and deserve further investigation.

In summary, although much work has focused on the ways in which real-time language systems fail, it is important to distinguish failure in general from lack of grammatical precision. A good deal of evidence supports the notion that the real-time systems are, in fact, highly grammatically precise. This conclusion is entirely expected if the real-time system is the grammar. To the extent that a real-time analysis system (i.e., parser or producer) is able to capture all of the distinctions required of the grammar, it becomes less clear why there is a separate need for an independent grammar that does not operate in real time.

#3: Grammars Fail to Explain Ambiguity Resolution Phenomena. A further source of evidence for assuming the existence of multiple structure-building systems comes from investigations of parsing. At least since the late 1960s and early 1970s, it has commonly been assumed that the parser incorporates mechanisms and principles that are by their nature specialized for the task of parsing. This is implicit in the "heuristics and strategies" approach proposed by Bever and colleagues (Bever, 1970; Fodor, Bever, & Garrett, 1974; see also Townsend & Bever, 2001), which incorporates a series of parsing heuristics (e.g., NP V → subject verb) that are specifically tailored for the task of parsing unambiguous input. Meanwhile, principles such as *Minimal Attachment, Late Closure*, and the *Active Filler Strategy* proposed later by Frazier and colleagues (Frazier, 1987a, 1987b; Frazier & Fodor, 1978) are designed specifically for resolving structural ambiguities that arise during parsing. If these assumptions are correct—and what is important here is the general approach that they represent, rather than the specifics of the individual models[17]—then they

---

[16]Note that Ferreira and colleagues are aware of this kind of possibility and construct an ingenious control study in which optionally transitive verbs like *hunt* in (44) are replaced with transitive/reflexive verbs like *bathe, scratch,* and *hide*. Importantly, when these verbs are used without an overt direct object, they must be understood as reflexive: *John bathed* means that John bathed himself, not that he bathed something or other. Ferreira and colleagues showed that speakers still hold onto incorrect interpretations in sentences with this type of verb. I agree that this shows that the persistent misinterpretations do not simply arise from inferential processes (e.g., "he hunted something, and a deer is mentioned, so he probably hunted a deer"), and it also shows that speakers do not reliably *reinterpret* the first clause after syntactic reanalysis. However, I am not sure that this shows that speakers maintain an impossible syntactic representation.

[17]In particular, this argument does not depend on the modular, "syntax first" property of Frazier's model, which has been highly controversial in language-processing research. All that is required for this argument is that there be some parser-specific structural constraints regardless of how they interact with other sources of information in ambiguity resolution.

provide another good reason to distinguish systems for parsing, production, and grammar.

However, even in this area there is reason for optimism. Bever's heuristics and strategies were designed to handle the parsing of unambiguous input given that grammars available at the time did not seem equal to that task. As we have already seen, we now have grammars that can more plausibly be deployed for real-time processes. Meanwhile, the literature on structural ambiguity resolution now contains a number of alternatives to the parsing-specific strategies proposed by Frazier and colleagues. Of particular interest are suggestions that the parsing biases that at one time appeared to be the result of general structural simplicity metrics are in fact the result of the need to satisfy lexical and grammatical requirements.[18] One example from our recent work shows that it is not only possible to replace parsing-specific strategies with independently motivated principles; it is in fact preferable to do so. This example involves a cross-language comparison of parsing in English and Japanese (Aoshima, Phillips, & Weinberg, in press).

In English *wh*-questions, *wh*-phrases such as *who, what,* or *which dog* appear in sentence-initial position, displaced from their canonical argument position. It is well known that when English speakers process *wh*-questions, they attempt to associate the *wh*-phrase with the verb in the main clause provided that the verb is semantically compatible. In standard parlance, they attempt to locate the *gap* position from which the *filler wh*-phrase was displaced. The relationship between the surface position of the *wh*-phrase and the gap is known as a *filler-gap dependency.* Thus, when speakers incrementally process a sentence like (45), they initially interpret the *wh*-phrase filler as the object of the main verb *say* (45a) and are then forced to revise this analysis when they encounter the complementizer *that,* which signals the presence of an embedded clause. The *wh*-phrase is ultimately interpreted as the object of the embedded verb *read* (45b).

(45) a. What did you say ＿＿＿＿
     b. What did you say that Bill read ＿＿＿＿

The generalization that speakers attempt to posit a gap for the fronted phrase at the first available opportunity is well established and has been

---

[18]This claim is independent of the question of how parsing decisions are affected by nonsyntactic cues based on plausibility, frequency, prosody, and so on. For this reason, the kind of principle-based parsing mechanisms that I describe here may be understood as the syntactic subcomponent of the constraint-based parsing architectures that currently dominate psychological research on sentence comprehension (Gibson & Pearlmutter, 1998; MacDonald, Pearlmutter, & Seidenberg, 1994).

documented in a number of languages (de Vincenzi, 1991; Frazier & Flores d'Arcais, 1989; Schlesewsky et al., 2000). To capture this generalization, Frazier and colleagues proposed that there is a parsing-specific strategy that leads the parser to create a gap for a displaced phrase in the first possible position (*Active Filler Strategy*: de Vincenzi, 1991; Frazier, 1987b). An alternative approach to this generalization argues that there is no specialized strategy for creating filler-gap dependencies. Rather, the observed effects arise as a direct consequence of the need to satisfy thematic role assignment constraints as soon as possible (Gibson, Hickok, & Schütze, 1994; Pritchett, 1992). A *wh*-phrase is preferably associated with a gap position in the main clause because that is the first position where thematic role assignment is possible.

Unfortunately, these two approaches to the processing of filler-gap relations make similar predictions in English, and so it is hard to distinguish between them empirically. However, the two approaches make clearly different predictions in Japanese due to the strongly verb-final word order of Japanese. As illustrated in (46), the main verb of a multiclause sentence is the final word of the sentence. The embedded clause precedes the main verb, with the consequence that the first verb in the sentence is the most deeply embedded verb, in contrast to English, where the first verb in the linear order of the sentence is typically the least deeply embedded verb.

(46) John-wa Mary-ga sono hon-o nakusita-to omotteiru.
John-top Mary-nom that book-acc lost-that thinks
"John thinks that Mary lost that book."

To explain the key predictions, some preliminaries on Japanese word order are needed. In Japanese, *wh*-phrases may appear either in their canonical argument position (i.e., Japanese is a "wh-in-situ" language) or may be displaced leftward ("scrambling"), including to sentence-initial position. Whereas in English the position of the *wh*-phrase indicates whether the question is a direct or indirect question (47), in Japanese the position of the *wh*-phrase does not indicate whether the question is a direct or indirect question. This is instead indicated by the position of a question particle suffix *-ka* on either the main clause verb (direct question: 48a) or the embedded verb (indirect question: 48b). This device is common cross-linguistically. If the *wh*-phrase appears in the main clause, but the question particle is in the embedded clause, the sentence is understood as an indirect question (48c).

(47) a. Who did John say that Mary saw?   *direct question*
     b. John said who Mary saw.   *indirect question*

(48) a. John-wa [Mary-ga dare-ni sono hon-o ageta-to] itta-no?
   John-top Mary-nom whom-dat that book-acc gave-Comp said-Q
   "Who did John say Mary gave that book to?"
   b. John-wa [Mary-ga dare-ni sono hon-o ageta-ka] itta.
   John-top Mary-nom whom-dat that book-acc gave-Q said
   "John said who Mary gave that book to."
   c. Dare-ni John-wa [Mary-ga sono hon-o ageta-ka] itta.
   whom-dat John-top Mary-nom that book-acc gave-Q said
   "John said to whom Mary gave that book."

These properties of Japanese word order make it possible to distinguish the predictions of the two approaches to parsing *wh*-phrases outlined earlier. In the sentence in (49), the fronted dative *wh*-phrase could be associated with either of the two gap positions marked. The gap position that is closest to the *wh*-phrase is in the main clause, but the gap position that allows earliest satisfaction of thematic role assignment requirements is in the embedded clause because the embedded verb is the first verb.

(49) Dono-seito-ni tannin-wa _____gap1 [koocyoo-ga _____gap2
   which student-dat class teacher-top principal-nom
   hon-o yonda-ka] tosyositu-de sisyo-ni iimasita
   book-acc read-Q library-at librarian-dat told
   "The class teacher told the librarian at the library which student the principal read a book for."

Therefore, the account of parsing *wh*-phrases that is based on independently motivated grammatical principles makes the striking prediction that Japanese speakers should prefer to interpret the sentence-initial *wh*-phrase in (49) as if it is displaced from the *most deeply embedded clause* of the sentence. In fact this is exactly what Japanese speakers do, as we have shown in three different experiments (Aoshima et al., in press). In contrast, if Japanese speakers were simply trying to create a gap position as soon as possible, due to a parser-specific routine such as the Active Filler Strategy, there would be no reason for them to interpret the *wh*-phrase in the embedded clause.

Our example from Japanese reiterates the value of cross-language comparisons and shows just one example of a situation where parsing-specific mechanisms can be replaced by independently motivated grammatical principles. Of course this is just one example, and much more evidence is needed to show that parsing-specific syntactic mechanisms are unnecessary in general. However, as I outlined previously, there are currently fewer reasons to assume a set of task-specific parsing strategies than there may have been 25 years ago. This is good news for attempts to unify the different subcomponents of linguistic knowledge.

#4: Parsing and Production Are Fast, Grammaticality Judgment Is Slow.

A fourth argument for separation of systems is based on the fact that many grammaticality judgments, particularly ones involving subtle semantic contrasts, are slow and difficult. This would appear to fit naturally with the assumption that the grammar operates in a different time domain from systems for real-time parsing and production. Again this apparently compelling argument does not survive closer scrutiny. For this argument to go through, it would need to be shown that grammaticality judgment involves a slow process that follows a *different sequence of operations* than parsing or production. I am not aware of evidence of this kind.

Much of the available evidence points to a different conclusion. A number of different experimental paradigms based on violation detection indicate that grammaticality violations are detected within a few hundred milliseconds of the presentation of the offending word. This can be observed in studies that have used a "stops making sense" task, in which participants read a sentence word by word and respond as soon as they detect an anomaly. This technique has been used to show rapid detection of violations involving verb–argument structure (e.g., Boland et al., 1995). More fine-grained information about the speed of violation detection is provided by speed-accuracy trade-off studies, in which participants are required to make well-formedness judgments under varying degrees of time pressure. This technique has shown rapid detection of violations involving verb–argument structure (McElree & Griffith, 1995) and constraints on long-distance dependencies (McElree & Griffith, 1998). Even more fine-grained information comes from electrophysiological studies of syntactic anomaly detection. Studies using this technique have shown detection of violations within 300 to 600 milliseconds in areas such as word order (Friederici, Pfeifer, & Hahne, 1993; Neville et al., 1991), subject–verb agreement (Hagoort, Brown, & Groothusen, 1993; Osterhout & Holcomb, 1992), case marking (Coulson, King, & Kutas, 1998), verb–argument structure (Friederici & Frisch, 2000; Osterhout, Holcomb, & Swinney, 1994), coreference (Osterhout & Mobley, 1995), and question formation (Kluender & Kutas, 1993; Neville et al., 1991), to list but a few. Based on all of these studies, it seems clear that a good number of grammaticality judgments—negative judgments at least—can be delivered extremely quickly.

Of course there remain many situations where grammaticality judgments are reliable, but slow. These are the cases that give rise to the assumption that grammaticality judgments are the product of a system that operates on an independent time scale from normal parsing or production. However, even slow judgments do not entail a separate system. It is important to consider why such judgments take a long time. I suspect that the slowness of such judgments simply reflects repeated attempts to reparse the sentence, which may be necessary for at least two reasons.

Reparsing may be necessary to avoid an irrelevant initial parse. For example, there is a robust contrast between (50a) and (50b) in the availability of an interpretation in which the question word *why* is construed with the embedded verb *fix* (i.e., as a question about the reason for fixing the drain). The embedded clause interpretation is available in (50a), but not in (50b). The unavailability of this interpretation in (50b) reflects a characteristic of a factive verb like *remember* (i.e., a verb that gives rise to the presupposition that its complement is true; Cinque, 1990; Kiparsky & Kiparsky, 1971; Melvold, 1991). Although the contrast between (50a) and (50b) is robust, it typically takes time for a speaker to make this judgment because reparsing is necessary to avoid the dominant, but irrelevant, reading in which *why* is interpreted with the main clause verb.

(50) a. Why did you think that John fixed the drain?
     b. Why did you remember that John fixed the drain?

A second situation where reparsing may be needed is when the speaker attempts to construct a mental scenario that makes the target reading felicitous. This is particularly relevant in sentences that involve scope ambiguities. For example, (51) and (52) illustrate a well-known contrast in the interpretations available for sentences that contain a *wh*-phrase and a quantifier: (51) exhibits a scope ambiguity that is not available in (52). Specifically, (51) can be understood as a question that invites a list of answers (the so-called *pair-list reading*), documenting who each person met.[19] In contrast, (52) can only be understood as a question about which individuals met every single member of the group and does not allow the pair-list reading (May, 1985).

(51) Who did everyone meet?
     a. *Who is the person such that everyone met him?*
     b. *For each person, who is the person that he met?*

(52) Who met everyone?
     a. *Who is the person such that he met everyone?*
     b. **For each person, who met him?*

---

[19]Questions with the form of (51) are commonly used in naturally occurring speech with the expectation of a pair-list reading. Imagine, for example, a teacher asking a group of students on Monday morning, *What did everybody do on the weekend?* This is understood as an invitation for each student to list what he or she did on the weekend, and not as a question about what all the students did in common on the weekend.

Although this contrast in scope possibilities is clear and consistent across speakers of English, it may take some time for any individual to confirm this judgment for him or herself because the judgment typically requires the speaker to first construct in his mind an appropriate context for each of the scope readings under consideration, and then judge whether the sentence could be used in that context. For each context, the judgment step itself does not take long. It takes a long while to judge whether a question contains a scope ambiguity because this judgment involves a number of subtasks requiring construction of multiple contexts and a separate judgment of the appropriateness of the question form for each different context. Trained semanticists can often make these judgments quickly—not because they have out-of-the-ordinary language processing abilities, but because they are experienced at imagining exactly the right kinds of contexts that are needed to test such judgments.

I see little reason at present to assume that grammaticality judgments, however long they might take, reflect the operation of a separate syntactic system that follows a different time course from real-time parsing and production systems. Furthermore, I am not aware of any evidence that sentences are constructed in a different sequence of steps depending on whether they are being parsed or judged on their well formedness.

Another observation that is sometimes used to motivate a grammar–parser distinction is that there are many ungrammatical sentences that are readily comprehensible, such as violations of subject–verb agreement (53), violations of restrictions on double object constructions (54), or so-called *that-trace* effects (55).

(53) *The cats likes fish.

(54) *The millionaire donated the museum a painting.

(55) *Who do you think that __ appreciates hockey?

The examples in (53) to (55) can be accounted for easily without recourse to separate structure-building systems. All that is required is to assume that the grammar can use its standard structure-building mechanisms to construct combinations of words and phrases that are *almost* fully compatible in their lexical-grammatical features (e.g., number mismatch in [53]) and somehow mark the fact that the ungrammatical feature combination is recognized to be illicit. In fact it would be unhelpful to treat (53) to (55) as evidence for a separate parsing system because that move would beg the question of why it is that speakers are so good at identifying and diagnosing the anomalies in the sentences.

More troubling are sentences that appear at first to be entirely natural, but that turn out, on further reflection, to be ungrammatical and even incomprehensible. Sentence (56) is a notorious example due to Mario Montalbetti (1984), which sounds seductively natural until one stops to reflect on what it actually means. Surely the fact that speakers can readily parse sentences that turn out to be both ungrammatical and uninterpretable implies the existence of a real-time structure-building system that is distinct from the grammar (see Townsend & Bever, 2001, for an explicit argument to that effect).

(56) *More people have visited Russia than I have.

Although I cannot present a full account at present of why such sentences sound so good, it is interesting to note that there are minimally different sentences that either have a fairly clear interpretation (57) or are much more quickly detected as odd (58). This indicates that whatever is special about (56) is subject to detailed grammatical restrictions, and therefore cannot be simply the reflection of a *dumb* first-pass parsing mechanism.

(57) More Italians have visited Rome than Germans have.

(58) *More people have visited Russia than I have visited.[20]

In summary, the double dissociation between grammaticality and parsability appears at first glance to present a compelling case for distinguishing a grammar and parser. I was convinced by this argument at one time (cf. Phillips, 1995a). However, the argument does not go through particularly if we assume that the structure-building system may be able to construct representations that it recognizes to be illicit in a specific way. Therefore, grammaticality judgment does not eliminate the possibility of a single real-time grammar. Nevertheless, this does not change the fact that our current understanding of the process of grammaticality judgment is extremely limited, and there is a clear need for more systematic work on this topic (see Schütze, 1996, for a detailed review of existing studies of grammaticality judgment).

---

[20]Note that a reading of (58) is available for some speakers, in which the elided object of the second verb is understood as dependent on the subject of the first verb. Under this reading, the sentence asserts that the number of people that have visited Russia is greater than the number of people that I have visited.

#5: *Speaking and Understanding Are Different.* A fifth argument for separation of systems derives from the fact that there are differences between speaking and understanding. Classic models of parsing and production look quite different from one another (parsing: Frazier & Fodor, 1978; Kimball, 1973; production: Garrett, 1976), and the kinds of errors that have attracted most attention in parsing—namely, garden path sentences—look rather different from the kinds of errors that have attracted most attention in production—namely, slips of the tongue. Also research on language disorders commonly turns up cases where comprehension and production appear to be affected differently. These observations are widely taken to motivate independent structure-building systems for comprehension and production. Furthermore, to the extent that parsing and production draw on different syntactic systems, there is also a need for an additional syntactic system—the grammar—to capture whatever is shared between parsing and production. Although the possibility of parser–producer parallels has not been investigated in great depth, both theoretical and empirical considerations suggest that uniting the syntactic aspect of these two systems may be more feasible now than previously thought.

The theoretical consideration is that differences between the *outcomes* of parsing and production tasks do not entail that the tasks are carried out by independent systems. The different outcomes may reflect a single sentence-generation system, which always incrementally generates structures that link up the sound of a sentence with its meaning. Such a system can be expected to encounter different types of bottleneck depending on whether it faces a production task, in which a meaning is given, and the task is to generate a compatible syntax and phonology, or a comprehension task, in which a phonological input is provided, and the task is to generate a compatible syntax and semantics. In both situations, the task is to generate a structure to match a prespecified semantic or phonological representation, but the more open-ended part of the problem is different in the two situations.

It is interesting to note that in the area of lexical processing there are many differences between the tasks of picture naming and word recognition, yet this does not typically lead to the conclusion that there are different lexicons for speaking and understanding. Rather, it is generally assumed that a single lexicon responds differently when deployed in different task situations. The same conclusion deserves more serious consideration in the area of sentence structure.

The empirical motivation for closing the gap between parsing and production is that research in the two areas has been undergoing a quiet convergence for a number of years. Traditional approaches to sentence production tended to emphasize the role of clause-sized templates, into which lexical material was inserted, to explain systematicities in slips of the tongue (e.g., Fromkin, 1971; Garrett, 1976). Such an approach is hard to reconcile with models of sentence comprehension, which have almost always assumed that structures are built up more incrementally on a word-by-word basis. However, recent sentence-production research has moved beyond a focus on speech errors and has uncovered evidence for more incremental encoding of structure (e.g., Ferreira, 1996; Ferreira & Dell, 2000). To the extent that syntactic encoding in production is shown to proceed incrementally, rather than by the filling in of larger templates, it is more feasible to view the syntactic aspects of comprehension and speaking as products of the same system.

Of course these observations fall well short of demonstrating that a single structure-building system can capture the syntactic component of parsing and production. They show only that this is a feasible goal. Clearly, much work needs to be done to show whether this goal can actually be realized. (For some interesting computational models that move in this direction, see Kempen & Hoenkamp, 1987; Vosse & Kempen, 2000.)

#6: The Implications of the "Derivational Theory of Complexity." Finally, there is an additional reason that grammar, parsing, and production have been investigated as independent systems. This reason has exerted a more powerful influence on the field than should have been the case.

In the mid-1960s, collaborative efforts between George Miller and Noam Chomsky and their students gave rise to a famous set of experiments that suggested a close relationship between the mechanisms of transformational grammar and real-time sentence processing. This was followed by an equally famous set of experiments that led to widespread disillusionment about this enterprise, and substantial divergence between the fields of syntactic theory and language processing.

The crux of the matter was a specific linking suggestion by Miller and Chomsky (1963, p. 481) that the perceptual complexity of a sentence, presumably reflected in its processing time, might be predicted by the complexity of its derivation in a transformational grammar. For example, if it is assumed that active, declarative sentences are "kernel" structures, and that passive sentences and questions are derived from the corresponding kernels by means of a transformation, then passive sentences should take longer to process than active sentences, questions should take longer than declaratives, and passive questions should take even longer. This linking hypothesis came to be known as the *Derivational Theory of Complexity* (DTC). The initial experiments focused on transformations such as passivization, question-formation, and negation, and they produced results that were quite encouraging, even "breathtaking" by some accounts

(Townsend & Bever, 2001, p. 29). However, subsequent studies on a broader set of constructions produced results that appeared less consistent with the DTC hypothesis, and the DTC quickly acquired a reputation as a classic error in psycholinguistic theorizing. Although the DTC was just one specific linking hypothesis, and the problematic results appear much less problematic from a current perspective (see Phillips, 1996, for a detailed review), in practice the demise of the DTC had a chilling effect on attempts to provide clear linking hypotheses among grammar, parser, and producer, and it was instrumental in creating the separation between the fields of syntactic theory and sentence processing.

Since the demise of the DTC over 30 years ago, research in grammatical theory and sentence processing has been carried out by largely disparate groups of people who, in most cases, occupy different academic departments. As a result, there has been only limited contact between the two subfields, and the divisions between them have become self-perpetuating. In this climate, it is perhaps not surprising that a consensus should have emerged that the two fields are investigating different systems.

Neither the conclusions about the DTC from the 1960s nor the separation of disciplines that they engendered amount to real arguments for the existence of multiple syntactic systems. It is unfortunate that they have had such a powerful effect on thinking about language, and in particular about the relation between linguistic knowledge and real-time processes.

I should emphasize that it is not my goal to revive the specific linking hypotheses that were entertained in the 1960s. There are good reasons not to do this. For example, the DTC provided only an index of perceptual complexity—something that does not amount to an explicit account of parsing or production. However, it is my goal to revive the objectives of the 1960s work, which was to take seriously the relationship between linguistic models and real-time models of comprehension and production.

IMPLICATIONS

If we want to understand how specific neural structures (and the genes that give rise to them) support human language, it should go without saying that we need to have a proper understanding of human language. The same is clearly true for efforts to understand DLDs. If we misconstrue the nature of a language disorder at the behavioral or cognitive level, we run the risk of asking the wrong questions at the neural or genetic levels.

In the first part of the chapter, I presented a series of examples from normal language development of how we can better understand the kinds of errors that children make—if we take into account either the detailed structure of the target adult language or facts about cross-language typology and universals of language. In each case, the children showed a highly systematic pattern of errors, which made more sense in light of detailed investigations of adult languages. The distribution of children's root infinitive clauses across languages appeared much less arbitrary once we observed the parallels with embedded infinitival clauses in the children's own target language. In the examples of English children's locative verb production and Russian children's pronoun interpretation, we saw that children make errors in areas that are subject to cross-language variation, but fail to make errors in closely related areas where all adult languages behave alike. In the case of Russian aspect, in particular, we saw that if we had only focused on children's interpretation of simple sentences, we could have severely underestimated the semantic sophistication of the children. In fact there was a period in the evolution of this project where we did just that. It was only when our attention was drawn to a little-discussed detail of adult Dutch, and we tested Russian 3-year-olds on more complex sentences, that we were able to find that the children know a good deal more about the semantics of aspect than we had previously suspected.

If the DLDs discussed elsewhere in this volume reflect language abilities that are fundamentally normal, but delayed, as many have argued, we should expect the details of linguistic structure and linguistic typology to have a similar impact on our understanding of language disorders.

In the second part of the chapter, I argued that it is feasible to develop an account of sentence-structure building that operates in real time and uses a single syntactic system that underlies speaking, understanding, and grammaticality judgment alike. I also argued that it is well worth the effort to pursue this possibility because it will make the goal of developing and testing explicit linking hypothesis for brain and language a good deal more attainable. This is because it represents our best chance of developing linguistic models that can match the temporal granularity of the tools that we can already use to observe the brain in action.

However, it should have been clear that most of my arguments in that section included demonstrations of what *would* need to be explained *if* we were to develop an explicit linking hypothesis for brain and language, and that in doing so I issued a number of promissory notes. Therefore, a good deal remains to be done to more fully develop a dynamic model of structure building and connect a linguistic model of this kind with studies in cognitive neuroscience and computational neuroscience. This is a project that we are currently engaged in, and we expect that it will take some time. However, I am confident that if this effort is at all successful in understanding how normally developed brains support normally acquired language, it will provide many new possibilities for understanding how atypical brain development leads to atypical language outcomes.

ACKNOWLEDGMENTS

This work was supported in part by grants from the National Science Foundation (#BCS-0196004), the Human Frontiers Science Program (#RGY-0134), and the McDonnell-Pew Cognitive Neuroscience program (#CNS99-31), and by a Semester Research Award from the University of Maryland. The studies described here could not have been completed without the help of many people. In particular, Sachiko Aoshima, Nina Kazanina, and Meesook Kim deserve special thanks for their contributions.

REFERENCES

Aoshima, S., Phillips, C., & Weinberg, A. (in press). Processing filler-gap dependencies in a head-final language. *Journal of Memory and Language.*

Avrutin, S., & Reuland, E. (2002). *Backward anaphora and tense interpretation.* Unpublished manuscript, Utrecht University.

Baker, M. (1991). On some subject-object non-asymmetries in Mohawk. *Natural Language and Linguistic Theory, 9,* 537–576.

Bar-Shalom, E. (in press). Tense and aspect in early child Russian. *Language Acquisition.*

Bar-Shalom, E., Snyder, W., & Boro, J. (1996). Evidence for the optional infinitive stage in Russian. In A. Halbert & K. Matsuoka (Eds.), *Papers on acquisition and processing.* Storrs, CT: University of Connecticut Working Papers in Linguistics.

Behrens, H. (1993). *Temporal reference in German child language.* Unpublished doctoral dissertation, University of Amsterdam.

Bever, T. G. (1970). The cognitive basis for linguistic structures. In J. R. Hayes (Ed.), *Cognition and the development of language* (pp. 279–352). New York: Wiley.

Boland, J., Tanenhaus, M. K., Garnsey, S. M., & Carlson, G. N. (1995). Verb argument structure in parsing and interpretation: Evidence from *wh*-questions. *Journal of Memory and Language, 34,* 774–806.

Bowerman, M. (1982). Reorganizational processes in lexical and syntactic development. In E. Wanner & L. R. Gleitman (Eds.), *Language acquisition: The state of the art.* New York: Cambridge University Press.

Bresnan, J. (2000). *Lexical-functional syntax.* Malden, MA: Blackwell.

Brody, M. (1995). *Lexico-logical form.* Cambridge, MA: MIT Press.

Brun, D., Avrutin, S., & Babyonyshev, M. (1999). Aspect and its temporal interpretation during the optional infinitive stage in Russian. In A. Greenhill, H. Littlefield, & C. Tano (Eds.), *Proceedings of the 23rd Annual Boston University Conference on Language Development* (pp. 120–131). Somerville, MA: Cascadilla Press.

Chomsky, N. (1981). *Lectures on government and binding.* Dordrecht: Foris.

Chomsky, N. (1995). *The minimalist program.* Cambridge, MA: MIT Press.

Christianson, K., Hollingworth, A., Halliwell, J., & Ferreira, F. (2001). Thematic roles assigned along the garden path linger. *Cognitive Psychology, 42,* 368–407.

Cinque, G. (1990). *Types of A' dependencies.* Cambridge, MA: MIT Press.

Clahsen, H., Kursawe, C., & Penke, M. (1996). Introducing CP: wh-questions and subordinate clauses in German child language. In C. Koster & F. Wijnen (Eds.), *Proceedings of the Groningen assembly on language acquisition* (pp. 5–22). Groningen: Center for Language and Cognition.

Coulson, S., King, J. W., & Kutas, M. (1998). Expect the unexpected: Event-related brain response to morphosyntactic violations. *Language and Cognitive Processes, 13,* 21–58.

Crain, S., & McKee, C. (1985). The acquisition of structural restrictions on anaphora. In S. Berman, J. Choe, & J. McDonough (Eds.), *Proceedings of NELS15.* Amherst, MA: GLSA Publications.

Crain, S., & Thornton, R. (1998). *Investigations in universal grammar.* Cambridge, MA: MIT Press.

de Vincenzi, M. (1991). *Syntactic parsing strategies in Italian.* Dordrecht, The Netherlands: Kluwer Academic Publishers.

Dowty, D. (1979). *Word meaning and montague grammar.* Dordrecht, Netherlands: Kluwer Academic Publishers.

Ferreira, F., Bailey, K. G. D., & Ferraro, V. (2002). Good-enough representations in language comprehension. *Current Directions in Psychological Science, 11,* 11–15.

Ferreira, F., Christianson, K., & Hollingworth, A. (2001). Misinterpretations of garden-path sentences: Implications for models of reanalysis. *Journal of Psycholinguistic Research, 30,* 3–20.

Ferreira, F., & Henderson, J. (1991). Recovery from misanalyses of garden path sentences. *Journal of Memory and Language, 30,* 725–745.

Ferreira, V. S. (1996). Is it better to give than to donate? Syntactic flexibility in language production. *Journal of Memory and Language, 35,* 724–755.

Ferreira, V. S., & Dell, G. S. (2000). Effect of ambiguity and lexical availability of syntactic and lexical production. *Cognitive Psychology, 40,* 296–340.

Fodor, J. A., Bever, T. G. B., & Garrett, M. (1974). *The psychology of language.* New York: McGraw-Hill.

Frazier, L. (1987a). Sentence processing: A tutorial review. In M. Coltheart (Ed.), *Attention and Performance XII* (pp. 559–586). Hillsdale, NJ: Lawrence Erlbaum Associates.

Frazier, L. (1987b). Syntactic processing: Evidence from Dutch. *Natural Language and Linguistic Theory, 5,* 519–560.

Frazier, L., & Flores d'Arcais, G. B. (1989). Filler-driven parsing: A study of gap filling in Dutch. *Journal of Memory and Language, 28,* 331–344.

Frazier, L., & Fodor, J. D. (1978). The Sausage Machine: A new two-stage parsing model. *Cognition, 6,* 291–326.

Frazier, L., & Rayner, K. (1982). Making and correcting errors in sentence comprehension: Eye-movements in the analysis of structurally ambiguous sentences. *Cognitive Psychology, 14,* 178–210.

Friederici, A. D., & Frisch, S. (2000). Verb argument structure processing: The role of verb specific and argument specific information. *Journal of Memory and Language, 43,* 476–507.

Friederici, A. D., Pfeifer, E., & Hahne, A. (1993). Event-related brain potentials during natural speech processing: Effects of semantic, morphological, and syntactic violations. *Cognitive Brain Research, 1,* 183–192.

Fries, N. (1983). *Syntaktische und semantische Studien zum frei verwendeten Infinitiv und zu verwandten Erscheinungen im Deutschen.* Tübingen: Narr (Studien zur deutschen Grammatik 21).

Fromkin, V. (1971). The non-anomalous nature of anomalous utterances. *Language, 47,* 27–52.

Garrett, M. F. (1976). Syntactic processes in sentence production. In G. Bower (Ed.), *Psychology of learning and motivation* (Vol. 9, pp. 231–256). New York: Academic Press.

Gibson, E., Hickok G., & Schütze, C. T. (1994). Processing empty categories: A parallel approach. *Journal of Psycholinguistic Research, 23,* 381–405.

Gibson, E., & Pearlmutter, N. (1998). Constraints on sentence processing. *Trends in Cognitive Science, 2,* 262–268.

Gropen, J., Pinker, S., Hollander, M., & Goldberg, R. (1991a). The role of lexical semantics in the acquisition of verb argument structure. *Cognition, 41,* 153–195.

Gropen, J., Pinker, S., Hollander, M., & Goldberg, R. (1991b). Syntax and semantics in the acquisition of locative verbs. *Journal of Child Language, 18,* 115–151.

Guimaraes, M. (1999). *Deriving prosodic structure from dynamic top-down syntax.* Unpublished manuscript, University of Maryland, College Park.

Gvozdev, A. N. (1961). *Voprosy Izuchenija Detskoj Rechi.* Moscow: Academia Pedagogicheskix Nauk.

Haegeman, L. (1995). Root infinitives, tense and truncated structures. *Language Acquisition, 4,* 205–255.

Hagoort, P., Brown, C., & Groothusen, J. (1993). The Syntactic Positive Shift (SPS) as an ERP-measure of syntactic processing. *Language and Cognitive Processes, 8,* 439–484.

Hamann, C., & Plunkett, K. (1998). Subjectless sentences in child Danish. *Cognition, 69,* 35–72.

Holmberg, A. (1986). *Word order and syntactic features in the Scandinavian languages and English.* Unpublished doctoral dissertation, University of Stockholm.

Jonas, D. (1995). On the acquisition of verb syntax in child Faroese. In C. Schütze, J. Ganger, & K. Broihier (Eds.), *Papers on language acquisition and processing: MIT working papers in linguistics* (Vol. 26, pp. 265–280). Department of Linguistics and Philosophy, MIT.

Julien, M. (2001). *On optional "have" in Swedish and Norwegian.* Talk presented at the 16th Comparative Germanic Syntax Workshop, McGill University, Montreal, Canada.

Kazanina, N., & Phillips, C. (2001). Conference in child Russian: Distinguishing syntactic and discourse constraints. In A. Do, L. Domínguez, & A. Johansen (Eds.), *Proceedings of the 25th Annual Boston University Conference on Language Development* (pp. 413–424). Somerville, MA: Cascadilla.

Kazanina, N., & Phillips, C. (2003a). Russian children's knowledge of aspectual distinctions. In *Proceedings of the 27th Annual Boston University Conference on Language Development.* Medford, MA: Cascadilla.

Kazanina, N., & Phillips, C. (2003b). Imperfective paradox in acquisition. In *Proceedings of the 22nd West Coast Conference on Formal Linguistics.* Medford, MA: Cascadilla.

Kempen, G., & Hoenkamp, E. (1987). An incremental procedural grammar for sentence production. *Cognitive Science, 11,* 201–258.

Kempson, R., Meyer-Viol, W., & Gabbay, D. (2001). *Dynamic syntax: The flow of language understanding.* Malden, MA: Blackwell.

Kim, M. (1999). *A cross-linguistic perspective on the acquisition of locative verbs.* Unpublished doctoral dissertation, University of Delaware.

Kim, M., Landau, B., & Phillips, C. (1999). Cross-linguistic differences in children's syntax for locative verbs. In A. Greenhill, H. Littlefield, & C. Tano (Eds.), *Proceedings of the 23rd Annual Boston University Conference on Language Development* (pp. 337–348). Somerville, MA: Cascadilla.

Kimball, J. (1973). Seven principles of surface structure parsing in natural language. *Cognition, 2,* 15–47.

Kiparsky, P., & Kiparsky, C. (1971). Fact. In D. Steinberg & L. Jakobovits (Eds.), *Semantics: An interdisciplinary reader in philosophy, linguistics, and psychology* (pp. 143–173). Cambridge, United Kingdom: Cambridge University Press.

Klein, W. (1995). A time-relational analysis of Russian aspect. *Language, 71,* 669–695.

Kluender, R., & Kutas, M. (1993). Bridging the gap: Evidence from ERPs on the processing of unbounded dependencies. *Journal of Cognitive Neuroscience, 5,* 196–214.

Krämer, I. (1993). The licensing of subjects in early child language. In C. Phillips (Ed.), *Papers on Case & Agreement: II. MIT Working Papers in Linguistics 19,* 197–212.

Legate, J. (1999). The morphosyntax of Irish agreement. In K. Arregi, B. Bruening, C. Krause, & V. Lin (Eds.), *Papers on morphology and syntax, Cycle One: MIT Working Papers in Linguistics* (Vol. 33, pp. 219–240). Department of Linguistics and Philosophy, MIT.

Leonard, L. (2003). Specific language impairment: Characterizing the deficit. In Y. Levy & J. Schaeffer (Eds.), *Towards a definition of SLI* (pp. 209–231). Mahwah, NJ: Lawrence Erlbaum Associates.

Levelt, W. J. M. (1974). *Formal grammars in linguistics and psycholinguistics* (3 volumes). The Hague: Mouton.

MacDonald, M. C., Pearlmutter, N. J., & Seidenberg, M. S. (1994). The lexical nature of syntactic ambiguity resolution. *Psychological Review, 89*, 483–506.

May, R. (1985). *Logical form.* Cambridge, MA: MIT Press.

McElree, B., & Griffith, T. (1995). Syntactic and thematic processing in sentence comprehension: Evidence for a temporal dissociation. *Journal of Experimental Psychology: Learning, Memory & Cognition, 21*, 134–157.

McElree, B., & Griffith, T. (1998). Structural and lexical constraints on filling gaps during sentence processing: A time-course analysis. *Journal of Experimental Psychology: Learning, Memory, & Cognition, 24*, 432–460.

Melvold, J. (1991). Factivity and definiteness. In L. Cheng & H. Demirdash (Eds.), *More Papers on Wh-Movement: MIT Working Papers in Linguistics* (Vol. 15, pp. 97–117). Cambridge, MA: Department of Linguistics and Philosophy, MIT.

Miller, G., & Chomsky, N. (1963). Finitary models of language users. In R. D. Luce, R. R. Bush, & E. Galanter (Eds.), *Handbook of mathematical psychology* (Vol. 2, pp. 419–491). New York: Wiley.

Milward, D. (1994). Dynamic dependency grammar. *Linguistics and Philosophy, 17*, 561–605.

Montalbetti, M. (1984). *After binding. On the interpretation of pronouns.* Unpublished doctoral dissertation, MIT.

Neville, H., Nicol, J., Barss, A., Forster, K. I., & Garrett, M. I. (1991). Syntactically based sentence processing classes: Evidence from event related brain potentials. *Journal of Cognitive Neuroscience, 3*, 151–165.

Nicol, J., & Swinney, D. (1989). The role of structure in coreference assignment during sentence processing. *Journal of Psycholinguistic Research, 18*, 5–19.

Osterhout, L., & Holcomb, P. J. (1992). Event-related brain potentials elicited by syntactic anomaly. *Journal of Memory and Language, 31*, 785–806.

Osterhout, L., Holcomb, P. J., & Swinney, D. A. (1994). Brain potentials elicited by garden path sentences: Evidence of the application of verb information during parsing. *Journal of Experimental Psychology. Learning, Memory and Cognition, 28*, 786–803.

Osterhout, L., & Mobley, L. A. (1995). Event-related brain potentials elicited by failure to agree. *Journal of Memory and Language, 34*, 739–773.

Parsons, T. (1991). *Events in the semantics of English: A study in subatomic semantics.* Cambridge, MA: MIT Press.

Phillips, C. (1995a). Right association in parsing and grammar. In C. Schütze, J. Ganger, & K. Broihier (Eds.), *Papers on language processing and acquisition, MIT Working Papers in Linguistics* (Vol. 26, pp. 37–93). Department of Linguistics and Philosophy, MIT.

Phillips, C. (1995b). Syntax at age two: Cross-linguistic differences. In C. Schütze, J. Ganger, & K. Broihier (Eds.), *Papers on language processing and acquisition. MIT Working Papers in Linguistics* (Vol. 26, pp. 225–282). Department of Linguistics and Philosophy, MIT.

Phillips, C. (1996). *Order and structure.* Unpublished doctoral dissertation, MIT.

Phillips, C. (2001). Levels of representation in the electrophysiology of speech perception. *Cognitive Science, 25*, 711–731.

Phillips, C. (2003). Linear order and constituency. *Linguistic Inquiry, 34*, 37–90.

Phillips, C., Edgar, E., & Kabak, B. (2000, March). *Lexical access and syntactic search: The case of dative (non-)alternations.* Poster presented at the 13th Annual CUNY Sentence Processing Conference, La Jolla, CA.

Phillips, C., Rabbin, B., Pablos, L., & Wong, K. (2003, March). *The real-time status of island constraints.* Talk presented at the 16th annual CUNY Sentence Processing Conference, MIT.

Pinker, S. (1989). *Learnability and cognition.* Cambridge, MA: MIT Press.

Poeppel, D., & Wexler, K. (1993). The full competence hypothesis of clause structure in early German. *Language, 69,* 1–33.

Pollard, C., & Sag, I. (1994). *Head driven phrase structure grammar.* Stanford, CA: CSLI Publications.

Pritchett, B. L. (1992). Parsing with grammar: Islands, heads, and garden paths. In H. Goodluck & M. Rochemont (Eds.), *Island constraints: Theory, acquisition, and processing* (pp. 321–350). Dordrecht: Kluwer.

Reis, M. (2002). What are we doing with *wh*-infinitivals in German? *Georgetown University Working Papers in Theoretical Linguistics, 2,* 287–341.

Rice, M., Wexler, K., & Cleave, P. (1995). Specific language impairment as a period of extended optional infinitive. *Journal of Speech and Hearing Research, 38,* 850–863.

Richards, N. (1999). Dependency formation and directionality of tree construction. In V. Lin, C. Krause, B. Bruening, & K. Arregi (Eds.), *Papers on morphology and syntax, Cycle Two: MIT Working Papers in Linguistics* (Vol. 34, pp. 67–105). Department of Linguistics and Philosophy, MIT.

Richards, N. (2002). Very local A′ movement in a root first derivation. In S. Epstein & D. Seely (Eds.), *Derivation and explanation in the Minimalist Program* (pp. 227–248). Malden, MA: Blackwell.

Rizzi, L. (1994). Some notes on linguistic theory and language development: The case of root infinitives. *Language Acquisition, 3,* 371–393.

Roeper, T., & Rohrbacher, B. (2000). Null subjects in early child English and the theory of economy of projection. In C. Hamann & S. Powers (Eds.), *The acquisition of scrambling and cliticization* (pp. 345–396). Dordrecht, Netherlands: Kluwer Academic Publishers.

Santelmann, L. (1994, November). *Topicalization, CP and licensing in the acquisition of Swedish.* Paper presented at the Boston University Conference on Language Development.

Schlenker, P. (1999). Adjective inflection in German: Morphology from top-to-bottom. *Recherches Linguistiques de Vincennes* 28.

Schlesewsky, M., Fanselow, G., Kliegl, R., & Krems, J. (2000). The subject preference in the processing of locally ambiguous *wh*-questions in German. In B. Hemforth & L. Konieczny (Eds.), *German sentence processing* (pp. 65–93). Dordrecht, The Netherlands: Kluwer Academic Publishers.

Schütze, C. (1996). *The empirical base of linguistics.* Chicago, IL: University of Chicago Press.

Schütze, C. (1997). *INFL in child and adult language: Agreement, case and licensing.* Unpublished doctoral dissertation, Massachusetts Institute of Technology.

Schütze, C., & Wexler, K. (2000). An elicitation study of young English children's knowledge of tense: Semantic and syntactic properties of optional infinitives. In S. C. Howell, S. A. Fish, & T. Keith-Lucas (Eds.), *Proceedings of the 24th annual Boston University Conference on Language Development* (pp. 669–683). Somerville, MA: Cascadilla.

Sigurjónsdottir, S. (1999). Root infinitives and null subjects in early Icelandic. In A. Greenhill, H. Littlefield, & C. Tano (Eds.), *Proceedings of the 23rd annual Boston University Conference on Language Development* (pp. 630–641). Somerville, MA: Cascadilla.

Steedman, M. (2000). *The syntactic process.* Cambridge, MA: MIT Press.

Steinbach, M. (2002). *Middle voice: A comparative study in the syntax–semantics interface in German.* Amsterdam: John Benjamins.

Stephany, U. (1997). The acquisition of Greek. In D. I. Slobin (Ed.), *The cross linguistic study of language acquisition* (pp. 183–333). Mahwah, NJ: Lawrence Erlbaum Associates.

Stowe, L. A. (1986). Parsing *WH*-constructions: Evidence for on-line gap location. *Language and Cognitive Processes, 1,* 227–245.

Sturt, P. (2003). The time course of the application of binding constraints in reference resolution. *Journal of Memory and Language, 48,* 542–562.

Sturt, P., Pickering, M., & Crocker, M. (1999). Structural change and reanalysis difficulty in language comprehension. *Journal of Memory and Language, 40,* 136–150.

Townsend, D., & Bever, T. (2001). *Sentence comprehension: The integration of habits and rules.* Cambridge, MA: MIT Press.

Traxler, M., & Pickering, M. (1996). Plausibility and the processing of unbounded dependencies: An eye-tracking study. *Journal of Memory and Language, 35,* 454–475.

van der Feest, S., & van Hout, A. (2002). Tense comprehension in child Dutch. *Proceedings of BUCLD, 26,* 734–745.

Varlokosta, S., Vainikka, A., & Rohrbacher, B. (1998). Functional projections, markedness, and "root infinitives" in early child Greek. *The Linguistic Review, 15,* 187–207.

Vikner, S. (1995). *Verb movement and expletive subjects in the germanic languages.* New York: Oxford University Press.

Vinnitskaya, I., & Wexler, K. (2001). The role of pragmatics in the development of Russian aspect. *First Language, 21,* 143–186.

Vosse, T., & Kempen, G. (2000). Syntactic structure assembly in human parsing: A computational model based on competitive inhibition and a lexicalist grammar. *Cognition, 75,* 105–143.

Weissenborn, J. (1994). Constraining the child's grammar: Local well-formedness in the development of verb movement in German and French. In B. Lust, M. Suñer, & J. Whitman (Eds.), *Syntactic theory and first language acquisition* (pp. 215–247). Hillsdale, NJ: Lawrence Erlbaum Associates.

Wexler, K. (1994). Optional infinitives, head movement, and economy of derivation. In N. Hornstein & D. Lightfoot (Eds.), *Verb movement* (pp. 305–350). Cambridge, United Kingdom: Cambridge University Press.

Wexler, K., Schütze, C., & Rice, M. (1998). Subject case in children with SLI and unaffected controls: Evidence for the Agr/Tense omission model. *Language Acquisition, 7,* 317–344.

III

NEURAL, GENETIC, AND BEHAVIORAL ELEMENTS OF INHERITED FACTORS

Genes, Language Disorders, and Developmental Archaeology: What Role Can Neuroimaging Play?

Ralph-Axel Müller
San Diego State University &
University of California, San Diego

GRAMMAR MODULES AND LANGUAGE GENES

Historically, language has often been conceived as something "out there," in the outside world, rather than a system of mind or brain (Sampson, 1980). For a relatively recent example, Saussure (1915/1972) defined "langue" as a socially constituted system of signs. When B. F. Skinner (1957) adapted the behaviorist approach to the study of language, he described the rules of language in terms of reinforcement and conditioning (i.e., as fully determined by external parameters of stimulus and response). It was Chomsky's (1959) groundbreaking criticism of Skinner's book that launched the study of language as a mental system. Chomsky's early work on syntax as a mental system of quasi-mathematical rules (Chomsky, 1957, 1965) was an integral part of the newly developing "cognitive sciences" (Gardner, 1987). Later, Chomsky went a step further and reunited linguistics with biology. According to his views, language was a "mental organ" that would mature based on biological necessity (rather than environmental contingency) in the course of child development, in similar ways as a heart or lung would mature (Chomsky, 1980). At the time, these views were radical compared with competing behaviorist and Piagetian views that granted experience an important role in language development (Piattelli-Palmarini, 1980). Chomsky's views were also radical with respect to the role they allotted genetic information. Chomsky believed that "universal grammar," a set of abstract principles determining acquisition of any possible human language, was fully specified in the human genome. Not only did this imply that *Homo sapiens* was radically different from nonhuman primates with respect to linguistic capacities, but also that the core language system developed autonomously in mind/ brain and that other domains of developing cognition (e.g., object recognition, visual spatial thinking, attention, memory) played no crucial role in language acquisition.

Since Chomsky first formulated this framework of ideas, the fields of psycho- and neurolinguistics have progressed dramatically. Nonetheless, his general ideas are still considered by many the most promising approach to the cognitive neuroscience of language. Traditional psycholinguistic arguments in favor of the Chomskian view relate to claims according to which, for example, language acquisition follows universal principles that cannot be inferred from typical language input children receive (Crain, 1991). More recent approaches, however, also include clinical and biological evidence. For instance, the existence of developmental disorders such as specific language impairment (SLI) and Williams syndrome is taken as evidence that language can be dissociated from other cognitive domains (Stromswold, 2000). As Pinker (1995) interpreted such apparent modular dissociations in rather crude terms, there can be "intelligence without language" (SLI) and "language without intelligence" (Williams syndrome). In the following section, we examine the former type of disorder in more detail.

Genotype–Phenotype Divergence: Developmental Language Disorders

One important set of evidence that has developed in the context of questions raised by Chomsky relates to developmental language disorders (DLDs), often referred to as specific language impairments (SLI). A growing literature has related these disorders to identifiable neural features, such as atypical morphology and hemispheric asymmetry in perisylvian regions. In normal adults, postmortem and in vivo imaging studies indicate that asymmetries in posterior (Foundas et al., 1994; Tzourio et al., 1998; Witelson & Kigar, 1992) and anterior (Foundas et al., 1996) perisylvian anatomy are related to language dominance. Although there are some inconsistencies in findings regarding the planum temporale (Habib, 2000), most studies on DLD (Clark & Plante, 1998; Gauger et al., 1997; Jackson & Plante, 1996; Plante et al., 1991) and dyslexia (Eckert et al., 2003; Kushch et al., 1993; Leonard et al., 1993; Robichon et al., 2000) identified some pattern of atypical morphology or asymmetry in or around perisylvian cortex. This is consistent with functional neuroimaging studies in children with DLD (Lou et al., 1990; Shaywitz et al., 2002; Tzourio et al.,

1994) and adults with a history of dyslexia (Horwitz et al., 1998; Paulesu et al., 2001; Rumsey et al., 1997; Shaywitz et al., 1998) showing various types of abnormalities in perisylvian regions.

Of particular interest here is the question of whether brain-based DLDs can be traced back to genetics. The studies that probably received the widest attention concern familial aggregation of SLI in family KE (Gopnik, 1990; Gopnik & Crago, 1991). Speech disorder in this family is an autosomal-dominant trait involving a single gene on Chromosome 7 (Fisher et al., 1998; Lai et al., 2001). Findings from family KE corroborate evidence for genetic factors in the DLD population at large (Bishop, 2002; Tomblin & Buckwalter, 1994). Initial studies in this family by Gopnik and colleagues also suggested a highly selective linguistic deficit restricted to certain aspects of morphosyntax (e.g., past tense formation), compatible with the notion of modular linguistic subsystems and an autonomous neurofunctional organization of language vis-à-vis other cognitive domains (Chomsky, 1981; Pinker, 1991). However, more comprehensive testing by Vargha-Khadem and colleagues has shown that deficits in affected family members are not exclusively morphosyntactic. Not only did affected family members show significantly lower *performance* IQ scores than unaffected members, but also evidence of orofacial apraxia and impaired phonological working memory (Vargha-Khadem et al., 1995; Watkins et al., 2002). Voxel-based morphometry of structural MRI identified perirolandic sensorimotor cortex and the caudate nuclei as primary sites of gray matter reduction in affected members compared with normal controls (Watkins et al., 2002). The caudate nuclei are considered an "associative" region within the striatum, with multimodal connectivity from neocortex of all four lobes of the forebrain (Yelnik, 2002). There have been some reports of language-related impairments in basal ganglia patients (Wallesch et al., 1997; Wallesch & Wyke, 1985). However, Nadeau and Crosson (1997) concluded from a review of the clinical literature on patients with subcortical lesion that the basal ganglia do not play a specific linguistic role. The MRI findings in family KE are thus consistent with behavioral findings suggesting that basic impairments are probably nonlinguistic and morphosyntactic deficits are secondary to orofacial motor, phonemic, and other impairments.

The above evidence suggests that single-gene mutations can have detrimental effects on morphosyntactic aspects of language acquisition. However, these effects are *pleiotropic* (i.e., multiple other functional domains are also affected). Pleiotropy is a principle of *divergence* in genotype-phenotype relationships (Fig. 12.1A). A striking example of pleiotropy with neurological relevance is phenylketonuria (PKU)—a single-gene defect associated with a severe disorder of amino acid metabolism and toxic accumulation of phenylalanine. PKU is phenotypically characterized not

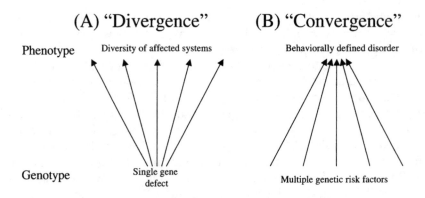

FIG. 12.1. Schematic depiction of divergent and convergent principles in genotype–phenotype relations. (A) Divergence corresponds to pleiotropy in single-gene mutations, which have multiple effects in different (brain and non-brain) systems of the mature phenotype. (B) Convergence relates to phenotypically defined symptoms or disorders that may be caused by multiple different genetic alterations or by combinations of multiple genetic risk factors.

only by mental retardation and microcephaly, but also by social behavioral deficits, seizures, stunted bodily growth, and dermatological symptoms (Brenton & Pietz, 2000; Følling, 1994; Scriver & Waters, 1999). Another example is Rett syndrome—a disorder seen only in girls that is associated with apparently normal development up to age 6 to 18 months, followed by regression. In a large majority of cases, the disorder is caused by sporadic mutation of the *MECP2* gene on the X chromosome (Amir & Zoghbi, 2000). Females with Rett syndrome have been described as autistic-like. What is relevant in the present discussion is the wide array of phenotypic traits associated with this single-gene mutation, including language and motor impairment, stereotypic behaviors, deficits in social interaction; disturbances of breathing, peripheral blood circulation, and sleep patterns; stunted growth and reduced head size; and widespread neuroanatomic and cellular abnormalities (Shahbazian & Zoghbi, 2002; Weaving et al., 2003). In both the examples of PKU and Rett syndrome, a single gene mutation results in phenotypic manifestations that are *pleiotropic*, affecting numerous biological systems.

Genotype–Phenotype Convergence: Autism

Pleiotropy enhances the complexity of gene–behavior relationships. However, there is another, seemingly antagonistic principle that further complicates these relationships and is certainly also involved in developmental disorders of language. This is a principle of *convergence* in genotype–phenotype relationships (Fig. 12.1B). A prime example of a developmental disorder that appears to be governed by polygenic (or multigenic) principles of convergence is autism (Korvatska et al., 2002). Autism is a neurodevelopmental disorder with an estimated prevalence of 1 to 4 individuals in 1,000 (Charman, 2002). The disorder is pervasive, affecting numerous domains of cognitive, sensorimotor, and sociobehavioral function (Tager-Flusberg et al., 2001). Delayed language acquisition is one of the diagnostic criteria for autism (American Psychiatric Association, 2000). Twin studies demonstrate strong genetic factors (Bailey et al., 1995; Greenberg et al., 2001; Rutter, 2000). Recent evidence indicates potential links between genetic and cognitive subtypes in autism (Silverman et al., 2002) and heritability of general symptom severity (Spiker et al., 2002) as measured by the Autism Diagnostic Interview–Revised (Lord et al., 1994). Regarding language, genetic variation within the disorder may correlate with onset of phrase speech (Silverman et al., 2002), with a potential role of a site on Chromosome 2 (Shao et al., 2002a).

Despite such preliminary evidence, the current genetic linkage literature on autism appears confusing and fraught with inconsistencies. Although there is partial convergence regarding Chromosomes 7 (Folstein & Rosen-Sheidley, 2001; Hutcheson et al., 2003) and 15 (Shao et al., 2003; Sutcliffe et al., 2003), no sites of susceptibility for autism have been firmly established. In fact the number of suspected genetic loci of susceptibility is extremely large (Folstein & Rosen-Sheidley, 2001; Shao et al., 2002b; Veenstra-Vanderweele et al., 2003). Reviewing the impact of the human genome project on the study of autism and other psychiatric disorders, Cowan and colleagues (2002) acknowledge a "sense of disappointment and frustration" (p. 25) in view of the multitude of candidate sites and the inconsistencies across studies.

Further complicating the picture is the possibility that nongenetic events may, in some cases, mimic genetic effects in autistic pathogenesis. Claims implicating MMR vaccines in autism (Wakefield, 1999) are not supported by the bulk of available evidence (Korvatska et al., 2002). However, viral infections (Lotspeich & Ciaranello, 1993; Tanoue et al., 1988) or neurotoxic exposure in utero (Edelson & Cantor, 1998; Mason-Brothers et al., 1990; Rodier et al., 1997; Stromland et al., 1994) cannot be ruled out as risk factors in autism. Some studies also suggest links between perinatal risk factors and autism (Hultman et al., 2002), although it remains unclear whether these factors are causative or secondary to autistic pathology.

Taking all this together, it appears likely that numerous genes are involved in autism and multiple genetic and environmental risk factors converge in autistic development (Jones & Szatmari, 2002). Language deficits in autism are unlikely to be linked to one or a few genes. There have been suggestions of involvement of common genetic sites in autism and DLD based on the proximity of susceptibility loci in region 7q31 for both disorders (Bradford, 2001; Folstein & Mankoski, 2000). This proposal is consistent with greater than expected comorbidity between autism and DLD and findings of symptom overlap between the two disorders (Bishop, 1989; Howlin et al., 2000; Mawhood et al., 2000). Folstein and Mankoski (2000) suggested there could be "a single gene on 7q31 that is involved in both autism and specific language impairment" (p. 279). Despite initial excitement that one of the prime candidates, the FOXP2 gene (Lai et al., 2001), "may have a causal role in the development of the normal brain circuitry that underlies language and speech" (Pinker, 2001, p. 465), recent studies have not yielded any evidence for involvement of this gene in either autism or DLD (Newbury et al., 2002; Wassink et al., 2002).

The discussion of this section should not create the impression that DLDs and autism are exclusively characterized by pleiotropic and polygenic principles, respectively. Divergent and convergent principles are at work in both types of disorder. For instance, although one locus on Chromosome 7 has been linked to language impairment in family KE and one unrelated case (Lai et al., 2001), a number of other loci have been identified for other DLD populations, including sites on Chromosomes 16 and 19 (SLI-Consortium, 2002), as well as 13 and possibly 2 (Bartlett et al., 2002).

All in all, there is substantial evidence indicating the importance of genetic factors in language acquisition. As a first approximation, the Chomskian hypothesis of genetic foundations for the human language capacity is therefore correct. On closer examination, however, this hypothesis and its implications become more problematic. First, the study of DLDs shows that most likely a multitude of genes may be involved in such disorders. Second, genetic defects (and, in particular, single-gene defects) do not result in modular or highly selective language deficits, but typically also affect nonlinguistic cognitive and sensorimotor domains. The evidence on language impairments from behavior genetics may appear tantalizing because it indicates clear links between genes and language, but does not yield a true understanding of how exactly the two relate during development. Giving all this a more positive spin, the following conclusion can be drawn: A better understanding of the causal links between genes and language requires adequate consideration of developmental neuroscience. A brief discussion of some of the basic principles that may bridge genes and cognitive development follows in the next section. The final sections are dedicated to the role of functional neuroimaging in the study of these developmental neuroscientific principles.

INTRINSIC, ACTIVITY-DRIVEN, AND EXPERIENTIAL EFFECTS IN BRAIN DEVELOPMENT

The developing brain is shaped through interactions of constructive (Quartz & Sejnowski, 1997) and regressive (or selectional) events (Changeux, 1986; Pennington, 2001; Rakic, 1989). Early "exuberance" of neurons and synapses is followed by selective stabilization and loss. Whereas prenatal neuronal loss (apoptosis) is predominantly determined by endogenous neurotrophic factors (Jessell & Sanes, 2000), experience and environmental interaction play important roles in postnatal synaptic survival and loss (Katz & Shatz, 1996). Synaptic connectivity is overly abundant in the first years of life and is subject to subsequent pruning and selective stabilization (Caviness et al., 1997; Huttenlocher & Dabholkar, 1997; Pennington, 2001). Experiential and activity-dependent effects on the number and efficacy of synaptic connections have been shown in invertebrates (Kandel et al., 2000) and mammals (Greenough & Bailey, 1988; Kleim et al., 1996).

Enriched environments have a positive influence on cortical thickness presumably because they are more stimulating and offer greater opportunities for interaction and manipulation (Kolb & Gibb, 2001). Increased cortical thickness has also been shown following motor skill learning in rats (Anderson et al., 2002). Besides synaptic effects mentioned earlier, gray matter thickness is probably affected by an increase in glial cells, neuronal survival, and dendritic complexity due to environmental enrichment (van Praag et al., 2000). Although much of the supporting data come from animal studies, there is some evidence from research with human subjects. For instance, structural MRI has demonstrated greater depth of the central sulcus in professional musicians (compared to nonmusicians; Amunts et al., 1997). This measure, which reflects the size of primary motor cortex, was significantly correlated with the age at which musicians began keyboard or string instrument training. Human postmortem findings also suggest that laminar and cellular architecture in perisylvian language areas correlated with language experience and skills (Amunts et al., in press) and educational level (Jacobs et al., 1993). Corroborating evidence from functional imaging is discussed in the following section.

The generation and loss of neurons and synaptic connections are governed by both intrinsic mechanisms and environmental factors, although in different ways and at different stages of brain development. For example, early phases of synaptogenesis (gestational weeks 6–17 in humans) are probably driven by genetic factors, but environmental and activity-dependent mechanisms play important roles in later postnatal stages of synaptogenesis and selective loss (Pennington, 2001). Whereas plasticity may not be at work in early stages of neuronogenesis, apoptosis, and synaptogenesis, later stages are certainly affected by plasticity, which results in environmentally based variability of individuals, but also in resilience in the face of brain damage.

Considering effects of early damage, a similar duality of genetic and environmental effects can be observed, albeit on a more macroscopic level. Recent studies have demonstrated the astounding genetic impact on brain morphology (Thompson et al., 2001) and cognitive abilities (Plomin & Kosslyn, 2001; Plomin et al., 1994). Nonetheless, it is also well established that neocortical differentiation into functionally specialized areas is not strictly predetermined genetically, but characterized by equally astounding malleability (O'Leary et al., 1994). In a recent review of experimental manipulations of early brain development in animals, Pallas (2001) distinguished between early *regionalization*, which is under relatively tight genetic control, and subsequent *arealization*, which is dependent on extrinsic and activity-driven factors. Knockout studies of regulatory genes provide evidence for the first part of the model. For example, *Emx2* expression shows a gradient in antero-posterior and lateral-medial directions in embryonic mice. *Emx2* knockout results in distorted regionalization, with more anterior (somatosensory, auditory) regions expanding at the expense of posterior visual regions (see reviews in Cecchi, 2002; Pallas, 2001). However, the view of genetic and epigenetic influences on cortical differentiation occurring as a chronological sequence is probably oversimplified. More likely, they present interacting principles in the sense that activity-dependent thalamo-cortical effects underlie genetic factors and may, in turn, influence cortical gene expression (O'Leary & Nakagawa, 2002).

Evidence for extrinsic effects on regionalization comes mostly from transplantation and rewiring studies. Schlaggar and O'Leary (1991) transplanted embryonic occipital cortex into the postcentral region in neonatal rats and observed almost normal formation of barrelfields in transplanted cortex. This shows that occipital cortex, which assumes visual functions in normal development, has the capacity to develop somatosensory functions in response to somatosensory thalamo-cortical afferents (Schlaggar et al., 1993). Such cross-modal plasticity of developing cortical tissue has also been demonstrated in rewiring experiments by Sur and colleagues (1990). Inducing retinal afferents in newborn ferrets to connect to the medial geniculate nucleus (MGN, normally an auditory structure connecting to auditory cortex), they found that both MGN and primary auditory cortex responded to visual stimulation (Sur et al., 1988). More recent experiments with such rewired animals also show that this response is indeed functionally relevant and contributes to stimulus-appropriate behavior (von Melchner et al., 2000).

In summary, the functional architecture of the developing brain is probably subject to numerous interacting factors. Some of these are more directly related to genetic information, whereas others heavily involve activity of afferent connections, which in turn relates to (interaction with) the environment. This scenario greatly complicates the study of developmental disorders of language. First, it is unlikely that polymodal brain regions known to be important for language processing (Broca's area, Wernicke's area) achieve functional specialization based on one or a few genes alone. Therefore, we cannot expect any simple links between gene defects and specific or modular language disorders. Second, any developmental abnormality is potentially compensated by developmental plasticity and reorganization, or possibly aggravated by developmental vulnerability and misconstruction. Links between sites of brain abnormality and symptom complexes inferred from the study of adult lesion patients are thus unlikely to apply to developmental populations. In the words of Thomas and Karmiloff-Smith (in press), the assumption of "residual normality"—dubious even in adult patients—is clearly inadequate in developmental disorders (Müller, in press).

INSIGHTS FROM FUNCTIONAL NEUROIMAGING

Functional neuroimaging techniques were first applied to developmental populations in the 1980s. Positron emission tomography (PET) and single photon emission tomography (SPECT) require radioactive tracers, and their use in children is tightly restricted for ethical reasons (Morton et al., 1996). Nonetheless, these techniques have generated evidence that is relevant to the issues of brain developmental changes and plasticity discussed earlier. In the first systematic study of developmental changes in brain metabolism, Chugani and colleagues presented children who had received PET scans because a neurological disorder was suspected (Chugani & Phelps, 1986; Chugani et al., 1987). Among a large group of such children, 29 turned out to be neurologically normal. In these children, age-related changes in glucose metabolic rate could be identified that resembled synaptic density curves in animal and human postmortem studies (Huttenlocher & Dabholkar, 1997). Glucose metabolism showed a steep increase in the first 2 postnatal years, plateaued at two to three times higher than adult levels between ages 3 and 8, and then slowly declined through the second decade of life (Fig. 12.2A [see color panel]). These findings were corroborated in later PET and SPECT studies of glucose me-

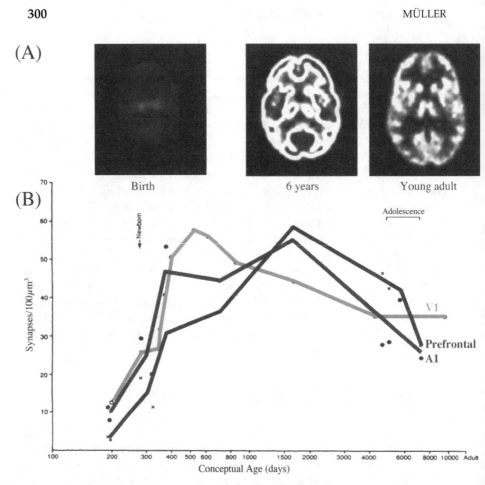

FIG. 12.2. Developmental curves of glucose metabolism and synaptic density. (A) The top part of the figure (adapted from Chugani, 1991) shows global glucose metabolism in a 6-year-old child at levels two to three times higher than seen in adults. The period of elevated glucose metabolism is seen between ages 2 and 10 years. This developmental curve corresponds well to changes in synaptic density during childhood. The lower part of the figure (B) shows synaptic density for primary visual, primary auditory, and prefrontal cortex. Adapted from Huttenlocher and Dabholkar (1997). (See Color Panel 1.)

tabolism (Bentourkia et al., 1998) and brain perfusion (Chiron et al., 1992). The dramatic changes in glucose metabolism and resting blood flow throughout childhood and adolescence predominantly reflect changes in synaptic density (Fig. 12.2B), which are in turn based on the constructive and regressive principles discussed in the previous section. Functional neuroimaging has thus been able to confirm neurohistological evidence of changes in synaptic connectivity underlying developmental plasticity.

Experiential Effects

More recently, neuroimaging studies have also been able to highlight such plasticity and the importance of experiential factors in studies of adults. One set of evidence comes from functional neuroimaging studies in adults with specific areas of expertise, such as professional musicians (Münte et al., 2002). Consistent with findings of structural effects related to musical expertise (Amunts et al., 1997; Schlaug et al., 1995), functional studies demonstrate more extensive functional representation of left-hand digits (Elbert et al., 1995) and greater motor learning-related short-term plasticity (Hund-Georgiadis & von Cramon, 1999) in primary motor cortex of professional musicians.

A second set of evidence highlighting experiential effects on neurofunctional organization concerns subjects with absence of peripheral sensory input in the auditory or visual modality. Grossly speaking, these studies have shown that in early-onset blindness or deafness, the functional representation of intact modalities expands into territory normally occupied by the missing modality. For instance, in congenitally deaf subjects, the superior temporal cortex is activated during comprehension of sign language (Neville et al., 1995). This region also responds to nonverbal visual stimulation in early deaf subjects (Finney et al., 2001). Analogously, in early blind subjects, occipital cortex has been shown to participate in tactile Braille reading (Sadato et al., 1998). Occipital cortex in the congenitally blind also activates during auditory localization in regions corresponding to those involved in visual localization in seeing subjects (Weeks et al., 2000). These studies of normal and clinical plasticity in humans therefore underline the effects of afferent information and experience on regional functional differentiation in cerebral cortex. Sadato and colleagues (2002) also showed more recently that such cross-modal plasticity effects are subject to critical periods. In their study, "primary visual" cortex was activated during tactile discrimination only in subjects with blindness onset before age 16, but not with onset at a later age.

Plasticity Caused by Brain Damage

Further evidence regarding neurofunctional development and its plasticity comes from imaging studies in children with brain damage. Brain damage in adults tends to result in persistent region-specific deficits (such as aphasia following left perisylvian lesion; Caplan et al., 1996; Pedersen et al., 1995). In children however, early left lesion or left hemispherectomy is often associated with good long-term language outcome if the right hemisphere remains intact (Basser, 1962; Boatman et al., 1999; Curtiss et al., 2001; Vargha-Khadem et al., 1997; Vargha-Khadem & Mishkin, 1997).

These differences may be related to critical periods of language plasticity and are thought to reflect an enhanced developmental potential for inter-hemispheric reorganization.

More recently, such effects have been demonstrated directly in imaging studies. In one PET study, 21 children with unilateral lesion and first risk within the first 6 years of life were examined (Müller et al., 1998b). Left-hemisphere patients showed robust right-hemisphere involvement in simple language processes. In a follow-up study, effects of lesion onset were examined more directly in patients with unilateral left-hemisphere lesion involving perisylvian language regions (Müller et al., 1999b). When verbal auditory stimulation (listening to sentences) was compared to rest, perisylvian areas showed leftward asymmetry in healthy adults (Müller et al., 1997a). This asymmetry was reduced in patients with late lesion and reversed in those with early lesion (Fig. 12.3). These findings were com-

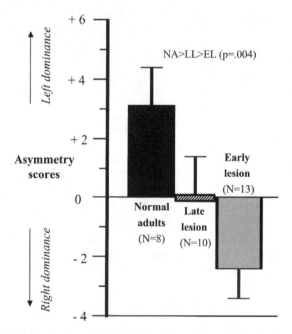

FIG. 12.3.   Asymmetry of regional blood flow changes (left minus right) in frontotemporal perisylvian cortex during verbal auditory stimulation (listening to sentences). Blood flow increases (activations) show leftward asymmetry in normal adults, bilaterality in patients with late-onset left-hemisphere lesion, and reversed asymmetry (right-hemisphere dominance) in patients with early onset left-hemisphere lesion. The findings support the hypothesis of an overall greater potential for interhemispheric reorganization in the first years of life, compared with adolescence and adulthood. Adapted from Müller et al. (1999b).

patible overall with expected lesion onset effects, showing reduced left dominance for language-related processing in left-lesion patients compared with normal adults and overall greater interhemispheric reorganization in patients with early lesion compared to those with lesion acquired in adulthood. Concordant differences in perisylvian regions could also be shown for expressive language functions associated with sentence generation in a study that roughly matched small samples of early and late-lesion patients for chronological age, lesion site, and verbal intelligence quotient (VIQ; Müller et al., 1999a; Fig. 12.4 [see color panel]). Nonetheless, inspection of rCBF changes in each patient showed considerable individual variation, most likely related to a host of clinical and demographic variables (such as underlying pathology, seizure disorder, and sex).

The use of PET in pediatric studies of reorganization is limited by the lack of age-appropriate normal control data (because healthy children are not usually studied with PET). FMRI studies, considered noninvasive and minimal risk, do not underlie the same restrictions, but unfortunately only few such studies on developmental plasticity for language have been published. One reason lies in the much greater motion sensitivity of fMRI compared with PET, which makes it difficult to acquire artifact-free fMRI data from young children (Eden & Zeffiro, 2000). A few studies examined the usefulness of fMRI for identification of eloquent language cortex in neurosurgery patients, but without directly addressing issues of reorganization (Benson et al., 1996; Hertz-Pannier et al., 1997; Lehericy et al., 2000; Stapleton et al., 1997). In one more recent study, language reorganization was assessed in a single child with Rasmussen's encephalitis (Hertz-Pannier et al., 2002). Word generation was associated with left frontal and inferior parietal activation before surgery, but with extensive right-hemisphere activation after left hemispherotomy (extrathalamic white matter disconnection and callosotomy). Another study (Staudt et al., 2002) reported right-hemisphere activations largely homotopic with left perisylvian language areas for silent word generation in a small sample of adult patients with a history of congenital left periventricular lesions.

These neuroimaging studies of atypical language organization in patients with early onset left-hemisphere lesion demonstrate plasticity guided by basic reorganizational principles. Although premorbid and clinical variability is surely reflected in differences of neurofunctional outcome, certain types of postlesional reorganization appear common, whereas others are not seen. As discussed previously, in studies of cross-modal plasticity of early deaf or blind subjects, one sensory modality can invade the territory of another modality that does not receive peripheral stimulation. Language reorganization even in cases of congenital or early postnatal lesion onset does not seem to include the potential for such invasion of unimodal sensorimotor cortex. In fact the evidence for intrahemispheric reorganiza-

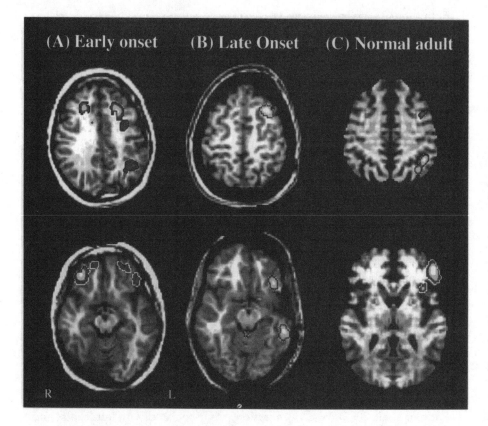

FIG. 12.4.   Single-case examples of brain activations during an expressive language task (sentence generation), in which subjects create and overtly produce a sentence based on a stimulus sentence and a prompt word (e.g., "He listened to the radio—*television,*" with expected response: "He watched television"). The control condition was sentence repetition. (A) An 8-year-old male subject with a progressive calcification of congenital origin in the left hemisphere (Sturge–Weber syndrome) shows extensive right-hemisphere frontal and parietal activation. (B) In contrast, a 17-year-old female intractable epilepsy patient with seizure onset at age 10 and resection of left temporal epileptogenic tissue at age 13 years shows exclusively left-hemispheric activation in fronto-temporal areas during sentence generation. These activations resemble those seen in a group of nine healthy adults (C). Adapted from Müller et al. (1997a, 1999a). (See Color Panel 2.)

tion into ipsilesional territory adjacent to the site of damage is inconsistent. Conversely, evidence for a potential of interhemispheric reorganization is abundant. Here again the target sites of reorganization seem to be governed by strict principles, and atypically strong activation is almost always seen in brain regions homotopic to those expected in healthy brains. Interestingly, these principles of language organization are different from those observed for the motor domain. In the latter, atypical ipsilateral activation of primary motor cortex is not as pronounced, whereas interhemispheric reorganization and lesion onset effects are mostly seen in secondary motor regions (Graveline et al., 1998; Müller et al., 1997b, 1998c).

Functional neuroimaging in pediatric patients thus supports the hypothesis of enhanced plasticity for language during the first decade of life. It also suggests that factors specific to each functional network affect the patterns of plasticity and postlesional reorganization. Thus, the differences observed between language and motor domains may be related to the earlier organization of motor circuits and the fact that humans start developing motor behaviors in utero (D'Elia et al., 2001), based on intrinsically driven processes that are much more directly under genetic control than is the case in language development. Motor circuitry becomes established relatively early in infants (Clearfield & Thelen, 2001), as opposed to language networks that develop much later and are characterized by a prolonged "critical period." However, the available functional imaging literature is suggestive rather than conclusive in all these respects.

One fundamental question remains to be addressed: How do different patterns of postlesional reorganization relate to cognitive compensation and long-term outcome for language? This question has only been examined in adult lesion patients recovering from aphasia. Greater than normal right perisylvian activations have been interpreted as beneficial (Calvert et al., 2000; Gold & Kertesz, 2000; Silvestrini et al., 1995; Thulborn et al., 1999; Weiller et al., 1995). However, none of the above studies directly compared patients with matched left-hemisphere lesions that only differed in the degree of recovery. In a number of recent studies (Belin et al., 1996; Cao et al., 1999; Heiss et al., 1999; Rosen et al., 2000; Thomas et al., 1997; Warburton et al., 1999), good recovery from aphasia was found to be associated with reestablished activations in the perilesional perisylvian cortex of the left hemisphere. The issue of how interhemispheric reorganization relates to language recovery is thus not fully resolved in adults. In children, this question has not yet been addressed in neuroimaging studies.

Neural Underpinnings of Developmental Plasticity

A further question concerns the degree to which clinical studies of language plasticity can shed light on plasticity in normal development. Is malleability of functional organization a potential that is exclusively realized under abnormal circumstances (e.g., when crucial tissue substrates are damaged), or is this malleability a general characteristic of neurofunctional development? A simple but reasonable model of developmental language plasticity relates to the changes in synaptic density described before. Exuberant density in early development may imply excessive interregional and interhemispheric connectivity. This could be associated with a less distinctive or absent hemispheric asymmetry for language in the toddler (Fig. 12.5A).

Such an assumption would be overly simple because it is known that some potentially language-relevant asymmetries already exist in the neonate. These concern leftward asymmetries of the planum temporale (observed in the fetus), as well as auditory asymmetries detected in event-related potential (ERP) and dichotic listening studies of neonates and infants (Werker & Vouloumanos, 2001). Nonetheless, there is evidence pointing at greater right-hemisphere language involvement during early

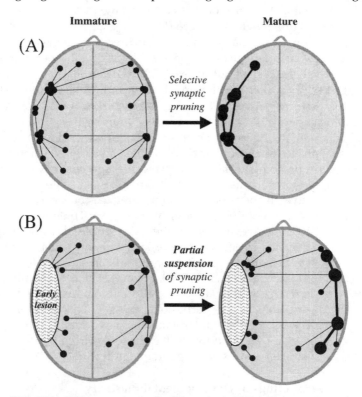

FIG. 12.5.   Diagrammatic sketch of hypothesized links between synaptic pruning and regional and hemispheric organization for language. During synaptic abundance in early childhood, language processing involves numerous frontal, parietal, and temporal regions in both hemispheres (A). Some of these interregional connections stabilize and strengthen during development, resulting in the typical left perisylvian organization for language in the mature brain. However, when left perisylvian regions are damaged early in life (B), some of the normal synaptic pruning is suspended, and alternative connectivity, especially in homotopic right-hemisphere regions, becomes selectively stabilized.

stages of language acquisition. For instance, Mills and colleagues found that ERPs distinguishing known from unknown words were broadly distributed bilaterally in 13- to 17-month-old infants, but more localized over left temporo-parietal sites in 20-month-olds (Mills et al., 1997). Neville and Mills (1997) further observed that a leftward asymmetry of ERPs to closed class (grammatical function) words, as found in adults, is absent or reversed in children under age 3. Studying children ages 5 years and older, Holcomb and colleagues (1992) found that ERP asymmetries observed in adults for semantic processing of sentence-final words are absent or inconsistent in children and become established only around age 13 years.

There is also limited neuroimaging evidence relevant to the question of right-hemisphere language involvement in children. Balsamo and colleagues (2002) recently reported robust left dominance in lateral temporal areas for auditory response naming in children ages 7 to 9 years. However, this study did not directly compare children to adults. In contrast, Gaillard et al. (2000) found significantly greater overall right-hemisphere involvement for verb generation in 8- to 13-year-old children compared with young adults. Holland and coworkers (2001) studied subjects of a wider age range (7–18 years) and found a significant negative correlation between age and number of voxels activated in the right hemisphere overall. Laterality indices of activation were significantly correlated with age, indicating increasing left-hemisphere dominance in older children and adolescents (for supportive evidence, see also Saccuman et al., 2002).

In agreement with these imaging studies, clinical evidence shows that in young children lexical comprehension is more strongly affected by right- (compared with left-) hemisphere lesion (Bates, 1999; Thal et al., 1991; Vicari et al., 2000). Applying the hypothesis of synaptic pruning and neurofunctional changes to lesion patients, loss of part of the initially rather distributed and bilateral network would result in stabilization of those parts of the network that remain intact. A left perisylvian lesion may thus result in suspended normal synaptic pruning and compensatory stabilization of synapses in right perisylvian regions (Fig. 12.5B).

The developing language network, and in particular increasing left-hemisphere lateralization for language in childhood, may thus be considered a reflection of the general principle of synaptic pruning and stabilization. As discussed earlier, these synaptic changes are predominantly related to activity, stimulation, and interaction with environment, rather than being specified in the genome. Changes in the hemispheric organization for language, both in clinical lesion patients and healthy children, thus epitomize the importance of epigenetic factors on neural and cognitive organization for language.

CAN DEVELOPMENTAL PATHOLOGY
BE STUDIED WITH fMRI?

In the previous section, a number of imaging approaches were reviewed
that elucidate neurofunctional development and the plasticity of the child
brain. As mentioned, PET is hampered by ethical issues resulting in a lack
of normative data. Although PET continues to be of great promise for the
study of brain biochemistry (Herscovitch & Ernst, 2000; Morris et al.,
2000), its use in the imaging of task-related activation is limited by additional methodological disadvantages. In comparison with functional MRI,
PET has a lower spatial and temporal resolution. In particular, recent advances in event-related fMRI make it possible to study multiple conditions or trial types in randomized order with a temporal resolution of a
few seconds (Miezin et al., 2000) or even less (Hernandez et al., 2002).
Nonetheless, fMRI still has its limits in the study of developmental disorders. The mentioned sensitivity to motion artifacts makes it virtually impossible to study children under the age of 4 or 5 during task performance
in the awake state. MR imaging during natural sleep is possible (Courchesne et al., 2000), but the range of cognitive processes that can be examined through passive stimulation is narrow.

As discussed earlier, child language disorders in DLD or autism are
associated with strong genetic factors. It is likely that pathogenesis begins before birth in these disorders. Even if the age limit in fMRI can be
lowered with more sophisticated head restraints and motion correction
algorithms, imaging data will still primarily reflect outcome of initial
pathogenic events. A pessimistic approach might discard functional neuroimaging as irrelevant in such genetically anchored disorders. However, the picture is much less bleak when the mechanisms that determine
neurofunctional organization are taken into account. From the previous
discussion, it is clear that functional organization in the mature brain
largely reflects developmental processes (genetically driven regionalization, activity-driven arealization, fine-tuning through experience-driven
synaptic pruning and stabilization). Therefore, any aberration of these
normal developmental processes can equally be expected to manifest itself in the more mature brain, in terms of atypical functional organization. The application of fMRI can then be considered archaeological because it may uncover developmental abnormalities that occurred long
before the time of study.

Archaeological fMRI in the Study of Autism

This section describes a hypothetical model of neurofunctional abnormalities in autism that illustrates how fMRI findings in older children and
adults can shed light on pathological changes occurring much earlier in

Color Panel 1

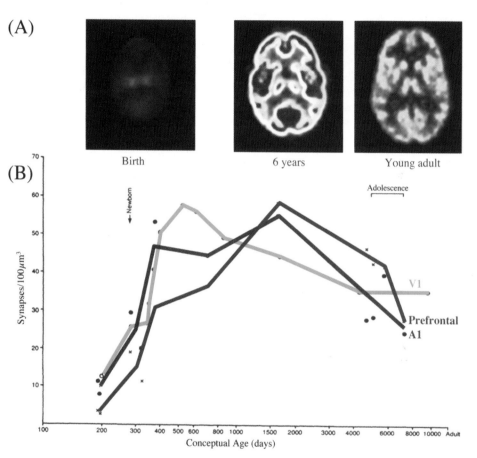

FIG. 12.2. Developmental curves of glucose metabolism and synaptic density. (A) The top part of the figure (adapted from Chugani, 1991) shows global glucose metabolism in a 6-year-old child at levels two to three times higher than seen in adults. The period of elevated glucose metabolism is seen between ages 2 and 10 years. This developmental curve corresponds well to changes in synaptic density during childhood. The lower part of the figure (B) shows synaptic density for primary visual, primary auditory, and prefrontal cortex. Adapted from Huttenlocher and Dabholkar (1997).

Color Panel 2

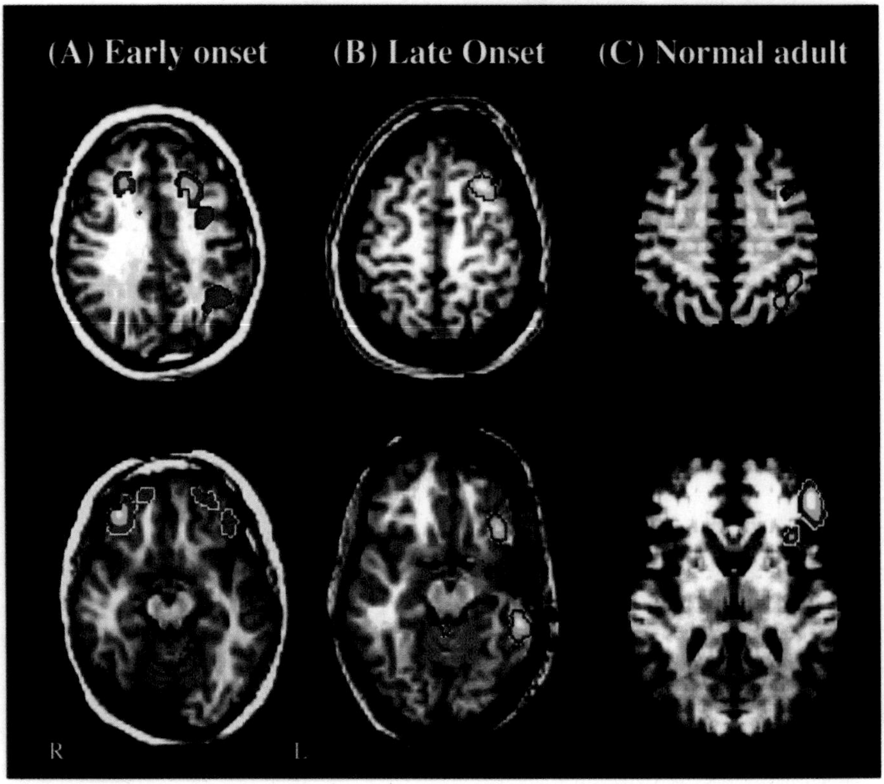

FIG. 12.4. Single-case examples of brain activations during an expressive language task (sentence generation), in which subjects create and overtly produce a sentence based on a stimulus sentence and a prompt word (e.g., "He listened to the radio—*television*," with expected response: "He watched television"). The control condition was sentence repetition. (A) An 8-year-old male subject with a progressive calcification of congenital origin in the left hemisphere (Sturge–Weber syndrome) shows extensive right-hemisphere frontal and parietal activation. (B) In contrast, a 17-year-old female intractable epilepsy patient with seizure onset at age 10 and resection of left temporal epileptogenic tissue at age 13 years shows exclusively left-hemispheric activation in fronto-temporal areas during sentence generation. These activations resemble those seen in a group of nine healthy adults (C). Adapted from Müller et al. (1997a, 1999a).

Color Panel 3

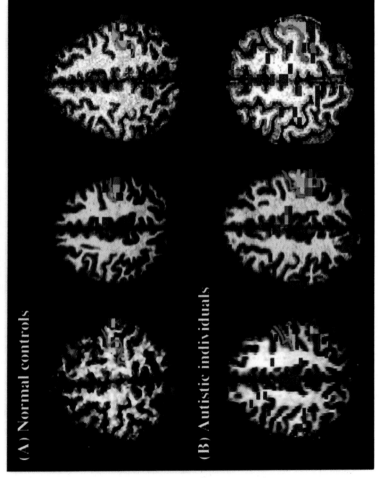

(A) Normal controls

(B) Autistic individuals

FIG. 12.6. Typical examples of activations seen during visually prompted index finger movement. (A) In normal controls, focal activations are seen in primary motor and somatosensory cortex along the central sulcus (green lines), with some additional activity in mediofrontal supplementary motor area (subject upper row, center). (B) Autistic individuals also show activations in these areas, but their activation patterns are more scattered, with distributed activation in parietal and prefrontal areas.

development when functional maps first emerge. The hypothesis ties together structural and functional findings in the cerebellum with atypical functional maps seen in cerebral cortex.

Autism is most commonly thought of in terms of impairments of language and social communication. Yet motor impairments have also been observed by many investigators (Bauman, 1992; Eisenmajer et al., 1998; Ghaziuddin & Butler, 1998; Haas et al., 1996; Hughes, 1996; V. Jones & Prior, 1985; Rapin, 1997; Rinehart et al., 2001). Stereotypic behavior, which is a characteristic of autism, can be observed on the cognitive level (e.g., as obsessive interest in unusual objects), but also on a motor level (e.g., as hand flapping seen in many patients). Interestingly, a study by Teitelbaum and colleagues (1998) suggested that abnormalities of elementary motor behaviors (e.g., righting, sitting, crawling) may be observed in the first months of life in children later diagnosed as autistic. A more recent retrospective study (Osterling et al., 2002) found additional behavioral markers (looking preferences, gestures, etc.) that distinguished 1-year-old infants later diagnosed as autistic from those with mental retardation, but also identified repetitive motor behavior as one of the discriminating variables. Motor impairments thus emerge earlier or in parallel with sociocommunicative, linguistic, and cognitive deficits, which may suggest an elementary role of motor impairments in autism. As mentioned, simple motor behavior normally begins in the fetus (D'Elia et al., 2001; Forssberg, 1999; Hepper, 1995). This indicates that neurofunctional organization of the motor system probably develops early during phases when autistic pathogenesis emerges.

Several fMRI studies looked at motor organization in autism from different angles. The first two examined extremely simple motor behavior (single-finger movement). In one study (Allen & Courchesne, 2003), subjects performed button presses with the thumb. Only the cerebellum and posterior cerebrum were imaged. Cerebellar activity overall was greater in autistic patients. In particular, many patients showed activations scattered beyond the site of activation seen in normal adults (the anterior cerebellum ipsilateral to the movement). A second study (Müller et al., 2001) extended these observations to the cerebrum. Again subjects performed simple finger movements (visually paced button presses with the index finger). When fMRI data were analyzed for whole groups of eight normal and eight autistic subjects each, few striking differences were apparent. Activations in typical motor regions (primary motor cortex, premotor cortex, supplementary motor area, basal ganglia) were simply less pronounced in the autism group.

Such groupwise analyses in Talairach space are common procedure in studies of autism and Asperger syndrome. Our study showed that this procedure might severely limit the ability to detect abnormalities in patients. When we analyzed imaging data on a subject-by-subject basis in native space (i.e., without warping to standardized space), we found that each control subject showed expected activation clusters along the central sulcus in primary motor and somatosensory cortex. Autistic individuals also showed activation in this site, but most patients showed unusual additional activation outside typical motor areas (e.g., in prefrontal cortex and in the superior parietal lobe; Fig. 12.6 [see color panel]). The overall picture was thus highly similar to the scattered and unusually distributed activation patterns in the cerebellum seen in the first motor study.

Similar analysis procedures were applied in a study on face perception (Pierce et al., 2001). In groupwise analyses, normal activation in fusiform gyrus was absent in autistic patients. Inspection of single patient data in native space, however, demonstrated that loci around the fusiform gyrus (the site of main activation in normal adults) were activated in the majority of patients, although these activations were scattered and individually highly variable.

A third motor study looked at more complex visually driven motor sequence learning (Müller et al., 2003). Again we found unusual variability across autistic individuals with regard to the spatial loci of major activation foci in premotor and superior parietal lobes (the main sites of activation during early stages of digit sequence learning). In addition, groupwise abnormalities were also consistent with a general hypothesis of "hierarchical crowding" that was derived from the findings of the two motor studies described earlier. This hypothesis is based on the assumption that neural tissue has a generally reduced processing capacity in autism. (For supportive evidence, see Casanova et al., 2002, and the following discussion.) This impaired processing capacity would imply that early developing functional systems (e.g., visual and motor) require more processing territory than in the normal brain. Those additional territories will then be less available to later emerging higher polymodal cognition.

The results from the study on simple finger movement (Müller et al., 2001) were consistent with this model because autistic individuals showed activation scattered beyond primary pericentral regions in the frontal and parietal cortex (Fig. 12.7A). Findings on more complex visually driven motor learning (Müller et al., 2003) were also consistent in that the autism group showed reduced activation in sites that were most robustly activated in normal adults (premotor and superior parietal cortex), but enhanced activation in prefrontal and more inferior parietal regions that are typically not involved in visuomotor coordination and digit sequence learning (Fig. 12.7B). These findings could explain why autistic patients show impairments of executive processing and delays of language

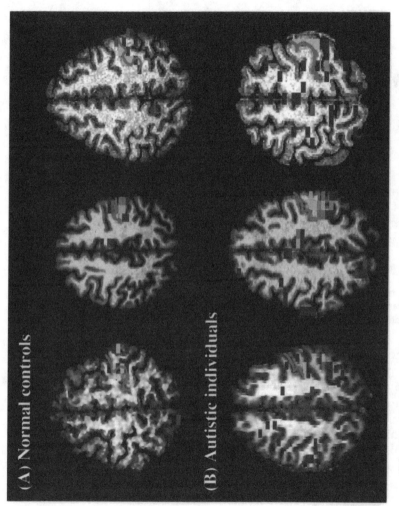

FIG. 12.6. Typical examples of activations seen during visually prompted index finger movement. (A) In normal controls, focal activations are seen in primary motor and somatosensory cortex along the central sulcus (green lines), with some additional activity in mediofrontal supplementary motor area (subject upper row, center). (B) Autistic individuals also show activations in these areas, but their activation patterns are more scattered, with distributed activation in parietal and prefrontal areas. (See Color Panel 3.)

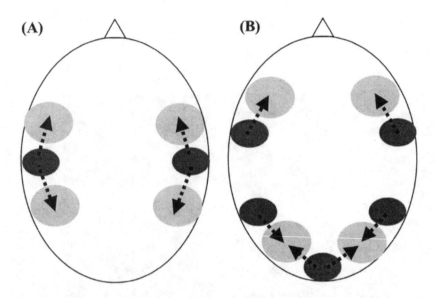

FIG. 12.7. Schematic diagram of hypothesized effects of scattered functional maps in autism. (A) Simple motor execution scenario (corresponding to the findings in Müller et al., 2001). (B) Motor learning scenario corresponding to findings of Müller et al. (2003). Dark shaded circles indicate regions of stronger activation in normal adults, light shaded circles those of stronger activation in autistic patients. Dotted arrows indicate direction of scatter beyond regions of normal primary activations observed in autistic patients. Adapted from Müller et al. (2003).

acquisition (because prefrontal and inferior parietal lobes are partly "invaded" by simpler functional domains such as visuomotor coordination).

The hypothesis of hierarchical crowding implies that abnormal emergence of functional maps early in development is reflected by persistent abnormalities in the adult autistic brain. This hypothesis is quite general and requires more specific neuroscientific support. One line of evidence relates to the parallel findings of activation scatter in autistic cerebellum and cerebrum described before. Although there is much inconsistency regarding sites of volumetric abnormality in the autistic brain (reviewed in Cody et al., 2002), many studies have found evidence for cerebellar abnormalities (Courchesne et al., 2001; Courchesne et al., 1994; Courchesne et al., 1988; Gaffney et al., 1987; Hardan et al., 2001; Hashimoto et al., 1995; Murakami et al., 1989; Otsuka et al., 1999). Nonetheless, nonreplications should be noted (Filipek, 1995; Holttum et al., 1992; Piven et al., 1997), as should methodological issues regarding IQ matching that may confound cerebellar effects (Cody et al., 2002; Piven & Arndt, 1995; Yeung-Courchesne & Courchesne, 1997). In a postmortem study including six brains

(Bailey et al., 1998), the most consistent finding was abnormality involving cerebellar Purkinje neurons. Reduced cerebellar measures in autism are associated with deficits of attention (Harris et al., 1999; Townsend et al., 1996) and reduced exploratory behavior (Pierce & Courchesne, 2001). Cerebellar hypoplasia presumably reflects reduced numbers of Purkinje neurons, which may set in prenatally (Courchesne, 1997) or in early postnatal stages (Bailey et al., 1998). PET studies have also identified abnormalities of serotonin synthesis in the cerebellar dentate nucleus in autistic boys (Chugani et al., 1997).

As discussed previously, animal work (O'Leary et al., 1994) has demonstrated the importance of thalamocortical afferents for neocortical differentiation and the development of adult maps of functional specialization. The cerebellum is heavily interconnected via the thalamus with almost all neocortical regions in topographic and functionally specific ways (Schmahmann, 1996). Cerebello-thalamo-cortical fibers originate almost exclusively from deep cerebellar nuclei (in particular the dentate nuclei), which in turn receive synaptic inputs from inhibitory Purkinje cells in cerebellar cortex (Altman & Bayer, 1997). Cerebellar afferents to the thalamus terminate in ventrolateral "motor" nuclei (Altman & Bayer, 1997, p. 71ff), but also in a variety of nonmotor thalamic nuclei (Middleton & Strick, 1994; Schmahmann, 1996).

As noted, postmortem histological studies of autistic brains show reduced numbers of Purkinje cells (Bailey et al., 1998; Bauman & Kemper, 1986). Reduced cerebellar levels of Reelin and Bcl-2, as observed in autistic postmortem brains, may be related to disturbances in migration, cortical lamination, and apoptosis (Fatemi et al., 2001), although it must be noted that these findings from adult brains do not directly establish developmental abnormalities. Finally, absence of "empty" basket cells suggests that Purkinje cell reduction in adults is due to reduced neuronogenesis rather than subsequent loss (Bailey et al., 1998; Courchesne, 1997). Growth interaction between basket and Purkinje cells takes place before the differentiation of Purkinje cells is completed (around postnatal day 8 in the rat; Altman & Bayer, 1997), which roughly corresponds to the end of the second trimester in human gestation (Clancy et al., 2001).

Early Purkinje cell loss may thus affect thalamocortical afferents from deep cerebellar nuclei. This could in turn have indirect effects on functional differentiation of cerebral cortex in autism (misconstruction). Inhibitory synapses of Purkinje cells in deep cerebellar nuclei probably form around the beginning of the third trimester in humans (Clancy et al., 2001; Garin & Escher, 2001). In the thalamus, afferents from deep cerebellar nuclei are present at birth in the rat (i.e., preceding the previously mentioned events; Asanuma et al., 1988). Early Purkinje cell loss in autism may thus impair developing cerebello-thalamo-cortical connectivity and cerebral cortical functional differentiation as reflected in abnormally scattered fMRI activation patterns.

Based on the hypothesis of aberrant cerebello-thalamo-cortical pathways in autism, one would have to expect evidence for thalamic abnormalities. Although the evidence is limited to date, a few studies have reported reduced thalamic perfusion in autistic patients (Starkstein et al., 2000) and reduced correlation of glucose metabolic rates between thalamus and fronto-parietal regions, which may be an index of impaired thalamocortical networks (Horwitz et al., 1988). A recent MR spectroscopy study found reductions of the neuronal marker N-acetyl aspartate in the thalamus bilaterally in autistic children ages 3 to 4 years (Friedman et al., 2003). In a PET study using a serotonin precursor as a tracer, Chugani et al. (1999, 1997) observed a characteristic pattern of increased serotonin synthesis in the cerebellar dentate nucleus, accompanied by decreases in contralateral thalamus and frontal cortex in autistic boys (but not girls). Serotonin plays an important role in neuronal differentiation and synaptogenesis. In particular, serotonin is crucially involved in the establishment of thalamo-cortical connectivity (Bennett-Clarke et al., 1996; D'Amato et al., 1987; Lauder, 1990; Lieske et al., 1999). The findings of the PET studies by Chugani and colleagues came from children ages 2 years and older and therefore do not conclusively demonstrate that serotonergic abnormalities are present when thalamocortical afferents are first established. Interestingly, a PET activation study in male autistic adults yielded some preliminary evidence for persistent functional impairments of dentato-thalamo-cortical pathways during language processing, albeit in a small sample (Müller et al., 1998a).

The scenario described above would imply that developmental abnormalities of cerebello-thalamo-cortical afferents result in persistent neurofunctional abnormalities of autistic cerebral cortex. This scenario is not meant to be a comprehensive neurocognitive model of autism, but may account for some aspects of autistic pathogenesis. Other mechanisms are certainly involved. For example, a recent postmortem study suggests abnormal columnar architecture in frontal and temporal areas of the autistic brain (Casanova et al., 2002). These would probably require explanation in terms of neuromigrational disturbances. For another example, MR volumetric work (Courchesne et al., 2001) demonstrates rather diffuse brain growth disturbances in autism, with greater than normal growth up to ages 2 to 4 years (as also reported by Sparks et al., 2002) and subsequent reduced or stunted growth especially in white matter. These results may be related to findings of abnormal brain growth factors in neonates later diagnosed as autistic, which were however not specific for autism in comparison with nonautistic mental retardation (Nelson et al., 2001). All in all, it is likely that potential cerebello-thalamo-cortical abnormalities are accompanied by more global neurodevelopmental disturbances.

It is unclear at this point how these different types of disturbances may interact in causing typical autistic impairments, such as language delays and deficits. In any case, the hypothesis of developmental cerebello-thalamo-cortical disturbances causing abnormalities in cerebral cortical functional maps serves, in the present context, as an illustration of how functional neuroimaging in older children and adults can shed light on much earlier occurring developmental events that are characteristic of an emerging language disorder. It also underlines that in autism, as in developmental language disorders (with the possible exception of rare cases such as family KE), direct lines of causality between genes and language impairments are improbable (Gottlieb & Halpern, 2002; Pennington, 2001). Instead the effects of suspected genetic risk factors and their interactions must be examined in the developing nervous system, in particular with regard to changes in normal activity-driven formation of the functional organization of cerebral cortex.

CONCLUSION

One of the goals of this review was to illuminate why relationships between genotypes and language-related phenotypic traits are unlikely to be simple and linear. This caveat applies to normal development as much as to developmental disorders. Divergence as well as convergence of genotype–phenotype links complicate the study of developmental disorders. We cannot expect simple genetic explanations for developmental disorders of language that are diagnosed with respect to diverse sets of consensus-based behavioral outcome criteria.

Without regard for the basic epigenetic principles of neurofunctional development, the search for one or a few genes that may "explain" language impairment in such disorders is almost certainly futile. While this may sound pessimistic, a realistic neurodevelopmental perspective, on the contrary, opens up experimental windows that have not previously been explored. One example is the use of functional neuroimaging in older children and adults with developmental disorders. The principles of activity-based neurofunctional organization of cerebral cortex allow us to interpret functional maps in patients as reflections of disturbances that occurred early in development. The traces of fetal and early postnatal abnormalities are therefore not entirely lost, but may be recovered even at later stages when patients become available for functional neuroimaging.

ACKNOWLEDGMENTS

Supported by the National Institutes of Health (1R01-NS43999, 1R01-DC6155).

REFERENCES

Allen, G., & Courchesne, E. (2003). Differential effects of developmental cerebellar abnormality on cognitive and motor functions in the cerebellum: An fMRI study of autism. *American Journal of Psychiatry, 160,* 262–273.

Altman, J., & Bayer, S. A. (1997). *Development of the cerebellar system.* Boca Raton: CRC Press.

American Psychiatric Association. (2000). *Diagnostic and statistical manual of mental disorders–IV–TR.* Washington, DC: American Psychiatric Association.

Amir, R. E., & Zoghbi, H. Y. (2000). Rett syndrome: Methyl-Cpg-binding protein 2 mutations and phenotype-genotype correlations. *American Journal of Medical Genetics, 97,* 147–152.

Amunts, K., Schlaug, G., Jänicke, L., Steinmetz, H., Schleicher, A., Dabringhaus, A., & Zilles, K. (1997). Motor cortex and hand motor skills: Structural compliance in the human brain. *Human Brain Mapping, 5,* 206–215.

Amunts, K., Schleicher, A., & Zilles, K. (in press). Outstanding language competence and cytoarchitecture in Broca's speech region. *Brain and Language.*

Anderson, B. J., Eckburg, P. B., & Relucio, K. I. (2002). Alterations in the thickness of motor cortical subregions after motor-skill learning and exercise. *Learning and Memory, 9,* 1–9.

Asanuma, C., Ohkawa, R., Stanfield, B. B., & Cowan, W. M. (1988). Observations on the development of certain ascending inputs to the thalamus in rats: I. Postnatal development. *Brain Research, 469,* 159–170.

Bailey, A., Le Couteur, A., Gottesman, I., Bolton, P., Simonoff, E., Yuzda, E., & Rutter, M. (1995). Autism as a strongly genetic disorder: Evidence from a British twin study. *Psychological Medicine, 25,* 63–77.

Bailey, A., Luthert, P., Dean, A., Harding, B., Janota, I., Montgomery, M., Rutter, M., & Lantos, P. (1998). A clinicopathological study of autism. *Brain, 121,* 889–905.

Balsamo, L. M., Xu, B., Grandin, C. B., Petrella, J. R., Braniecki, S. H., Elliott, T. K., & Gaillard, W. D. (2002). A functional magnetic resonance imaging study of left hemisphere language dominance in children. *Archives of Neurology, 59,* 1168–1174.

Bartlett, C. W., Flax, J. F., Logue, M. W., Vieland, V. J., Bassett, A. S., Tallal, P., & Brzustowicz, L. M. (2002). A major susceptibility locus for specific language impairment is located on 13q21. *American Journal of Human Genetics, 71,* 45–55.

Basser, L. S. (1962). Hemiplegia of early onset and the faculty of speech with special reference to the effects of hemispherectomy. *Brain, 85,* 427–460.

Bates, E. (1999). Plasticity, localization and language development. In S. H. Broman & J. M. Fletcher (Eds.), *The changing nervous system: Neurobehavioral consequences of early brain disorders* (pp. 214–253). New York: Oxford University Press.

Bauman, M. L. (1992). Motor dysfunction in autism. In A. B. Joseph & R. R. Young (Eds.), *Movement disorders in neurology and psychiatry* (pp. 660–663). Boston: Blackwell.

Bauman, M. L., & Kemper, T. L. (1986). Developmental cerebellar abnormalities: A consistent finding in early infantile autism. *Neurology, 36,* 190.

Belin, P., Van Eeckhout, P., Zilbovicius, M., Remy, P., François, C., Guillaume, S., Chain, F., Rancurel, G., & Samson, Y. (1996). Recovery from nonfluent aphasia after melodic intonation therapy: A PET study. *Neurology, 47,* 1504–1511.

Bennett-Clarke, C. A., Chiaia, N. L., & Rhoades, R. W. (1996). Thalamocortical afferents in rat express high-affinity serotonin uptake sites. *Brain Research, 733,* 301–306.

Benson, R. R., Logan, W. J., Cosgrove, G. R., Cole, A. J., Jiang, H., LeSueur, L. L., Buchbinder, B. R., Rosen, B. R., & Caviness, V. S., Jr. (1996). Functional MRI localization of language in a 9-year-old child. *Canadian Journal of Neurological Sciences, 23,* 213–219.

Bentourkia, M., Michel, C., Ferriere, G., Bol, A., Coppens, A., Sibomana, M., Bausart, R., Labar, D., & De Volder, A. G. (1998). Evolution of brain glucose metabolism with age in epileptic infants, children and adolescents. *Brain and Development, 20,* 524–529.

Bishop, D. V. (1989). Autism, Asperger's syndrome and semantic-pragmatic disorder: Where are the boundaries? *British Journal of Disorders of Communication, 24,* 107–121.

Bishop, D. V. (2002). The role of genes in the etiology of specific language impairment. *Journal of Communication Disorders, 35,* 311–328.

Boatman, D., Freeman, J., Vining, E., Pulsifer, M., Miglioretti, D., Minahan, R., Carson, B., Brandt, J., & McKhann, G. (1999). Language recovery after left hemispherectomy in children with late-onset seizures. *Annals of Neurology, 46,* 579–586.

Bradford, Y. (2001). Incorporating language phenotypes strengthens evidence of linkage to autism. *American Journal of Medical Genetics, 105,* 539–547.

Brenton, D. P., & Pietz, J. (2000). Adult care in phenylketonuria and hyperphenylalaninaemia: The relevance of neurological abnormalities. *European Journal of Pediatrics, 159* (Suppl. 2), S114–S120.

Calvert, G. A., Brammer, M. J., Morris, R. G., Williams, S. C., King, N., & Matthews, P. M. (2000). Using fMRI to study recovery from acquired dysphasia. *Brain and Language, 71,* 391–399.

Cao, Y., Vikingstad, E. M., George, K. P., Johnson, A. F., & Welch, K. M. (1999). Cortical language activation in stroke patients recovering from aphasia with functional MRI. *Stroke, 30,* 2331–2340.

Caplan, D., Hildebrandt, N., & Makris, N. (1996). Location of lesions in stroke patients with deficits in syntactic processing in sentence comprehension. *Brain, 119,* 933–949.

Casanova, M. F., Buxhoeveden, D. P., Switala, A. E., & Roy, E. (2002). Minicolumnar pathology in autism. *Neurology, 58,* 428–432.

Caviness, V. S., Kennedy, D. N., Bates, J. F., & Makris, N. (1997). The developing human brain: A morphometric profile. In R. W. Thatcher, G. R. Lyon, J. Rumsey, & N. Krasnegor (Eds.), *Developmental neuroimaging* (pp. 3–14). San Diego: Academic Press.

Cecchi, C. (2002). Emx2: A gene responsible for cortical development, regionalization and area specification. *Gene, 291,* 1–9.

Changeux, J.-P. (1986). *Neuronal man.* New York: Oxford University Press.

Charman, T. (2002). The prevalence of autism spectrum disorders: Recent evidence and future challenges. *European Child and Adolescent Psychiatry, 11,* 249–256.

Chiron, C., Raynaud, C., Mazière, B., Zilbovicius, M., Laflamme, L., Masure, M.-C., Dulac, O., Bourguignon, M., & Syrota, A. (1992). Changes in regional cerebral blood flow during brain maturation in children and adolescents. *Journal of Nuclear Medecine, 33,* 696–703.

Chomsky, N. (1957). *Syntactic structures.* s'-Gravenhage: Mouton.

Chomsky, N. (1959). Review of B. F. Skinner "Verbal Behavior." *Language, 35,* 26–58.

Chomsky, N. (1965). *Aspects of the theory of syntax.* Cambridge, MA: MIT Press.

Chomsky, N. (1980). *Rules and representations.* New York: Columbia University Press.

Chomsky, N. (1981). *Lectures on government and binding.* Dordrecht: Foris.

Chugani, D. C., Muzik, O., Behen, M., Rothermel, R., Janisse, J. J., Lee, J., & Chugani, H. T. (1999). Developmental changes in brain serotonin: Synthesis capacity in autistic and nonautistic children. *Annals of Neurology, 45,* 287–295.

Chugani, D. C., Muzik, O., Rothermel, R. D., Behen, M. E., Chakraborty, P. K., Mangner, T. J., da Silva, E. A., & Chugani, H. T. (1997). Altered serotonin synthesis in the dentato-thalamo-cortical pathway in autistic boys. *Annals of Neurology, 14,* 666–669.

Chugani, H. T. (1991). Childhood epilepsy: Anatomical and functional neuroimaging. In S. Ohtahara & J. Roger (Eds.), *New trends in pediatric epileptology* (pp. 17–29). Osaka: Dainippon Pharmaceutical.

Chugani, H. T., & Phelps, M. E. (1986). Maturational changes in cerebral function in infants determined by 18-FDG positron emission tomography. *Science, 231,* 840–843.

Chugani, H. T., Phelps, M. E., & Mazziotta, J. C. (1987). Positron emission tomography study of human brain functional development. *Annals of Neurology, 22,* 487–497.

Clancy, B., Darlington, R. B., & Finlay, B. L. (2001). Translating developmental time across mammalian species. *Neuroscience, 105,* 7–17.

Clark, M. M., & Plante, E. (1998). Morphology of the inferior frontal gyrus in developmentally language-disordered adults. *Brain and Language, 61,* 288–303.

Clearfield, M. W., & Thelen, E. (2001). Stability and flexibility in the acquisition of skilled movement. In C. A. Nelson & M. Luciana (Eds.), *Handbook of developmental cognitive neuroscience* (pp. 253–266). Cambridge, MA: MIT Press.

Cody, H., Pelphrey, K., & Piven, J. (2002). Structural and functional magnetic resonance imaging of autism. *International Journal of Developmental Neuroscience, 20,* 421–438.

Courchesne, E. (1997). Brainstem, cerebellar and limbic neuroanatomical abnormalities in autism. *Current Opinion in Neurobiology, 7,* 269–278.

Courchesne, E., Chisum, H., Townsend, J., Cowles, A., Covington, J., Egaas, B., Hinds, S., & Press, G. (2000). Normal brain development and aging: Quantitative analysis at in vivo MR imaging in healthy volunteers. *Radiology, 216,* 672–682.

Courchesne, E., Karns, C. M., Davis, H. R., Ziccardi, R., Carper, R. A., Tigue, Z. D., Chisum, H. J., Moses, P., Pierce, K., Lord, C., Lincoln, A. J., Pizzo, S., Schreibman, L., Haas, R. H., Akshoomoff, N. A., & Courchesne, R. Y. (2001). Unusual brain growth patterns in early life in patients with autistic disorder: An MRI study. *Neurology, 57,* 245–254.

Courchesne, E., Saitoh, O., Yeung-Courchesne, R., Press, G. A., Lincoln, A. J., Haas, R. H., & Schreibman, L. (1994). Abnormality of cerebellar vermian lobules VI and VII in patients with infantile autism: Identification of hypoplastic and hyperplastic subgroups with MR imaging. *American Journal of Roentgenology, 162,* 123–130.

Courchesne, E., Yeung-Courchesne, R., Press, G. A., Hesselink, J. R., & Jernigan, T. L. (1988). Hypoplasia of cerebellar vermal lobules VI and VII in autism. *New England Journal of Medicine, 318,* 1349–1354.

Cowan, W. M., Kopnisky, K. L., & Hyman, S. E. (2002). The human genome project and its impact on psychiatry. *Annual Reviews in Neuroscience, 25,* 1–50.

Crain, S. (1991). Language acquisition in the absence of experience. *Behavioral and Brain Sciences, 14,* 597–650.

Curtiss, S., de Bode, S., & Mathern, G. W. (2001). Spoken language outcomes after hemispherectomy: Factoring in etiology. *Brain and Language, 79,* 379–396.

D'Amato, R. J., Blue, M. E., Largent, B. L., Lynch, D. R., Ledbetter, D. J., Molliver, M. E., & Snyder, S. H. (1987). Ontogeny of the serotonergic projection to rat neocortex: Transient expression of a dense innervation to primary sensory areas. *Proceedings of the National Academy of Sciences of the USA, 84,* 4322–4326.

D'Elia, A., Pighetti, M., Moccia, G., & Santangelo, N. (2001). Spontaneous motor activity in normal fetuses. *Early Human Development, 65,* 139–147.

Eckert, M. A., Leonard, C. M., Richards, T. L., Aylward, E. H., Thomson, J., & Berninger, V. W. (2003). Anatomical correlates of dyslexia: Frontal and cerebellar findings. *Brain, 126,* 482–494.

Edelson, S. B., & Cantor, D. S. (1998). Autism: Xenobiotic influences. *Toxicology and Industrial Health, 14,* 553–563.

Eden, G. F., & Zeffiro, T. A. (2000). Functional magnetic resonance imaging. In M. Ernst & J. Rumsey (Eds.), *The foundation and future of functional neuroimaging in child psychiatry* (pp. 45–58). New York: Cambridge University Press.

Eisenmajer, R., Prior, M., Leekam, S., Wing, L., Ong, B., Gould, J., & Welham, M. (1998). Delayed language onset as a predictor of clinical symptoms in pervasive developmental disorders. *Journal of Autism and Developmental Disorders, 28,* 527–533.

Elbert, T., Pantev, C., Wienbruch, C., Rockstroh, B., & Taub, E. (1995). Increased cortical representation of the fingers of the left hand in string players. *Science, 270,* 305–307.

Fatemi, S. H., Stary, J. M., Halt, A. R., & Realmuto, G. R. (2001). Dysregulation of Reelin and Bcl-2 proteins in autistic cerebellum. *Journal of Autism and Developmental Disorders, 31,* 529–535.

Filipek, P. A. (1995). Neurobiologic correlates of developmental dyslexia: How do dyslexics' brains differ from those of normal readers? *Journal of Child Neurology, 10,* S62–S69.

Finney, E. M., Fine, I., & Dobkins, K. R. (2001). Visual stimuli activate auditory cortex in the deaf. *Nature Neuroscience, 4,* 1171–1173.

Fisher, S. E., Vargha-Khadem, F., Watkins, K. E., Monaco, A. P., & Pembrey, M. E. (1998). Localisation of a gene implicated in a severe speech and language disorder. *Nature Genetics, 18,* 168–170.

Følling, I. (1994). The discovery of phenylketonuria. *Acta Paediatrica Supplement, 407,* 4–10.

Folstein, S. E., & Mankoski, R. E. (2000). Chromosome 7q: Where autism meets language disorder? *American Journal of Human Genetics, 67,* 278–281.

Folstein, S. E., & Rosen-Sheidley, B. (2001). Genetics of autism: Complex aetiology for a heterogeneous disorder. *Nature Reviews of Genetics, 2,* 943–955.

Forssberg, H. (1999). Neural control of human motor development. *Current Opinion in Neurobiology, 9,* 676–682.

Foundas, A. L., Leonard, C. M., Gilmore, R., Fennell, E., & Heilman, K. M. (1994). Planum temporale asymmetry and language dominance. *Neuropsychologia, 32,* 1225–1231.

Foundas, A. L., Leonard, C. M., Gilmore, R. L., Fennell, E. B., & Heilman, K. M. (1996). Pars triangularis asymmetry and language dominance. *Proceedings of the National Academy of Sciences of the United States of America, 93,* 719–722.

Friedman, S. D., Shaw, D. W., Artru, A. A., Richards, T. L., Gardner, J., Dawson, G., Posse, S., & Dager, S. R. (2003). Regional brain chemical alterations in young children with autism spectrum disorder. *Neurology, 60,* 100–107.

Gaffney, G. R., Tsai, L. Y., Kuperman, S., & Minchin, S. (1987). Cerebellar structure in autism. *American Journal of Diseases of Children, 141,* 1330–1332.

Gaillard, W. D., Hertz-Pannier, L., Mott, S. H., Barnett, A. S., LeBihan, D., & Theodore, W. H. (2000). Functional anatomy of cognitive development: fMRI of verbal fluency in children and adults. *Neurology, 54,* 180–185.

Gardner, H. (1987). *The mind's new science.* New York: Basic Books.

Garin, N., & Escher, G. (2001). The development of inhibitory synaptic specializations in the mouse deep cerebellar nuclei. *Neuroscience, 105,* 431–441.

Gauger, L. M., Lombardino, L. J., & Leonard, C. M. (1997). Brain morphology in children with specific language impairment. *Journal of Speech, Language, and Hearing Research, 40,* 1272–1284.

Ghaziuddin, M., & Butler, E. (1998). Clumsiness in autism and Asperger syndrome: A further report. *Journal of Intellectual Disability Research, 42*(Pt. 1), 43–48.

Gold, B. T., & Kertesz, A. (2000). Right hemisphere semantic processing of visual words in an aphasic patient: An fMRI study. *Brain and Language, 73,* 456–465.

Gopnik, M. (1990). Feature blindness: A case study. *Language Acquisition: A Journal of Developmental Linguistics, 1,* 139–164.

Gopnik, M., & Crago, M. B. (1991). Familial aggregation of a developmental language disorder. *Cognition, 39,* 1–50.

Gottlieb, G., & Halpern, C. T. (2002). A relational view of causality in normal and abnormal development. *Developmental Psychopathology, 14,* 421–435.

Graveline, C. J., Mikulis, D. J., Crawley, A. P., & Hwang, P. A. (1998). Regionalized sensorimotor plasticity after hemispherectomy fMRI evaluation. *Pediatric Neurology, 19,* 337–342.

Greenberg, D. A., Hodge, S. E., Sowinski, J., & Nicoll, D. (2001). Excess of twins among affected sibling pairs with autism: Implications for the etiology of autism. *American Journal of Human Genetics, 69,* 1062–1067.

Greenough, W. T., & Bailey, C. H. (1988). The anatomy of a memory: Convergence of results across a diversity of tests. *Trends in Neuroscience, 11,* 142–147.

Haas, R. H., Townsend, J., Courchesne, E., Lincoln, A. J., Schreibman, L., & Yeung-Courchesne, R. (1996). Neurologic abnormalities in infantile autism. *Journal of Child Neurology, 11,* 84–92.

Habib, M. (2000). The neurological basis of developmental dyslexia: An overview and working hypothesis. *Brain, 123*(Pt. 12), 2373–2399.

Hardan, A. Y., Minshew, N. J., Harenski, K., & Keshavan, M. S. (2001). Posterior fossa magnetic resonance imaging in autism. *Journal of the American Academy of Child and Adolescent Psychiatry, 40,* 666–672.

Harris, N. S., Courchesne, E., Townsend, J., Carper, R. A., & Lord, C. (1999). Neuroanatomic contributions to slowed orienting of attention in children with autism. *Cognitive Brain Research, 8,* 61–71.

Hashimoto, T., Tayama, M., Murakawa, K., Yoshimoto, T., Miyazaki, M., Harada, M., & Kuroda, Y. (1995). Development of the brainstem and cerebellum in autistic patients. *Journal of Autism and Developmental Disorders, 25,* 1–18.

Heiss, W. D., Kessler, J., Thiel, A., Ghaemi, M., & Karbe, H. (1999). Differential capacity of left and right hemispheric areas for compensation of poststroke aphasia. *Annals of Neurology, 45,* 430–438.

Hepper, P. G. (1995). The behavior of the fetus as an indicator of neural functioning. In J.-P. Lecanuet, W. P. Fifer, N. A. Krasnegor, & W. P. Smotherman (Eds.), *Fetal development* (pp. 405–417). Hillsdale, NJ: Lawrence Erlbaum Associates.

Hernandez, L., Badre, D., Noll, D., & Jonides, J. (2002). Temporal sensitivity of event-related fMRI. *Neuroimage, 17,* 1018–1026.

Herscovitch, P., & Ernst, M. (2000). Functional brain imaging with PET and SPECT. In M. Ernst & J. Rumsey (Eds.), *The foundation and future of functional neuroimaging in child psychiatry* (pp. 3–26). New York: Cambridge University Press.

Hertz-Pannier, L., Chiron, C., Jambaque, I., Renaux-Kieffer, V., Van de Moortele, P. F., Delalande, O., Fohlen, M., Brunelle, F., & Le Bihan, D. (2002). Late plasticity for language in a child's non-dominant hemisphere: A pre- and post-surgery fMRI study. *Brain, 125,* 361–372.

Hertz-Pannier, L., Gaillard, W. D., Mott, S. H., Cuenod, C. A., Bookheimer, S. Y., Weinstein, S., Conry, J., Papero, P. H., Schiff, S. J., LeBihan, D., & Theodore, W. H. (1997). Noninvasive assessment of language dominance in children and adolescents with functional MRI: A preliminary study. *Neurology, 48,* 1003–1012.

Holcomb, P. J., Coffey, S. A., & Neville, H. J. (1992). Visual and auditory sentence processing: A developmental analysis using event-related brain potentials. *Developmental Neuropsychology, 8,* 203–241.

Holland, S. K., Plante, E., Weber Byars, A., Strawsburg, R. H., Schmithorst, V. J., & Ball, W. S., Jr. (2001). Normal fMRI brain activation patterns in children performing a verb generation task. *Neuroimage, 14,* 837–843.

Holttum, J. R., Minshew, N. J., Sanders, R. S., & Phillips, N. E. (1992). Magnetic resonance imaging of the posterior fossa in autism. *Biological Psychiatry, 32,* 1091–1101.

Horwitz, B., Rumsey, J. M., & Donohue, B. C. (1998). Functional connectivity of the angular gyrus in normal reading and dyslexia. *Proceedings of the National Academy of Sciences of the United States of America, 95,* 8939–8944.

Horwitz, B., Rumsey, J. M., Grady, C. L., & Rapoport, S. I. (1988). The cerebral metabolic landscape in autism: Intercorrelations of regional glucose utilization. *Archives of Neurology, 45,* 749–755.

Howlin, P., Mawhood, L., & Rutter, M. (2000). Autism and developmental receptive language disorder—a follow-up comparison in early adult life: II. Social, behavioural, and psychiatric outcomes. *Journal of Child Psychology and Psychiatry, 41,* 561–578.

Hughes, C. (1996). Brief report: Planning problems in autism at the level of motor control. *Journal of Autism and Developmental Disorders, 26,* 99–107.

Hultman, C. M., Sparen, P., & Cnattingius, S. (2002). Perinatal risk factors for infantile autism. *Epidemiology, 13,* 417–423.

Hund-Georgiadis, M., & von Cramon, D. Y. (1999). Motor-learning-related changes in piano players and non-musicians revealed by functional magnetic-resonance signals. *Experimental Brain Research, 125,* 417–425.

Hutcheson, H. B., Bradford, Y., Folstein, S. E., Gardiner, M. B., Santangelo, S. L., Sutcliffe, J. S., & Haines, J. L. (2003). Defining the autism minimum candidate gene region on chromosome 7. *American Journal of Medical Genetics, 117B,* 90–96.

Huttenlocher, P. R., & Dabholkar, A. S. (1997). Regional differences in synaptogenesis in human cerebral cortex. *Journal of Comparative Neurology, 387,* 167–178.

Jackson, T., & Plante, E. (1996). Gyral morphology in the posterior sylvian region in families affected by developmental language disorder. *Neuropsychology Review, 6,* 81–94.

Jacobs, B., Schall, M., & Scheibel, A. B. (1993). A quantitative dendritic analysis of Wernicke's area in humans: II. Gender, hemispheric, and environmental factors. *Journal of Comparative Neurology, 327,* 97–111.

Jessell, T. M., & Sanes, J. N. (2000). The generation and survival of nerve cells. In E. R. Kandel, J. H. Schwartz, & T. M. Jessell (Eds.), *Principles of neural science* (4th ed., pp. 1042–1062). New York: Elsevier.

Jones, M. B., & Szatmari, P. (2002). A risk-factor model of epistatic interaction, focusing on autism. *American Journal of Medical Genetics, 114,* 558–565.

Jones, V., & Prior, M. (1985). Motor imitation abilities and neurological signs in autistic children. *Journal of Autism and Developmental Disorders, 15,* 37–45.

Kandel, E. R., Jessell, T. M., & Sanes, J. R. (2000). Sensory experience and the fine tuning of synaptic connections. In E. R. Kandel, J. H. Schwartz, & T. M. Jessell (Eds.), *Principles of neural science* (4th ed., pp. 1115–1130). New York: Elsevier.

Katz, L. C., & Shatz, C. J. (1996). Synaptic activity and the construction of the cortical circuits. *Science, 274,* 1133–1138.

Kleim, J. A., Lussnig, E., Schwarz, E. R., Comery, T. A., & Greenough, W. T. (1996). Synaptogenesis and Fos expression in the motor cortex of the adult rat after motor skill learning. *Journal of Neuroscience, 16,* 4529–4535.

Kolb, B., & Gibb, R. (2001). Early brain injury, plasticity, and behavior. In C. A. Nelson & M. Luciana (Eds.), *Handbook of developmental cognitive neuroscience* (pp. 175–190). Cambridge, MA: MIT Press.

Korvatska, E., Van de Water, J., Anders, T. F., & Gershwin, M. E. (2002). Genetic and immunologic considerations in autism. *Neurobiology of Disease, 9,* 107–125.

Kushch, A., Gross-Glenn, K., Jallad, B., Lubs, H., Rabin, M., Feldman, E., & Duara, R. (1993). Temporal lobe surface area measurements on MRI in normal and dyslexic readers. *Neuropsychologia, 31,* 811–821.

Lai, C. S., Fisher, S. E., Hurst, J. A., Vargha-Khadem, F., & Monaco, A. P. (2001). A forkhead-domain gene is mutated in a severe speech and language disorder. *Nature, 413,* 519–523.

Lauder, J. M. (1990). Ontogeny of the serotonergic system in the rat: Serotonin as a developmental signal. *Annals of the New York Academy of Sciences, 600,* 297–314.

Lehericy, S., Cohen, L., Bazin, B., Samson, S., Giacomini, E., Rougetet, R., Hertz-Pannier, L., Le Bihan, D., Marsault, C., & Baulac, M. (2000). Functional MR evaluation of temporal and frontal language dominance compared with the Wada test. *Neurology, 54,* 1625–1633.

Leonard, C. M., Voeller, K. K. S., Lombardino, L. J., Morris, M. K., Hynd, G. W., Alexander, A. W., Andersen, H. G., Garofalakis, M., Honeyman, J. C., Mao, J., Agee, F., & Staab, E. V. (1993). Anomalous cerebral structure in dyslexia revealed with magnetic resonance imaging. *Neurology, 50*, 461–469.

Lieske, V., Bennett-Clarke, C. A., & Rhoades, R. W. (1999). Effects of serotonin on neurite outgrowth from thalamic neurons in vitro. *Neuroscience, 90*, 967–974.

Lord, C., Rutter, M., & Le Couteur, A. (1994). Autism diagnostic interview-revised: A revised version of a diagnostic interview for caregivers of individuals with possible pervasive developmental disorders. *Journal of Autism and Developmental Disorders, 24*, 659–685.

Lotspeich, L. J., & Ciaranello, R. D. (1993). The neurobiology and genetics of infantile autism. *International Review of Neurobiology, 35*, 87–129.

Lou, H. C., Henriksen, L., & Bruhn, P. (1990). Focal cerebral dysfunction in developmental learning disabilities. *Lancet, 335*, 8–11.

Mason-Brothers, A., Ritvo, E. R., Pingree, C., Petersen, P. B., Jenson, W. R., McMahon, W. M., Freeman, B. J., Jorde, L. B., Spencer, M. J., & Mo, A. (1990). The UCLA-University of Utah epidemiologic survey of autism: Prenatal, perinatal, and postnatal factors. *Pediatrics, 86*, 514–519.

Mawhood, L., Howlin, P., & Rutter, M. (2000). Autism and developmental receptive language disorder—a comparative follow-up in early adult life: I. Cognitive and language outcomes. *Journal of Child Psychology and Psychiatry, 41*, 547–559.

Middleton, F. A., & Strick, P. L. (1994). Anatomical evidence for cerebellar and basal ganglia involvement in higher cognitive function. *Science, 266*, 458–461.

Miezin, F. M., Maccotta, L., Ollinger, J. M., Petersen, S. E., & Buckner, R. L. (2000). Characterizing the hemodynamic response: Effects of presentation rate, sampling procedure, and the possibility of ordering brain activity based on relative timing. *Neuroimage, 11*, 735–759.

Mills, D. L., Coffey-Corina, S. A., & Neville, H. J. (1997). Language comprehension and cerebral specialization from 13 to 20 months. *Developmental Neuropsychology, 13*, 397–445.

Morris, E. D., Muzic, R. F., Christian, B. C., Endres, C. J., & Fisher, R. E. (2000). Modeling of receptor images in PET and SPECT. In M. Ernst & J. Rumsey (Eds.), *The foundation and future of functional neuroimaging in child psychiatry* (pp. 27–44). New York: Cambridge University Press.

Morton, C. T., Casey, B., Cohen, J., Zametkin, A., Schwartz, D., Ernst, M., & Cohen, R. (1996). Is research in normal and ill children involving radiation exposure ethical? [letter and replies]. *Archives of General Psychiatry, 53*, 1059–1061.

Müller, R.-A. (in press). Weak evidence for a strong case against modularity in developmental disorders [Commentary on Thomas and Karmiloff-Smith]. *Behavioral and Brain Sciences.*

Müller, R.-A., Behen, M. E., Rothermel, R. D., Muzik, O., Chakraborty, P. K., & Chugani, H. T. (1999a). Brain organization for language in children, adolescents, and adults with left hemisphere lesion: A PET study. *Progress in Neuropsychopharmacology and Biological Psychiatry, 23*, 657–668.

Müller, R.-A., Chugani, D. C., Behen, M. E., Rothermel, R. D., Muzik, O., Chakraborty, P. K., & Chugani, H. T. (1998a). Impairment of dentato-thalamo-cortical pathway in autistic men: Language activation data from positron emission tomography. *Neuroscience Letters, 245*, 1–4.

Müller, R.-A., Kleinhans, N., Pierce, K., Kemmotsu, N., & Courchesne, E. (2003). Abnormal variability and distribution of functional maps in autism: An fMRI study of visuomotor coordination. *American Journal of Psychiatry, 160*, 1847–1862.

Müller, R.-A., Pierce, K., Ambrose, J. B., Allen, G., & Courchesne, E. (2001). Atypical patterns of cerebral motor activation in autism: A functional magnetic resonance study. *Biological Psychiatry, 49*, 665–676.

Müller, R.-A., Rothermel, R. D., Behen, M. E., Muzik, O., Chakraborty, P. K., & Chugani, H. T. (1999b). Language organization in patients with early and late left hemisphere lesion: A PET study. *Neuropsychologia, 37,* 545–557.

Müller, R.-A., Rothermel, R. D., Behen, M. E., Muzik, O., Mangner, T. J., Chakraborty, P. K., & Chugani, H. T. (1997a). Receptive and expressive language activations for sentences: A PET study. *Neuroreport, 8,* 3767–3770.

Müller, R.-A., Rothermel, R. D., Behen, M. E., Muzik, O., Mangner, T. J., Chakraborty, P. K., & Chugani, H. T. (1998b). Brain organization of language after early unilateral lesion: A PET study. *Brain and Language, 62,* 422–451.

Müller, R.-A., Rothermel, R. D., Behen, M. E., Muzik, O., Mangner, T. J., & Chugani, H. T. (1998c). Differential patterns of language and motor reorganization following early left hemisphere lesion: A PET study. *Archives of Neurology, 55,* 1113–1119.

Müller, R.-A., Rothermel, R. D., Muzik, O., Behen, M. E., Chakraborty, P. K., & Chugani, H. T. (1997b). Plasticity of motor organization in children and adults. *Neuroreport, 8,* 3103–3108.

Münte, T. F., Altenmüller, E., & Jäncke, L. (2002). The musician's brain as a model of neuroplasticity. *Nature Reviews of Neuroscience, 3,* 473–478.

Murakami, J. W., Courchesne, E., Press, G. A., Yeung-Courchesne, R., & Hesselink, J. R. (1989). Reduced cerebellar hemisphere size and its relationship to vermal hypoplasia in autism. *Archives of Neurology, 46,* 689–694.

Nadeau, S. E., & Crosson, B. (1997). Subcortical aphasia. *Brain and Language, 58,* 355–402.

Nelson, K. B., Grether, J. K., Croen, L. A., Dambrosia, J. M., Dickens, B. F., Jelliffe, L. L., Hansen, R. L., & Phillips, T. M. (2001). Neuropeptides and neurotrophins in neonatal blood of children with autism or mental retardation. *Annals of Neurology, 49,* 597–606.

Neville, H., & Mills, D. (1997). Epigenesis of language. *Mental Retardation and Developmental Disabilities Research Reviews, 3,* 282–292.

Neville, H. J., Corina, D., Bavelier, D., Clark, V., Jezzard, P., Prinster, A., Padmanabhan, S., Braun, A., Rauschecker, J., & Turner, R. (1995). Effects of early experience on cerebral organization for language: An fMRI study on sentence processing in English and ASL by hearing and deaf subjects. *Human Brain Mapping*(Suppl. 1), 278.

Newbury, D. F., Bonora, E., Lamb, J. A., Fisher, S. E., Lai, C. S., Baird, G., Jannoun, L., Slonims, V., Stott, C. M., Merricks, M. J., Bolton, P. F., Bailey, A. J., & Monaco, A. P. (2002). FOXP2 is not a major susceptibility gene for autism or specific language impairment. *American Journal of Human Genetics, 70,* 1318–1327.

O'Leary, D. D., & Nakagawa, Y. (2002). Patterning centers, regulatory genes and extrinsic mechanisms controlling arealization of the neocortex. *Current Opinions in Neurobiology, 12,* 14–25.

O'Leary, D. D. M., Schlaggar, B. L., & Tuttle, R. (1994). Specification of neocortical areas and thalamocortical connections. *Annual Review of Neuroscience, 17,* 419–439.

Osterling, J. A., Dawson, G., & Munson, J. A. (2002). Early recognition of 1-year-old infants with autism spectrum disorder versus mental retardation. *Developmental Psychopathology, 14,* 239–251.

Otsuka, H., Harada, M., Mori, K., Hisaoka, S., & Nishitani, H. (1999). Brain metabolites in the hippocampus-amygdala region and cerebellum in autism: An 1H-MR spectroscopy study. *Neuroradiology, 41,* 517–519.

Pallas, S. L. (2001). Intrinsic and extrinsic factors that shape neocortical specification. *Trends in Neuroscience, 24,* 417–423.

Paulesu, E., Demonet, J. F., Fazio, F., McCrory, E., Chanoine, V., Brunswick, N., Cappa, S. F., Cossu, G., Habib, M., Frith, C. D., & Frith, U. (2001). Dyslexia: Cultural diversity and biological unity. *Science, 291,* 2165–2167.

Pedersen, P. M., Jørgensen, H. S., Nakayama, H., Raaschou, H. O., & Olsen, T. S. (1995). Aphasia in acute stroke: Incidence, determinants, and recovery. *Annals of Neurology, 38,* 659–666.

Pennington, B. F. (2001). Genetic methods. In C. A. Nelson & M. Luciana (Eds.), *Handbook of developmental cognitive neuroscience* (pp. 149–158). Cambridge, MA: MIT Press.

Piattelli-Palmarini, M. (Ed.). (1980). *Language and learning*. Cambridge, MA: Harvard University Press.

Pierce, K., & Courchesne, E. (2001). Evidence for a cerebellar role in reduced exploration and stereotyped behavior in autism. *Biological Psychiatry, 49,* 655–664.

Pierce, K., Müller, R.-A., Ambrose, J. B., Allen, G., & Courchesne, E. (2001). Face processing occurs outside the "fusiform face area" in autism: Evidence from functional MRI. *Brain, 124,* 2059–2073.

Pinker, S. (1991). Rules of language. *Science, 253,* 530–535.

Pinker, S. (1995). Facts about human language relevant to its evolution. In J.-P. Changeux & J. Chavaillon (Eds.), *Origins of the human brain* (pp. 262–283). New York: Clarendon.

Pinker, S. (2001). Talk of genetics and vice versa. *Nature, 413,* 465–466.

Piven, J., & Arndt, S. (1995). The cerebellum and autism. *Neurology, 45,* 398–402.

Piven, J., Saliba, K., Bailey, J., & Arndt, S. (1997). An MRI study of autism: The cerebellum revisited. *Neurology, 49,* 546–551.

Plante, E., Swisher, L., Vance, R., & Rapcsak, S. (1991). MRI findings in parents and siblings of specifically language-impaired boys. *Brain and Language, 40,* 52–66.

Plomin, R., & Kosslyn, S. M. (2001). Genes, brain and cognition. *Nature Neuroscience, 4,* 1153–1154.

Plomin, R., Owen, M. J., & McGuffin, P. (1994). The genetic basis of complex human behaviors. *Science, 264,* 1733–1739.

Quartz, S. R., & Sejnowski, T. J. (1997). The neural basis of cognitive development: A constructivist manifesto. *Behavioral and Brain Sciences, 20,* 537–596.

Rakic, P. (1989). Competitive interactions during neuronal synaptic development. In A. M. Galaburda (Ed.), *From reading to neurons* (pp. 443–459). Cambridge, MA: MIT Press.

Rapin, I. (1997). Autism. *New England Journal of Medicine, 337,* 97–104.

Rinehart, N. J., Bradshaw, J. L., Brereton, A. V., & Tonge, B. J. (2001). Movement preparation in high-functioning autism and Asperger Disorder: A serial choice reaction time task involving motor reprogramming. *Journal of Autism and Developmental Disorders, 31,* 79–88.

Robichon, F., Levrier, O., Farnarier, P., & Habib, M. (2000). Developmental dyslexia: Atypical cortical asymmetries and functional significance. *European Journal of Neurology, 7,* 35–46.

Rodier, P. M., Ingram, J. L., Tisdale, B., & Croog, V. J. (1997). Linking etiologies in humans and animal models: Studies of autism. *Reproductive Toxicology, 11,* 417–422.

Rosen, H. J., Petersen, S. E., Linenweber, M. R., Snyder, A. Z., White, D. A., Chapman, L., Dromerick, A. W., Fiez, J. A., & Corbetta, M. D. (2000). Neural correlates of recovery from aphasia after damage to left inferior frontal cortex. *Neurology, 55,* 1883–1894.

Rumsey, J. M., Nace, K., Donohue, B., Wise, D., Maisog, J. M., & Andreason, P. (1997). A positron emission tomographic study of impaired word recognition and phonological processing in dyslexic men. *Archives of Neurology, 54,* 562–573.

Rutter, M. (2000). Genetic studies of autism: From the 1970s into the millennium. *Journal of Abnormal Child Psychology, 28,* 3–14.

Saccuman, C., Dick, F., Bates, E., Müller, R.-A., Bussiere, J., Krupa-Kwiatkowski, M., & Wulfeck, B. (2002). Lexical access and sentence processing: A developmental fMRI study of language processing. *Journal of Cognitive Neuroscience* (Suppl.).

Sadato, N., Okada, T., Honda, M., & Yonekura, Y. (2002). Critical period for cross-modal plasticity in blind humans: A functional MRI study. *Neuroimage, 16,* 389–400.

Sadato, N., Pascual-Leone, A., Grafman, J., Deiber, M., Ibanez, V., & Hallett, M. (1998). Neural networks for Braille reading by the blind. *Brain, 121,* 1213–1229.

Sampson, G. (1980). *Schools of linguistics*. Stanford: Stanford University Press.

Saussure, F. (1915/1972). *Cours de linguistique générale*. Paris: Payot.

Schlaggar, B., & O'Leary, D. (1991). Potential of visual cortex to develop an array of functional units unique to somatosensory cortex. *Science, 252,* 1556–1560.

Schlaggar, B. L., Fox, K., & O'Leary, D. D. (1993). Postsynaptic control of plasticity in developing somatosensory cortex. *Nature, 364,* 623–626.

Schlaug, G., Jänicke, L., Huang, Y., & Steinmetz, H. (1995). In vivo evidence of structural brain asymmetry in musicians. *Science, 267,* 699–701.

Schmahmann, J. D. (1996). From movement to thought: Anatomic substrates of the cerebellar contribution to cognitive processing. *Human Brain Mapping, 4,* 174–198.

Scriver, C. R., & Waters, P. J. (1999). Monogenic traits are not simple: Lessons from phenylketonuria. *Trends in Genetics, 15,* 267–272.

Shahbazian, M. D., & Zoghbi, H. Y. (2002). Rett syndrome and MeCP2: Linking epigenetics and neuronal function. *American Journal of Human Genetics, 71,* 1259–1272.

Shao, Y., Cuccaro, M. L., Hauser, E. R., Raiford, K. L., Menold, M. M., Wolpert, C. M., Ravan, S. A., Elston, L., Decena, K., Donnelly, S. L., Abramson, R. K., Wright, H. H., DeLong, R. G., Gilbert, J. R., & Pericak-Vance, M. A. (2003). Fine mapping of autistic disorder to chromosome 15q11-q13 by use of phenotypic subtypes. *American Journal of Human Genetics, 72,* 539–548.

Shao, Y., Raiford, K. L., Wolpert, C. M., Cope, H. A., Ravan, S. A., Ashley-Koch, A. A., Abramson, R. K., Wright, H. H., DeLong, R. G., Gilbert, J. R., Cuccaro, M. L., & Pericak-Vance, M. A. (2002a). Phenotypic homogeneity provides increased support for linkage on chromosome 2 in autistic disorder. *American Journal of Human Genetics, 70,* 1058–1061.

Shao, Y., Wolpert, C. M., Raiford, K. L., Menold, M. M., Donnelly, S. L., Ravan, S. A., Bass, M. P., McClain, C., von Wendt, L., Vance, J. M., Abramson, R. H., Wright, H. H., Ashley-Koch, A., Gilbert, J. R., DeLong, R. G., Cuccaro, M. L., & Pericak-Vance, M. A. (2002b). Genomic screen and follow-up analysis for autistic disorder. *American Journal of Medical Genetics, 114,* 99–105.

Shaywitz, B. A., Shaywitz, S. E., Pugh, K. R., Mencl, W. E., Fulbright, R. K., Skudlarski, P., Constable, R. T., Marchione, K. E., Fletcher, J. M., Lyon, G. R., & Gore, J. C. (2002). Disruption of posterior brain systems for reading in children with developmental dyslexia. *Biological Psychiatry, 52,* 101–110.

Shaywitz, S. E., Shaywitz, B. A., Pugh, K. R., Fulbright, R. K., Constable, R. T., Mencl, W. E., Shankweiler, D. P., Liberman, A. M., Skudlarski, P., Fletcher, J. M., Katz, L., Marchione, K. E., Lacadie, C., Gatenby, C., & Gore, J. C. (1998). Functional disruption in the organization of the brain for reading in dyslexia. *Proceedings of the National Academy of Sciences of the United States of America, 95,* 2636–2641.

Silverman, J. M., Smith, C. J., Schmeidler, J., Hollander, E., Lawlor, B. A., Fitzgerald, M., Buxbaum, J. D., Delaney, K., & Galvin, P. (2002). Symptom domains in autism and related conditions: Evidence for familiality. *American Journal of Medical Genetics, 114,* 64–73.

Silvestrini, M., Troisis, E., Matteis, M., Cupini, L. M., & Caltagirone, C. (1995). Involvement of the healthy hemisphere in recovery from aphasia and motor deficit in patients with cortical ischemic infarction: A transcranial Doppler study. *Neurology, 45,* 1815–1820.

Skinner, B. F. (1957). *Verbal behavior.* New York: Appleton-Century-Crofts.

SLI-Consortium. (2002). A genomewide scan identifies two novel loci involved in specific language impairment. *American Journal of Human Genetics, 70,* 384–398.

Sparks, B. F., Friedman, S. D., Shaw, D. W., Aylward, E. H., Echelard, D., Artru, A. A., Maravilla, K. R., Giedd, J. N., Munson, J., Dawson, G., & Dager, S. R. (2002). Brain structural abnormalities in young children with autism spectrum disorder. *Neurology, 59,* 184–192.

Spiker, D., Lotspeich, L. J., Dimiceli, S., Myers, R. M., & Risch, N. (2002). Behavioral phenotypic variation in autism multiplex families: Evidence for a continuous severity gradient. *American Journal of Medical Genetics, 114,* 129–136.

Stapleton, S. R., Kiriakopoulos, E., Mikulis, D., Drake, J. M., Hoffman, H. J., Humphreys, R., Hwang, P., Otsubo, H., Holowka, S., Logan, W., & Rutka, J. T. (1997). Combined utility of functional MRI, cortical mapping, and frameless stereotaxy in the resection of lesions in eloquent areas of brain in children. *Pediatric Neurosurgery, 26,* 68–82.

Starkstein, S. E., Vazquez, S., Vrancic, D., Nanclares, V., Manes, F., Piven, J., & Plebst, C. (2000). SPECT findings in mentally retarded autistic individuals. *Journal of Neuropsychiatry: Clinical Neuroscience, 12,* 370–375.

Staudt, M., Lidzba, K., Grodd, W., Wildgruber, D., Erb, M., & Krageloh-Mann, I. (2002). Right-hemispheric organization of language following early left-sided brain lesions: Functional MRI topography. *Neuroimage, 16,* 954–967.

Stromland, K., Nordin, V., Miller, M., Akerstrom, B., & Gillberg, C. (1994). Autism in thalidomide embryopathy: A population study. *Developmental Medicine & Child Neurology, 36,* 351–356.

Stromswold, K. (2000). The cognitive neuroscience of language acquisition. In M. S. Gazzaniga (Ed.), *The new cognitive neurosciences* (pp. 909–932). Boston: MIT Press.

Sur, M., Garraghty, P. E., & Roe, A. W. (1988). Experimentally induced visual projections into auditory thalamus and cortex. *Science, 242,* 1437–1441.

Sur, M., Pallas, S. L., & Roe, A. W. (1990). Cross-modal plasticity in cortical development: Differentiation and specification of sensory neocortex. *Trends in Neuroscience, 13,* 227–233.

Sutcliffe, J. S., Nurmi, E. L., & Lombroso, P. J. (2003). Genetics of childhood disorders: XLVII. Autism, part 6: Duplication and inherited susceptibility of chromosome 15q11-q13 genes in autism. *Journal of the American Academy of Child and Adolescent Psychiatry, 42,* 253–256.

Tager-Flusberg, H., Joseph, R., & Folstein, S. (2001). Current directions in research on autism. *Mental Retardation and Developmental Disabilities Research Reviews, 7,* 21–29.

Tanoue, Y., Oda, S., Asano, F., & Kawashima, K. (1988). Epidemiology of infantile autism in southern Ibaraki, Japan: Differences in prevalence in birth cohorts. *Journal of Autism and Developmental Disorders, 18,* 155–166.

Teitelbaum, P., Teitelbaum, O., Nye, J., Fryman, J., & Maurer, R. G. (1998). Movement analysis in infancy may be useful for early diagnosis of autism. *Proceedings of the National Academy of Sciences of the United States of America, 95,* 13982–13987.

Thal, D., Marchman, V., Stiles, J., Aram, D., Trauner, D., Nass, R., & Bates, E. (1991). Early lexical development in children with focal brain injury. *Brain and Language, 40,* 491–527.

Thomas, C., Altenmüller, E., Marckmann, G., Kahrs, J., & Dichgans, J. (1997). Language processing in aphasia: Changes in lateralization patterns during recovery reflect cerebral plasticity in adults. *Electroencephalography and Clinical Neurophysiology, 102,* 86–97.

Thomas, M., & Karmiloff-Smith, A. (in press). Are developmental disorders like cases of adult brain damage? Implications from connectionist modeling. *Behavioral and Brain Sciences, 26.*

Thompson, P. M., Cannon, T. D., Narr, K. L., van Erp, T., Poutanen, V. P., Huttunen, M., Lonnqvist, J., Standertskjold-Nordenstam, C. G., Kaprio, J., Khaledy, M., Dail, R., Zoumalan, C. I., & Toga, A. W. (2001). Genetic influences on brain structure. *Nature Neuroscience, 4,* 1253–1258.

Thulborn, K. R., Carpenter, P. A., & Just, M. A. (1999). Plasticity of language-related brain function during recovery from stroke. *Stroke, 30,* 749–754.

Tomblin, J. B., & Buckwalter, P. R. (1994). Studies of genetics of specific language impairment. In R. V. Watkins & M. L. Rice (Eds.), *Specific language impairments in children* (pp. 17–34). Baltimore: Paul H. Brookes.

Townsend, J., Courchesne, E., & Egaas, B. (1996). Slowed orienting of covert visual-spatial attention in autism: Specific deficits associated with cerebellar and parietal abnormality. *Development and Psychopathology, 8,* 563–584.

Tzourio, N., Crivello, F., Mellet, E., Nkanga-Ngila, B., & Mazoyer, B. (1998). Functional anatomy of dominance for speech comprehension in left handers vs. right handers. *Neuroimage, 8,* 1–16.

Tzourio, N., Heim, A., Zilbovicius, M., Gerard, C., & Mazoyer, B. (1994). Abnormal regional cerebral blood flow in dysphasic children during a language task. *Pediatric Neurology, 10,* 20–26.

van Praag, H., Kempermann, G., & Gage, F. H. (2000). Neural consequences of environmental enrichment. *Nature Reviews of Neuroscience, 1,* 191–198.

Vargha-Khadem, F., Carr, L. C., Isaacs, E., Brett, E., Adams, C., & Mishkin, M. (1997). Onset of speech after left hemispherectomy in a nine-year-old boy. *Brain, 120,* 159–182.

Vargha-Khadem, F., & Mishkin, M. (1997). Speech and language outcome after hemispherectomy in childhood. In I. Tuxhorn, H. Holthausen, & H. E. Boenigk (Eds.), *Paediatric epilepsy syndromes and their surgical treatment* (pp. 774–784). John Libbey.

Vargha-Khadem, F., Watkins, K., Alcock, K., Fletcher, P., & Passingham, R. (1995). Praxic and nonverbal cognitive deficits in a large family with a genetically transmitted speech and language disorder. *Procedures of the National Academy of Science USA, 92,* 930–933.

Veenstra-Vanderweele, J., Cook, E., Jr., & Lombroso, P. J. (2003). Genetics of childhood disorders: XLVI. Autism, part 5: Genetics of autism. *Journal of the American Academy of Child and Adolescent Psychiatry, 42,* 116–118.

Vicari, S., Albertoni, A., Chilosi, A. M., Cipriani, P., Cioni, G., & Bates, E. (2000). Plasticity and reorganization during language development in children with early brain injury. *Cortex, 36,* 31–46.

von Melchner, L., Pallas, S. L., & Sur, M. (2000). Visual behaviour mediated by retinal projections directed to the auditory pathway. *Nature, 404,* 871–876.

Wakefield, A. J. (1999). MMR vaccination and autism. *Lancet, 354,* 949–950.

Wallesch, C. W., Johannsen-Horbach, H., Bartels, C., & Herrmann, M. (1997). Mechanisms of and misconceptions about subcortical aphasia [comment]. *Brain and Language, 58,* 403–409.

Wallesch, C. W., & Wyke, M. A. (1985). Language and the subcortical nuclei. In S. Newman & R. Epstein (Eds.), *Current perspectives in dysphasia* (pp. 182–197). Edinburgh: Churchill Livingstone.

Warburton, E., Price, C. J., Swinburn, K., & Wise, R. J. (1999). Mechanisms of recovery from aphasia: Evidence from positron emission tomography studies. *Journal of Neurology, Neurosurgery and Psychiatry, 66,* 155–161.

Wassink, T. H., Piven, J., Vieland, V. J., Pietila, J., Goedken, R. J., Folstein, S. E., & Sheffield, V. C. (2002). Evaluation of FOXP2 as an autism susceptibility gene. *American Journal of Medical Genetics, 114,* 566–569.

Watkins, K. E., Dronkers, N. F., & Vargha-Khadem, F. (2002). Behavioural analysis of an inherited speech and language disorder: Comparison with acquired aphasia. *Brain, 125,* 452–464.

Watkins, K. E., Vargha-Khadem, F., Ashburner, J., Passingham, R. E., Connelly, A., Friston, K. J., Frackowiak, R. S., Mishkin, M., & Gadian, D. G. (2002). MRI analysis of an inherited speech and language disorder: Structural brain abnormalities. *Brain, 125,* 465–478.

Weaving, L. S., Williamson, S. L., Bennetts, B., Davis, M., Ellaway, C. J., Leonard, H., Thong, M. K., Delatycki, M., Thompson, E. M., Laing, N., & Christodoulou, J. (2003). Effects of MECP2 mutation type, location and X-inactivation in modulating Rett syndrome phenotype. *American Journal of Medical Genetics, 118A,* 103–114.

Weeks, R., Horwitz, B., Aziz-Sultan, A., Tian, B., Wessinger, C. M., Cohen, L. G., Hallett, M., & Rauschecker, J. P. (2000). A positron emission tomographic study of auditory localization in the congenitally blind. *Journal of Neuroscience, 20,* 2664–2672.

Weiller, C., Isensee, C., Rijntjes, M., Huber, W., Müller, S., Bier, D., Dutschka, K., Woods, R. P., Noth, J., & Diener, H. C. (1995). Recovery from Wernicke's Aphasia: A Positron Emission Tomographic Study. *Annals of Neurology, 37,* 723–732.

Werker, J. F., & Vouloumanos, A. (2001). Speech and language processing in infancy: A neurocognitive approach. In C. A. Nelson & M. Luciana (Eds.), *Handbook of developmental cognitive neuroscience* (pp. 269–280). Cambridge, MA: MIT Press.

Witelson, S. F., & Kigar, D. L. (1992). Sylvian fissure morphology and asymmetry in men and women: Bilateral differences in relation to handedness in men. *Journal of Comparative Neurology, 323,* 326–340.

Yelnik, J. (2002). Functional anatomy of the basal ganglia. *Movement Disorders, 17*(Suppl. 3), S15–S21.

Yeung-Courchesne, R., & Courchesne, E. (1997). From impasse to insight in autism research: From behavioral symptoms to biological explanations. *Development and Psychopathology, 9,* 389–419.

13

Localization and Identification of Genes Affecting Language and Learning

Shelley D. Smith
University of Nebraska Medical Center

Serious language and learning problems occur in as much as 10% of school children, but the underlying causes are unknown, making it difficult to develop specific diagnostic criteria and tailor appropriate remediation. Family and twin studies indicate that genetic factors influence the most common disorders—specific language impairment (SLI), dyslexia, and attention deficit/hyperactivity disorder (ADHD)—but environmental factors are also important. These nature and nurture influences may be present to different degrees in different individuals and their families, and they may even interact. Furthermore, the genetic influences may differ because there is evidence for multiple genes affecting these conditions. Identification of either the environmental or genetic mechanisms would help sort this heterogeneous population into subgroups with similar etiologies so that the mechanisms can be investigated and understood. The complexity of these traits has made the identification of specific genes challenging, but recent developments in molecular and statistical technologies are promising, giving hope that genes for these conditions will finally be identified.

Identification of mutations in genes affecting complex cognitive disorders could have practical advantages, although these should not be overstated. Preclinical diagnosis would be possible, allowing the identification of at-risk children and the development of effective means of remediation before the children experience frustration and failure. However, the actual application of such screening depends on the proportion of cases that are due to mutations in a given gene, the ease of screening for mutations in that gene, and the penetrance of the mutations (the proportion of individuals with a gene mutation who actually manifest the disorder). If a gene is found to be commonly involved in a disorder, there are only a few mutations of that gene, and the mutations have high penetrance, screening may be a possibility. Conversely, if there are many genes that would have to be tested, preclinical testing may only be practical within families in which the mutation has already been defined in a family member. Specific medical or genetic therapy may also be possible depending on the gene's function and when it is active; a disorder in neural transmission may be helped by a specific drug, for example, but a condition resulting from an abnormality in embryologic brain development may be more difficult to address.

The most important contributions of gene identification will likely be in the definition of etiologic subtypes, which could help clarify the contradictory results of studies looking at specific neurologic and behavioral phenotypes (Fisher & DeFries, 2002). If an underlying neurologic or cognitive deficit could be related to a specific gene, educational methods could be developed to effectively target those deficits in individuals with the gene. Finally, the functions of the genes and their pathways would reveal the processes necessary for the normal development of language and learning skills, and this could be the most far-reaching benefit.

METHODS OF GENE LOCALIZATION
AND IDENTIFICATION

The most direct method to identify a gene that might cause a disorder is to select a set of candidate genes whose function, time, and place of expression are consistent with the etiology of the disorder. If it is known that the disorder is characterized by a given metabolic abnormality, for example, genes involved in that metabolic pathway would be appropriate candidates. This kind of information is rarely available for complex cognitive disorders, however. An exception would be disorders that respond to medication, such as ADHD, in which the efficacy of medications that affect dopamine-mediated neural transmission have led to the testing of variations in and around genes involved in dopamine pathways, such as receptors (DRD2, DRD3, DRD4) and transmitters (DAT1; for a review, see Biederman & Faraone, 2002). Similarly, a gene causing a severe form of speech and language disorder in a few families—the SPCH1 gene—is a candidate for SLI because less disruptive allelic mutations could cause milder phenotypes (Fisher & DeFries, 2002). Unfortunately, these particular examples have not identified major genes, and a prominent complication in the identification of genes influencing complex cognitive disorders is the lack of knowledge of the potential causes. Often there are few reliable criteria for narrowing down the overall set of 30,000 to 50,000 human genes into a manageable set of candidate genes that can be screened for mutations in affected individuals. The alternative is to use methods that narrow down the candidates to those in a small chromosomal region. This gene localization is generally accomplished through two different statistical procedures—linkage analysis and association analysis—or more rarely through a structural chromosomal abnormality. These procedures can differ in the types of populations and subjects that are required and in the laboratory technologies that are used.

Linkage and association analysis are both based on the fundamental principle that genes are arrayed in consistent order on chromosomes, their order and distance are maintained from generation to generation, and the occurrence of recombination between genes on homologous chromosomes is proportional to their distance. To briefly review, genes are encoded in the DNA within 23 pairs of chromosomes, with one chromosome from each pair inherited from one parent and the other chromosome in a pair (the homolog) inherited from the other parent. Genes that are close together on the same chromosome tend to be inherited together and are said to be linked. Genes often have heritable differences in their codes, termed *alleles*, and the allele for a given gene can be used to trace the segregation of its segment of chromosome through a family.

Similarly, the set of alleles for linked genes on a given homolog constitutes its haplotype. During the formation of germ cells in meiosis, homologs pair and exchange portions of DNA through a process of crossing over. This recombination can be detected as a disruption of a linked haplotype; that is, alleles that were formerly on the same homolog are subsequently on opposite homologs, indicating that a cross-over event has occurred between two genes. The probability that a cross-over will occur between two genes is proportional to the distance between them, so that the frequency of recombination can be taken as an estimate of their distance. If genes are far apart on a chromosome or are on separate chromosomes, recombination between them will be random. The percent recombination is often expressed in units of genetic measurement called *centimorgans* (cM), with random recombination equal to 50% recombination or 50 cM. This may also be expressed as the proportion of recombination, θ, with $\theta = 0.5$ indicative of nonlinkage.

Linkage between two genes is detected when their recombination is significantly less than 50%. This is generally observed by following the transmission of the alleles of the genes through related individuals. The transmission of a phenotypic trait can be followed along with the transmission of alleles in relatives. If the trait is found to segregate significantly with the alleles of a known gene, it is evidence that an unknown gene influencing the trait is linked to the known gene. The chromosomal location of the known gene gives the location of the unknown gene, and the rate of recombination between them estimates their distance. In practice, to maximize the probability that a known gene will be close enough to the trait gene to be detected by linkage analysis, a series of markers are used, which are heritable variations in DNA code that are unique to a certain position (locus) in the chromosomes. Ideally, markers are highly polymorphic, meaning that they have at least two alleles that are frequent enough that there is a good probability that an individual will be heterozygous for the alleles so that their two homologs can be identified and their transmission through the family can be followed. If the whole genome is being screened for linkage, the markers should be spaced across all of the chromosomes at sufficient density so that at least one will be close enough to the trait gene to show linkage in the population studied. There are several types of markers that fit these criteria, but the most commonly used are microsatellite repeat markers, in which short segments of DNA, usually two to four bases, are tandemly repeated, with the number of repeats constituting the different alleles. These have the advantage of having many alleles, making them polymorphic, and they are amenable to automated typing. A panel of about 400 markers will cover the genome with about 10 cM spacing.

Association differs from linkage in that a particular allele of the known (marker) gene is consistently transmitted with the trait. This is almost always due to linkage disequilibrium, in which certain alleles in a haplotype are found together in a population significantly more often than would be predicted by chance. This is most commonly due to a *founder effect*, meaning that the haplotype represents an ancestral chromosomal region that is common in the population and most easily seen in relatively inbred or isolated populations. However, it has been increasingly observed that there are regions of preserved haplotypes covering relatively small segments of DNA even in apparently heterogeneous populations. Because regions of linkage disequilibrium are small, association of a trait with a given allele or haplotype can imply close linkage, thus narrowing the chromosomal region containing the gene. Conversely, however, because association may exist only over a short distance, the number of markers needed to cover the whole genome would be large, so genome searches using association analysis have not been practical thus far. Markers must also be close together to adequately cover the short distances, and suitable microsatellite markers used for linkage analysis may not have sufficient density. This has led to the development of maps of single-nucleotide polymorphisms (SNPs), which are variations in a single base at locus. These are much more frequent across the genome and are genetically stable, but are inherently less polymorphic because there are usually only two options for the base that can be present at the locus. Grouping closely linked SNPs into haplotypes may provide sufficient heterozygosity to differentiate associated and nonassociated DNA segments, however.

Overall, association analysis can be much more powerful than linkage analysis, requiring smaller sample sizes to obtain significant results, particularly in genes with modest effects on the phenotype (Risch & Merikangas, 1996). Disadvantages of association analysis include the number and type of markers that are needed, particularly for a genome search, the need to match populations in a case-control design, and the underlying requirement for a founder mutation that remains in linkage disequilibrium with the trait locus and exists with sufficient frequency in the population to be detectable. For this reason, association analysis is particularly suitable for genetically homogeneous populations and isolates.

Within linkage and association analyses, there are different statistical procedures that require different study designs and sample collections. The choice of the analytical procedure for a study depends largely on the characteristics of the phenotype.

STUDY DESIGN: LINKAGE ANALYSIS

The primary characteristics of the phenotype that need to be considered are (a) the formulation of a definition that is sensitive and specific; (b) the evidence that it has a detectable genetic component; (c) the optimal means of measurement; (d) the mode of inheritance; (e) the number of genes involved and their frequency; (f) the evidence for candidate genes; and (g) the selection of a suitable population for study. In most cases, not all of these parameters are known, but strategies exist to allow their estimation or to bypass them if necessary.

Phenotype Definition

Definition of a phenotype is critical to identify a population that is as etiologically homogeneous as possible because etiologic and genetic heterogeneity decrease the power of linkage and association analysis to detect genes. Misdiagnosis disrupts the relationship between the trait and the gene, so it is important that the definition of the trait is not too broad or too narrow. In practice, several strategies have been used, including the use of several different diagnostic criteria or the creation of phenotypic subtypes or endophenotypes that may relate to specific biologic mechanisms, and designs may be used that only include clearly affected individuals.

Examples of these approaches in studies of complex cognitive disorders demonstrate the importance of careful phenotype selection. Dyslexia is probably the most completely studied complex learning disorder, but there is still no concise definition. It is generally characterized as a disability in learning to read and spell that is greater than would be expected based on age, intelligence, and opportunity, but exactly how severe the disability should be and whether a discrepancy with IQ is required has been a source of debate (see Smith, Gilger, & Pennington, 2002, for review). Over the past 10 to 15 years, there has been a general consensus that the basic defect is in phonologic processing, and this has led to somewhat greater comparability between studies. In an effort to further characterize the phenotype, studies such as those by Olson et al. (1989) looked at component phenotypes such as phonemic awareness, phonological decoding, and orthographic coding. Results of linkage analysis with these phenotypes were reported by Grigorenko et al. (1997) and appeared to show that a locus on Chromosome 6 had an influence on phonologic decoding, whereas a locus on Chromosome 15 had a more global effect measured by single-word reading. In an accompanying editorial, however, Pennington (1997) cautioned against overinterpreting differences in the magnitude of linkage for highly correlated phenotypes and suggested that these may not be separable components. This concern was verified by subsequent studies that did not show differential linkage of these component phenotypes, particularly to Chromosome 6p (Fisher et al., 1999; Gayán et al., 1999; Grigorenko et al., 2000). However, definition of a subtype of autism characterized by "insistence on sameness" appears to have strengthened earlier suggestions of linkage to Chromosome 15q (Shao et al., 2003).

Evidence for a Genetic Component

Careful family and/or twin studies should be conducted to demonstrate that familial occurrence of the trait is due to genetic rather than solely environmental influences. These would include estimates of heritability or determination of the mode of inheritance through segregation analysis. All of these have been accomplished for dyslexia (e.g., DeFries & Alarcón, 1996; Pennington et al., 1991), SLI (e.g., Bishop et al., 1995; Tomblin, 1989), autism (e.g., Folstein & Piven, 1991; Smalley et al., 1988), and ADHD (reviewed in Faraone & Biederman, 1998). In fact these analyses can be used to select the best phenotype for linkage and association. Gayán and Olson (2001) showed that their component phenotypes of dyslexia, phonemic awareness, phonologic decoding, orthographic coding, and reading recognition all have significant heritabilities, verifying their usefulness for linkage and association analysis. Wijsman and colleagues took another approach, examining a variety of phenotypes for familial aggregation and segregation to objectively identify the phenotypes most suitable for further analysis (Hsu et al., 2002; Raskind et al., 2000).

Trait Measurement: Quantitative Versus Affection Status

A decision also has to be made about the most suitable measurement of the trait—as either a quantitative, continuous variable or a qualitative, dichotomous diagnosis of affected or unaffected status. A quantitative measure that accurately reflects the variation due to genetic effects can be more powerful than a dichotomous definition based on an arbitrary cutoff in a score (e.g., Fisher et al., 1999). Conversely, if the tests that compose the continuous measure are only distantly related to the underlying biology of the condition, an insightful clinical diagnosis may be more appropriate.

Inherent in the selection of quantitative traits, as well as the determination of the point of cutoff for a dichotomous trait, is the determination of the importance of the phenotype's severity. Selection for more severely affected individuals may produce a more homogeneous subgroup especially if the mutation of a gene does not influence variation in the normal range, but, as discussed more fully later, the resulting population may not fit the distributional assumptions necessary for some analysis techniques and the decrease in sample size may affect the power of the study. Selection for severity generally will create greater power, however, so a smaller sample can still provide evidence for linkage (Cardon et al., 1995). This has been observed in studies of dyslexia, in which selected samples have provided the greatest evidence for linkage to 6p21.3 (Cardon et al., 1994, 1995; Gayán et al., 1999).

Mode of Inheritance and Penetrance

The mode of inheritance—that is, whether a causal mutation is dominant or recessive—and its penetrance can be valuable if known because inclusion of these parameters in linkage analysis increases its power. Unfortunately, one of the hallmarks of complex cognitive traits is that these parameters are unknown. This has led to the characterization of methods of linkage analysis, which are either primarily *parametric* or *nonparametric*. Both approaches can be appropriate for complex traits, whether measured qualitatively or quantitatively, although generally parametric analyses have been used for qualitative traits with higher penetrance and nonparametric analyses have been used for quantitative trait loci (QTLs) that produce susceptibility for a trait.

Classic parametric analysis utilizes extended families in which phenotypes and genotypes are available on as many individuals as possible, and the frequency and mode of inheritance of the causal allele are included (possibly estimated by segregation analysis). The trait gene is character-ized as having two alleles, one associated with affection status, and the mode of inheritance is indicated by the penetrances for each genotype (ho-mozygous for the allele associated with affectation, heterozygous, and ho-mozygous for the nonsusceptibility allele) at the trait locus. The segrega-tion of the genotypes and phenotypes in each family is assessed to determine the maximum likelihood estimate of the recombination frac-tion, θ, between each marker and the trait. The probability that the trans-mission in a family would be observed given a certain value of θ is com-pared to the probability that the recombination fraction is 0.5—that is, the null hypothesis of no linkage. The log of the ratio of these probabilities is termed the *log* of *od*ds of linkage (LOD) score. LOD scores are generally computed for a range of values of θ from 0 to 0.5 for each family, and then the LODs for each value of θ are summed across families. The recombina-tion fraction with the maximum LOD score indicates the most likely dis-tance between the marker and trait. By convention, a LOD score of 3.0 has been accepted as significant evidence for linkage (2.0 for X-linked traits), between 1.9 and 3 is considered suggestive of linkage, and a LOD of –2 re-jects the hypothesis of linkage, with intermediate values inconclusive (Morton, 1955). When a whole genome screen is performed, Lander and Kruglyak (1995) proposed that a LOD of 3.3 be required to compensate for multiple testing. One distinct advantage of the LOD score method is that a single large family with multiple affected members may contain enough information to localize a gene. This means that smaller numbers of indi-viduals need to be genotyped and phenotyped, and can allow identifica-tion of single genes in heterogeneous disorders, but the caveat is that this may identify rare genes. Software packages typically used for this type of analysis include LINKAGE (Lathrop et al., 1984), FASTLINK (Cottingham et al., 1993), and VITESSE (O'Connell & Weeks, 1995).

The LOD score method with extended families and dichotomous phe-notypes inherited in Mendelian fashion (dominant or recessive) has been responsible for the majority of gene localizations for clinical genetic disor-ders. Because complex traits do not show clear Mendelian inheritance, are often continuous variables, may not be easily diagnosed in all age groups, and have unknown penetrances, parametric analysis has been thought to be less appropriate for such conditions, and nonparametric methods have been favored. However, parametric methods may still be useful and have the advantage of being able to utilize information from multiple family members. It has been shown that the allele frequency and penetrance pa-rameters do not need to be precise, and reasonable estimates will not pro-duce false-positive linkage results, although the power may be decreased and estimates of the recombination fraction may not be accurate (William-son & Amos, 1990). Furthermore, analyses can be run using different models with appropriate correction for multiple tests (Abreu et al., 1999). Because there is likely to be genetic heterogeneity within the population studied, the parameters are necessarily estimates across linked and unlinked families, meaning that they are inherently inaccurate, and the resulting recombination fraction is probably too large (Ott, 2001).

Nonparametric methods were developed particularly for the identification of genes that confer susceptibility to complex traits. They basically fall into two types: allele-sharing methods and variance component methods. Allele-sharing methods are derived from the 1972 publication by Haseman and Elston and are based on the assumption that the phenotypic similarity of two siblings will be related to their genetic similarity at markers linked to the trait locus. In other words, siblings who are more alike phenotypically will be more alike genetically at the linked loci, having greater identity by descent (IBD) for the marker alleles. An allele that is IBD in two siblings is one that is inherited on the same parental chromosome. Full siblings may have 0, 1, or both alleles identical by descent, expressed as IBD values of 0, 0.5, and 1, with a mean value of 0.5. In some cases, it may be difficult to determine whether an allele is identical by descent (e.g., if a parent is homozygous, if an allele could be inherited from either parent, or if genotypes are not available for one or both parents). In those cases, the IBD value must be estimated from the parental genotypes or allele frequencies in the population.

Haseman and Elston (1972) used regression analysis to relate the squared phenotypic difference between siblings to the IBD value for a marker. If there is no relationship between the phenotype and genotype, the regression slope is flat, but if decreasing phenotypic differences are related to increasing IBD values, the slope of the regression is negative, with significant deviation indicative of linkage. This method has the advantage of only requiring phenotypic and genotypic information on siblings, who are of similar age and may be more easily ascertained and tested, although as noted before, genotypic information on parents will increase the accuracy of IBD estimates. Parental genotypes can also help ensure the accuracy of genotyping and can identify siblings who are actually half-sibs. Software packages that include the Haseman Elston methodology include SIBPAL in the S.A.G.E. (2001) package, GENEHUNTER 2 (Kruglyak et al., 1996), and GAS (Young, 1995).

DeFries and Fulker (1985) developed a slightly different method of analysis based on their work with monozygotic and dizygotic twin pairs in which regression analysis of the phenotypic score of an affected proband twin with their co-twin's score was used to measure heritability. It is expected that the co-twin scores will tend to regress toward the mean, but that regression will be less for MZ co-twins than DZ co-twins if there is a genetic influence on the phenotype. The degree of relationship (0.5 for DZ twins and 1.0 for MZ twins) was used as the coefficient in the regression equation. This was adapted for linkage analysis in nonidentical sibling pairs (DZ twins or singletons) by substituting a marker's IBD value for the coefficient of relatedness (Fulker et al., 1991). The program QMS2 (Lessem & Cherny, 2001) uses a SAS macro for the DeFries–Fulker (D–F) multipoint analysis.

The level of significance considered indicative of linkage has been a source of debate. Particularly for complex phenotypes in which the evidence for genetic influence is less clear and when many markers are tested as part of a genome search, it has been argued that the traditional requirement of a LOD of 3.0 (basically equivalent to $p = .001$) is not sufficiently rigorous. Lander and Kruglyak (1995) proposed that a p value of .00002 (LOD = 3.6) be considered as evidence for linkage in a single nonparametric study. In practice, this may be difficult to achieve, so replication of results with lower significance in several independent studies is also accepted. Thomson (1994) proposed three levels of significance and the requirements for replication: (a) weak linkage or association ($p < .05$) obtained in at least three independent data sets, (b) moderate linkage ($p < .01$) obtained in at least two data sets, or (c) strong linkage or association ($p < .001$) in one or in the overall data set. The requirement for replication has been used to verify that results are not random, but Vieland (2001) pointed out that replication in an independent sample may not be possible if a linkage is characteristic of a particular population. In that case, nonreplication would be due to genetic heterogeneity and not to false linkage.

Because each sib pair contributes a small amount of information, a large number of pairs may be needed to reach significance levels that confirm linkage. If the relative risk of the disorder in siblings is low (indicating low penetrance and/or multiple genes and environmental affects involved), hundreds or even thousands of sib pairs may be required (Risch & Merikangas, 1996). Selection of sib pairs can help decrease the overall sample size necessary for sufficient power to detect linkage, and thus decrease the time and expense of the studies to manageable levels. One of the most common approaches used to counteract the problem of decreased penetrance (and thus misdiagnosis of a sibling carrying a susceptible genotype) is to restrict the population to affected sib pairs (ASP). As noted previously, selection for more severely affected siblings can increase the power (Cardon et al., 1995), and selection for extremely discordant siblings (Risch & Zhang, 1996) can be even more powerful, although one must ensure that such discordance is not due to the fact that the siblings are actually half-sibs (Allison, 1996). Finally, Forrest and Feingold (2000) demonstrated that inclusion of both discordant and concordant siblings can give adequate power, particularly if the discordant pairs are only moderately discordant. Fortunately, regression methods are robust to the deviations from normal distributions of phenotypes created by such selection.

Inclusion of multiple siblings in a family can also keep the overall sample size lower by increasing the value of each genotype because multiple pairings can be made within a sibship. However, these pairs are not independent, so evidence for linkage may be inflated. The results from such a sibship can be weighted to try to correct for this, but the available methods appear to be too conservative. Thus, in practice, both weighted and unweighted results are generally reported (Fisher et al., 1999) or it is specified which method has been utilized. Other variations of the sib pair method include other pairs of affected relatives (affected pedigree member, APM). Because the expected IBD value is less for pairs who are not as closely related, increased IBD levels in affected relatives can be important. Accurate estimation of marker IBD is essential, however. Because intervening relatives may not be genotyped, the IBD estimation may be heavily dependent on accurate marker allele frequencies in the population from which the families are drawn, and these values generally are not available.

There has also been considerable debate recently regarding the best statistic to use to measure the phenotypic similarity between pairs of relatives. The squared difference in scores used in the original Haseman–Elston (H–E) procedure does not give complete information about the phenotype, and a number of methods have been proposed to produce a statistic with more information. Wright (1997) proposed including the sum of the siblings' trait scores as well as their squared difference, and subsequent studies have investigated ways to combine the regressions of both the trait sum and trait difference values. The revised Haseman–Elston approach is one of these, in which the mean-corrected product of the trait values is used to produce a more powerful method of linkage detection (Elston et al., 2000; implemented in SIBPAL in the SAGE [2001] package and in QMS2). Palmer et al. (2000) noted that the revised H–E can actually be less powerful, however, if sibling correlations are high. Feingold (2001, 2002) provided thorough reviews of these methods, including subsequently developed procedures that tried to compensate for the problems that arose with high sib correlations. These generally involved methods of weighting the regressions, but such procedures may require knowledge of the normal population variance and/or mean. These parameters may not be known, however, and cannot be reliably estimated from selected samples. In some cases, then, the original H–E method may be just as powerful as the newer methods and would have the advantage of being robust in selected samples. Most recently, Sham et al. (2002) described a multivariate regression-based procedure that treats the IBD value as the dependent variable and the phenotypic score as the independent variable in the equation. This may have increased power especially because extended families can be used without correction for nonindependence and have been implemented in the program MERLIN (Abecasis et al., 2002).

The other primary type of nonparametric method used for linkage analysis is the variance components approach. In this method, family data are used to model the components of phenotypic variation—that is, the variation due to genetic (additive as well as dominant) and environmental factors. By including the IBD value and recombination fraction for a marker as covariates, it can be determined whether the genotype at the marker affects the estimates of the genetic components for a phenotype when compared to the unconstrained model. This is tested by the ratio of the log likelihoods of the two models given the family data (Amos, 1994). This method has greater power than regression-based analyses because it utilizes data from entire families, and it can also be expanded to include additional genetic and environmental covariates.

Modifications by Almasy and Blangero (1998) included multipoint and multivariate analyses (e.g., several QTLs) for extended pedigrees implemented in the program SOLAR. However, variance component methods assume multivariate normality of the probability distributions for the phenotype values, which is not the case with samples that have been selected for presence of a disorder, particularly if there is selection for severity (Feingold, 2001). In this way, variance components methods are not totally nonparametric, in that the trait distributions must be known (Ghosh et al., 2002). There have been attempts to compensate for non-normality by transformation of data or by conditioning on the probability of ascertainment in a selected sample, but these still require knowledge of the phenotype distribution in the unselected population. In cases where the parameters of the unconstrained model cannot be determined, another approach has been to verify the significance of a result by comparison to repeated simulations of random genotypes within the structure of the study population (e.g., Fisher et al., 1999).

In addition to the single-point analyses described earlier, in which the phenotype is compared to each marker individually, both parametric and nonparametric analyses can be done in multipoint fashion, in which groups of closely linked markers are considered simultaneously, and linkage of the phenotype is tested at intervals between the markers (e.g., LINKAGE and FASTLINK for parametric methods; QMS2 for H-E and D-F regression-based methods; GENEHUNTER2 for H-E, NPL, and variance components; and SOLAR for variance components methods). This can result in increased marker information because a single marker, taken in isolation, may be uninformative (due to homozygosity in the sibs or a parent), but consideration of the haplotype formed by adjacent markers can increase the information available. Also variations in informativeness of single markers affect the magnitude of the significance of linkage, so direct comparison of LOD scores or significance levels of single-point analyses may not accurately indicate the marker that is most closely linked to the trait gene, whereas multipoint analysis can more accurately place the gene. However, multipoint analyses are more susceptible to errors in genotyping, incorrect estimates of distance between markers, or misspecification of the order of the markers along the chromosome. Fortunately, examination of the haplotypes for increased rates of crossing over between markers can be used to detect errors in genotyping and marker order, and maps are becoming increasingly accurate as the genome sequence is finalized.

Heterogeneity

The degree of genetic heterogeneity, as reflected by the number of genes involved and their relative frequency in the population, has a profound effect on the power of a study to detect linkage or association. At the same time, prior to the identification of the causal genes, gene localization is uniquely able to prove the presence of genetic heterogeneity by establishing that there are linked and unlinked families for a given locus or by confirming multiple localizations. Aside from merely increasing the sample size to detect genes within a heterogeneous population, there are also statistical means to estimate the proportion of linked families (α). The resulting LOD scores, which have been maximized over α, are termed HLODs and may be single or multipoint. These may be calculated using the results of parametric analyses, as with the program HOMOG (Ott, 1986), or with nonparametric NPL scores in GENEHUNTER 2. HLODs may be particularly valuable and may outperform standard LOD and NPL methods if genetic heterogeneity is suspected, but there are no clear means to stratify the population as by phenotypic or ethnic criteria (Greenberg & Abreu, 2001; Hodge et al., 2002). Multipoint methods may be especially powerful (Greenberg & Abreu, 2001). Although the resulting estimates for α and θ may not be accurate, the significance of the linkage result of an HLOD analysis is appropriate (Vieland & Logue, 2002). As summarized by Huang and Vieland (2001),

> It is thus a cautionary tale for statisticians working in genetics research that a statistic with such messy and inelegant statistical properties, such as we

have presented here, might nevertheless in some applications prove to be the best tool for the job. (p. 220)

Whole Genome Search Versus Candidate Genes

As noted earlier, suitable candidate genes for complex cognitive disorders are rare. Linkage analysis is ideal for whole genome searches, which then narrow down to specific candidate regions. Typically, a two-stage analysis is done. The first stage is performed with markers spaced about every 10 cM, and any regions with evidence for linkage above an arbitrary threshold (such as a LOD > 1.0) are followed up by fine mapping with more closely spaced markers in the second stage. If the linkage is real, the markers in the fine mapping will also indicate linkage, and multipoint mapping can help place the trait locus. Examination of the haplotypes in affected individuals in a family (and unaffected individuals if the genotype has high penetrance) can also narrow the critical region containing the trait locus by detecting crossovers that serve to include or exclude part of the region. This is primarily feasible in extended families in which the phase of the haplotypes (i.e., the alleles that belong together on a chromosome) can be determined with confidence and in which the phenotype allows discrimination of affected versus unaffected family members. Haplotypes can be constructed by hand or through automated methods as in GENEHUNTER2. The resolution of linkage analysis is limited, however, by the spacing of adequately polymorphic markers and by the quantitative nature of complex phenotypes, so that it would be difficult to define a critical region smaller than 1 cM (roughly 1 megabase). As a result, the critical region could still contain hundreds of genes even after fine mapping.

Population Selection

The structure of families with the trait influences how a linkage study is designed, and this in turn is produced by the frequency and penetrance of the causal genes. If a gene has high penetrance and is fairly common, and if the phenotype is reliably measured across age groups, extended families may be fairly easy to ascertain and will have greater power than small families. LOD score and variance component methods would take advantage of such family information. Conversely, nuclear families may be more appropriate to detect loci that are somewhat less frequent or have smaller effects, or in which age is a factor in diagnosis (e.g., later onset disorders such as dementia, where parents of an affected individual may not be available and their children have not yet reached the age of onset, or disorders such as dyslexia or SLI, where adults may have partially compensated for earlier deficits). Because sib pair analyses may require several hundred families, the available population must be large enough to contain the appropriate families particularly if selection is used to further limit the families to specific configurations, such as those containing affected siblings within a certain age range or highly discrepant sibs. It is not surprising that national and international consortia have been formed to pool such families to have enough power to detect linkage—for example, the SLI-Consortium (2002), the International Molecular Genetic Study of Autism Consortium (2001) studying autism, or the joint US/UK study of dyslexia (Fisher & DeFries, 2002).

STUDY DESIGN: ASSOCIATION ANALYSIS

Many of the concerns for linkage analysis are the same for association analysis, such as the optimal definition of the phenotype, evidence for a genetic component, and measurement of the phenotype. In particular, the use of quantitative versus qualitative phenotypes is important because some approaches, such as case-control analysis, are best suited for dichotomous traits. The mode of inheritance and penetrance do not need to be specified for association analysis, although decreased penetrance will affect methods that include unaffected siblings. Because association analysis is looking for allele frequency differences related to phenotype variation, extended families are not required. This can make ascertainment of subjects for association studies much easier than linkage studies, but the heterogeneity of the population can be a concern. The primary decisions to be made in the design of an association analysis involve the extent of the genome to be included and the population to be ascertained.

Whole Genome Search Versus Candidate Genes Versus Candidate Region

Linkage disequilibrium (i.e., the maintenance of a linked haplotype over a number of generations without intervening crossovers) generally exists over fairly short distances of less than 10 up to around 150 kilobases (Patil et al., 2001; Zhang et al., 2002). Hence, a dense map of markers is needed for a genome screen to ensure that several markers are close enough to the trait gene to detect allelic association. The finding that the genome can be divided into haplotype blocks of linkage disequilibrium has helped in the choice of markers, which just need to characterize a block of DNA rather than completely cover it at regular intervals, and some believe that this will decrease the number of markers needed from over 1 million to as few as several hundred thousand (Judson et al., 2002). If only markers in coding regions of genes are utilized, the estimate could be as low as 50,000

(Botstein & Risch, 2003). At this time, SNP markers are the only ones known to occur with sufficient frequency across the genome, and typing for so many markers is prohibitively expensive for most laboratories. Technological advances may well change that, however, such as micro-array methods, which can type thousands of SNPs simultaneously. The location of haplotype blocks and the SNPs within them may be population-specific, however, so selection of SNPs appropriate for each block will have to be known for the target population (Tabor et al., 2002). Multipoint methods, which treat several SNPs together as a haplotype, can compensate for uninformative individual markers and increase the ability to detect linkage disequilibrium. The program Graphical Overview of Linkage Disequilibrium (GOLD; Abecasis & Cookson, 2000) can aid in the definition of haplotype blocks of linkage disequilibrium in a population.

Candidate gene studies are much less expensive because a gene may be adequately covered by a few markers and may be especially powerful if the marker polymorphism used in the analysis is actually a causal mutation. Careful selection of candidate genes and markers is critical, and Tabor et al. (2002) noted that early studies may have suffered from a paucity of potential candidates and less than optimal markers. They advocate the use of procedures from epidemiology to select and rank a set of candidate genes, taking advantage of what is known about gene function and expression, the relevance of the function to the pathology of the disorder, and whether the gene has been evaluated with respect to any other phenotypes. They pointed out that, with the development of more complete genome maps, SNPs and other polymorphisms can be identified within particular regions of genes that are most likely to be causal, such as in coding or conserved regulatory regions of genes, and such mutations could be detected in pooled samples rather than genotyping every individual (Botstein & Risch, 2003). However, it may still be much more probable that a polymorphism will be linked to a mutation rather than being the mutation, and restriction to potentially causal markers that may be of low frequency would hinder the chance of finding linkage disequilibrium (Müller-Myhsok & Abel, 1997).

As noted earlier, another source of candidate genes for complex traits are those known to be involved in more severe Mendelian disorders that include the trait phenotype. The SPCH1 gene is one example of a gene involved in a severe disorder in which milder mutations might be found to cause SLI. Similarly, chromosomal abnormalities can disrupt several contiguous genes and cause a more severe phenotype that includes characteristics of a trait such as dyslexia or autism, thus suggesting that genes influencing the trait are located in the involved region. In some cases, presumably when the gene or genes involved in the rearrangement are not critical, the phenotype may not be severe. Translocations involving Chromosome 15 have been found in families with dyslexia, for example (Nopola-Hemmi et al., 2000).

Because candidate genes are not known for most complex cognitive traits, but a whole genome search with association analysis is impractical, association analysis is often used as a follow-up to linkage analysis to cover a critical region identified by those studies, but too small for further resolution by linkage alone. With a smaller region to cover, it becomes more practical to characterize the haplotype blocks in the population being studied, select markers that cover coding and conserved regions of known genes, and adequately characterize the haplotype blocks.

Population Selection

Because association exists on a population basis, it has the advantage of being detectable by comparison of the frequencies of marker alleles of affected individuals with those of unaffected individuals, avoiding the need for ascertainment and typing of family members. This case-control approach can be powerful, requiring fewer numbers of individuals and thus cutting down on the expense of such studies. However, this only holds if the two populations are otherwise matched; in particular, ethnic stratification can produce false association. If there are ethnic differences between the affected and unaffected populations, differences in allele frequencies between the two may be related to ethnicity rather than affected status. In addition to the use of careful epidemiological characterization of the populations to ensure that they are comparable, the comparison of allele frequencies for the affected and control populations for a battery of as few as 32 unrelated polymorphic markers can be used to demonstrate that they are probably drawn from the same gene pool (Hoggart et al., 2003).

To avoid the concerns of population stratification altogether, family-based methods of analysis have been developed. With this approach, the control population is the parental alleles that are not transmitted to affected offspring. The first application of this principle was the haplotype-based haplotype relative risk (HHRR) method (Falk & Rubinstein, 1987; Terwilliger & Ott, 1992), in which the frequency with which a given allele was transmitted by each parent to an affected child was compared with the frequency of that same allele in the parental homolog that was not transmitted to the child. To confirm that the association was due to linkage disequilibrium between an associated allele and a disorder, Spielman et al. (1993) modified the procedure to include an analysis of the segregation of a specific allele compared to the other alleles at the marker locus, utilizing only the affected offspring of a heterozygous parent. This is known as the Transmission Disequilibrium Test (TDT). As in the HHRR test, the frequency with which the affected child inherited the associated allele is compared to the frequency with which a nonassociated allele was transmitted; deviation from the expected 50% is tested by χ^2. This approach has been further modified to allow for markers with more than two alleles and/or quantitative traits, some including covariates, as well as multiple siblings (Allison, 1997; Allison et al., 1999; Rabinowitz, 1997). These methods have been implemented in programs such as ETDT (Sham & Curtis, 1995), which allows for multiple marker alleles with dichotomous traits; FBAT, which can handle both dichotomous and quantitative traits and can also include haplotype analyses (Horvath et al., 2001); and GENEHUNTER2, which can also perform multilocus TDT.

Another family-based approach for detecting association has been to apply a sib-pair variance-components approach to test for both linkage and association simultaneously. The model for the covariance structure includes within- and between-pair components, with the test for association being the within-pair component. As with linkage analysis, genotypes for the parents are helpful in determining the IBD estimates for the marker. This method can accommodate multiple alleles at a marker and expanded sibships and is implemented (along with approaches based on Allison and Rabinowitz procedures) in the program QTDT (Abecasis et al., 2000). However, for now the caveat remains that variance-components methods may not do well with selected samples (Sham et al., 2000).

Another caveat for any association analysis that has been touched on earlier is the assumption that there are a limited number of founder mutations in a population, so there are only one or a few haplotypes in linkage disequilibrium with a causal mutation. If the population comes from different ethnic groups, or if there are many recent mutations in the population, there may not be sufficient linkage disequilibrium for detection. For that reason, association analyses are ideal for homogeneous populations such as specific ethnic groups, or from historically isolated regions such as Iceland or parts of Finland.

There have been concerns in the last few years that association studies have identified many associations of markers with various phenotypes that have not been replicated in subsequent studies, suggesting that the results may be unreliable. Ioannidis et al. (2001) presented a meta-analysis of association studies and found that nonreplication was most common when the initial study had a small sample size. Other factors affecting nonreplication would be differences in phenotype definition and measurement and differences in the genetic structure of the populations being studied. The point has been made that population differences in linkage disequilibrium are lessened when the marker is actually a causal mutation, but it is also quite possible for populations to show allelic heterogeneity, with different mutations being common in different populations. Thus, nonreplication of association does not necessarily indicate that the initial results were wrong for that phenotype and population (Tabor et al., 2002; Vieland, 2001). As Vieland (2001) noted, ". . . this leaves open the pressing question of how we are to proceed scientifically based only on (frequently modest) linkage or association evidence for which independent replication is not forthcoming" (p. 245).

EVALUATION OF CANDIDATE GENES

Once the critical region has been narrowed as much as possible by linkage and/or association analyses, available databases can be searched to identify genes or putative gene sequences in the region. The Web sites at the National Center for Biotechnology Information (http://www.ncbi.nlm. nih.gov/mapview/map_search.cgi) and the University of California at Santa Cruz (http://genome.ucsc.edu/cgi-bin/hgGateway) are excellent sources for this information. To prioritize genes in the region for analysis, each one should be researched to determine its function, the tissues in which it is expressed and the timing of expression, and any genetic disorders it may already be associated with or has been evaluated for in humans or animals (particularly mice). If precise information about function is unknown, especially for putative genes (i.e., regions of DNA, which have the coding characteristics of genes), the function can sometimes be inferred by regions within the gene that have similarity in sequence (homology) to other known genes, such as regions known to bind DNA characteristic of transcription factors or regions that appear to be transmembrane domains that may assist in transport to or from the cell. Because sections of DNA are conserved between humans and mice, the region of the mouse genome that is known to be equivalent to the critical region can also be searched for genes that have been identified and may be associated with mutant phenotypes.

Once a gene is identified as a plausible candidate, it can be screened for mutations in affected probands. For a quantitative trait, it might be preferable to start with those scoring toward the more severe tail of the distribution. The coding sequences and intron–exon boundaries are sequenced along with known regulatory regions to determine whether there are deviations from the known sequence (or the sequence in controls or less severely affected individuals). Any deviations that are found need to be evaluated to determine whether they are likely to be causal. Mutations that are particularly disruptive and likely to have effects on function include insertions or deletions of DNA, which change the "reading frame" of the codons so that the amino acid sequence that results is incorrect or a codon coding for a stop is created and truncates the protein prematurely.

Similarly, a change in a single nucleotide may change its codon to a stop codon, or it may result in the substitution of an amino acid with different charge or size characteristics that interfere with the structure of the protein. Location of a mutation in a conserved region of a gene (i.e., in a part of the gene that shows very little variation in sequence across gene families or in other species such as mouse) can also indicate that a mutation is significant. Other mutations produce more subtle changes, and it can be difficult to predict whether they would cause a functional disruption of the resulting protein. Botstein and Risch (2003) provided a full discussion of the prioritization of genes and any mutations that are found. In the case of mutations causing susceptibility to language and learning disorders, it is quite possible that the mutations will not be as disruptive as those that cause frank clinical disorders inherited in Mendelian fashion, and there may be more mutations in regulatory regions that control the amount or timing of protein produced. Unfortunately, regulatory regions are not well characterized currently, and mutations may be difficult to evaluate.

Important tests of a mutation are to see whether they segregate with the disorder in families (if family data are available) and if it occurs with reduced frequency in a control population. Because susceptibility alleles for common disorders probably occur in the general population and may have decreased penetrance, a mutation may be found in unaffected individuals, but it should be more common in affected individuals or, in the case of a quantitative trait, the phenotype distributions should be different for those carrying the mutation versus those who do not. If a specific mutation is not common in the affected population, it may not be possible to reliably determine its effect on the phenotype. Yet if several different mutations of the same gene are found in affected individuals, it would also suggest that the gene is important to the phenotype especially if at least one of the mutations is predicted to be particularly disruptive (Botstein & Risch, 2003). Finally, replication of the finding of mutations of the gene in a similar population is encouraging that the gene is involved with the phenotype.

The most convincing evidence is functional assays showing that the mutation does indeed disrupt the translation of the gene resulting in decreased levels of protein or decreased functional ability. This can be done by various in vitro techniques that measure the results of mutation of the gene or alterations in its expression on cell function or by in vivo methods such as the genetic engineering of mouse models with alterations in the gene and examination of the resulting phenotype. Although study of mouse models may seem dubious in the case of disorders like dyslexia or SLI, it is quite possible that other forms of learning in the mouse could be affected and observed. Similarly, putative mouse models of hyperactivity and autism have been described (e.g., Cox et al., 2003; Wassink et al., 2001; Winslow & Insel, 2002).

CONCLUSIONS

Localization and isolation of genes for language and learning disorders are difficult, but ongoing improvements in statistical analysis and molecular technology make it more likely that at least the more common and penetrant genes will be identified. Studies of dyslexia are particularly encouraging, with the replication of several localizations including 2p, 3c, 6p, 15q, and 18p (see Fisher & DeFries, 2002, for a recent review). A genome-wide scan of SLI produced possible linkages to 16q and 19q (SLI-Consortium, 2002), but candidate gene studies of *SPCH1* have been less clear. Suggestion of linkage to the region has been reported by O'Brien et al. (2003), but not in other studies, and direct analysis of the *FOXP2* gene did not find mutations in any of the studies (e.g., Newbury et al., 2002). Analysis of surrounding markers by O'Brien et al. indicates that another gene or genes in the region around *FOXP2* might be involved, however.

Some of the comorbidity between disorders may be explained by particular genes that may affect both phenotypes, such as a region of 13q affecting SLI and dyslexia (Bartlett et al., 2002) and a locus or loci in 6p affecting dyslexia and ADHD (Willcutt et al., 2002). Similarly, genome scans of ADHD have indicated possible linkages to 16p (Ogdie et al., 2003; Smalley et al., 2002) and 5p (Ogdie et al., 2003) in the same regions identified by autism studies (International Molecular Genetic Study of Autism Consortium, 2001; Liu et al., 2001; Philippe et al., 1999). Thus, finding the genes affecting any one of these disorders may not only reveal the pathogenesis of that condition, but could lead to the understanding of other language and learning disorders as well.

REFERENCES

Abecasis, G. R., Cardon, L. R., & Cookson, W. O. C. (2000). A general test of association for quantitative traits in nuclear families. *American Journal of Human Genetics, 66,* 279–292.

Abecasis, G. R., Cherny, S. S., Cookson, W. O., & Cardon, L. R. (2002). Merlin—rapid analysis of dense genetic maps using sparse gene flow trees. *Nature Genetics, 30,* 97–101.

Abecasis, G. R., & Cookson, W. O. (2000). GOLD—graphical overview of linkage disequilibrium. *Bioinformatics, 16,* 182–183.

Abreu, P. C., Greenberg, D. A., & Hodge, S. E. (1999). Direct power comparisons between simple lod scores and NPL scores for linkage analysis in complex disease. *American Journal of Human Genetics, 65,* 847–857.

Allison, D. B. (1996). The use of discordant sibling pairs for finding genetic loci linked to obesity: Practical considerations. *International Journal on Obesity, 20*, 553–560.

Allison, D. B. (1997). Transmission-disequilibrium tests for quantitative traits. *American Journal of Human Genetics, 60*, 676–690.

Allison, D. B., Heo, M., Kaplan, N., & Martin, E. R. (1999). Sibling-based tests of linkage and association for quantitative traits. *American Journal of Human Genetics, 64*, 1754–1764.

Almasy, L., & Blangero, J. (1998). Multipoint quantitative-trait linkage analysis in general pedigrees. *American Journal of Human Genetics, 62*, 1198–1211.

Amos, C. I. (1994). Robust variance-components approach for assessing genetic linkage in pedigrees. *American Journal of Human Genetics, 54*, 535–543.

Bartlett, C. W., Flax, J. F., Logue, M. W., Vieland, V. J., Bassett, A. S., Tallal, P., & Brzustowicz, L. M. (2002). A major susceptibility locus for specific language impairment is located on 13q21. *American Journal of Human Genetics, 71*, 45–55.

Biederman, J., & Faraone, S. V. (2002). Current concepts on the neurobiology of Attention-Deficit/Hyperactivity Disorder. *Journal of Attention Disorders, 6* (Suppl.) 1, S7–S16.

Bishop, D. V., North, T., & Donlan, C. (1995). Genetic basis of specific language impairment: Evidence from a twin study. *Developmental Medicine and Child Neurology, 37*, 56–71.

Botstein, D., & Risch, N. (2003). Discovering genotypes underlying human phenotypes: Past successes for mendelian disease, future approaches for complex disease. *Nature Genetics, Supplement 33*, 228–237.

Cardon, L. R., Fulker, D. W., & Cherny, S. S. (1995). Linkage analysis of a common oligogenic disease using selected sib pairs. *Genetics of Epidemiology, 12*(6), 741–746.

Cardon, L. R., Smith, S. D., Fulker, D. W., Kimberling, W. J., Pennington, B. F., & DeFries, J. C. (1995). Quantitative trait locus for reading disability: A correction. *Science, 268*, 1553.

Cardon, L. R., Smith, S. D., Fulker, D. W., Pennington, B. F., Kimberling, W. J., & DeFries, J. C. (1994). Quantitative trait locus on chromosome 6 predisposing to reading disability. *Science, 266*, 276–279.

Cottingham, R. W., Jr., Idury, R. M., & Schäffer, A. A. (1993). Faster sequential genetic linkage computations. *American Journal of Human Genetics, 53*, 252–263.

Cox, P. R., Fowler, V., Xu, B., Sweatt, J. D., Paylor, R., & Zoghbi, H. Y. (2003). Mice lacking Tropomodulin-2 show enhanced long-term potentiation, hyperactivity, and deficits in learning and memory. *Molecular and Cellular Neuroscience, 23*, 1–12.

DeFries, J. C., & Alarcón, M. (1996). Genetics of specific reading disability. *Mental Retardation and Developmental Disabilities Research Reviews, 2*, 39–47.

DeFries, J. C., & Fulker, D. W. (1985). Multiple regression analysis of twin data. *Behavior Genetics, 15*, 467–473.

Elston, R. C., Buxbaum, S., Jacobs, K. B., & Olson, J. M. (2000). Haseman and Elston revisited. *Genetics of Epidemiology, 19*, 1–17.

Falk, C. T., & Rubinstein, P. (1987). Haplotype relative risks: An easy reliable way to construct a proper control sample for risk calculations. *Annals of Human Genetics, 51*, 227–233.

Faraone, S. V., & Biederman, J. (1998). Neurobiology of attention-deficit hyperactivity disorder. *Biological Psychiatry, 44*, 951–958.

Feingold, E. (2001). Methods of linkage analysis of quantitative trait loci in humans. *Theoretical Population Biology, 60*, 167–180.

Feingold, E. (2002). Invited editorial: Regression-based quantitative-trait-locus mapping in the 21st century. *American Journal of Human Genetics, 71*, 217–222.

Fisher, S. E., & DeFries, J. C. (2002). Developmental dyslexia: Genetic dissection of a complex cognitive trait. *Nature Reviews: Neuroscience, 3*, 767–780.

Fisher, S. E., Marlow, A. J., Lamb, J., Maestrini, E., Williams, D. F., Richardson, A. J., Weeks, D. E., Stein, J. F., & Monaco, A. P. (1999). A quantitative-trait locus on chromosome 6p influences different aspects of developmental dyslexia. *American Journal of Human Genetics, 64*, 146–156.

Folstein, S. E., & Piven, J. (1991). Etiology of autism: Genetic influences. *Pediatrics, 87,* 767–773.

Forrest, W. F., & Feingold, E. (2000). Composite statistics for QTL mapping with moderately discordant sibling pairs. *American Journal of Human Genetics, 66*(5), 1642–1660.

Fulker, D. W., Cardon, L. R., DeFries, J. C., Kimberling, W. J., Pennington, B. F., & Smith, S. D. (1991). Multiple regression analysis of sib pair data on reading to detect quantitative trait loci. *Reading and Writing: An Interdisciplinary Journal, 3,* 299–313.

Gayán, J., & Olson, R. K. (2001). Genetic and environmental influences on orthographic and phonological skills in children with reading disabilities. *Developmental Neuropsychology, 20,* 483–507.

Gayán, J., Smith, S. D., Cherny, S. S., Cardon, L., Fulker, D. W., Brower, A. M., Olson, R. K., Pennington, B. F., & DeFries, J. C. (1999). Quantitative trait locus for specific language and reading disability on chromosome 6p. *American Journal of Human Genetics, 64,* 157–164.

Ghosh, S., Reich, T., & Majumder, P. P. (2002). Linkage mapping of quantitative trait loci in humans: An overview. *Annals of Human Genetics, 66,* 431–438.

Greenberg, D. A., & Abreu, P. (2001). Determining trait locus position from multipoint analysis: Accuracy and power of three different statistics. *Genetics of Epidemiology, 21,* 299–314.

Grigorenko, E. L., Wood, F. B., Meyer, M. S., Hart, L. A., Speed, W. C., Shuster, A., & Pauls, D. L. (1997). Susceptibility loci for distinct components of developmental dyslexia on chromosomes 6 and 15. *American Journal of Human Genetics, 60,* 27–39.

Grigorenko, E. L., Wood, F. B., Meyer, M. S., & Pauls, D. L. (2000). Chromosome 6p influences on different dyslexia-related cognitive processes: Further confirmation. *American Journal of Human Genetics, 66,* 715–723.

Haseman, J. K., & Elston, R. C. (1972). The investigation of linkage between a quantitative trait and a marker locus. *Behavior Genetics, 2,* 3–19.

Hodge, S. E., Vieland, V. J., & Greenberg, D. A. (2002). HLODs remain powerful tools for detection of linkage in the presence of genetic heterogeneity. *American Journal of Human Genetics, 70,* 556–557.

Hoggart, C. J., Esteban, J., Parra, E. J., Shriver, M. D., Bonilla, C., Kittles, R. A., Clayton, D. G., & McKeigue, P. M. (2003). Control of confounding of genetic associations in stratified populations. *American Journal of Human Genetics, 72,* 1492–1504.

Horvath, S., Xu, X., & Laird, N. (2001). The family based association test method: Strategies for studying general genotype-phenotype associations. *European Journal of Human Genetics, 9,* 301–306.

Hsu, L., Wijsman, E. M., Berninger, V. W., Thomson, J. B., & Raskind, W. H. (2002). Familial aggregation of dyslexia phenotypes: II. Paired correlated measures. *American Journal of Medical Genetics (Neuropsychiatric Genetics), 114,* 471–478.

Huang, J., & Vieland, V. J. (2001). The null distribution of the heterogeneity lod score does depend on the assumed genetic model for the trait. *Human Heredity, 52,* 217–222.

International Molecular Genetic Study of Autism Consortium. (1998). A full genome screen for autism with evidence for linkage to a region on chromosome 7q. *Human Molecular Genetics, 7,* 71–578.

Ioannidis, J. P. A., Ntzani, E. E., Trikalinos, T. A., & Contopoulos-Ionnidis, D. G. (2001). Replication validity of genetic association studies. *Nature Genetics, 29,* 306–309.

Judson, R., Salisbury, B., Schneider, J., Windemuth, A., & Stephens, J. C. (2002). How many SNPs does a genome-wide haplotype map require? *Pharmacogenomics, 3,* 379–391.

Kruglyak, L., Daly, M. J., Reeve-Daly, M. P., & Lander, E. S. (1996). Parametric and nonparametric linkage analysis: A unified multipoint approach. *American Journal of Human Genetics, 58*(6), 1347–1363.

Lander, E. S., & Kruglyak, L. (1995). Genetic dissection of complex traits: Guidelines for interpreting and reporting linkage results. *Nature Genetics, 11,* 241–247.

Lathrop, G. M., Lalouel, J. M., Julier, C., & Ott, J. (1984). Strategies for multilocus linkage analysis in humans. *Proceedings of the National Academy of Science USA, 81*, 3443–3446.

Lessem, J. M., & Cherny, S. S. (2001). DeFries-Fulker Multiple Regression of Sibship QTL Data: A SAS Macro. *Bioinformatics, 17*, 371–372.

Liu, J., Nyholt, D. R., Magnussen, P., Parano, E., Pavone, P., Geschwind, D., Lord, C., Iversen, P., Hoh, J., Ott, J., & Gilliam, T. C. (2001). A genomewide screen for autism susceptibility loci. *American Journal of Human Genetics, 69*, 327–340.

Morton, N. E. (1955). Sequential tests for the detection of linkage. *American Journal of Human Genetics, 7*, 277–328.

Müller-Myhsok, B., & Abel, L. (1997). Letter in response to Risch and Merikangas, 1996. *Science, 275*, 1328–1329.

Newbury, D. F., Bonora, E., Lamb, J. A., Fisher, S. E., Lai, C. S., Baird, G., Jannoun, L., Slonims, V., Stott, M., Merricks, M. J., Bolton, P. F., Bailey, A. J., & Monaco, A. P. International Molecular Genetic Study of Autism Consortium (2002). FOXP2 is not a major susceptibility gene for autism or specific language impairment. *American Journal of Human Genetics, 70*(5), 1318–1327.

Nopola-Hemmi, J., Taipale, M., Haltia, T., Lehesjoki, A. E., Voutilainen, A., & Kere, J. (2000). Two translocations of chromosome 15q associated with dyslexia. *Journal of Medical Genetics, 37*, 771–775.

O'Brien, E. K., Zhang, X., Nishimura, C., Tomblin, J. B., & Murray, J. C. (2003). Association of specific language impairment (SLI) to the region of 7q31. *American Journal of Human Genetics, 72*, 1536–1543.

O'Connell, J. R., & Weeks, D. E. (1995). The VITESSE algorithm for rapid exact multilocus linkage analysis via genotype set-recoding and fuzzy inheritance. *Nature Genetics, 11*, 402–408.

Ogdie, M. N., Macphie, I. L., Minassian, S. L., Yang, M., Fisher, S. E., Francks, C., Cantor, R. M., McCracken, J. T., McGough, J. J., Nelson, S. F., Monaco, A. P., & Smalley, S. L. (2003). A genomewide scan for attention-deficit/hyperactivity disorder in an extended sample: Suggestive linkage on 17p11. *American Journal of Human Genetics, 72*, 1268–1279.

Olson, R., Wise, B., Conners, F., Rack, J., & Fulker, D. (1989). Specific deficits in component reading and language skills: Genetic and environmental influences. *Journal of Learning Disabilities, 22*, 339–348.

Ott, J. (1986). Linkage probability and its approximate confidence interval under possible heterogeneity. *Genetics of Epidemiology, Supplement 1*, 251–257.

Ott, J. (2001). Major strengths and weaknesses of the lod score method. *Advances in Genetics, 42*, 125–132.

Palmer, L. J., Jacobs, K. B., & Elston, R. C. (2000). Haseman and Elston revisited: The effects of ascertainment and residual familial correlations on power to detect linkage. *Genetics of Epidemiology, 19*, 456–460.

Patil, N., Berno, A. J., Hinds, D. A., Barrett, W. A., Doshi, J. M., Hacker, C. R., Kautzer, C. R., Lee, D. H., Marjoribanks, C., McDonough, D. P., Nguyen, B. T., Norris, M. C., Sheehan, J. B., Shen, N., Stern, D., Stokowski, R. P., Thomas, D. J., Trulson, M. O., Vyas, K. R., Frazer, K. A., Fodor, S. P., & Cox, D. R. (2001). Blocks of limited haplotype diversity revealed by high-resolution scanning of human chromosome 21. *Science, 294*, 1719–1723.

Pennington, B. F. (1997). Using genetics to dissect cognition. *American Journal of Human Genetics, 60*, 13–16.

Pennington, B. F., Gilger, J., Pauls, D., Smith, S. A., Smith, S. D., & DeFries, J. C. (1991). Evidence for Dominant Transmission of Developmental Dyslexia. *The Journal of the American Medical Association, 266*, 1527–1534.

Philippe, A., Martinez, M., Guilloud-Bataille, M., Gillberg, C., Rastam, M., Sponheim, E., Coleman, M., Zappella, M., Aschauer, H., Van Maldergem, L., Penet, C., Feingold, J.,

Brice, A., & Leboyer, M. (1999). Genome-wide scan for autism susceptibility genes. Paris Autism Research International Sibpair Study. *Human Molecular Genetics, 8,* 805–812.

Rabinowitz, D. (1997). A transmission disequilibrium test for quantitative trait loci. *Human Heredity, 47,* 342–350.

Raskind, W. H., Hsu, L., Berninger, V. W., Thomson, J. B., & Wijsman, E. M. (2000). Familial aggregation of dyslexia phenotypes. *Behavioral Genetics, 30,* 385–396.

Risch, N., & Merikangas, K. (1996). The future of genetic studies of complex human diseases. *Science, 273*(5281), 1516–1517.

Risch, N. J., & Zhang, H. (1996). Mapping quantitative trait loci with extreme discordant sib pairs: Sampling considerations. *American Journal of Human Genetics, 58,* 836–843.

S.A.G.E. (2001). *Statistical Package for Genetic Epidemiology, S.A.G.E. 4.2.* Computer program package available from the Department of Epidemiology and Biostatistics, Rammelkamp Center for Education and Research, MetroHealth Campus, Case Western Reserve University, Cleveland.

Sham, P. C., Cherny, S. S., Purcell, S., & Hewitt, J. K. (2000). Power of linkage versus association analysis of quantitative traits, by use of variance-components models, for sibship data. *American Journal of Human Genetics, 66,* 1616–1630.

Sham, P. C., & Curtis, D. (1995). Monte Carlo tests for associations between disease and alleles at highly polymorphic loci. *Annals of Human Genetics, 59,* 97–105.

Sham, P. C., Purcell, S., Cherny, S. S., & Abecasis, G. R. (2002). Powerful regression-based quantitative-trait linkage analysis of general pedigrees. *American Journal of Human Genetics, 71,* 238–253.

Shao, Y., Cuccaro, M. L., Hauser, E. R., Raiford, K. L., Menold, M. M., Wolpert, C. M., Ravan, S. A., Elston, L., Decena, K., Donnelly, S. L., Abramson, R. K., Wright, H. H., DeLong, G. R., Gilbert, J. R., & Pericak-Vance, M. A. (2003). Fine mapping of autistic disorder to chromosome 15q11-q13 by use of phenotypic subtypes. *American Journal of Human Genetics, 72,* 539–548.

SLI-Consortium. (2002). A genomewide scan identifies two novel loci involved in specific language impairment. *American Journal of Human Genetics, 70,* 384–398.

Smalley, S. L., Asarnow, R. F., & Spence, M. A. (1988). Autism and genetics: A decade of research. *Archives of General Psychiatry, 45,* 953–961.

Smalley, S. L., Kustanovich, V., Minassian, S. L., Stone, J. L., Ogdie, M. N., McGough, J. J., McCracken, J. T., MacPhie, I. L., Francks, C., Fisher, S. E., Cantor, R. M., Monaco, A. P., & Nelson, S. F. (2002). Genetic linkage of attention-deficit/hyperactivity disorder on chromosome 16p13, in a region implicated in autism. *American Journal of Human Genetics, 71,* 959–963.

Smith, S. D., Gilger, J. W., & Pennington, B. F. (2002). Dyslexia and other language/learning disorders. In D. L. Rimoin, J. M. Conner, & R. Pyeritz (Eds.), *Emery and Rimoin's Principles and Practice of Medical Genetics* (4th ed., pp. 2827–2865). New York: Churchill Livingstone.

Spielman, R. S., McGinnis, R. E., & Ewens, W. J. (1993). Transmission test for linkage disequilibrium: The insulin gene region and insulin-dependent diabetes mellitus (IDDM). *American Journal of Human Genetics, 52,* 506–516.

Tabor, H. K., Risch, N. J., & Myers, R. M. (2002). Candidate-gene approaches for studying complex genetic traits: Practical considerations. *Nature Reviews Genetics, 3,* 1–7.

Terwilliger, J. D., & Ott, J. (1992). A haplotype-based "haplotype relative risk" approach to detecting allelic associations. *Human Heredity, 42,* 337–346.

Thomson, G. (1994). Identifying complex disease genes: Progress and paradigms. *Nature Genetics, 8,* 108–110.

Tomblin, J. B. (1989). Familial concentration of developmental language impairment. *Journal of Speech and Hearing Disorders, 54,* 287–295.

Vieland, V. J. (2001). The replication requirement. *Nature Genetics, 29,* 244–245.

Vieland, V. J., & Logue, M. (2002). HLODs, trait models, and ascertainment: Implications of admixture for parameter estimation and linkage detection. *Human Heredity, 53,* 23–35.

Wassink, T. H., Piven, J., Vieland, V. J., Huang, J., Swiderski, R. E., Pietila, J., Braun, T., Beck, G., Folstein, S. E., Haines, J. L., & Sheffield, V. C. (2001). Evidence supporting WNT2 as an autism susceptibility gene. *American Journal of Medical Genetics, 105,* 406–413.

Willcutt, E. G., Pennington, B. F., Smith, S. D., Cardon, L. R., Gayán, J., Knopik, V. S., Olson, R. K., & DeFries, J. C. (2002). Quantitative trait locus for reading disability on chromosome 6p is pleiotropic for ADHD. *American Journal of Medical Genetics, 114,* 260–268.

Williamson, J. A., & Amos, C. I. (1990). On the asymptotic behavior of the estimate of the recombination fraction under the null hypothesis of no linkage with the model is misspecified. *Genetics of Epidemiology, 7,* 309–318.

Winslow, J. T., & Insel, T. R. (2002). The social deficits of the oxytocin knockout mouse. *Neuropeptides, 36,* 221–229.

Wright, F. A. (1997). The phenotypic difference discards sib-pair QTL linkage information. *American Journal of Human Genetics, 60,* 740–742.

Young, A. (1995). *Genetic Analysis System (GAS).* Oxford, England: Oxford University Press.

Zhang, K., Deng, M., Chen, T., Waterman, M. S., & Sun, F. (2002). A dynamic programming algorithm for haplotype block partitioning. *Proceedings of the National Academy of Science USA, 99,* 7335–7339.

14

Genotype–Phenotype Correlations: Lessons From Williams Syndrome Research

Colleen A. Morris
University of Nevada School of Medicine

Molecular genetics advances have accelerated the discovery of the genetic etiology of many syndromes and diseases, and progress has been made in sorting out the causes of more complex traits such as diabetes and mental illness. Genotype–phenotype correlation study is a powerful method used to link the DNA code (genotype) with observable, measurable characteristics (the phenotype). The traditional method of gene discovery has proceeded from the phenotype to the genotype, but new techniques of gene manipulation have allowed experiments in the opposite direction—from genotype to phenotype. This reverse genetics includes knocking out a candidate gene in an animal and measuring the effects on the organism and its development. In experimental animals, the gene can be knocked out in different strains, which also allows study of gene expression clues regarding modifying genes. In humans, genotype to phenotype study is possible when a rare chromosome anomaly such as a translocation or inversion disrupts a single gene, providing a candidate gene for the phenotype. Unlike animal studies, however, humans with particular genetic mutations or deletions do not have the same genetic background or environment, potentially clouding the interpretation of the phenotype. Many of these chromosomal syndromes include common complex conditions such as mental retardation as part of the phenotype. Discovery of a gene accounting or predisposing for mental retardation in a particular syndrome likely identifies one of the quantitative trait loci in the general population. Further, such an advance may lead to the discovery of a family of genes or a biologic pathway that contributes to normal neurodevelopment. However, the individual gene would probably account for only a small percentage of the variability of the trait in the general population with nonsyndromic mental retardation.

For human genetic syndromes, correlations are more often found by progressing from phenotype to genotype. First, it is important to carefully classify individuals in the study population as *affected*, *unaffected*, or *uncertain* using measurable, objective criteria. Once the genetic etiology is identified by linkage or mutation analysis, there are several practical consequences. Usually, it is possible to develop a diagnostic test to confirm the clinical diagnosis, which typically results in earlier diagnosis of affected individuals allowing for improved opportunities for intervention. Prenatal diagnosis becomes feasible as well. Confirmation of a genetic etiology accounting for the phenotype is of great importance to parents of affected individuals because it may relieve feelings of guilt. Identifying the responsible gene(s) for a condition results in the opportunity to explore the pathogenesis. Improved treatment and intervention strategies can be based on new understanding; implementation of those strategies allows measurement of environmental modifiers of the phenotype. Determination of the genetic etiology of the condition allows redefinition of the phenotype by examining individuals with the mutation and recording the phenotypic feature present. Thus, both mild and severe phenotypes (variable expression) may be defined. Investigation of the different genetic backgrounds of affected individuals leads to discovery of potential genetic modifiers of the phenotype. The effect of the mutant gene on different organ systems (pleiotropy) can be identified by study of affected individuals. By determining the frequency of the phenotype in the population with the mutation, penetrance of the trait is defined, which is important in providing genetic counseling.

Expression studies determine where and when the gene is active in a particular tissue. Different proteins may be produced in different tissues due to splice site variations within the gene. This is the mechanism by which one gene can serve different functions in the organism. Mutations in different parts of the gene may result in different phenotypes, which provides insight regarding protein structure and function.

In clinical genetics practice, making a correct syndrome diagnosis depends on the recognition of a distinctive pattern of malformations accompanied by the characteristic family, medical, developmental, and behavioral history. The task is complicated by phenotypic variability that may be due to environmental influences (including treatment), the unique set of genetic modifiers operative in each individual, or a combination of both. Thus, the clinician must be cognizant of the range of severity and the natural history of the syndrome. The clinical diagnosis is most likely to be uncertain at both the mild and severe extremes of the phenotype. For many genetic diseases, this problem has been alleviated by the recent availability of laboratory confirmation of the clinical diagnosis by direct analysis of the genotype. However, molecular biology may not yield a simple answer because often a one gene–one disease model does not apply. For instance, different mutations in the Fibroblast Growth Factor Receptor 3 gene (*FGFR3*) result in clinically distinct conditions, including the mild skeletal dysplasia, hypochondroplasia; the common dwarfing condition, achondroplasia; the most common lethal short-limbed dwarfing condition, thanatophoric dysplasia; and the craniosynostosis syndrome, Saethre–Chotzen syndrome. Similarly, a characteristic clinical phenotype does not guarantee a single genetic etiology either. The aforementioned Saethre–Chotzen syndrome can result from a mutation in *FGFR3*, but it is more commonly due to a mutation in another gene, *TWIST*. Such genotype–phenotype correlations advance the understanding of pathogenetic mechanisms. When different mutations of a single gene are found to cause different diseases, important clues regarding protein function result. When mutations in different genes are discovered to result in a single syndrome, final common pathways in development are elucidated.

Although genotype–phenotype analysis of rare syndromes is complicated, the problems are compounded in common multifactorial conditions such as diabetes, coronary artery disease (CAD), language impairment, attention deficit disorder (ADD), and mental retardation. For common phenotypes, it is likely that mutations in many different genes may cause the condition dependent on the interaction of multiple possible environmental modulators. Nevertheless, approaches that have been successful in determining the genetic etiology of rare conditions may prove useful in the search for genes involved in cognition and behavior. In this chapter, results of a multidisciplinary program of research on Williams syndrome demonstrate the utility of modern molecular/cytogenetic tools in determining genotype–phenotype relations.

THE WILLIAMS SYNDROME PHENOTYPE

Williams syndrome has an incidence between 1/10,000 and 1/20,000, and it affects multiple organ systems. It is characterized by dysmorphic facial features, mental retardation, supravalvar aortic stenosis (SVAS), growth deficiency, infantile hypercalcemia, an unusual cognitive profile characterized by relative strength in verbal short-term memory and extreme weakness in visuospatial constructive cognition, and a unique personality with empathy, sociability, and overfriendliness complicated by generalized anxiety. The specialists treating the individual presenting symptoms wrote the early reports of children with this syndrome. After an epidemic of infantile hypercalcemia in Britain caused by overfortification of foods with vitamin D, Stapleton, MacDonald, and Lightwood (1957) noted that some infants had persistent hypercalcemia with failure to thrive and developmental delay even after the intake of calcium and vitamin D was normalized. A cardiologist reported four children with SVAS who had mental retardation and resembled each other (Williams, Barratt-Boyes, & Lowe, 1961). Geneticists observed that SVAS, a rare cause of left outflow tract obstruction, could occur in families as an isolated abnormality or could occur sporadically when it was commonly associated with mental retardation (Merritt, Palmar, Lurie, & Petry, 1963). The varied presenting signs and symptoms were recognized as parts of a single entity in 1964 when Garcia, Friedman, Kaback, and Rowe noted SVAS in a child who was previously documented to have infantile hypercalcemia. Subsequent articles delineated the complete Williams syndrome medical phenotype (Beuren, 1972; Jones & Smith, 1975). Von Arnim and Engel (1964) drew attention to the characteristic Williams syndrome personality, and Bellugi, Marks, Bihrle, and Sabo (1988) explored the unique pattern of cognitive strengths and weaknesses. Morris and her colleagues (Morris, Dilts, Demsey, Leonard, & Blackburn, 1988) studied the natural history of Williams syndrome and reported the adult phenotype (Morris, Leonard, Dilts, & Demsey, 1990).

Williams syndrome is a multisystem disorder. The characteristic facial features of Williams syndrome include a broad forehead, bitemporal narrowing, low nasal root, periorbital fullness, stellate/lacy iris pattern, strabismus, bulbous nasal tip, malar flattening, long philtrum, full lips, wide mouth, full cheeks, dental malocclusion with small widely spaced teeth, small jaw, and prominent ear lobes (Fig. 14.1). Growth deficiency may be both pre- and postnatal, and puberty may occur early (Partsch et al., 1999), leading to final adult height that is less than the third percentile (Morris et al., 1988; Pankau, Partsch, Gosch, Opperman, & Wessel, 1992). Endocrine problems may include infantile hypercalcemia, hypothyroidism, and diabetes (Pober, Wang, Petersen, Osborne, & Caprio, 2001). Common neurological problems include hypotonia, hyperreflexia, and cerebellar dysfunction (Morris et al., 1990; Pober & Szekely, 1999). Neuroimaging studies show reduced cerebral volume with preservation of the cerebellar and superior temporal gyrus volumes (Reiss et al., 2000). Reduced stereoacuity, esotropia, and hyperopia are common ophthalmologic findings (Sadler, Olitsky, & Reynolds, 1996; Winter, Pankau, Amm, Gosch, & Wessel, 1996). Hypersensitivity to sound and chronic otitis media are often seen. The voice is typically hoarse or deep. Gastrointestinal/abdominal problems may include feeding difficulty, failure to thrive, gastroesophageal reflux, constipation, colon diverticulosis, and hernias (Morris

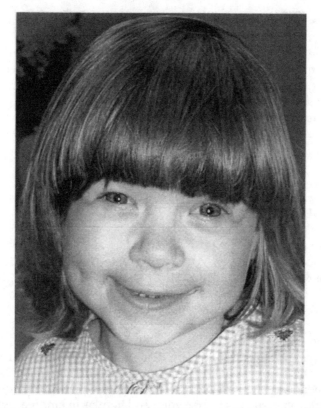

FIG. 14.1. This 4-year-old girl with WS shows typical facial features of WS including stellate irides, periorbital fullness, low nasal root, full nasal tip, flat mala, full cheeks, long philtrum, wide mouth, and small widely spaced teeth.

et al., 1988, 1990). Urinary tract abnormalities include renal structural defects, bladder diverticulae, and nephrocalcinosis (Pankau, Partsch, Winter, Gosch, & Wessel, 1996; Pober, Lacro, Rice, Mandell, & Teele, 1993). The musculoskeletal problems seen in Williams syndrome include a long neck, sloping shoulders, joint contractures, radioulnar synostosis, kyphosis, lordosis, and scoliosis, which lead to an abnormal posture and a stiff gait. The cardiovascular disease in Williams syndrome is responsible for the greatest morbidity and mortality. There is a diffuse arteriopathy, and vascular stenosis may occur at any point. The overall prevalence of detectable cardiovascular disease is 80% and includes SVAS, peripheral pulmonary stenosis, hypertension, and mitral valve prolapse (Kececioglu, Kotthoff, & Vogt, 1993).

Mean full-scale IQ in Williams syndrome is 58, with a range from 32 to 88 (Mervis, Robinson, Rowe, Becerra, & Klein-Tasman, in press). Some individuals have normal intelligence, but the majority have mental retardation ranging from severe to mild. The unusual Williams Syndrome Cognitive Profile (WSCP) is characterized by a relative strength in verbal short-term memory accompanied by extreme weakness in visuospatial constructive cognition (Mervis et al., 2000; see Mervis, chap. 8, this volume, for a detailed description). The characteristic Williams syndrome personality includes sociability, empathy, and generalized anxiety (Klein-Tasman & Mervis, 2003; Mervis & Klein-Tasman, 2000). ADD is common (Dilts, Morris, & Leonard, 1990).

FROM PHENOTYPE TO GENOTYPE IN SVAS AND WILLIAMS SYNDROME

Although most cases of Williams syndrome occur sporadically, dominant inheritance has been reported, including male–male transmission (Morris, Thomas, & Greenberg, 1993; Sadler, Robinson, Verdaasdonk, & Gingell, 1993). SVAS is also inherited in a dominant fashion (Eisenberg, Young, Jacobson, & Boito, 1964), and the histological abnormalities of the arterial wall in familial SVAS are identical to those seen in Williams syndrome (Conway, Noonan, Marion, & Steeg, 1990; O'Connor et al., 1985). This phenotypic overlap led to the speculation that Williams syndrome could be an "iceberg dominant"—that is, the most severe manifestation of the SVAS phenotype. Reports of some individuals with a few features of Williams syndrome, such as hoarse voice and hernias in kindreds with SVAS, provided some support for that hypothesis (Grimm & Wesselhoeft, 1980; Morris & Moore, 1991). To identify the genetic cause of SVAS, linkage studies were completed in large extended families with the cardiovascular disease. (For details regarding the techniques of gene localization, refer to Smith, chap. 13, this volume.) The SVAS phenotype was narrowly defined using quantitative measurements obtained by echocardiogram and Doppler analysis to classify individuals as *affected*, *unaffected*, or *uncertain*. For the purpose of linkage studies, it is best to exclude individuals who have a phenotype in the borderline range, although they might be classified as affected in a clinical setting.

Using these definitions, linkage for the cardiovascular phenotype to the *elastin* gene (*ELN*) on Chromosome 7 was demonstrated (Ewart, Morris, Ensing et al., 1993). The suitability of *ELN* as a candidate gene was reinforced when a three-generation SVAS family was found to have a 6;7 chromosome translocation that disrupted *ELN* in exon 27 cosegregating with the disease phenotype (Curran et al., 1993; Morris, Loker, Ensing, & Stock, 1993). Subsequent mutational analysis of *ELN* in additional SVAS kindreds identified point mutations in *ELN* exons 1–28 (Li, Toland, Boak, Atkinson, & Ensing, 1997; Metcalfe et al., 2000). *ELN* also passed the test of biologic plausibility as the gene responsible for the cardiovascular phenotype because the elastin protein comprises 90% of the elastic fiber, and elastic fibers are highly concentrated in arterial walls.

Identification of the causative gene in SVAS allowed the condition to be redefined by examining the individual phenotypes associated with the known *ELN* mutation. As is typical of dominant conditions, not everyone who had an *ELN* mutation had cardiovascular disease detectable by echocardiogram on the day they were studied. The modern echocardiogram with Doppler is a sensitive measure of arterial narrowing for the great arteries, but not every artery is evaluated by this method. An arterial biopsy would be a more sensitive tool, but would be too invasive. In this study, the penetrance (frequency of those with mutations who had positive echocardiograms) was 92%. Gene expression was also variable: 10% had severe disease (requiring surgical intervention), 25% were moderate, and 65% were mild. Two individuals who each had a bicuspid aortic valve (BAV) were coded as *uncertain* because it was unknown whether the valve abnormality was part of the SVAS phenotype. Because both individuals were found to have an *ELN* mutation, it is likely that BAV is part of the SVAS spectrum, thus expanding the clinical phenotype. Discovery of the causative gene also allowed analysis of the diverse effects (pleiotropy) of the *ELN* gene in affected individuals. Hernias, hoarse voice, and some dysmorphic facial features were detected in some affected individuals, implicating *ELN* mutation as the cause for other abnormalities in addition to cardiovascular disease. The study of SVAS kindreds identified *ELN* as a candidate gene that could be tested in the Williams syndrome population, which could not be evaluated by linkage analysis because large families are not available. One copy of *ELN* was deleted in 99% of individuals with the clinical diagnosis, leading to the conclusion that functional hemizygosity of *ELN* results in the cardiovascular disease seen in both SVAS and WS (Ewart, Morris, Atkinson et al., 1993; Lowery et al., 1995).

Additional phenotypic heterogeneity has been identified for *ELN*. Mutations in exons 30 and 32 have been found in individuals with a different dominant disorder—cutis laxa (Tassabehji et al., 1998; Zhang et al., 1999). Cutis laxa is characterized by soft lax skin that it is not hyperextensible or fragile, and may also be associated with a hoarse voice, long earlobes, and peripheral pulmonic stenosis. Tassabehji and colleagues (1998) showed that the *ELN* exon 32 mutation produced an abnormal elastin protein that resulted in abnormal dermal elastic fibers, suggesting a dominant-negative effect.

FROM GENOTYPE TO PHENOTYPE IN SVAS

The mechanism by which hemizygosity for *ELN* results in arterial stenosis has been studied in *ELN* knockout mice (Li, Brooke et al., 1998; Li, Faury et al., 1998). *ELN* codes for elastin protein, which forms elastic fibers by aligning and cross-linking on a scaffold of microfibrils. In arteries, elastic fibers are arranged in concentric lamellar units. Each elastic lamella alternates with a ring of smooth muscle. The elastic lamellae are thin in mice that are hemizygous for *ELN* because only 50% of the normal amount of the elastin protein is produced in these animals. The extensibility of the arteries is preserved, however, by an increase in the number of lamellar units by 25% (Li, Faury et al., 1998). In comparison, humans with SVAS show a 2.5-fold increase in the number of lamellar units in the affected aorta. Li, Faury et al. (1998) suggested that the focal thickening of the arteries leading to a discrete short-segment arterial stenosis could be the result of the medial wall being too thick for its blood supply, allowing fibrosis to occur.

GENOTYPE–PHENOTYPE CORRELATIONS IN WILLIAMS SYNDROME

Although the role of *ELN* in the phenotype of Williams syndrome is now understood, there are many other aspects of the Williams syndrome phenotype that are not explained by the *ELN* deletion, such as hypercalcemia and mental retardation. In addition to the deletion of *ELN* on Chromosome 7q11.23, another 20 contiguous genes are also deleted. The size of the deletion is approximately 1.6 Mb (Hillier et al., 2003). Most individuals with Williams syndrome have the same deletion breakpoints (Bayes, Magano, Rivera, Flores, & Perez-Jurado, 2003; Meng et al., 1998; Peoples et al., 2000). The deletion is the result of unequal crossing over occurring during meiosis due to the large number of repetitive sequences flanking the commonly deleted region (Bayes et al., 2003; Osborne et al., 2001). The deletion may be of maternal or paternal origin (Ewart, Morris, Atkinson et al., 1993; Urban et al., 1996). Of 200 individuals studied by Stock et al. (2003) who had ELN deletion and a clinical diagnosis of Williams syndrome, all but 6 had the common deletion size. Five had longer deletions, but none was large enough to detect on a standard karyotype. The average IQ for the long deletion group was significantly lower than the classic deletion group (Stock et al., 2003). One individual with an IQ of 95 had a shorter deletion of ~1Mb. This deletion had the typical centromeric Williams syndrome breakpoint, but did not include the two most telomeric genes in the common deletion region, GTF2IRD1 and GTF2I. These data suggest that one or more genes in the telomeric region of the Williams syndrome deletion and/or telomeric to the deletion may play a role in cognition (Morris et al., 1999; Stock et al., 2003). However, almost all individuals with Williams syndrome who have IQs greater than 85 have deletions of classic length (Karmiloff-Smith et al., 2003; Morris & Mervis, 2000). These individuals have lower IQs than their parents (Morris et al., in press). Thus, although deletion length may account for some of the variability of phenotype seen in WS, other factors must contribute as well.

To determine the role other deleted genes in the region have in the Williams syndrome phenotype, we studied five SVAS kindreds who have small deletions within the Williams syndrome region (Frangiskakis et al., 1996; Morris et al., in press). The deletions varied in size from 83.6 Kb to ~950 Kb; all deletions included *ELN* and *LIM-kinase 1* (*LIMK1*; see Fig. 14.2). Like other SVAS families, affected family members have cardiovascular disease; some additional connective tissue abnormalities such as hoarse voice, mitral valve prolapse, or hernias; and some Williams syndrome facial features, especially long philtrum, full cheeks, and periorbital fullness. Because these findings have also been reported in individuals with point mutations in SVAS (Li, Toland, Boak, Atkinson, & Ensing, 1997), it is likely that hemizygosity for *ELN* is the cause of these phenotypic features. Most affected family members in these kindreds with small deletions demonstrated the WSCP, and all had normal intelligence, with IQs (on the Kaufman Brief Intelligence Test [Kaufman & Kaufman, 1990], which does not include visuospatial construction) that did not differ significantly from unaffected family members. The smallest deletion among the five kindreds included the telomeric portion of *ELN* and all of *LIMK-1* (Frangiskakis et al., 1996).

The evidence suggests that *LIMK-1* is important in normal visuospatial constructive cognition. There is also evidence that visuospatial construction ability varies in the general population and likely follows a quantitative trait loci model (Mervis, Robinson, & Pani, 1999). *LIMK-1* is probably one of the genes important in this pathway. *LIMK-1* encodes a protein kinase that is expressed in the developing brain (Frangiskakis et al., 1996) and interacts with cofilin, a regulator of the actin cytoskeleton important in axonal growth of neurons (Yang et al., 1998). Only 2 of the 21 affected individuals in the 5 kindreds did not have the WSCP, which may represent variable expression. Tassabehji et al. (1999) studied three high-functioning individuals with short deletions in the Williams syndrome region including *LIMK-1*; none of them had the WSCP.

The deletions in the five families nearly span the Williams syndrome deletion region; only the most centromeric gene *FKBP6* and the most teleomeric gene *GTF2I* are not deleted in any of the families. Because no individual in these families has mental retardation, it is likely that one of

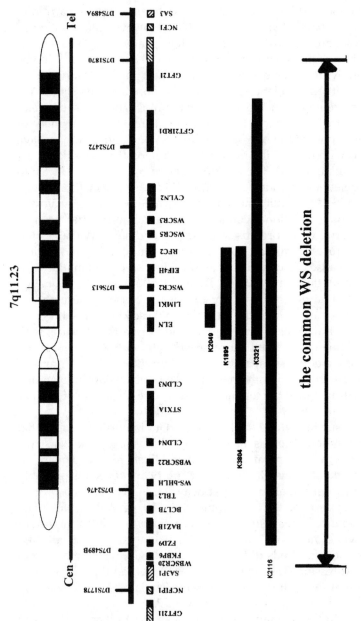

FIG. 14.2. The typical deletion in WS spans ~1.6 Mb (boundaries shown by arrows) and includes the following genes: *FKBP6*, FK506 binding protein; *FZD9*, Frizzled 9; *BAZ1B*, Williams syndrome transcription factor; *BCL7B*, B-cell lymphoma 7B; *WS-βTRP*, WS β-transducin repeats protein; *WSbHLH*, WS basic-helix-loop-helix leucine zipper; *CLDN4*, *Clostridium perfringens* enterotoxin receptor 1; *STX1A*, Syntaxin 1A; *CLDN3*, *Clostridium perfringens* enterotoxin receptor 2; *ELN*, Elastin; *LIMK1*, LIM kinase 1; *EIFH4*, Eukaryotic translation initiation factor 4H; *RFC2*, Replication factor C, subunit 2; *CYCLN2*, Cytoplasmic linker protein; *WBSCR11*, Williams–Beuren syndrome chromosome region 11; *GTF2I*, General transcription factor 2-I. Duplicated genes flanking the common deletion region are designated by filled bars and kindred numbers. The smaller deletions found in five SVAS families are indicated by filled bars and kindred numbers. The drawing is not to scale.

the genes in the breakpoint regions is involved in the mental retardation common in Williams syndrome (Morris et al., in press). Botta et al. (1999) reported a girl with moderate mental retardation who had a short deletion in the Williams syndrome region that included *GTF2I*. In contrast, Karmiloff-Smith et al. (2003) reported a girl with an IQ of 117 with a short deletion who did not have a deletion of *GTF2I*, but did have a deletion of *FKBP6*, suggesting that *FKBP6* deletion is not involved in the mental retardation. Taken together, this evidence supports a role for *GTF2I* in mental retardation in Williams syndrome. Even individuals with Williams syndrome who have IQs in the normal range and classic size deletions have lower IQs than their family members (Morris et al., in press). *GTF2I* is expressed in both fetal and adult tissues especially in the brain. The gene encodes two proteins; one of them, TFII-I, is a transcription factor that shuttles between the cell nucleus and cytoplasm activating other genes, and it also has a role in transcriptional repression (Hakimi et al., 2003).

Deletion mapping has been helpful in clarifying genotype–phenotype relations in Williams syndrome. However, the technique does have limitations. There are small numbers of affected individuals with short deletions in the Williams syndrome region. Each of the families has a different deletion, so it is not a homogeneous group genotypically. None of the families is related, and therefore interfamilial variability is difficult to interpret because the genetic background is heterogeneous. There are also potential confounds to the interpretation of the phenotype. For instance, some phenotypic features vary with age. The few Williams syndrome facial features that individuals within these kindreds had were often observed only in infancy, for instance (Morris et al., in press). IQ and socioeconomic status (SES) are two other factors that could impact the interpretation. Individuals with higher IQs are more likely to be able to devise compensatory strategies for dealing with cognitive weaknesses (Mervis et al., 1999). Ideally, to support an etiologic role for any of the genes in the region for the Williams syndrome phenotype, one would like to associate a point mutation in the gene that would result in a particular phenotypic feature in an otherwise normal individual. For example, if one were able to demonstrate an increase in *GTF2I* mutations in the general population of individuals with mental retardation, or if one could identify *LIMK-1* mutations in individuals with visuospatial construction difficulty, one could be more secure that the gene is responsible for the phenotype. Because it is likely that these genes account for a small percentage of the variability in these traits, extremely large sample sizes would be required. Investigating the phenotype of knockout mice for individual genes in the region will be helpful. If these genes are important in the neurodevelopment of experimental animals, that would provide supportive evidence.

The genotype–phenotype correlation studies have demonstrated that WS is a contiguous gene syndrome. Deletion of different genes account for different aspects of the phenotype. *Elastin* hemizygosity has been proved to cause the cardiovascular disease. There is strong evidence that *LIMK1* is important in visuospatial constructive cognition and that hemizygous *GTF2I* deletion negatively affects IQ in Williams syndrome.

Future studies should examine the role of other genes in the Williams syndrome region. Some do not contribute to the phenotype because for some gene pairs one working copy is sufficient for a normal phenotype. Hemizygosity of other deleted genes may contribute to anxiety and ADHD, which are common behavioral traits in the Williams syndrome population. Continued technological advances will refine the methods for determining deletion breakpoints, and study of additional rare families with unusual deletions in the Williams syndrome region will contribute to our knowledge of genotype–phenotype correlations in this region.

ACKNOWLEDGMENTS

Preparation of this manuscript was supported by grant #NS35102 from the National Institute of Neurological Disorders and Stroke. The research is made possible by the generous participation of families with genetic conditions, and by the collaboration of Carolyn Mervis, Holly Hobart, Ron Gregg, and Mark Keating.

REFERENCES

Bayes, M., Magano, L. F., Rivera, N., Flores, R., & Perez-Jurado, L. A. (2003). Mutational mechanisms of Williams–Beuren syndrome deletions. *American Journal of Human Genetics, 73*, 131–151.

Bellugi, U., Marks, S., Bihrle, A., & Sabo, H. (1988). Dissociation between language and cognitive functions in Williams syndrome. In D. Bishop & K. Mogford (Eds.), *Language development in exceptional circumstances* (pp. 177–189). London: Churchill Livingstone.

Beuren, A. J. (1972). Supravalvular aortic stenosis: A complex syndrome with and without mental retardation. *Birth Defects Original Article Series, 8*(5), 45–56.

Botta, A., Novelli, G., Mari, A., Novelli, A., Sabini, M., Korenberg, J., Osborne, L. R., Digilio, M. C., Giannotti, A., & Dallapiccola, B. (1999). Detection of an atypical 7q11.23 deletion in Williams syndrome patients which does not include the STX1A and FZD3 genes. *Journal of Medical Genetics, 36*, 478–480.

Conway, E. E., Noonan, J., Marion, R. W., & Steeg, C. N. (1990). Myocardial infarction leading to sudden death in the Williams syndrome: Report of three cases. *Journal of Pediatrics, 117*, 593–595.

Curran, M. E., Atkinson, D. L., Ewart, A. K., Morris, C. A., Leppert, M. F., & Keating, M. T. (1993). The *elastin* gene is disrupted by a translocation associated with supravalvar aortic stenosis. *Cell, 73*, 159–168.

Dilts, C., Morris, C. A., & Leonard, C. O. (1990). Hypothesis for development of a behavioral phenotype in Williams syndrome. *American Journal of Medical Genetics Supplement, 6,* 126–131.

Eisenberg, R., Young, D., Jacobson, B., & Boito, A. (1964). Familial supravalvar aortic stenosis. *American Journal of Diseases of Children, 108,* 341–347.

Ewart, A. K., Morris, C. A., Atkinson, D., Jin, W., Sternes, K., Spallone, P., Stock, A. D., Leppert, M., & Keating, M. T. (1993). Hemizygosity at the *elastin* locus in a developmental disorder, Williams syndrome. *Nature Genetics, 5,* 11–16.

Ewart, A. K., Morris, C. A., Ensing, G. J., Loker, J., Moore, C., Leppert, M., & Keating, M. T. (1993). A human vascular disorder, supravalvar aortic stenosis, maps to chromosome 7. *Proceedings of the National Academy of Sciences of the United States of America, 90,* 3226–3330.

Frangiskakis, J. M., Ewart, A. K., Morris, C. A., Mervis, C. B., Bertrand, J., Robinson, B. F., Klein, B. P., Ensing, G. J., Everett, L. A., Green, E. D., Pröschel, C., Gutowski, N., Noble, M., Atkinson, D. L., Odelberg, S., & Keating, M. T. (1996). LIM-kinase1 hemizygosity implicated in impaired visuospatial constructive cognition. *Cell, 86,* 59–69.

Garcia, R. E., Friedman, W. F., Kaback, M. M., & Rowe, R. D. (1964). Idiopathic hypercalcemia and supravalvular aortic stenosis. *New England Journal of Medicine, 271,* 117–120.

Grimm, T., & Wesselhoeft, H. (1980). The genetic aspects of Williams–Beuren syndrome and the isolated form of the supravalvular aortic stenosis. Investigation of 128 families. *Zeitschrift für Kardiologie, 69,* 168–172.

Hakimi, M. A., Dong, Y., Lane, W. S., Speicher, D. W., & Shiekhattar, R. (2003). A candidate X-linked mental retardation gene is a component of a new family of histone deacetylase-containing complexes. *Journal of Biological Chemistry, 278,* 7234–7239.

Hillier, L. W., Fulton, R. S., Fulton, L. A., Graves, T. A., Pepin, K. H., Wagner-McPherson, C., et al. (2003). The DNA sequence of chromosome 7. *Nature, 424,* 157–164.

Jones, K. L., & Smith, D. W. (1975). The Williams elfin facies syndrome. *Journal of Pediatrics, 86,* 718–723.

Karmiloff-Smith, A., Grant, J., Ewing, S., Carette, M. J., Metcalfe, K., Donnai, D., Read, A. P., & Tassabehji, M. (2003). Using case study comparisons to explore genotype–phenotype correlations in Williams–Beuren syndrome. *Journal of Medical Genetics, 40,* 136–140.

Kaufman, A. S., & Kaufman, N. L. (1990). *Kaufman Brief Intelligence Test.* Circle Pines, MN: American Guidance Services.

Kececioglu, D., Kotthoff, S., & Vogt, J. (1993). Williams–Beuren syndrome: A 30-year follow-up of natural and postoperative course. *European Heart Journal, 14,* 1458–1464.

Klein-Tasman, B. P., & Mervis, C. B. (2003). Distinctive personality characteristics of 8-, 9-, and 10-year-old children with Williams syndrome. *Developmental Neuropsychology, 23,* 271–292.

Li, D. Y., Brooke, B., Davis, E. C., Mecham, R. P., Sorensen, L. K., Boak, B. B., Eichwald, E., & Keating, M. T. (1998). Elastin is an essential determinant of arterial morphogenesis. *Nature, 393,* 276–280.

Li, D. Y., Faury, G., Taylor, D. G., Davis, E. C., Boyle, W. A., Mecham, R. P., Stenzel, P., Boak, B., & Keating, M. T. (1998). Novel arterial pathology in mice and humans hemizygous for *elastin.* *Journal of Clinical Investigation, 102,* 1783–1787.

Li, D. Y., Toland, A. E., Boak, B. B., Atkinson, D., & Ensing, G. J. (1997). *Elastin* point mutations cause an obstructive vascular disease, supravalvular aortic stenosis. *Human Molecular Genetics, 6,* 1021–1028.

Lowery, M. C., Morris, C. A., Ewart, A., Brothman, L., Zhu, X. L., Leonard, C. O., Carey, J. C., Keating, M. T., & Brothman, A. R. (1995). Strong correlations of *elastin* deletions, detected by FISH, with Williams syndrome: Evaluation of 235 patients. *American Journal of Human Genetics, 57,* 49–53.

Meng, X., Lu, X., Zhizhong, L., Green, E. D., Massa, H., Trask, B. J., Morris, C. A., & Keating, M. T. (1998). Complete physical map of the common deletion region in Williams syndrome and identification and characterization of three novel genes. *Human Genetics, 103,* 590–599.

Merritt, D. A., Palmar, C. G., Lurie, P. R., & Petry, E. L. (1963). Supravalvular aortic stenosis: Genetic and clinical studies. *Journal of Laboratory and Clinical Medicine, 62,* 995.

Mervis, C. B., & Klein-Tasman, B. P. (2000). Williams syndrome: Cognition, personality, and adaptive behavior. *Mental Retardation and Developmental Disabilities Research Reviews, 6,* 148–158.

Mervis, C. B., Robinson, B. F., Bertrand, J., Morris, C. A., Klein-Tasman, B. P., & Armstrong, S. C. (2000). The Williams Syndrome Cognitive Profile. *Brain and Cognition, 44,* 604–628.

Mervis, C. B., Robinson, B. F., & Pani, J. R. (1999). Visuospatial construction. *American Journal of Human Genetics, 65,* 1222–1229.

Mervis, C. B., Robinson, B. F., Rowe, M. L., Becerra, A. M., & Klein-Tasman, B. P. (in press). Language abilities of individuals with Williams syndrome. In L. Abbeduto (Ed.), *International review of research in mental retardation* (Vol. 27). Orlando, FL: Academic Press.

Metcalfe, K., Rucka, A. K., Smoot, L., Hofstadler, G., Tuzler, G., McKeown, P., Siu, V., Rauch, A., Dean, J., Dennis, N., Ellis, I., Reardon, W., Cytrynbaum, C., Osborne, L., Yates, J. R., Read, A. P., Donnai, D., & Tassabehji, M. (2000). Elastin: Mutational spectrum in supravalvular aortic stenosis. *European Journal of Human Genetics, 8,* 955–963.

Morris, C. A., Dilts, C., Demsey, S. A., Leonard, C. O., & Blackburn, B. (1988). The natural history of Williams syndrome: Physical characteristics. *Journal of Pediatrics, 113,* 318–326.

Morris, C. A., Leonard, C. O., Dilts, C., & Demsey, S. A. (1990). Adults with Williams syndrome. *American Journal of Medical Genetics. Supplement, 6,* 102–107.

Morris, C. A., Loker, J., Ensing, G., & Stock, A. D. (1993). Supravalvular aortic stenosis cosegregates with a familial 6;7 translocation which disrupts the *elastin* gene. *American Journal of Medical Genetics, 46,* 737–744.

Morris, C. A., & Mervis, C. B. (2000). Williams syndrome and related disorders. *Annual Review of Genomics and Human Genetics, 1,* 461–484.

Morris, C. A., Mervis, C. B., Hobart, H. H., Gregg, R. G., Bertrand, J., Ensing, G. J., Sommer, A., Moore, C. A., Hopkin, R. J., Spallone, P., Keating, M. T., Osborne, L., Kimberley, K. W., & Stock, A. D. (in press). GTF2I hemizygosity implicated in mental retardation in Williams syndrome: Genotype/phenotype analysis of 5 families with deletions in the Williams syndrome region. *American Journal of Medical Genetics.*

Morris, C. A., & Moore, C. A. (1991). The inheritance of Williams syndrome. *Proceedings of the Greenwood Genetics Center, 10,* 81–82.

Morris, C. A., Pober, B., Wang, P., Levinson, M., Sadler, L., Kaplan, P., Lacro, R., & Greenberg, F. (1999). *Medical guidelines for Williams syndrome* [Williams Syndrome Association web site]. Available at: http://www.williams-syndrome.org.

Morris, C. A., Thomas, I. T., & Greenberg, F. (1993). Williams syndrome: Autosomal dominance. *American Journal of Medical Genetics, 47,* 478–481.

O'Connor, W., Davis, J., Geissler, R., Cottrill, C., Noonan, J., & Todd, E. P. (1985). Supravalvular aortic stenosis: Clinical and pathologic observations in six patients. *Archives of Pathology & Laboratory Medicine, 109,* 179–185.

Osborne, L. R., Li, M., Pober, B., Chitayat, D., Bodurtha, J., Mandel, A., Costa, T., Grebe, T., Cox, S., Tsui, L. C., & Scherer, S. W. (2001). A 1.5 million-base pair inversion polymorphism in families with Williams-Beuren syndrome. *Nature Genetics, 29,* 321–325.

Pankau, R., Partsch, C.-J., Gosch, A., Oppermann, H. C., & Wessel, A. (1992). Statural growth in Williams-Beuren syndrome. *European Journal of Pediatrics, 151,* 751–755.

Pankau, R., Partsch, C.-J., Winter, M., Gosch, A., & Wessel, A. (1996). Incidence and spectrum of renal abnormalities in Williams-Beuren syndrome. *American Journal of Medical Genetics, 63,* 301–304.

Partsch, C.-J., Dreyer, G., Gosch, A., Winter, M., Schneppenheim, R., Wessel, A., & Pankau, R. (1999). Longitudinal evaluation of growth, puberty, and bone maturation in children with Williams Syndrome. *Journal of Pediatrics, 134*, 82–89.

Peoples, R., Franke, Y., Wang, Y., Perez-Jurado, L., Paperna, T., Cisco, M., & Francke, U. (2000). A physical map, including a BAC/PAC clone contig, of the Williams-Beuren Syndrome-deletion region at 7q11.23. *American Journal of Medical Genetics, 66*, 47–68.

Pober, B. R., Lacro, R. V., Rice, C., Mandell, V., & Teele, R. L. (1993). Renal findings in 40 individuals with Williams syndrome. *American Journal of Medical Genetics, 46*, 271–274.

Pober, B. R., & Szekely, A. M. (1999). Distinct neurological profile in Williams syndrome. *American Journal of Human Genetics. Supplement, 65*(4), A70.

Pober, B. R., Wang, E., Petersen, K., Osborne, L., & Caprio, S. (2001). Impaired glucose tolerance in Williams Syndrome. *American Journal of Medical Genetics, 69*(4), 302A.

Reiss, A. L., Eliez, S., Schmitt, J. E., Straus, E., Lai, Z., Jones, W., & Bellugi, U. (2000). IV. Neuroanatomy of Williams syndrome: A high-resolution MRI study. *Journal of Cognitive Neuroscience, 12*(Suppl. 1), 65–73.

Sadler, L. S., Olitsky, S. E., & Reynolds, J. D. (1996). Reduced stereoacuity in Williams syndrome. *American Journal of Medical Genetics, 66*, 287–288.

Sadler, L. S., Robinson, L. K., Verdaasdonk, K. R., & Gingell, R. (1993). The Williams syndrome: Evidence for possible autosomal dominant inheritance. *American Journal of Medical Genetics, 47*, 468–470.

Stapleton, T., MacDonald, W. B., & Lightwood, R. (1957). The pathogenesis of idiopathic hypercalcemia in infancy. *American Journal of Clinical Nutrition, 5*, 533–542.

Stock, A. D., Spallone, P. A., Dennis, T. R., Netski, D., Morris, C. A., Mervis, C. B., & Hobart, H. H. (2003). *Heat Shock Protein 27* Gene: Chromosomal and molecular location and relationship to Williams syndrome. *American Journal of Medical Genetics, 120A*, 320–325.

Tassabehji, M., Metcalfe, K., Hurst, J., Ashcroft, G. S., Kielty, C., Wilmot, C., Donnai, D., Read, A. P., & Jones, C. J. (1998). An *elastin* gene mutation producing abnormal tropoelastin and abnormal elastic fibres in a patient with autosomal dominant cutis laxa. *Human Molecular Genetics, 7*, 1021–1028.

Tassabehji, M., Metcalfe, K., Karmiloff-Smith, A., Carette, M. J., Grant, J., Dennis, N., Reardon, W., Splitt, M., Read, A. P., & Donnai, D. (1999). Williams syndrome: Use of chromosomal microdeletions as a tool to dissect cognitive and physical phenotypes. *American Journal of Human Genetics, 64*, 118–125.

Urban, Z., Helms, C., Fekete, G., Csiszar, K., Bonnet, D., Munnich, A., Donis-Keller, H., & Boyd, C. D. (1996). 7q11.23 deletions in Williams syndrome arise as a consequence of unequal meiotic crossover. *American Journal of Human Genetics, 59*, 958–962.

Von Arnim, G., & Engel, P. (1964). Mental retardation related to hypercalcemia. *Developmental Medicine and Child Neurology, 6*, 366–377.

Williams, J. C. P., Barratt-Boyes, B. G., & Lowe, J. B. (1961). Supravalvular aortic stenosis. *Circulation, 24*, 1311–1318.

Winter, M., Pankau, R., Amm, M., Gosch, A., & Wessel, A. (1996). The spectrum of ocular features in the Williams-Beuren syndrome. *Clinical Genetics, 49*, 28–31.

Yang, N., Higuchi, O., Ohashi, K., Nagata, K., Wada, A., Kangawa, K., Nishida, E., & Mizuno, K. (1998). Cofilin phosphorylation by LIM-kinase 1 and its role in Rac-mediated actin reorganization. *Nature, 393*, 809–812.

Zhang, M. C., He, L., Giro, M., Yong, S. L., Tiller, G. E., & Davidson, J. M. (1999). Cutis laxa arising from frameshift mutations in exon 30 of the *elastin* gene (*ELN*). *Journal of Biological Chemistry, 274*, 981–986.

IV

RESEARCH ACTION STEPS FOR THE SHORT AND LONG TERM

15

Next Steps in the Study of Genetics and Language Disorders

Peggy McCardle
National Institute of Child Health and Human Development

Judith Cooper
National Institute on Deafness and Other Communication Disorders

Investigation of the question of the genetic bases of language and language disorders requires information across various topics, including the clear delineation of behavioral phenotypes, identification of neurocognitive substrates, synthesis of emerging discoveries across different clinical diagnoses (e.g., Williams syndrome, fragile X, autism, specific language impairment [SLI]), new models of genetic mechanisms, new methods of gene discovery, and new quantitative techniques for estimation of genetic effects and effect sizes. Breakthrough discoveries are underway in each of these areas of investigation, but often they are developing in ways that make it difficult for scientists to be well informed. Several factors have impeded access to this information: distributed sources of funding, traditional disciplinary boundaries, and reliance on relatively circumscribed communication networks among scientists.

To address this need for increased communication and the naturally ensuing collaborations, it is important to bring together scientists from various disciplines, to share and synthesize emerging discoveries, and to begin developing innovative, hybrid methods to be applied to the search for the genetic mechanisms operative in the human language capacity. This would ideally include recognition of how this capacity can be limited

The opinions expressed herein are those of the authors alone and should not be construed as official or representing the National Institute of Child Health and Human Development, the National Institute on Deafness and Other Communication Disorders, the National Institutes of Health, or the Department of Health and Human Services.

in some individuals, how this is reflected in the abilities of young children, how language capacity and abilities change over time, and how other areas of language-related abilities such as reading and learning more generally are affected. Ultimately, success in unraveling genetic contributions to language impairment can be applied to the development of effective and efficient teaching and intervention methods that take into account the interaction of individual aptitudes, environment, and instructional methods.

The May 2002 Merrill Conference, "The Relationship of Genes, Environments, and Developmental Language Disorders: Research for the 21st Century," provided an important initial step in bringing together a small group of interdisciplinary scholars to begin the enhancement of communication across disciplines about this important area. The conference was not only informative and important, but also raised key issues we must hold in mind as we move forward to increase the knowledge base in language and genetics. During discussions, four major points emerged.

First, we must remember the big picture—that language abilities fall along a continuum. This continuum ranges from typical language development, which can be observed in monolingual children, bilingual children, and deaf children of deaf parents, through the spectrum of children with language impairments, some related to specific syndromes and others of as-yet unknown etiologies. Although much of what was presented at this conference were data that addressed the language characteristics of specific disorders, an overriding fact that came out of this conference is that language impairments vary more in quantity than quality. As we look for differences—distinct features that help us define these conditions—we must also remember that there is a foundational similarity. These language impairments vary in timing and severity, but all seem to fall on the developmental continuum, showing slowed, arrested, or regressed development, but not showing characteristics that are totally foreign to what we know of some period of typical language development. Thus, even as we are forced to be "splitters" by the demands of research to describe and define the features of specific disorders, we must also be "lumpers" across disorders as we seek clues to the role of genetics in language development and its disorders. This may be especially challenging as we seek to define ever more narrow behavioral phenotypes in our search for genetic bases for language disorders, and it may be that we must split even more finely before we can lump again. For intervention and theories of what underlies language disorders, we must do both.

Second, we must lay out a plan for investigation. A few fundamental questions from the conference that must be held in mind, although we know parts of the answer, are: How can we go about studying the genetics of language and language disorders in a coordinated way? What kinds of data do we need? In which instances should we bring various data sources and analyses together? Given the genetic information that we have available now and the methods and approaches that are constantly being developed, is there a basic rule of thumb to guide the collection of data for those who would like to solve the genetics puzzle as it relates to language disorders? Clearly those clinicians who treat children with language disorders could be gathering data that might lend themselves to later analyses, and this type of effort could be far more fruitful if it were clear what specific data would be helpful to researchers. How best can language and cognition researchers and genetics researchers collaborate in their efforts at data collection? How can researchers minimize the impact on participants and maximize what we can learn from those data?

Third, we must move the diagnosis of language disorders from art to science. We can move toward this goal by addressing a few big research issues that are crucial to the study of language and language disorders, but that are also foundational to the study of the genetic contributions to language and language disorders. We need to give continued attention to issues of definition, measurement, design, and analytic methods. This need overlaps significantly with the second point—the plan of investigation. We need to generally agree on what to measure (key constructs), how to measure (which instruments to use), and how to collect, analyze, and interpret the data (design and methods). To accomplish this, we must increase communication and collaboration across disciplines as well as across syndromes and conditions being studied.

Finally, we must find a way to sustain these research efforts. We have a responsibility to attract and train the next generation of scientists who will carry on the work that we have begun. We must train our successors to be open and responsible collaborators, to work cooperatively to investigate in an integrated way those research participants whom so many different scientists in various fields want to study. We must serve as models for young researchers as we develop methods to archive and share for future study the precious data we collect so that we can learn as much as possible from it. We have this responsibility not only to our scientific colleagues, but also to the participants who allow us to study them in detail and the parents who trust us to scrutinize the behaviors, brains, and tissues of their children.

What do we need to do to move forward? There are several key areas, mentioned earlier, that the meeting participants agreed should receive the attention of the research community to ensure a coordinated, serious research effort in the genetics of language and language disorders. These are outlined next and then summarized as Next Steps.

WHAT SHOULD WE MEASURE?

First, we should agree on a core of important constructs. Some would consider it ideal to have a single protocol that all researchers would use in collecting their data, or to have common measures that could be used so that data could be pooled to examine questions with larger numbers of subjects. Yet we know that child development is messy—that it changes over time and presents serious measurement challenges. We are interested in studying language across a large range of ages, from infancy through preschool and school age into adolescence and adulthood. No measure can cover even a large part of such an age range. Therefore, we try to find instruments that measure the same construct over time. Likewise, we often seek within research networks and across studies to agree on common constructs—when it may not be possible or practical to use common measures. We often elect to use multiple measures of the same construct to examine different aspects of it or to gain convergent data. Thus, some agreement on what key constructs should form a core for investigations of the genetics of particular language disorders is important to advancing the field. What these core constructs should be is an important topic for future discussion, to lay the foundation for a more systematic science of the genetics of language and language disorders.

In addition, we must continue and improve our efforts to measure typical language development. As we develop new measures, we must gather normative data on today's children. Today's children may not look like the children of 30 or 40 years ago for various reasons—maybe they are smarter and developing faster than they did before. Many older instruments were never normed on the various racial and ethnic groups that now make up a large proportion of the U.S. population. Thus, in some cases, the typical language development of these children has not been thoroughly studied. We have also not examined certain aspects of language development in the detailed ways that we are able to now.

Finally, we must measure both change over time and the effects of intervention. The measurement of intervention must include how it is implemented, for whom, and for which children it is effective under what conditions. What is the optimal timing and intensity of that intervention?

HOW SHOULD WE MEASURE?

Often no single measure can be relied on to adequately measure a construct. There may be constructs that we want to measure for which no instruments exist, or extant instruments may not be psychometrically sound or do not lend themselves to the types of analyses we wish to use. We sometimes find ourselves using measures that were developed for clinical purposes or were developed long ago and normed on populations quite different from those for whom we are now using them. Rather than force our research efforts into a Procrustean bed, where the sleeper's legs were cut off to fit the bed, we should focus on adapting measures to better fit our research needs or developing new measures.

In some instances, we may need tools to perform more fine-grained analyses. One example is Lord's development of new instruments to be used in conjunction with existing ones to better capture early language development and investigate the much discussed phenomenon of language loss or regression in a subset of autistic children. This is also an example that illustrates the need to remain mindful of the continuum of abilities in language from normal through disordered—it may well be that there is a fluctuation of appearance, disappearance, and reappearance of vocabulary in the early stages of typical language development. This is not a phenomenon that has been clearly documented, at least in part because we have not examined early language development in quite this way—we have not asked the detailed questions that Lord is asking of the parents of autistic children. Thus, piloting measures with a normative sample and using comparison groups in studies are crucially important. In a similar vein, the complex syntactic tasks developed by Zukowski to elicit relative object clauses in individuals with Williams syndrome are also tasks that are difficult for some individuals with typically developing or developed language; they are tasks that will likely reveal new information about language abilities in general.

Both qualitative and quantitative measures are needed if we are to fully capture language behavior in specific areas. Pragmatics is a notable area where both methods are needed. Although there are some measures of the social use of language, most are qualitative, and such measures do not exist for certain age groups. Because it would be useful to measure this construct over time, new instruments are needed.

HOW SHOULD WE COLLECT, ANALYZE, AND INTERPRET THE DATA?

The careful characterization of research participants is critical to clearly defining phenotypes that are key to unlocking some of the genetic puzzles that tantalize researchers in child language and language disorders. We need innovative methods and designs for the collection of data that will characterize the groups and subgroups that we study. For example, Mervis has made use of behavioral profiling in Williams syndrome to better define her research subjects.

We must ensure that our samples represent the diversity of the U.S. population within the various syndromes that include language disorders, and that our samples cross socioeconomic strata. We cannot study only those families that are sufficiently sophisticated to have sought out services—we must find a way to reach those who currently may go undiagnosed to gain the full spectrum of severity of the disorders we study. Observing the full spectrum may also lead us to look for subgroups within syndromes or disorders. The careful characterization of each research participant and comparison participants is crucial to the identification of patterns, be they patterns of symptoms or patterns of response (or non-response) to interventions.

NEXT STEPS

To accomplish or even approach the goals laid out in this stimulating conference, certain steps are recommended:

• We must continue the conversations that were, if not begun, then strengthened and enlivened at the 2002 Merrill conference, "Genes, Environments, and Developmental Language Disorders." We should establish collaborative relationships across disciplines, institutions, and disorders. We should bring together fields such as genetics, cognitive neuroscience, and developmental psychology with those studying language. These are just a few of the disciplines that might have significant input into the collaborations needed to solve this puzzle.

• We must focus on measurement and methodology, working to adapt or re-norm existing measures and develop new measures where none exist or where those that do exist do not meet the research needs. We must find ways to use or adapt for use methods not typically used in language research, and develop innovative research designs and analytic procedures.

• We must provide clear guidance for how the field can progress most rapidly—by outlining core constructs and optimal designs to study various disorders so that data can ultimately be pooled and/or compared.

• We must attract and train the most talented students and beginning scientists in various disciplines as our replacement cadre to carry on the research that we have begun.

• We must develop a culture of data archiving and data sharing and make the most of the valuable, detailed, well-documented data that we are already collecting and will continue to collect.

Throughout the Merrill conference, it was evident that these recommendations are being taken quite seriously already. Researchers have begun cross-discipline conversations and have begun to establish the types of collaborations that are crucial to moving the research forward. The enthusiasm for a greater focus on measurement and methodologies, and for increased interdisciplinary collaboration, is a positive indicator that these recommendations will result in an increase in the amount and quality of research focused on genetics and language disorders. In fact these recommendations are consistent with what has been done fruitfully in other areas. Thus, there is reason to be quite optimistic that we can make significant progress. The momentum that was begun at this conference must not be lost.

Author Index

A

Aakalu, G., 135, *147*
Abbeduto, L., 78, 82, 83, 84, 85, 86, 90, *94, 95, 96,* 131, *143,* 193, 194, *203*
Abecasis, G. R., 340, 344, 346, *349, 353*
Abel, L., 344, *352*
Abitbol, M., *143*
Abrams, B., 127, *144*
Abrams, M. T., 124, 125, 135, *146, 147, 148*
Abramson, R., *47, 325*
Abreu, P. C., 337, 341, *349, 351*
Achenbach, T. M., 89, *95*
Acuna, J. M., 122, *145*
Adams, C., 56, *74,* 213, 220, *236, 327*
Adolphs, R., 133, *143*
Adrien, K. T., *49*
Agee, F., *322*
AGRE Consortium, *26,* 46, *47* (or Autism Genetic Resource Exchange Consortium)
Agulhon, C., 123, *143*
Akerstrom, B., *326*
Akshoomoff, N. A., 27, *318*
Alarcón, M., 9, *26,* 46, *47,* 121, *145,* 334, *350*
Albertoni, A., *327*

Alcock, K., *327*
Alexander, A. W., *322*
Allen, D., 33, 34, 36, *47, 75*
Allen, G., 309, *316, 322*
Allen, R., 190, *206*
Allison, D. B., 338, 346, *350*
Almasy, L., 340, *350*
Almazan, M., 102, *118*
Altenmüller, E., *323, 326*
Altman, J., 313, *316*
Altshul-Stark, D., 129, *147*
Ambros, V., 207, *236*
Ambrose, J. B., *322, 324*
Ament, N., 127, *143,* 194, *203*
American Psychiatric Association, 295, *316*
American Psychological Association, 31, *47*
Amir, R. E., 294, *316*
Amiri, K., 124, *145*
Amm, M., 358, *369*
Amos, C. I., 336, 340, *350, 354*
Amunts, K., 297, 301, *316*
Anders, T. F., *321*
Andersen, H. G., *322*
Anderson, B. J., 297, *316*
Anderson, G. M., *150*
Anderson, K., 125, *149*
Anderson, M., 32, *51*
Andreasen, N. C., *148*

Andreason, P., 324
Andrew, C., 149
Aoshima, S., 271, 273, 282
Aram, D. M., 54, 55, 59, 74, 75, 326
Arbelle, S., 132, 145
Arber, S., 160, 183
Ardnt, S., 127, 148
Arin, D., 39, 48
Armstrong, S. C., 119, 184, 368
Arndt, S., 148, 312, 324
Artru, A. A., 319, 325
Asano, F., 326
Asanuma, C., 313, 316
Asarnow, R. F., 353
Aschauer, H., 352
Ashburner, J., 52, 327
Ashcroft, G. S., 369
Ashley-Koch, A., 45, 47, 325
Assel, M. A., 188, 204
Atkinson, D. L., 184, 361, 362, 363, 366, 367
Avrutin, S., 256, 282
Aylsworth, A., 47, 127, 147
Aylward, E., 48, 135, 148, 318, 325
Aziz-Sultan, A., 327

B

Babyonyshev, M., 282
Baddeley, A. D., 37, 49, 177, 180, 184
Badre, D., 320
Bahr, D., 198, 204
Bailey, A., 27, 28, 34, 44, 45, 47, 48, 49, 50, 148, 237, 295, 313, 316, 323, 352
Bailey, C. H., 297, 320
Bailey, D. B., 79, 81, 95, 124, 125, 126, 127, 128, 130, 139, 143, 146, 149, 194, 203
Bailey, J., 148, 324
Bailey, K. G. D., 268, 283
Baird, G., 50, 52, 237, 323, 352
Bakardjiev, A., 49
Baker, D. E., 119
Baker, L., 32, 48
Baker, M., 255, 282
Bakker, C. E., 123, 143, 147
Baldwin, C. D., 190, 204
Ball, W. S., Jr., 320
Balla, D., 9, 29
Balsamo, L. M., 307, 316
Baltaxe, C. A. M., 32, 47

Baranek, G. T., 124, 146
Barbayannis, F. A., 183
Barbour, N., 191, 204
Barkley, R. A., 134, 143
Barnard, K. E., 193, 204
Barnett, A. S., 319
Baron-Cohen, S., 86, 95, 117, 118, 119, 133, 134, 143, 149
Barratt-Boyes, B. G., 358, 369
Barrett, W. A., 352
Bar-Shalom, E., 245, 246, 258, 282
Barss, A., 285
Bartak, L., 32, 33, 47
Bartels, C., 327
Bartlett, C., 46, 47, 214, 230, 236, 239, 296, 316, 349, 350
Bass, M. P., 325
Basser, L. S., 301, 316
Bassett, A., 47, 236, 316, 350
Basu, S., 47
Bates, E., 59, 79, 74, 184, 203, 307, 316, 324, 326, 327
Bates, J. E., 190, 203
Bates, J. F., 317
Bates, K. E., 96
Baulac, M., 321
Bauman, M. L., 309, 313, 316
Baumgardner, T., 127, 129, 134, 144, 147
Bauminger, N., 79, 88, 96
Baumwell, L., 190, 205
Bausart, R., 317
Bavelier, D., 323
Bayer, S. A., 313, 316
Bayes, M., 362, 366
Bayley, N., 161, 183
Bazin, B., 321
Becerra, A. M., 102, 119, 163, 184, 359, 368
Beck, G., 354
Beckel-Mitchener, A., 79, 95
Bedore, L. M., 38, 47, 219, 236, 237
Beeghly, M., 74
Beery, K. E., 180, 183
Behen, M. E., 317, 322, 323
Behrens, H., 245, 246, 282
Belin, P., 304, 316
Bell, R., 198, 203
Bellocq, J. P., 123, 145
Bellugi, U., 102, 109, 117, 118, 119, 154, 180, 183, 358, 366, 369
Belser, R. C., 125, 131, 133, 134, 138, 144, 149
Bemporad, J., 148

Benedetto, E., 87, *97*
Bennett-Clarke, C. A., 314, *317, 322*
Bennetto, L., 129, 135, *144*
Bennetts, B., *327*
Benson, G., 84, *94*
Benson, R. R., 303, *317*
Bentourkia, M., 299, *317*
Bernard, O., *183*
Bernier, R., *28*
Berninger, V. W., *318, 351, 353*
Berno, A. J., *352*
Bertheas, M. F., *148*
Berthoud, I., *119*
Bertrand, J., *119*, 161, *184, 185, 367, 368*
Beuren, A. J., 358, *366*
Bever, T. G., 265, 266, 268, 270, 277, 280,
    282, 283, 287
Biancalana, V., *143*
Biber, M. E., 62, *75*
Bick, P., *148*
Biederman, J., 330, 334, *350*
Bier, D., *327*
Bihrle, A., 102, *118, 183*, 358, *366*
Bishop, D. V. M., 33, 34, 37, 44, 47, *51*, 54,
    56, 61, 62, 73, *74*, 103, 104, *118*, 122,
    144, 192, 213, 220, *236, 238*, 293, 296,
    316, 334, *350*
Bishop, K., *206*
Blacher, J., 191, *205*
Blackburn, B., 358, *368*
Blanchet, P., *143*
Blangero, J., 340, *350*
Blasey, C., 135, *145, 146*
Bless, D., 83, *96*
Blonden, L., *150*
Bloom, L., 59, *74*
Blue, M. E., *318*
Boak, B. B., 361, 363, *367*
Boatman, D., 301, *317*
Bobée, S., 135, *144*
Boccia, M. L., 125, 132, 140, *149*
Bodfish, J. W., 127, *144*
Bodurtha, J., *119, 185, 368*
Boito, A., 360, *367*
Bol, A., *317*
Boland, J., 269, *282*
Bolton, P., 11, *27*, 44, *47, 49, 50, 148, 237*,
    316, 323, 352
Bonilla, C., *351*
Bonnet, D., *369*
Bonora, E., *50, 237, 323, 352*
Bontekoe, C., *150*

Bookheimer, S. Y., *320*
Borer, H., 230, *236*
Borghgraef, M., 128, *144*
Borkowski, J. G., 190, *204*
Bornstein, M. H., 190, 193, *203, 205*
Boro, J., 245, 246, *282*
Botstein, D., 344, 348, *350*
Botta, A., 365, *366*
Botting, N., 33, 37, *48, 55, 75*, 213, 219, *236*
Boue, J., *148*
Bouillon, M., *145*
Bourguignon, M., *317*
Bowerman, M., 252, *282*
Bowler, D., 33, *48*
Boyce, G. C., 189, *205*
Boyce, L. K., 189, *205*
Boyd, C. D., *369*
Boyle, C., *29*
Boyle, W. A., *367*
Braden, M., 126, 131, *146*
Bradford, Y., 9, *27*, 296, *317, 321*
Bradshaw, J. L., *324*
Brammer, M. J., *317*
Branden, M., *147*
Brandt, J., *317*
Braniecki, S. H., *316*
Braummer, M., *149*
Braun, A., *323*
Braun, T., *27, 354*
Bregman, W. R., 125, *148*
Breiter, S. N., 135, *146*
Brenton, D. P., 294, *317*
Brereton, A. V., *324*
Bresnan, J., 264, *282*
Bretherton, I., *74*
Brett, E., *327*
Brice, A., *352*
Briscoe, J., 213, *238*
Brody, M., 264, *282*
Broks, P., 33, *51*
Brook, S. L., 33, *48*
Brooke, B., 362, *367*
Brooks, J., *144*
Brothman, A. R., *367*
Brothman, L., *367*
Brower, A. M., *351*
Brown, C., 274, *284*
Brown, E., *145*
Brown, W. T., 79, *95*, 126, 133, *144*
Brownell, H., *119*
Bruhn, P., *322*
Brun, D., 258, *282*

Brunelle, F., *320*
Brunswick, N., *323*
Bryan, R. N., 135, *148*
Bryson, S. E., *29*
Brzustowicz, L., *47, 236, 239, 316, 350*
Buchbinder, B. R., *317*
Buckner, R. L., *322*
Buckwalter, P., 37, 44, *51, 52,* 225, *240,* 293, *326*
Buhen, M., *317*
Bullmore, E. T., *149*
Burack, J. A., 87, *97*
Burchinal, M., 125, *149,* 190, *204*
Bussiere, J., *324*
Butler, E., 309, *319*
Buxbaum, J. D., 9, *27, 325*
Buxbaum, S., *350*
Buxhoeveden, D. P., *317*
Bygrave, A., *143*

C

Calkins, S. D., 190, *203*
Callias, M., 87, *95,* 135, *146*
Caltagirone, C., *325*
Calvert, G. A., 304, *317*
Campbell, M., 127, *144*
Campbell, T. F., 37, 39, *48, 62, 75*
Cannon, T. D., 194, *203, 326*
Cantor, D. S., 295, *318*
Cantor, R. M., *26, 46, 47, 352, 353*
Cantwell, D., 32, *48*
Cao, Y., 304, *317*
Capirci, O., 102, 103, *119*
Caplan, D., 301, *317*
Cappa, S. F., *323*
Caprio, S., 358, *369*
Cardon, L. R., 335, 338, *349, 350, 351, 354*
Carette, M. J., *367, 369*
Carey, J. C., *367*
Carlson, G. N., *282*
Caroni, P., *183*
Carpenter, P. A., *326*
Carper, R. A., *318, 320*
Carr, L. C., *327*
Carrington, J. C., 207, *236*
Carrow-Woolfolk, E., 83, *95*
Carson, B., *317*
Carta, J., 192, *205*
Casanova, M. F., 310, 314, *317*

Caselli, M. C., 102, *119*
Casey, B., *322*
Caskey, C. T., *150*
Cassavant, T., *27*
Caston, J., 136, *144*
Catts, H. W., 62, *74, 76,* 214, 225, *236, 239*
Cavalli-Sforza, L. L., *149*
Caviness, V. S., Jr., 42, *48, 49, 50,* 297, *317*
Cawthon, S. W., *95*
Cayer, M., *29*
Cecchi, C., 298, *317*
Chabris, C. F., *49*
Chain, F., *316*
Chakrabarti, S., 23, *27*
Chakraborty, P. K., *317, 322, 323*
Chamberlain, W. D., 123, *150*
Chandler, M. J., 191, *205*
Chandler, M. P., 136, *145*
Changeux, J. -P., 297, *317*
Chanoine, V., *323*
Chapman, L., *324*
Chapman, R. S., 77, 78, 79, 83, 85, 93, *95*
Charman, T., 295, *317*
Chastain, J., *150*
Chen, T., *354*
Chen, W., 52, 124, *147*
Cherny, S. S., 338, *349, 350, 351, 352, 353*
Chiaia, N. L., *317*
Childress, D., 44, *50*
Chilosi, A. M., *327*
Chiotti, C., *149*
Chipcase, B., 37, *51*
Chiron, C., 300, *317, 320*
Chisum, H. J., *27, 318*
Chitayat, D., *119, 185, 368*
Chomsky, N., 230, *236,* 255, 264, 279, *282, 285, 291, 293, 317*
Choroco, M. C., *144*
Christian, B. C., *322*
Christianson, K., 269, *282, 283*
Christodoulou, J., *327*
Chugani, D. C., 313, 314, *317*
Chugani, H. T., 299, 300, *317, 318, 322, 323*
Churchill, D. W., 32, *48*
Churchill, J. D., 79, *95*
Chynoweth, J. G., 37, *52*
Ciaranello, R. D., 295, *322*
Cicchetti, D., 9, *29,* 194, *203*
Cinque, G., 275, *282*
Cioni, G., *327*
Cipriani, P., *327*
Cisco, M., *369*

Clahsen, H., 102, *118*, 245, *282*
Clancy, B., 313, *318*
Clark, H. H., 89, *95*
Clark, M. M., 292, *318*
Clark, R. D., 125, *143*, *146*
Clark, V., *323*
Clayton, D. G., *351*
Clearfield, M. W., 304, *318*
Cleave, P. L., 38, *51*, 59, *75*, 215, 217, 219, *239*, 251, *286*
Clincke, G., *147*
Cnattingius, S., *321*
Cocchi, R., 198, *203*
Cody, H., 312, *318*
Coffey, S. A., *320*
Coffey-Corina, S. A., *322*
Cohen, D., 32, *50*, 86, *95*, 125, 126, 127, 132, 139, *144*, *147*, *148*, *150*
Cohen, I. L., 127, 130, 133, 140, *144*, *145*, *150*
Cohen, J., 168, *183*, *322*
Cohen, L., *321*, *327*
Cohen, R., *322*
Cohen, W. I., 188, *203*
Cole, A. J., *317*
Cole, K. N., 57, 59, 74, *75*
Coleman, M., *352*
Collaborative Linkage Study of Autism, 46, *48*
Colledge, E., 59, 62, *74*
Collings, D. L., *52*
Collins, F. S., 142, *144*
Collins, W., 193, *203*
Comery, T. A., *321*
Condouris, K., 39, 40, 41, *48*, 220, *236*
Connelly, A., *52*, *327*
Conners, F., *352*
Conry, J., *320*
Constable, R. T., *325*
Conti-Ramsden, G., 33, 37, 38, *48*, 55, *75*, 213, 219, *236*, *237*
Contopoulos-Ionnidis, D. G., *351*
Conway, E. E., 360, *366*
Cook, E. H., 25, *27*, 28, *50*, 121, *144*, *327*
Cookson, W. O. C., 344, *349*
Cooper, J., 37, *51*, 58, *75*, 213, 220, *239*
Cope, H. A., *325*
Coppens, A., *317*
Corbetta, M. D., *324*
Corbin, F., 123, *145*
Corfield, D. R., 136, *145*
Corina, D., *323*

Cornish, K. M., 124, 133, *145*, *148*, *150*
Corona, R., 132, 139, *145*
Corsiglia, J., 41, *49*
Corter, C., 190, *203*
Cosgrove, G. R., *317*
Cossu, G., *323*
Costa, T., *119*, *185*, *368*
Cote, F., *147*
Cottingham, R. W., Jr., 336, *350*
Cottrill, C., *368*
Coulson, S., 274, *283*
Courchesne, E., 25, *27*, 308, 309, 312, 313, 314, *316*, *318*, *320*, *322*, *323*, *324*, *326*, *328*
Courchesne, R. Y., *27*
Covington, J., *318*
Cowan, W. M., 295, *316*, *318*
Cowles, A., *318*
Cox, A., 32, *47*
Cox, D. R., *352*
Cox, P. R., 349, *350*
Cox, S., *119*, *185*, *368*
Coy, K., 190, *204*
Crago, M. G., 122, *146*, 230, *238*, 293, *319*
Craig, H., 33, 45, *48*
Craig, I., *50*, 213, *237*
Crain, S., 101, 104, *118*, 256, 260, *283*, 292, *318*
Cras, P., *143*
Crawford, D. C., 122, *145*
Crawley, A. P., *320*
Critchley, H. D., 134, 136, *145*
Crivello, F., *326*
Crocker, M., 269, *287*
Croen, L. A., *323*
Cronister, A., 124, *145*
Croog, V. J., *324*
Cross, G., 124, *145*
Crosson, B., 293, *323*
Crowson, M., *27*, *48*
Crutchley, A., 55, *75*
Csiszar, K., *369*
Cuccaro, M. L., *47*, *325*, *353*
Cuenod, C. A., *320*
Cupini, L. M., *325*
Curran, M. E., 360, *366*
Curtis, D., 346, *353*
Curtiss, S., *150*, 213, *239*, 301, *318*
Cuskelly, M., 199, *203*
Cytrynbaum, C., *368*

D

Dabholkar, A. S., 297, 299, 300, *321*
Dabringhaus, A., *316*
Dager, S., *48, 319, 325*
Dail, R., *326*
Dale, P., 45, *50, 203*
Dale, P. S., 57, 59, *74, 75, 184*, 213, 237
Dallapiccola, B., *366*
Daly, M. J., *351*
Daly, T., 16, *28*
D'Amato, R. J., 314, *318*
Dambrosia, J. M., *323*
Danysz, W., 142, *145*
Darby, J. K., *143*
Darlington, R. B., *318*
Da Silva, E. A., *317*
David, H. R., *27*
Davidson, J. M., *369*
Davies, B., 192, *206*
Davies, M., *119*
Davis, E. C., *367*
Davis, E. P., 80, *97*
Davis, H. R., *318*
Davis, J., *368*
Davis, K. L., *27*
Davis, M., *327*
Dawson, G., 25, *28, 29*, 46, *48*, 132, 133,
    139, *145, 319, 323, 325*
Dean, A., *316*
Dean, J., *368*
de Bode, S., *318*
Deboulle, K., *143*
Decena, K., *325*
Dedeyn, P. P., *143*
Dedrick, C. F., 191, *204*
De Fossé, L., 42, *48*
DeFries, J. C., 121, *145*, 330, 334, 337, 343,
    349, *350, 351, 352, 354*
Deiber, M., *324*
Delalande, O., *320*
Delaney, K., *325*
Delatycki, M., *327*
D'Elia, A., 304, 309, *318*
Dell, G. S., 279, *283*
DeLon, G., *47*
DeLong, R. G., *325*
Demonet, J. F., *323*
Demsey, S. A., 358, *368*
Denckla, M. B., 135, *147*
Deng, M., *354*

Dennis, N., *368, 369*
Dennis, T. R., *369*
Denton, D., *148*
de Villiers, J., 211, 212, 230, *236, 239*
de Vincenzi, M., 272, *283*
De Volder, A. G., *317*
Devys, D., 123, *145, 147, 148*
Dhooge, R., *143, 147*
Dichgans, J., *326*
Dick, F., *324*
Dickens, B. F., *323*
Dielkens, A., 128, *144*
Diener, H. C., *327*
Digilio, M. C., *366*
DiLavore, P. C., 19, 22, *28*
DiLavore, P. S., *50*
Dilts, C., 358, 360, *367, 368*
Dimiceli, S., *149, 325*
Dinno, N., 25, *29*
Dissanayake, C., 132, *145*
Dobkins, K. R., *319*
Docherty, Z., *52*
Dodge, K. A., 190, *203*
Doernberg, N., *29*
Dolan, R. J., 136, *145*
Dolan, T., 78, *95*, 193, *203*
Dolish, J., 84, *94*
Dollaghan, C., 37, 39, *48*, 62, *75*
Dong, Y., *367*
Donis-Keller, H., *369*
Donlan, C., 37, 44, *47, 48, 350*
Donnai, D., *367, 368, 369*
Donnelly, S., *47, 325*
Donohue, B. C., *320, 324*
Doshi, J. M., *352*
Douglas, J. M., 219, *237*
Dowd, M., *29*
Dowty, D., 258, *283*
Drake, J. M., *326*
Dreyer, G., *369*
Dromerick, A. W., *324*
Dronkers, N. F., *327*
Duara, R., *321*
Dulac, O., *317*
Dunn, A., 215, *236*
Dunn, D., 33, 34, 55, *75*
Dunn, L. E., 169, 172, *183*
Dunn, L. M., 7, *27, 28*, 62, *75*
Dunn, M., *51, 75*
Dutschka, K., *327*
Dyer, P. N., *150*
Dyer-Friedman, J., *146*

Dykens, E., *45, 77, 79,* 80, 89, 93, *95,* 125, 126, 127, 129, 135, *146, 148*

E

Eadie, P. A., 219, 220, *237*
Eberhart, D., 123, *145*
Echelard, D., *325*
Eckburg, P. B., *316*
Eckert, M. A., 292, *318*
Edelson, S. B., 295, *318*
Eden, G. F., 303, *318*
Edgar, E., 269, *285*
Edmundson, A., 54, *74*
Edwards, J., 38, *48*
Egaas, B., *318, 326*
Egan, G., *148*
Eichwald, E., *367*
Eisenberg, R., 360, *367*
Eisenberg, S. L., 222, *237*
Eisenmajer, R., 9, 27, 309, *319*
Elbert, T., 301, *319*
Eley, T. C., *74*
Eliez, S., 135, *145*
Ellaway, C. J., *327*
Elliez, S., *369*
Elliott, C. D., 8, 27, 157, *183*
Elliott, G. R., 7, *28,* 157, *185*
Elliott, S., 62, *75*
Elliott, T. K., *316*
Ellis, I., *368*
Elston, R. C., *325,* 337, 339, *350, 351, 352*
Endres, C. J., *322*
Engel, P., 358, *369*
Ensing, G. J., *184, 185,* 360, 361, 363, *367, 368*
Erb, M., *326*
Erel, O., 87, *97*
Ernst, M., 308, *320, 322*
Erwick-Roberts, J., 190, *204*
Escher, G., 313, *319*
Eschler, J., 7, *28*
Esteban, J., *351*
Eure, K. F., 41, *49*
Eussen, B., *150*
Evancie, L., 40, 41, *48,* 220, *236*
Evans, A. C., 33, *52*
Evans, J., *48,* 78, *95,* 193, *203*
Everett, L. A., *184, 367*
Ewart, A. K., *184,* 360, 361, 362, *366, 367*

Ewens, W. J., *353*
Ewing, S., *367*
Eyer, J., 219, *237*

F

Falk, C. T., 345, *350*
Falls, D. L., *185*
Falzi, G., 41, *49*
Fanselow, G., *286*
Faragher, B., 37, *48,* 213, 219, *236*
Faraone, S. V., 330, 334, *350*
Farnarier, P., *324*
Farrar, M. J., 190, *205*
Fatemi, S. H., 313, *319*
Faucon, N., *143*
Faury, G., 362, *367*
Favuto, M., 198, *203*
Fazio, F., *323*
Fein, D., *75*
Feingold, E., 338, 339, 340, *350, 351*
Feingold, J., *352*
Feinstein, C., 81, *95*
Fekete, G., *369*
Feldman, E., *321*
Feng, Y., 123, *145, 146*
Fennel, E., *319*
Fenson, L., 25, 27, 164, *184,* 196, *203*
Ferguson, J., *149*
Ferrari, P., *150*
Ferraro, V., 268, *283*
Ferreira, F., 268, 269, *282, 283*
Ferreira, V. S., 279, *283*
Ferriere, G., *316*
Fersko, T. M., 222, *237*
Fey, M. E., 214, 219, *236, 237*
Fiese, B. H., 121, *149,* 191, 194, *205*
Fiez, J. A., *324*
Filipek, P. A., 27, 42, *50,* 312, *319*
Fine, I., *319*
Finlay, B. L., *318*
Finney, E. M., 301, *319*
Finucane, B., 77, *95,* 133, *145, 149*
Fisch, G., 126, *144, 145*
Fisher, R. E., *322*
Fisher, S. E., 44, 45, 46, *49, 50,* 207, 213, 214, *237,* 293, *319, 321, 323,* 330, 334, 335, 339, 340, 343, 349, *350, 352, 353*
Fitzgerald, M., 27, *325*
Flax, J., *47, 236, 239, 316, 350*

Fletcher, J. M., 66, *75, 237, 325*
Fletcher, P., *327*
Flores, R., 362, *366*
Flores d'Arcais, G. B., 272, *283*
Fodor, J. A., 265, 266, 270, 278, *283*
Fodor, J. D., *283*
Fodor, S. P., *352*
Fohlen, M., *320*
Folling, I., 294, *319*
Folstein, S., 9, *27, 29,* 44, 45, *48, 51, 52,*
    137, *149,* 295, 296, *319, 321, 326, 327,*
    334, *351, 354*
Fombonne, E., 23, 25, *27,* 44, *49*
Foorman, B. R., 66, *75*
Forman, D. R., 190, *204*
Forrest, W. F., 338, *351*
Forssberg, H., 309, *319*
Forste, K. I., *285*
Fortin, A., *145, 147*
Foundas, A. L., 41, *49,* 292, *319*
Fowler, V., *350*
Fox, K., *325*
Fox, P. T., *148*
Frackowiak, R. S. J., *52, 327*
Francis, D. J., 66, *75,* 231, 234, *237*
Francke, U., *369*
Francks, C., *352, 353*
François, C., *316*
Frangiskakis, J. M., 160, 182, *184, 363, 367*
Franke, Y., *369*
Frazer, K. A., *352*
Frazier, L., 269, 270, 272, 278, *283*
Freeman, B., 126, 127, *145, 322*
Freeman, J., *317*
French, J., *144*
Frenzel, K. E., *185*
Freund, L., 80, *97,* 125, 127, 128, 129, 130,
    134, 135, *144, 145, 146, 147, 148*
Frick, R. W., 171, *184*
Friederici, A. D., 274, *283*
Friedman, E., *144*
Friedman, J. M., 188, *206*
Friedman, S., *48,* 314, *319, 325*
Friedman, W. F., 358, *367*
Fries, N., 249, *283*
Frisch, S., 274, *283*
Fristoe, M., 215, *237*
Friston, K. J., *52, 327*
Frith, C. D., 134, *146, 323*
Frith, U., 117, *118, 149, 323*
Fromkin, W., 279, *283*
Frye, D., 87, *97*

Fryman, J., *326*
Fryns, J., 128, *144*
Fu, Y., *150*
Fulbright, R. K., *325*
Fulker, D. W., 337, 338, *350, 351, 352*
Fulton, L. A., *184*
Fulton, R. S., *184, 367*

G

Gabbay, D., 268, *284*
Gadian, D. G., *52, 327*
Gaffney, G. R., 312, *319*
Gage, F. H., *327*
Gaillard, W. D., 307, *316, 319, 320*
Galaburda, A. M., 41, 42, *49, 50*
Galjaard, H., *150*
Gallaway, C., 191, *203*
Galves, R., *79, 96*
Galvin, P., *325*
Gane, L. W., 123, *150*
Garcia, R. E., 358, *367*
Gardiner, M., *27, 321*
Gardner, H., 291, *319*
Gardner, J., *319*
Garin, N., 313, *319*
Garner, C., 87, *95,* 135, *146*
Garner, P. W., 190, *204*
Garnsey, S. M., *282*
Garofalakis, M., *322*
Garraghty, P. E., *326*
Garrett, M., 265, 266, 270, 278, 279, *283,*
    285
Gartner, G., 190, *203*
Gatenby, C., *325*
Gathercole, S. E., 37, *49*
Gauger, L. M., 41, *49,* 292, *319*
Gayán, J., 334, 335, *354*
Gehring, W. J., 207, *237*
Geissler, R., *368*
Genesee, F., 230, *238*
George, K. P., *317*
Gerard, C., *327*
Gerber, E., 38, *50*
Gershwin, M. E., *321*
Gertner, B. L., 225, *237*
Geschwind, D. H., *26,* 46, 47, *352*
Ghaemi, M., *320*
Ghaziuddin, M., 309, *319*
Ghosh, S., 340, *351*

Giacheti, C., 125, *149*
Giacomini, E., *321*
Giannotti, A., *366*
Gibb, R., 297, *321*
Gibson, E., 272, *283*
Gibson, T., 103, *118, 271, 283*
Giedd, J. N., *325*
Gilbert, J. R., *47, 325, 353*
Gilger, J., *334, 352, 353*
Gill, K. L., 190, *203*
Gillberg, C., 12, *28*, 44, *51, 326, 352*
Gilliam, T. C., *26*, 46, *47, 352*
Gilmore, R., *319*
Gingell, R., 360, *369*
Giro, M., *369*
Glaser, B., *146*
Glucksberg, S., 90, *96*
Godfrey, T. E., 123, *150*
Goedken, R. J., *52, 327*
Gold, B. T., 304, *319*
Goldberg, R., *283, 284*
Goldberg, S., 190, *203*
Goldberg, W. A., 25, *27*
Goldman, R., 215, *237*
Goode, S., 7, 9, *27, 28*, 45, *48, 49*
Goodluck, H., 103, *118*
Goodman, J., 199, *204*
Gopnik, M., 122, *146*, 293, *319*
Gore, J.C., *325*
Gosch, A., 358, 359, *368, 369*
Gottesman, I., *28*, 45, *47, 49, 316*
Gottfried, A. W., 192, *203*
Gottlieb, G., 315, *319*
Goudie, J., *28*
Gould, J., *27, 319*
Grady, C. L., *321*
Graesser, A. C., 90, *96*
Grafman, J., *324*
Graham, P., 126, *150*
Grandin, C. B., *316*
Grant, J., 117, *119, 367, 369*
Graveline, C. J., 304, *320*
Graves, T. A., *184, 367*
Grebe, T., *119, 185, 368*
Green, E. D., *184, 367*
Greenberg, D. A., *27*, 295, *319*, 341, *349, 351*
Greenberg, F., 360, *368*
Greenlaw, R., 135, *148*
Greenough, W. T., 79, *95, 96*, 123, *150*, 297, *319, 321*
Greenwood, C., 192, *205*

Gregg, R. G., *185, 368*
Grela, B. G., 219, *237*
Gresham, F., 62, *75*
Grether, J. K., *323*
Griffith, T., 274, *285*
Grigorenko, E. L., *334, 351*
Grimm, T., 360, *367*
Grodd, W., *326*
Groothusen, J., 274, *284*
Gropen, J., 252, *283, 284*
Gross-Glenn, K., *321*
Gruber, C., 9, *28*
Guasti, M., 109, *118*, 218, 230, *237*
Guillaume, S., *316*
Guilloud-Bataille, M., *352*
Guimaraes, M., 268, *284*
Gullion, C., 127, *147*
Gunn, P., 198, *203*
Gunnar, M., 80, *97, 146*
Guralnik, D., 187, *205*
Gutekunst, C., 123, *145*
Guthrie, D., *145*
Gutowski, N., *184, 367*
Guyán, J., *351*
Gvozdev, A. N., 258, *284*

H

Haas, R. H., *27*, 309, *318, 320*
Habib, M., 292, *320, 323, 324*
Hacker, C. R., *352*
Hadley, P., 33, *49*, 225, *237*
Haegeman, L., 218, *237*, 245, *284*
Hafeman, L., 45, *51*
Hagerman, P. J., 123, *150*
Hagerman, R. J., 77, 79, 82, 85, 88, *96*, 123, 124, 125, 126, 129, 131, 133, 135, *143, 144, 145, 146, 147, 149, 150*, 194, *203*
Hagoort, P., 274, *284*
Hahn, K., *52*
Hahne, A., 274, *283*
Haines, J., *27, 321, 354*
Hakimi, M. A., 365, *367*
Hall, L. M., *150*
Hall, S., 32, *50*
Hallett, M., *324, 327*
Halliwell, J., 269, *282*
Hallmayer, J., *149*
Halpern, C. T., 315, *319*
Halt, A. R., *319*

Haltia, T., *352*
Hamann, C., 248, *284*
Hamburger, H., 104, *118*
Hammill, D., 62, *76*, 215, *237*
Hanauer, A., *148*
Haney, K. R., 38, *51*, 213, 216, 222, *238*
Hansen, R. L., *323*
Hanser, H., *183*
Hanson, D., *144*
Happé, F. G., 22, 26, 27, 32, *49*, *74*, 129, 134, *146*
Harada, M., *320*, *323*
Harcum, E. R., 168, *184*
Hardan, A. Y., 312, *320*
Harding, B., *316*
Harenski, K., *320*
Hargett-Beck, M. Q., 125, *146*
Harper, C., *149*
Harper, J., 127, *148*
Harper, L., 198, *203*
Harris, G., *48*, *49*
Harris, N. S., 313, *320*
Hart, B., 192, 193, *204*, *205*
Hart, L. A., *351*
Hartung, J., *184*, *203*
Haseman, J. K., 337, *351*
Hashimoto, T., 312, *320*
Hastie, T., 135, *145*, *146*
Hatton, D. D., 79, 81, *95*, 124, 125, 127, *143*, *146*, *149*, 194, *203*
Hauser, E. R., *325*, *353*
Hauser-Cram, P., 190, 192, *204*
Havercamp, S., *148*
He, L., *369*
Heavey, L., 44, *47*
Hedrick, D., 173, *184*
Hegerl, U., *52*
Heilman, K. M., 41, *49*, *319*
Heim, A., *327*
Heiss, W. D., 304, *320*
Heitz, D., *148*
Hellgren, L., 44, *51*
Helms, C., *369*
Henderson, J., 269, *283*
Henriksen, L., *322*
Henry, A., 213, *237*
Heo, M., *350*
Hepper, P. G., 309, *320*
Herbert, J., *149*
Herbert, M. R., 42, 43, *49*
Hermon, S., 102, *119*
Hernandez, L., 308, *320*

Herrmann, M., *327*
Hersch, S., 123, *145*
Herscovitch, P., 308, *320*
Hersh, J., 163, *184*
Hershberger, S., 215, 219, 224, 225, *239*
Hertzig, M. E., *150*
Hertz-Pannier, L., 303, *319*, *320*, *321*
Hesketh, L. J., 77, 78, 79, 83, 85, *95*
Hesselink, J. R., *318*, *323*
Hessl, D., 133, *146*
Hetherington, E., 193, *203*
Hewes, A. K., 180, *184*
Hewitt, J. K., *353*
Heysek, P. J., 190, *204*
Hickok, G., 272, *283*
Higgins, E. T., 90, *96*
Higuchi, O., *185*, *369*
Hildebrandt, N., *317*
Hillier, L. W., 159, *184*, 362, *367*
Hinds, D., *149*, *352*
Hinds, S., *318*
Hiramatsu, K., 114, *118*
Hirsch, L. S., *239*
Hirstein, W., 132, *146*
Hisaoka, S., *323*
Hobart, H. H., *185*, *368*, *369*
Hodapp, R., 77, 93, *95*, *96*, 129, *145*
Hodge, S., *48*, *319*, 341, *349*, *351*
Hodgson, S., *52*
Hodsgon, J., *49*
Hoehn-Saric, R., 133, *147*
Hoenkamp, E., 279, *284*
Hoffman, H. J., *326*
Hoffman, L., 222, 223, *238*, *239*
Hofstadler, G., *368*
Hoggart, C. J., 345, *351*
Hoh, J., *352*
Holcomb, P. J., 274, *285*, 307, *320*
Holland, S. K., 307, *320*
Hollander, E., 27, *325*
Hollander, M., *283*, *284*
Hollingworth, A., 269, *282*, *283*
Holmberg, A., 248, *284*
Holowka, S., *326*
Holttum, J. R., 312, *320*
Honda, M., *324*
Honeyman, J. C., *322*
Hoogeveen, A. T., *143*, *150*
Hooper, S., 124, *146*, 190, *204*
Hopkin, R. J., *185*, *368*
Horohov, J. E., 219, *238*
Horvath, S., 346, *351*

Horwitz, B., 293, 314, *320, 321, 327*
Howlin, P., 7, 9, *27, 119*, 296, *321, 322*
Hsu, L., 335, *351, 353*
Hsu, W., *28*
Huang, J., 341, *351, 354*
Huang, W., *27*
Huang, Y., *325*
Huber, W., *327*
Huffman, L. C., 80, *97*
Hughes, C., 309, *321*
Hughes, S., 32, *50*
Hultman, C. M., 295, *321*
Humphreys, R., *326*
Hund-Georgiadis, M., 301, *321*
Hurst, J., 45, *49*, 213, *237, 321, 369*
Hutcheson, H., *27*, 295, *321*
Hutchinson, T. A., 131, *150*
Huttenlocher, P. R., 297, 299, 300, *321*
Huttunen, M., *326*
Hwang, P. A., *320, 326*
Hyman, S. E., *318*
Hyman, S. L., *28*
Hynd, G. W., *322*

I

Ibanez, V., *324*
Idury, R. M., *350*
Ikeo, K., 207, *237*
Ikle, D. N., 124, *150*
Imbert, G., 123, *146*
IMGSAC, 9, 10, *27*, 45, *49, 237*, 343, 349,
         351, 352 (or International Molecular
         Genetic Study of Autism Consor-
         tium)
Ingram, J. L., *324*
Insel, T. R., 349, *354*
Ioannidis, J. P. A., 346, *351*
Irwin, S.A., 79, *96*
Isaacs, E., *327*
Isensee, C., *327*
Iversen, P., 132, *146, 352*

J

Jackendoff, R., 154, *184*
Jackson, A. W., 126, *146*
Jackson, T., 292, *321*
Jacobi, D., 44, *50*

Jacobs, B., 297, *321*
Jacobs, K. B., *350, 352*
Jacobs, W. B., *52*
Jacobson, B., 360, *367*
Jallad, B., *321*
Jambaque, I., *320*
Jänicke, L., *316, 325*
Janisse, J. J., *317*
Jannoun, L., *50*, 237, *323, 352*
Janota, I., *316*
Jarrold, C., 177, 180, *184*
Jelliffe, L. L., *323*
Jenkins, E., 133, *144*
Jenson, W. R., *322*
Jernigan, T. L., 154, *183, 318*
Jessell, T. M., 297, *321*
Jezzard, P., *323*
Jiang, H., *317*
Jin, W., *367*
Johannsen-Horbach, H., *327*
Johnson, A. F., *317*
Johnson, M. C., 190, *203*
Johnson, W., 132, 139, *144*
Johnston, J. R., 59, *75*, 223, *237*
Jonas, D., 247, *284*
Jones, C. J., *369*
Jones, K. L., 358, *367*
Jones, M., 37, 38, 41, *49, 52*, 295, *321*
Jones, V., 309, *321*
Jones, W., 180, *183, 369*
Jonides, J., *320*
Jordan, H., 44, *49*
Jorde, L. B., *322*
Jorgensen, H. S., *323*
Joseph, K. L., 8, 219, *237*
Joseph, R. M., 22, *27*, 40, 43, *48, 51*, 134,
         146, 326
Joshi, P. K., 135, *148*
Judson, R., 343, *351*
Julien, M., 248, *284*
Julier, C., *352*
Just, M. A., *326*

K

Kaback, M. M., 358, *367*
Kabak, B., 269, *285*
Kadish, W., *148*
Kafantaris, V., *144*
Kahrs, J., *326*

Kaiser, A. P., 196, *204*
Kalaydjieva, L., *149*
Kandel, E. R., 297, *321*
Kangawa, K., *185, 369*
Kanner, L., 34, *49*
Kaplan, C. S., 37, *51*
Kaplan, N., *350*
Kaplan, P., *368*
Kaprio, J., *326*
Karadottir, S., *95*
Karapurkar, T., *29*
Karbe, H., *320*
Karmiloff, K., 110, *118*
Karmiloff-Smith, A., 102, 103, 110, 117, *118, 119,* 299, *326,* 363, 365, *367, 369*
Karns, C. M., *27, 318*
Kasari, C., 79, 88, *96,* 131, *148*
Kates, W., 134, 135, *146, 147*
Kathmann, N., *52*
Katz, L. C., 297, *321, 325*
Kau, A. S., 127, *146*
Kaufman, A. S., 103, *119,* 160, *184,* 363, *367*
Kaufman, N. L., 103, *119,* 160, *184,* 363, *367*
Kaufman, P., 135, *146*
Kaufman, W. E., 124, 135, *146, 147*
Kautzer, C. R., *352*
Kawashima, K., *326*
Kay-Raining Bird, E., 83, *95*
Kazanina, N., 254, 256, 257, 261, *284*
Keating, M. T., *184, 185, 366, 367, 368*
Kececioglu, D., 359, *367*
Keetz, A., 196, *204*
Kelly, J. F., 193, *204*
Kemmotsu, N., *322*
Kempen, G., 279, *284, 287*
Kemper, M. B., 129, 135, *147*
Kemper, T. L., 313, *316*
Kempermann, G., *327*
Kempson, R., 268, *284*
Kennedy, D.N., 42, *48, 49, 50,* 317
Kere, J., *352*
Kertesz, A., 304, *319*
Keshavan, M. S., *320*
Kesin, M., *95*
Kessler, J., *320*
Keysor, C., 79, 80, *96,* 125, *147*
Khaledy, M., *326*
Khandjian, E. W., 123, *145, 147*
Kielty, C., *369*
Kigar, D. L., 292, *328*
Kilifarski, M., *27*

Kim, M., 252, 253, *284*
Kimball, J., 278, *284*
Kimberley, K. W., *185, 368*
Kimberling, W. J., *350, 351*
King, J. W., 274, *283*
King, N., *317*
Kiparsky, C., 275, *284*
Kiparsky, P., 275, *284*
Kiriakopoulos, E., *326*
Kittles, R. A., *351*
Kjelgaard, M. M., 22, 26, *28,* 31, 34, 38, 39, 41, *49,* 131, *147*
Kleim, J. A., 297, *321*
Klein, B. P., 102, *119,* 169, 170, 171, 172, *184,* 220, *239, 367*
Klein, W., 258, *284*
Kleinhans, N., *322*
Klein-Tasman, B. P., 102, *119,* 183, *184,* 359, 360, *367, 368*
Kliegl, R., *286*
Klima, E., 117, *119*
Klin, A., 133, *147*
Klinsova, A. Y., 79, *96*
Kluender, R., 274, *284*
Knopik, V. S., *354*
Kobetz, A., *143*
Kochanska, G., 190, *204*
Koeppen-Schomerus, G., *74*
Kolb, B., 297, *321*
Kootz, J., *147*
Kooy, R. F., 123, *147*
Kopnisky, K. L., *318*
Korenberg, J., *366*
Korvatska, E., 295, *321*
Kosslyn, S. M., 298, *324*
Kotthoff, S., 359, *367*
Kraemer, H. C., *149,* 157, *185*
Krageloh-Mann, I., *326*
Krämer, I., 245, 246, *284*
Krauss, M., 190, *204*
Krauss, R., 90, *96*
Krems, J., *286*
Kretz, C., *148*
Kruglyak, L., 336, 337, 338, *351*
Krupa-Kwiatkowski, M., *324*
Kuh, D. L., 188, *204*
Kuhl, D., *150*
Kulynych, J. J., *41, 49*
Kumin, L., 85, 93, *96,* 198, *204*
Kunst, C., *150*
Kuperman, S., *319*
Kurita, H., 25, *28,* 31, *49*

Kuroda, Y., *320*
Kursawe, C., 245, *282*
Kushch, A., 292, *321*
Kustanovich, V., *353*
Kutas, M., 274, *283, 284*

L

Labar, D., *317*
Lacadie, C., *325*
Lachiewicz, A., 123, 127, 129, *147, 150*
Lacro, R., 359, *368, 369*
Laflamme, L., *317*
Lahey, M., *48, 57, 75*
Lai, C., 44, 45, *49, 50,* 213, 237, 293, 296, 321, 323, *352*
Lai, Z., 180, *183, 369*
Laing, N., *327*
Laird, N., *351*
Lalouel, J. M., *352*
Lamb, J., *50, 237,* 323, *350, 352*
Lambrecht, L., *28, 50*
Lampe, M., *147, 150*
Lancaster, J., *148*
Lanchiewicz, A., *145*
Landa, R., 44, *50*
Landau, B., 252, 253, *284*
Lander, E. S., 336, 338, *351*
Landry, S., 32, *50,* 188, 189, 190, 191, 193, *204, 205*
Lane, W. S., *367*
Lange, N. T., *49*
Lantos, P., *316*
Largent, B. L., *318*
Lathrop, G. M., 336, *352*
Lauder, J. M., 314, *321*
Laulhere, T. M., *27*
Lawlor, B. A., *27,* 325
Leadholm, B., 215, *237*
Le Bihan, D., *319, 320, 321*
Leboyer, M., *352*
Leckman, J., 125, 129, *145, 146, 148*
Le Couteur, A., 10, 11, 12, *28, 33,* 44, 45, *47, 49, 50, 148,* 316, *322*
Ledbetter, D. J., *318*
Lee, D. H., *352*
Lee, J., 135, *148, 317*
Leekam, S., *27, 319*
Legate, J., 268, *284*
Lehericy, S., 303, *321*

Lehesjoki, A. E., *352*
Leinsinger, G., *52*
Lender, W., 199, *204*
Lenneberg, E., 230, 234, *237*
Leonard, C. M., 41, *49,* 292, *318, 319, 322*
Leonard, C. O., 358, 360, *367, 368*
Leonard, H., *327*
Leonard, L. B., 38, 40, *47, 50,* 57, 58, *75, 76,* 211, 216, 217, 219, 224, *236, 237,* 251, *285*
Leppert, M. F., *366, 367*
Lerch, J. P., *52*
Leslie, A., 117, *118,* 134, *147*
Lessem, J. M., 338, *352*
LeSueur, L. L., *317*
Levelt, W. J. M., 265, *285*
Leventhal, B. L., *28, 50*
Levinson, M., *368*
Levitas, A., 126, 131, *146, 147*
Levrier, O., *324*
Levy, Y., 102, *119*
Lewis, B., 44, *50*
Lewis, M. H., 126, *144*
Lewy, A., 132, 139, *145*
Li, D. Y., 361, 362, 363, *367*
Li, M., *119, 185, 368*
Liberman, A. M., *325*
Lichtenberger, L., 180, *183*
Lidzba, K., *326*
Lieske, V., 314, *322*
Lightwood, R., 358, *369*
Lillo-Martin, D., 114, *118*
Lin, A., *149*
Lincoln, A. J., *27, 318, 320*
Linenweber, M. R., *324*
Linn, M., 199, *204*
Liu, J., *26, 46, 47,* 349, *352*
Loban, W., *96*
Locascio, J. J., *144*
Loesch, D. Z., 123, *150*
Logan, W. J., *317, 326*
Logue, M., *47, 236,* 316, 341, *350, 354*
Lojkasek, M., 190, *203*
Loker, J., 360, *367, 368*
Lombardino, L. J., 41, *49, 319, 322*
Lombroso, P. J., *326, 327*
Lonnqvist, J., *326*
Lookadoo, R., 79, *96*
Lopez, S. R., 191, *205*
Lord, C., 7, 8, 10, 11, 12, 14, 16, 19, 22, 23, 25, *27, 28, 29,* 31, 33, 34, *50,* 295, *318, 320, 322, 352*

Lotspeich, L. J., *149*, 295, 322, *325*
Lotter, V., *28*
Lou, H. C., 292, *322*
Lovaas, O. I., 195, *204*
Loveland, K., 32, *50*
Lowe, J. B., 358, *369*
Lowery, M. C., 361, *367*
Lu, X., *367*
Lubs, H., *321*
Luevano, L. F., 41, *49*
Lundgren, C., 222, *237*
Lurie, P. R., 358, *368*
Lussnig, E., *321*
Luthert, P., *316*
Lutz, N., 123, *145*
Luyster, R., 24, 25, *28*
Lynch, D. R., *318*
Lyon, G. R., *325*

M

Maccoby, E., 193, *203*
Maccotta, L., *322*
Macdonald, H., 27, *48, 148*
MacDonald, M. C., 271, *285*
MacDonald, W. B., 358, *369*
MacMillan, M., 127, *148*
Macphie, I. L., *352, 353*
Madnick, M. E., 188, *203*
Maestrini, E., *350*
Magano, L. F., 362, *366*
Magnussen, P., *352*
Maisog, J. M., *324*
Makris, N., 42, *48, 49, 317*
Malafosse, A., *143*
Malone, R. P., *144*
Mandel, A., *119, 185, 368*
Mandel, J., 123, *145, 146, 147, 148*
Mandell, V., 359, *369*
Manes, F., *326*
Mangner, T. J., *317, 323*
Mankoski, R. E., 9, 27, *29, 296, 319*
Mao, J., *322*
Maravilla, K. R., *325*
Marchant, D., *143*
Marchione, K. E., *325*
Marchman, V. A., 40, *50, 219, 237, 326*
Marckmann, G., *326*
Marcus, G. F., 207, 214, 235, *237*
Marfo, K., 191, *204*

Mari, A., *366*
Mariette, E., 135, *144*
Marinelli, B., 132, *147*
Marion, R. W., 360, *366*
Marjoribanks, C., *352*
Marks, S., 102, *118*, 154, *183*, 358, *366*
Marlow, A. J., *350*
Marquis, J., 215, 219, 225, *239*
Marsault, C., *321*
Martin, E. R., *350*
Martin, J. J., *143*
Martinez, M., *352*
Mason-Brothers, A., 295, *322*
Massa, H., *367*
Masure, M. -C., *317*
Mathern, G. W., *318*
Mathias, C. J., 136, *145*
Matteis, M., *325*
Matthews, P. M., *317*
Matus, I., 131, *147*
Maurer, R. G., *326*
Mawhood, L., 9, *27, 32, 48, 296, 321, 322*
May, R., 275, *285*
Mayhew, L., 125, *143*
Maziade, M., *29*
Maziere, B., *317*
Mazoyer, B., *326, 327*
Mazziotta, J. C., *318*
Mazzocco, M. M., 77, 79, 80, *96*, 124, 125, 134, 135, 136, *147*, 201, *204*
McBogg, P., 131, *147*
McBride, P. A., *150*
McCague, P., *149*
McCarthy, D., 169, *184*
McCathren, R. B., 189, *204*
McClain, C., *325*
McCracken, J. T., *352, 353*
McCrory, E., *323*
McDaniel, D., 104, *119*
McDonald, J. L., 38, *50, 219, 238*
McDonough, D. P., *352*
McElree, B., 274, *285*
McEvoy, R., 32, *50*
McGee, G. G., 16, *28*
McGinnis, R. E., *353*
McGough, J. J., *352, 353*
McGrath, J., *147*
McGrath, L., 29, 41, *48*
McGuckian, M., 213, *237*
McGuffin, P., *324*
McIntosh, D., *147*
McKee, C., 104, *119*, 256, *283*

McKeigue, P. M., *351*
McKeown, P., *368*
McKhann, G., *317*
McKinley, M., *148*
McKusick, V. A., 142, *144*
McLeod, D. R., 133, *147*
McMahon, W. M., *28, 149, 322*
McNew, S., *74*
McSweeny, J. L., 213, *239*
Meaburn, E., 45, *50*, 213, *237*
Mecham, R. P., *367*
Mehta, P., 66, *75*
Meisenzahl, E. M., *52*
Mellet, E., *326*
Meltzoff, A. N., 133, *145*
Melvold, J., 275, *285*
Mencl, W. E., *325*
Meng, X., 362, *367*
Menold, M., *47*, 325, *353*
Merenstein, S. A., 124, 125, 127, 133, *147*
Merette, C., *29*
Merikangas, K., 333, 338, *353*
Merricks, M., *50, 237, 323, 352*
Merrill, E. C., 79, *96*
Merritt, D. A., 358, *368*
Mervis, C. B., 101, 102, 103, *119*, 155, 157,
   158, 159, 161, 163, 168, 169, 170, 171,
   172, 175, 183, *184, 185*, 220, *239*, 359,
   360, 363, 365, *367, 368, 369*
Mesibov, G., 125, 127, 128, *143*, 194, *203*
Mesulam, M. M., 135, *147*
Metcalfe, K., 361, *367, 368, 369*
Meyer, J. W., 42, *48*
Meyer, M. S., *351*
Meyer, W. A., 127, *146*
Meyer-Viol, W., 268, *284*
Michel, C., *317*
Middleton, F. A., 313, *322*
Miezin, F. M., 308, *322*
Miglioretti, D., *317*
Mikkelsen, E., *148*
Mikulis, D. J., *320, 326*
Miller, C., 38, *50, 76*, 190, *204*
Miller, G., 279, *285*
Miller, J., 40, *50*, 215, *237*
Miller, L., 125, 133, *147*
Miller, M., *326*
Miller, S., *239*
Miller-Loncar, C. L., 189, 190, *204*
Mills, D. L., 307, *322, 323*
Mills, K. K., 90, *96*
Mills, P. E., 57, *74*

Milward, D., 268, *285*
Minahan, R., *317*
Minassian, S. L., *352, 353*
Minchin, S., *319*
Minshew, N., *28, 320*
Mirrett, P., 124, 125, 127, 131, *149*
Mishkin, M., *52*, 301, *327*
Miyazaki, M., *320*
Mizuno, K., *185, 369*
Mo, A., *322*
Mobley, L. A., 274, *285*
Moccia, G., *318*
Moller, H. -J., *52*
Molliver, M. E., *318*
Monaco, A., 44, 45, *49, 50*, 213, *237, 319*,
   321, 323, 350, 352, 353
Montalbetti, M., 277, *285*
Montgomery, J. W., 37, *50, 316*
Moore, C. A., *185*, 360, *367, 368*
Moraine, C., *143*
Mori, K., *323*
Morin, S., *145*
Morrier, M. J., 16, *28*
Morris, C. A., 101, *119*, 159, 160, 163, 164,
   182, *184, 185*, 358, 360, 361, 362, 363,
   365, *366, 367, 368, 369*
Morris, E. D., 308, *322*
Morris, K., *52*
Morris, M. K., *322*
Morris, R., *75, 317*
Morton, C. T., 299, *322*
Morton, N. E., 336, *352*
Moses, P., *27, 318*
Mostofsky, S. H., 135, 136, *147*
Mott, S. H., *319, 320*
Mujumder, P. P., *351*
Mullen, E., 9, *28*, 161, *185*
Müller, R. -A., 299, 302, 303, 304, 305, 309,
   310, 312, 314, *322, 323, 324*
Müller, S., *327*
Müller-Myhsok, B., 344, *352*
Mundy, P., 131, *148*
Munir, F., 124, 135, *145, 148*
Munnich, A., *369*
Munson, J. A., *323, 325*
Münte, T. F., 301, *323*
Murakami, J. W., 312, *323*
Murakawa, K., *320*
Murphy, C., *29*
Murphy, M. M., 78, 82, 85, *95, 96*
Murray, J., 45, *50, 238, 352*
Muthen, B. O., 68, *75*

Muthen, L. K., 68, *75*
Music, R. F., *322*
Muzik, O., *317, 322, 323*
Myers, R. M., *149, 325, 353*

N

Nace, K., *324*
Nadeau, S. E., 293, *323*
Nadel, L., 188, *203*
Naeem, L., *47*
Nagata, K., *185, 369*
Nagels, G., *143, 147*
Nakagawa, Y., 298, *323*
Nakayama, H., *323*
Nanclares, V., *326*
Narr, K. L., *326*
Nass, R., *326*
Nation, J., 54, 55, *74*
National Research Council and Institute of Medicine, 188, *205*
Neebe, E., 125, *149*, 190, *204*
Neelin, P., *52*
Neiderhiser, J. M., 121, *148*, 188, 194, 195, *205*
Neitzel, K., *147*
Nelson, D., 123, 124, *143, 146, 150*
Nelson, K., 59, *75*, 314, *323*
Nelson, S. F., *352, 353*
Netski, D., *369*
Neufeldt, V., 187, *205*
Neville, H., 274, *285*, 301, 307, *320, 322, 323*
Newbury, D., 45, 46, *50*, 213, 214, *237*, 296, *323*, 349, *352*
Newcomer, P. L., 215, *238*
Nguyen, B. T., *352*
Nguyen, L., *149*
Nicholas, P., *149*
Nicol, J., 269, *285*
Nicoll, D., *320*
Ninio, A., 86, *96*
Nishida, E., *185, 369*
Nishimura, C., 45, *50, 238, 352*
Nishitani, H., *323*
Nkanga-Ngila, B., *326*
Noble, M., *184, 367*
Noll, D., *320*
Noonan, J., 360, *366, 368*
Nopola-Hemmi, J., 345, *352*

Norbury, C. F., 33, *47*, 56, *74*, 213, *238*
Nordin, V., 12, *28, 326*
Norris, M. C., *352*
North, T., 37, 44, *47, 48, 350*
Noth, J., *327*
Nouri, N., *149*
Novelli, G., *366*
Ntzani, E. E., *351*
Nurmi, E. L., *326*
Nye, J., *326*
Nyholt, D. R., *352*

O

Oberle, I., 123, *148*
O'Brien, A., *95*
O'Brien, E., 45, *50*, 214, *237, 349, 352*
O'Brien, M., 45, *51, 239*
O'Connell, J. R., 336, *352*
O'Connor, R., *145*
O'Connor, W., 360, *368*
Oda, S., *326*
Odelberg, S., *184, 367*
Oerlemans, F., *143*
Oetting, J. B., 38, *50*, 219, *238*
Ogdie, M. N., 349, *352, 353*
Ohashi, K., *185, 369*
Ohkawa, R., *316*
Okada, T., *324*
O'Leary, D. D., 298, 313, *323, 325*
Olitsky, S. E., 358, *369*
Ollinger, J. M., *322*
Olsen, T. S., *323*
Olson, J. M., 334, *350*
Olson, R. K., 334, *351, 352, 354*
Ong, B., 27, *319*
Oostra, B., 79, *96*, 123, *143, 147, 148, 150*
Oppermann, H. C., 358, *368*
Ort, S., *145, 146*
Osann, K., *27*
Osborne, L., 101, *119*, 159, *185*, 358, 362, *366, 368, 369*
Osofsky, J., 190, 191, *205*
Osterhout, L., 274, *285*
Osterling, J., 25, *28, 29*, 133, *145*, 309, *323*
Otsubo, H., *326*
Otsuka, H., 312, *323*
Ott, J., 337, 345, *352, 353*
Overall, J. E., *144*
Owen, M. J., *324*

Ozonoff, S., 134, *148*

P

Pablos, L., 269, *285*
Padmanabhan, S., *323*
Palferman, S., 44, *47*
Pallas, S. L., 298, *323, 326, 327*
Palmar, C. G., 358, *368*
Palmer, L. J., 339, *352*
Palmer, P., 44, *50,* 127, *148*
Pani, J. R., 363, *368*
Pankau, R., 358, 359, *368, 369*
Pantev, C., *319*
Paperna, T., *369*
Papero, P. H., *320*
Paradis, J., 230, *238*
Parano, E., *352*
Parker, D. E., 127, *144*
Parra, E. J., *351*
Parsons, C. L., 219, *237*
Parsons, L. M., 136, *148*
Parsons, T., 258, *285*
Partsch, C. -J., 358, 359, *368, 369*
Pascual-Leone, A., *324*
Passingham, R. E., *52,* 327
Paterson, S., 168, *185*
Patil, N., 343, *352*
Paul, R., 31, 32, 34, *50,* 125, *148,* 216, *238*
Paulesu, E., 293, *323*
Pauls, D. L., *351, 352*
Paus, T., *52*
Pavetto, M., *95*
Pavonne, P., *352*
Paylor, R., *350*
Pearlmuter, N. J., 271, *283, 285*
Pedersen, P. M., 301, *323*
Pelphrey, K., *318*
Pembrey, M. E., 45, *49,* 319
Penet, C., *352*
Penke, M., 245, *282*
Pennington, B. F., 129, 135, *144, 147,* 297, 298, 315, *324,* 334, *350, 351, 352, 353, 354*
Peoples, R., 362, *369*
Pepin, K. H., *184,* 367
Perez-Jurado, L. A., 362, *366, 369*
Pericak-Vance, M., *47,* 325, *353*
Perner, J., 86, *96*
Perrone, P., 41, *49*
Peters, A., 59, *75*

Petersen, B. P., *149*
Petersen, K., 358, *369*
Petersen, P. B., *322*
Petersen, S. E., *322, 324*
Pethick, S., *184, 203*
Petrella, J. R., *316*
Petry, E. L., 358, *368*
Pettit, G. S., 190, *203*
Pezzini, G., 103, *119*
Pfadt, A., 133, *144*
Pfeifer, E., 274, *283*
Phelps, M. E., 299, *318*
Philippe, A., 349, *352*
Phillips, C., 177, 180, *184,* 243, 247, 249, 250, 252, 253, 254, 256, 257, 261, 265, 266, 268, 269, 271, 277, 280, *282, 284, 285*
Phillips, N. E., *320*
Phillips, T. M., *323*
Phillips, W., 3, *47*
Piattelli-Palmarini, M., 291, *324*
Pickering, K., 19, *29*
Pickering, M., 269, *287*
Pickles, A., 7, 12, 19, *27, 28, 29,* 45, *48, 49, 50,* 137, *148*
Pierce, K., 27, 310, 313, *318, 322, 324*
Pieretti, M., *150*
Pietila, J., *52,* 327, *354*
Pietz, J., 294, *317*
Pighetti, M., *318*
Pingree, C., *149,* 322
Pinker, S., 46, *50,* 154, *185,* 252, *283, 284, 286,* 292, 293, 296, *324*
Pitts, T., *149*
Piven, J., *27,* 44, *50, 52,* 127, 133, 136, *143, 148,* 312, *318, 324, 326, 327,* 334, *351, 354*
Pizzo, S., *27,* 318
Pizzuti, A., *150*
Plante, E., 42, *50,* 57, 75, 122, *148,* 213, *238,* 292, *318, 320, 321, 324*
Plebst, C., *326*
Pliner, C., 7, *28*
Plomin, R., 45, *50,* 74, 194, 198, *205,* 213, *237, 324*
Plunkett, K., *284*
Pober, B., *119, 185,* 358, 359, *368, 369*
Poeppel, D., 245, 250, *286*
Polakoff, S., *148*
Pollard, C., 264, *286*
Porter, D., 135, *144*
Posse, S., *319*
Poutanen, V. P., *326*

Powell, C., *47*
Power, C., 188, *204*
Prather, E., 173, *184*
Prather, P., *119*
Press, G., *318, 323*
Preuss, U. W., *52*
Price, C. J., *327*
Price, T. S., *74*
Prinster, A., *323*
Prior, J., 44, *49*
Prior, M., 27, 127, *148*, 309, *319, 321*
Pritchett, B. L., 272, *286*
Prizant, B. M., 62, *76*, 131, *150*
Pröschel, C., *184, 367*
Pueschel, S. M., 79, 89, *96*
Pugh, K. R., *325*
Pulsifer, M., *317*
Purcell, S., *353*
Purnell, B., 207, *238*
Putnam, S., *29*
Pyck, K., 128, *144*

Q

Quartz, S. R., 297, *324*
Quinton, D., 190, *205*
Qumsiyeh, M., *47*

R

Raaschou, H. O., *323*
Rabbin, B., 269, *285*
Rabin, M., *321*
Rabinowitz, D., 346, *353*
Rack, J., *352*
Rademacher, J., 42, *50*
Raelpe-Bonilla, T., *239*
Raguthu, S., *144*
Raiford, K. L., *325, 353*
Rakic, P., 297, *324*
Ramachandran, V. S., 132, *146*
Rancurel, G., *316*
Rapcsak, S., 42, *50, 148, 324*
Rapin, I., 33, 34, 36, *47, 51*, 55, *75*, 309, *324*
Rapoport, J. L., 127, *149*
Rapoport, S. I., *321*
Rashotte, C., 39, *52*
Raskind, W. H., 335, *351, 353*
Rasmussen, S. A., 188, *206*

Rastam, M., *352*
Ratey, J. J., 132, 139, *148*
Rauch, A., *368*
Rauschecker, J. P., *237, 323*
Ravan, S., *47, 325, 353*
Raynaud, C., *317*
Rayner, K., 269, *283*
Read, A. P., *367, 368, 369*
Realmuto, G. R., *319*
Reardon, W., *368, 369*
Records, N. L., 212, *240*
Redmond, S. M., 215, 219, 222, 223, 225, 226, *238, 239*
Reeve-Daly, M. P., *351*
Reich, T., *351*
Reichert, J., *27*
Reider, E. E., 127, *146*
Reilly, J., *184, 203*
Reinberg, J., *119*
Reiner, O., *150*
Reis, M., 249, *286*
Reiss, A. L., 80, 81, *95, 97*, 121, 124, 125, 127, 128, 129, 130, 134, 135, *144, 145, 146, 147, 148*, 188, 358, *369*
Reiss, D., 194, 195, *205*
Relucio, K. I., *316*
Remy, P., *316*
Renaux-Kieffer, V., *320*
Rescorla, L., 216, 219, *238*
Reuland, E., 256, *282*
Revelle, W., 53, *75*
Reynell, J., 9, *28*
Reyniers, E., *143, 147*
Reynolds, J. D., 358, *369*
Reznick, J. S., *184*
Reznick, S., *203*
Rhoades, R. W., *317, 322*
Rice, C., 29, 359, *369*
Rice, K. J., 220, 222, 223, *239*
Rice, M. L., 38, 39, 40, *49, 50*, 59, *75, 76*, 208, 210, 212, 213, 215, 216, 217, 218, 219, 220, 221, 222, 223, 224, 225, 226, 227, 228, 229, 230, 235, 237, *238, 239*, 251, *286, 287*
Richards, B. J., 191, *203*
Richards, N., 268, *286*
Richards, S., *150*
Richards, T., *48, 318, 319*
Richardson, A. J., *350*
Richieri-Costa, A., 125, *149*
Richler, J., *28*
Richman, W. A., *239*

Richmond, E. K., 95
Riddle, J. E., 124, 147
Riggins, G., 150
Rijntjes, M., 327
Rilea, S., 79, 96
Rimland, B., 126, 131, 146, 147
Rinaldi, J., 133, 145
Rinehart, N. J., 309, 324
Ring, H. A., 134, 143, 149
Rios, P., 27, 48
Risch, N., 137, 149, 325, 333, 338, 344, 348, 350, 353
Risi, S., 28, 50
Risley, T., 192, 193, 204
Risucci, D., 57, 76
Ritvo, E., 145, 322
Rivera, N., 362, 366
Rizzi, L., 250, 286
Roberts, J., 39, 51, 219, 220, 238, 239
Roberts, J. E., 124, 125, 127, 131, 132, 140, 143, 149
Roberts, J. P., 124, 146
Robertson, S., 28, 45, 49
Robichon, F., 292, 324
Robinson, B. F., 102, 119, 155, 168, 169, 170, 172, 175, 183, 184, 359, 360, 363, 367, 368
Robinson, L. K., 369
Rocha, A., 125, 149
Rockstroh, B., 319
Rodgers, B., 188, 204
Rodier, P. M., 295, 324
Roe, A. W., 326
Roeper, T., 212, 239, 251, 286
Rogers, S. J., 28, 82, 96, 125, 126, 128, 139, 149
Rogers, T., 149
Rohrbacher, B., 230, 236, 244, 251, 286, 287
Rosen, B. R., 317
Rosen, G. D., 41, 49
Rosen, H. J., 304, 324
Rosenbloom, L., 33, 48
Rosen-Sheidley, B., 295, 319
Rosin, M., 83, 96
Ross, R., 213, 239
Rothermel, R., 317, 322, 323
Rougetet, R., 321
Rousseau, F., 145, 147, 148
Rouyer, J., 123, 145
Rowe, M., 102, 119, 163, 184, 358, 359, 368
Rowe, R. D., 367
Roy, E., 317

Roy, M. A., 29
Rozien, N. J., 77, 78, 96
Rubinstein, P., 345, 350
Rucka, A. K., 368
Rumsey, J. M., 127, 134, 149, 293, 320, 321, 324
Ruskin, E., 131, 149, 153, 155, 168, 169, 185
Rusucci, E., 76
Rutka, J. T., 326
Rutter, M., 7, 9, 10, 11, 12, 16, 27, 28, 32, 33, 34, 44, 45, 47, 48, 49, 50, 51, 126, 148, 149, 188, 190, 194, 205, 295, 316, 321, 322, 324

S

Sabaratnam, M., 136, 149
Sabbadini, L., 103, 119
Sabini, M., 366
Sabo, H., 102, 118, 154, 183, 358, 366
Saccuman, C., 307, 324
Sadato, N., 301, 324
Sadler, L., 358, 360, 368, 369
Sag, I., 264, 286
Saitoh, O., 318
Saliba, K., 324
Salisbury, B., 351
Salmon, B., 149
Sameroff, A. J., 121, 149, 191, 194, 205
Sampson, G., 291, 324
Samson, S., 321
Samson, Y., 316
Sanders, R. S., 320
Sanes, J. N., 297, 321
Sanes, J. R., 321
Santangelo, N., 318
Santangelo, S., 27, 44, 50, 51, 137, 149, 321
Santelmann, L., 245, 286
Sarda, P., 143
Saussure, F., 291, 324
Sceery, W. R., 127, 149
Schäffer, A. A., 350
Schall, M., 321
Schatschneider, C., 66, 75
Scheibel, A. B., 321
Schellenberg, G., 48
Scherer, S. W., 119, 185, 368
Schiff, S. J., 320
Schlaggar, B. L., 298, 323, 325
Schlaug, G., 301, 316, 325
Schleicher, A., 316

Schlenker, P., *286*
Schlesewsky, M., 272, *286*
Schmahmann, J. D., 313, *325*
Schmeidler, J., *325*
Schmithorst, V. J., *320*
Schmitt, J. E., *369*
Schneider, C., *183*
Schneider, J., *351*
Schneppenheim, R., *369*
Schopler, E., 7, *28, 29,* 126, *149*
Schreibman, L., *27, 318, 320*
Schroth, P., *145*
Schumacher, K., 38, *49*
Schütze, C. T., 247, 251, 272, 277, *283, 286,*
    287
Schwartz, D., *322*
Schwartz, S. E., 83, *95*
Schwarz, E. R., *321*
Scriver, C. R., 294, *325*
Sears, L., 133, *143*
Secord, W., 62, *76,* 173, *185*
Seidenberg, M. S., 271, *285*
Sejnowski, T. J., 297, *324*
Semel, E., 62, *76,* 173, 175, *185*
Serratrice, L., 219, *237*
Seung, H. -K., 83, *95*
Seymour, H. N., 212, *239*
Shade, R., *148*
Shah, A., *149*
Shahbazian, M. D., 294, *325*
Shaked, M., 87, *97*
Sham, P. C., 339, 346, *353*
Shankweiler, D. P., *325*
Shao, Y., 295, *325,* 334, *353*
Shapiro, J., 191, *205*
Shatz, C. J., 297, *321*
Shaw, D. W., *319, 325*
Shaywitz, B. A., *237,* 292, 293, *325*
Shaywitz, S. E., *247, 325*
Sheehan, J. B., *352*
Sheffield, V., *27, 52, 327, 354*
Shen, N., *352*
Sherman, G. F., 41, *49*
Sherman, S., 79, *96,* 122, *145*
Shiekhattar, R., *367*
Shields, J., 33, *51*
Shonkoff, J., 190, *204*
Shore, C., 59, *74, 75*
Short, K., 84, *94*
Short-Meyerson, K., 78, *95*
Shriberg, L. D., 213, *239*
Shriver, M. D., *351*

Shulman, C., 19, 22, *28*
Shuster, A., *351*
Shyu, V., *147*
Sibomana, M., *317*
Siegel, B., 7, *28,* 157, *185*
Sigman, M., *28,* 131, 132, *145, 148, 149,*
    153, 155, 168, 169, *185*
Sigurjónsdottir, S., 248, *286*
Silverman, J. M., *27,* 295, *325*
Silverman, W., 130, *150*
Silvestrini, M., 304, *325*
Sim, C. H., *148*
Simon, E. W., 133, *149*
Simonoff, E., *47,* 316
Simpson, A., 33, *51*
Sims, K., *119*
Sittler, A., *143*
Siu, V., *368*
Skinner, B. F., 291, *325*
Skinner, M., 79, 81, *95,* 124, 125, 127, *143,*
    146, 149, 194, *203*
Skudlarski, P., *325*
SLI Consortium, 213, 214, *239,* 296, *325,*
    343, 349, *353*
Slonims, V., *50, 237, 323, 352*
Smalley, S. L., 334, 349, *352, 353*
Smith, C. J., *27, 325*
Smith, C. L., 190, *203*
Smith, D. W., 358, *367*
Smith, E., *240*
Smith, J. L., 39, *48*
Smith, K. E., 188, 189, 190, 193, *204, 205*
Smith, S. A., *352*
Smith, S. D., 334, *350, 351, 352, 353, 354*
Smoot, L., *368*
Snedeker, J., 104, *119*
Snow, C. E., 86, *96,* 192, *205*
Snow, M. E., *150*
Snowling, J., 37, *51*
Snyder, A. Z., *324*
Snyder, L., *74*
Snyder, S. H., *318*
Snyder, W., 245, 246, *282*
Sobesky, W. E., 124, *147*
Sokolov, J. L., 192, *205*
Solomon, C., 190, *206*
Solomonica-Levi, D., 87, *97*
Sommer, A., *185, 368*
Sorensen, L. K., *367*
Sorgi, P., *148*
Sowinski, J., *320*
Spallone, P., *185, 367, 368, 369*

Sparen, P., *321*
Sparks, B. F., 314, *325*
Sparrow, S., 9, *29*, *146*
Speed, W. C., *351*
Speicher, D. W., *367*
Spence, M. A., *27*, *28*, *353*
Spencer, E. K., *144*
Spencer, M. J., *322*
Spielman, R. S., 345, *353*
Spiker, D., *149*, 189, *205*, 295, *325*
Spinelli, M., 125, *149*
Spiridigliozzi, G., 127, *145*, 147
Splitt, M., *369*
Sponheim, E., *352*
Sridhar, S. N., 107, *119*
Staab, E. V., *322*
Stackhouse, T., *147*
Standertskjold-Nordenstam, C. G., *326*
Stanfield, B. B., *316*
Stanyon, C. A., *183*
Stapleton, T., 303, *326*, 358, *369*
Stark, R., 57, *75*
Starkstein, S. E., 314, *326*
Stary, J. M., *319*
Staudt, M., 303, *326*
Steedman, M., 268, *286*
Steeg, C. N., 360, *366*
Steele, S., *48*
Steffenburg, S., 44, *51*
Stein, J. F., *350*
Steinbach, M., 247, *286*
Steinberg, L., 193, *203*
Steinmetz, H., *316*, *325*
Stenzel, P., *367*
Stephany, U., 244, *286*
Stephens, J. C., *351*
Stern, D., *352*
Sternes, K., *367*
St. George, M., 180, *183*
Stiles, J., *326*
Stock, A. D., *185*, 360, 362, 363, *367*, *368*, *369*
Stokowski, R. P., *352*
Stollwerck, L., 122, *150*, 213, *240*
Stone, J. L., *353*
Storm, K., *147*
Storoschuk, S., *28*
Stothard, S. E., 37, *51*
Stott, C., *50*, 237, *323*
Stott, M., *352*
Stowe, L. A., 269, *286*
Straus, E., *369*
Strauss-Swan, R., *27*

Strawsburg, R. H., *320*
Strayer, D. L., 134, *148*
Strick, P. L., 313, *322*
Stromland, K., 295, *326*
Stromswold, K., 292, *326*
Stuebing, K. K., *237*
Sturt, P., 269, *286*, *287*
Sudhalter, V., 125, 130, 131, 133, 134, 138, *144*, *149*, *150*
Sullivan, K., 32, *51*, 87, 88, *97*, 117, *119*, 125, *146*
Sun, F., *354*
Sur, M., 298, *326*, *327*
Sutcliffe, J. S., *150*, 295, *321*, *326*
Swank, P. R., 188, 189, 190, 193, *204*, *205*
Sweatt, J. D., *350*
Swiderski, R. E., *354*
Swift, E., 83, *96*
Swinburn, K., *327*
Swinney, D., *119*, 269, 274, *285*
Swisher, L., 42, *50*, *148*, *324*
Switala, A. E., *317*
Symons, F. S., 127, *144*
Syrota, A., *317*
Szatmari, P., 12, *29*, 295, *321*
Szekely, A. M., 358, *369*

T

Tabor, H. K., 344, 347, *353*
Tadevosyan-Leyfer, O., 11, *29*
Tager-Flusberg, H., 8, 22, 26, *27*, *28*, *29*, 31, 32, 34, 37, 38, 39, 40, 41, 43, *48*, *49*, *50*, *51*, 58, *75*, 86, 87, 88, *95*, *96*, *97*, 117, *119*, 127, 131, 138, *147*, *150*, 213, 220, *236*, *239*, 295, *326*
Taipale, M., *352*
Takeoka, M., *49*
Tallal, P., *47*, 57, *75*, 122, *150*, 213, 214, *236*, *239*, *316*, *350*
Tamanini, F., 123, *150*
Tamis-LeMonda, C. S., 190, *205*
Tanenhaus, M. K., *282*
Tanoue, Y., 295, *326*
Tassabehji, M., 361, *367*, *368*, *369*
Tassone, F., 79, *95*, 123, 124, *143*, *147*, *150*, 194, *203*
Taub, E., *319*
Tavakolian, S., 103, *118*
Tayama, M., *320*

Taylor, A., 19, 26, *29, 147*
Taylor, A. K., 79, *95,* 123, 124, 135, *143, 144, 147, 150,* 194, *203*
Taylor, D. G., *367*
Taylor, J., *52*
Teele, R. L., 359, *369*
Teitelbaum, O., 309, *326*
Teitelbaum, P., *326*
Temple, C., 102, *118*
Terwilliger, J. D., 345, *353*
Thal, D., *184, 203,* 307, *326*
Thelen, E., 304, *318*
Theodore, W. H., *319, 320*
Thibodeau, A., *147*
Thiel, A., *320*
Thivierge, J., *29*
Thomas, C., 304, *326*
Thomas, D. J., *352*
Thomas, I. T., 360, *368*
Thomas, M., *326*
Thompson, E. M., *327*
Thompson, L., 44, *50, 150*
Thompson, M., 190, 191, *205*
Thompson, P. M., 298, *326*
Thomson, G., 338, *353*
Thomson, J. B., *318, 351, 353*
Thong, M. K., *327*
Thornton, R., 101, 109, 111, *118, 119,* 256, 260, *283*
Thorpe, D., *149*
Thulborn, K. R., 304, *326*
Tian, B., *327*
Tigue, Z. D., *27, 318*
Tiller, G. E., *369*
Tisdale, B., *324*
Tobin, A., 173, *184*
Todd, E. P., *368*
Todd, J., 190, *205*
Toga, A. W., *326*
Toland, A. E., 361, 363, *367*
Tomasello, M., 190, *205*
Tomblin, J. B., 37, 44, 45, *50, 51, 52,* 55, 57, 58, 59, 60, 73, *76,* 212, 213, 214, 225, 228, *236, 238, 239, 240,* 293, *326,* 334, *352, 353*
Tonge, B. J., *324*
Tonick, I., *145*
Tordjman, S., 132, 139, *150*
Torgesen, J., 39, *52*
Townsend, D., 265, 268, 270, 277, 280, *287*
Townsend, J., *150,* 313, *318, 320, 326*
Tran, H. X., 124, *147*

Trask, B. J., *367*
Trauner, D., *326*
Traxler, M., 269, *287*
Tremblay, S., *147*
Tremblay-Leveau, H., 135, *144*
Trikalinos, T. A., *351*
Troisis, E., *325*
Trulson, M. O., *352*
Tsai, L. Y., *319*
Tseng, J. E., 135, *148*
Tsui, L. C., *119, 185, 368*
Tunali, B., 32, *50*
Turk, J., 87, *95,* 126, 133, 135, *146, 150*
Turner, M., 127, *150*
Turner, N. D., *119*
Turner, R., *323*
Tuttle, R., *323*
Tuzler, G., *368*
Tyler, L. K., *119*
Tzourio, N., 292, *326, 327*

U

Udwin, O., *119*
Urban, Z., 362, *369*

V

Vainikka, A., 244, *287*
Vance, J., 42, 47, *325*
Vance, R., *50, 148, 324*
Van de Moortele, P. F., *320*
van Den Berghe, H., 128, *144*
van der Feest, S., 260, *287*
Van de Water, J., *321*
van der Lely, H. K. J., 122, *150, 213, 234, 240*
Van Eeckhout, P., *316*
van Erp, T., *326*
van Hout, A., 260, *287*
Van Maldergem, L., *352*
van Ommen, G., *150*
van Praag, H., 297, *327*
Van Unen, L., *150*
Van Velzen, D., *143*
Vanderhelm, R., *143*
Vargha-Khadem, F., 45, *49, 52,* 213, *237,* 293, 301, *319, 321, 327*
Varley, R., 33, *51*
Varlokosta, S., 244, *287*
Vazquez, S., *326*

Veenstra-Vanderweele, J., 295, *327*
Vellet, S., 188, *204*
Venter, A., 7, 26, *29*
Verdaasdonk, K. R., 360, *369*
Verheij, C., *143*
Verkerk, A., *150*
Vermeer, S., *149*
Vermey, M., *143*
Vetter, D., 83, *96*
Vicari, S., 103, *119*, 307, *327*
Victoria, M., *150*
Vieland, V., 27, 47, *52*, 236, 316, *327*, 338, 341, 347, *350, 351, 353, 354*
Vietze, P. M., 133, *144*
Vignolo, L. A., 41, *49*
Vikingstad, E. M., *317*
Vikner, S., 248, 250, *287*
Vining, E., *317*
Vinnitskaya, I., 259, *287*
Vladar, K., 41, *49*
Voeller, K. K. S., *322*
Vogt, J., 359, *367*
Voice, K., *119*
Volkmar, F., 28, 126, *145*
Volterra, V., 102, 103, *119*
Von Arnim, G., 358, *369*
Von Cramon, D. Y., 301, *321*
von Melchner, L., 299, *327*
von Wendt, L., *325*
Vosse, T., 279, *287*
Vouloumanos, A., 306, *327*
Voutilainen, A., *352*
Vrancic, D., *326*
Vukicevic, J., 157, *185*
Vyas, K. R., *352*

W

Wada, A., *185, 369*
Wagner, R., 39, *52*
Wagner-McPherson, C., *184, 367*
Wake, L., *145*
Wakefield, A. J., 295, *327*
Walker, D., 191, 192, *205*
Wallace, G., 62, *76*
Wallesch, C. W., 293, *327*
Wang, E., 358, *369*
Wang, J. Y., 160, *185*
Wang, K., *27*
Wang, P. P., 154, *183, 368*
Wang, Y., *369*

Warburton, E., 304, *327*
Warburton, P., 45, *52*
Warfield, M., 190, *204*
Warren, S., 123, *145, 150*, 189, 191, 192, 196, 197, 198, 199, 200, *204, 205, 206*
Warren, S. T., *146*
Waserman, G. A., 190, *206*
Warsofsky, I. S., 135, *147*
Wassink, T., 46, *52*, 296, *327, 349, 354*
Waterhouse, L., *75*
Waterman, M. S., *354*
Waters, P. J., 294, *325*
Watkins, K. E., 41, 42, 45, 49, *52*, 293, 319, *327*
Watson, M., 125, *148*
Weaving, L. S., 294, *327*
Webb, S., *48*
Weber Byars, A., *320*
Wechsler, D., 64, *76*, 157, *185*
Weeks, D. E., 336, *350, 352*
Weeks, R., 301, *327*
Wehner, D. E., 82, *96*
Wehner, E. A., 125, *149*
Weiler, I. J., 79, *95, 96*, 123, *150*
Weiller, C., 304, *327*
Weinberg, A., 271, *282*
Weinberger, D. R., 41, *49*
Weinbruch, C., *319*
Weinstein, S., *320*
Weismer, S. E., 37, 38, 40, 49, *50, 52, 76*, 219, *237*
Weissenborn, J., 250, *287*
Weissman, M. D., *95*
Welch, K. M., *317*
Welham, M., 27, *319*
Wellington, P., 132, *145*
Wen, D., *185*
Werker, J. F., 306, *327*
Werner, E., 25, *29*
Wessel, A., 358, 359, *368, 369*
Wesselhoeft, H., 360, *367*
Wessinger, C. M., *327*
Wetherby, A., 32, *52*, 62, *76*, 131, *150*
Wexler, K., 38, 40, *51*, 59, *75*, 109, *118*, 212, 213, 215, 216, 217, 218, 219, 220, 224, 225, 226, 227, 230, 235, *238, 239, 240*, 244, 245, 247, 250, 251, 259, *286, 287*
Wheeler, A., 125, *146*
Wheelwright, S., *149*
White, D. A., *324*
Whitman, T. L., 190, *204*
Wiese-Slater, S., *149*

Wiig, E., 62, *76,* 173, *185*
Wijsman, E. M., *351, 353*
Wildgruber, D., *326*
Wilding, J., 124, *148*
Wilkinson, K., 131, *150*
Willcutt, E. G., 349, *354*
Willems, P. J., *143, 147*
Willemsen, R., *143, 150*
Williams, D. F., *350*
Williams, J. C. P., 358, *369*
Williams, K. T., 176, *185*
Williams, S. C., *149, 317*
Williamson, J. A., 336, *354*
Williamson, S. L., *327*
Wilmot, C., *369*
Wilson, B. C., 57, *76*
Windemuth, A., *351*
Wing, L., 27, *319*
Wingfield, A., *119*
Winklosky, B., *29*
Winslow, J. T., 349, *354*
Winter, M., 358, 359, *368, 369*
Wisbeck, J. M., 80, *97*
Wise, B., *352*
Wise, D., *324*
Wise, R. J., *327*
Wisniewski, K., *144*
Witelson, S. F., 292, *328*
Wittenberger, M., 124, *145*
Wolf-Schein, E. G., *144, 150*
Wolpert, C., *47, 325, 353*
Wong, D. L., *149*
Wong, K., 269, *285*
Wood, F. B., *351*
Woods, R. P., *327*
Worsley, K. J., *52*
Wright, F. A., 339, *354*
Wright, H., *47, 325*
Wulfeck, B., 40, *50, 150,* 219, *237, 324*
Wyke, M. A., 293, *327*

X

Xu, B., *316, 350*
Xu, X., *351*

Y

Yang, J., *149*

Yang, M., *352*
Yang, N., 160, *185,* 363, *369*
Yang, Q., 188, *206*
Yates, J. R., *368*
Yeargin-Allsopp, M., 16, *29*
Yelnik, J., 293, *328*
Yeung-Courchesne, R., 312, *318, 320, 323, 328*
Yi, H., 123, *145*
Yirmiya, N., 87, 93, *97*
Yoder, P. J., 189, 191, 192, 196, 197, 198, 199, 200, *204, 205, 206*
Yonekura, Y., *324*
Yong, S. L., *369*
Yoshimoto, T., *320*
Young, A., 337, *354*
Young, D., 360, *367*
Young, H., *149*
Yuzda, E., *47, 316*

Z

Zametkin, A., *322*
Zappella, M., *352*
Zeffiro, T. A., 303, *318*
Zeisel, S., 190, *204*
Zelazo, P. D., 87, 93, *97*
Zelinsky, D., *146*
Zetzsche, T., 41, *52*
Zhang, H., *353*
Zhang, K., 343, *354*
Zhang, M. C., 361, *369*
Zhang, X., 37, 44, 45, *50, 52,* 55, 57, 58, 59, 60, 73, *76, 150,* 212, 214, *225, 236, 238, 239, 240, 352*
Zhizhong, L., *367*
Zhu, X. L., *367*
Zibovicius, M., *317*
Ziccardi, R., *318*
Ziegler, D. A., *49*
Zijdenbos, A., *52*
Zilbovicius, M., *316, 327*
Zilles, K., *316*
Zoghbi, H. Y., 294, *316, 325, 350*
Zoumalan, C. I., *326*
Zuckerman, H. S., *148*
Zukowski, A., 103, 105, 109, 110, 113, 117, *119*
Zurif, E., 103, *119*
Zwaan, R. A., 90, *96*

Subject Index

A

Acquisition of language, 58–67, 207–211,
    229–231, 291–296
  articulation, 59–60
  Chomsky and cognitive sciences,
    291–296
  expressive-gestalt style, 59
  individual differences, 72–73
  lexical learners, 59
  maturational models of acquisition,
    230–231
    unique checking constraint, 230
  morphosyntax, 217–218
    grammatical marker, timing, 221
  onset and growth, 209–211, 229–230
  referential-analytic, 59
Autism, 7–26, 31–46, 121–142, 294–295,
    308–315
  acquisition of language, 20–22
    phonological processing, 33, 35–36
      semantic skills, 36
    receptive and expressive disorders, 13,
      21–22, 26, 32–33
    syntax, 33
    vocabulary, 33, 37
  arousal, 132, 139–140
    inhibitory control, deficit, 134

Autism Genetic Resource Exchange
    Consortium (AGRE), 46
  brain development, 25, 312–315
    executive function deficits, 134
    Purkinje cell loss, 313–314
  communication, 131
    articulation, 35–36
    first words, 10, 23
    joint attention and signaling, 131, 156
  delay, early language, 7–9, 13, 34
  diagnosis, 14–16, 31, 137
    behavioral, 16
    clinical observation, 14, 137, 140
    definition of autism, 16, 140
    language delay, 12–14, 22
    nonverbal, 16, 19–20
    PDD-NOS, 14, 15–16, 22–23, 56
  Down syndrome, comparison with, 133
  etiology, 138, 140, 156
    fragile X as cause, 126
    risk factors, 25, 295
  fragile X syndrome, comparison with,
    see fragile X syndrome, 126–143
  mental retardation, 16, 138
  nonverbal children, 16, 18–19
    verbal-nonverbal discrepancy, 20–21
  nonverbal mental age, 22

Autism *(cont.)*
  pragmatic impairments, 32–33
    Pragmatic Language Impairment
      (PLI), 56
  prevalence, 16–17, 295
    Autism, due to, 126
  regression, 22–26
    frontal lobe failure, 25
    social behavior, 25–26
    word loss, 20–26, 377
  Specific Language Impairment, compari-
    son with, 36–37
  social functioning, 25, 133
    aloofness, 133, 138
  stereotypic behaviors, 309
    echolalia, 32, 39, 131
    repetitive motor, 309
  sticky ceilings and language measure-
    ment, 19–20
  subtype, language impaired, 43–44
    hyperarousal, 139–140
  genetic studies, 46
Autism Diagnostic Interview–Revised
    (ADI–R), 10, 12, 16–19, 33, 128, 295,
    377
Autism Diagnostic Observation Schedule
    (ADOS), 14–17, 19, 33, 128

B

Bailey Scales of Mental Development, 161
Brain development, 297–300
  asymmetries, 306–307
    language acquisition, 306–307
    Specific Language Impairment, 41–42,
      292
  Brocas' and Wernicke's areas, 41, 299
  early neural development, 297, 305–306,
    313
    fMRP, 79, 123
    synaptic pruning, 297, 306–307
  enriched environments, affect on, 297
  interhemispheric reorganization and
    plasticity, 298–299, 301–307

C

Child Behavior Checklist (CBCL), 89

Clinical Evaluation of Language Funda-
    mentals (CELF) test, 35, 173–174
Communication and Symbolic Behavior
    Scales Developmental Profile, 62
Communication Development Inventory,
    196
Comprehensive Test of Phonological Proc-
    essing (CTOPP), 39, 66

D

Developmental language disorders (DLD),
    53–74, 121–122, 141–143
  delay, definition of, 196
  genetics, 122, 140–141, 296
  individual differences, 60, 73–74
  pragmatics, 56, 61, 73
  semantics, 56, 73–74
  subtypes, 55, 60, 73
  treatment, 141
Differential Ability Scales, 157
Down syndrome, 77–93, 198–202
  articulation, 85
  auditory short-term memory, 79
  communication, prelinguistic, 198–199
    commenting, 199
    requesting, 198–199
  diagnosis by treatment interactions, 199
  fragile X, comparison with, 77–94
    language delay, 83–86
      expressive, 84–85
      MLU, 86
      receptive, 83–84
      syntax, 86
    maladaptive behavior, 88–89, 93
    social cognition, 93
      noncomprehension signaling, 92
      referential talk, 90–91
  hypotoncity, 198
  life expectancy, 188
  mental retardation, 79, 188
  prevalence, 78

E

Environment—*see also* Intervention,
    187–202
  maternal responsivity, 189–192

child development, affect on, 189–190
  child with disabilities, 190–192
  cognitive development, 191
  cumulative deficits, environmental,
    192
  fragile X, 193–194
    mother with symptoms, 194
    parent behavior shaped by child's,
      193–194
  transactional model of development,
    191–192, 196
  linguistic mapping, 191

F

Fragile X syndrome (FXS), 121–143
  anxiety, 133–134
  arousal, 125, 134
  autism, comparison of fragile X with,
    126–143
    age-related changes, 128
    arousal, 132–134, 137
    attention, 127
    brain size, 136
    communication, 131, 138
      gaze, 130
      social communication, 131
      tangential speech, 134, 138
    development, 126–135
      cognitive, 126–127, 129
        executive function, 135
        sequential versus contextual
          information, 129
        theory of mind, 135
      delays, 130, 139
      flat profile, 130, 139
      language, 131
    diagnosis, 137–138
      arousal, 137
      clinical versus genetic, 137
      social awareness, 137–138
    neurobiological pathways, 135–136
    repetitive behaviors, 127, 130, 133, 138
    social skills, 127, 130, 133–134
  brain abnormalities, 135
  cognitive skills, 128–129
    executive function, 135
    visuospatial skills, 128
  communication, 131–134
    cause of deficits, 134

joint attention and signaling, 131
  symbolic play, 131
  tangential speech, 131, 134
diagnosis, 79, 122
  autism and fragile X, 128, 136
Down syndrome, comparison with, 77–94
IQ, 124
  decline in, 129
language delay, 124, 131
maladaptive behaviors, 80, 89, 125
mental retardation, 79–80, 127–129
  prevalence, 79, 122, 200–201
  with autism, 81–82, 128
social behavior, 130
speech characteristics, 125
  articulation, 131
treatment, 141–142
  gene therapy, 142
  medication, 142

G

Genetics, 1, 291–296, 329–349, 355–366
  ADHD, 329, 330, 334, 357
  association analysis, 331, 332–333,
    343–347
  autism, 9–10, 121, 137, 140, 295–296
    and ADHD, 349
    broader autism phenotype, 44
    heritability rate, 44
    twins, 295
    language impairment, 45
    and Specific Language Impairment,
      45, 296
  candidate genes, 330–331, 344, 355
    autism and SLI, 45–46
    ELN for Williams syndrome, 360–361
    evaluation of, 347–349
    SPCH1 for Specific Language Impair-
      ment, 330
  cerebral cortex and functional organiza-
    tion, 315
  CFTR gene, 45, 214
  Collaborative Linkage Study of Autism
    (CLSA), 46
  complex traits, 335, 338, 344–345, 355
  deletion mapping, 364–366
  developmental language disorders, 242,
    296

Genetics *(cont.)*
  dyslexia, 334, 342, 344–345, 348–349
    and ADHD, 349
    and Specific Language Impairment,
      232, 349
  environment, 208
    dormant genes, activating, 195
    and gene expression, 188–189
      intervention, 202–203
  environmental trigger, 188
  fMRP, 123–124, 141
    ADD and ADHD, 141
    fragile X, 141–142
    severity of disability, 124, 141
  FOXP2, 45, 213–214, 233, 235, 296, 349
  gene therapy, 142
  genotype, 362–366
  heterogeneity, 341, 346, 361
  HHRR method (haplotype relative risk),
    345
  International Molecular Genetic Study of
    Autism Consortium (AMGSAC),
    9–10, 45, 343, 349
  knockout studies, 123, 298, 355, 362, 365
  linkage analysis, 46, 331–332, 335–336,
    338–340, 342–343, 346, 356, 360
    malleability, environmental compo-
      nents, 195
  morphosyntax, affect of genetics on, 293
  penetrance, 335–336, 338, 342, 348–349,
    361
  pharmacogenetics, 142
  pleiotropy, 293–294, 361
  quantitative trait locus (QTL), 335,
    347–348, 355
  regression analysis, 337–340
  screening for DLD's, 329–330
  Specific Language Impairment (SLI),
    44–45, 213–216, 330–349
    family aggregation, 216
      prevalence rate in families, 44
      twins, 44, 213
    grammatical marker, 213
    SPCH1 gene, 330, 344, 349
  TDT test (transmission disequilibrium),
    345
  timing, language, 207–208, 234–235
  variance components approach, 340
  whole genome search, 342–345
  Williams syndrome, 101, 159
    and ADHD, 366

    elastin deletion (ELN), 160, 360–363,
      366
    genetic etiology, 164
    GTF2I, 362–366
      IQ, 164, 366
    LIM-kinase 1 (LIMK–1), 160–161, 182,
      362–366
    visuospatial deficits, 164, 366
  X-linked disorders, 79
    fragile X syndrome, 79, 122–124, 137,
      235
      FMR1 gene, 79, 123–124
Goldman-Fristoe Test of Articulation (GF),
  34

I

Intervention, 187–202
  communication and language targets,
    199
  cumulative deficits, 192
  intervention as experiment, 194–199
    identifying phenotype, 194–195
    malleable traits, 195
  maternal responsiveness, 189–193, 197
    child with mental retardation, affect
      on, 190–192
      cognitive development, 191
      language development, 198
  maturational change points, in language,
    234
  MLU, 199
  phenotype and the learning environ-
    ment, 193–194
  Prelinguistic Milieu Teaching (PMT),
    196, 197–199
  responsive small group, 196
  syndrome-specific, 94

K, L

KE family in England, 213, 233, 293, 296
  frontal cortex, 42
  morphosyntactic deficits, MRI findings,
    293
Language Impairments, 20–26, 53–74,
    82–86, 99–117, 207–232

grammar, 37–38, 102–117, 207–211—*see also* Specific Language Impairment, 37–38, 217–233
  clinical tense marker, 37–38, 217–218, 221, 235
  SLI, Down, and Williams syndrome, 220
  universal constraints, 262
linguistic mapping, 191
Nonspecific Language Impairment (NLI) compared with SLI, 228–229
phonologic processing, 55, 334
reading, 235
timing mechanisms, 208–210, 231–232, 234, 374
  general delay in language, 210, 221
  delayed and disrupted language, 210–211, 217, 226
  late talkers, 216–217, 233
  hierarchical linear modeling of growth, 225
Linguistics and child language, 1–2, 241–281
  cross-language variation, 244–262
  root infinitives, 244–251, 281
  derivational theory of complexity (DTC), 279–280
  exceptional case marking, 247, 251
  grammatical aspect, 257–261
  grammaticality judgment, 274–277
  locative verb syntax, 252–254
  pronouns, constraints on, 254–257

target variables, 175
intervention studies, 200–202, 376
  longitudinal design, when to use, 200
  sample size, 200–202
  single-subject designs, 200
missing data, 11
MLU as matching variable, 222–223
Nonlinear Vocabulary Growth Cognitive-Linguistic Profile (NVGP), 164–166
normative sample, 377
null hypothesis, 167–170
parent reports, retrospective, 10, 23–26, 233, 377
population sampling method, 61
profiling method, 154, 156–167, 377
  for genotype/phenotype research, 154
  joint attention, example of, 156–157
  sensitivity (se), 157, 163, 165–167, 182, 212
  specificity (sp), 157, 159, 162–163, 165–167, 182, 212
  target group, 157, 182
  Williams Syndrome Cognitive Profile (WSCP), 157–164, 182
raw scores, use of, 172–175
regression, instrument to study, 377
signal detection analysis, 154, 157
Mullen Scales of Early Learning, 13, 161–163

M

MacArthur Communicative Development Inventory, 25, 164
Methodology and measurement, 153–182, 375–378
  cluster analysis, 67–72
  cognitive-linguistic profiles, 154–167
  dependent variable, 155
  elicited production, 100–101, 103–106, 111–115, 116–117, 377
  factor analysis, 54, 64–67
  group-matching designs, 167–181
    age equivalent scores (AE), 173–182
    CA range, 182
    control variable, 170–172, 176–181
    nonverbal mental age, 81

N

Neuroimaging, 291–315
  autism studies, 309–311
    asymmetries of brain, 42
    cerebellar abnormalities, 134, 312–314
    motor organization, 309–312
  dyslexia studies, 292–293
  EEG, 263
  fMRI, 263, 308–312
  fragile X studies, 135
  PET, 263, 299–300, 302–303, 308, 313, 314
  plasticity, studies of, 301–307
    children with brain lesion, 301–303
    developmental language plasticity, 305
    interhemispheric reorganization, 303–304

Neuroimaging *(cont.)*
  Specific Language Impairment studies,
    42–43
  SPECT, 299–300
  Williams syndrome studies, 358

P

Phenotypes, 1, 187, 202, 333, 355–356
  autism, 31–32
  clinical diagnosis, 356–357
  Down syndrome, 79, 188
    behavioral, 92–93
  dyslexia, 334
  environment, affect on phenotype,
    93–94, 187–188, 192–194
    maternal responsivity, 188, 192–193
  fragile X, 124–125
    behavioral, 92–93, 125
    cognitive profile, compared to autism,
      128–129
    communication, 131
  grammar, 264
  growth markers, language impairment,
    234–235
  profiling methods, 182
  Specific Language Impairment, 37, 220
  Williams syndrome, 101–102, 357–360,
    365–366
    ELN, 361–362
    LIMK-1, 363–366
    SVAS phenotype, related to, 358,
      360–363
Pragmatic Language Impairment (PLI),
  33–34, 74
  autism with, 34
Prelinguistic Milieu Teaching—*see* Intervention

S

Sequenced Inventory of Communicative
  Development (SICD), 173
Specific Language Impairment (SLI),
  33–34, 37–46, 207–235
  autism, comparison with, 32–46
    asymmetries, brain development, 44
    neurobiological basis, language, 43
    nonword repetition tasks, 39, 41

phonological processing deficits, 39
tense-marking deficits, 40
  finite-verb morphology, 40–41, 220
clinical markers, 37–38, 217–221
  dialects, 38
  growth curves, 222, 224–225, 227–229,
    231
  MLU, 223
  morphosyntax, 217–218, 223–226
    Extended Optional Infinitive, 38,
      209, 217–220, 227, 233, 251
    finiteness marking, 38, 217–219, 225,
      227
  phonological processing, 33, 37–39
cross-language delay, 251
diagnosis, 37, 57, 211–213
  exclusionary criteria, 212–213
  inclusionary criteria, 211–212
  speech impairments, 213
Down syndrome, comparison with, 220
IQ, 57, 229
  Nonspecific Language Impaired (NLI),
    57–58, 61–67, 70–74, 228–229
maturational model, 230–231, 234
reading, 225
SLI Consortium, 214, 343
Williams syndrome, comparison with,
  220–221

T

Test for Auditory Comprehension of Language (TACL), 83
Test for Reception of Grammar (TROG),
  103–104
Theory of mind, 86
  autism, 25–26, 134–135
  Down syndrome, 87–88, 93
  fragile X, 87–88, 93, 135

V, W

Vineland Adaptive Behavior Scales, 13–14
Williams syndrome, 99–117, 157–167,
  355–366
  attention, 114
  auditory rote memory, 100, 110, 115
  diagnosis, 101–102, 159–160
    clinical, 159

etiology, cognitive, 164
incidence, 101, 357
language, 102–114
  delays, 102
    morphology, grammatical, 102,
      220–221
  expressive, 102
  syntax, 100–114
    questions, 108–115

    negatives, 110–114
  relative clauses, 100, 102–108
    mapping errors, 107, 114–115
    object gap relatives, 105–108, 114
    subject gap relatives, 105–108, 114
mental retardation, 358, 360, 362–363,
  365
  IQ, 359–360, 362–363
personality, 360